Marketing Classics

DATE DUE			

Ben M. Enis
University of Missouri, Columbia

Keith K. Cox
University of Houston

MARKETING CLASSICS /

A Selection of Influential Articles

FOURTH EDITION

Allyn and Bacon, Inc.

Boston · London · Sydney · Toronto

Library of Congress Cataloging in Publication Data

Enis, Ben M   comp.
   Marketing classics.

   Bibliography: p.
   Includes index.
      1. Marketing—Addresses, essays, lectures.
I. Cox, Keith Kohn.   II. Title.
HF5415.E67   1981   658.8   80–29115

ISBN 0–205–07325–5

Printed in the United States of America.

10 9 8 7 6 5 4 3 2 1   85 84 83 82 81

Contributors

Russell L. Ackoff

Lee Adler

Wroe Alderson

Leo V. Aspinwall

Richard P. Bagozzi

Raymond A. Bauer

Neil H. Borden

Louis P. Bucklin

Victor P. Buell

Gilbert Burck

Robert D. Buzzell

Harry L. Davis

George S. Day

Peter F. Drucker

James R. Emshoff

Foundation for Research
on Human Behavior

John Kenneth Galbraith

Bradley T. Gale

Paul E. Green

Stephen A. Greyser

Mason Haire

Russell I. Haley

Stanley C. Hollander

John A. Howard

Shelby D. Hunt

Richard M. Johnson

George Katona

Robert J. Keith

Philip Kotler

Robert J. Lavidge

Theodore Levitt

Sidney J. Levy

Bruce Mallen

Edgar A. Pessemier

Al Ries

Everett M. Rogers

Jagdish N. Sheth

Alvin J. Silk

Wendell R. Smith

Gary A. Steiner

Frederick N. Sturdivant

Ralph G.M. Sultan

Jack Trout

Frederick E. Webster, Jr.

William D. Wells

William L. Wilkie

Yoram Wind

Contents

Preface

When this book was conceived, we commented in the Preface:

Marketing is that phase of human activity that produces economic want-satisfaction by matching consumers' needs and the resources of business firms. From the firm's point of view, consumer-satisfaction is the result of its marketing strategy. Strategy is based on marketing philosophy and is derived from the analysis of consumers and their functional interrelationships with such market forces as economic conditions, competitors' actions, institutional change, and other environmental factors. This volume is a compilation of articles that provide broad insight into the field of marketing.

The authors consider these works to be among the classics of marketing literature. These articles are generally recognized by marketing scholars as being of enduring significance to marketing thought. They are widely quoted, have led to new directions in marketing research, and reflect the views of influential scholars. Consequently, these are works with which serious marketing students should be familiar, and to which they should have ready access. We believe the book will be a useful supplement to advanced undergraduate courses in marketing management and marketing strategy and to graduate courses in marketing fundamentals and marketing theory. The practitioner might also enjoy having these familiar works in his library.

The articles in this volume were chosen on the basis of extensive research in marketing literature, and the authors were fortunate to obtain the suggestions of a number of colleagues. Nevertheless, it would be presumptuous to imply that we have compiled *the* classic works of marketing. Marketing is too rich, too complex, too diverse a discipline to be subsumed in one volume. Our selections reflect our own perceptions of and biases about marketing. . . .

The fourth edition of *Marketing Classics* reflects our continuing attempt to match this concept to the needs of marketing students. Responses to questionnaires sent to some adopters of the third edition revealed that this anthology is used in a variety of courses, ranging from introductory marketing to doctoral-level seminars.

This edition includes several new articles that have stood the test of time and deletes a few genuine *classics* that our research indicates are no longer frequently assigned to students for various reasons. In addition, we have included several types of *comprehension aids*. These aids are described in the following section, "To the Reader."

Again, we are most grateful to the authors and publishers who granted permission to reprint their work. Our list of competent secretarial help includes Gwen Florence and Rebecca Davis on the first edition; Betty Wolfe and Marleen Vickers on the second edition; Jelka Woodard on the third edition; and Wanda Reeves and Kathleen P. King on this fourth edition. In spite of all this assistance, errors of commission and omission no doubt appear in the anthology. We are, of course, responsible for these errors and would very much appreciate having them called to our attention.

BME
KKC

TO THE READER

The purpose of a readings book is to present the work of various authorities in the field in convenient form. *Marketing Classics* represents, in our judgment, the best that the marketing discipline has to offer. To aid you in efficiently comprehending these articles, we have added the following material:

1. A suggested procedure for systematically evaluating an article
2. A key relating the articles to standard textbooks in marketing
3. Short introductions to each part of the book
4. Brief biographical sketches of each author
5. Suggestions for further reading
6. An index

Please make whatever use of these comprehension aids that you deem appropriate.

Critical Evaluation
of an Article:
A Suggested Procedure

1. *Who is the author?* (What are his qualifications for writing on this topic?)
    Scholarly achievements
    Business or administrative experience
    Other published work

2. *What is the author's message?*
    Major theme (in one sentence, if possible)
    Purpose of the message
    Author's viewpoint

3. *What evidence is offered to support this theme?*
    Three of four key points supported by references, facts, quotes, etc.

4. *How well is the argument presented?*
    Logical consistency
    Limitations and/or assumptions
    Completeness

5. *How does this article relate to other work in this area of marketing?*
    Other authorities (articles, books, etc.)
    Personal experience

6. *What is the significance of this article for marketing management?*
    Managerial usefulness of ideas presented
    Future direction of work in this area

Marketing principles textbooks correlated with Marketing Classics

Marketing Classics article number

Chapter in text	Enis	Kotler Principles	Markin	McCarthy	Pride	Stanton
1	1, 4, 5, 7; 8	1, 2, 4, 5, 6, 7, 8	1, 2, 4, 5, 6, 7, 8	2, 5, 6	1, 4, 8	1, 2, 5, 6, 8
2	2, 3, 6, 28	18, 28		1, 4, 8, 7	6, 7	4, 7, 27
3	27	19, 27	18, 27, 28, 29	18, 28, 29	13, 14	13, 14
4	13		17, 20, 21, 29	10	11, 14, 15, 17	20, 21
5	24, 34	13	9, 11, 12, 14, 15		18, 20, 21	15, 16
6		30	13	9, 11, 14, 15	22	11, 17
7	9, 10	10	16, 22, 30	12	16, 30	12
8	11, 14, 15, 16, 17	9, 11, 14, 15, 17		17, 20, 21	26, 35	16, 22, 30
9	20, 21	12	23, 33		33	18, 19
10	18	20, 21, 29	24, 34	16, 30		
11		16			24, 34	26
12	26, 35	22	31, 32	22, 23, 34		
13	19, 22, 29, 30	26, 35	25	33	13, 29	35
14	23, 25, 31, 32	33	35	24	31, 32	23, 24, 34
15	23, 33	24, 34	26		25	
16		23	3		36	33
17		31, 32	10, 36			
18	36	25		25	2	28, 29
19		3		31, 32	18, 19, 27	26
20				26, 35	12	31, 32
21		36			5	1, 7
22					3	5, 6
23				19, 27		3
24						18, 27
25				3		
26				13		10
27						36
28				36		

Enis, Ben, *Marketing Principles*, 3rd ed. (Goodyear Publishing, 1980).
Kotler, Philip, *Principles of Marketing* (Prentice-Hall, 1980).
Markin, Rom, *Marketing* (John Wiley, 1979).
McCarthy, Jerome, *Basic Marketing*, 6th ed. (Richard D. Irwin, 1978).
Pride, William, and O. C. Ferrell, *Marketing: Basic Concepts and Decisions*, 2nd ed. (Houghton Mifflin, 1980).
Stanton, William, *Fundamentals of Marketing*, 6th ed. (McGraw-Hill, 1981).

Marketing management textbooks correlated with Marketing Classics

Marketing Classics article number

Chapter in text	Cravens et al.	Hughes	Kotler, 4th ed.	Marcus	Rewoldt
1	2, 4, 7	1, 4, 6, 8	2, 6, 8	1, 2 ,4, 10	1, 4, 5, 7, 8
2	1, 5, 6, 8	27, 28	1, 4, 5, 7	27, 28	3, 6, 18
3	3, 9		7, 28	9, 11, 15	13, 14, 18
4		18	18, 19, 28	14, 17	9, 11, 15, 17
5	20	19, 30	10		12
6	11, 14	7, 11, 13	9, 11, 14, 15, 22	20, 21	20, 21
7	13	20, 21	12	18, 19	16, 19, 28, 30
8	21	12	17, 20, 21	13, 14	33
9	18, 27, 28	34		22	23, 24
10	19, 22	36	27	16	29
11	30	28		30	31, 32
12	23, 24	16, 19, 22	16	23, 29	
13	33	26, 35		31, 32	26
14	26, 35	33		25	35
15	29	29, 31, 32	26, 35	26	
16	31, 32	25	24, 33, 34	35	
17	25	23, 24		33	
18		3	23	34	
19		18, 19, 27	31, 32	27	
20				28	
21	36		25		
22	10		30	3	
23			13	36	
24				1, 5, 10	
25			3		
26			26		
27					

Cravens, David, Gerald Hills, and Robert Woodruff, *Marketing Decision Making: Concepts and Strategy*, rev. ed. (Richard D. Irwin, 1980).

Hughes, David, *Marketing Management: A Planning Approach* (Addison-Wesley, 1978).

Kotler, Philip, *Marketing Management: Analysis, Planning, and Control*, 4th ed. (Prentice-Hall, 1980).

Marcus, Burton, et al., *Modern Marketing Management*, rev. ed. (Random House, 1980).

Rewoldt, James, James Scott, and Martin Warshaw, *Introduction to Marketing Management*, 3rd ed. (Richard D. Irwin, 1977).

I / MARKETING PHILOSOPHY

Any discipline or area of human inquiry is based on a philosophy, a set of principles that provide the rationale for the existence of the discipline. The articles in Part I present a cross-section of the philosophy of marketing.

Levitt's article sets the stage. It vividly demonstrates the need for a broad interpretation of the marketing function and is perhaps the discipline's single best definitive statement. Levitt's thoughts on the continuing relevance of his paper are also included in this edition. Wroe Alderson, in his trenchant style, provides an overview of the marketing discipline. He envisions the discipline as based in the economics of imperfect competition, composed of the problem-solving activities of consumers and firms, and illuminated by concepts from the social sciences. The articles by Drucker and by Keith each illustrate Levitt's viewpoint and Alderson's framework. Drucker focuses on the macro, or societal, role that marketing performs in promoting economic growth and individual freedom. Keith's paper complements Drucker's; it emphasizes marketing's micro or managerial role in the operation of a business firm.

The following four articles in this section reflect the increasing sophistication of marketing thought in the 70s. Kotler and Levy began the decade with the article that has proved to be perhaps the discipline's most provocative to date. They argue that marketing concepts and techniques, hitherto limited exclusively to economic goods and services, are in fact applicable to all organizations. Marketing, they maintain, is a pervasive social activity. Kotler subsequently delineated more clearly, in "The Generic Concept of Marketing," the nature of the tasks and responsibilities performed by marketing managers. The thinking of Kotler and Levy was "deepened" by the rigorous work of their student Bagozzi, as he thoughtfully and precisely set out the conditions for exchange. Finally, Hunt focused the tools of philosophy of science on the discipline, devising the three-dichotomies taxonomy for describing the domain of marketing activities. These articles provide a firm philosophical foundation for the marketing discipline.

1 / MARKETING MYOPIA /
Theodore Levitt

Every major industry was once a growth industry. But some that are now riding a wave of growth enthusiasm are very much in the shadow of decline. Others which are thought of as seasoned growth industries have actually stopped growing. In every case the reason growth is threatened, slowed, or stopped is *not* because the market is saturated. It is because there has been a failure of management.

FATEFUL PURPOSES

The failure is at the top. The executives responsible for it, in the last analysis, are those who deal with broad aims and policies. Thus:

The railroads did not stop growing because the need for passenger and freight transportation declined. That grew. The railroads are in trouble today not because the need was filled by others (cars, trucks, airplanes, even telephones), but because it was *not* filled by the railroads themselves. They let others take customers away from them because they assumed themselves to be in the railroad business rather than in the transportation business. The reason they defined their industry wrong was because they were railroad-oriented instead of transportation-oriented; they were product-oriented instead of customer-oriented.

Hollywood barely escaped being totally ravished by television. Actually, all the established film companies went through drastic reorganizations. Some simply disappeared. All of them got into trouble not because of TV's inroads but because of their own myopia. As with the railroads, Hollywood defined its business incorrectly. It thought it was in the movie business when it was actually in the entertainment business. "Movies" implied a specific, limited product. This produced a fatuous contentment which from the beginning led producers to view TV as a threat. Hollywood scorned and rejected TV when it should have welcomed it as an opportunity—an opportunity to expand the entertainment business.

Today TV is a bigger business than the old narrowly defined movie business ever was. Had Hollywood been customer-oriented (providing entertainment), rather than product-oriented (making movies), would it have gone through the

Theodore Levitt, a professor in the Harvard Business School, is the author of many widely-read publications, including *Innovation in Marketing* and numerous articles. He received his B.A. from Antioch College and the Ph.D. in economics from Ohio State University. His best known book is *Marketing for Business Growth.*

fiscal purgatory that it did? I doubt it. What ultimately saved Hollywood and accounted for its recent resurgence was the wave of new young writers, producers, and directors whose previous success in television had decimated the old movie companies and toppled the big movie moguls.

There are other less obvious examples of industries that have been and are now endangering their futures by improperly defining their purposes. I shall discuss some in detail later and analyze the kind of policies that lead to trouble. Right now it may help to show what a thoroughly customer-oriented management *can* do to keep a growth industry growing, even after the obvious opportunities have been exhausted; and here there are two examples that have been around for a long time. They are nylon and glass—specifically, E. I. duPont de Nemours & Company and Corning Glass Works:

Both companies have great technical competence. Their product orientation is unquestioned. But this alone does not explain their success. After all, who was more pridefully product-oriented and product-conscious than the erstwhile New England Textile companies that have been so thoroughly massacred? The duPonts and the Cornings have succeeded not primarily because of their product or research orientation but because they have been thoroughly customer-oriented also. It is constant watchfulness for opportunities to apply their technical know-how to the creation of customer-satisfying uses which accounts for their prodigious output of successful new products. Without a very sophisticated eye on the customer, most of their new products might have been wrong, their sales methods useless.

Aluminum has also continued to be a growth industry, thanks to the efforts of two wartime-created companies which deliberately set about creating new customer-satisfying uses. Without Kaiser Aluminum & Chemical Corporation and Reynolds Metals Company, the total demand for aluminum today would be vastly less than it is.

Error of Analysis

Some may argue that it is foolish to set the railroads off against aluminum or the movies off against glass. Are not aluminum and glass naturally so versatile that the industries are bound to have more growth opportunities than the railroads and movies? This view commits precisely the error I have been talking about. It defines an industry, or a product, or a cluster of know-how so narrowly as to guarantee its premature senescence. When we mention "railroads," we should make sure we mean "transportation." As transporters, the railroads still have a good chance for very considerable growth. They are not limited to the railroad business as such (though in my opinion rail transportation is potentially a much stronger transportation medium than is generally believed).

What the railroads lack is not opportunity, but some of the same managerial imaginativeness and audacity that made them great. Even an amateur like Jacques Barzun can see what is lacking when he says:

I grieve to see the most advanced physical and social organization of the last century go down in shabby disgrace for lack of the same comprehensive imagination that built it up. [What is lacking is] the will of the companies to survive and to satisfy the public by inventiveness and skill.[1]

SHADOW OF OBSOLESCENCE

It is impossible to mention a single major industry that did not at one time qualify for the magic appellation of "growth industry." In each case its assumed strength lay in the apparently unchallenged superiority of its product. There appeared to be no effective substitute for it. It was itself a runaway substitute for the product it so triumphantly replaced. Yet one after another of these celebrated industries has come under a shadow. Let us look briefly at a few more of them, this time taking examples that have so far received a little less attention:

Dry cleaning.   This was once a growth industry with lavish prospects. In an age of wool garments, imagine being finally able to get them safely and easily clean. The boom was on.

Yet here we are 30 years after the boom started and the industry is in trouble. Where has the competition come from? From a better way of cleaning? No. It has come from synthetic fibers and chemical additives that have cut the need for dry cleaning. But this is only the beginning. Lurking in the wings and ready to make chemical dry cleaning totally obsolescent is that powerful magician, ultrasonics.

Electric utilities.   This is another one of those supposedly "no-substitute" products that has been enthroned on a pedestal of invincible growth. When the incandescent lamp came along, kerosene lights were finished. Later the water wheel and the steam engine were cut to ribbons by the flexibility, reliability, simplicity, and just plain easy availability of electric motors. The prosperity of electric utilities continues to wax extravagant as the home is converted into a museum of electric gadgetry. How can anybody miss by investing in utilities, with no competition, nothing but growth ahead?

But a second look is not quite so comforting. A score of nonutility companies are well advanced toward developing a powerful chemical fuel cell which could sit in some hidden closet of every home silently ticking off electric power. The electric lines that vulgarize so many neighborhoods will be eliminated. So will the endless demolition of streets and service interruptions during storms. Also on the horizon is solar energy, again pioneered by nonutility companies.

Who says that the utilities have no competition? They may be natural monopolies now, but tomorrow they may be natural deaths. To avoid this prospect, they too will have to develop fuel cells, solar energy, and other power sources. To survive, they themselves will have to plot the obsolescence of what now produces their livelihood.

Grocery stores.   Many people find it hard to realize that there ever was a thriving establishment known as the "corner grocery store." The supermarket has taken over with a powerful effectiveness. Yet the big food chains of the 1930's narrowly escaped being completely wiped out by the aggressive expansion of independent supermarkets. The first genuine supermarket was opened in 1930, in Jamaica, Long Island.

By 1933 supermarkets were thriving in California, Ohio, Pennsylvania, and elsewhere. Yet the established chains pompously ignored them. When they chose to notice them, it was with such derisive descriptions as "cheapy," "horse-and-buggy," "cracker-barrel store-keeping," and "unethical opportunities."

The executive of one big chain announced at the time that he found it "hard to believe that people will drive for miles to shop for foods and sacrifice the personal service chains have perfected and to which Mrs. Consumer is accustomed." [2] As late as 1936, the National Wholesale Grocers convention and the New Jersey Retail Grocers Association said there was nothing to fear. They said that the supers' narrow appeal to the price buyer limited the size of their market. They had to draw from miles around. When imitators came, there would be wholesale liquidations as volume fell. The current high sales of the supers was said to be partly due to their novelty. Basically people wanted convenient neighborhood grocers. If the neighborhood stores "cooperate with their suppliers, pay attention to their costs, and improve their services," they would be able to weather the competition until it blew over. [3]

It never blew over. The chains discovered that survival required going into the supermarket business. This meant the wholesale destruction of their huge investments in corner store sites and in established distribution and merchandising methods. The companies with "the courage of their convictions" resolutely stuck to the corner store philosophy. They kept their pride but lost their shirts.

Self-Deceiving Cycle

But memories are short. For example, it is hard for people who today confidently hail the twin messiahs of electronics and chemicals to see how things could possibly go wrong with these galloping industries. They probably also cannot see how a reasonably sensible businessman could have been as myopic as the famous Boston millionaire who 50 years ago unintentionally sentenced his heirs to poverty by stipulating that his entire estate be forever invested exclusively in electric streetcar securities. His posthumous declaration, "There will always be a big demand for efficient urban transportation," is no consolation to his heirs who sustain life by pumping gasoline at automobile filling stations.

Yet, in a casual survey I recently took among a group of intelligent business executives, nearly half agreed that it would be hard to hurt their heirs by tying their estates forever to the electronics industry. When I then confronted them with the Boston street car example, they chorused unanimously, "That's different!" But is it? Is not the basic situation identical?

In truth, *there is no such thing* as a growth industry, I believe. There are only companies organized and operated to create and capitalize on growth opportunities. Industries that assume themselves to be riding some automatic growth escalator invariably descend into stagnation. The history of every dead and dying "growth" industry shows a self-deceiving cycle of bountiful expansion and undetected decay. There are four conditions which usually guarantee this cycle:

1. The belief that growth is assured by an expanding and more affluent population.
2. The belief that there is no competitive substitute for the industry's major product.

3. Too much faith in mass production and in the advantages of rapidly declining unit costs as output rises.
4. Preoccupation with a product that lends itself to carefully controlled scientific experimentation, improvement, and manufacturing cost reduction.

I should like now to begin examining each of these conditions in some detail. To build my case as boldly as possible, I shall illustrate the points with reference to three industries—petroleum, automobiles, and electronics—particularly petroleum, because it spans more years and more vicissitudes. Not only do these three have excellent reputations with the general public and also enjoy the confidence of sophisticated investors, but their managements have become known for progressive thinking in areas like financial control, product research, and management training. If obsolescence can cripple even these industries, it can happen anywhere.

POPULATION MYTH

The belief that profits are assured by an expanding and more affluent population is dear to the heart of every industry. It takes the edge off the apprehensions everybody understandably feels about the future. If consumers are multiplying and also buying more of your product or service, you can face the future with considerably more comfort than if the market is shrinking. An expanding market keeps the manufacturer from having to think very hard or imaginatively. If thinking is an intellectual response to a problem, then the absence of a problem leads to the absence of thinking. If your product has an automatically expanding market, then you will not give much thought to how to expand it.

One of the most interesting examples of this is provided by the petroleum industry. Probably our oldest growth industry, it has an enviable record. While there are some current apprehensions about its growth rate, the industry itself tends to be optimistic. But I believe it can be demonstrated that it is undergoing a fundamental yet typical change. It is not only ceasing to be a growth industry, but may actually be a declining one, relative to other business. Although there is widespread unawareness of it, I believe that within 25 years the oil industry may find itself in much the same position of retrospective glory that the railroads are now in. Despite its pioneering work in developing and applying the present-value method of investment evaluation, in employee relations, and in working with backward countries, the petroleum business is a distressing example of how complacency and wrongheadedness can stubbornly convert opportunity into near disaster.

One of the characteristics of this and other industries that have believed very strongly in the beneficial consequences of an expanding population, while at the same time being industries with a generic product for which there has appeared to be no competitive substitute, is that the individual companies have sought to outdo their competitors by improving on what they are already doing. This makes sense, of course, if one assumes that sales are tied to the country's population strings, because the customer can compare products only on a feature-by-feature basis. I believe it is significant, for example, that not since John D. Rockefeller sent free kerosene lamps to China has the oil industry done anything really outstanding to create a demand for its product. Not even in product improvement has it showered itself with eminence. The greatest single improvement, namely, the development of tetraethyl lead, came from outside the industry, specifically from General Motors and duPont. The big contributions made by the industry itself are confined to the technology of oil exploration, production, and refining.

Asking for Trouble

In other words, the industry's efforts have focused on improving the *efficiency* of getting and making its product, not really on improving the generic product or its marketing. Moreover, its chief product has continuously been defined in the narrowest possible terms, namely, gasoline, not energy, fuel, or transportation. This attitude has helped assure that:

Major improvements in gasoline quality tend not to originate in the oil industry. Also, the development of superior alternative fuels comes from outside the oil industry, as will be shown later.

Major innovations in automobile fuel marketing are originated by small new oil companies that are not primarily preoccupied with production or refining. These are the companies that have been responsible for the rapidly expanding multipump gasoline stations, with their successful emphasis on large and clean layouts, rapid and efficient driveway service, and quality gasoline at low prices.

Thus, the oil industry is asking for trouble from outsiders. Sooner or later, in this land of hungry inventors and entrepreneurs, a threat is sure to come. The possibilities of this will become more apparent when we turn to the next dangerous belief of many managements. For the sake of continuity, because this second belief is tied closely to the first, I shall continue with the same example.

Idea of Indispensability

The petroleum industry is pretty much persuaded that there is no competitive substitute for its major product, gasoline—or if there is, that it will continue to be a derivative of crude oil, such as diesel fuel or kerosene jet fuel.

There is a lot of automatic wishful thinking in this assumption. The trouble is that most refining companies own huge amounts of crude oil reserves. These have value only if there is a market for products into which oil can be converted—hence the tenacious belief in the continuing competitive superiority of automobile fuels made from crude oil.

This idea persists despite all historic evidence against it. The evidence not only shows that oil has never been a superior product for any purpose for very long, but it also shows that the oil industry has never really been a growth industry. It has been a succession of different businesses that have gone through the usual historic cycles of growth, maturity, and decay. Its over-all survival is owed to a series of miraculous escapes from total obsolescence, of last minute and unexpected reprieves from total disaster reminiscent of the Perils of Pauline.

Perils of Petroleum

I shall sketch in only the main episodes:

First, crude oil was largely a patent medicine. But even before that fad ran out, demand was greatly expanded by the use of oil in kerosene lamps. The prospect of lighting the world's lamps gave rise to an extravagant promise of growth. The prospects were similar to those the industry now holds for gasoline in other parts of the world. It can hardly wait for the underdeveloped nations to get a car in every garage.

In the days of the kerosene lamp, the oil companies competed with each other and against gaslight by trying to improve the illuminating characteristics of kerosene. Then suddenly the impossible happened. Edison invented a light which was totally nondependent on crude oil. Had it not been for the growing use of kerosene in space heaters, the incandescent lamp would have completely finished oil as a growth industry at that time. Oil would have been good for little else than axle grease.

Then disaster and reprieve struck again. Two great innovations occurred, neither originating in the oil industry. The successful development of coal-burning domestic central-heating systems made the space heater obsolescent. While the industry reeled, along came its most magnificent boost yet—the internal combustion engine, also invented by outsiders. Then when the prodigious expansion for gasoline finally began to level off in the 1920's, along came the miraculous escape of a central oil heater. Once again, the escape was provided by an outsider's invention and development. And when that market weakened, wartime demand for aviation fuel came to the rescue. After the war the expansion of civilian aviation, the dieselization of railroads, and the explosive demand for cars and trucks kept the industry's growth in high gear.

Meanwhile centralized oil heating—whose boom potential had only recently been proclaimed—ran into severe competition from natural gas. While the oil companies themselves owned the gas that now competed with their oil, the industry did not originate the natural gas revolution, nor has it to this day greatly profited from its gas ownership. The gas revolution was made by newly formed transmission companies that marketed the product with an aggressive ardor. They started a magnificent new industry, first against the advice and then against the resistance of the oil companies.

By all the logic of the situation, the oil companies themselves should have made the gas revolution. They not only owned the gas; they also were the only people experienced in handling, scrubbing, and using it, the only people experienced in pipeline technology and transmission, and they understood heating problems. But, partly because they knew that natural gas would compete with their own sale of heating oil, the oil companies pooh-poohed the potentials of gas.

The revolution was finally started by oil pipeline executives who, unable to persuade their own companies to go into gas, quit and organized the spectacularly successful gas transmission companies. Even after their success became painfully evident to the oil companies, the latter did not go into gas transmission. The multibillion dollar business which should have been theirs went to others. As in the past, the industry was blinded by its narrow preoccupation with a specific product and the value of its reserves. It paid little or no attention to its customers' basic needs and preferences.

The postwar years have not witnessed any change. Immediately after World War II the oil industry was greatly encouraged about its future by the rapid expansion of demand for its traditional line of products. In 1950 most companies projected annual rates of domestic expansion of around 6% through at least 1975. Though the ratio of crude oil reserves to demand in the Free World was about 20 to 1, with 10 to 1 being usually considered a reasonable working ratio in the United States, booming demand sent oil men searching for more without sufficient regard to what the future really promised. In 1952 they "hit" in the Middle East; the ratio skyrocketed to 42 to 1. If gross additions to reserves continue at the average rate of the past five years (37 billion barrels annually), then by 1970 the reserve ratio will be up to 45 to 1. This abundance of oil has weakened crude and product prices all over the world.

Uncertain Future

Management cannot find much consolation today in the rapidly expanding petrochemical industry, another oil-using idea that did not originate in the leading firms. The total United States production of petrochemicals is equivalent to about 2% (by volume) of the demand for all petroleum products. Although the petrochemical industry is now expected to grow by about 10% per year, this will not offset other drains on the growth of crude oil consumption. Furthermore, while petrochemical products are many and growing, it is well to remember that there are nonpetroleum sources of the basic raw material, such as coal. Besides, a lot of plastics can be produced with relatively little oil. A 50,000-barrel-per-day oil refinery is now considered the absolute minimum size for efficiency. But a 50,000-barrel-per-day chemical plant is a giant operation.

Oil has never been a continuously strong growth industry. It has grown by fits and starts, always miraculously saved by innovations and developments not of its own making. The reason it has not grown in a smooth progression is that each time it thought it had a superior product safe from the possibility of competitive substitutes, the product turned out to be inferior and notoriously subject to obsolescence. Until now, gasoline (for motor fuel, anyhow) has escaped this fate. But, as we shall see later, it too may be on its last legs.

The point of all this is that there is no guarantee against product obsolescence. If a company's own research does not make it obsolete, another's will. Unless an industry is especially lucky, as oil has been until now, it can easily go down in a sea of red figures—just as the railroads have, as the buggy whip manufacturers have, as the corner grocery chains have, as most of the big movie companies have, and indeed as many other industries have.

The best way for a firm to be lucky is to make its own luck. That requires knowing what makes a business successful. One of the greatest enemies of this knowledge is mass production.

PRODUCTION PRESSURES

Mass-production industries are impelled by a great drive to produce all they can. The prospect of steeply declining unit costs as output rises is more than most companies can usually resist. The profit possibilities look spectacular. All effort focuses on production. The result is that marketing gets neglected.

John Kenneth Galbraith contends that just the opposite occurs.[4] Output is so prodigious that all effort concentrates on trying to get rid of it. He says this accounts for singing commercials, desecration of the countryside with advertising signs, and other wasteful and vulgar practices. Galbraith has a finger on something real, but he misses the strategic point. Mass production does indeed generate great pressure to "move" the product. But what usually gets emphasized is selling, not marketing. Marketing, being a more sophisticated and complex process, gets ignored.

The difference between marketing and selling is more than semantic. Selling focuses on the needs of the seller, marketing on the needs of the buyer. Selling is preoccupied with the seller's need to convert his product into cash; marketing with the idea of satisfying the needs of the customer by means of the product and the whole cluster of things associated with creating, delivering, and finally consuming it.

In some industries the enticements of full mass production have been so powerful that for many years top management in effect has told the sales departments, "You get rid of it; we'll worry about profits." By contrast, a truly marketing-minded firm tries to create value-satisfying goods and services that consumers will want to buy. What it offers for sale includes not only the generic product or service, but also how it is made available to the customer, in what form, when, under what conditions, and at what terms of trade. Most important, what it offers for sale is determined not by the seller but by the buyer. The seller takes his cues from the buyer in such a way that the product becomes a consequence of the marketing effort, not vice versa.

Lag in Detroit

This may sound like an elementary rule of business, but that does not keep it from being violated wholesale. It is certainly more violated than honored. Take the automobile industry:

Here mass production is most famous, most honored, and has the greatest impact on the entire society. The industry has hitched its fortune to the relentless requirements of the annual model change, a policy that makes customer orientation an especially urgent necessity. Consequently the auto companies annually spend millions of dollars on consumer research. But the fact that the new compact cars are selling so well in their first year indicates that Detroit's vast researchers have for a long time failed to reveal what the customer really wanted. Detroit was not persuaded that he wanted anything different from what he had been getting until it lost millions of customers to other small car manufacturers.

How could this unbelievable lag behind consumer wants have been perpetuated so long? Why did not research reveal consumer preferences before consumers' buying decisions themselves revealed the facts? Is that not what consumer research is for—to find out before the fact what is going to happen? The answer is that Detroit never really researched the customer's wants. It only researched his preferences between the kinds of things which it had already decided to offer him. For Detroit is mainly product-oriented, not customer-oriented. To the extent that the customer is recognized as having needs that the manufacturer should try to satisfy, Detroit usually acts as if the job can be done entirely by product changes. Occasionally attention gets paid to financing, too, but that is done more in order to sell than to enable the customer to buy.

As for taking care of other customer needs, there is not enough being done to write about. The areas of the greatest unsatisfied needs are ignored, or at best get stepchild attention. These are at the point of sale and on the matter of automotive repair and maintenance. Detroit views these problem areas as being of secondary importance. That is underscored by the fact that the retailing and servicing ends of this industry are neither owned and operated nor controlled by the manufacturers. Once the car is produced, things are pretty much in the dealer's inadequate hands. Illustrative of Detroit's arm's-length attitude is the fact that, while servicing holds enormous sales-stimulating, profit-building opportunities, only 57 of Chevrolet's 7,000 dealers provide night maintenance service.

Motorists repeatedly express their dissatisfaction with servicing and their apprehensions about buying cars under the present selling setup. The anxieties and problems they encounter during the auto buying and maintenance processes are probably more intense and widespread today than 30 years ago. Yet the automobile companies do not *seem* to listen to or take their cues from the anguished consumer. If they do listen, it must be through the filter of their own preoccupation with production. The marketing effort is still viewed as a necessary consequence of the product, not vice versa, as it should be. That is the legacy of mass production, with its parochial view that profit resides essentially in low-cost full production.

What Ford Put First

The profit lure of mass production obviously has a place in the plans and strategy of business management, but it must always follow hard thinking about the customer. This is one of the most important lessons that we can learn from the contradictory behavior of Henry Ford. In a sense Ford was both the most brilliant and the most senseless marketer in American history. He was senseless because he refused to give the customer anything but a black car. He was brilliant because he fashioned a production system designed to fit market needs. We habitually celebrate him for the wrong reason, his production genius. His real genius was marketing. We think he was able to cut his selling price and therefore sell millions of $500 cars because his invention of the assembly line had reduced the costs. Actually he invented the assembly line because he had concluded that at $500 he could sell millions of cars. Mass production was the *result* not the cause of his low prices.

Ford repeatedly emphasized this point, but a nation of production-oriented business managers refuses to hear the great lesson he taught. Here is his operating philosophy as he expressed it succinctly:

Our policy is to reduce the price, extend the operations, and improve the article. You will notice that the reduction of price comes first. We have never considered any costs as fixed. Therefore we first reduce the price to the point where we believe more sales will result. Then we go ahead and try to make the prices. We do not bother about the costs. The new price forces the costs down. The more usual way is to take the costs and then determine the price, and although that method may be scientific in the narrow sense; it is not scientific in the broad sense, because what earthly use is it to know the cost if it tells you that you cannot manufacture at a price at which the article can be sold? But more to the point is the fact that, although one may calculate what a cost is, and of course all of our costs are carefully calculated, no one knows what a cost ought to be. One of the ways of discovering . . . is to name a price so low as to force everybody in the place to the highest point of efficiency. The low price makes everybody dig for profits. We make more discoveries concerning manufacturing and selling under this forced method than by any method of leisurely investigation.[5]

Product Provincialism

The tantalizing profit possibilities of low unit production costs may be the most seriously self-deceiving attitude that can afflict a company, particularly a "growth" company where an apparently assured expansion of demand already tends to undermine a proper concern for the importance of marketing and the customer.

The usual result of this narrow preoccupation with so-called concrete matters is that instead of growing, the industry declines. It usually means that the product fails to adapt to the constantly changing patterns of consumer needs and tastes, to new and modified marketing institutions and practices, or to product developments in competing or complementary industries. The industry has its eyes so firmly on its own specific product that it does not see how it is being made obsolete.

The classical example of this is the buggy whip industry. No amount of product improvement could stave off its death sentence. But had the industry defined itself as being in the transportation business rather than the buggy whip business, it might have survived. It would have done what survival always entails, that is, changing. Even if it had only defined its business as providing a stimulant or catalyst to an energy source, it might have survived by becoming a manufacturer of, say, fanbelts or air cleaners.

What may some day be a still more classical example is again, the oil industry. Having let others steal marvelous opportunities from it (e.g., natural gas, as already mentioned, missile fuels, and jet engine lubricants), one would expect it to have taken steps never to let that happen again. But this is not the case. We are now getting extraordinary new developments in fuel systems specifically designed to power automobiles. Not only are these developments concentrated in firms outside the petroleum industry, but petroleum is almost systematically ignoring them, securely content in its wedded bliss to oil. It is the story of the kerosene lamp versus the incandescent lamp all over again. Oil is trying to improve hydrocarbon fuels rather than to develop *any* fuels best suited to the needs of their users, whether or not made in different ways and with different raw materials from oil.

Here are some of the things which nonpetroleum companies are working on:

Over a dozen such firms now have advanced working models of energy systems which, when perfected, will replace the internal combustion engine and eliminate the demand for gasoline. The superior merit of each of these systems is their elimination of frequent, time-consuming, and irritating refueling stops. Most of these systems are fuel cells designed to create electrical energy directly from chemicals without combustion. Most of them use chemicals that are not derived from oil, generally hydrogen and oxygen.

Several other companies have advanced models of electric storage batteries designed to power automobiles. One of these is an aircraft producer that is working jointly with several electric utility companies. The latter hope to use off-peak generating capacity to supply overnight plug-in battery regeneration. Another company, also using the battery approach, is a medium-size electronics firm with extensive small-battery experience that it developed in connection with its work on hearing aids. It is collaborating with an automobile manufacturer. Recent improvements arising from the need for high-powered miniature power storage plants in rockets have put us within reach of a relatively small battery capable of withstanding great overloads or surges of power. Germanium diode applications and batteries using sintered-plate and nickel-cadmium techniques promise to make a revolution in our energy sources.

Solar energy conversion systems are also getting increasing attention. One usually cautious Detroit auto executive recently ventured that solar-powered cars might be common by 1980.

As for the oil companies, they are more or less "watching developments," as one research director put it to me. A few are doing a bit of research on fuel cells, but almost always confined to developing cells powered by hydrocarbon chemicals. None of them are enthusiastically researching fuel cells, batteries, or solar power plants. None of them are spending a fraction as much on research in these profoundly important areas as they are on the usual run-of-the-mill things like reducing combustion chamber deposit in gasoline engines. One major integrated petroleum company recently took a tentative look at the fuel cell and concluded that although "the companies actively working on it indicate a belief in ultimate success . . . the timing and magnitude of its impact are too remote to warrant recognition in our forecasts."

One might, of course, ask: Why should the oil companies do anything different? Would not chemical fuel cells, batteries, or solar energy kill the present product lines? The answer is that they would indeed, and that is precisely the reason for the oil firms having to develop these power units before their competitors, so they will not be companies without an industry.

Management might be more likely to do what is needed for its own preservation if it thought of itself as being in the energy business. But even that would not be enough if it persists in imprisoning itself in the narrow grip of its tight product orientation. It has to think of itself as taking care of customer needs, not finding, refinings, or even selling oil. Once it genuinely thinks of its business as taking care of people's transportation needs, nothing can stop it from creating its own extravagantly profitable growth.

Creative Destruction

Since words are cheap and deeds are dear, it may be appropriate to indicate what this kind of thinking involves and leads to. Let us start at the beginning—the customer. It can be shown that motorists strongly dislike the bother, delay, and experience of buying gasoline. People actually do not buy gasoline. They cannot see it, taste it, feel it, appreciate it, or really test it. What they buy is the right to continue driving their cars. The gas station is like a tax collector to whom people are compelled to pay a periodic toll as the price of using their cars. This makes the gas station a basically unpopular institution. It can never be made popular or pleasant, only less unpopular, less unpleasant.

To reduce its unpopularity completely means eliminating it. Nobody likes a tax collector, not even a pleasantly cheerful one. Nobody likes to interrupt a trip to buy a phantom product, not even from a handsome Adonis or a seductive Venus. Hence, companies that are working on exotic fuel substitutes which will eliminate the need for frequent refueling are heading directly into the outstretched arms of the irritated motorists. They are riding a wave of inevitability, not because they are creating something which is technologically superior or more sophisticated, but because they are satisfying a powerful customer need. They are also eliminating noxious odors and air pollution.

Once the petroleum companies recognize the customer-satisfying logic of what another power system can do, they will see that they have no more choice about working on an efficient, long-lasting fuel (or some way of delivering present fuels without bothering the motorist) than the big food chains had a choice about going into the supermarket business, or the vacuum tube companies had a choice about making semiconductors. For their own good the oil firms will have to destroy their own highly profitable assets. No amount of wishful thinking can save them from the necessity of engaging in this form of "creative destruction."

I phrase the need as strongly as this because I think management must make quite an effort to break itself loose from conventional ways. It is all too easy in this day and age for a company or industry to let its sense of purpose become dominated by the economies of full production and to develop a dangerously lopsided product orientation. In short, if management lets itself drift, it invariably drifts in the direction of thinking of itself as producing goods and services, not customer satisfactions. While it probably will not descend to the depths of telling its salesmen, "You get rid of it; we'll worry about profits," it can, without knowing it, be practicing precisely that formula for withering decay. The historic fate of one growth industry after another has been its suicidal product provincialism.

DANGERS OF R & D

Another big danger to a firm's continued growth arises when top management is wholly transfixed by the profit possibilities of technical research and development. To illustrate I shall turn first to a new industry—electronics—and then return once more to the oil companies. By comparing a fresh example with a familiar one, I hope to emphasize the prevalence and insidiousness of a hazardous way of thinking.

Marketing Shortchanged

In the case of electronics, the greatest danger which faces the glamorous new companies in this field is not that they do not pay enough attention to research and development, but that they pay *too much* attention to it. And the fact that the fastest growing electronics firms owe their eminence to their heavy emphasis on technical research is completely beside the point. They have vaulted to affluence on a sudden crest of unusually strong general receptiveness to new technical ideas. Also, their success has been shaped in the virtually guaranteed market of military subsidies and by military orders that in many cases actually preceded the existence of facilities to make the products. Their expansion has, in other words, been almost totally devoid of marketing effort.

Thus, they are growing up under conditions that come dangerously close to creating the illusion that a superior product will sell itself. Having created a successful company by making a superior product, it is not surprising that management continues to be oriented toward the product rather than the people who consume it. It develops the philosophy that continued growth is a matter of continued product innovation and improvement.

A number of other factors tend to strengthen and sustain this belief:

1. Because electronic products are highly complex and sophisticated, managements become top-heavy with engineers and scientists. This creates a selective bias in favor of research and production at the expense of marketing. The organization tends to view itself as making things rather than satisfying customer needs. Marketing gets treated as a residual activity, "something else" that must be done once the vital job of product creation and production is completed.
2. To this bias in favor of product research, development, and production is added the bias in favor of dealing with controllable variables. Engineers and scientists are at home in the world of concrete things like machines, test tubes, production lines, and even balance sheets. The abstractions to which they feel kindly are those which are testable or manipulatable in the laboratory, or, if not testable, then functional, such as Euclid's axioms. In short, the managements of the new glamour-growth companies tend to favor those business activities which lend themselves to careful study, experimentation, and control—the hard, practical, realities of the lab, the shop, the books.

What gets shortchanged are the realities of the *market*. Consumers are unpredictable, varied, fickle, stupid, shortsighted, stubborn, and generally bothersome. This is not what the engineer-managers say, but deep down in their consciousness it is what they believe. And this accounts for their concentrating on what they know and what they can control, namely, product research, engineering, and production. The emphasis on production becomes particularly attractive when the product can be made at declining unit costs. There is no more inviting way of making money than by running the plant full blast.

Today the top-heavy science-engineering-production orientation of so many electronics companies works reasonably well because they are pushing into new frontiers in which the armed services have pioneered virtually assured markets. The companies are in the felicitous position of having to fill, not find markets; of not having to discover what the customer needs and wants, but of having the customer voluntarily come forward with specific new product demands. If a team of consultants had been assigned specifically to design a business situation calculated to prevent the emergence and development of a customer-oriented marketing viewpoint, it could not have produced anything better than the conditions just described.

Stepchild Treatment

The oil industry is a stunning example of how science, technology, and mass production can divert an entire group of companies from their main task. To the extent the consumer is studied at all (which is not much), the focus is forever on getting information which is designed to help the oil companies improve what they are now doing. They try to discover more convincing advertising themes, more effective sales promotional drives, what the market shares of the various companies are, what people like or dislike about service station dealers and oil companies, and so forth. Nobody seems as interested in probing deeply into the basic human needs that the industry might be trying to satisfy as in probing into the basic properties of the raw material that the companies work with in trying to deliver customer satisfactions.

Basic questions about customers and markets seldom get asked. The latter occupy a stepchild status. They are recognized as existing, as having to be taken care of, but not worth very much real thought or dedicated attention. Nobody gets as excited about the customers in his own backyard as about the oil in the Sahara Desert. Nothing illustrates better the neglect of marketing than its treatment in the industry press:

The centennial issue of the *American Petroleum Institute Quarterly*, published in 1959 to celebrate the discovery of oil in Titusville, Pennsylvania, contained 21 feature articles proclaiming the industry's greatness. Only one of these talked about its achievements in marketing, and that was only a pictorial record of how service station architecture has changed. The issue also contained a special section on "New Horizons," which was devoted to showing the magnificent role oil would play in America's future. Every reference was ebulliently optimistic, never implying once that oil might have some hard competition. Even the reference to atomic energy was a cheerful catalogue of how oil would help make atomic energy a success. There was not a single apprehension that the oil industry's affluence might be threatened or a suggestion that one "new horizon" might include new and better ways of serving oil's present customers.

But the most revealing example of the stepchild treatment that marketing gets was still another special series of short articles on "The Revolutionary Potential of Electronics." Under that heading this list of articles appeared in the table of contents:
"In the Search for Oil"
"In Production Operations"
"In Refinery Processes"
"In Pipeline Operations"

Significantly, every one of the industry's major functional areas is listed, *except* marketing. Why? Either it is believed that electronics holds no revolutionary potential for petroleum marketing (which is palpably wrong), or the editors forgot to discuss marketing (which is more likely, and illustrates its stepchild status).

The order in which the four functional areas are listed also betrays the alienation of the oil industry from the consumer. The industry is implicitly defined as beginning with the search for oil and ending with its distribution from the refinery. But the truth is, it seems to me, that the industry begins with the needs of the customer for its products. From that primal position its definition moves steadily backstream to areas of progressively lesser importance, until it finally comes to rest at the "search for oil."

Beginning & End

The view that an industry is a customer-satisfying process, not a goods-producing process, is vital for all businessmen to understand. An industry begins with the customer and his needs, not with a patent, a raw material, or a selling skill. Given the customer's needs, the industry develops backwards, first concerning itself with the physical *delivery* of customer satisfactions. Then it moves back further to *creating* the things by which these satisfactions are in part achieved. How these materials are created is a matter of indifference to the customer, hence the particular form of manufacturing, processing, or what-have-you cannot be considered as a vital aspect of the industry. Finally, the industry moves back still further to *finding* the raw materials necessary for making its products .

The irony of some industries oriented toward technical research and development is that the scientists who occupy the high executive positions are totally unscientific when it comes to defining their companies' over-all needs and purposes. They violate the first two rules of the scientific method—being aware of and defining their companies' problems, and then developing testable hypotheses about solving them. They are scientific only about the convenient things, such as laboratory and product experiments. The reason that the customer (and the satisfaction of his deepest needs) is not considered as being "the problem" is not because there is any certain belief that no such problem exists, but because an organizational lifetime has conditioned management to look in the opposite direction. Marketing is a stepchild.

I do not mean that selling is ignored. Far from it. But selling, again, is not marketing. As already pointed out, selling concerns itself with the tricks and techniques of getting people to exchange their cash for your product. It is not concerned with the values that the exchange is all about. And it does not, as marketing invariably does, view the entire business process as consisting of a tightly integrated effort to discover, create, arouse, and satisfy customer needs. The customer is somebody "out there" who, with proper cunning, can be separated from his loose change.

Actually, not even selling gets much attention in some technologically minded firms. Because there is a virtually guaranteed market for the abundant flow of their new products, they do not actually know what a real market is. It is as if they lived in a planned economy, moving their products routinely from factory to retail outlet. Their successful concentration on products tends to convince them of the soundness of what they have been doing, and they fail to see the gathering clouds over the market.

CONCLUSION

Less than 75 years ago American railroads enjoyed a fierce loyalty among astute Wall Streeters. European monarchs invested in them heavily. Eternal wealth was thought to be the benediction for anybody who could scrape a few thousand dollars together to put into rail stocks. No other form of transportation could compete with the railroads in speed, flexibility, durability, economy, and growth potentials. As Jacques Barzun put it, "By the turn of the century it was an institution, an image of man, a tradition, a code of honor, a source of poetry, a nursery of boyhood desires, a sublimest of toys, and the most solemn machine—next to the funeral hearse —that marks the epochs in man's life." [6]

Even after the advent of automobiles, trucks, and airplanes, the railroad tycoons remained imperturbably self-confident. If you had told them 60 years ago that in 30 years they would be flat on their backs, broke, and pleading for government subsidies, they would have thought you totally demented. Such a future was simply not considered possible. It was not even a discussable subject, or an askable question, or a matter which any sane person would consider worth speculating about. The very thought was insane. Yet a lot of insane notions now have matter-of-fact acceptance—for example, the idea of 100-ton tubes of metal moving smoothly through the air 20,000 feet above the earth, loaded with 100 sane and solid citizens casually drinking martinis—and they have dealt cruel blows to the railroads.

What specificially must other companies do to avoid this fate? What does customer orientation involve? These questions have in part been answered by the preceding examples and analysis. It would take another article to show in detail what is required for specific industries. In any case, it should be obvious that building an effective customer-oriented company involves far more than good intentions or promotional tricks; it involves profound matters of human organization and leadership. For the present, let me merely suggest what appear to be some general requirements.

Visceral Feel of Greatness

Obviously the company has to do what survival demands. It has to adapt to the requirements of the market, and it has to do it sooner rather than later. But mere survival is a so-so aspiration. Anybody can survive in some way or other, even the skid-row bum. The trick is to survive gallantly, to feel the surging impulse of commercial mastery; not just to experience the sweet smell of success, but to have the visceral feel of enterpreneurial greatness.

No organization can achieve greatness without a vigorous leader who is driven onward by his own pulsating *will to succeed*. He has to have a vision of grandeur, a vision that can produce eager followers in vast numbers. In business, the followers are the customers. To produce these customers, the entire corporation must be viewed as a customer-creating and customer-satisfying organism. Management must think of itself not as producing products but as providing customer-creating value satisfactions. It must push this idea (and everything it means and requires) into every nook and cranny of the organization. It has to do this continuously and with the kind of flair that excites and stimulates the people in it. Otherwise, the company will be merely a series of pigeonholed parts, with no consolidating sense of purpose or direction.

In short, the organization must learn to think of itself not as producing goods or services but as *buying customers,* as doing the things that will make people *want* to do business with it. And the chief executive himself has the inescapable responsibility for creating this environment, this viewpoint, this attitude, this aspiration. He himself must set the company's style, its direction, and its goals. This means he has to know precisely where he himself wants to go, and to make sure the whole organization is enthusiastically aware of where that is. This is a first requisite of leadership, for *unless he knows where he is going, any road will take him there.*

If any road is okay, the chief executive might as well pack his attaché case and go fishing. If an organization does not know or care where it is going, it does not need to advertise that fact with a ceremonial figurehead. Everybody will notice it soon enough.

1975: RETROSPECTIVE COMMENTARY

Amazed, finally, by his literary success, Isaac Bashevis Singer reconciled an attendant problem: "I think the moment you have published a book, it's not any more your private property . . . . If it has value, everybody can find in it what he finds, and I cannot tell the man I did not intend it to be so." Over the past 15 years, "Marketing Myopia" has become a case in point. Remarkably, the article spawned a legion of loyal partisans—not to mention a host of unlikely bedfellows.

Its most common and, I believe, most influential consequence is the way certain companies for the first time gave serious thought to the question of what businesses they are really in.

The strategic consequences of this have in many cases been dramatic. The best-known case, of course, is the shift in thinking of oneself as being in the "oil business" to being in the "energy business." In some instances the payoff has been spectacular (getting into coal, for example) and in others dreadful (in terms of the time and money spent so far on fuel cell research). Another successful example is a company with a large chain of retail shoe stores that redefined itself as a retailer of moderately priced, frequently purchased, widely assorted consumer specialty products. The result was a dramatic growth in volume, earnings, and return on assets.

Some companies, again for the first time, asked themselves whether they wished to be masters of certain technologies for which they would seek markets, or be masters of markets for which they would seek customer-satisfying products and services.

Choosing the former, one company has declared, in effect, "We are experts in glass technology. We intend to improve and expand that expertise with the object of creating products that will attract customers." This decision has forced the company into a much more systematic and customer-sensitive look at possible markets and users, even though its stated strategic object has been to capitalize on glass technology.

Deciding to concentrate on markets, another company has determined that "we want to help people (primarily women) enhance their beauty and sense of youthfulness." This company has expanded its line of cosmetic products, but has also entered the fields of proprietary drugs and vitamin supplements.

All these examples illustrate the "policy" results of "Marketing Myopia." On the operating level, there has been, I think, an extraordinary heightening of sensitivity to customers and consumers. R&D departments have cultivated a greater "external" orientation toward uses, users, and markets—balancing thereby the previously one-sided "internal" focus on materials and methods; upper management has realized that marketing and sales departments should be somewhat more willingly accommodated than before; finance departments have become more receptive to the legitimacy of budgets for market research and experimentation in marketing; and salesmen have been better trained to listen to and understand customer needs and problems, rather than merely to "push" the product.

A Mirror, Not a Window

My impression is that the article has had more impact in industrial-products companies than in consumer-products companies—perhaps because the former had lagged most in customer orientation. There are at least two reasons for this lag: (1) industrial-products companies tend to be more capital intensive, and (2) in the past, at least, they have had to rely heavily on communicating face-to-face the technical character of what they made and sold. These points are worth explaining.

Capital-intensive businesses are understandably preoccupied with magnitudes, especially where the capital, once invested, cannot be easily moved, manipulated, or modified for the production of a variety of products—e.g., chemical plants, steel mills, airlines, and railroads. Understandably, they seek big volumes and operating efficiencies to pay off the equipment and meet the carrying costs.

At least one problem results: corporate power becomes disproportionately lodged with operating or financial executives. If you read the charter of one of the nation's largest companies, you will see that the chairman of the finance committee, not the chief executive officer, is the "chief." Executives with such backgrounds have an almost trained incapacity to see that getting "volume" may require understanding and serving many discrete and sometimes small market segments, rather than going after a perhaps mythical batch of big or homogeneous customers.

These executives also often fail to appreciate the competitive changes going on around them. They observe the changes, all right, but devalue their significance or underestimate their ability to nibble away at the company's markets.

Once dramatically alerted to the concept of segments, sectors, and customers, though, managers of capital-intensive businesses have become more responsive to the necessity of balancing their inescapable preoccupation with "paying the bills" or breaking even with the fact that the best way to accomplish this may be to pay more attention to segments, sectors, and customers.

The second reason industrial-products companies have probably been more influenced by the article is that, in the case of the more technical industrial products or services, the necessity of clearly communicating product and service characteristics to prospects results in a lot of face-to-face "selling" effort. But precisely because the product is so complex, the situation produces salesmen who know the product more than they know the customer, who are more adept at explaining what they have and what it can do than learning what the customer's needs and problems are. The result has been a narrow product orientation rather than a liberating customer orientation, and "service" often suffered. To be sure, sellers said, "We have to provide service," but they tended to define service by looking into the mirror rather than out the window. They *thought* they were looking out the window at the customer, but it was actually a mirror—a reflection of their own product-oriented biases rather than a reflection of their customers' situations.

A Manifesto, Not a Prescription

Not everything has been rosy. A lot of bizarre things have happened as a result of the article:

- Some companies have developed what I call "marketing mania"—they've become obsessively responsive to every fleeting whim of the customer. Mass production operations have been converted to approximations of job shops, with cost and price consequences far exceeding the willingness of customers to buy the product.
- Management has expanded product lines and added new lines of business without first establishing adequate control systems to run more complex operations.
- Marketing staffs have suddenly and rapidly expanded themselves and their research budgets without either getting sufficient prior organizational support or, thereafter, producing sufficient results.
- Companies that are functionally organized have converted to product, brand, or market-based organizations with the expectation of instant and miraculous results. The outcome has been ambiguity, frustration, confusion, corporate infighting, losses, and finally a reversion to functional arrangements that only worsened the situation.
- Companies have attempted to "serve" customers by creating complex and beautifully efficient products or services that buyers are either too risk-averse to adopt or incapable of learning how to employ—in effect, there are now steam shovels for people who haven't yet learned to use spades. This problem has happened repeatedly in the so-called service industries (financial services, insurance, computer-based services) and with American companies selling in less-developed economies.

"Marketing Myopia" was not intended as analysis or even prescription; it was intended as manifesto. It did not pretend to take a balanced position. Nor was it a new idea—Peter F. Drucker, J. B. McKitterick, Wroe Alderson, John Howard, and Neil Borden had each done more original and balanced work on "the marketing concept." My scheme, however, tied marketing more closely to the inner orbit of business policy. Drucker—especially in The Concept of the Corporation and The Practice of Management—originally provided me with a great deal of insight.

My contribution, therefore, appears merely to have been a simple, brief, and useful way of communicating an existing way of thinking. I tried to do it in a very direct, but responsible, fashion, knowing that few readers (customers), especially managers and leaders, could stand much equivocation or hesitation. I also knew that the colorful and lightly documented affirmation works better than the tortuously reasoned explanation.

But why the enormous popularity of what was actually such a simple pre-existing idea? Why its appeal throughout the world to resolutely restrained scholars, implacably temperate managers, and high government officials, all accustomed to balanced and thoughtful calculation? Is it that concrete examples, joined to illustrate a simple idea and presented with some attention to literacy, communicate better than massive analytical reasoning that reads as though it were translated from the German? Is it that provocative assertions are more memorable and persuasive than restrained and balanced explanations, no matter who the audience? Is it that the character of the message is as much the message as its content? Or was mine not simply a different tune, but a new symphony? I don't know.

Of course, I'd do it again and in the same way, given my purposes, even with what more I now know—the good and the bad, the power of facts and the limits of rhetoric. If your mission is the moon, you don't use a car. Don Marquis's cockroach, Archy, provides some final consolation: "an idea is not responsible for who believes in it."

NOTES

[1] Jacques Barzun, "Trains and the Mind of Man," *Holiday* February 1960, p. 21.
[2] For more details see M. M. Zimmerman, *The Super Market: A Revolution in Distribution* (New York, McGraw-Hill Book Company, Inc. 1955), p. 48.
[3] Ibid., pp. 45–47.
[4] *The Affluent Society* (Boston, Houghton-Mifflin Company, 1958), pp. 152–160.
[5] Henry Ford, *My Life and Work* (New York, Doubleday, Page & Company, 1923), pp. 146–147.
[6] Op. cit., p. 20.

SOME SUGGESTIONS FOR FURTHER READING

Enis, B. M. and M. P. Mokwa (1979), "The Marketing Management Matrix: A Taxonomy for Strategy Comprehension," in *Conceptual and Theoretical Developments in Marketing*, O. C. Ferrell, S. W. Brown, and C. M. Lamb, eds., Chicago: American Marketing Association.

Kotler, P. (1972), "What Consumerism Means for Marketers," *Harvard Business Review* (May–June), 48–57.

————— (1973), "The Major Tasks of Marketing Management," *Journal of Marketing* (October), 42–49.

Levitt, T. (1974), *Marketing for Business Growth*, New York: McGraw-Hill.

2 / THE ANALYTICAL FRAMEWORK FOR MARKETING / Wroe Alderson

My assignment is to discuss the analytical framework for marketing. Since our general purpose here is to consider the improvement of the marketing curriculum, I assume that the paper I have been asked to present might serve two functions. The first is to present a perspective of marketing which might be the basis of a marketing course at either elementary or advanced levels. The other is to provide some clue as to the foundations in the social sciences upon which an analytical framework for marketing may be built.

Economics has some legitimate claim to being the original science of markets. Received economic theory provides a framework for the analysis of marketing functions which certainly merits the attention of marketing teachers and practitioners. It is of little importance whether the point of view I am about to present is a version of economics, a hybrid of economics and sociology, or the application of a new emergent general science of human behavior to marketing problems. The analytical framework which I find congenial at least reflects some general knowledge of the social sciences as well as long experience in marketing analysis. In the time available I can do no more than present this view in outline or skeleton form and leave you to determine how to classify it or whether you can use it.

An advantageous place to start for the analytical treatment of marketing is with the radical heterogeneity of markets. Heterogeneity is inherent on both the demand and the supply sides. The homogeneity which the economist assumes for certain purposes is not an antecedent condition for marketing. Insofar as it is ever realized, it emerges out of the marketing process itself.

The materials which are useful to man occur in nature in heterogeneous mixtures which might be called conglomerations since these mixtures have only a random relationship to human needs and activities. The collection of goods in the possessions of a household or an individual also constitutes a heterogeneous supply, but it might be called an assortment since it is related to anticipated patterns of future behavior. The whole economic process may be described as a series of transformations from meaningless to meaningful heterogeneity. Marketing produces as much homogeneity as may be needed to facilitate some of the intermediate economic processes but homogeneity has limited significance or utility for consumer behavior or expectations.

Reprinted from Delbert Duncan (ed.), *Proceedings: Conference of Marketing Teachers from Far Western States* (Berkeley: University of California, 1958), pp. 15–28.

Wroe Alderson was, until his death, professor at the Wharton School of Finance and Commerce at the University of Pennsylvania and director of that school's Management Science Center. He also founded a management consulting firm and served as president of the American Marketing Association. He studied at the George Washington University, the University of Pennsylvania, and the Massachusetts Institute of Technology and was author or editor of several books on marketing. His *Marketing Behavior and Executive Action* is hailed as a landmark in marketing thought.

The marketing process matches materials found in nature or goods fabricated from these materials against the needs of households or individuals. Since the consuming unit has a complex pattern of needs, the matching of these needs creates an assortment of goods in the hands of the ultimate consumer. Actually the marketing process builds up assortments at many stages along the way, each appropriate to the activities taking place at that point. Materials or goods are associated in one way for manufacturing, in another way for wholesale distribution, and in still another for retail display and selling. In between the various types of heterogeneous collections relatively homogeneous supplies are accumulated through the process of grading, refining, chemical reduction and fabrication.

Marketing brings about the necessary transformations in heterogeneous supplies through a multiphase process of sorting. Matching of every individual need would be impossible if the consumer had to search out each item required or the producer had to find the users of a product one by one. It is only the ingenious use of intermediate sorts which make it possible for a vast array of diversified products to enter into the ultimate consumer assortments as needed. Marketing makes mass production possible first by providing the assortment of supplies needed in manufacturing and then taking over the successive transformations which ultimately produce the assortment in the hands of consuming units.

To some who have heard this doctrine expounded, the concept of sorting seems empty, lacking in specific behavioral content, and hence unsatisfactory as a root idea for marketing. One answer is that sorting is a more general and embracing concept than allocation, which many economists regard as the root idea of their science. Allocation is only one of the four basic types of sorting, all of which are involved in marketing. Among these four, allocation is certainly no more significant than assorting, one being the breaking down of a homogeneous supply and the other the building up of a heterogeneous supply. Assorting, in fact, gives more direct expression to the final aim of marketing but allocation performs a major function along the way.

There are several basic advantages in taking sorting as a central concept. It leads directly to a fundamental explanation of the contribution of marketing to the overall economy of human effort in producing and distributing goods. It provides a key to the unending search for efficiency in the marketing function itself. Finally, sorting as the root idea of marketing is consistent with the assumption that heterogeneity is radically and inherently present on both sides of the market and that the aim of marketing is to cope with the heterogeneity of both needs and resources

At this stage of the discussion it is the relative emphasis on assorting as contrasted with allocation which distinguishes marketing theory from at least some versions of economic theory. This emphasis arises naturally from the preoccupation of the market analyst with consumer behavior. One of the most fruitful approaches to understanding what the consumer is doing is the idea that she is engaged in building an assortment, in replenishing or extending an inventory of goods for use by herself and her family. As evidence that this paper is not an attempt to set up a theory in opposition to economics it is acknowledged that the germ of this conception of consumer behavior was first presented some eighty years ago by the Austrian economist Böhm-Bawerk.

The present view is distinguished from that of Böhm-Bawerk in its greater emphasis on the probabilistic approach to the study of market behavior. In considering items for inclusion in her assortment the consumer must make judgments concerning the relative probabilities of future occasions for use. A product in the assortment is intended to provide for some aspect of future behavior. Each such occasion for use carries a rating which is a product of two factors, one a judgment as to the probability of its incidence and the other a measure of the urgency of the need in case it should arise. Consumer goods vary with respect to both measures. One extreme might be illustrated by cigarettes with a probability of use approaching certainty but with relatively small urgency or penalty for deprivation on the particular occasion for use. At the other end of the scale would be a home fire extinguisher with low probability but high urgency attaching to the expected occasion of use.

All of this means that the consumer buyer enters the market as a problem-solver. Solving a problem, either on behalf of a household or on behalf of a marketing organization means reaching a decision in the face of uncertainty. The consumer buyer and the marketing executive are opposite numbers in the double search which pervades marketing; one looking for the goods required to complete an assortment, the other looking for the buyers who are uniquely qualified to use his goods. This is not to say that the behavior of either consumers or executives can be completely characterized as rational problem-solvers. The intention rather is to assert that problem-solving on either side of the market involves a probabilistic approach to heterogeneity on the other side. In order to solve his own problems arising from the heterogeneous demand, the marketing executive should understand the processes of consumer decisions in coping with heterogeneous supplies.

The viewpoint adopted here with respect to the competition among sellers is essentially that which is associated in economics with such names as Schumpeter, Chamberlin and J. M. Clark and with the emphasis on innovative competition, product differentiation and differential advantage. The basic assumption is that every firm occupies a position which is in some respects unique, being differentiated from all others by characteristics of its products, its services, its geographic location or its specific combination of these features. The survival of a firm requires that for some group of buyers it should enjoy a differential advantage over all other suppliers. The sales of any active marketing organization come from a core market made up of buyers with a preference for this source and a fringe market which finds the source acceptable, at least for occasional purchases.

In the case of the supplier of relatively undifferentiated products or services such as the wheat farmer, differential advantage may pertain more to the producing region than to the individual producer. This more diffused type of differential advantage often becomes effective in the market through such agencies as the marketing cooperative. Even the individual producer of raw materials, however, occupies a position in the sense that one market or buyer provides the customary outlet for his product rather than another. The essential point for the present argument is that buyer and seller are not paired at random even in the marketing of relatively homogeneous products but are related to some scale of preference or priority.

Competition for differential advantage implies goals of survival and growth for the marketing organization. The firm is perenially seeking a favorable place to stand and not merely immediate profits from its operations. Differential advantage is subject to change and neutralization by competitors. In dynamic markets differential advantage can only be preserved through continuous innovation. Thus competition presents an analogy to a succession of military campaigns rather than to the pressures and attrition of a single battle. A competitor may gain ground through a successful campaign based on new product features or merchandising ideas. It may lose ground or be forced to fall back on its core position because of the successful campaigns of others. The existence of the core position helps to explain the paradox of survival in the face of the destructive onslaughts of innovative competition.

Buyers and sellers meet in market transactions, each side having tentatively identified the other as an answer to its problem. The market transaction consumes much of the time and effort of all buyers and sellers. The market which operates through a network of costless transactions is only a convenient fiction which economists adopt for certain analytical purposes. Potentially the cost of transactions is so high that controlling or reducing this cost is a major objective in market analysis and executive action. Among economists John R. Commons has given the greatest attention to the transaction as the unit of collective action. He drew a basic distinction between strategic and routine transactions which for present purposes may best be paraphrased as fully negotiated and routine transactions.

The fully negotiated transaction is the prototype of all exchange transactions. It represents a matching of supply and demand after canvassing all of the factors which might affect the decision on either side. The routine transaction proceeds under a set of rules and assumptions established by previous negotiation or as a result of techniques of pre-selling which take the place of negotiation. Transactions on commodity and stock exchanges are carried out at high speed and low cost but only because of carefully established rules governing all aspects of trading. The economical routines of self-service in a supermarket are possible because the individual items on display have been pre-sold. The routine transaction is the end-result of previous marketing effort and ingenious organization of institutions and processes. Negotiation is implicit in all routine transactions. Good routines induce both parties to save time and cost by foregoing explicit negotiation.

The negotiated transaction is the indicated point of departure for the study of exchange values in heterogeneous markets. Many considerations enter into the decision to trade or not to trade on either side of the market. Price is the final balancing or integrating factor which permits the deal to be made. The seller may accept a lower price if relieved from onerous requirements. The buyer may pay a higher price if provided with specified services. The integrating price is one that assures an orderly flow of goods so long as the balance of other considerations remains essentially unchanged. Some economists are uneasy about the role of the negotiated transaction in value determination since bargaining power may be controlling within wide bargaining limits. These limits as analyzed by Commons are set by reference to the best alternatives available to either partner rather than by the automatic control of atomistic competition. This analysis overlooks a major constraint on bargaining in modern markets. Each side has a major stake in a deal that the other side can live with. Only in this way can a stable supply relationship be established so as to achieve the economics of transactional routines. Negotiation is not a zero sum game since the effort to get the best of the other party transaction by transaction may result in a loss to both sides in terms of mounting transactional cost.

In heterogeneous markets price plays an important role in matching a segment of supply with the appropriate segment of demand. The seller frequently has the option of producing a stream-lined product at a low price, a deluxe product at a high price or selecting a price-quality combination somewhere in between. There are considerations which exert a strong influence on the seller toward choosing the price line or lines which will yield the greatest dollar volume of sales. Assuming that various classes of consumers have conflicting claims on the productive capacity of the supplier, it might be argued that the price-quality combination which maximized gross revenue represented the most constructive compromise among these claims. There are parallel considerations with respect to the claims of various participants in the firm's activities on its operating revenue. These claimants include labor, management, suppliers of raw materials and stockholders. Assuming a perfectly fluid situation with respect to bargaining among these claimants, the best chance for a satisfactory solution is at the level of maximum gross revenue. The argument becomes more complicated when the claims of stockholders are given priority, but the goal would still be maximum gross revenue as suggested in a recent paper by William J. Baumol. My own intuition and experience lead me to believe that the maximization of gross revenue is a valid goal of marketing management in heterogeneous markets and adherence to this norm appears to be widely prevalent in actual practice.

What has been said so far is doubtless within the scope of economics or perhaps constitutes a sketch of how some aspects of economic theory might be reconstructed on the assumption of heterogeneity rather than homogeneity as the normal and prevailing condition of the market. But there are issues raised by such notions as enterprise survival, expectations, and consumer behavior, which in my opinion cannot be resolved within the present boundaries of economic science. Here marketing must not hesitate to draw upon the concepts and techniques of the social sciences for the enrichment of its perspective and for the advancement of marketing as an empirical science.

The general economist has his own justifications for regarding the exchange process as a smoothly functioning mechanism which operates in actual markets or which should be taken as the norm and standard to be enforced by government regulation. For the marketing man, whether teacher or practitioner, this Olympian view is untenable. Marketing is concerned with those who are obliged to enter the market to solve their problems, imperfect as the market may be. The persistent and rational action of these participants is the main hope for eliminating or moderating some of these imperfections so that the operation of the market mechanism may approximate that of the theoretical model.

To understand market behavior the marketing man takes a closer look at the nature of the participants. Thus he is obliged, in my opinion, to come to grips with the organized behavior system. Market behavior is primarily group behavior. Individual action in the market is most characteristically action on behalf of some group in which the individual holds membership. The organized behavior system is related to the going concern of John R. Commons but with a deeper interest in what keeps it going. The organized behavior system is also a much broader concept including the more tightly organized groups acting in the market such as business firms and households and loosely connected systems such as the trade center and the marketing channel.

The marketing man needs some rationale for group behavior, some general explanation for the formation and persistence of organized behavior systems. He finds this explanation in the concept of expectations. Insofar as conscious choice is involved, individuals operate in groups because of their expectations of incremental satisfactions as compared to what they could obtain operating alone. The expected satisfactions are of many kinds, direct and indirect. In a group that is productive activity is held together because of an expected surplus over individual output. Other groups such as households and purely social organizations expect direct satisfactions from group association and activities. They also expect satisfactions from future activities facilitated by the assortment of goods held in common. Whatever the character of the system, its vitality arises from the expectations of the individual members and the vigor of their efforts to achieve them through group action. While the existence of the group is entirely derivative, it is capable of operating as if it had a life of its own and was pursuing goals of survival and growth.

Every organized behavior system exhibits a structure related to the functions it performs. Even in the simplest behavior system there must be some mechanism for decision and coordination of effort if the system is to provide incremental satisfaction. Leadership emerges at an early stage to perform such functions as directing the defense of the group. Also quite early is the recognition of the rationing function by which the leader allocates the available goods or satisfactions among the members of the group.

As groups grow in size and their functions become more complex functional specialization increases. The collection of individuals forming a group with their diversified skills and capabilities is a meaningful heterogeneous ensemble vaguely analogous to the assortment of goods which facilitates the activities of the group. The group, however, is held together directly by the generalized expectations of its members. The assortment is held together by a relatively weak or derivative bond. An item "belongs" to the assortment only so long as it has some probability of satisfying the expectations of those who possess it.

This outline began with an attempt to live within the framework of economics or at least within an economic framework amplified to give fuller recognition to heterogeneity on both sides of the market. We have now plunged into sociology in order to deal more effectively with the organized behavior system. Meanwhile we attempt to preserve the line of communication to our origins by basing the explanations of group behavior on the quasi-economic concept of expectations.

The initial plunge into sociology is only the beginning since the marketing man must go considerably further in examining the functions and structure of organized behavior systems. An operating group has a power structure, a communication structure and an operating structure. At each stage an effort should be made to employ the intellectual strategy which has already been suggested. That is, to relate sociological notions to the groundwork of marketing economics through the medium of such concepts as expectations and the processes of matching and sorting.

All members of an organized behavior system occupy some position or status within its power structure. There is a valid analogy between the status of an individual or operating unit within the system and the market position of the firm as an entity. The individual struggles for status within the system having first attained the goal of membership. For most individuals in an industrial society, status in some operating system is a prerequisite for satisfying his expectations. Given the minimal share in the power of the organization inherent in membership, vigorous individuals may aspire to the more ample share of power enjoyed by leadership. Power in the generalized sense referred to here is an underlying objective on which the attainment of all other objectives depends. This aspect of organized behavior has been formulated as the power principle, namely, "The rational individual will act in such a way to promote the power to act." The word *promote* deliberately glosses over an ambivalent attitude toward power, some individuals striving for enhancement and others being content to preserve the power they have.

Any discussion which embraces power as a fundamental concept creates uneasiness for some students on both analytical and ethical ground. My own answer to the analytical problem is to define it as control over expectations. In these terms it is theoretically possible to measure and evaluate power, perhaps even to set a price on it. Certainly it enters into the network of imputations in a business enterprise. Management allocates or rations status and recognition as well as or in lieu of material rewards. As for the ethical problem, it does not arise unless the power principle is substituted for ethics as with Machiavelli. Admitting that the power principle is the essence of expediency, the ethical choice of values and objectives is a different issue. Whatever his specific objectives, the rational individual will wish to serve them expediently.

If any of this discussion of power seems remote from marketing let it be remembered that the major preoccupation of the marketing executive, as pointed out by Oswald Knauth, is with the creation or the activation of organized behavior systems such as marketing channels and sales organizations. No one can be effective in building or using such systems if he ignores the fundamental nature of the power structure.

The communication structure serves the group in various ways. It promotes the survival of the system by reinforcing the individual's sense of belonging. It transmits instructions and operating commands or signals to facilitate coordinated effort. It is related to expectations through the communication of explicit or implied commitments. Negotiations between suppliers and customers and much that goes on in the internal management of a marketing organization can best be understood as a two-way exchange of commitments. A division sales manager, for example, may commit himself to produce a specified volume of sales. His superior in turn may commit certain company resources to support his efforts and make further commitments as to added rewards as an incentive to outstanding performance.

For some purposes it is useful to regard marketing processes as a flow of goods and a parallel flow of informative and persuasive messages. In these terms the design of communication facilities and channels becomes a major aspect of the creation of marketing systems. Marketing has yet to digest and apply the insights of the rapidly developing field of communication theory which in turn has drawn freely from both engineering and biological and social sciences. One stimulating idea expounded by Norbert Wiener and others is that of the feedback of information in a control system. Marketing and advertising research are only well started on the task of installing adequate feedback circuits for controlling the deployment of marketing effort.

Social psychology is concerned with some problems of communication which are often encountered in marketing systems. For example, there are the characteristic difficulties of vertical communication which might be compared to the transmission of telephone messages along a power line. Subordinates often hesitate to report bad news to their superiors fearing to take the brunt of emotional reactions. Superiors learn to be cautious in any discussion of the subordinate's status for fear that a casual comment will be interpreted as a commitment. There is often a question as to when a subordinate should act and report and when he should refer a matter for decision upstream. Progress in efficiency, which is a major goal in marketing, depends in substantial part on technological improvement in communication facilities and organizational skill in using them.

The third aspect of structure involved in the study of marketing systems is operating structure. Effective specialization within an organization requires that activities which are functionally similar be placed together but properly coordinated with other activities. Billing by wholesaler grocers, for example, has long been routinized in a separate billing department. In more recent years the advances in mechanical equipment have made it possible to coordinate inventory control with billing, using the same set of punch cards for both functions. Designing an operating structure is a special application of sorting. As in the sorting of goods to facilitate handling, there are generally several alternative schemes for classifying activities presenting problems of choice to the market planner.

Functional specialization and the design of appropriate operating structures is a constant problem in the effective use of marketing channels. Some functions can be performed at either of two or more stages. One stage may be the best choice in terms of economy or effectiveness. Decisions on the placement of a function may have to be reviewed periodically since channels do not remain static. Similar considerations arise in the choice of channels. Some types of distributors or dealers may be equipped to perform a desired service while others may not. Often two or more channels with somewhat specialized roles are required to move a product to the consumer. The product's sponsor can maintain perspective in balancing out these various facilities by thinking in terms of a total operating system including his own sales organization and the marketing channels employed.

The dynamics of market organization pose basic problems for the marketing student and the marketing executive in a free enterprise economy. Reference has already been made to the competitive pursuit of differential advantage. One way in which a firm can gain differential advantage is by organizing the market in a way that is favorable to its own operations. This is something else than the attainment of a monopolistic position in relation to current or potential competitors. It means creating a pattern for dealing with customers or suppliers which persists because there are advantages on both sides. Offering guarantees against price declines on floor stocks is one example of market organization by the seller. Attempts to systematize the flow of orders may range from various services offered to customers or suppliers all the way to complete vertical integration. Another dynamic factor affecting the structure of markets may be generalized under the term "closure." It frequently happens that some marketing system is incomplete or out of balance in some direction. The act of supplying the missing element constitutes closure, enabling the system to handle a greater output or to operate at a new level of efficiency. The incomplete system in effect cries out for closure. To observe this need is to recognize a form of market opportunity. This is one of the primary ways in which new enterprises develop, since there may be good reasons why the missing service cannot be performed by the existing organizations which need the service. A food broker, for example, can cover a market for several accounts of moderate size in a way that the individual manufacturer would not be able to cover it for himself.

There is a certain compensating effect between closure as performed by new or supplementary marketing enterprises and changes in market organization brought about by the initiative of existing firms in the pursuit of differential advantage. The pursuit of a given form of advantage, in fact, may carry the total marketing economy out of balance in a given direction creating the need and opportunity for closure. Such an economy could never be expected to reach a state of equilibrium, although the tendency toward structural balance is one of the factors in its dynamics. Trade regulation may be embraced within this dynamic pattern as an attempt of certain groups to organize the market to their own advantage through political means. Entering into this political struggle to determine the structure of markets are some political leaders and some administrative officials who regard themselves as representing the consumer's interests. It seems reasonable to believe that the increasing sophistication and buying skill of consumers is one of the primary forces offsetting the tendency of the free market economy to turn into something else through the working out of its inherent dynamic forces. This was the destiny foreseen for the capitalistic system by Schumpeter, even though he was one of its staunchest advocates.

The household as an organized behavior system must be given special attention in creating an analytical framework for marketing. The household is an operating entity with an assortment of goods and assets and with economic functions to perform. Once a primary production unit, the household has lost a large part of these activities to manufacturing and service enterprises. Today its economic operations are chiefly expressed through earning and spending. In the typical household there is some specialization between the husband as primary earner and the wife as chief purchasing agent for the household. It may be assumed that she becomes increasingly competent in buying as she surrenders her production activities such as canning, baking and dressmaking, and devotes more of her time and attention to shopping. She is a rational problem solver as she samples what the market has to offer in her effort to maintain a balanced inventory or assortment of goods to meet expected occasions of use. This is not an attempt to substitute Economic Woman for the discredited fiction of Economic Man. It is only intended to assert that the decision structure of consumer buying is similar to that for industrial buying. Both business executive and housewife enter the market as rational problem solvers, even though there are other aspects of personality in either case.

An adequate perspective on the household for marketing purposes must recognize several facets of its activities. It is an organized behavior system with its aspects of power, communication, and operating structure. It is the locus of forms of behavior other than instrumental or goal-seeking activities. A convenient three-way division, derived from the social sciences, recognizes instrumental, congenial, and symptomatic behavior. Congenial behavior is that kind of activity engaged in for its own sake and presumably yielding direct satisfactions. It is exemplified by the act of consumption as compared to all of the instrumental activities which prepare the way for consumption. Symptomatic behavior reflects maladjustment and is neither pleasure-giving in itself nor an efficient pursuit of goals. Symptomatic behavior is functional only to the extent that it serves as a signal to others that the individual needs help.

Some studies of consumer motivation have given increasing attention to symptomatic behavior or to the projection of symptoms of personality adjustment which might affect consumer buying. The present view is that the effort to classify individuals by personality types is less urgent for marketing than the classification of families. Four family types with characteristically different buying behavior have been suggested growing out of the distinction between the instrumental and congenial aspects of normal behavior. Even individuals who are fairly well adjusted in themselves will form a less than perfect family if not fully adapted to each other.

On the instrumental side of household behavior it would seem to be desirable that the members be well coordinated as in any other operating system. If not, they will not deliver the maximum impact in pursuit of family goals. On the congenial side it would appear desirable for the members of a household to be compatible. That means enjoying the same things, cherishing the same goals, preferring joint activities to solitary pursuits or the company of others. These two distinctions yield an obvious four-way classification. The ideal is the family that is coordinated in its instrumental activities and compatible in its congenial activities. A rather joyless household which might nevertheless be well managed and prosperous in material terms is the coordinated but incompatible household. The compatible but uncoordinated family would tend to be happy-go-lucky and irresponsible with obvious consequences for buying behavior. The household which was both uncoordinated and incompatible would usually be tottering on the brink of dissolution. It might be held together formally by scruples against divorce, by concern for children, or by the dominant power of one member over the others. This symptomology of families does not exclude an interest in the readjustment of individuals exhibiting symptomatic behavior. Such remedial action lies in the sphere of the psychiatrist and the social worker, whereas the marketer is chiefly engaged in supplying goods to families which are still functioning as operating units.

All of the discussion of consumers so far limits itself to the activities of the household purchasing agent. Actually the term *consumption* as it appears in marketing and economic literature nearly always means consumer buying. Some day marketing may need to look beyond the act of purchasing to a study of consumption proper. The occasion for such studies will arise out of the problems of inducing consumers to accept innovations or the further proliferation of products to be included in the household assortment. Marketing studies at this depth will not only borrow from the social sciences but move into the realm of esthetic and ethical values. What is the use of a plethora of goods unless the buyer derives genuine satisfaction from them? What is the justification of surfeit if the acquisition of goods serves as a distraction from activities which are essential to the preservation of our culture and of the integrity of our personalities?

It has been suggested that a study of consumption might begin with the problem of choice in the presence of abundance. The scarce element then is the time or capacity for enjoyment. The bookworm confronted with the thousands of volumes available in a great library must choose in the face of this type of limitation.

The name *hedonomics* would appear to be appropriate for this field of study suggesting the management of the capacity to enjoy. Among the problems for hedonomics is the pleasure derived from the repetition of a familiar experience as compared with the enjoyment of a novel experience or an old experience with some novel element. Another is the problem of direct experience versus symbolic experience, with the advantages of intensity on the one hand and on the other the possibility of embracing a greater range of possible ideas and sensations by relying on symbolic representations. Extensive basic research will probably be necessary before hedonomics can be put to work in marketing or for the enrichment of human life through other channels.

This paper barely suffices to sketch the analytical framework for marketing. It leaves out much of the area of executive decision-making in marketing on such matters as the weighing of uncertainties and the acceptance of risk in the commitment of resources. It leaves out market planning which is rapidly becoming a systematic discipline centering in the possibilities for economizing time and space as well as resources. It leaves out all but the most casual references to advertising and demand formation. Advertising is certainly one of the most difficult of marketing functions to embrace within a single analytical framework. It largely ignores the developing technology of physical distribution. Hopefully what it does accomplish is to show how the essentially economic problems of marketing may yield to a more comprehensive approach drawing on the basic social sciences for techniques and enriched perspective.

SOME SUGGESTIONS FOR FURTHER READING

Alderson, W. (1957), *Marketing Behavior and Executive Action,* Homewood, IL: Richard D. Irwin, Inc.

———— and L. Martin (1965), "Toward a Formal Theory of Transactions and Transvections," *Journal of Marketing Research* (May), 117–127.

Glaser, S. and M. I. Halliday (1979), "A Systems Foundation for Alderson's Functionalism," in *Macromarketing Evolution of Thought,* G. Fisk, R. Nason, and P. White, eds., Boulder, CO: University of Colorado, 71–81.

Nicosia, F. M. (1962), "Marketing and Alderson's Functionalism," *Journal of Business,* Volume 35, 403–13.

Verdoorn, P. J. (1956), "Marketing from the Producer's Point of View," *Journal of Marketing* (January), 221–235.

3 / MARKETING AND ECONOMIC DEVELOPMENT / Peter F. Drucker

MARKETING AS A BUSINESS DISCIPLINE

The distinguished pioneer of marketing, whose memory we honor today, was largely instrumental in developing marketing as a systematic business discipline—in teaching us how to go about, in an orderly, purposeful and planned way to find and create customers; to identify and define markets; to create new ones and promote them; to integrate customers' needs, wants, and preferences, and the intellectual and creative capacity and skills of an industrial society, toward the design of new and better products and of new distributive concepts and processes.

On this contribution and similar ones of other Founding Fathers of marketing during the last half century rests the rapid emergence of marketing as perhaps the most advanced, certainly the most "scientific" of all functional business disciplines.

But Charles Coolidge Parlin also contributed as a Founding Father toward the development of marketing as a *social discipline*. He helped give us the awareness, the concepts, and the tools that make us understand marketing as a dynamic process of society through which business enterprise is integrated productively with society's purposes and human values. It is in marketing, as we now understand it, that we satisfy individual and social values, needs, and wants—be it through producing goods, supplying services, fostering innovation, or creating satisfaction. Marketing, as we have come to understand it, has its focus on the customer, that is, on the individual making decisions within a social structure and within a personal and social value system. Marketing is thus the process through which economy is integrated into society to serve human needs.

I am not competent to speak about marketing in the first sense, marketing as a functional discipline of business. I am indeed greatly concerned with marketing in this meaning. One could not be concerned, as I am, with the basic institutions of industrial society in general and with the management of business enterprise in particular, without a deep and direct concern with marketing. But in this field I am a consumer of marketing alone—albeit a heavy one. I am not capable of making a contribution. I would indeed be able to talk about the wants and needs I have which I, as a consumer of marketing, hope that you, the men of marketing,

Reprinted from the *Journal of Marketing*, published by the American Marketing Association (January, 1958), pp. 252–259. This article is based on the Charles Coolidge Parlin Memorial Lecture sponsored by the Philadelphia Chapter of the American Marketing Association in 1957.

Peter F. Drucker, an internationally recognized management consultant and professor at Claremont Graduate School, is perhaps best known for his widely read management books, including *Managing for Results* and *Management: Tasks, Responsibilities, Practices*. A native of Vienna, he holds an LL.D. degree from the University of Frankfurt and honorary degrees from two American universities and from one in Japan.

will soon supply:—a theory of pricing, for instance, that can serve, as true theories should, as the foundation for actual pricing decisions and for an understanding of price behavior; or a consumer-focused concept and theory of competition. But I could not produce any of these "new products" of marketing which we want. I cannot contribute myself. To use marketing language, I am not even "effective demand," in these fields as yet.

THE ROLE OF MARKETING

I shall today in my remarks confine myself to the second meaning in which marketing has become a discipline: The role of marketing in economy and society. And I shall single out as my focus the role of marketing in the economic development, especially of underdeveloped "growth" countries.

My thesis is very briefly as follows. Marketing occupies a critical role in respect to the development of such "growth" areas. Indeed marketing is the most important "multiplier" of such development. It is in itself in every one of these areas the least developed, the most backward part of the economic system. Its development, above all others, makes possible economic integration and the fullest utilization of whatever assets and productive capacity an economy already possesses. It mobilizes latent economic energy. It contributes to the greatest needs: that for the rapid development of entrepreneurs and managers, and at the same time it may be the easiest area of managerial work to get going. The reason is that, thanks to men like Charles Coolidge Parlin, it is the most systematized and, therefore, the most learnable and the most teachable of all areas of business management and entrepreneurship.

INTERNATIONAL AND INTERRACIAL INEQUALITY

Looking at this world of ours, we see some essentially new facts.

For the first time in man's history the whole world is united and unified. This may seem a strange statement in view of the conflicts and threats of suicidal wars that scream at us from every headline. But conflict has always been with us. What is new is that today all of mankind shares the same vision, the same objective, the same goal, the same hope, and believes in the same tools. This vision might, in gross over-simplification, be called "industrialization."

It is the belief that it is possible for man to improve his economic lot through systematic, purposeful, and directed effort—individually as well as for an entire society. It is the belief that we have the tools at our disposal—the technological, the conceptual, and the social tools—to enable man to raise himself, through his own efforts, at least to a level that we in this country would consider poverty, but which for most of our world would be almost unbelievable luxury.

And this is an irreversible new fact. It has been made so by these true agents of revolution in our times: the new tools of communication—the dirt road, the truck, and the radio, which have penetrated even the furthest, most isolated and most primitive community.

This is new, and cannot be emphasized too much and too often. It is both a tremendous vision and a tremendous danger in that catastrophe must result if it cannot be satisfied, at least to a modest degree.

But at the same time we have a new, unprecedented danger, that of international and interracial inequality. We on the North American continent are a mere tenth of the world population, including our Canadian friends and neighbors. But we have at least 75 per cent of the world income. And the 75 per cent of the world population whose income is below $100 per capita a year receive together perhaps no more than 10 per cent of the world's income. This is inequality of income, as great as anything the world has ever seen. It is accompanied by very high equality of income in the developed countries, especially in ours where we are in the process of proving that an industrial society does not have to live in extreme tension between the few very rich and the many very poor as lived all earlier societies of man. But what used to be national inequality and economic tension is now rapidly becoming international (and unfortunately also interracial) inequality and tension.

This is also brand new. In the past there were tremendous differences between societies and cultures: in their beliefs, their concepts, their ways of life, and their knowledge. The Frankish knight who went on Crusade was an ignorant and illiterate boor according to the standards of the polished courtiers of Constantinople or of his Moslem enemies. But economically his society and theirs were exactly alike. They had the same sources of income, the same productivity of labor, the same forms and channels of investment, the same economic institutions, and the same distribution of income and wealth. Economically the Frankish knight, however much a barbarian he appeared, was at home in the societies of the East; and so was his serf. Both fitted in immediately and without any difficulty.

And this has been the case of all societies that went above the level of purely primitive tribe.

The inequality in our world today, however, between nations and races, is therefore a new—and a tremendously dangerous—phenomenon.

What we are engaged in today is essentially a race between the promise of economic development and the threat of international worldwide class war. The economic development is the opportunity of this age. The class war is the danger. Both are new. Both are indeed so new that most of us do not even see them as yet. But they are the essential economic realities of this industrial age of ours. And whether we shall realize the opportunity or succumb to danger will largely decide not only the economic future of this world—it may largely decide its spiritual, its intellectual, its political, and its social future.

SIGNIFICANCE OF MARKETING

Marketing is central in this new situation. For marketing is one of our most potent levers to convert the danger into the opportunity.

To understand this we must ask: What do we mean by "under-developed"?

The first answer is, of course, that we mean areas of very low income. But income is, after all, a result. It is a result first of extreme agricultural over-population in which the great bulk of the people have to find a living on the land which, as a result, cannot even produce enough food to feed them, let alone produce a surplus. It is certainly a result of low productivity. And both, in a vicious circle, mean that there is not enough capital for investment and very low productivity of what is being invested—owing largely to misdirection of investment into unessential and unproductive channels.

All this we know today and understand. Indeed we have learned during the last few years a very great deal both about the structure of an under-developed economy and about the theory and dynamics of economic development.

What we tend to forget, however, is that the essential aspect of an "under-developed" economy and the factor of absence which keeps it "under-developed," is the inability to organize economic efforts and energies, to bring together resources, wants, and capacities, and so to convert a self-limiting static system into creative, self-generating organic growth.

And this is where marketing comes in.

Lack of Development in "Under-developed" Countries

First, in every "under-developed" country I know of, marketing is the most under-developed—or the least developed—part of the economy, if only because of the strong, pervasive prejudice against the middle-man.

As a result, these countries are stunted by inability to make effective use of the little they have. Marketing might by itself go far toward changing the entire economic tone of the existing system—without any change in methods of production, distribution of population, or of income.

It would make the producers capable of producing marketable products by providing them with standards, with quality demands, and with specifications for their product. It would make the product capable of being brought to markets instead of perishing on the way. And it would make the consumer capable of discrimination, that is, of obtaining the greatest value for his very limited purchasing power.

In every one of these countries, marketing profits are characteristically low. Indeed, the people engaged in marketing barely eke out a subsistence living. And "mark-ups" are minute by our standards. But marketing costs are outrageously high. The waste in distribution and marketing, if only from spoilage or from the accumulation of unsalable inventories that clog the shelves for years, has to be seen to be believed. And marketing service is by and large all but non-existent.

What is needed in any "growth" country to make economic development realistic, and at the same time produce a vivid demonstration of what economic development can produce, is a marketing system:—a system of physical distribution, a financial system to make possible the distribution of goods, and finally actual marketing, that is, an actual system of integrating wants, needs, and purchasing power of the consumer with capacity and resources of production.

This need is largely masked today because marketing is so often confused with the traditional "trader and merchant" of which every one of these countries has more than enough. It would be one of our most important contributions to the development of "under-developed" countries to get across the fact that marketing is something quite different.

It would be basic to get across the triple function of marketing—the function of crystallizing and directing demand for maximum productive effectiveness and efficiency; the function of guiding production purposefully toward maximum consumer satisfaction and consumer value; the function of creating discrimination that then gives rewards to those who really contribute excellence, and that then also penalizes the monopolist, the slothful, or those who only want to take but do not want to contribute or to risk.

Utilization by the Entrepreneur

Marketing is also the most easily accessible "multiplier" of managers and entrepreneurs in an "under-developed" growth area. And managers and entrepreneurs are the foremost need of these countries. In the first place, "economic development" is not a force of nature. It is the result of the action, the purposeful, responsible, risk-taking action, of men as entrepreneurs and managers.

Certainly it is the entrepreneur and manager who alone can convey to the people of these countries an understanding of what economic development means and how it can be achieved.

Marketing can convert latent demand into effective demand. It cannot, by itself, create purchasing power. But it can uncover and channel all purchasing power that exists. It can, therefore, create rapidly the conditions for a much higher level of economic activity than existed before, can create the opportunities for the entrepreneur.

It then can create the stimulus for the development of modern, responsible, professional management by creating opportunity for the producer who knows how to plan, how to organize, how to lead people, how to innovate.

In most of these countries markets are of necessity very small. They are too small to make it possible to organize distribution for a single-product line in any effective manner. As a result, without a marketing organization, many products for which there is an adequate demand at a reasonable price cannot be distributed; or worse, they can be produced and distributed only under monopoly conditions. A marketing system is needed which serves as the joint and common channel for many producers if any of them is to be able to come into existence and to stay in existence.

This means in effect that a marketing system in the "under-developed" countries is the *creator of small business,* is the only way in which a man of vision and daring can become a businessman and an entrepreneur himself. This is thereby also the only way in which a true middle class can develop in the countries in which the habit of investment in productive enterprise has still to be created.

Developer of Standards

Marketing in an "under-developed" country is the developer of standards—of standards for product and service as well as of standards of conduct, of integrity, of reliability, of foresight, and of concern for the basic long-range impact of decisions on the customer, the supplier, the economy, and the society.

Rather than go on making theoretical statements let me point to one illustration: The impact Sears Roebuck has had on several countries of Latin America. To be sure, the countries of Latin America in which Sears operates—Mexico, Brazil, Cuba, Venezuela, Colombia, and Peru—are not "under-developed" in the same sense in which Indonesia or the Congo are "under-developed." Their average income, although very low by our standards, is at least two times, perhaps as much as four or five times, that of the truly "under-developed" countries in which the bulk of mankind still live. Still in every respect except income level these Latin American countries are at best "developing." And they have all the problems of economic development—perhaps even in more acute form than the countries of Asia and Africa, precisely because their development has been so fast during the last ten years.

It is also true that Sears in these countries is not a "low-price" merchandiser. It caters to the middle class in the richer of these countries, and to the upper middle class in the poorest of these countries. Incidentally, the income level of these groups is still lower than that of the worker in the industrial sector of our economy.

Still Sears is a mass-marketer even in Colombia or Peru. What is perhaps even more important, it is applying in these "under-developed" countries exactly the same policies and principles it applies in this country, carries substantially the same merchandise (although most of it produced in the countries themselves), and applies the same concepts of marketing it uses in Indianapolis or Philadelphia. Its impact and experience are, therefore, a fair test of what marketing principles, marketing knowledge, and marketing techniques can achieve.

The impact of this one American business which does not have more than a mere handful of stores in these countries and handles no more than a small fraction of the total retail business of these countries is truly amazing. In the first place, Sears' latent purchasing power has fast become actual purchasing power. Or, to put it less theoretically, people have begun to organize their buying and to go out for value in what they do buy.

Secondly, by the very fact that it builds one store in one city, Sears forces a revolution in retailing throughout the whole surrounding area. It forces store modernization. It forces consumer credit. It forces a different attitude toward the customer, toward the store clerk, toward the supplier, and toward the merchandise itself. It forces other retailers to adopt modern methods of pricing, of inventory control, of training, of window display, and what have you.

The greatest impact Sears has had, however, is the multiplication of new industrial business for which Sears creates a marketing channel. Because it has had to sell goods manufactured in these countries rather than import them (if only because of foreign exchange restrictions), Sears has been instrumental in getting established literally hundreds of new manufacturers making goods which, a few years ago, could not be made in the country, let alone be sold in adequate quantity. Simply to satisfy its own marketing needs, Sears has had to insist on standards of workmanship, quality, and delivery—that is, on standards of production management, of technical management, and above all of the management of people—which, in a few short years, have advanced the art and science of management in these countries by at least a generation.

I hardly need to add that Sears is not in Latin America for reasons of philanthropy, but because it is good and profitable business with extraordinary growth potential. In other words, Sears is in Latin America because marketing is the major opportunity in a "growth economy"—precisely because its absence is a major economic gap and the greatest need.

The Discipline of Marketing

Finally, marketing is critical in economic development because marketing has become so largely systematized, so largely both learnable and teachable. It is the discipline among all our business disciplines that has advanced the furthest.

I do not forget for a moment how much we still have to learn in marketing. But we should also not forget that most of what we have learned so far we have learned in a form in which we can express it in general concepts, in valid principles and, to a substantial degree, in quantifiable measurements. This, above all others, was the achievement of that generation to whom Charles Coolidge Parlin was leader and inspiration.

A critical factor in this world of ours is the learnability and teachability of what it means to be an entrepreneur and manager. For it is the entrepreneur and the manager who alone can cause economic development to happen. The world needs them, therefore, in very large numbers; and it needs them fast.

Obviously this need cannot be supplied by our supplying entrepreneurs and managers, quite apart from the fact that we hardly have the surplus. Money we can supply. Technical assistance we can supply, and should supply more. But the supply of men we can offer to the people in the "under-developed" countries is of necessity a very small one.

The demand is also much too urgent for it to be supplied by slow evolution through experience, or through dependence on the emergence of "naturals." The danger that lies in the inequality today between the few countries that have and the great many countries that have not is much too great to permit a wait of centuries. Yet it take centuries if we depend on experience and slow evolution for the supply of entrepreneurs and managers adequate to the needs of a modern society.

There is only one way in which man has ever been able to short-cut experience, to telescope development, in other words, to *learn something*. That way is to have available the distillate of experience and skill in the form of knowledge, of concepts, of generalization, of measurement—in the form of *discipline*, in other words.

THE DISCIPLINE OF ENTREPRENEURSHIP

Many of us today are working on the the fashioning of such a discipline of entrepreneurship and management. Maybe we are further along than most of us realize.

Certainly in what has come to be called "Operation Research and Synthesis" we have the first beginnings of a systematic approach to the entrepreneurial task of purposeful risk-taking and innovation—so far only an approach, but a most promising one, unless indeed we become so enamored with the gadgets and techniques as to forget purpose and aim.

We are at the beginning perhaps also of an understanding of the basic problems of organizing people of diversified and highly advanced skill and judgment together in one effective organization, although again no one so far would, I am convinced, claim more for us than that we have begun at last to ask intelligent questions.

But marketing, although it only covers one functional area in the field, has something that can be called a discipline. It has developed general concepts, that is, theories that explain a multitude of phenomena in simple statements. It even has measurements that record "facts" rather than opinions. In marketing, therefore, we already possess a learnable and teachable approach to this basic and central problem not only of the "under-developed" countries but of all countries. All of us have today the same survival stake in economic development. The risk and danger of international and interracial inequality are simply too great.

Marketing is obviously not a cure-all, not a panacea. It is only one thing we need. But it answers a critical need. At the same time marketing is most highly developed.

Indeed without marketing as the hinge on which to turn, economic development will almost have to take the totalitarian form. A totalitarian system can be defined economically as one in which economic development is being attempted without marketing, indeed as one in which marketing is suppressed. Precisely because it first looks at the values and wants of the individual, and because it then develops people to act purposefully and responsibly—that is, because of its effectiveness in developing a free economy—marketing is suppressed in a totalitarian system. If we want economic development in freedom and responsibility, we have to build it on the development of marketing.

In the new and unprecedented world we live in, a world which knows both a new unity of vision and growth and a new and most dangerous cleavage, marketing has a special and central role to play. This role goes beyond "getting the stuff out the back door," beyond "getting the most sales with the least cost," beyond "the optimal integration of our values and wants as customers, citizens, and persons, with our productive resources and intellectual achievements"—the role marketing plays in a developed society.

In a developing economy, marketing is, of course, all of this. But in addition, in an economy that is striving to break the age-old bondage of man to misery, want, and destitution, marketing is also the catalyst for the transmutation of latent resources into actual resources, of desires into accomplishments, and the development of responsible economic leaders and informed economic citizens.

SOME SUGGESTIONS FOR FURTHER READING

Clark, Thomas B. and Robert M. Fulmer (1973), "The Limits to *The Limits of Growth,*" *Business Horizons* (June), 88–96.

Drucker, P. F. (1980), *Managing in Turbulent Times,* New York: Harper & Row.

Enis, Ben M. and Norman Kangun (1976), "Zero Economic Growth: A Marketing Perspective and Public Policy Implications," *Proceedings,* Macro-Marketing Conference, Boulder, CO.: American Marketing Ass'n.

Kahn, Herman, W. Browne, and L. Martel (1976), "The Next 200 Years: *A Scenario for America and the World,*" New York: William Morrow and Company.

Meadows, Donnella and others (1972), *The Limits to Growth,* New York: Universe Books.

Mesarovic, Mihajlo and Eduard Pestel (1974), *Mankind at the Turning Point,* New York: E. P. Dutton & Company.

Van Dam, A. (1977), "Marketing in the New International Economic Order," *Journal of Marketing* (January), 19–23.

4 / THE MARKETING REVOLUTION /
Robert J. Keith

The consumer, not the company, is in the middle.

In today's economy the consumer, the man or woman who buys the product, is at the absolute dead center of the business universe. Companies revolve around the customer, not the other way around.

Growing acceptance of this consumer concept has had, and will have, far-reaching implications for business, achieving a virtual revolution in economic thinking. As the concept gains ever greater acceptance, marketing is emerging as the most important single function in business.

A REVOLUTION IN SCIENCE

A very apt analogy can be drawn with another revolution, one that goes back to the sixteenth century. At that time astronomers had great difficulty predicting the movements of the heavenly bodies. Their charts and computations and celestial calendars enabled them to estimate the approximate positions of the planets on any given date. But their calculations were never exact—there was always a variance.

Then a Polish scientist named Nicolaus Copernicus proposed a very simple answer to the problem. If, he proposed, we assume that the sun, and not the earth, is at the center of our system, and that the earth moves around the sun instead of the sun moving around the earth, all our calculations will prove correct.

The Pole's idea raised a storm of controversy. The earth, everyone knew, was at the center of the universe. But another scientist named Galileo put the theory to test—and it worked. The result was a complete upheaval in scientific and philosophic thought. The effects of Copernicus's revolutionary idea are still being felt today.

A REVOLUTION IN MARKETING

In much the same way American business in general—and Pillsbury in particular—is undergoing a revolution of its own today: a marketing revolution.

This revolution stems from the same idea stated in the opening sentence of

Reprinted from the *Journal of Marketing*, published by the American Marketing Association (January, 1960), pp. 35–38.
The late Robert J. Keith was president of The Pillsbury Company and a director of Pillsbury and other national companies. During his 25 years with Pillsbury, his responsibility centered around the grocery products division and the refrigerated-products division.

this article. No longer is the company at the center of the business universe. Today the customer is at the center.

Our attention has shifted from problems of production to problems of marketing, from the product we *can* make to the product the consumer *wants* us to make, from the company itself to the market place.

The marketing revolution has only begun. It is reasonable to expect that its implications will grow in the years to come, and that lingering effects will be felt a century, or more than one century, from today.

So far the theory has only been advanced, tested, and generally proved correct. As more and more businessmen grasp the concept, and put it to work, our economy will become more truly marketing oriented.

PILLSBURY'S PATTERN: FOUR ERAS

Here is the way the marketing revolution came about at Pillsbury. The experience of this company has followed a typical pattern. There has been nothing unique, and each step in the evolution of the marketing concept has been taken in a way that is more meaningful because the steps are, in fact, typical.

Today in our company the marketing concept finds expression in the simple statement, "Nothing happens at Pillsbury until a sale is made." This statement represents basic reorientation on the part of our management. For, not too many years ago, the ordering of functions in our business placed finances first, production second, and sales last.

How did we arrive at our present point of view? Pillsbury's progress in the marketing revolution divides neatly into four separate eras—eras which parallel rather closely the classic pattern of development in the marketing revolution.

1st ERA—PRODUCTION ORIENTED

First came the era of manufacturing. It began with the formation of the company in 1869 and continued into the 1930s. It is significant that the *idea* for the formation of our company came from the *availability* of high-quality wheat and the *proximity* of water power—and not from the availability and proximity of growing major market areas, or the demand for better, less expensive, more convenient flour products.

Of course, these elements were potentially present. But the two major elements which fused in the mind of Charles A. Pillsbury and prompted him to invest his modest capital in a flour mill were, on the one hand, wheat, and, on the other hand, water power. His principal concern was with production, not marketing.

His thought and judgment were typical of the business thinking of his day, And such thinking was adequate and proper for the times.

Our company philosophy in this era might have been stated this way: "We are professional flour millers. Blessed with a supply of the finest North American wheat, plenty of water power, and excellent milling machinery, we produce flour of the highest quality. Our basic function is to mill high-quality flour, and of course (and almost incidentally) we must hire salesmen to sell it, just as we hire accountants to keep our books."

The young company's first new product reveals an interesting example of the thinking of this era. The product was middlings, the bran left over after milling. Millfeed, as the product came to be known, proved a valuable product because it was an excellent nutrient for cattle. But the impetus to launch the new product came not from a consideration of the nutritional needs of cattle or a marketing analysis. It came primarily from the desire to dispose of a by-product! The new product decision was production oriented, not marketing oriented.

2nd ERA—SALES ORIENTED

In the 1930s Pillsbury moved into its second era of development as a marketing company. This was the era of sales. For the first time we began to be highly conscious of the consumer, her wants, and her prejudices, as a key factor in the business equation. We established a commercial research department to provide us with facts about the market.

We also became more aware of the importance of our dealers, the wholesale and retail grocers who provided a vital link in our chain of distribution from the mill to the home. Knowing that consumers and dealers as well were vital to the company's success, we could no longer simply mark them down as unknowns in our figuring. With this realization, we took the first step along the road to becoming a marketing company.

Pillsbury's thinking in this second era could be summed up like this: "We are a flour-milling company, manufacturing a number of products for the consumer market. We must have a first-rate sales organization which can dispose of all the products we can make at a favorable price. We must back up this sales force with consumer advertising and market intelligence. We want our salesmen and our dealers to have all the tools they need for moving the output of our plants to the consumer."

Still not a marketing philosophy, but we were getting closer.

3rd ERA—MARKETING ORIENTED

It was at the start of the present decade that Pillsbury entered the marketing era. The amazing growth of our consumer business as the result of introducing baking mixes provided the immediate impetus. But the groundwork had been laid by key men who developed our sales concepts in the middle forties.

With the new cake mixes, products of our research program, ringing up sales on the cash register, and with the realization that research and production could produce literally hundreds of new and different products, we faced for the first time the necessity for selecting the best new products. We needed a set of criteria for selecting the kind of products we would manufacture. We needed an organization to establish and maintain these criteria, and for attaining maximum sale of the products we did select.

We needed, in fact, to build into our company a new management function which would direct and control all the other corporate functions from procurement to production to advertising to sales. This function was marketing. Our solution was to establish the present marketing department.

This department developed the criteria which we would use in determining which products to market. *And these criteria were, and are, nothing more nor less than those of the consumer herself.* We moved the mountain out to find out what Mahomet, and Mrs. Mahomet, wanted. The company's purpose was no longer to mill flour, nor to manufacture a wide variety of products, but to satisfy the needs and desires, both actual and potential, of our customers.

If we were to restate our philosophy during the past decade as simply as possible, it would read: "We make and sell products for consumers."

The business universe, we realized, did not have room at the center for Pillsbury or any other company or groups of companies. It was already occupied by the customers.

This is the concept at the core of the marketing revolution. How did we put it to work for Pillsbury?

The Brand-manager Concept

The first move was to transform our small advertising department into a marketing department. The move involved far more than changing the name on organizational charts. It required the introduction of a new, and vitally important, organizational concept—the brand-manager concept.

The brand-manager idea is the very backbone of marketing at Pillsbury. The man who bears the title, brand manager, has total accountability for results. He directs the marketing of his product as if it was his own business. Production does its job, and finance keeps the profit figures. Otherwise, the brand manager has total responsibility for marketing his product. This responsibility encompasses pricing, commercial research, competitive activity, home service and publicity coordination, legal details, budgets, advertising plans, sales promotion, and execution of plans. The brand manager must think first, last, and always of his sales target, the consumer.

Marketing permeates the entire organization. Marketing plans and executes the sale—all the way from the inception of the product idea, through its development and distribution, to the customer purchase. Marketing begins and ends with the consumer. New product ideas are conceived after careful study of her wants and needs, her likes and dislikes. Then marketing takes the idea and marshals all the forces of the corporation to translate the idea into product and the product into sales.

In the early days of the company, consumer orientation did not seem so important. The company made flour, and flour was a staple—no one would question the availability of a market. Today we must determine whether the American housewife will buy lemon pudding cake in preference to orange angel food. The variables in the equation have multiplied just as the number of products on the grocers' shelves have multiplied from a hundred or so into many thousands.

When we first began operating under this new marketing concept, we encountered the problems which always accompany any major reorientation. Our people were young and frankly immature in some areas of business; but they were men possessed of an idea and they fought for it. The idea was almost too powerful. The marketing concept proved its worth in sales, but it upset many of the internal balances of the corporation. Marketing-oriented decisions resulted in peaks and valleys in production, schedules, labor, and inventories. But the system worked. It worked better and better as maverick marketing men became motivated toward tonnage and profit.

4th ERA—MARKETING CONTROL

Today marketing is coming into its own. Pillsbury stands on the brink of its fourth major era in the marketing revolution.

Basically, the philosophy of this fourth era can be summarized this way: "We are moving from a company which has the marketing concept to a marketing company."

Marketing today sets company operating policy short-term. It will come to influence long-range policy more and more. Where today consumer research, technical research, procurement, production, advertising, and sales swing into action under the broad canopy established by marketing, tomorrow capital and financial planning, ten-year volume and profit goals will also come under the aegis of marketing. More than any other function, marketing must be tied to top management.

Today our marketing people know more about inventories than anyone in top management. Tomorrow's marketing man must know capital financing and the implications of marketing planning on long-range profit forecasting.

Today technical research receives almost all of its guidance and direction from marketing. Tomorrow marketing will assume a more creative function in the advertising area, both in terms of ideas and media selection.

Changes in the Future

The marketing revolution has only begun. There are still those who resist its basic idea, just as there are always those who will resist change in business, government, or any other form of human institution.

As the marketing revolution gains momentum, there will be more changes. The concept of the customer at the center will remain valid; but business must adjust to the shifting tastes and likes and desires and needs which have always characterized the American consumer.

For many years the geographical center of the United States lay in a small Kansas town. Then a new state, Alaska, came along, and the center shifted to the north and west. Hawaii was admitted to the Union and the geographical midpoint took another jump to the west. In very much the same way, modern business must anticipate the restless shifting of buying attitudes, as customer preferences move north, south, east, or west from a liquid center. There is nothing static about the marketing revolution, and that is part of its fascination. The old order has changed, yielding place to the new—but the new order will have its quota of changes, too.

At Pillsbury, as our fourth era progresses, marketing will become the basic motivating force for the entire corporation. Soon it will be true that every activity of the corporation—from finance to sales to production—is aimed at satisfying the needs and desires of the consumer. When that stage of development is reached, the marketing revolution will be complete.

SOME SUGGESTIONS FOR FURTHER READING

Bell, M. L. and C. W. Emory (1971), "The Faltering Marketing Concept," *Journal of Marketing* (October), 37–42.

Enis, B. M. and M. P. Mokwa (1981), "The Development Department: Next Stage in the Evolution of the Marketing Concept," *BUSINESS,* forthcoming.

Galbraith, J. R. (1974), "Organizational Design: An Information Processing View," *Interface,* 4 (May), 28–36.

Myers, James H. (1979), "Reorganizing the Marketing Concept," working paper, Claremont, CA: Claremont Graduate School of Business Administration.

Nonaka, I. and F. M. Nicosia (1979), "Marketing Management, Its Environment and Information Processing: A Problem of Organizational Design," *Journal of Business Research* (Fall).

5 / BROADENING THE CONCEPT OF MARKETING / Philip Kotler and Sidney J. Levy

The term *marketing* connotes to most people a function peculiar to business firms. Marketing is seen as the task of finding and stimulating buyers for the firm's output. It involves product development, pricing, distribution, and communication; and in the more progressive firms, continuous attention to the changing needs of customers and the development of new products, with product modifications and services to meet these needs. But whether marketing is viewed in the old sense of "pushing" products or in the new sense of "customer satisfaction engineering," it is almost always viewed and discussed as a business activity.

It is the authors' contention that marketing is a pervasive societal activity that goes considerably beyond the selling of toothpaste, soap, and steel. Political contests remind us that candidates are marketed as well as soap; student recruitment by colleges reminds us that higher education is marketed; and fund raising reminds us that "causes" are marketed. Yet these areas of marketing are typically ignored by the student of marketing. Or they are treated cursorily as public relations or publicity activities. No attempt is made to incorporate these phenomena in the body proper of marketing thought and theory. No attempt is made to redefine the meaning of product development, pricing, distribution, and communication in these newer contexts to see if they have a useful meaning. No attempt is made to examine whether the principles of "good" marketing in traditional product areas are transferable to the marketing of services, persons and ideas.

The authors see a great opportunity for marketing people to expand their thinking and to apply their skills to an increasingly interesting range of social activity. The challenge depends on the attention given to it; marketing will either take on a broader social meaning or remain a narrowly defined business activity.

"Broadening the Concept of Marketing," by Philip Kotler and Sidney J. Levy. Reprinted from the *Journal of Marketing* (January 1969), pp. 10–15, published by the American Marketing Association. This article received the 1969 Alpha Kappa Psi award as outstanding article of the year.

Philip Kotler, Harold T. Martin professor of marketing at Northwestern University, received his Ph.D. in economics from Massachusetts Institute of Technology. He did post doctoral work in mathematics and behavioral sciences at Harvard and the University of Chicago respectively. His articles have appeared in numerous scholarly journals; several have won best article awards. His *Marketing Management: Analysis, Planning and Control*, now in its fourth edition, is widely used.
Sidney J. Levy is professor of marketing at Northwestern University and vice president of Social Research, Inc. He earned his Ph.D. in psychology at the University of Chicago. He is the author of *Promotion: A Behavioral View* and many articles. His latest book is *Marketplace Behavior—Its Meaning for Management*.

THE RISE OF ORGANIZATIONAL MARKETING

One of the most striking trends in the United States is the increasing amount of society's work being performed by organizations other than business firms. As a society moves beyond the stage where shortages of food, clothing, and shelter are the major problems, it begins to organize to meet other social needs that formerly had been put aside. Business enterprises remain a dominant type of organization, but other types of organizations gain in conspicuousness and in influence. Many of these organizations become enormous and require the same rarefied management skills as traditional business organizations. Managing the United Auto Workers, Defense Department, Ford Foundation, World Bank, Catholic Church, and University of California has become every bit as challenging as managing Proctor and Gamble, General Motors, and General Electric. These nonbusiness organizations have an increasing range of influence, affect as many livelihoods, and occupy as much media prominence as major business firms.

All of these organizations perform the classic business functions. Every organization must perform a financial function insofar as money must be raised, managed, and budgeted according to sound business principles. Every organization must perform a production function in that it must conceive of the best way of arranging inputs to produce the outputs of the organization. Every organization must perform a personnel function in that people must be hired, trained assigned, and promoted in the course of the organization's work. Every organization must perform a purchasing function in that it must acquire materials in an efficient way through comparing and selecting sources of supply.

When we come to the marketing function, it is also clear that every organization performs marketing-like activities whether or not they are recognized as such. Several examples can be given.

The police department of a major U.S. city, concerned with the poor image it has among an important segment of its population, developed a campaign to "win friends and influence people." One highlight of this campaign is a "visit your police station" day in which tours are conducted to show citizens the daily operations of the police department, including the crime laboratories, police lineups, and cells. The police department also sends officers to speak at public schools and carries out a number of other activities to improve its community relations.

Most museum directors interpret their primary responsibility as "the proper preservation of an artistic heritage for posterity."[1] As a result, for many people museums are cold marble mausoleums that house miles of relics that soon give way to yawns and tired feet. Although museum attendance in the United States advances each year, a large number of citizens are uninterested in museums. Is this indifference due to failure in the manner of presenting what museums have to offer? This nagging question led the new director of the Metropolitan Museum of Art to broaden the museum's appeal through sponsoring contemporary art shows and "happenings." His marketing philosophy of museum management led to substantial increases in the Met's attendance.

The public school system in Oklahoma City sorely needed more public support and funds to prevent a deterioration of facilities and exodus of teachers. It recently resorted to television programming to dramatize the work the public schools were doing to fight the high school dropout problem, to develop new teaching techniques, and to enrich the children. Although an expensive medium, television quickly reached large numbers of parents whose response and interest were tremendous.

Nations also resort to international marketing campaigns to get across important points about themselves to the citizens of other countries. The junta of Greek colonels who seized power in Greece in 1967 found the international publicity surrounding their cause to be extremely unfavorable and potentially disruptive of international recognition. They hired a major New York public relations firm and soon full-page newspaper ads appeared carrying the headline "Greece Was Saved From Communism," detailing in small print why the takeover was necessary for the stability of Greece and the world.[2]

An anti-cigarette group in Canada is trying to press the Canadian legislature to ban cigarettes on the grounds that they are harmful to health. There is widespread support for this cause but the organization's funds are limited, particularly measured against the huge advertising resources of the cigarette industry. The group's problem is to find effective ways to make a little money go a long way in persuading influential legislators of the need for discouraging cigarette consumption. This group has come up with several ideas for marketing anti-smoking to Canadians, including television spots, a paperback book featuring pictures of cancer and heart disease patients, and legal research on company liability for the smoker's loss of health.

What concepts are common to these and many other possible illustrations of organizational marketing? All of these organizations are concerned about their "product" in the eyes of certain "consumers" and are seeking to find "tools" for furthering their acceptance. Let us consider each of these concepts in general organizational terms.

Products

Every organization produces a "product" of at least one of the following types:

Physical products.   "Product" first brings to mind everyday items like soap, clothes, and food, and extends to cover millions of *tangible* items that have a market value and are available for purchase.

Services.   Services are *intangible* goods that are subject to market transaction such as tours, insurance, consultation, hairdos, and banking.

Persons.   Personal marketing is an endemic *human* activity, from the employee trying to impress his boss to the statesman trying to win the support of the public. With the advent of mass communications, the marketing of persons has been turned over to professionals. Hollywood stars have their press agents, political candidates their advertising agencies, and so on.

Organizations. Many organizations spend a great deal of time marketing themselves. The Republican Party has invested considerable thought and resources in trying to develop a modern look. The American Medical Association decided recently that it needed to launch a campaign to improve the image of the American doctor.[3] Many charitable organizations and universities see selling their *organization* as their primary responsibility.

Ideas. Many organizations are mainly in the business of selling *ideas* to the larger society. Population organizations are trying to sell the idea of birth control, and the Women's Christian Temperance Union is still trying to sell the idea of prohibition.

Thus the "product" can take many forms, and this is the first crucial point in the case for broadening the concept of marketing.

Consumers

The second crucial point is that organizations must deal with many groups that are interested in their products and can make a difference in its success. It is vitally important to the organization's success that it be sensitive to, serve, and satisfy these groups. One set of groups can be called the *suppliers*. *Suppliers* are those who provide the management group with the inputs necessary to perform its work and develop its product effectively. Suppliers include employees, vendors of the materials, banks, advertising agencies, and consultants.

The other set of groups are the *consumers* of the organization's product, of which four sub-groups can be distinguished. The *clients* are those who are the immediate consumers of the organization's product. The clients of a business firm are its buyers and potential buyers; of a service organization those receiving the services, such as the needy (from the Salvation Army) or the sick (from County Hospital); and of a protective or a primary organization, the members themselves. The second group is the *trustees* or *directors,* those who are vested with the legal authority and responsibility for the organization, oversee the management, and enjoy a variety of benefits from the "product." The third group is the active *publics* that take a specific interest in the organization. For a business firm, the active publics include consumer rating groups, governmental agencies, and pressure groups of various kinds. For a university, the active publics include alumni and friends of the university, foundations, and city fathers. Finally, the fourth consumer group is the *general public.* These are all the people who might develop attitudes toward the organization that might affect its conduct in some way. Organizational marketing concerns the programs designed by management to create satisfactions and favorable attitudes in the organization's four consuming groups: clients, trustees, active publics, and general public.

Marketing Tools

Students of business firms spend much time studying the various tools under the firm's control that affect product acceptance: product improvement, pricing, distribution, and communication. All of these tools have counterpart applications to nonbusiness organizational activity.

Nonbusiness organizations to various degrees engage in product improvement, especially when they recognize the competition they face from other organizations. Thus, over the years churches have added a host of nonreligious activities to their basic religious activities to satisfy members seeking other bases of human fellowship. Universities keep updating their curricula and adding new student services in an attempt to make the educational experience relevant to the students. Where they have failed to do this, students have sometimes organized their own courses and publications, or have expressed their dissatisfaction in organized protest. Government agencies such as license bureaus, police forces, and taxing bodies are often not responsive to the public because of monopoly status; but even here citizens have shown an increasing readiness to protest mediocre services, and more alert bureaucracies have shown a growing interest in reading the user's needs and developing the required product services.

All organizations face the problem of pricing their products and services so that they cover costs. Churches charge dues, Universities charge tuition, governmental agencies charge fees, fund-raising organizations send out bills. Very often specific product charges are not sufficient to meet the organization's budget, and it must rely on gifts and surcharges to make up the difference. Opinions vary as to how much the users should be charged for the individual services and how much should be made up through general collection. If the university increases its tuition, it will have to face losing some students and putting more students on scholarship. If the hospital raises its charges to cover rising costs and additional services, it may provoke a reaction from the community. All organizations face complex pricing issues although not all of them understand good pricing practice.

Distribution is a central concern to the manufacturer seeking to make his goods conveniently accessible to buyers. Distribution also can be an important marketing decision area for nonbusiness organizations. A city's public library has to consider the best means of making its books available to the public. Should it establish one large library with an extensive collection of books, or several neighborhood branch libraries with duplication of books? Should it use bookmobiles that bring the books to the customers instead of relying exclusively on the customers coming to the books? Should it distribute through school libraries? Similarly the police department of a city must think through the problem of distributing its protective services efficiently through the community. It has to determine how much protective service to allocate to different neighborhoods; the respective merits of squad cars, motorcycles, and foot patrolmen; and the positioning of emergency phones.

Customer communication is an essential activity of all organizations although many nonmarketing organizations often fail to accord it the importance it deserves. Managements of many organizations think they have fully met their communication responsibilities by setting up advertising and/or public relations departments. They fail to realize that *everything about an organization talks.* Customers form impressions of an organization from its physical facilities, employees, officers, stationery, and a hundred other company surrogates. Only when this is appreciated do the members of the organization recognize that they all are in marketing, whatever else they do. With this understanding they can assess realistically the impact of their activities on the consumers.

CONCEPTS FOR EFFECTIVE MARKETING MANAGEMENT IN NONBUSINESS ORGANIZATIONS

Although all organizations have products, markets, and marketing tools, the art and science of effective marketing management have reached their highest state of development in the business type of organization. Business organizations depend on customer goodwill for survival and have generally learned how to sense and cater to their needs effectively. As other types of organizations recognize their marketing roles, they will turn increasingly to the body of marketing principles worked out by business organizations and adapt them to their own situations.

What are the main principles of effective marketing management as they appear in most forward-looking business organizations? Nine concepts stand out as crucial in guiding the marketing effort of a business organization.

Generic Product Definition

Business organizations have increasingly recognized the value of placing a broad definition on their products, one that emphasizes the basic customer need(s) being served. A modern soap company recognizes that its basic product is cleaning, not soap; a cosmetics company sees its basic product as beauty or hope, not lipsticks and makeup; a publishing company sees its basic product as information, not books.

The same need for a broader definition of its business is incumbent upon nonbusiness organizations if they are to survive and grow. Churches at one time tended to define their product narrowly as that of producing religious services for members. Recently, most churchmen have decided that their basic product is human fellowship. There was a time when educators said that their product was the three R's. Now most of them define their product as education for the whole man. They try to serve the social, emotional, and political needs of young people in addition to intellectual needs.

Target Groups Definition

A generic product definition usually results in defining a very wide market, and it is then necessary for the organization, because of limited resources, to limit its product offering to certain clearly defined groups within the market. Although the generic product of an automobile company is transportation, the company typically sticks to cars, trucks, and buses, and stays away from bicycles, airplanes, and steamships. Furthermore, the manufacturer does not produce every size and shape of car but concentrates on producing a few major types to satisfy certain substantial and specific parts of the market.

In the same way, nonbusiness organizations have to define their target groups carefully. For example, in Chicago the YMCA defines its target groups as men, women and children who want recreational opportunities and are willing to pay $20 or more a year for them. The Chicago Boys Club, on the other hand, defines its target group as poorer boys within the city boundaries who are in want of recreational facilities and can pay $1 a year.

Differentiated Marketing

When a business organization sets out to serve more than one target group, it will be maximally effective by differentiating its product offerings and communications. This is also true for nonbusiness organizations. Fund-raising organizations have recognized the advantage of treating clients, trustees, and various publics in different ways. These groups require differentiated appeals and frequency of solicitation. Labor unions find that they must address different messages to different parties rather than one message to all parties. To the company they may seem unyielding, to the conciliator they may appear willing to compromise, and to the public they seek to appear economically exploited.

Customer Behavior Analysis

Business organizations are increasingly recognizing that customer needs and behavior are not obvious without formal research and analysis; they cannot rely on impressionistic evidence. Soap companies spend hundreds of thousands of dollars each year researching how Mrs. Housewife feels about her laundry, how, when, and where she does her laundry, and what she desires of a detergent.

Fund raising illustrates how an industry has benefited by replacing stereotypes of donors with studies of why people contribute to causes. Fund raisers have learned that people give because they are getting something. Many give to community chests to relieve a sense of guilt because of their elevated state compared to the needy. Many give to medical charities to relieve a sense of fear that they may be struck by a disease whose cure has not yet been found. Some give to feel pride. Fund raisers have stressed the importance of identifying the motives operating in the marketplace of givers as a basis for planning drives.

Differential Advantages

In considering different ways of reaching target groups, an organization is advised to think in terms of seeking a differential advantage. It should consider what elements in its reputation or resources can be exploited to create a special value in the minds of its potential customers. In the same way Zenith has built a reputation for quality and International Harvester a reputation for service, a nonbusiness organization should base its case on some dramatic value that competitive organizations lack. The small island of Nassau can compete against Miami for the tourist trade by advertising the greater dependability of its weather; the Heart Association can compete for funds against the Cancer Society by advertising the amazing strides made in heart research.

Multiple Marketing Tools

The modern business firm relies on a multitude of tools to sell its product, including product improvement, consumer and dealer advertising, salesman incentive programs, sales promotions, contests, multiple-size offerings, and so forth. Likewise nonbusiness organizations also can reach their audiences in a variety of ways. A church can sustain the interest of its members through discussion groups, newsletters, news releases, campaign drives, annual reports, and retreats. Its "salesmen" include the religious head, the board members, and the present members in terms of attracting potential members. Its advertising includes announcements of weddings, births and deaths, religious pronouncements, and newsworthy developments.

Integrated Marketing Planning

The multiplicity of available marketing tools suggests the desirability of overall coordination so that these tools do not work at cross purposes. Over time, the business firms have placed under a marketing vice-president activities that were previously managed in a semi-autonomous fashion, such as sales, advertising, and marketing research. Nonbusiness organizations typically have not integrated their marketing activities. Thus, no single officer in the typical university is given total responsibility for studying the needs and attitudes of clients, trustees, and publics, and undertaking the necessary product development and communication programs to serve these groups. The university administration instead includes a variety of "marketing" positions such as dean of students, director of alumni affairs, director of public relations, and director of development; coordination is often poor.

Continuous Marketing Feedback

Business organizations gather continuous information about changes in the environment and about their own performance. They use their salesmen, research department, specialized research services, and other means to check on the movement of goods, actions of competitors, and feelings of customers to make sure they are progressing along satisfactory lines. Nonbusiness organizations typically are more casual about collecting vital information on how they are doing and what is happening in the marketplace. Universities have been caught off guard by underestimating the magnitude of student grievance and unrest, and so have major cities underestimated the degree to which they were failing to meet the needs of important minority constituencies.

Marketing Audit

Change is a fact of life, although it may proceed almost invisibly on a day-to-day basis. Over a long stretch of time, it might be so fundamental as to threaten organizations that have not provided for periodic reexaminations of their purposes. Organizations can grow set in their ways and unresponsive to new opportunities or problems. Some great American companies are no longer with us because they did not change definitions of their businesses, and their products lost relevance in a changing world. Political parties become unresponsive after they enjoy power for a while and every so often experience a major upset. Many union leaders grow insensitive to new needs and problems until one day they find themselves out of office. For an organization to remain viable, its management must provide for periodic audits of its objectives, resources, and opportunities. It must reexamine its basic business, target groups, differential advantage, communication channels, and messages in the light of current trends and needs. It might recognize when change is needed and make it before it is too late.

IS ORGANIZATIONAL MARKETING A SOCIALLY USEFUL ACTIVITY?

Modern marketing has two different meanings in the minds of people who use the term. One meaning of marketing conjures up the terms selling, influencing, persuading. Marketing is seen as a huge and increasingly dangerous technology, making it possible to sell persons on buying things, propositions, and causes they either do not want or which are bad for them. This was the indictment in Vance Packard's *Hidden Persuaders* and numerous other social criticisms, with the net effect that a large number of persons think of marketing as immoral or entirely self-seeking in its fundamental premises. They can be counted on to resist the idea of organizational marketing as so much "Madison Avenue."

The other meaning of marketing unfortunately is weaker in the public mind; it is the concept of sensitively *serving and satisfying human needs*. This was the great contribution of the marketing concept that was promulgated in the 1950s, and that concept now counts many business firms as its practitioners. The marketing concept holds that the problem of all business firms in an age of abundance is to develop customer loyalties and satisfaction, and the key to this problem is to focus on the customer's needs.[4] Perhaps the short-run problem of business firms is to sell people on buying the existing products, but the long-run problem is clearly to create the products that people need. By this recognition that effective marketing requires a consumer orientation instead of a product orientation, marketing has taken a new lease on life and tied its economic activity to a higher social purpose.

It is this second side of marketing that provides a useful concept for all organizations. All organizations are formed to serve the interest of particular groups: hospitals serve the sick, schools serve the students, governments serve the citizens, and labor unions serve the members. In the course of evolving, many organizations lose sight of their original mandate, grow hard, and become self-serving. The bureaucratic mentality begins to dominate the original service mentality. Hospitals may become perfunctory in their handling of patients, schools treat their students as nuisances, city bureaucrats behave like petty tyrants toward the citizens, and labor unions try to run instead of serve their members. All of these actions tend to build frustration in the consuming groups. As a result some withdraw meekly from these organizations, accept frustration as part of their condition, and find their satisfactions elsewhere. This used to be the common reaction of ghetto Negroes and college students in the face of indifferent city and university bureaucracies. But new possibilities have arisen, and now the same consumers refuse to withdraw so readily. Organized dissent and protest are seen to be an answer, and many organizations thinking of themselves as responsible have been stunned into recognizing that they have lost touch with their constituencies. They had grown unresponsive.

Where does marketing fit into this picture? Marketing is that function of the organization that can keep in constant touch with the organization's consumers, read their needs, develop "products" that meet these needs, and build a program of communications to express the organization's purposes. Certainly selling and influencing will be large parts of organizational marketing; but, properly seen, selling follows rather than precedes the organization's drive to create products to satisfy its consumers.

CONCLUSION

It has been argued here that the modern marketing concept serves very naturally to describe an important facet of all organizational activity. All organizations must develop appropriate products to serve their sundry consuming groups and must use modern tools of communication to reach their consuming publics. The business heritage of marketing provides a useful set of concepts for guiding all organizations.

The choice facing those who manage nonbusiness organizations is not whether to market or not to market, for no organization can avoid marketing. The choice is whether to do it well or poorly, and on this necessity the case for organizational marketing is basically founded.

NOTES

[1] This is the view of Sherman Lee, Director of the Cleveland Museum, quoted in *Newsweek*, Vol. 71 (April 1, 1968), p. 55.
[2] "PR for Colonels," *Newsweek*, Vol. 71 (March 18, 1968), p. 70.
[3] "Doctors Try an Image Transplant," *Business Week*, No. 2025 (June 22, 1968), p. 64.
[4] Theodore Levitt, "Marketing Myopia," *Harvard Business Review*, Vol. 38 (July–August, 1960), pp. 45–56.

SOME SUGGESTIONS FOR FURTHER READING

Enis, B. M. (1973), "Deepening the Concept of Marketing," *Journal of Marketing* (October), 57–62.

Kotler, P. and S. J. Levy (1969), "A New Form of Marketing Myopia: Rejoiner to Professor Luck," *Journal of Marketing* (July), 56–8.

Luck, D. J. (1969), "Broadening the Concept of Marketing—Too Far," *Journal of Marketing* (July), 53–55

────── (1974), "Social Marketing: Confusion Compounded," *Journal of Marketing* (October), 70–72.

Zaltman, G. and P. Kotler (1971), "Social Marketing: An Approach to Planned Social Change," *Journal of Marketing* (July), 3–12.

6 / A GENERIC CONCEPT OF MARKETING / Philip Kotler

One of the signs of the health of a discipline is its willingness to reexamine its focus, techniques, and goals as the surrounding society changes and new problems require attention. Marketing has shown this aptitude in the past. It was originally founded as a branch of *applied economics* devoted to the study of distribution channels. Later marketing became a *management discipline* devoted to engineering increases in sales. More recently, it has taken on the character of an *applied behavioral science* that is concerned with understanding buyer and seller systems involved in the marketing of goods and services.

The focus of marketing has correspondingly shifted over the years. Marketing evolved through a *commodity focus* (farm products, minerals, manufactured goods, services); an *institutional focus* (producers, wholesalers, retailers, agents); a *functional focus* (buying, selling, promoting, transporting, storing, pricing); a *managerial focus* (analysis, planning, organization, control); and a *social focus* (market efficiency, product quality, and social impact). Each new focus had its advocates and its critics. Marketing emerged each time with a refreshed and expanded self-concept.

Today marketing is facing a new challenge concerning whether its concepts apply in the nonbusiness as well as the business area. In 1969, this author and Professor Levy advanced the view that *marketing is a relevant discipline for all organizations insofar as all organizations can be said to have customers and products*.[1] This "broadening of the concept of marketing" proposal received much attention, and the 1970 Fall Conference of the American Marketing Association was devoted to this theme.

Critics soon appeared who warned that the broadening concept could divert marketing from its true purposes and dilute its content. One critic did not deny that marketing concepts and tools could be useful in fund raising, museum membership drives, and presidential campaigns, but he felt that these were extracurricular applications of an intrinsical business technology.[2]

Several articles have been published which describe applications of marketing ideas to nonbusiness areas such as health services, population control, recycling of solid wastes, and fund raising.[3] Therefore, the underlying issues should be reexamined to see whether a more generic concept of marketing can be established.

"A Generic Concept of Marketing," Philip Kotler, Vol. (April 1972), pp. 46–54. Reprinted from the *Journal of Marketing,* published by the American Marketing Association. This article won the Alpha Kappa Psi Award as best article of the year.
Philip Kotler, Harold T. Martin professor of Marketing at Northwestern University, received his Ph.D. in Economics from the Massachusetts Institute of Technology. He did post doctoral work in the Mathematics and Behavior Science at Harvard and the University of Chicago respectively. His textbook, *Marketing Management: Analysis, Planning, and Control,* now in its fourth edition, is widely used.

This author concludes that the traditional conception of marketing would relegate this discipline to an increasingly narrow and pedestrian role in a society that is growing increasingly postindustrial. In fact, this article will argue that the broadening proposal's main weakness was not that it went too far but that it did not go far enough.

This article is organized into five parts. The first distinguishes three stages of consciousness regarding the scope of marketing. The second presents an axiomatic treatment of the generic concept of marketing. The third suggests three useful marketing typologies that are implied by the generic concept of marketing. The fourth describes the basic analytical, planning, organization, and control tasks that make up the logic of marketing management. The fifth discusses some interesting questions raised about the generic concept of marketing.

THREE STAGES OF MARKETING CONSCIOUSNESS

Three different levels of consciousness can be distinguished regarding the boundaries of marketing. The present framework utilizes Reich's consciousness categories without his specific meanings.[4] The traditional consciousness, that marketing is essentially a business subject, will be called *consciousness one*. Consciousness one is the most widely held view in the mind of practitioners and the public. In the last few years, a marketing *consciousness two* has appeared among some marketers holding that marketing is appropriate for all organizations that have customers. This is the thrust of the original broadening proposal and seems to be gaining adherents. Now it can be argued that even consciousness two expresses a limited concept of marketing. One can propose *consciousness three* that holds that marketing is a relevant subject for all organizations in their relations with all their publics, not only customers. The future character of marketing will depend on the particular consciousness that most marketers adopt regarding the nature of their field.

Consciousness One

Consciousness one is the conception that marketing is essentially a business subject. It maintains that marketing is concerned with *sellers, buyers,* and *"economic" product and services.* The sellers offer goods and services, the buyers have purchasing power and other resources, and the objective is an exchange of goods for money or other resources.

The core concept defining marketing consciousness one is that of *market transactions.* A market transaction involves the transfer of ownership or use of an economic good or service from one party to another in return for a payment of some kind. For market transactions to occur in a society, six conditions are necessary:

1. Two or more parties
2. A scarcity of goods

3. Concept of private property
4. One party must want a good held by another
5. The "wanting" party must be able to offer some kind of payment for it
6. The "owning" party must be willing to forego the good for the payment.

These conditions underlie the notion of a market transaction, or more loosely, economic exchange.

Market transactions can be contrasted with nonmarket transactions. Nonmarket transactions also involve a transfer of resources from one party to another, *but without clear payment by the other*. Giving gifts, paying taxes, receiving free services are all examples of nonmarket transactions. If a housekeeper is paid for domestic services, this is a market transaction; if she is one's wife, this is a nonmarket transaction. Consciousness one marketers pay little or no attention to nonmarket transactions because they lack the element of explicit payment.

Consciousness Two

Consciousness two marketers do not see *payment* as a necessary condition to define the domain of marketing phenomena. Marketing analysis and planning are relevant in all organizations producing products and services for an intended consuming group, whether or not payment is required.

Table 1 lists several nonbusiness organizations and their "products" and "customer groups." All of these products, in principle, can be priced and sold. A price can be charged for museum attendance ,safe driving lessons, birth control information, and education. The fact that many of these services are offered "free" should not detract from their character as products. A product is something that has value to someone. Whether a charge is made for its consumption is an incidental rather than essential feature defining value. In fact, most of these social goods are "priced," although often not in the normal fashion. Police services are paid for by taxes, and religious services are paid for by donations.

Each of these organizations faces marketing problems with respect to its product and customer group. They must study the size and composition of their market and consumer wants, attitudes, and habits. They must design their products to appeal to their target markets. They must develop distribution and communication programs that facilitate "purchase" and satisfaction. They must develop customer feedback systems to ascertain market satisfaction and needs.

Table 1. Some Organizations and Their Products and Customer Groups

Organization	Product	Customer Group
Museum	Cultural appreciation	General public
National Safety Council	Safer driving	Driving public
Political candidate	Honest government	Voting public
Family Planning Foundation	Birth control	Fertile public
Police department	Safety	General public
Church	Religious experience	Church members
University	Education	Students

Thus consciousness two replaces the core concept of *market transactions* with the broader concept of *organization-client transactions*. Marketing is no longer restricted only to transactions involving parties in a two-way exchange of economic resources. Marketing is a useful perspective for any organization producing products for intended consumption by others. *Marketing consciousness two states that marketing is relevant in all situations where one can identify an organization, a client group, and products broadly defined.*

Consciousness Three

The emergence of a marketing consciousness three is barely visible. Consciousness three marketers do not see why marketing technology should be confined only to an organization's transactions with its client group. An organization—or more properly its management—may engage in marketing activity not only with its customers but also with all other publics in its environment. A management group has to market to the organization's supporters, suppliers, employees, government, the general public, agents and other key publics. *Marketing consciousness three states that marketing applies to an organization's attempts to relate to all of its publics, not just its consuming public.* Marketing can be used in multiple institutional contexts to effect transactions with multiple targets.

Marketing consciousness three is often expressed in real situations. One often hears a marketer say that his real problem is not *outside marketing* but *inside marketing;* for example, getting others in his organization to accept his ideas. Companies seeking a preferred position with suppliers or dealers see this as a problem of marketing themselves. In addition, companies try to market their viewpoint to congressmen in Washington. These and many other examples suggest that marketers see the marketing problem as extending far beyond customer groups.

The concept of defining marketing in terms of *function* rather than *structure* underlies consciousness three. To define a field in terms of function is to see it as a process or set of activities. To define a field in terms of structure is to identify it with some phenomena such as a set of institutions. Bliss pointed out that many sciences are facing this choice.[5] In the field of political science, for example, there are those who adopt a structural view and define political science in terms of political institutions such as legislatures, government agencies, judicial courts, and political parties. There are others who adopt a functional view and define political science as the study of *power* wherever it is found. The latter political scientists study power in the family, in labor-management relations, and in corporate organizations.

Similarly, marketing can be defined in terms of functional rather than structural considerations. Marketing takes places in a great number of situations, including executive recruiting, political campaigning, church membership drives, and lobbying. Examining the marketing aspects of these situations can yield new insights into the generic nature of marketing. The payoff may be higher than from continued concentration in one type of structural setting, that of business.

It is generally a mistake to equate a science with a certain phenomenon.

For example, the subject of *matter* does not belong exclusively to physics, chemistry, or biology. Rather physics, chemistry, and biology are logical systems that pose different questions about matter. Nor does *human nature* belong exclusively to psychology, sociology, social psychology, or anthropology. These sciences simply raise different questions about the same phenomena. Similarly, traditional business subjects should not be defined by institutional characteristics. This would mean that finance deals with banks, production with factories, and marketing with distribution channels. Yet each of these subjects has a set of core ideas that are applicable in multiple institutional contexts. An important means of achieving progress in a science is to try to increase the generality of its concepts.

Consider the case of a hospital as an institution. A production-minded person will want to know about the locations of the various facilities, the jobs of the various personnel, and in general the arrangement of the elements to produce the product known as health care. A financial-minded person will want to know the hospital's sources and applications of funds and its income and expenses. A marketing-minded person will want to know where the patients come from, why they appeared at this particular hospital, and how they feel about the hospital care and services. Thus the phenomena do not create the questions to be asked; rather the questions are suggested by the disciplined view brought to the phenomena.

What then is the disciplinary focus of marketing? The core concept of marketing is the *transaction.. A transaction is the exchange of values between two parties.* The things-of-values need not be limited to goods, services, and money; they include other resources such as time, energy, and feelings. Transactions occur not only between buyers and sellers, and organizations and clients, but also between any two parties. A transaction takes place, for example, when a person decides to watch a television program; he is exchanging his time for entertainment. A transaction takes place when a person votes for a particular candidate; he is exchanging his time and support for expectations of better government. A transaction takes place when a person gives money to a charity; he is exchanging money for a good conscience. *Marketing is specifically concerned with how transactions are created, stimulated, facilitated, and valued.* This is the generic concept of marketing.

THE AXIOMS OF MARKETING

The generic concept of marketing will now be more rigorously developed. Marketing can be viewed as a *category of human action* distinguishable from other categories of human action such as voting, loving, consuming, or fighting. As a category of human action, it has certain characteristics which can be stated in the form of axioms. A sufficient set of axioms about marketing would provide unambiguous criteria about what marketing is, and what it is not. Four axioms, along with corollaries, are proposed in the following section.

Axiom 1. *Marketing involves two or more social units, each consisting of one or more human actors.*
  Corollary 1.1. The social units may be individuals, groups, organizations, communities, or nations.

Two important things follow from this axiom. First, marketing is not an activity found outside of the human species. Animals, for example, engage in production and consumption, but do not engage in marketing. They do not exchange goods, set up distribution systems, and engage in persuasive activity. Marketing is a peculiarly human activity.

Second, the referent of marketing activity is another social unit. Marketing does not apply when a person is engaged in an activity in reference to a *thing* or *himself.* Eating, driving, and manufacturing are not marketing activities, as they involve the person in an interactive relationship primarily with things. Jogging, sleeping, and daydreaming are not marketing activities, as they involve the person in an interactive relationship primarily with himself. An interesting question does arise as to whether a person can be conceived of marketing something to himself, as when he undertakes effort to change his own behavior. Normally, however, marketing involves actions by a person directed toward one or more other persons.

Axiom 2. *At least one of the social units is seeking a specific response from one or more other units concerning some social object.*

Corollary 2.1. The social unit seeking the response is called the *marketer,* and the social unit whose response is sought is called the *market.*

Corollary 2.2. The social object may be a product, service, organization, person, place, or idea.

Corollary 2.3. The response sought from the market is some behavior toward the social object, usually acceptance but conceivably avoidance (More specific descriptions of responses sought are purchase, adoption, usage, consumption, or their negatives. Those who do or may respond are called buyers, adopters, users, consumers, clients, or supporters.)

Corollary 2.4. The marketer is normally aware that he is seeking the specific response.

Corollary 2.5. The response sought may be expected in the short or long run.

Corollary 2.6. The response has value to the marketer.

Corollary 2.7. *Mutual marketing* describes the case where two social units simultaneously seek a response from each other. Mutual marketing is the core situation underlying bargaining relationships.

Marketing consists of actions undertaken by persons to bring about a response in other persons concerning some specific social object. A social object is any entity or artifact found in society, such as a product, service, organization, person, place, or idea. The marketer normally seeks to influence the market to accept this social object. The notion of marketing also covers attempts to influence persons to avoid the object, as in a business effort to discourage excess demand or in a social campaign designed to influence people to stop smoking or overeating.[6] *The marketer is basically trying to shape the level and composition of demand for his product.* The marketer undertakes these influence actions because he values their consequences. The market may also value the consequences, but this is not a necessary condition for defining the occurrence of marketing activity. The marketer is normally conscious that he is attempting to influence a market, but it is also possible to interpret as marketing activity cases where the marketer is not fully conscious of his ends and means.

Axiom 2 implies that "selling" activity rather than "buying" activity is closer to the core meaning of marketing. The merchant who assembles goods for the purpose of selling them is engaging in marketing, insofar as he is seeking a purchase response from others. The buyer who comes into his store and pays the quoted price is engaging in buying, not marketing, in that he does not seek to produce a specific response in the seller, who has already put the goods up for sale. If the buyer decides to bargain with the seller over the terms, he too is involved in marketing, or if the seller had been reluctant to sell, the buyer has to market himself as an attractive buyer. The terms "buyer" and "seller" are not perfectly indicative of whether one, or both, of the parties are engaged in marketing activity.

Axiom 3. *The market's response probability is not fixed.*
>   Corollary 3.1. The probability that the market will produce the desired response is called the *market's response probability*.
>   Corollary 3.2. The market's response probability is greater than zero; that is, the market is capable of producing the desired response.
>   Corollary 3.3. The market's response probability is less than one; that is, the market is not internally compelled to produce the desired response.
>   Corollary 3.4. The market's response probability can be altered by marketer actions.

Marketing activity makes sense in the context of a market that is free and capable of yielding the desired response. If the target social unit *cannot respond* to the social object, as in the case of no interest or no resources, it is not a market. If the target social unit *must respond* to the social object, as in the case of addiction or perfect brand loyalty, that unit is a market but there is little need for marketing activity. In cases where the market's response probability is fixed in the short run but variable in the long run, the marketer may undertake marketing activity to prevent or reduce the erosion in the response probability. Normally, marketing activity is most relevant where the market's response probability is less than one and highly influenced by marketer actions.

Axiom 4. *Marketing is the attempt to produce the desired response by creating and offering values to the market.*
>   Corollary 4.1. The marketer assumes that the market's response will be voluntary.
>   Corollary 4.2. The essential activity of marketing is the creation and offering of value. Value is defined subjectively from the market's point of view.
>   Corollary 4.3. The marketer creates and offers value mainly through configuration, valuation, symbolization, and facilitation. (Configuration is the act of designing the social object. Valuation is concerned with placing terms of exchange on the object. Symbolization is the association of meanings with the object. Facilitation consists of altering the accessibility of the object.)
>   Corollary 4.4. *Effective marketing* means the choice of marketer actions that are calculated to produce the desired response in the market. *Efficient marketing* means the choice of *least cost* marketer actions that will produce the desired response.

Marketing is an approach to producing desired responses in another party that lies mid-way between *coercion* on the one hand and *brainwashing* on the other.

Coercion involves the attempt to produce a response in another by forcing or threatening him with agent-inflicted pain. Agent-inflicted pain should be distinguished from object-inflicted pain in that the latter may be used by a marketer as when he symbolizes something such as cigarettes as potentially harmful to the smoker. The use of agent-inflicted pain is normally not a marketing solution to a response problem. That is not to deny that marketers occasionally resort to arranging a "package of threats" to get or keep a customer. For example, a company may threaten to discontinue purchasing from another company if the latter failed to behave in a certain way. But normally, marketing consists of noncoercive actions to induce a response in another.

Brainwashing lies at the other extreme and involves the attempt to produce a response in another by profoundly altering his basic beliefs and values. Instead of trying to persuade a person to see the social object as serving his existing values and interests, the agent tries to shift the subject's values in the direction of the social object. Brainwashing, fortunately, is a very difficult feat to accomplish. It requires a monopoly of communication channels, operant conditioning, and much patience. Short of pure brainwashing efforts are attempts by various agents to change people's basic values in connection with such issues as racial prejudice, birth control, and private property. Marketing has some useful insights to offer to agents seeking to produce basic changes in people, although its main focus is on creating products and messages attuned to existing attitudes and values. It places more emphasis on preference engineering than attitude conditioning, although the latter is not excluded.

The core concern of marketing is that of producing desired responses in free individuals by the judicious creation and offering of values. The marketer is attempting to get value from the market through offering value to it. The marketer's problem is to create attractive values. Value is completely subjective and exists in the eyes of the beholding market. Marketers must understand the market in order to be effective in creating value. This is the essential meaning of the marketing concept.

The marketer seeks to create value in four ways. He can try to design the social object more attractively (configuration); he can put an attractive terms on the social object (valuation); he can add symbolic significance in the social object symbolization); and he can make it easier for the market to obtain the social object (facilitation). He may use these activities in reverse if he wants the social object to be avoided. These four activities have a rough correspondence to more conventional statements of marketing purpose, such as the use of product, price, promotion, and place to stimulate exchange.

The layman who thinks about marketing often overidentifies it with one or two major component activities, such as facilitation or symbolization. In *scarcity economies,* marketing is often identified with the facilitation function. Marketing is the problem of getting scarce goods to a marketplace. There is little concern with configuration and symbolization. In *affluent economies,* marketing is often identified with the symbolization function. In the popular mind, marketing is seen as the task of encoding persuasive messages to get people to buy more goods. Since most people resent persuasion attempts, marketing has picked up a negative image in the minds of many people. They forget or overlook the marketing work involved in creating values through configuration, valuation, and facilitation. In the future postindustrial society concern over the quality of life becomes paramount, and the public understanding of marketing is likely to undergo further change, hopefully toward an appreciation of all of its functions to create and offer value.

TYPOLOGIES OF MARKETING

The new levels of marketing consciousness make it desirable to reexamine traditional classifications of marketing activity. Marketing practitioners normally describe their type of marketing according to the *target market or product*. A *target-market classification* of marketing activity consists of consumer marketing, industrial marketing, government marketing, and international marketing.

A *product* classification consists of durable goods marketing, nondurable goods marketing, and service marketing.

With the broadening of marketing, the preceding classifications no longer express the full range of marketing application. They pertain to business marketing, which is only one type of marketing. More comprehensive classifications of marketing activity can be formulated according to the *target market, product,* or *marketer.*

Target Market Typology

A *target-market classification* of marketing activity distinguishes the various *publics* toward which an organization can direct its marketing activity. *A public is any group with potential interest and impact on an organization.* Every organization has up to nine distinguishable publics (Figure 1). There are three *input publics* (supporters, employees, suppliers), two *output publics* (agents, consumers), and four *sanctioning publics* (government, competitors, special publics, and general public). The organization is viewed as a resource conversion machine which takes the resources of supporters (e.g., stockholders, directors), employees, and suppliers and converts these into products that go directly to consumers or through agents. The organization's basic input-output activities are subject to the watchful eye of sanctioning publics such as government, competitors, special publics, and the general public. All of these publics are targets for organizational marketing activity because of their potential impact on the resource converting efficiency of the organization. Therefore, a *target-market classification* of marketing activity consists of supporter-directed marketing, employee-directed marketing, supplier-directed marketing, agent-directed marketing, consumer-directed marketing, general-public-directed marketing, special-public-directed marketing, government-directed marketing, and competitor-directed marketing.

Product Typology

A typology of marketing activity can also be constructed on the basis of the *product* marketed. Under the broadened concept of marketing, the product is no longer

Figure 1. An organization's publics

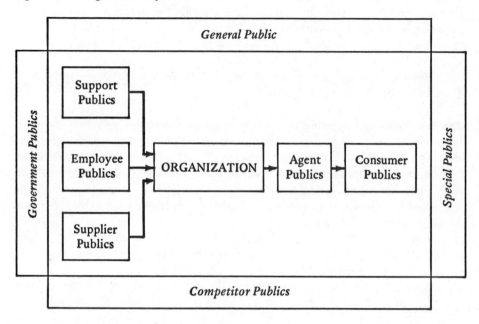

restricted to commercial goods and services. An organization can try to market to a public up to six types of products or social objects. A product classification of marketing consists of goods marketing, service marketing, organization marketing, person marketing, place marketing, and idea marketing.

Goods and service marketing, which made up the whole of traditional marketing, reappear in this classification. In addition, marketers can specialize in the marketing of organizations (e.g., governments, corporations, or universities), persons (e.g., political candidates, celebrities), places (e.g., real estate developments, resort areas, states, cities), and ideas (e.g., family planning, Medicare, antismoking, safe driving).

Marketer Typology

A typology can also be constructed on the basis of the *marketer*, that is, the organization that is carrying on the marketing. A first approximation would call for distinguishing between business and nonbusiness organization marketing. Since there are several types of nonbusiness organizations with quite different products and marketing tasks, it would be desirable to build a marketer classification that recognizes the different types of organizations. This leads to the following classifications: Business organization marketing, political organization marketing, social organization marketing, religious organization marketing, cultural organization marketing, and knowledge organization marketing.

Organizations are classified according to their primary or formal character. Political organizations would include political parties, government agencies, trade unions, and cause groups. Social organizations would include service clubs, fraternal organizations, and private welfare agencies. Religious organizations would include churches and evangelical movements. Cultural organizations would include museums, symphonies, and art leagues. Knowledge organizations would include public schools, universities, and research organizations. Some organizations are not easy to classify. Is a nonprofit hospital a business or a social organization? Is an employee credit union a political or a social organization? The purpose of the classification is primarily to guide students of marketing to look for regularities that might characterize the activities of certain basic types of organizations.

In general, the purpose of the three classifications of marketing activity is to facilitate the accumulation of marketing knowledge and its transfer from one marketing domain to another. Thus political and social organizations often engage in marketing ideas, and it is desirable to build up generic knowledge about idea marketing. Similarly, many organizations try to communicate a program to government authorities, and they could benefit from the accumulation of knowledge concerning idea marketing and government-directed marketing.

BASIC TASKS OF MARKETING MANAGEMENT

Virtually all persons and organizations engage in marketing activity at various times. They do not all engage in marketing, however, with equal skill. A distinction can be drawn between *marketing* and *marketing management*. *Marketing* is a descriptive science involving the study of how transactions are created, stimulated, facilitated, and valued. *Marketing management* is a normative science involving the efficient creation and offering of values to stimulate desired transactions. Marketing management is essentially a disciplined view of the task of achieving specific responses in others through the creation and offering of values.

Marketing management is not a set of answers so much as an orderly set of questions by which the marketer determines what is best to do in each situation. Effective marketing consists of intelligently analyzing, planning, organizing, and controlling marketing effort.

The marketer must be skilled at two basic analytical tasks. The first is *marketing analysis*. He must be able to identify the market, its size and location, needs and wants, perceptions and values. The second analytical skill is *product analysis*. The marketer must determine what products are currently available to the target, and how the target feels about each of them.

Effective marketing also calls for four major planning skills. The first is *product development*, i.e., configuration. The marketer should know where to look for appropriate ideas, how to choose and refine the product concept, how to stylize and package the product, and how to test it. The second is *pricing*, i.e., valuation. He must develop an attractive set of terms for the product. The third is *distribution*, i.e., facilitation. The marketer should determine how to get the product into circulation and make it accessible to its target market. The fourth is *promotion*, i.e., symbolization. The marketer must be capable of stimulating market interest in the product.

Effective marketing also requires three organizational skills. The first is *orga-

nizational design. The marketer should understand the advantages and disadvantages of organizing market activity along functional, product, and market lines. The second is *organizational staffing.* He should know how to find, train, and assign effective comarketers. The third is *organizational motivation.* He must determine how to stimulate the best marketing effort by his staff.

Finally, effective marketing also calls for two control skills. The first is *market results measurement,* whereby the marketer keeps informed of the attitudinal and behavioral responses he is achieving in the marketplace. The second is *marketing cost measurement,* whereby the marketer keeps informed of his costs and efficiency in carrying out his marketing plans.

SOME QUESTIONS ABOUT GENERIC MARKETING

The robustness of the particular conception of marketing advocated in this article will be known in time through testing the ideas in various situations. The question is whether the logic called marketing really helps individuals such as educational administrators, public officials, museum directors, or church leaders to better interpret their problems and construct their strategies. If these ideas are validated in the marketplace, they will be accepted and adopted.

However, academic debate does contribute substantially to the sharpening of the issues and conceptions. Several interesting questions have arisen in the course of efforts by this author to expound the generic concept of marketing. Three of these questions are raised and discussed below.

1. Isn't generic marketing really using influence as the core concept rather than exchange?

It is tempting to think that the three levels of consciousness of marketing move from *market transactions* to *exchange* to *influence* as the succeeding core concepts. The concept of influence undeniably plays an important role in marketing thought. Personal selling and advertising are essentially influence efforts. Product design, pricing, packaging, and distribution planning make extensive use of influence considerations. It would be too general to say, however, that marketing is synonymous with interpersonal, intergroup, or interorganizational influence processes.

Marketing is a particular way of looking at the problem of achieving a valued response from a target market. It essentially holds that exchange values must be identified, and the marketing program must be based on these exchange values. Thus the anticigarette marketer analyzes what the market is being asked to give up and what inducements might be offered. The marketer recognizes that every action by a person has an opportunity cost. The marketer attempts to find ways to increase the person's perceived rate of exchange between what he would receive and what he would give up in *freely* adopting that behavior. The marketer is a specialist at understanding human wants and values and knows what it takes for someone to act.

2. How would one distinguish between marketing and a host of related activities such as lobbying, propagandizing, publicizing, and negotiating?

Marketing and other influence activities and tools share some common characteristics as well as exhibit some unique features. Each influence activity has to be examined separately in relation to marketing. *Lobbying,* for example, is one aspect of government-directed marketing. The lobbyist attempts to evoke support from a legislator through offering values to the legislator (e.g., information, votes, friendship, and favors). A lobbyist thinks through the problem of marketing his legislation as carefully as the business marketer thinks through the problem of marketing his product or service. *Propagandizing* is the marketing of a political or social idea to a mass audience. The propagandist attempts to package the ideas in such a way as to constitute values to the target audience in exchange for support. *Publicizing* is the effort to create attention and interest in a target audience. As such it is a tool of marketing. *Negotiation* is a face-to-face mutual marketing process. In general, the broadened concept of marketing underscores the kinship of marketing with a large number of other activities and suggests that marketing is a more endemic process in society than business marketing alone suggests.

3. Doesn't generic marketing imply that a marketer would be more capable of managing political or charitable campaigns than professionals in these businesses?

A distinction should be drawn between marketing as a *logic* and marketing as a *competence.* Anyone who is seeking a response in another would benefit from applying marketing logic to the problem. Thus a company treasurer seeking a loan, a company recruiter seeking a talented executive, a conservationist seeking an antipollution law, would all benefit in conceptualizing their problem in marketing terms. In these instances, they would be donning a marketer's hat although they would not be performing as professional marketers. A professional marketer is someone who (1) regularly works with marketing problems in a specific area and (2) has a specialized knowledge of this area. The political strategist, to the extent he is effective, is a professional marketer. He has learned how to effectively design, package, price, advertise, and distribute his type of product in his type of market. A professional marketer who suddenly decides to handle political candidates would need to develop competence and knowledge in this area just as he would if he suddenly decided to handle soap or steel. Being a marketer only means that a person has mastered the logic of marketing. To master the particular market requires additional learning and experience.

SUMMARY AND CONCLUSION

This article has examined the current debate in marketing concerning whether its substance belongs in the business area, or whether it is applicable to all areas in which organizations attempt to relate to customers and other publics. Specifically, *consciousness one marketing* holds that marketing's core idea is *market transactions,* and therefore marketing applies to buyers, sellers, and commercial products and services. *Consciousness two marketing* holds that marketing's core idea is *organization-client transactions,* and therefore marketing applies in any organization that can recognize a group called customers. *Consciousness three marketing* holds that marketing's core area is *transactions,* and therefore marketing applies to any social unit seeking to exchange values with other social units.

This broadest conception of marketing can be called *generic marketing.* Generic marketing takes a functional rather than a structural view of marketing. Four axioms define generic marketing.

Axiom 1. *Marketing involves two or more social units.*
Axiom 2. *At least one of the social units is seeking a specific response from one or more other units concerning some social object.*
Axiom 3. *The market's response probability is not fixed.*
Axiom 4. *Marketing is the attempt to produce the desired response by creating and offering values to the market.*

These four axioms and their corollaries are intended to provide unambiguous criteria for determining what constitutes a marketing process.

Generic marketing further implies that marketing activity can be classed according to the *target market* (marketing directed to supporters, employees, suppliers, agents, consumers, general public, special publics, government, and competitors); the *product* (goods, services, organizations, persons, places, and ideas); and the *marketer* (business, political, social, religious, cultural, and knowledge organizations).

Marketers face the same tasks in all types of marketing. Their major analytical tasks are *market analysis* and *product analysis.* Their major planning tasks are *product development, pricing, distribution,* and *promotion.* Their major organizational tasks are *design, staffing,* and *motivation.* Their major control tasks are *marketing results measurement* and *marketing cost measurement.*

Generic marketing is a logic available to all organizations facing problems of market response. A distinction should be drawn between applying a marketing point of view to a specific problem and being a marketing professional. Marketing logic alone does not make a marketing professional. The professional also acquires competence, which along with the logic, allows him to interpret his problems and construct his marketing strategies in an effective way.

NOTES

[1] Philip Kotler and Sidney J. Levy, "Broadening the Concept of Marketing," *Journal of Marketing,* Vol. 33 (January, 1969), pp. 10–15.

[2] David Luck, "Broadening the Concept of Marketing—Too Far," *Journal of Marketing,* Vol. 33 (July, 1969), pp. 53–54.

[3] *Journal of Marketing,* Vol. 35 (July, 1971).

[4] Charles A. Reich, *The Greening of America* (New York: Random House, 1970).

[5] Perry Bliss, *Marketing Management and the Behavioral Environment* (Englewood Cliffs, N.J.: Prentice-Hall, Inc., 1970), pp. 106–108, 119–120.

[6] See Philip Kotler and Sidney J. Levy, "Demarketing, Yes, Demarketing," *Harvard Business Review,* Vol. 49 (November–December, 1971), pp. 71–80.

SOME SUGGESTIONS FOR FURTHER READING

Arndt, J. (1978), "How Broad Should the Marketing Concept Be?"*Journal of Marketing* (January), 101–104.

Carman, J. M. (1973), "On the Universality of Marketing," *Journal of Contemporary Business* (Autumn), 1–16.

———— (1980), "Paradigms for Marketing Theory," *Research in Marketing* (Volume 3), 1–36.

Levy, S. J. and G. Zaltman (1975), *Marketing, Society and Conflict*, Englewood Cliffs, N.J.: Prentice-Hall.

Tucker, W. J., "Future Directions in Marketing Theory," *Journal of Marketing* (April), 30–35.

7 / MARKETING AS EXCHANGE /
Richard P. Bagozzi

The exchange paradigm has emerged as a framework useful for conceptualizing marketing behavior. Indeed, most contemporary definitions of marketing explicitly include exchange in their formulations.[1] Moreover, the current debate on "broadening" centers on the very notion of exchange: on its nature, scope, and efficacy in marketing.

This article analyzes a number of dimensions of the exchange paradigm that have not been dealt with in the marketing literature. First, it attempts to show that what marketers have considered as exchange is a special case of exchange theory that focuses primarily on direct transfers of tangible entities between two parties. In reality, marketing exchanges often are indirect, they may involve intangible and symbolic aspects, and more than two parties may participate. Second, the media and meaning of exchange are discussed in order to provide a foundation for specifying underlying mechanisms in marketing exchanges. Finally, social marketing is analyzed in light of the broadened concept of exchange.

The following discussion proceeds from the assumptions embodied in the generic concept of marketing as formulated by Kotler, Levy, and others.[2] In particular, it is assumed that marketing theory is concerned with two questions: (1) Why do people and organizations engage in exchange relationships? and (2) How are exchanges created, resolved, or avoided? The domain for the subject matter of marketing is assumed to be quite broad, encompassing all activities involving "exchange" and the cause and effect of phenomena associated with it. As in the social and natural sciences, marketing owes its definition to the outcome of debate and competition between divergent views in an evolutionary process that Kuhn terms a "scientific revolution."[3] Although the debate is far from settled, there appears to be a growing consensus that exchange forms the core phenomenon for study in marketing. Whether the specific instances of exchange are to be limited to economic institutions and consumers in the traditional sense or expanded to all organizations in the broadened sense deserves further attention by marketing scholars and practitioners. Significantly, the following principles apply to exchanges in both senses.

THE TYPES OF EXCHANGE

In general, there are three types of exchange: restricted, generalized, and complex.[4] Each of these is described below.

"Marketing as Exchange," Richard P. Bagozzi, Vol. 39 (October 1975), pp. 32–39. Reprinted from the *Journal of Marketing,* published by the American Marketing Association.
Richard Bagozzi is a professor of marketing at The Massachusetts Institute of Technology. He received his Ph.D. from Northwestern University and has taught at the University of California at Berkeley. His latest book is *Causal Models in Marketing.*

Restricted Exchange

Restricted exchange refers to two-party reciprocal relationships which may be represented diagrammatically as A ⟷ B, where "⟷" signifies "gives to and receives from" and A and B represent social actors such as consumers, retailers, salesmen, organizations, or collectivities.[5] Most treatments of, and references to, exchanges in the marketing literature have implicitly dealt with restricted exchanges; that is, they have dealt with customer-salesman, wholesaler-retailer, or other such dyadic exchanges.

Restricted exchanges exhibit two characteristics:

First, there is a great deal of attempt to maintain equality. This is especially the case with repeatable social exchange acts. Attempts to gain advantage at the expense of the other is [*sic*] minimized. Negatively, the breach of the rule of equality quickly leads to emotional reactions. . . . Secondly, there is a *quid pro quo* mentality in restricted exchange activities. Time intervals in mutual reciprocities are cut short and there is an attempt to balance activities and exchange items as part of the mutual reciprocal relations.[6]

The "attempt to maintain equality" is quite evident in restricted marketing exchanges. Retailers, for example, know that they will not obtain repeat purchases if the consumer is taken advantage of and deceived. The "breach" in this rule of equality—which is a central tenet of the marketing concept—has led to picketing, boycotts, and even rioting. Finally, the fact that restricted marketing exchanges must involve a *quid pro quo* notion (something of value in exchange for something of value) has been at the heart of Luck's criticism of broadening the concept of marketing.[7] However, as will be developed below, there are important exceptions to the *quid pro quo* requirement in many marketing exchanges.

Generalized Exchange

Generalized exchange denotes univocal, reciprocal relationships among at least three actors in the exchange situation. Univocal reciprocity occurs "if the reciprocations involve at least three actors and if the actors do not benefit each other directly but only indirectly."[8] Given three social actors, for instance, generalized exchange may be represented as A→B→C→A, where "→" signifies "gives to." In generalized exchange, the social actors form a system in which each actor gives to another but receives from someone other than to whom he gave. For example, suppose a public bus company (B) asks a local department store chain (A) to donate or give a number of benches to the bus company. Suppose further that, after the department store chain (A) gives the benches to the bus company (B), the company (B) then places the benches at bus stops for the convenience of its riders (C). Finally, suppose that a number of the riders (C) see the advertisements placed on the benches by the department store chain (A) and later patronize the store as a result of this exposure. This sequence of exchange, A→B→C→A, is known as generalized exchange; while it fails to conform to the usual notions of *quid pro quo*, it certainly constitutes a marketing exchange of interest.

Complex Exchange

Complex exchange refers to a system of mutual relationships between at least three parties. Each social actor is involved in at least one direct exchange, while the entire system is organized by an interconnecting web of relationships.

Perhaps the best example of complex exchange in marketing is the channel of distribution. Letting A represent a manufacturer, B a retailer, and C a consumer, it is possible to depict the channel as A⟷B⟷C. Such open-ended sequences of direct exchanges may be designated *complex chain exchanges*.

But many marketing exchanges involve relatively closed sequences of relationships. For example, consider the claim made by Kotler that a "transaction takes place . . . when a person decides to watch a television program." [9] Recently, Carman and Luck have criticized this assertion, maintaining that it may not exhibit an exchange.[10] The differences stem from: (1) a disagreement on whether exchange must consist of transfers of tangible (as opposed to intangible) things of value, and (2) a neglect of the possibility of systems of exchange. Figure 1 illustrates the exchange between a person and a television program and how it may be viewed as a link in a system termed *complex circular exchange*.[11] In this system of exchange, the person experiences a direct transfer of intangibles between himself and the program. That is, he gives his attention, support (for example, as measured by the Nielsen ratings), potential for purchase, and so on, and receives entertainment, enjoyment, product information, and other intangible entities. The person also experiences an indirect exchange with the television program via a sequence of direct, tangible exchanges. Thus, after being informed of the availability of a book through an exchange with the television program and its advertising, a person

Figure 1. An example of complex circular exchange

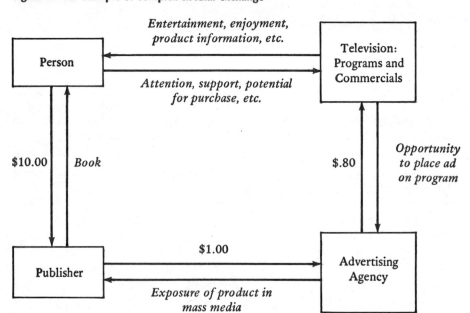

may purchase it for, say, $10.00. The book's publisher, in turn, may purchase the services of an advertiser, paying what amounts to a percentage of each sale, say, $1.00. Finally, the advertiser receives the opportunity to place a commercial on the air from the television network in exchange for what amounts to a percentage of each sale, say, $.80. In this particular example, the occurrence of the direct intangible exchange was a necessary prerequisite for the development of the series of indirect tangible exchanges. Thus, an exchange *can* occur between a person and a television program.

Complex chain and complex circular exchanges involve predominantly conscious systems of social and economic relationships. In this sense, there is an overt coordination of activities and expectations, which Alderson called an organized behavioral system and which he reserved for the household, the firm, and the channel of distribution.[12] However, it should be evident that the designation "organized" is a relative one and that other exchange systems, such as the one shown in Figure 1, also evidence aspects of overt coordination in an economic, social, and symbolic sense.

Generalized and complex exchanges are also present in relatively unconscious systems of social and economic relationships. Thus, a modern economy may experience a covert coordination of activities through exchanges that occur when many individuals, groups, and firms pursue their own self-interest. This is what Adam Smith meant by his reference to an "invisible hand."[13] Similarly, in his analysis of primitive societies and marketing systems, Frazer has shown that exchange and the pursuit of self-interest can be the foundation for the web of kinship, economic, and social institutions.[14] The recent exchange theories of Homans and Blau are also based on this individualistic assumption of self-interest.[15] It should be stressed, however, that the exchange tradition developed by Levi-Strauss is not an individualistic one but rather is built on social, collectivistic assumptions associated with generalized exchange.[16] These differences will become more apparent when social marketing is analyzed below.

THE MEDIA AND MEANING OF EXCHANGE

In order to satisfy human needs, people and organizations are compelled to engage in social and economic exchanges with other people and organizations. This is true for primitive as well as highly developed societies. Social actors obtain satisfaction of their needs by complying with, or influencing, the behavior of other actors. They do this by communicating and controlling the media of exchange which, in turn, comprise the links between one individual and another, between one organization and another. Significantly, marketing exchanges harbor meanings for individuals that go beyond the mere use of media for obtaining results in interactions.

The Media of Exchange

The media of exchange are the vehicles with which people communicate to, and influence, others in the satisfaction of their needs. These vehicles include money, persuasion, punishment, power (authority), inducement, and activation of normative or ethical commitments.[17] Products and services are also media of exchange. In consumer behavior research, marketers have extensively studied the effects of these vehicles on behavior. Moreover, it has been suggested that a number of these vehicles be used in conjunction with sociopsychological processes to explain the customer-salesman relationship.[18] It should be noted, however, that marketing is not solely concerned with influence processes, whether these involve manufacturers influencing consumers or consumers influencing manufacturers. Marketing is also concerned with meeting existing needs and anticipating future needs, and these activities do not necessarily entail attempts to influence or persuade.

To illustrate the multivariate nature of media in marketing exchanges, consider the example of the channel of distribution, a complex chain exchange. The firms in a channel of distribution are engaged in an intricate social system of behavioral relationships that go well beyond the visible exchange of products and money.[19] Typically, the traditional channel achieves its conscious coordination of effort through the mutual expectations of profit. In addition, each firm in the channel may influence the degree of cooperation and compliance of its partners by offering inducements in the form of services, deals, or other benefits or by persuading each link in the channel that it is in its own best interest to cooperate. A firm may also affect the behavior or decisions of another firm through the use of the power it may possess. Wilkinson has studied five bases of power in the channel of distribution—reward, coercive, legitimate, referent, and expert power—and has tested aspects of these relationships between firms.[20] Finally, a firm may remind a delinquent member in the channel of its contractual obligations or even threaten the member with legal action for a breach of agreement. This influence medium is known as the activation of commitments.

The Meaning of Exchange

Human behavior is more than the outward responses or reactions of people to stimuli. Man not only reacts to events or the actions of others but he self-generates his own acts.[21] His behavior is purposeful, intentional. It is motivated. Man is an information seeker and generator as well as an information processor. In short, human behavior is a conjunction of meaning with action and reaction.

Similarly, exchange is more than the mere transfer of a product or service for money. To be sure, most marketing exchanges are characterized by such a transfer. But the reasons behind the exchange—the explanation of its occurrence—lie in the social and psychological significance of the experiences, feelings, and meanings of the parties in the exchange. In general, marketing exchanges may exhibit one of three classes of meanings: utilitarian, symbolic, or mixed.

Utilitarian exchange. A utilitarian exchange is an interaction whereby goods are given in return for money or other goods and the motivation behind the actions lies in the anticipated use or tangible characteristics commonly associated with the objects in the exchange. The utilitarian exchange is often referred to as an economic exchange, and most treatments of exchange in marketing implicitly rely on this usage. As Bartels notes with regard to the identity crisis in marketing:

Marketing has initially and generally been associated exclusively with the distributive part of the *economic* institution and function. . . .

The question, then, is whether marketing is identified by the *field* of economics in which the marketing techniques have been developed and generally applied, or by the socalled marketing *techniques,* wherever they may be applied.

If marketing relates to the distributive function of the economy, providing goods and services, that *physical* function differentiates it from all other social institutions.[22]

Most marketers have traditionally conceptualized the subject matter of the discipline in these terms, and they have proceeded from the assumptions embodied in utilitarian exchange.

In general, utilitarian exchange theory is built on the foundation of *economic man.*[23] Thus, it is assumed that:

1. Men are rational in their behavior.
2. They attempt to maximize their satisfaction in exchanges.
3. They have complete information on alternatives available to them in exchanges.
4. These exchanges are relatively free from external influence.

Coleman has developed an elaborate mathematical framework for representing exchange behavior that assumes many of the features of economic man.[24] His model is based on the theory of purposive action, which posits that each "actor will choose that action which according to his estimate will lead to an expectation of the most beneficial consequences." [25] Among other things, the theory may be used to predict the outcomes and degree of control social actors have for a set of collective actions in an exchange system.

Symbolic exchange. Symbolic exchange refers to the mutual transfer of psychological, social, or other intangible entities between two or more parties. Levy was one of the first marketers to recognize this aspect of behavior, which is common to many everyday marketing exchanges:

. . . *symbol* is a general term for all instances where experience is mediated rather than direct; where an object, action, word, picture, or complex behavior is understood to mean not only itself but also some *other* ideas or feelings.

The less concern there is with the concrete satisfactions of a survival level of existence, the more abstract human responses become. As behavior in the market place is increasingly elaborated, it also becomes increasingly symbolic. This idea needs some examination, because it means that sellers of goods are engaged, whether willfully or not, in selling *symbols,* as well as practical merchandise. It means that marketing managers must attend to more than the relatively superficial facts with which they usually concern themselves when they do not think of their goods as having symbolic significance. . . . *People buy things not only for what they can do, but also for what they mean.*[26]

Mixed exchange. Marketing exchanges involve both utilitarian and symbolic aspects, and it is often very difficult to separate the two. Yet, the very creation and resolution of marketing exchanges depend on the nature of the symbolic and utilitarian mix. It has only been within the past decade or so that marketers have investigated this deeper side of marketing behavior in their studies of psychographics, motivation research, attitude and multiattribute models, and other aspects of buyer and consumer behavior. Out of this research tradition has emerged a picture of man in his true complexity as striving for both economic and symbolic rewards. Thus, we see the emergence of *marketing man*, perhaps based on the following assumptions:

1. Man is sometimes rational, sometimes irrational.
2. He is motivated by tangible as well as intangible rewards, by internal as well as external forces.[27]
3. He engages in utilitarian as well as symbolic exchanges involving psychological and social aspects.
4. Although faced with incomplete information, he proceeds the best he can and makes at least rudimentary and sometimes unconscious calculations of the costs and benefits associated with social and economic exchanges.
5. Although occasionally striving to maximize his profits, marketing man often settles for less than optimum gains in his exchanges.
6. Finally, exchanges do not occur in isolation but are subject to a host of individual and social constraints: legal, ethical, normative, coercive, and the like.

The important research question to answer is: *What are the forces and conditions creating and resolving marketing exchange relationships?* The processes involved in the creation and resolution of exchange relationships constitute the subject matter of marketing, and these processes depend on, and cannot be separated from, the fundamental character of human and organizational needs.

SOCIAL MARKETING

The marketing literature is replete with conflicting definitions of *social marketing*. Some have defined the term to signify the *use* of marketing skills in social causes,[28] while others have meant it to refer also to "the *study* of markets and marketing activities within a total social system." [29] Bartels recently muddied the waters with still a new definition that is vastly different from those previously suggested. For him, social marketing designates "the *application* of marketing techniques to *nonmarketing* fields." [30] Since these definitions cover virtually everything in marketing and even some things outside of marketing, it is no wonder that one author felt compelled to express his "personal confusion" and "uncomfortable" state of mind regarding the concept.[31]

But what is social marketing? Before answering this question, we must reject the previous definitions for a number of reasons. First, we must reject the notion that social marketing is merely the "use" or "application" of marketing techniques or skills to other areas. A science or discipline is something more than its technologies. "Social marketing" connotes what is social and what is marketing, and to limit the definition to the tools of a discipline is to beg the question of the meaning of marketing. Second, social marketing is not solely the study of marketing within the frame of the total social system, and it is even more than the subject matter of the discipline. Rather, the meaning of social marketing—like that of marketing itself—is to be found in the unique *problems* that confront the discipline. Thus, as the philosopher of science, Popper, notes:

The belief that there is such a thing as physics, or biology, or archaeology, and that these "studies" or "disciplines" are distinguishable by the subject matter which they investigate, appears to me to be a residue from the time when one believed that a theory had to proceed from a definition of its own subject matter. But subject matter, or kinds of things, do not, I hold, constitute a basis for distinguishing disciplines. Disciplines are distinguished partly for historical reasons and reasons of administrative convenience (such as the organization of teaching and of appointments), and partly because the theories which we construct to solve our problems have a tendency to grow into unified systems. But all this classification and distinction is a comparatively unimportant and superficial affair. *We are not students of some subject matter but students of problems.* And problems may cut right across the borders of any subject matter or discipline.[32]

Social marketing, then, addresses a particular type of problem which, in turn, is a subset of the generic concept of marketing. That is, social marketing is the answer to a particular question: Why and how are *exchanges* created and resolved in *social* relationships? Social relationships (as opposed to economic relationships) are those such as family planning agent-client, welfare agent-indigent, social worker-poor person, and so on.[33] Social marketing attempts to determine the dynamics and nature of the exchange behavior in these relationships.

But is there an exchange in a social relationship? Luck, for example, feels that "a person who receives a free service is not a buyer and has conducted no exchange of values with the provider of the service."[34] It is the contention in this article that there is most definitely an exchange in social marketing relationships, but the exchange is not the simple *quid pro quo* notion characteristic of most economic exchanges. Rather, social marketing relationships exhibit what may be called generalized or complex exchanges. They involve the symbolic transfer of both tangible and intangible entities, and they invoke various media to influence such exchanges.

Figure 2 illustrates a typical social marketing exchange. In this system, society authorizes government—through its votes and tax payments—to provide needed social services such as welfare. In return, the members of society receive social insurance against common human maladies. Government, in turn, pays the salaries of social workers, gives them authority to provide social services, and so on. It also distributes welfare payments directly to the needy. These relatively contemporaneous transfers make this marketing system one of generalized exchange. In addition, a number of symbolic and delayed transfers occur that make the system also one of complex exchange. For example, as shown by dotted lines in the figure, in many cases the needy and dependent have given to the government in the past, since they may have paid taxes and voted. Moreover, members of society anticipate that they, or a number of their members, will become dependent and that social services represent an investment as well as an obligation. Hence, in one sense there is a mutual exchange between society and the needy separated, in part, by the passage of time. Finally, it should be noted that there are other tangential exchanges and forces occurring in this social marketing system that, depending on their bal-

Figure 2.   Social marketing and exchange

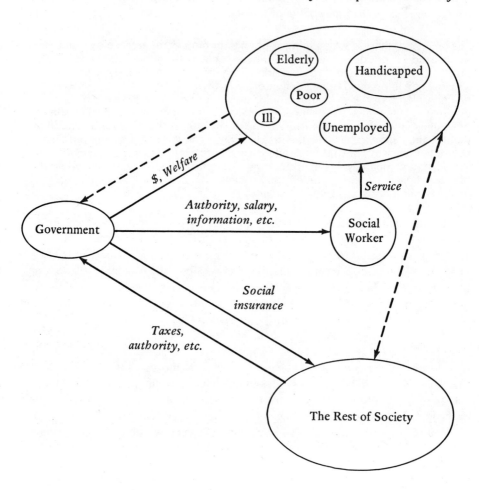

The Needy and Dependent in Society

ance, give it stability or promote change. The system achieves stability due, first, to the presence of the exchanges described above, which create mutual dependencies and univocal reciprocities; and, second, to symbolic exchanges, which reinforce the overt transfers. For example, the social worker gives to the needy but also receives back gratitude and feelings of accomplishment. The system undergoes change due to the dynamics of competing interests, as is exemplified in the efforts of lobbies and pressure groups to bring their needs to bear on the legislative process.

Thus, social marketing is really a subset of the generic concept of marketing in that it deals with the creation and resolution of exchanges in social relationships. Marketers can make contributions to other areas that contain social exchanges by providing theories and techniques for the understanding and control of such transactions. They do not usurp the authority of specialists in areas such as social work, but rather they aid and complement the efforts of these social scientists.

It is not so much the fact that the subject matter of marketing overlaps with that of other disciplines as it is that the problems of marketing are universal. In answer to Bartels' query, "Is marketing a specific function with general applicability or a general function that is specifically applied?"[35]—one may state that it is neither. Rather, marketing is a general function of universal applicability. It is the discipline of exchange behavior, and it deals with problems related to this behavior.

CONCLUSIONS AND IMPLICATIONS

A number of broad research questions may be posed:

1. Why do marketing exchanges emerge? How do people and organizations satisfy their needs through exchange?
2. Why do some marketing exchanges persist in ongoing relationships while others fall apart?
3. What are the processes leading to changes in marketing exchange relationships? How do the social actors or third parties influence or control an exchange?
4. What are the consequences of imbalances in power, resources, knowledge, and so on, in a marketing exchange? What is an equitable exchange?
5. What are the relationships between conflict, cooperation, competition, and exchange?
6. At what level may marketing exchanges be analyzed? What are the consequences of viewing exchanges as single dyads or complex systems of relation ships? What are the consequences of employing the individualistic reductionism of Homans versus the collectivistic orientation of Levi-Strauss for understanding exchange behavior?
7. Is the exchange paradigm universal? Does it apply to the free-enterprise countries of the western world, the planned economies of the communist countries, and the primitive economies of the third world?
8. How well does the exchange paradigm meet the requirements for theory as specified by philosophy of science criteria?

Although marketing seems to defy simple definition and circumspection, it is essential that marketers locate the distinctive focus (or foci) of the discipline. Failure to do so impedes both the growth of the discipline and the character of its performance. Exchange is a central concept in marketing, and it may well serve as the foundation for that elusive "general theory of marketing." This article has attempted to explore some of the key concepts in the exchange paradigm. Future research and discussion must search for specific social and psychological processes that create and resolve marketing exchanges.

NOTES

[1] See, for example, Marketing Staff of The Ohio State University, "A Statement of Marketing Philosophy," *Journal of Marketing,* Vol. 29 (January 1965), pp. 43–44; E. Jerome McCarthy, *Basic Marketing,* 5th ed. (Homewood, Ill.: Richard D. Irwin, 1975); Philip Kotler,

Marketing Management, 2nd ed. (Englewood Cliffs, N.J.: Prentice-Hall, 1972), p. 12; and Ben M. Enis, *Marketing Principles* (Pacific Palisades, Calif.: Goodyear Publishing Co., 1974), p. 21.

[2] Philip Kotler, "A Generic Concept of Marketing," *Journal of Marketing,* Vol. 36 (April 1972), pp. 46–54; and Philip Kotler and Sidney J. Levy, "Broadening the Concept of Marketing," *Journal of Marketing,* Vol. 33 (January 1969), pp. 10–15.

[3] Thomas S. Kuhn, *The Structure of Scientific Revolutions,* 2nd ed. (Chicago: The University of Chicago Press, 1970).

[4] The distinction between restricted and generalized exchange was first made by anthropologist Claude Levi-Strauss in *The Elementary Structures of Kinship* (Boston: Beacon Press, 1969). An extended critical analysis of restricted and generalized exchange may be found in Peter P. Ekeh, *Social Exchange Theory: The Two Traditions* (Cambridge, Mass.: Harvard University Press, 1974), Chap. 3.

[5] Ekeh, same reference as footnote 4, p. 50.

[6] Ekeh, same reference as footnote 4, pp. 51–52.

[7] David J. Luck, "Broadening the Concept of Marketing—Too Far," *Journal of Marketing,* Vol. 33 (January 1969), pp. 10–15; and Luck, "Social Marketing: Confusion Compounded," *Journal of Marketing,* Vol. 38 (October 1974), pp. 70–72.

[8] Ekeh, same reference as footnote 4, pp. 48, 50.

[9] Kotler, same reference as footnote 2, p. 48.

[10] James M. Carman, "On the Universality of Marketing," *Journal of Contemporary Business,* Vol. 2 (Autumn 1973), p. 5; and Luck, "Social Marketing," same reference as footnote 7, p. 72.

[11] A form of circular exchange in primitive societies was first suggested by Bronislaw Malinowski in *Argonauts of the Western Pacific* (London: Routledge and Kegan Paul, 1922), p. 93; but in his concept the same physical items were transmitted to all parties, while in complex circular exchange as defined here different tangible or symbolic entities may be transferred.

[12] Wroe Alderson, *Dynamic Marketing Behavior* (Homewood, Ill.: Richard D. Irwin, 1965), Chap. 1.

[13] For a modern treatment of Adam Smith's contribution to exchange theory, see Walter Nord, "Adam Smith and Contemporary Social Exchange Theory," *The American Journal of Economics and Sociology,* Vol. 32 (October 1974), pp. 421–436.

[14] Sir James G. Frazer, *Folklore in the Old Testament,* Vol. 2 (London: Macmillan & Co., 1919).

[15] George C. Homans, *Social Behavior: Its Elementary Forms,* rev. ed. (New York: Harcourt Brace Jovanovich, 1974); and Peter M. Blau, *Exchange and Power in Social Life* (New York: John Wiley & Sons, 1964).

[16] Levi-Strauss, same reference as footnote 4. See also, Ekeh, same reference as footnote 4, Chaps. 3 and 4.

[17] Talcott Parsons, "On the Concept of Influence," *Public Opinion Quarterly,* Vol. 27 (Spring 1963), pp. 37–62; and Parsons, "On the Concept of Political Power," *Proceedings of the American Philosophical Society,* Vol. 107 (June 1963), pp. 232–262. See also, Richard Emerson, "Power Dependence Relations," *American Sociological Review,* Vol. 27 (February 1962), pp. 31–40.

[18] Richard P. Bagozzi, "Marketing as an Organized Behavioral System of Exchange," *Journal of Marketing,* Vol. 38 (October 1974), pp. 77–81.

[19] See, for example, Louis W. Stern, *Distribution Channels: Behavioral Dimensions* (New York: Houghton Mifflin Co., 1969).

[20] Ian Wilkinson, "Power in Distribution Channels," *Cranfield Research Papers in Marketing and Logistics,* Session 1973–1974 (Cranfield School of Management, Cranfield, Bedfordshire, England); and Wilkinson, "Researching the Distribution Channels for Consumer and Industrial Goods: the Power Dimension," *Journal of the Market Research Society,* Vol. 16 (No. 1, 1974), pp. 12–32.

[21] This dynamic, as opposed to mechanistic, image of human behavior is described nicely in R. Harré and P. F. Secord, *The Explanation of Social Behavior* (Totawa, N.J.: Littlefield, Adams & Co., 1973).

[22] Robert Bartels, "The Identity Crisis in Marketing," *Journal of Marketing,* Vol. 38 (October 1974), p. 75. Emphasis added.

[23] For a modern treatment of economic man, see Harold K. Schneider, *Economic Man* (New York: The Free Press, 1974).

[24] James S. Coleman, "Systems of Social Exchange," *Journal of Mathematical Sociology,* Vol. 2 (December 1972).

[25] James S. Coleman, *The Mathematics of Collective Action* (Chicago: Aldine-Atherton, 1973).

[26] Sidney J. Levy, "Symbols for Sale," *Harvard Business Review,* Vol. 37 (July–August 1959), pp. 117–119.

[27] It should be stressed that man is motivated by the hope or anticipation of *future* rewards, and these may consist of classes of benefits not necessarily experienced in the past. See Homans's individualistic exchange theory, a learning perspective, same reference as footnote 15; Levi-Strauss's collectivistic, symbolic perspective, same reference as footnote 4; and Ekeh, same reference as footnote 4, pp. 118–124, 163.

[28] Philip Kotler and Gerald Zaltman, "Social Marketing: An Approach to Planned Social Change," *Journal of Marketing,* Vol. 35 (July 1971), p. 5.

[29] William Lazer and Eugene J. Kelley, eds., *Social Marketing: Perspectives and Viewpoints* (Homewood, Ill.: Richard D. Irwin, 1973), p. 4. Emphasis added.

[30] Same reference as footnote 22. Emphasis added.

[31] Luck, "Social Marketing," same reference as footnote 7, p. 70.

[32] Karl R. Popper, *Conjectures and Refutations* (New York: Harper & Row, 1963), p. 67.

[33] For a conceptual framework comparing marketing and other social relationships, see Richard P. Bagozzi, "What is a Marketing Relationship?" *Der Markt,* No. 51, 1974, pp. 64–69.

[34] Luck, "Social Marketing," same reference as footnote 7, p. 71.

[35] Same reference as footnote 22, p. 73.

SOME SUGGESTIONS FOR FURTHER READING

Bagozzi, R. P. (1978), "Marketing as Exchange: A Theory of Transactions in the Marketplace," *American Behavioral Scientist* (March–April), 535–556.

——, T. V. Bonoma, and G. Zaltman (1977), "The Dyadic Paradigm in Marketing Thought," in T. V. Bonoma and G. Zaltman, eds., *Organization Buying Behavior,* Chicago: American Marketing Association.

Kaikati, J. G. (1976), "The Reincarnation of Barter Trade as a Marketing Tool," *Journal of Marketing* (April), 17–24.

Ohio State University Marketing Staff, (1965), "A Statement of Marketing Philosophy," *Journal of Marketing* (January), 43–44.

Weigand, R. E. (1977), "International Trade Without Money," *Harvard Business Review* (November–December), 28ff.

8 / THE NATURE AND SCOPE OF MARKETING / Shelby D. Hunt

During the past three decades, two controversies have overshadowed all others in the marketing literature. The first is the "Is marketing a science?" controversy sparked by an early *Journal of Marketing* article by Converse entitled "The Development of a Science of Marketing."[1] Other prominent writers who fueled the debate included Bartels, Hutchinson, Baumol, Buzzell, Taylor, and Halbert.[2] After raging throughout most of the '50s and '60s, the controversy has since waned. The waning may be more apparent than real, however, because many of the substantive issues underlying the marketing science controversy overlap with the more recent "nature of marketing" (broadening the concept of marketing) debate. Fundamental to both controversies are some radically different perspectives on the essential characteristics of both *marketing* and *science*.

The purpose of this article is to develop a conceptual model of the scope of marketing and to use that model to analyze (1) the approaches to the study of marketing, (2) the "nature of marketing" controversy, and (3) the marketing science debate. Before developing the model, some preliminary observations on the controversy concerning the nature of marketing are appropriate.

THE NATURE OF MARKETING

What is marketing? What kinds of phenomena are appropriately termed *marketing phenomena*? How do marketing activities differ from nonmarketing activities? What is a marketing system? How can marketing processes be distinguished from other social processes? Which institutions should one refer to as marketing institutions? *In short, what is the proper conceptual domain of the construct labeled "marketing"?*

The American Marketing Association defines marketing as "the performance of business activities that direct the flow of goods and services from producer to consumer or user."[3] This position has come under attack from various quarters as being too restrictive and has prompted one textbook on marketing to note: "Marketing is not easy to define. No one has yet been able to formulate a clear, concise definition that finds universal acceptance."[4]

"The Nature and Scope of Marketing," Shelby D. Hunt, Vol. 40 (July 1976), pp. 17–28. Reprinted from the *Journal of Marketing,* published by the American Marketing Association. This article won the Maynard Award as best theoretical article of the year.
Shelby Hunt is Professor of Marketing at Texas Technological University. He received his Ph.D. from Michigan State University and has written extensively in the area of marketing theory.
The author wishes to gratefully acknowledge the constructive criticisms of earlier drafts of this article by Professors George W. Brooker and John R. Nevin, both of the University of Wisconsin–Madison.

Although vigorous debate concerning the basic nature of marketing has alternately waxed and waned since the early 1900s, the most recent controversy probably traces back to a position paper by the marketing staff of the Ohio State University in 1965. They suggested that marketing be considered "the process in a society by which the demand structure for economic goods and services is anticipated or enlarged and satisfied through the conception, promotion, exchange, and physical distribution of goods and services." [5] Note the conspicuous absence of the notion that marketing consists of a set of *business activities* (as in the AMA definition). Rather, they considered marketing to be a *social process*.

Next to plunge into the semantical battle were Kotler and Levy. Although they did not specifically propose a new definition of marketing, Kotler and Levy in 1969 suggested that the concept of marketing be broadened to include nonbusiness organizations. They observed that churches, police departments, and public schools have products and customers, and that they use the normal tools of the marketing mix. Therefore, Kotler and Levy conclude that these organizations perform marketing, or at least marketing-like, activities. Thus,

the choice facing those who manage nonbusiness organizations is not whether to market or not to market, for no organization can avoid marketing. The choice is whether to do it well or poorly, and on this necessity the case for organizational marketing is basically founded.[6]

In the same issue of the *Journal of Marketing,* Lazer discussed the changing boundaries of marketing. He pleaded that: "What is required is a broader perception and definition of marketing than has hitherto been the case—one that recognizes marketing's societal dimensions and perceives of marketing as more than just a technology of the firm." [7] Thus, Kotler and Levy desired to broaden the notion of marketing by including not-for-profit organizations, and Lazer called for a definition of marketing that recognized the discipline's expanding societal dimensions.

Luck took sharp issue with Kotler and Levy by insisting that marketing be limited to those business processes and activities that ultimately result in a *market* transaction.[8] Luck noted that even thus bounded, marketing would still be a field of enormous scope and that marketing specialists could still render their services to nonmarketing causes. Kotler and Levy then accused Luck of a new form of myopia and suggested that, "The crux of marketing lies in a *general idea of exchange* rather than the narrower thesis of market transactions." [9] They further contended that defining marketing "too narrowly" would inhibit students of marketing from applying their expertise to the most rapidly growing sectors of the society.

Other marketing commentators began to espouse the dual theses that (1) marketing be broadened to include nonbusiness organizations, and (2) marketing's societal dimensions deserve scrutiny. Thus, Ferber prophesied that marketing would diversify into the social and public policy fields.[10] And Lavidge sounded a similar call to arms by admonishing marketers to cease evaluating new products solely on the basis of whether they *can* be sold. Rather, he suggested, they should evaluate new products from a societal perspective, that is, *should* the product be sold?

The areas in which marketing people can, and must, be of service to society have broadened. In addition, marketing's functions have been broadened. Marketing no longer can be defined adequately in terms of the activities involved in buying, selling, and transporting goods and services.[11]

The movement to expand the concept of marketing probably became irreversible when the *Journal of Marketing* devoted an entire issue to marketing's changing social/environmental role. At that time, Kotler and Zaltman coined the term *social marketing,* which they defined as "the design, implementation and control of programs calculated to influence the acceptability of social ideas and involving considerations of product planning, pricing, communication, distribution, and marketing research."[12] In the same issue, marketing technology was applied to fund raising for the March of Dimes, health services, population problems, and the recycling of solid waste.[13] Further, Dawson chastised marketers for ignoring many fundamental issues pertaining to the social relevance of marketing activities:

Surely, in these troubled times, an appraisal of marketing's actual and potential role in relation to such [societal] problems is at least of equal importance to the technical aspects of the field. Yet, the emphasis upon practical problem-solving within the discipline far outweighs the attention paid to social ramifications of marketing activity.[14]

Kotler has since reevaluated his earlier positions concerning broadening the concept of marketing and has articulated a "generic" concept of marketing. He proposes that the essence of marketing is the *transaction,* defined as the exchange of values between two parties. Kotler's generic concept of marketing states: "Marketing is specifically concerned with how transactions are created, stimulated, facilitated and valued."[15] Empirical evidence indicates that, at least among marketing educators, the broadened concept of marketing represents a *fait accompli.* A recent study by Nichols showed that 95% of marketing educators believed that the scope of marketing should be broadened to include nonbusiness organizations. Similarly 93% agreed that marketing goes beyond just economic goods and services, and 83% favored including in the domain of marketing many activities whose ultimate result is not a market transaction.[16]

Although the advocates of extending the notion of marketing appear to have won the semantic battle, their efforts may not have been victimless. Carman notes that the definition of marketing plays a significant role in directing the research efforts of marketers. He believes that many processes (e.g., political processes) do not involve an exchange of values and that marketing should not take such processes under its "disciplinary wing."[17] Bartels has also explored the so-called identity crises in marketing and has pointed out numerous potential disadvantages to broadening the concept of marketing. These *potential* disadvantages include: (1) turning the attention of marketing researchers away from important problems in the area of physical distribution, (2) emphasizing methodology rather than substance as the content of marketing knowledge, and (3) an increasingly esoteric and abstract marketing literature. Bartels concluded: "If 'marketing' is to be regarded as so broad as to include both economic and noneconomic fields of application, perhaps marketing as originally conceived will ultimately reappear under another name."[18]

Similarly, Luck decries the "semantic jungle" that appears to be growing in marketing.[19] Citing conflicting definitions of *marketing* and *social marketing* in the current literature, Luck suggests that this semantic jungle has been impeding the efforts of marketers to think clearly about their discipline. He has challenged the American Marketing Association to create a special commission to clear up the definitional problems in marketing. Finally, a recent president of the American Marketing Association set the development of a consistent standard definition of marketing as a primary goal of the association.[20]

Three questions appear to be central to the "nature [broadening the concept] of marketing" controversy. First, what kinds of phenomena and issues *do* the various marketing writers perceive to be included in the scope of marketing? Second, what kinds of phenomena and issues *should* be included in the scope of marketing? Third, how can marketing be defined to both systematically encompass all the phenomena and issues that should be included and, at the same time, systematically exclude all other phenomena and issues? That is, a good definition of marketing must be both properly inclusive and exclusive. To rigorously evaluate these questions requires a conceptual model of the scope of marketing.

THE SCOPE OF MARKETING

No matter which definition of marketing one prefers, the scope of marketing is unquestionably broad. Often included are such diverse subject areas as consumer behavior, pricing, purchasing, sales management, product management, marketing communications, comparative marketing, social marketing, the efficiency/productivity of marketing systems, the role of marketing in economic development, packaging, channels of distribution, marketing research, societal issues in marketing, retailing, wholesaling, the social responsibility of marketing, international marketing, commodity marketing, and physical distribution. Though lengthy, this list of topics and issues does not exhaust the possibilities. Not all writers would include all the topics under the general rubric of marketing. The point deserving emphasis here, however, is that different commentators on marketing would *disagree* as to which topics should be excluded. The disagreement stems from fundamentally different perspectives and can best be analyzed by attempting to develop some common ground for classifying the diverse topics and issues in marketing.

The most widely used conceptual model of the scope of marketing is the familiar "4 Ps" model popularized by McCarthy in the early '60s.[21] The model is usually represented by three concentric circles. The inner circle contains the consumer, since this is the focal point of marketing effort. The second circle contains the marketing mix ("controllable factors") of price, place, promotion, and product. Finally, the third circle contains the uncontrollable factors of political and legal environment, economic environment, cultural and social environment, resources and objectives of the firm, and the existing business situation. As is readily apparent, many of the subject areas previously mentioned have no "home" in the 4 Ps model. For example, where does social marketing or efficiency of marketing systems or comparative marketing belong?

During a presentation at the 1972 Fall Conference of the American Marketing Association, Kotler made some observations concerning the desirability of classifying marketing phenomena using the concepts of *micro, macro, normative,* and *positive.*[22] These observations spurred the development of the conceptual model detailed in Table 1. The schema proposes that all marketing phenomena, issues, problems, models, theories, and research can be categorized using the three categorical dichotomies of (1) profit sector/nonprofit sector, (2) micro/macro, and (3) positive/normative. The three categorical dichotomies yield $2 \times 2 \times 2 = 8$ classes or cells in the schema. Thus, the first class includes all marketing topics that are

Table 1. The scope of marketing

		Positive	*Normative*

Profit Sector	**Micro**	(1) Problems, issues, theories, and research concerning:
		  a. Individual consumer buyer behavior
		  b. How firms determine prices
		  c. How firms determine products
		  d. How firms determine promotion
		  e. How firms determine channels of distribution
		  f. Case studies of marketing practices
			(2) Problems, issues, normative models, and research concerning how firms *should:*
			  a. Determine the marketing mix
			  b. Make pricing decisions
			  c. Make product decisions
			  d. Make promotion decisions
			  e. Make packaging decisions
			  f. Make purchasing decisions
			  g. Make international marketing decisions
			  h. Organize their marketing departments
			  i. Control their marketing efforts
			  j. Plan their marketing strategy
			  k. Apply systems theory to marketing problems
			  l. Manage retail establishments
			  m. Manage wholesale establishments
			  n. Implement the marketing concept

	Macro	(3) Problems, issues, theories, and research concerning:
		  a. Aggregate consumption patterns
		  b. Institutional approach to marketing
		  c. Commodity approach to marketing
		  d. Legal aspects of marketing
		  e. Comparative marketing
		  f. The efficiency of marketing systems
		  g. Whether the poor pay more
		  h. Whether marketing spurs or retards economic development
		  i. Power and conflict relationships in channels of distribution
		  j. Whether marketing functions are universal
		  k. Whether the marketing concept is consistent with consumers' interests
			(4) Problems, issues, normative models, and research concerning:
			  a. How marketing can be made more efficient
			  b. Whether distribution costs too much
			  c. Whether advertising is socially desirable
			  d. Whether consumer sovereignty is desirable
			  e. Whether stimulating demand is desirable
			  f. Whether the poor should pay more
			  g. What kinds of laws regulating marketing are optimal
			  h. Whether vertical marketing systems are socially desirable
			  i. Whether marketing should have special social responsibilities

	Positive	Normative
Micro	(5) Problems, issues, theories, and research concerning: a. Consumers' purchasing of public goods b. How nonprofit organizations determine prices c. How nonprofit organizations determine products d. How nonprofit organizations determine promotion e. How nonprofit organizations determine channels of distribution f. Case studies of public goods marketing	(6) Problems, issues, normative models, and research concerning how nonprofit organizations *should:* a. Determine the marketing mix (social marketing) b. Make pricing decisions c. Make product decisions d. Make promotion decisions e. Make packaging decisions f. Make purchasing decisions g. Make international marketing decisions (e.g., CARE) h. Organize their marketing efforts i. Control their marketing efforts j. Plan their marketing strategy k. Apply systems theory to marketing problems
Macro	(7) Problems, issues, theories, and research concerning: a. The institutional framework for public goods b. Whether television advertising influences elections c. Whether public service advertising influences behavior (e.g., "Smokey the Bear") d. Whether existing distribution systems for public goods are efficient e. How public goods are recycled	(8) Problems, issues, normative models, and research concerning: a. Whether society should allow politicians to be "sold" like toothpaste b. Whether the demand for public goods should be stimulated c. Whether "low informational content" political advertising is socially desirable (e.g., ten-second "spot" commercials) d. Whether the U.S. Army should be allowed to advertise for recruits

Nonprofit Sector

micro-positive and in the profit sector. Similarly, the second class includes all marketing activities that are micro-normative and in the profit sector, and so on throughout the table.

Some definitions are required to properly interpret the schema presented in Table 1. *Profit sector* encompasses the study and activities of organizations or other entities whose stated objectives include the realization of profit. Also applicable are studies that adopt the *perspective* of profit-oriented organizations. Conversely, *nonprofit* sector encompasses the study and perspective of all organizations and entities whose stated objectives do not include the realization of profit.

The *micro/macro* dichotomy suggests a classification based on the level of aggregation. *Micro* refers to the marketing activities of individual units, normally individual organizations (firms) and consumers or households. *Macro* suggests a higher level of aggregation, usually marketing systems or groups of consumers.

The *positive/normative* dichotomy provides categories based on whether the focus of the analysis is primarily descriptive or prescriptive. *Positive* marketing adopts the perspective of attempting to describe, explain, predict, and understand the marketing activities, processes, and phenomena that actually exist. This perspective examines *what is*. In contrast, normative marketing adopts the perspective of attempting to prescribe what marketing organizations and individuals ought to do or what kinds of marketing systems a society ought to have. That is, this perspective examines what *ought to be* and what organizations and individuals *ought to do.*

ANALYZING APPROACHES TO MARKETING

An examination of Table 1 reveals that most of the early (circa 1920) approaches to the study of marketing reside in cell 3: profit sector/macro/positive. The institutional, commodity, and functional approaches analyzed existing (positive) business activities (profit sector) from a marketing systems (macro) perspective. However, not all the early marketing studies were profit/macro/positive. Weld's 1920 classic *The Marketing of Farm Products* not only examined existing distribution systems for farm commodities, but also attempted to evaluate such normative issues as: "Are there too many middlemen in food marketing?" [23] Thus, Weld's signally important work was both profit/macro/positive and profit/macro/normative. Similarly, the Twentieth Century Fund study *Does Distribution Cost Too Much?* took an essentially profit/macro/normative perspective. [24] Other important works that have combined the profit/macro/positive and the profit/macro/normative perspectives include those of Barger, Cox, and Borden. [25]

Although the profit/micro/normative (cell 2) orientation to marketing can be traced at least back to the 1920s and the works of such notables as Reed and White, [26] the movement reached full bloom in the early 1960s under proponents of the *managerial approach* to marketing, such as McCarthy. [27] The managerial approach adopts the perspective of the marketing manager, usually the marketing manager in a large manufacturing corporation. Therefore, the emphasis is micro and in the profit sector. The basic question underlying the managerial approach is: "What is the optimal marketing mix?" Consequently, the approach is unquestionably normative.

During the middle 1960s, writers such as Lazer, Kelley, Adler, and Fisk began advocating a *system approach* to marketing. [28] Sometimes the systems approach used a profit/micro/normative perspective and simply attempted to apply to marketing certain sophisticated optimizing models (like linear and dynamic programming) developed by the operations researchers. Other writers used the systems approach in a profit/macro/positive fashion to analyze the complex interactions among marketing institutions. Finally, some used the systems approach in a profit/macro/normative fashion:

The method used in this book is called the general systems approach. In this approach the goals, organization, inputs, and outputs of marketing are examined to determine how efficient and *how effective marketing is.* Constraints, including competition and government, are also studied because they affect both the level of efficiency and the kinds of effects obtained. [29]

During the late 1960s, the *environmental approach* to marketing was promulgated by writers such as Holloway, Hancock, Scott, and Marks. [30] This approach emphasized an essentially descriptive analysis of the environmental constraints on marketing activities. These environments included consumer behavior, culture, competition, the legal framework, technology, and the institutional framework. Consequently, this approach may be classified as profit/macro/positive.

Two trends are evident in contemporary marketing thought. The first is the trend toward *social marketing* as proposed by Kotler, Levy, and Zaltman[31] and as promulgated by others.[32] Social marketing, with its emphasis on the marketing problems of nonprofit organizations, is nonprofit/micro/normative. The second trend can be termed *societal issues*. It concerns such diverse topics as consumerism, marketing and ecology, the desirability of political advertising, social responsibility, and whether the demand for public goods should be stimulated.[33] All these works share the common element of *evaluation*. They attempt to evaluate the desirability or propriety of certain marketing activities or systems and, therefore, should be viewed as either profit/macro/normative or nonprofit/macro/normative.

In conclusion, it is possible to classify all the approaches to the study of marketing and all the problems, issues, theories, models, and research usually considered within the scope of marketing using the three categorial dichotomies of profit sector/nonprofit sector, positive/normative, and micro/macro. This is not meant to imply that reasonable people cannot disagree as to which topics should fall within the scope of marketing. Nor does it even imply that reasonable people cannot disagree as to which cell in Table 1 is most appropriate for each issue or particular piece of research. For example, a study of the efficiency of marketing systems may have *both* positive and normative aspects; it may both *describe* existing marketing practices and *prescribe* more appropriate practices. Rather, the conceptual model of the scope of marketing presented in Table 1 provides a useful framework for analyzing fundamental differences among the various approaches to marketing and, as shall be demonstrated, the nature of marketing and marketing science controversies.

ANALYZING THE NATURE OF MARKETING AND MARKETING SCIENCE

The previous discussion on the scope of marketing now enables us to clarify some of the issues with respect to the "nature [broadening the concept] of marketing" controversy and the "Is marketing a science?" debate. Most marketing practitioners and some marketing academicians perceive the entire scope of marketing to be profit/micro/normative (cell 2 of Table 1). That is, practitioners often perceive the entire domain of marketing to be the analysis of how to improve the decision-making processes of marketers. This perspective is exemplified by the definition of marketing Canton has suggested [34] and, somewhat surprisingly, by the definition proffered by Kotler in the first edition of *Marketing Management:* "Marketing is the analyzing, organizing, planning, and controlling of the firm's customer-impinging resources, policies, and activities with a view to satisfying the needs and wants of chosen customer groups at a profit." [35]

Most marketing academicians would chafe at delimiting the entire subject matter of marketing to simply the profit/micro/normative dimensions. Most would, at the very least, include all the phenomena, topics, and issues indicated in the top half of Table 1 (that is, cells 1 through 4). Kotler and others now wish to include in the definition of marketing *all* eight cells in Table 1.

Other fields have experienced similar discipline-definitional problems. Several decades ago, a debate raged in philosophy concerning the definition of philosophy and philosophy of science. Some philosophers chose a very narrow definition of their discipline. Popper's classic rejoinder should serve to alert marketers to the danger that narrowly circumscribing the marketing discipline may trammel marketing inquiry:

> ... the theory of knowledge was inspired by the hope that it would enable us not only to know more about knowledge, but also to contribute to the advance of knowledge—of scientific knowledge, that is.... Most of the philosophers who believe that the characteristic method of philosophy is the analysis of ordinary language seem to have lost this admirable optimism which once inspired the rationalist tradition. Their attitude, it seems, has become one of resignation, if not despair. They not only leave the advancement of knowledge to the scientists: they even define philosophy in such a way that it becomes, by definition, incapable of making any contribution to our knowledge of the world. The self-mutilation which this so surprisingly persuasive definition requires does not appeal to me. There is no such thing as an essence of philosophy, to be distilled and condensed into a definition. *A definition of the word* philosophy *can only have the character of a convention, of an agreement; and I, at any rate, see no merit in the arbitrary proposal to define the word* philosophy *in a way that may well prevent a student of philosophy from trying to contribute, qua philosopher, to the advancement of our knowledge of the world.*[36]

Four conclusions seem warranted. First, definitions of the nature of marketing differ in large part because their authors perceive the total scope of marketing to be different portions of Table 1. Second, there is a growing consensus that the total scope of marketing should appropriately include all eight cells of Table 1. Third, it may be very difficult to devise a definition of marketing that would both systematically *include* all eight cells of Table 1 and, at the same time, systematically *exclude* all other phenomena. Especially difficult will be the task of including in a single definition both the normative dimensions of the *practice* of marketing and the positive dimensions of the *discipline* or *study* of marketing.

The fourth conclusion deserves special emphasis and elaboration. There is now a consensus among marketers that most nonprofit organizations, such as museums, zoos, and churches, engage in numerous activities (pricing, promoting, and so forth) that are very similar to the marketing activities of their profit-oriented cousins. There is also consensus that the marketing procedures that have been developed for profit-oriented organizations are equally applicable to nonprofit concerns. These are the two major, substantive issues involved in the debate over the nature (broadening the concept) of marketing. On these two issues there now exists substantial agreement.

The remaining two points of *disagreement* among marketers concerning the nature of marketing are minor when compared to the points of agreement. Issue one is essentially whether the activities of nonprofit organizations should be referred to as *marketing* activities or *marketing-like* activities. Given the agreement among marketers concerning the two previously cited substantive issues, the problem of distinguishing between marketing activities and marketing-like activities must be considered trivial to the extreme. The second issue on which disagreement exists concerns developing a definition of marketing. Although certainly nontrivial in nature, on this issue marketers would be well advised to take a cue from the discipline of philosophy, which has been around much longer and has yet to develop a consensus definition. That is, the discipline of marketing should not be overly alarmed about the difficulty of generating a consensus *definition* of marketing as long as there appears to be a developing consensus concerning its total *scope.*

The preceding analysis notwithstanding, there does remain a major, unresolved, substantive issue concerning the nature of marketing. Although *marketers* now recognize that nonprofit organizations (1) have marketing or marketing-like problems, (2) engage in marketing or marketing-like activities to solve these problems, and (3) can use the marketing policies, practices, and procedures that profit-oriented organizations have developed to solve marketing problems, we must candidly admit that most *nonmarketers* have yet to perceive this reality. Sadly, most administrators of nonprofit organizations and many academicians in other areas still do not perceive that many problems of nonprofit organizations are basically marketing in nature, and that there is an extant body of knowledge in marketing academia and a group of trained marketing practitioners that can help resolve these problems. Until administrators of nonprofit organizations perceive that they have marketing problems, their marketing decision making will inevitably suffer. Thus, the major *substantive* problem concerning broadening the concept of marketing lies in the area of *marketing* marketing to nonmarketers.

IS MARKETING A SCIENCE?

Returning to the "Is marketing a science?" controversy, the preceding analysis suggests that a primary factor explaining the nature of the controversy is the widely disparate notions of marketing held by the participants. The common element shared by those who hold that marketing is not (and cannot) be a science is the belief that the entire conceptual domain of marketing is cell 2: profit/micro/normative. Hutchinson clearly exemplifies this position:

There is a real reason, however, why the field of marketing has been slow to develop an unique body of theory. It is a simple one: marketing is not a science. It is rather an art or a practice, and as such much more closely resembles engineering, medicine and architecture than it does physics, chemistry or biology. The medical profession sets us an excellent example, if we would but follow it; its members are called "practitioners" and not scientists. It is the work of physicians, as it is of any practitioner, to apply the findings of many sciences to the solution of problems. . . . It is the drollest travesty to relate the scientist's search for knowledge to the market research man's seeking after customers.[37]

If, as Hutchinson implies, the entire conceptual domain of marketing is profit/micro/normative, then marketing is not and (more importantly) probably *cannot* be a science. If, however, the conceptual domain of marketing includes both micro/positive and macro/positive phenomena, then marketing *could* be a science. That is, if phenomena such as consumer behavior, marketing institutions, marketing channels, and the efficiency of systems of distribution are included in the conceptual domain of marketing (and there appears to be a consensus to so include them), there is no reason why the study of these phenomena could not be deserving of the designation *science*.

Is marketing a science? Differing perceptions of the scope of marketing have been shown to be a primary factor underlying the debate on this question. The second factor contributing to the controversy is differing perceptions concerning the basic nature of science, a subject that will now occupy our attention.

The Nature of Science

The question of whether marketing is a science cannot be adequately answered without a clear understanding of the basic nature of science. So, what is a science? Most marketing writers cite the perspective proposed by Buzzell. A science is:

> ... a classified and systematized body of knowledge, ... organized around one or more central theories and a number of general principles, ... usually expressed in quantitative terms, ... knowledge which permits the prediction and, under some circumstances, the control of future events.[38]

Buzzell then proceeded to note that marketing lacks the requisite central theories to be termed a science.

Although the Buzzell perspective on science has much to recommend it, the requirement "organized around one or more central theories" seems overly restrictive. This requirement confuses the *successful culmination* of scientific efforts with *science itself*. Was the study of chemistry not a science before discoveries like the periodic table of elements? Analogously, would not a pole vaulter still be a pole vaulter even if he could not vault fifteen feet? As Homans notes, "What makes a science are its aims, not its result."[39] The major purpose of science is to discover (create? invent?) laws and theories to explain, predict, understand, and control phenomena. Withholding the label *science* until a discipline has "central theories" would not seem reasonable.

The previous comments notwithstanding, requiring a science to be organized around one or more central theories is not completely without merit. There are strong *honorific* overtones in labeling a discipline a science.[40] These semantical overtones are so positive that, as Wartofsky has observed, even areas that are nothing more than systematized superstition attempt to usurp the term.[41] Thus, there are treatises on such subjects as the "Science of Numerology" and the "Science of Astrology." In part, the label *science* is conferred upon a discipline to signify that it has "arrived" in the eyes of other scientists, and this confirmation usually occurs only when a discipline has matured to the extent that it contains several "central theories."[42] Thus, chronologically, physics achieved the status of science before psychology, and psychology before sociology. However, the total conceptual content of the term *science* is decidedly not just honorific. Marketing does not, and should not, have to wait to be knighted by others to be a science. How, then, do sciences differ from other disciplines, if not by virtue of having central theories?

Consider the discipline of chemistry—unquestionably a science. Chemistry can be defined as "the science of substances—their structure, their properties, and the reactions that change them into other substances."[43] Using chemistry as an illustration, three observations will enable us to clarify the distinguishing characteristics of sciences. First, a science must have a distinct subject matter, a set of real-world phenomena that serve as a focal point for investigation. The subject matter of chemistry is *substances,* and chemistry attempts to understand, explain, predict, and control phenomena related to substances. Other disciplines, such as physics, are also interested in substances. However, chemistry can meaningfully lay claim to being a separate science because physics does not *focus on* substances and their reactions.

What is the basic subject matter of marketing? Most marketers now perceive the ultimate subject matter to be the *transaction.* Some subscribe to the *narrower thesis of marketing* and wish to delimit the basic subject matter to the *market* transaction. Others propose the *liberalized thesis of marketing* and wish to include within the subject matter of marketing all transactions that involve any form of *exchange of values* between parties.

Harking back to the chemistry analogue, marketing can be viewed as the *science of transactions*—their structure, their properties, and their relationships with other phenomena. Given this perspective, the subject matter of marketing would certainly overlap with other disciplines, notably economics, psychology, and sociology. The analysis of transactions is considered in each of these disciplines. Yet, only in marketing is the transaction the focal point. For example, transactions remain a tangential issue in economics, where the primary focus is on the allocation of scarce resources.[44] Therefore, the first distinguishing characteristic is that any science must have a distinct subject matter. Given that the *transaction* is the basic subject matter of marketing, marketing would seem to fulfill this requirement. Note that this conclusion is *independent* of whether one subscribes to the narrower or more liberal thesis of marketing.

A distinct subject matter alone is not sufficient to distinguish sciences from other disciplines, because all disciplines have a subject matter (some less distinct than others). The previously cited perspective of chemistry provides a second insight into the basic nature of science. Note the phrase, "their structure, their properties, and their reactions." Every science seeks to describe and classify the structure and properties of its basic subject matter. Likewise, the term *reactions* suggests that the phenomena comprising the basic subject matter of chemistry are presumed to be systematically interrelated. Thus, another distinguishing characteristic: *Every science presupposes the existence of underlying uniformities or regularities among the phenomena that comprise its subject matter. The discovery of these underlying uniformities yields empirical regularities, lawlike generalizations (propositions), and laws.*

Underlying uniformities and regularities are necessary for science because (1) a primary goal of science is to provide responsibly supported explanations of phenomena,[45] and (2) the scientific explanation of phenomena requires the existence of laws or lawlike generalizations.[46] Uniformities and regularities are also a requisite for theory development since theories are systematically related sets of statements, *including some lawlike generalizations,* that are empirically testable.[47]

The basic question for marketing is not whether there presently exist several "central theories" that serve to unify, explain, and predict marketing phenomena, as Buzzell suggests. Rather, the following should be asked: "Are there underlying uniformities and regularities among the phenomena comprising the subject matter of marketing?" This question can be answered affirmatively on two grounds—one *a priori* and one empirical. Marketing is a discipline that investigates human behavior. Since numerous uniformities and regularities have been observed in other behavioral sciences,[48] there is no *a priori* reason for believing that the subject matter of marketing will be devoid of uniformities and regularities. The second ground for believing that the uniformities exist is empirical. The quantity of scholarly research conducted on marketing phenomena during the past three decades probably exceeds the total of *all* prior research in marketing. Substantial research has been conducted in the area of channels of distribution. Also, efforts in the consumer behavior dimension of marketing have been particularly prolific. Granted, some of the research has been less than profound, and the total achievements may not be commensurate with the efforts expended. Nevertheless, who can deny that *some* progress has been made or that *some* uniformities have been identified? In short, who can deny that there exist uniformities and regularities interrelating the subject matter of marketing? I, for one, cannot.

The task of delineating the basic nature of science is not yet complete. Up to this point we have used chemistry to illustrate that all sciences involve (1) a distinct subject matter and the description and classification of that subject matter, and (2) the presumption that underlying the subject matter are uniformities and regularities that science seeks to discover. The chemistry example provides a final observation. Note that "chemistry is the *science* of. . . ." This suggests that sciences can be differentiated from other disciplines by the method of analysis. At the risk of being somewhat tautologous: sciences employ a set of procedures commonly referred to as the scientific method. As Bunge suggests, "No scientific method, no science." [49] The historical significance of the development and acceptance of the method of science cannot be overstated. It has been called "the most significant intellectual contribution of Western civilization." [50] Is the method of science applicable to marketing?

Detailed explication of the scientific method is beyond the scope of this article and is discussed elsewhere.[51] Nevertheless, the cornerstone requirement of the method of science must be monitored. The word *science* has its origins in the Latin verb *scire,* meaning "to know." Now, there are many ways to *know* things. The methods of tenacity, authority, faith, intuition, and science are often cited.[52] The characteristic that separates scientific knowledge from other ways to "know" things is the notion of *intersubjective certification.*

Scientific knowledge, in which theories, laws, and explanations are primal, must be *objective* in the sense that its truth content must be *intersubjectively certifiable.*[53] Requiring that theories, laws, and explanations be empirically testable ensures that they will be intersubjectively certifiable since different (but reasonably competent) investigators with differing attitudes, opinions, and beliefs will be able to make observations and conduct experiments to ascertain their truth content. "Science strives for objectivity in the sense that its statements are to be capable of public tests with results that do not vary essentially with the tester." [54] Scientific knowledge thus rests on the bedrock of empirical testability.

There is no reason whatsoever to presume that the scientific method of analysis is any less appropriate to marketing phenomena than to other disciplines. Similarly, scholarly researchers in marketing, although sometimes holding rather distorted notions concerning such topics as the role of laws and theories in research, seem to be at least as technically proficient as researchers in other areas. Finally, although some marketing researchers continue to cite "proprietary studies" as evidentiary support for their positions, the extent of this practice is now extremely small.

In summary, sciences (1) have a distinct subject matter drawn from the real world which is described and classified, (2) presume underlying uniformities and regularities interrelating the subject matter, and (3) adopt intersubjectively certifiable procedures for studying the subject matter. This perspective can be appropriately described as a consensus composite of philosophy of science views on science.[55] For example, Wartofsky suggests that a science is

... an organized or systematic body of knowledge, using general laws or principles; that it is knowledge about the world; and that it is that kind of knowledge concerning which universal agreement can be reached by scientists sharing a common language (or languages) and common criteria for the *justification* of knowledge claims and beliefs.[56]

Is Marketing a Science? A Conclusion

The scope of the area called marketing has been shown to be exceptionally broad. Marketing has micro/macro dimensions, profit sector/nonprofit sector dimensions, and positive/normative dimensions. Reasonable people may disagree as to which combination of these dimensions represents the *appropriate* total scope of marketing, although a consensus seems to be developing to include all eight cells in Table 1. If marketing is to be restricted to *only* the profit/micro/normative dimension (as many practitioners would view it), then marketing is not a science and could not become one. All sciences involve the explanation, prediction, and understanding of phenomena.[57] These explanations and predictions frequently serve as useful guides for developing normative decision rules and normative models. Such rules and models are then *grounded* in science.[58] Nevertheless, any discipline that is *purely* evaluative or prescriptive (normative) is not a science. At least for marketing academe, restricting the scope of marketing to its profit/micro/normative dimension is unrealistic, unnecessary, and, without question, undesirable.

Once the appropriate scope of marketing has been expanded to include at least some *positive* dimensions (cells 1, 3, 5, and 7 in Table 1), the explanation, prediction, and understanding of these phenomena could be a science. The question then becomes whether the study of the positive dimensions of marketing has the requisite characteristics of a science. Aside from the strictly honorific overtones of *nonmarketers* accepting marketing as a science, the substantive characteristics differentiating sciences from other disciplines have been shown to be (1) a distinct subject matter drawn from the real world and the description and classification of that subject matter, (2) the presumption of underlying uniformities and regularities interrelating the subject matter, and (3) the adoption of the method of science for studying the subject matter.

The *positive* dimensions of marketing have been shown to have a subject matter properly distinct from other sciences. The marketing literature is replete with description and classification. There have been discoveries (however tentative) of uniformities and regularities among marketing phenomena. Finally, although Longman deplores "the rather remarkable lack of scientific method employed by scientists of marketing," [59] researchers in marketing are at least as committed to the method of science as are researchers in other disciplines. Therefore, the study of the *positive* dimensions of marketing can be appropriately referred to as *marketing science*.

NOTES

[1] Paul D. Converse, "The Development of a Science of Marketing," *Journal of Marketing*, Vol. 10 (July 1945), pp. 14–23.

[2] Robert Bartels, "Can Marketing Be a Science?" *Journal of Marketing*, Vol. 15 (January 1951), pp. 319–328; Kenneth D. Hutchinson, "Marketing as a Science: An Appraisal," *Journal of Marketing*, Vol. 16 (January 1952), pp. 286–293; W. J. Baumol, "On the Role of Marketing Theory," *Journal of Marketing*, Vol. 21 (April 1957), pp. 413–419; Robert D. Buzzell, "Is Marketing a Science?" *Harvard Business Review*, Vol. 41 (January–February 1963), pp. 32–48; Weldon J. Taylor, "Is Marketing a Science? Revisited," *Journal of Marketing*, Vol. 29 (July 1965), pp. 49–53; and M. Halbert, *The Meaning and Sources of Marketing Theory* (New York: McGraw-Hill Book Co., 1965).

[3] Committee on Terms, *Marketing Definitions: A Glossary of Marketing Terms* (Chicago: American Marketing Assn., 1960).

[4] Stewart H. Rewoldt, James D. Scott, and Martin R. Warshaw, *Introduction to Marketing Management* (Homewood, Ill.: Richard D. Irwin, 1973), p. 3.

[5] Marketing Staff of the Ohio State University, "Statement of Marketing Philosophy," *Journal of Marketing*, Vol. 29 (January 1965), pp. 43–44.

[6] Philip Kotler and Sidney J. Levy, "Broadening the Concept of Marketing," *Journal of Marketing*, Vol. 33 (January 1969), p. 15.

[7] William Lazer, "Marketing's Changing Social Relationships," *Journal of Marketing*, Vol. 33 (January 1969), p. 9.

[8] David Luck, "Broadening the Concept of Marketing—Too Far," *Journal of Marketing*, Vol. 33 (July 1969), p. 54.

[9] Philip Kotler and Sidney Levy, "A New Form of Marketing Myopia: Rejoinder to Professor Luck," *Journal of Marketing*, Vol. 33 (July 1969), p. 57.

[10] Robert Ferber, "The Expanding Role of Marketing in the 1970's," *Journal of Marketing*, Vol. 34 (January 1970), pp. 29–30.

[11] Robert J. Lavidge, "The Growing Responsibilities of Marketing," *Journal of Marketing*, Vol. 34 (January 1970), p. 27.

[12] Philip Kotler and Gerald Zaltman, "Social Marketing: An Approach to Planned Social Change," *Journal of Marketing*, Vol. 35 (July 1971), p. 5.

[13] *Journal of Marketing*, Vol. 35 (July 1971): William A. Mindak and H. Malcolm Bybee, "Marketing's Application to Fund Raising," pp. 13–18; Gerald Zaltman and Ilan Vertinsky, "Health Services Marketing: A Suggested Model," pp. 19–27; John U. Farley and Harold J. Leavitt, "Marketing and Population Problems," pp. 28–33; and William G. Zikmund and William J. Stanton, "Recycling Solid Wastes: A Channels-of-Distribution Problem," pp. 34–39.

[14] Leslie Dawson, "Marketing Science in the Age of Aquarius," *Journal of Marketing,* Vol. 35 (July 1971), p. 71.

[15] Philip Kotler, "A Generic Concept of Marketing,' *Journal of Marketing,* Vol. 36 (April 1972), p. 49.

[16] William G. Nichols, "Conceptual Conflicts in Marketing," *Journal of Economics and Business,* Vol. 26 (Winter 1974), p. 142.

[17] James M. Carman, "On the Universality of Marketing," *Journal of Contemporary Business,* Vol. 2 (Autumn 1973), p. 14.

[18] Robert Bartels, "The Identity Crisis in Marketing," *Journal of Marketing,* Vol. 38 (October 1974), p. 76.

[19] David J. Luck, "Social Marketing: Confusion Compounded," *Journal of Marketing,* Vol. 38 (October 1974), pp. 2–7.

[20] Robert J. Eggert, "Eggert Discusses Additional Goals for His Administration, Seeks Help in Defining Marketing," *Marketing News,* September 15, 1974.

[21] E. J. McCarthy, *Basic Marketing* (Homewood, Ill.: Richard D. Irwin, 1960).

[22] These observations were apparently extemporaneous since they were not included in his published paper: Philip Kotler, "Defining the Limits of Marketing," in *Marketing Education and the Real World,* Boris W. Becker and Helmut Becker, eds. (Chicago: American Marketing Assn., 1972).

[23] L. D. H. Weld, *The Marketing of Farm Products* (New York: Macmillan, 1920).

[24] Paul W. Stewart, *Does Distribution Cost Too Much?* (New York: Twentieth Century Fund, 1939).

[25] Harold Barger, *Distribution's Place in the Economy Since 1869* (Princeton: Princeton University Press, 1955); Reavis Cox, *Distribution in a High Level Economy* (Englewood Cliffs, N.J.: Prentice-Hall, 1965); and Neil Borden, *The Economic Effects of Advertising* (Chicago: Richard D. Irwin ,1942).

[26] Virgil Read, *Planned Marketing* (New York: Ronald Press, 1930); and P. White and W. S. Hayward, *Marketing Practice* (New York: Doubleday, Page & Co., 1924).

[27] Same reference as footnote 21.

[28] William Lazer and Eugene Kelley, "Systems Perspective of Marketing Activity," in *Managerial Marketing: Perspectives and Viewpoints,* rev. ed. (Homewood, Ill.: Richard D. Irwin, 1962); Lee Adler, "Systems Approach to Marketing," *Harvard Business Review,* Vol. 45 (May–June, 1967); and George Fisk, *Marketing Systems: An Introductory Analysis* (New York: Harper & Row, 1967).

[29] Fisk, same reference as footnote 28; p. 3.

[30] Robert J. Holloway and Robert S. Hancock, *The Environment of Marketing Behavior* (New York: John Wiley & Sons, 1964); Robert J. Holloway and Robert S. Hancock, *Marketing in a Changing Environment* (New York: John Wiley & Sons, 1968); and Richard A. Scott and Norton E. Marks, *Marketing and Its Environment* (Belmont: Wadsworth, 1968).

[31] Kotler and Levy, same reference as footnote 6; Kotler and Zaltman, same reference as footnote 12; and Kotler, same reference as footnote 15.

[32] Mindak and Bybee, same reference as footnote 13; Farley and Leavitt, same reference as footnote 13; Zikmund and Stanton, same reference as footnote 13; Carman, same reference as footnote 17; and Donald P. Robin, "Success in Social Marketing," *Journal of Business Research,* Vol. 3 (July 1974), pp. 303–310.

[33] Lazer, same reference as footnote 7; Dawson, same reference as footnote 14; David S. Aaker and George Day, *Consumerism* (New York: Free Press, 1971); Norman Kangun, *Society and Marketing* (New York: Harper & Row, 1972); Frederick E. Webster, Jr., *Social Aspects of Marketing* (Englewood Cliffs, N.J.: Prentice-Hall, 1974); Reed Moyer, *Macro-Marketing* (New York: John Wiley & Sons, 1972); John R. Wish and Stephen H. Gamble, *Marketing and Social Issues* (New York: John Wiley & Sons, 1971); Ross L. Goble and Roy Shaw, *Controversy and Dialogue in Marketing* (Englewood Cliffs, N.J.: Prentice-Hall, 1975); Ronald R. Gist, *Marketing and Society* (New York: Holt, Rinehart & Winston, 1971); and William Lazer and Eugene Kelley, *Social Marketing* (Homewood, Ill.: Richard D. Irwin, 1973)

[34] Irving D. Canton, "A Functional Definition of Marketing," *Marketing News,* July 15, 1973.

[35] Philip Kotler, *Marketing Management* (Englewood Cliffs, N.J.: Prentice-Hall, 1967), p. 12.

[36] Karl R. Popper, *The Logic of Scientific Discovery* (New York: Harper & Row, 1959), p. 19. [Emphasis added.]

[37] Hutchinson, same reference as footnote 2.

[38] Buzzell, same reference as footnote 2, p. 37.

[39] George C. Homans, *The Nature of Social Science* (New York: Harcourt, Brace & World, 1967), p. 4.

[40] Ernest Nagel, *The Structure of Science* (New York: Harcourt, Brace & World, 1961), p. 2.

[41] Marx W. Wartofsky, *Conceptual Foundations of Scientific Thought* (New York: Macmillan Co., 1968), p. 44.

[42] Thomas S. Kuhn, *The Structure of Scientific Revelations* (Chicago: University of Chicago Press, 1970), p. 161.

[43] Linus Pauling, *College Chemistry* (San Francisco: W. H. Freeman & Co., 1956), p. 15.

[44] Richard H. Leftwich, *The Price System and Resource Allocation* (New York: Holt, Rinehart & Winston, 1966), p. 2.

[45] Same reference as footnote 40, p. 15.

[46] Carl G. Hempel, *Aspects of Scientific Explanation* (New York: Free Press ,1965), p. 354–364.

[47] Richard S. Rudner, *The Philosophy of Social Science* (Englewood Cliffs, N.J.: Prentice-Hall, 1966), p. 10; and Shelby D. Hunt, "The Morphology of Theory and the General Theory of Marketing," *Journal of Marketing*, Vol. 35 (April 1971), pp. 65–68.

[48] Bernard Berelson and Gary Steiner, *Human Behavior: An Inventory of Scientific Findings* (New York: Harcourt, Brace & World, 1964).

[49] Mario Bunge, *Scientific Research I: The Search for System* (New York: Springer-Verlag, 1967), p. 12.

[50] Charles W. Morris, "Scientific Empiricism," in *Foundations of the Unity of Science,* Vol. 1, Otto Newrath, Rudolf Carnap and Charles Morris, eds. (Chicago: University of Chicago Press, 1955), p. 63.

[51] Shelby D. Hunt, *Marketing Theory: Conceptual Foundation of Research in Marketing* (Columbus, Ohio: Grid Publishing Co., 1976).

[52] Morris R. Cohen and Ernest Nagel, *Logic and the Scientific Method* (New York: Harcourt, Brace & World, 1934), p. 193.

[53] Same reference as footnote 36, p. 44.

[54] Carl G. Hempel, "Fundamentals of Concept Formation in Empirical Science," in *Foundations of the Unity of Science,* Vol. 2, Otto Newrath, ed. (Chicago: University of Chicago Press, 1970), p. 695.

[55] See, for example: Nagel, same reference as footnote 40, p. 4; May Brodbeck, *Readings in the Philosophy of the Social Sciences* (New York: Macmillan Co., 1968), pp. 1–11; Richard B. Braithwaite, *Scientific Explanation* (Cambridge: Cambridge University Press, 1951), pp. 1–21; B. F. Skinner, *Science and Human Behavior* (New York: Macmillan Co., 1953), pp. 14–22; Rudner, same reference as footnote 47, pp. 7–9; Abraham Kaplan, *The Conduct of Inquiry* (Scranton, Pa.: Chandler Publishing Co., 1964), p. 32; Popper, same reference as footnote 36, pp. 44–48; and Hempel, same reference as footnote 54, p. 672.

[56] Same reference as footnote 41, p. 23.

[57] Nagel, same reference as footnote 40, p. 15; Henry E. Kyburg, Jr., *Philosophy of Science* (New York: Macmillan Co., 1968), p. 3; Carl G. Hempel, "The Theoretician's Dilemma," in *Aspects of Scientific Explanation* (New York: Free Press, 1965), p. 173; and Nicholas Rescher, *Scientific Explanation* (New York: Free Press, 1970), p. 4.

[58] Mario Bunge, *Scientific Research II: The Search for Truth* (New York: Springer-Verlag, 1967), p. 132.

[59] Kenneth A. Longman, "The Management Challenge to Marketing Theory," in *New Essays in Marketing Theory,* George Fisk, ed. (Boston: Allyn & Bacon, 1971), p. 10.

SOME SUGGESTIONS FOR FURTHER READING

Hunt, Shelby D. (1979), "Positive vs. Normative Theory in Marketing: The Three Dichotomies Model as a General Paradigm for Marketing," in O. C. Ferrell, S. W. Brown, C. W. Lamb (eds.) *Conceptual and Theoretical Developments in Marketing,* Chicago, IL: American Marketing Association, 567–576.

—— (1978), "A General Paradigm of Marketing: In Support of the '3-Dichotomies Model,' " *Journal of Marketing* (April), 107–110.

—— 1976), *Marketing Theory: Conceptual Foundations of Research in Marketing,* Columbus, Ohio: Grid Publishing, Inc.

Levy, S. J. (1976), "Marcology 101 or the Domain of Marketing," *Proceedings,* American Marketing Association Educators' Conference.

Nickels, William G. (1974), "Conceptual Conflicts in Marketing," *Journal of Economics and Business* (Winter), 140–143.

Robin, D. P. (1978), "A Useful Scope for Marketing," *Journal of the Academy of Marketing Science* (Summer), 22ff.

II / BUYER BEHAVIOR

The marketing objectives of any firm are to identify potential customers and to convince them that the firm's products will satisfy their needs. These objectives imply an understanding of human behavior, especially of the behavioral role of "buyer." The articles in Part II are some of marketing's most significant attempts to analyze buyer behavior.

The normative framework for analyzing the buyer is provided by economic theory. Katona has led the movement to integrate economic theory and the behavioral sciences in order to arrive at a sound theory of rational economic behavior. At the time this article was written, the power of marketing as a driving force of the economic system was just beginning to be evident. Galbraith, with extraordinary foresight and a provocative style, acknowledges these benefits of marketing but focuses on the difficulties engendered by marketing successes. Although we now know that buyer behavior is more complex than Galbraith postulates, this paper remains one of the most quoted in the literature.

A number of marketing scholars attempted to explain more completely the nature of buyer behavior. Two of the best attempts are included here. First is "The Theory of Buyer Behavior" by Howard and Sheth. This article is the most widely acclaimed general model of buyer behavior; it has been extensively debated and subjected to numerous empirical tests. Webster and Wind offer an essentially similar model but focus on the behavior of the organizational buyer rather than of the consumer.

Conceptual articles such as these have inspired considerable empirical research. Haire's work with projective techniques pioneered in applying scientific research methodology to consumer analysis. Later came considerably more sophisticated work, dominated by applications of multi-attribute models derived from the work of Fishbein and Rosenberg. This body of literature is critically reviewed in Wilkie and Pessemier's oft-quoted paper.

The remaining three articles in Part II examine the influence of interpersonal relationships on buyer behavior. The original general theory of group influence in marketing appears in the paper by the Foundation For Research on Human Behavior. One major stream of research resulting from this theory is the innovation and diffusion work of Everett Rogers. His recent article, "New Product Adoption and Diffusion," represents a summary and synthesis of his contributions. The final paper in this part is the review article on psychographics by Wells. It serves as a summary and integration of many of the concepts and empirical techniques that marketers use in studying buyer behavior.

9 / RATIONAL BEHAVIOR AND ECONOMIC BEHAVIOR / George Katona

While attempts to penetrate the boundary lines between psychology and sociology have been rather frequent during the last few decades, psychologists have paid little attention to the problems with which another sister discipline, economics, is concerned. One purpose of this paper is to arouse interest among psychologists in studies of economic behavior. For that purpose it will be shown that psychological principles may be of great value in clarifying basic questions of economics and that the psychology of habit formation, of motivation, and of group belonging may profit from studies of economic behavior.

A variety of significant problems, such as those of the business cycle or inflation, of consumer saving or business investment, could be chosen for the purpose of such demonstration. This paper, however, will be concerned with the most fundamental assumption of economics, the principle of rationality. In order to clarify the problems involved in this principle, which have been neglected by contemporary psychologists, it will be necessary to contrast the most common forms of methodology used in economics with those employed in psychology and to discuss the role of empirical research in the social sciences.

THEORY AND HYPOTHESES

Economic theory represents one of the oldest and most elaborate theoretical structures in the social sciences. However, dissatisfaction with the achievements and uses of economic theory has grown considerably during the past few decades on the part of economists who are interested in what actually goes on in economic life. And yet leading sociologists and psychologists have recently declared, "Economics is today, in a theoretical sense, probably the most highly elaborated sophisticated, and refined of the disciplines dealing with action." [1]

To understand the scientific approach of economic theorists, we may divide them into two groups. Some develop an a priori system from which they deduce propositions about how people *should* act under certain assumptions. Assuming that the sole aim of businessmen is profit maximization, these theorists deduce propositions about marginal revenues and marginal costs, for example, that are not

George Katona, a native of Hungary, received a Ph.D. in psychology from Gottingen University and has pioneered in combining psychology and economics. He is program director of the Survey Research Center and professor of economics and psychology at the University of Michigan. His two best-known books are *The Powerful Consumer* and *Mass Consumption Society*. *Psychological Economics*, published in 1975, synthesizes his contributions.

meant to be suited for testing. In developing formal logics of economic action, one of the main considerations is elegance of the deductive system, based on the law of parsimony. A wide gap separates these theorists from economic research of an empirical-statistical type which registers what they call aberrations or deviations, due to human frailty, from the norm set by theory.

A second group of economic theorists adheres to the proposition that it is the main purpose of theory to provide hypotheses that can be tested. This group acknowledges that prediction of future events represents the most stringent test of theory. They argue, however, that reality is so complex that it is necessary to begin with simplified propositions and models which are known to be unreal and not testable.[2] Basic among these propositions are the following three which traditionally have served to characterize the economic man or the rational man:

1. The principle of complete information and foresight. Economic conditions— demand, supply, prices, etc.—are not only given but also known to the rational man. This applies as well to future conditions about which there exists no uncertainty, so that rational choice can always be made. (In place of the assumption of certainty of future developments, we find nowadays more frequently the assumption that risks prevail but the probability of occurrence of different alternatives is known; this does not constitute a basic difference.)
2. The principle of complete mobility. There are no institutional or psychological factors which make it impossible, or expensive, or slow, to translate the rational choice into action.
3. The principle of pure competition. Individual action has no great influence on prices because each man's choice is independent from any other person's choice and because there are no "large" sellers or buyers. Action is the result of individual choice and is not group-determined.

Economic theory is developed first under these assumptions. The theorists then introduce changes in the assumptions so that the theory may approach reality. One such step consists, for instance, of introducing large-scale producers, monopolists, and oligopolists, another of introducing time lags, and still another of introducing uncertainty about the probability distribution of future events. The question raised in each case is this: Which of the original propositions needs to be changed, and in what way, in view of the new assumptions?

The fact that up to now the procedure of gradual approximation to reality has not been completely successful does not invalidate the method. It must be acknowledged that propositions were frequently derived from unrealistic economic models which were susceptible to testing and stimulated empirical research. In this paper, we shall point to a great drawback of this method of starting out with a simplified a priori system and making it gradually more complex and more real— by proceeding in this way one tends to lose sight of important problems and to disregard them.

The methods most commonly used in psychology may appear at first sight to be quite similar to the methods of economics which have just been described. Psychologists often start with casual observations, derive from them hypotheses, test those through more systematic observations, reformulate and revise their hypotheses accordingly, and test them again. The process of hypotheses-observations-hypotheses-observations often goes on with no end in sight. Differences from the approach of economic theory may be found in the absence in psychological research of detailed systematic elaboration prior to any observation. Also, in psychological research, findings and generalizations in one field of behavior are often considered as hypotheses in another field of behavior. Accordingly, in analyzing economic behavior[3] and trying to understand rationality, psychologists can draw on (a) the theory of learning and thinking, (b) the theory of group belonging, and (c) the theory of motivation. This will be done in this paper.

HABITUAL BEHAVIOR AND GENUINE DECISION MAKING

In trying to give noneconomic examples of "rational calculus," economic theorists have often referred to gambling. From some textbooks one might conclude that the most rational place in the world is the Casino in Monte Carlo where odds and probabilities can be calculated exactly. In contrast, some mathematicians and psychologists have considered scientific discovery and the thought processes of scientists as the best examples of rational or intelligent behavior.[4] An inquiry about the possible contributions of psychology to the analysis of rationality may then begin with a formulation of the differences between (a) associative learning and habit formation and (b) problem solving and thinking.

The basic principle of the first form of behavior is repetition. Here the argument of Guthrie holds: "The most certain and dependable information concerning what a man will do in any situation is information concerning what he did in that situation on its last occurrence."[5] This form of behavior depends upon the frequency of repetition as well as on its recency and on the success of past performances. The origins of habit formation have been demonstrated by experiments about learning nonsense syllables, lists of words, mazes, and conditioned responses. Habits thus formed are to some extent automatic and inflexible.

In contrast, problem-solving behavior has been characterized by the arousal of a problem or question, by deliberation that involves reorganization and "direction," by understanding of the requirements of the situation, by weighing of alternatives and taking their consequences into consideration and, finally, by choosing among alternative courses of action.[6] Scientific discovery is not the only example of such procedures; they have been demonstrated in the psychological laboratory as well as in a variety of real-life situations. Problem solving results in action which is new rather than repetitive; the actor may have never behaved in the same way before and may not have learned of any others having behaved in the same way.

Some of the above terms, defined and analyzed by psychologists, are also being used by economists in their discussion of rational behavior. In discussing, for example, a manufacturer's choice between erecting or not erecting a new factory, or raising or not raising his prices or output, reference is usually made to deliberation and to taking the consequences of alternative choices into consideration. Nevertheless, it is not justified to identify problem-solving behavior with rational behavior. From the point of view of an outside observer, habitual behavior may prove to be fully rational or the most appropriate way of action under certain

circumstances. All that is claimed here is that the analysis of two forms of behavior
—habitual versus genuine decision making—may serve to clarify problems of rationality. We shall proceed therefore by deriving six propositions from the psychological principles. To some extent, or in certain fields of behavior, these are findings or empirical generalizations; to some extent, or in other fields of behavior,
they are hypotheses.

1. Problem-solving behavior is a relatively rare occurrence. It would be incorrect
   to assume that everyday behavior consistently manifests such features as arousal
   of a problem, deliberation, or taking consequences of the action into consideration. Behavior which does not manifest these characteristics predominates
   in everyday life and in economic activities as well.
2. The main alternative to problem-solving behavior is not whimsical or impulsive
   behavior (which was considered the major example of "irrational" behavior by
   nineteenth-century philosophers). When genuine decision making does not
   take place, habitual behavior is the most usual occurrence: people act as they
   have acted before under similar circumstances, without deliberating and
   choosing.
3. Problem-solving behavior is recognized most commonly as a deviation from
   habitual behavior. Observance of the established routine is abandoned when
   in driving home from my office, for example, I learn that there is a parade in
   town and choose a different route, instead of automatically taking the usual
   one. Or, to mention an example of economic behavior: Many businessmen
   have rules of thumb concerning the timing for reorders of merchandise; yet
   sometimes they decide to place new orders even though their inventories have
   not reached the usual level of depletion (for instance, because they anticipate
   price increases), or not to order merchandise even though that level has been
   reached (because they expect a slump in sales).
4. Strong motivational forces—stronger than those which elicit habitual behavior
   —must be present to call forth problem-solving behavior. Being in a "cross-
   road situation," facing "choice points," or perceiving that something new has
   occurred are typical instances in which we are motivated to deliberate and
   choose. Pearl Harbor and the Korean aggression are extreme examples of "new"
   events; economic behavior of the problem-solving type was found to have pre-
   vailed widely after these events.
5. Group belonging and group reinforcement play a substantial role in changes
   of behavior due to problem solving. Many people become aware of the same
   events at the same time; our mass media provide the same information and
   often the same interpretation of events to groups of people (to businessmen,
   trade union members, sometimes to all Americans). Changes in behavior resulting from new events may therefore occur among very many people at the
   same time. Some economists[7] argued that consumer optimism and pessimism
   are unimportant because usually they will cancel out; in the light of sociopsychological principles, however, it is probable, and has been confirmed by
   recent surveys, that a change from optimistic to pessimistic attitudes, or vice
   versa, sometimes occurs among millions of people at the same time.
6. Changes in behavior due to genuine decision making will tend to be substantial and abrupt, rather than small and gradual. Typical examples of action that

results from genuine decisions are cessation of purchases or buying waves, the shutting down of plants or the building of new plants, rather than an increase or decrease of production by 5 or 10 per cent.[8]

Because of the preponderance of individual psychological assumptions in classical economics and the emphasis placed on group behavior in this discussion, the change in underlying conditions which has occurred during the last century may be illustrated by a further example. It is related—the author does not know whether the story is true or fictitious—that the banking house of the Rothschilds, still in its infancy at that time, was one of the suppliers of the armies of Lord Wellington in 1815. Nathan Mayer Rothschild accompanied the armies and was present at the Battle of Waterloo. When he became convinced that Napoleon was decisively defeated, he released carrier pigeons so as to transmit the news to his associates in London and reverse the commodity position of his bank. The carrier pigeons arrived in London before the news of the victory became public knowledge. The profits thus reaped laid, according to the story, the foundation to the outstanding position of the House of Rothschild in the following decades.

The decision to embark on a new course of action because of new events was then made by one individual for his own profit. At present, news of a battle, or of change of government, or of rearmament programs, is transmitted in short order by press and radio to the public at large. Businessmen—the manufacturers or retailers of steel or clothing, for instance—usually receive the same news about changes in the price of raw materials or in demand, and often consult with each other. Belonging to the same group means being subject to similar stimuli and reinforcing one another in making decisions. Acting in the same way as other members of one's group or of a reference group have acted under similar circumstances may also occur without deliberation and choice. New action by a few manufacturers will, then, frequently or even usually not be compensated by reverse action on the part of others. Rather the direction in which the economy of an entire country moves—and often the world economy as well—will tend to be subject to the same influences.

After having indicated some of the contributions which the application of certain psychological principles to economic behavior may make, we turn to contrasting that approach with the traditional theory of rationality. Instead of referring to the formulations of nineteenth-century economists, we shall quote from a modern version of the classical trend of thought. The title of a section in a recent article by Kenneth J. Arrow is "The Principle of Rationality." He describes one of the criteria of rationality as follows: "We can imagine the individual as listing, once and for all, all conceivable consequences of his actions in order of his preference for them."[9] We are first concerned with the expression "all conceivable consequences." This expression seems to contradict the principle of selectivity of human behavior. Yet habitual behavior is highly selective since it is based on (repeated) past experience, and problem-solving behavior likewise is highly selective since reorganization is subject to a certain direction instead of consisting of trial (and error) regarding all possible avenues of action.

Secondly, Arrow appears to identify rationality with consistency in the sense of repetition of the same choice. It is part and parcel of rational behavior, according to Arrow, that an individual "makes the same choice each time he is confronted with the same set of alternatives." [10] Proceeding in the same way on successive occasions appears, however, a characteristic of habitual behavior. Problem-solving behavior, on the other hand, is flexible. Rationality may be said to reflect adaptability and ability to act in a new way when circumstances demand it, rather than to consist of rigid or repetitive behavior.

Thirdly, it is important to realize the differences between the concepts, action, decision, and choice. It is an essential feature of the approach derived from considering problem-solving behavior that there is action without deliberate decision and choice. It then becomes one of the most important problems of research to determine under what conditions genuine decision and choice occur prior to an action. The three concepts are, however, used without differentiation in the classical theory of rationality and also, most recently, by Parsons and Shils. According to the theory of these authors, there are "five discrete choices (explicit or implicit) which every actor makes before he can act;" before there is action "a decision must always be made (explicitly or implicitly, consciously or unconsciously)." [11]

There exists, no doubt, a difference in terminology, which may be clarified by mentioning a simple case: Suppose my telephone rings: I lift the receiver with my left hand and say, "Hello." Should we then argue that I made several choices, for instance, that I decided not to lift the receiver with my right hand and not to say, "Mr. Katona speaking"? According to our use of the terms decision and choice, my action was habitual and did not involve "taking consequences into consideration." [12] Parsons and Shils use the terms *decision* and *choice* in a different sense, and Arrow may use the terms *all conceivable consequences* and *same set of alternatives* in a different sense from the one employed in this paper. But the difference between the two approaches appears to be more far-reaching. By using the terminology of the authors quoted, and by constructing a theory of rational action on the basis of this terminology, fundamental problems are disregarded. If every action by definition presupposes decision making, and if the malleability of human behavior is not taken into consideration, a one-sided theory of rationality is developed and empirical research is confined to testing a theory which covers only some of the aspects of rationality.

This was the case recently in experiments devised by Mosteller and Nogee. These authors attempt to test basic assumptions of economic theory, such as the rational choice among alternatives, by placing their subjects in a gambling situation (a variation of poker dice) and compelling them to make a decision, namely, to play or not to play against the experimenter. Through their experiments the authors prove that "it is feasible to measure utility experimentally," [13] but they do not shed light on the conditions under which rational behavior occurs or on the inherent features of rational behavior. Experiments in which making a choice among known alternatives is prescribed do not test the realism of economic theory.

MAXIMIZATION

Up to now we have discussed only one central aspect of rationality—means rather than ends. The end of rational behavior, according to economic theory, is maximization of profits in the case of business firms and maximization of utility in the case of people in general.

A few words, first, on maximizing profits. This is usually considered the simpler case because it is widely held (a) that business firms are in business to make profits and (b) that profits, more so than utility, are a quantitative, measurable concept.

When empirical research, most commonly in the form of case studies, showed that businessmen frequently strove for many things in addition to profits or in place of profits, most theorists were content with small changes in their systems. They redefined profits so as to include long-range profits and what has been called nonpecuniary or psychic profits. Striving for security or for power was identified with striving for profits in the more distant future; purchasing goods from a high bidder who was a member of the same fraternity as the purchaser, rather than from the lowest bidder—to cite an example often used in textbooks—was thought to be maximizing of nonpecuniary profits. Dissatisfaction with this type of theory construction is rather widespread. For example, a leading theorist wrote recently:

If *whatever* a business man does is explained by the principle of profit maximization—because he does what he likes to do, and he likes to do what maximizes the sum of his pecuniary and non-pecuniary profits—the analysis acquires the character of a system of definitions and tautologies, and loses much of its value as an explanation of reality.[14]

The same problem is encountered regarding maximization of utility. Arrow defines rational behavior as follows: "...among all the combinations of commodities an individual can afford, he chooses that combination which maximizes his utility or satisfaction" [15] and speaks of the "traditional identification of rationality with maximization of some sort." [16] An economic theorist has recently characterized this type of definition as follows:

The statement that a person seeks to maximize utility is (in many versions) a tautology: it is impossible to conceive of an observational phenomenon that contradicts it.... What if the theorem is contradicted by observation: Samuelson says it would not matter much in the case of utility theory; I would say that it would not make the slightest difference. For there is a free variable in his system: the tastes of consumers.... Any contradiction of a theorem derived from utility theory can always be attributed to a change of tastes, rather than to an error in the postulates or logic of the theory.[17]

What is the way out of this difficulty? Can psychology, and specifically the psychology of motivation, help? We may begin by characterizing the prevailing economic theory as a single-motive theory and contrast it with a theory of multiple motives. Even in case of a single decision of one individual, multiplicity of motives (or of vectors or forces in the field), some reinforcing one another and some conflicting with one another, is the rule rather than the exception. The motivational patterns prevailing among different individuals making the same decision need not be the same; the motives of the same individual who is in the same external situation at different times may likewise differ. This approach opens the way (a) for a study of the relation of different motives to different forms of behavior and (b) for an investigation of changes in motives. Both problems are disregarded by postulating a single-motive theory and by restricting empirical studies to attempts to confirm or contradict that theory.

The fruitfulness of the psychological approach may be illustrated first by a brief reference to business motivation. We may rank the diverse motivational patterns of businessmen by placing the striving for high immediate profits (maximization of short-run profits, to use economic terminology; charging whatever the market can bear, to use a popular expression) at one extreme of the scale. At the other extreme we place the striving for prestige or power. In between we discern striving for security, for larger business volume, or for profits in the more distant future. Under what kinds of business conditions will motivational patterns tend to conform with the one or the other end of the scale? Preliminary studies would seem to indicate that the worse the business situation is, the more frequent is striving for high immediate profits, and the better the business situation is, the more frequent is striving for nonpecuniary goals.[18]

Next we shall refer to one of the most important problems of consumer economics as well as of business-cycle studies, the deliberate choice between saving and spending. Suppose a college professor receives a raise in his salary or makes a few hundred extra dollars through a publication. Suppose, furthermore, that he suggests thereupon to his wife that they should buy a television set while the wife argues that the money should be put in the bank as a reserve against a "rainy day." Whatever the final decision may be, traditional economic theory would hold that the action which gives the greater satisfaction was chosen. This way of theorizing is of little value. Under what conditions will one type of behavior (spending) and under what conditions will another type of behavior (saving) be more frequent? Psychological hypotheses according to which the strength of vectors is related to the immediacy of needs have been put to a test through nationwide surveys over the past six years.[19] On the basis of survey findings the following tentative generalization was established: Pessimism, insecurity, expectation of income declines or bad times in the near future promote saving (putting the extra money in the bank), while optimism, feeling of security, expectation of income increases, or good times promote spending (buying the television set, for instance).

Psychological hypotheses, based on a theory of motivational patterns which change with circumstances and influence behavior, thus stimulated empirical studies. These studies, in turn, yielded a better understanding of past developments and also, we may add, better predictions of forthcoming trends than did studies based on the classical theory. On the other hand, when conclusions about utility or rationality were made on an a priori basis, researchers lost sight of important problems.[20]

DIMINISHING UTILITY, SATURATION, AND ASPIRATION

Among the problems to which the identification of maximizing utility with rationality gave rise, the measurability of utility has been prominent. At present the position of most economists appears to be that while interpersonal comparison of several consumers' utilities is not possible, and while cardinal measures cannot be attached to the utilities of one particular consumer, ordinal ranking of the utilities of each individual can be made. It is asserted that I can always say either that

I prefer *A* to *B*, or that I am indifferent to having *A* or *B*, or that I prefer *B* to *A*. The theory of indifference curves is based on this assumption.

In elaborating the theory further, it is asserted that rational behavior consists not only of preferring more of the same goods to less ($2 real wages to $1, or two packages of cigarettes to one package, for the same service performed) but also of deriving diminishing increments of satisfaction from successive units of a commodity.[21] In terms of an old textbook example, one drink of water has tremendous value to a thirsty traveler in a desert; a second, third, or fourth drink. may still have some value but less and less so; an *n*th drink (which he is unable to carry along) has no value at all. A generalization derived from this principle is that the more of a commodity or the more money a person has, the smaller are his needs for that commodity or for money, and the smaller his incentives to add to what he has.

In addition to using this principle of saturation to describe the behavior of the rational man, modern economists applied it to one of the most pressing problems of contemporary American economy. Prior to World War II the American people (not counting business firms) owned about 45 billion dollars in liquid assets (currency, bank deposits, government bonds) and these funds were highly concentrated among relatively few families; most individual families held no liquid assets at all (except for small amounts of currency). By the end of the year 1945, however, the personal liquid-asset holdings had risen to about 140 billion dollars and four out of every five families owned some bank deposits or war bonds. What is the effect of this great change on spending and saving? This question has been answered by several leading economists in terms of the saturation principle presented above. "The rate of saving is . . . a diminishing function of the wealth the indvidual holds"[22] because "the availability of liquid assets raises consumption generally by reducing the impulse to save."[23] More specifically: a person who owns nothing or very little will exert himself greatly to acquire some reserve funds, while a person who owns much will have much smaller incentives to save. Similarly, incentives to increase one's income are said to weaken with the amount of income. In other words, the strength of motivation is inversely correlated with the level of achievement.

In view of the lack of contact between economists and psychologists, it is hardly surprising that economists failed to see the relevance for their postulates of the extensive experimental work performed by psychologists on the problem of levels of aspiration. It is not necessary in this paper to describe these studies in detail. It may suffice to formulate three generalizations as established in numerous studies of goal-striving behavior:[24]

1. Aspirations are not static, they are not established once for all time.
2. Aspirations tend to grow with achievement and decline with failure.
3. Aspirations are influenced by the performance of other members of the group to which one belongs and by that of reference groups.

From these generalizations hypotheses were derived about the influence of assets on saving which differed from the postulates of the saturation theory. This is not the place to describe the extensive empirical work undertaken to test the hypotheses. But it may be reported that the saturation theory was not confirmed;

the level-of-aspiration theory likewise did not suffice to explain the findings. In addition to the variable "size of liquid-asset holdings," the studies had to consider such variables as income level, income change, and saving habits. (Holders of large liquid assets are primarily people who have saved a high proportion of their income in the past!)[25]

The necessity of studying the interaction of a great number of variables and the change of choices over time leads to doubts regarding the universal validity of a one-dimensional ordering of all alternatives. The theory of measurement of utilities remains an empty frame unless people's established preferences of A over B and of B over C provide indications about their probable future behavior. Under what conditions do people's preferences give us such clues, and under what conditions do they not? If at different times A and B are seen in different contexts— because of changed external conditions or the acquisition of new experiences— we may have to distinguish among several dimensions.

The problem may be illustrated by an analogy. Classic economic theory postulates a one-dimensional ordering of all alternatives; Gallup asserts that answers to questions of choice can always be ordered on a yes-uncertain (don't know)-no continuum; are both arguments subject to the same reservations? Specifically, if two persons give the same answer to a poll question (e.g., both say "Yes, I am for sending American troops to Europe" or "Yes, I am for the Taft-Hartley Act") may they mean different things so that their identical answers do not permit any conclusions about the similarity of their other attitudes and their behavior? Methodologically it follows from the last argument that yes-no questions need to be supplemented by open-ended questions to discern differences in people's level of information and motivation. It also follows that attitudes and preferences should be ascertained through a multi-question approach (or scaling) which serves to determine whether one or several dimensions prevail.

ON THEORY CONSTRUCTION

In attempting to summarize our conclusions about the respective merits of different scientific approaches, we might quote the conclusions of Arrow which he formulated for social science in general rather than for economics:

To the extent that formal theoretical structures in the social sciences have not been based on the hypothesis of rational behavior, their postulates have been developed in a manner which we may term *ad hoc*. Such propositions . . . depend, of course, on the investigator's intuition and common sense.[26]

The last sentence seems strange indeed. One may argue the other way around and point out that such propositions as "the purpose of business is to make profits" or "the best businessman is the one who maximizes profits" are based on intuition or supposed common sense, rather than on controlled observation. The main problem raised by the quotation concerns the function of empirical research. There exists an alternative to developing an axiomatic system into a full-fledged theoretical model in advance of testing the theory through observations. Controlled observations should be based on hypotheses, and the formulation of an integrated theory need not be delayed until all observations are completed. Yet theory construction is part of the process of hypothesis-observation-revised hypothesis and prediction-observation, and systematization should rely on some empirical research. The proximate aim of scientific research is a body of empirically validated generalizations and not a theory that is valid under any and all circumstances.

The dictum that "theoretical structures in the social sciences must be based on the hypothesis of rational behavior" presupposes that it is established what rational behavior is. Yet, instead of establishing the characteristics of rational behavior a priori, we must first determine the conditons a_1, b_1, c_1 under which behavior of the type x_1, y_1, z_1 and the conditions a_2, b_2, c_2 under which behavior of the type x_2, y_2, z_2 is likely to occur. Then, if we wish, we may designate one of the forms of behavior as rational. The contributions of psychology to this process are not solely methodological; findings and principles about noneconomic behavior provide hypotheses for the study of economic behavior. Likewise, psychology can profit from the study of economic behavior because many aspects of behavior, and among them the problems of rationality, may be studied most fruitfully in the economic field.

This paper was meant to indicate some promising leads for a study of rationality, not to carry such study to its completion. Among the problems that were not considered adequately were the philosophical ones (rationality viewed as a value concept), the psychoanalytic ones (the relationships between rational and conscious, and between irrational and unconscious), and those relating to personality theory and the roots of rationality. The emphasis was placed here on the possibility and fruitfulness of studying forms of rational behavior, rather than the characteristics of *the* rational man. Motives and goals that change with and are adapted to circumstances, and the relatively rare but highly significant cases of our becoming aware of problems and attempting to solve them, were found to be related to behavior that may be called truly rational.

NOTES

[1] T. Parsons and E. A. Shils, (Editors), *Toward a General Theory of Action* (Cambridge, Mass.: Harvard University Press, 1951).

[2] A variety of methods used in economic research differ, of course, from those employed by the two groups of economic theorists. Some research is motivated by dissatisfaction with the traditional economic theory; some is grounded in a systematization greatly different from traditional theory (the most important example of such systematization is national income accounting); some research is not clearly based on any theory; finally, some research has great affinity with psychological and sociological studies.

[3] The expression "economic behavior" is used in this paper to mean behavior concerning economic matters (spending, saving, investing, pricing, etc.) Some economic theorists use the expression to mean the behavior of the "economic man," that is, the behavior postulated in their theory of rationality.

[4] Reference should be made first of all to Max Wertheimer who in his book *Productive Thinking* uses the terms "sensible" and "intelligent" rather than "rational." Since we are mainly interested here in deriving conclusions from the psychology of thinking, the discussion of psychological principles will be kept extremely brief. See M. Wertheimer, *Productive Thinking* (New York: Harper, 1945); G. Katona, *Organizing and Memorizing* (New York:

Columbia University Press, 1940); and G. Katona, *Psychological Analysis of Economic Behavior* (New York: McGraw-Hill, 1951), especially Chapters 3 and 4.

[5] E. R. Guthrie, *Psychology of Learning* (New York: Harper, 1935), p. 228.

[6] Cf. the following statement by a leading psychoanalyst: "Rational behavior is behavior that is effectively guided by an understanding of the situation to which one is reacting." French adds two steps that follow the choice between alternative goals, namely, commitment to a goal and commitment to a plan to reach a goal. See T. M. French. *The Integration of Behavior* (Chicago: University of Chicago Press, 1952).

[7] J. M. Keynes, *The General Theory of Employment, Interest and Money* (New York: Harcourt, Brace, 1936), p. 95.

[8] Some empirical evidence supporting these six propositions in the area of economic behavior has been assembled by the Survey Research Center of the University of Michigan. See G. Katona, "Psychological Analysis of Business Decisions and Expectations," *American Economic Review* (1946), pp. 44–63.

[9] K. J. Arrow, "Mathematical Models in the Social Sciences," in D. Lerner and H. D. Lasswell (Editors), *The Policy Sciences* (Stanford: Stanford University Press, 1951), p. 135.

[10] In his recent book Arrow adds after stating that the economic man "will make the same decision each time he is faced with the same range of alternatives": "The ability to make consistent decisions is one of the symptoms of an integrated personality." See K. J. Arrow *Social Choice and Individual Values* (New York: Wiley, 1951), p. 2.

[11] T. Parsons and E. A. Shils, *op. cit.*

[12] If I have reason not to make known that I am at home, I may react to the ringing of the telephone by fright, indecision, and deliberation (should I lift the receiver or let the telephone ring?) instead of reacting in the habitual way. This is an example of problem-solving behavior characterized as deviating from habitual behavior. The only example of action mentioned by Parsons and Shils, "a man driving his automobile to a lake to go fishing," may be habitual or may be an instance of genuine decision making.

[13] F. Mosteller and P. Nogee, "An Experimental Measurement of Utility;" *Journal of Political Economy* (1951), pp. 371–405.

[14] F. Machlup, "Marginal Analysis and Empirical Research," *American Economic Review* (1946), p. 526.

[15] K. J. Arrow, *op cit.*

[16] K. J. Arrow, *Social Choice and Individual Values* (New York: Wiley, 1951). The quotation refers specifically to Samuelson's definition but also applies to that of Arrow.

[17] G. J. Stigler, "Review of P. A. Samuelson's Foundations of Economic Analysis," *Journal of American Statistical Association* (1948), p. 603.

[18] G. Katona, *Psychological Analysis of Economic Behavior* (New York: McGraw-Hill, 1951), pp. 193–213.

[19] In the Surveys of Consumer Finances, conducted annually since 1946 by the Survey Research Center of the University of Michigan for the Federal Reserve Board and reported in the *Federal Reserve Bulletin*. See a forthcoming publication of the Survey Research Center on consumer buying and inflation during 1950–52.

[20] It should not be implied that the concepts of utility and maximization are of no value for empirical research. Comparison between maximum utility as determined from the vantage point of an observer with the pattern of goals actually chosen (the "subjective maximum"), which is based on insufficient information, may be useful. Similar considerations apply to such newer concepts as "minimizing regrets" and the "minimax."

[21] This principle of diminishing utility was called a "fundamental tendency of human nature" by the great nineteenth century economist, Alfred Marshall.

[22] G. Haberler, *Prosperity and Depression*, 3rd ed. (Geneva: League of Nations, 1941), p. 199.

[23] The last quotation is from the publication of the U.S. Department of Commerce, *Survey of Current Business*, May 1950, p. 10.

[24] K. Lewin, et al., "Level of Aspiration," in J. Hunt (Editor), *Personality and the Behavior Disorders* (New York: Ronald, 1944).

[25] The empirical work was part of the economic behavior program of the Survey Research Center under the direction of the author.

[26] K. J. Arrow, "Mathematical Models in the Social Sciences," in D. Lerner and H. D. Lasswell (Editors), *The Policy Sciences* (Stanford: Stanford University Press, 1951), p. 137.

SOME SUGGESTIONS FOR FURTHER READING

Douglas, E. K. (1975), *Economics of Marketing,* New York: Harper & Row.

Katona, G. (1975), *Psychological Economics,* New York: Elsevier Scientific.

Lancaster, K. (1971), *Consumer Demand: A New Approach,* New York: Columbia University Press.

Ratchford, B. T. (1975), "The New Economic Theory of Consumer Behavior: An Interpretive Essay," *Journal of Consumer Research* (September), 65–75.

Sargent, T. J. and J. Wallace (1977), *Rational Expectations and the Theory of Economic Policy,* revised. Minneapolis, MN: Federal Reserve Bank.

10 / THE AFFLUENT SOCIETY /
John Kenneth Galbraith

INTRODUCTION

Wealth is not without its advantages and the case to the contrary, although it has often been made, has never proved widely persuasive. But, beyond doubt, wealth is the relentless enemy of understanding. The poor man has always a precise view of his problem and its remedy: he hasn't enough and he needs more. The rich man can assume or imagine a much greater variety of ills and he will be correspondingly less certain of their remedy. Also, until he learns to live with his wealth, he will have a well-observed tendency to put it to the wrong purposes or otherwise to make himself foolish.

As with individuals so with nations. And the experience of nations with well-being is exceedingly brief. Nearly all throughout all history have been very poor. The exception, almost insignificant in the whole span of human existence, has been the last few generations in the comparatively small corner of the world populated by Europeans. Here, and especially in the United States, there has been great and quite unprecedented affluence.

The ideas by which the people of this favored part of the world interpret their existence, and in measure guide their behavior, were not forged in a world of wealth. These ideas were the product of a world in which poverty had always been man's normal lot, and any other state was in degree unimaginable. This poverty was not the elegant torture of the spirit which comes from contemplating another man's more spacious possessions. It was the unedifying mortification of the flesh—from hunger, sickness, and cold. Those who might be freed temporarily from such burden could not know when it would strike again, for at best hunger yielded only perilously to privation. It is improbable that the poverty of the masses of the people was made greatly more bearable by the fact that a very few—those upon whose movements nearly all recorded history centers—were very rich.

No one would wish to argue that the ideas which interpreted this world of grim scarcity would serve equally well for the contemporary United States. Poverty was the all-pervasive fact of that world. Obviously it is not of ours. One would not expect that the preoccupations of a poverty-ridden world would be relevant in one

From THE AFFLUENT SOCIETY, Third Edition by John Kenneth Galbraith, published by Houghton Mifflin Company. Copyright © 1958, 1969, 1976 by John Kenneth Galbraith. Reprinted by permission of the publisher.
John Kenneth Galbraith, a noted economist and social critic, recently retired as professor of economics at Harvard University. He received M.S. and Ph.D. degrees from the University of California (Berkeley); was deputy administrator, Office of Price Administration during World War II, and Ambassador to India during 1961–63. In addition to *The Affluent Society,* his best known works are *American Capitalism: The Theory of Countervailing Power, The New Industrial State, Economics and the Public Purpose,* and *The Age of Uncertainty.*

where the ordinary individual has access to amenities—foods, entertainment, personal transportation, and plumbing—in which not even the rich rejoiced a century ago. So great has been the change that many of the desires of the individual are no longer even evident to him. They become so only as they are synthesized, elaborated, and nurtured by advertising and salesmanship, and these, in turn, have become among our most important and talented professions. Few people at the beginning of the nineteenth century needed an adman to tell them what they wanted.

It would be wrong to suggest that the economic ideas which once interpreted the world of mass poverty have made no adjustment to the world of affluence. There have been many adjustments, including some that have gone unrecognized or have been poorly understood. But there has also been a remarkable resistance. And the total alteration in underlying circumstances has not been squarely faced. As a result we are guided, in part, by ideas that are relevant to another world; and as a further result we do many things that are unnecessary, some that are unwise, and a few that are insane. We enhance substantially the risk of depression and thereby the threat to our affluence itself.

. . . .

No student of social matters in these days can escape feeling how precarious is the existence of that with which he deals. Western man has escaped for the moment the poverty which was for so long his all-embracing fate. The unearthly light of a handful of nuclear explosions would signal his return to utter deprivation if, indeed, he survived at all. I venture to think that the ideas here offered bear on our chances for escape from this fate. Illusion is a comprehensive ill. The rich man who deludes himself into behaving like a mendicant may conserve his fortune although he will not be very happy. The affluent country which conducts its affairs in accordance with rules of another and poorer age also foregoes opportunities. And in misunderstanding itself it will, in any time of difficulty, implacably prescribe for itself the wrong remedies. This the reader will discover is, to a disturbing degree, our present tendency.

Yet it would be a mistake to be too gravely depressed. The problems of an affluent world, which does not understand itself, may be serious, and they can needlessly threaten the affluence itself. But they are not likely to be as serious as those of a poor world where the simple exigencies of poverty preclude the luxury of misunderstanding but where, also and alas, no solutions are to be had.

. . . .

As Tawney observed, we are rarely conscious of the quality of the air we breathe. But in Los Angeles, where it is barely sufficient for its freight, we take it seriously. Similarly those who reside on a recently reclaimed desert see in the water in the canals the evidence of their unnatural triumph over nature. And the Chicagoan in Sarasota sees in his tanned belly the proof of his intelligence in escaping his dark and frozen habitat. But where sun and rain are abundant, though they are no less important, they are taken for granted. In the world of Ricardo goods were scarce. They were also closely related, if not to the survival, at least to the elemental comforts of man. They fed him, covered him when he was out of doors, and kept him warm when he was within. It is not surprising that the production by which these goods were obtained was central to men's thoughts.

Now goods are abundant. More die in the United States of too much food than of too little. Where the population was once thought to press on the food supply, now the food supply presses relentlessly on the population. No one can seriously suggest that the steel which comprises the extra four or five feet of purely decorative distance on our automobiles is of prime urgency. For many women and some men clothing has ceased to be related to protection from exposure and has become, like plumage, almost exclusively erotic. Yet production remains central to our thoughts. There is no tendency to take it, like sun and water, for granted; on the contrary, it continues to measure the quality and progress of our civilization.

Our preoccupation with production is, in fact, the culminating consequence of powerful historical and psychological forces—forces which only by an act of will we can hope to escape. Productivity, as we have seen, has enabled us to avoid or finesse the tensions anciently associated with inequality and its inconvenient remedies. It has become central to our strivings to reduce insecurity. And as we shall observe ... its importance is buttressed by a highly dubious but widely accepted psychology of want; by an equally dubious but equally accepted interpretation of national interest; and by powerful vested interest. So all embracing, indeed, is our sense of the importance of production as a goal that the first reaction to any questioning of this attitude will be, "What else is there?"

THE PARAMOUNT POSITION OF PRODUCTION

As with the bear and her cubs we must expect the reaction to be increasingly sharp as the danger becomes more threatening. In part it will take the form of a purely assertive posture. "There is still an economic problem"; "We still have poverty"; "It is human nature to want more"; "Without increasing production there will be stagnation"; "We must show the Russians." But the ultimate refuge will remain in the theory of consumer demand. This is a formidable structure; it has already demonstrated its effectiveness in defending the urgency of production. In a world where affluence is rendering the old ideas obsolete, it will continue to be the bastion against the misery of new ones.

The theory of consumer demand, as it is now widely accepted, is based on two broad propositions, neither of them quite explicit but both extremely important for the present value system of economists. The first is that the urgency of wants does not diminish appreciably as more of them are satisfied or, to put the matter more precisely, to the extent that this happens it is not demonstrable and not a matter of any interest to economists or for economic policy. When man has satisfied his physical needs, then psychologically grounded desires take over. These can never be satisfied or, in any case, no progress can be proved. The concept of satiation has very little standing in economics. It is neither useful nor scientific to speculate on the comparative cravings of the stomach and the mind.

The second proposition is that wants originate in the personality of the consumer or, in any case, that they are given data for the economist. The latter's task is merely to seek their satisfaction. He has no need to inquire how these wants are formed. His function is sufficiently fulfilled by maximizing the goods that supply the wants.

The examination of these two conclusions must now be pressed. The explanation of consumer behavior has its ancestry in a much older problem, indeed the oldest problem of economics, that of price determination. Nothing originally proved more troublesome in the explanation of prices, i.e., exchange values, than the indigestible fact that some of the most useful things had the least value in exchange and some of the least useful had the most. As Adam Smith observed: "Nothing is more useful than water; but it will purchase scarce anything; scarce anything can be had in exchange for it. A diamond, on the contrary, has scarce any value in use: but a very great quantity of other goods may frequently be had in exchange for it."

In explaining value, Smith thought it well to distinguish between "value in exchange" and "value in use" and sought thus to reconcile the paradox of high utility and low exchangeability. This distinction begged questions rather than solved them and for another hundred years economists sought for a satisfactory formulation. Finally, toward the end of the last century—though it is now recognized that their work had been extensively anticipated—the three economists of marginal utility (Karl Menger, an Austrian; William Stanley Jevons, an Englishman; and John Bates Clark, an American) produced more or less simultaneously the explanation which in broad substance still serves. The urgency of desire is a function of the quantity of goods which the individual has available to satisfy that desire. The larger the stock the less the satisfactions from an increment. And the less, also, the willingness to pay. Since diamonds for most people are in comparatively meager supply, the satisfaction from an additional one is great, and the potential willingness to pay is likewise high. The case of water is just the reverse. It also follows that where the supply of a good can be readily increased at low cost, its value in exchange will reflect that ease of reproduction and the low urgency of the marginal desires it thus comes to satisfy. This will be so no matter how difficult it may be (as with water) to dispense entirely with the item in question.

The doctrine of diminishing marginal utility, as it was enshrined in the economics textbooks, seemed to put economic ideas squarely on the side of the diminishing importance of production under conditions of increasing affluence. With increasing per capita real income, men are able to satisfy additional wants. These are of a lower order of urgency. This being so, the production that provides the goods that satisfy these less urgent wants must also be of smaller (and declining) importance. In Ricardo's England the supply of bread for many was meager. The satisfaction resulting from an increment in the bread supply—from a higher money income, bread prices being the same, or the same money income, bread prices being lower—was great. Hunger was lessened; life itself might be extended. Certainly any measure to increase the bread supply merited the deep and serious interest of the public-spirited citizen.

In the contemporary United States the supply of bread is plentiful and the supply of bread grains even redundant. The yield of satisfactions from a marginal increment in the wheat supply is small. To a Secretary of Agriculture it is indubitably negative. Measures to increase the wheat supply are not, therefore, a socially urgent preoccupation of publicly concerned citizens. These are more likely to be found spending their time devising schemes for the effective control of wheat production. And having extended their bread consumption to the point where its marginal utility is very low, people have gone on to spend their income on other things. Since these other goods entered their consumption pattern after bread, there is a presumption that they are not very urgent either—that *their* consumption has been carried, as with wheat, to the point where marginal utility is small or even negligible. So it must be assumed that the importance of marginal increments of all production is low and declining. The effect of increasing affluence is to minimize the importance of economic goals. Production and productivity become less and less important.

The concept of diminishing marginal utility was, and remains, one of the indispensable ideas of economics. Since it conceded so much to the notion of diminishing urgency of wants, and hence of production, it was remarkable indeed that the situation was retrieved. This was done—and brilliantly. The diminishing urgency of wants was not admitted.

THE DEPENDENCE EFFECT

The notion that wants do not become less urgent the more amply the individual is supplied is broadly repugnant to common sense. It is something to be believed only by those who wish to believe. Yet the conventional wisdom must be tackled on its own terrain. Intertemporal comparisons of an individual's state of mind do rest on doubtful grounds. Who can say for sure that the deprivation which afflicts him with hunger is more painful than the deprivation which afflicts him with envy of his neighbor's new car? In the time that has passed since he was poor his soul may have become subject to a new and deeper searing. And where a society is concerned, comparisons between marginal satisfactions when it is poor and those when it is affluent will involve not only the same individual at different times but different individuals at different times. The scholar who wishes to believe that with increasing affluence there is no reduction in the urgency of desires and goods is not without points for debate. However plausible the case against him, it cannot be proven. In the defense of the conventional wisdom this amounts almost to invulnerability.

However, there is a flaw in the case. If the individual's wants are to be urgent they must be original with himself. They cannot be urgent if they must be contrived for him. And above all they must not be contrived by the process of production by which they are satisfied. For this means that the whole case for the urgency of production, based on the urgency of wants, falls to the ground. One cannot defend production as satisfying wants if that production creates the wants.

Were it so that a man on arising each morning was assailed by demons which instilled in him a passion sometimes for silk shirts, sometimes for kitchenware, sometimes for chamber pots, and sometimes for orange squash, there would be every reason to applaud the effort to find the goods, however odd, that quenched this flame. But should it be that his passion was the result of his first having cultivated the demons, and should it also be that his effort to allay it stirred the demons to ever greater and greater effort, there would be question as to how rational was his solution. Unless restrained by conventional attitudes, he might wonder if the solution lay with more goods or fewer demons.

So it is that if production creates the wants it seeks to satisfy, or if the wants emerge *pari passu* with the production, then the urgency of the wants can no longer be used to defend the urgency of the production. Production only fills a void that it has itself created.

The point is so central that it must be pressed. Consumer wants can have bizarre, frivolous, or even immoral origins, and an admirable case can still be made for a society that seeks to satisfy them. But the case cannot stand if it is the process of satisfying wants that creates the wants. For then the individual who urges the importance of production to satisfy these wants is precisely in the position of the on-looker who applauds the efforts of the squirrel to keep abreast of the wheel that is propelled by his own efforts.

That wants are, in fact, the fruit of production will now be denied by few serious scholars. And a considerable number of economists, though not always in full knowledge of the implications, have conceded the point. In the observation cited at the end of the preceding chapter Keynes noted that needs of "the second class," i.e., those that are the result of efforts to keep abreast or ahead of one's fellow being "may indeed be insatiable; for the higher the general level the higher still are they." And emulation has always played a considerable role in the views of other economists of want creation. One man's consumption becomes his neighbor's wish. This already means that the process by which wants are satisfied is also the process by which wants are created. The more wants that are satisfied the more new ones are born.

However, the argument has been carried farther. A leading modern theorist of consumer behavior, Professor Duesenberry, has stated explicitly that "ours is a society in which one of the principal social goals is a higher standard of living.... [This] has great significance for the theory of consumption ... the desire to get superior goods takes on a life of its own. It provides a drive to higher expenditure which may even be stronger than that arising out of the needs which are supposed to be satisfied by that expenditure." The implications of this view are impressive. The notion of independently established need now sinks into the background. Because the society sets great store by ability to produce a high living standard, it evaluates people by the products they possess. The urge to consume is fathered by the value system which emphasizes the ability of the society to produce. The more that is produced the more that must be owned in order to maintain the appropriate prestige. The latter is an important point, for, without going as far as Duesenberry in reducing goods to the role of symbols of prestige in the affluent society, it is plain that his argument fully implies that the production of goods creates the want that the goods are presumed to satisfy.

The even more direct link between production and wants is provided by the institutions of modern advertising and salesmanship. These cannot be reconciled with the notion of independently determined desires, for their central function is to create desires—to bring into being wants that previously did not exist.[1] This is accomplished by the producer of the goods or at his behest. A broad empirical relationship exists between what is spent on production of consumers' goods and what is spent in synthesizing the desires for that production. A new consumer product must be introduced with a suitable advertising campaign to arouse an interest in it. The path for an expansion of output must be paved by a suitable expansion in the advertising budget. Outlays for the manufacturing of a product are not more important in the strategy of modern business enterprise than outlays for the manufacturing of demand for the product. None of this is novel. All would be regarded as elementary by the most retarded student in the nation's most primitive school of business administration. The cost of this want formation is formidable. In 1956 total advertising expenditure—though, as noted, not all of it may be assigned to the synthesis of wants—amounted to about ten billion dollars. For some years it had been increasing at a rate in excess of a billion dollars a year. Obviously, such outlays must be integrated with the theory of consumer demand. They are too big to be ignored.

But such integration means recognizing that wants are dependent on production. It accords to the producer the function both of making the goods and of making the desires for them. It recognizes that production, not only passively through emulation, but actively through advertising and related activities, creates the wants it seeks to satisfy.

The businessman and the lay reader will be puzzled over the emphasis which I give to a seemingly obvious point. The point is indeed obvious. But it is one which, to a singular degree, economists have resisted. They have sensed, as the layman does not, the damage to established ideas which lurks in these relationships. As a result, incredibly, they have closed their eyes (and ears) to the most obtrusive of all economic phenomena, namely modern want creation.

This is not to say that the evidence affirming the dependence of wants on advertising has been entirely ignored. It is one reason why advertising has so long been regarded with such uneasiness by economists. Here is something which cannot be accommodated easily to existing theory. More pervious scholars have speculated on the urgency of desires which are so obviously the fruit of such expensively contrived campaigns for popular attention. Is a new breakfast cereal or detergent so much wanted if so much must be spent to compel in the consumer demand the sense of want? But there has been little tendency to go on to examine the implications of this for the theory of consumer demand and even less for the importance of production and productive efficiency. These have remained sacrosanct. More often the uneasiness has been manifested in a general disapproval of advertising and advertising men, leading to the occasional suggestion that they shouldn't exist. Such suggestions have usually been ill received.

And so the notion of independently determined wants still survives. In the face of all the forces of modern salesmanship it still rules, almost undefiled, in the textbooks. And it still remains the economist's mission—and on few matters is the pedagogy so firm—to seek unquestioningly the means for filling these wants. This being so, production remains of prime urgency. We have here, perhaps, the ultimate triumph of the conventional wisdom in its resistance to the evidence of the eyes. To equal it one must imagine a humanitarian who was long ago persuaded of the grievous shortage of hospital facilities in the town. He continues to importune the passers-by for money for more beds and refuses to notice that the town doctor is deftly knocking over pedestrians with his car to keep up the occupancy.

And in unraveling the complex we should always be careful not to overlook the obvious. The fact that wants can be synthesized by advertising, catalyzed by salesmanship, and shaped by the discreet manipulations of the persuaders shows that they are not very urgent. A man who is hungry need never be told of his need for food. If he is inspired by his appetite, he is immune to the influence of Messrs. Batten, Barton, Durstine & Osborn. The latter are effective only with those who are so far removed from physical want that they do not already know what they want. In this state alone men are open to persuasion.

The general conclusion of these pages is of such importance for this essay that it had perhaps best be put with some formality. As a society becomes increasingly affluent, wants are increasingly created by the process by which they are satisfied. This may operate passively. Increases in consumption, the counterpart of increases in production, act by suggestion or emulation to create wants. Or producers may proceed actively to create wants through advertising and salesmanship. Wants thus come to depend on output. In technical terms it can no longer be assumed that welfare is greater at an all-round higher level of production than at a lower one. It may be the same. The higher level of production has, merely, a higher level of want creation necessitating a higher level of want satisfaction. There will be frequent occasion to refer to the way wants depend on the process by which they are satisfied. It will be convenient to call it the Dependence Effect.

We may now contemplate briefly the conclusions to which this analysis has brought us.

Plainly the theory of consumer demand is a peculiarly treacherous friend of the present goals of economics. At first glance it seems to defend the continuing urgency of production and our preoccupation with it as a goal. The economist does not enter into the dubious moral arguments about the importance or virtue of the wants to be satisfied. He doesn't pretend to compare mental states of the same or different people at different times and to suggest that one is less urgent than another. The desire is there. That for him is sufficient. He sets about in a workman-like way to satisfy desire, and accordingly he sets the proper store by the production that does. Like woman's his work is never done.

But this rationalization, handsomely though it seems to serve, turns destructively on those who advance it once it is conceded that wants are themselves both passively and deliberately the fruits of the process by which they are satisfied. Then the production of goods satisfies the wants that the consumption of these goods creates or that the producers of goods synthesize. Production induces more wants and the need for more production. So far, in a major *tour de force*, the implications have been ignored. But this obviously is a perilous solution. It cannot long survive discussion.

Among the many models of the good society no one has urged the squirrel wheel. Moreover, as we shall see presently, the wheel is not one that revolves with perfect smoothness. Aside from its dubious cultural charm, there are serious structural weaknesses which may one day embarrass us.

THE BILL COLLECTOR COMETH

The situation is this. Production for the sake of the goods produced is no longer very urgent. The significance of marginal increments (or decrements) in the supply of goods is slight. We sustain a sense of urgency only because of attitudes that trace to the world not of today but into which economics was born. These are reinforced by an untenable theory of consumer demand, an obsolete, erroneous, and even somewhat dangerous identification of production with military power, and by a system of vested interests which marries both liberals and conservatives to the importance of production.

At the same time production does remain important and urgent for its effect on economic security. When men are unemployed, society does not miss the goods they do not produce. The loss here is marginal. But the men who are without work *do* miss the income they no longer earn. Here the effect is not marginal. It involves all or a large share of the men's earnings and hence all or a large share of what they are able to buy. And, we note, high and stable production is the broad founda- tion of the economic security of virtually every other group—of farmers, white collar workers, and both large businessmen and small. The depression also remains the major uncovered risk of the modern large corporation. It is for reasons of economic security that we must produce at capacity.

The simple conclusions will not be well regarded by the conventional wisdom. To urge the importance of production because of its bearing on economic security, and to suggest that the product is in any way incidental, is disturbing. It brings the economic society to the brink of the dubious world of make-work and boondog- gling. One of the escapes from this world is to make all wants urgent, and no doubt we have here another reason for the obscurantist rationalization of consumer demand. It still seems more satisfactory to say that we need the goods than to stress the real point which is that social well-being and contentment require that we have enough production to provide income to the willing labor force. But if anyone has surviving doubts as to where the real priorities lie, let him apply a simple test. Let him assume that a President, or other candidate for re-election to major public office, has the opportunity of defending a large increase in man- hour productivity which has been divided equally between greatly increased total output and greatly increased unemployment. And let it be assumed that as an alternative he might choose unchanged productivity which has left everyone em- ployed. That full employment is more desirable than increased production com- bined with unemployment would be clear alike to the most sophisticated and the most primitive politician.

The foregoing provides the basic rule of procedure for the remainder of this essay. It shows that we need not be much concerned with the supply of goods for their own sake. The urgencies here are founded not on substance but on myth. And, indeed, our ultimate purpose is to see the opportunities that emerge as this myth is dispelled. But in all this we must be exceedingly conscious of the impor- tance of production for its bearing on the economic security of individuals. As a source of income for people its importance remains undiminished. This function of production must be carefully safeguarded.

But myth is rarely benign. And the system of illusions which causes us to attach such importance to production for its own sake is itself damaging or dangerous. One danger arises in the devices by which we fabricate wants and this, indeed nurtures a threat to the security of employment and income which production provides. Our failure to solve the problem of inflation is also the result of present attitudes toward the production of goods. And the way that present attitudes cause us to emphasize the supply of some as distinct from all goods and services is the source of deeper social dangers. To these problems, beginning with the dangers inherent in the present methods of manufacturing wants, the essay now turns.

. . . .

In a society in which the production and sale of goods seems sacrosanct there will be extreme hesitation over measures which will seem to restrain the financing of consumers' goods and hence their sale. Measures to prevent the competitive liberalization of consumer credit terms will encounter the heaviest resistance. When regarded in relation to the underlying interest in stability and economic security, such precautionary measures have a much stronger claim for attention. They promise to help keep the process of synthesizing demand and the purchasing power to make it effective from damaging the continuity of production and employment. The regulation of the terms and conditions of consumer credit, while it has been undertaken in the past in wartime, is not a power presently possessed by the United States government. It is, however, a commonplace in the United Kingdom.

However, the more substantial remedy lies deeper. Not all goods and services are subject to sale on the installment plan and to the attentions of the bill collector. Automobiles and radios and wall-to-wall carpeting are; the services of the schools, hospitals, and public libraries are not. To the extent that an economy concentrates its efforts on the first it will be subject to the vagaries of want-*cum*-debt creation. As it devotes its energies to serving itself with health, education, and other like services, it will reduce its danger. We have already seen that the preoccupation with production is a selective one. In particular it is heavily centered on those goods which by their character or by tradition are in the domain of private production. It concentrates energies, in other words, on producing the products which are subject to the greatest instability. It carries this indeed to the point where the manufacture of wants may itself be a tenuous process. A different arrangement for satisfying our needs—one, for example, that allotted a larger proportion of resources to those needs that are in the public domain—would thus be an important step toward stability. In one of the paradoxes with which economics is replete it might even, by contributing to the reliability of production, insure a greater total private product.

THE THEORY OF SOCIAL BALANCE

It is not till it is discovered that high individual incomes will not purchase the mass of mankind immunity from cholera, typhus, and ignorance, still less secure them the positive advantages of educational opportunity and economic security, that slowly and reluctantly, amid prophecies of moral degeneration and economic disaster, society begins to make collective provision for needs which no ordinary individual, even if he works overtime all his life, can provide himself.

—R. H. Tawney
Equality (4th revised ed.), pp. 134–35.

The final problem of the productive society is what it produces. This manifests itself in an implacable tendency to provide an opulent supply of some things and a niggardly yield of others. This disparity carries to the point where it is a cause of social discomfort and social unhealth. The line which divides our area of wealth from our area of poverty is roughly that which divides privately produced and marketed goods and services from publicly rendered services. Our wealth in the first is not only in startling contrast with the meagerness of the latter, but our wealth in privately produced goods is, to a marked degree, the cause of crisis in the supply of public services. For we have failed to see the importance, indeed the urgent need, of maintaining a balance between the two.

This disparity between our flow of private and public goods and services is no matter of subjective judgment. On the contrary, it is a source of the most extensive comment which only stops short of the direct contrast being made here. In the years following World War II, the papers of any major city—those of New York were an excellent example—told daily of the shortages and shortcomings in the elementary municipal and metropolitan services. The schools were old and overcrowded. The police force was under strength and underpaid. The parks and playgrounds were insufficient. Streets and empty lots were filthy, and the sanitation staff was underequipped and in need of men. Access to the city by those who work there was uncertain and painful and becoming more so. Internal transportation was overcrowded, unhealthful, and dirty. So was the air. Parking on the streets had to be prohibited, and there was no space elsewhere. These deficiencies were not in new and novel services but in old and established ones. Cities have long swept their streets, helped their people move around, educated them, kept order, and provided horse rails for vehicles which sought to pause. That their residents should have a nontoxic supply of air suggests no revolutionary dalliance with socialism.

The discussion of this public poverty competed, on the whole successfully, with the stories of ever-increasing opulence in privately produced goods. The Gross National Product was rising. So were retail sales. So was personal income. Labor productivity had also advanced. The automobiles that could not be parked were being produced at an expanded rate. The children, though without schools, subject in the playgrounds to the affectionate interest of adults with odd tastes, and disposed to increasingly imaginative forms of delinquency, were admirably equipped with television sets. We had difficulty finding storage space for the great surpluses of food despite a national disposition to obesity. Food was grown and packaged under private auspices. The care and refreshment of the mind, in contrast with the stomach, was principally in the public domain. Our colleges and universities were severely overcrowded and underprovided, and the same was true of the mental hospitals.

The contrast was and remains evident not alone to those who read. The family which takes its mauve and cerise air-conditioned, power-steered, and power-braked automobile out for a tour passes through cities that are badly paved, made hideous by litter, blighted buildings, billboards, and posts for wires that should long since have been put underground. They pass on into a countryside that has been rendered largely invisible by commercial art. (The goods which the latter advertise have an absolute priority in our value system. Such aesthetic considerations as a view of the countryside accordingly come second. On such matters we are consistent.) They picnic on exquisitely packaged food from a portable icebox by a polluted stream and go on to spend the night at a park which is a menace to public health and morals. Just before dozing off on an air mattress, beneath a nylon tent, amid the stench of decaying refuse, they may reflect vaguely on the curious unevenness of their blessings. Is this, indeed, the American genius?

ON SECURITY AND SURVIVAL

In our society the increased production of goods—privately produced goods—is, as we have seen, a basic measure of social achievement. This is partly the result of the great continuity of ideas which links the present with a world in which production indeed meant life. Partly it is a matter of vested interest. Partly it is a product of the elaborate obscurantism of the modern theory of consumer need. Partly it reflects an erroneous view of the problem of national security. And partly, we have seen, the preoccupation with production is forced quite genuinely upon us by tight nexus between production and economic security. However, it is a reasonable assumption that most people pressed to explain our concern for production—a pressure that is not often exerted—would be content to suggest that it serves the happiness of most men and women. That is sufficient.

The pursuit of happiness is admirable as a social goal. But the notion of happiness lacks philosophical exactitude; there is agreement neither on its substance nor its source.... A society has one higher task than to consider its goals, to reflect on its pursuit of happiness and harmony and its success in expelling pain, tension, sorrow, and the ubiquitous curse of ignorance. It must also, so far as this may be possible, insure its own survival.

The ideas with which this essay is concerned bear heavily on this considerable goal. The survival of a society rests on the same factors which make its survival worth while, for the simple but compelling reason that illusion is the enemy of both.

The nature of the deployment of the resources that would best serve our survival is beyond the scope of this essay. For myself I have little faith in the safety or security which derives from a never-ending arms race—from a competition to elaborate ever more agonizing weapons and to counter those of the enemy. If the possibility exists, the risks of negotiation and settlement, however great these may be, would still seem to provide a better prospect for survival than reliance on weapons which we can only hope are too terrible to use.

But whatever the paths to survival, the problem is the same. Were the Russians to disappear from the world, or become overnight as tractable as church mice, there would remain vast millions of hungry and discontented people in the world.

Without the promise of relief from that hunger and privation, disorder would still be inevitable. The promise of such relief requires that we have available or usable resources. The requirement is, of course, much more urgent in a world in which differing economic and political systems are in competition.

Even when the arms race ends, as it must, the scientific and technological frontier will remain. Either as an aspect of international competition, or in pursuit of the esteem and satisfaction which go with discovery, we shall want to seek to cross it and be in on the crossing. In the field of consumer satisfaction, as we should by now agree, there is little on which one can fault the American performance. But this is not all and, as we should now, hopefully, also agree, an economy that is preoccupied however brilliantly with the production of private consumer products is supremely ill fitted for many of these frontier tasks. Under the best of circumstances its research will be related to these products rather than to knowledge. The conventional wisdom will provide impressive arguments to the contrary. No one should be fooled.

And not only does a great part of modern scientific work lie outside the scope of the market and private enterprise but so does a large area of application and development. Private enterprise did not get us atomic energy. It has shown relatively slight interest in its development for power for the reason that it could not clearly be fitted into commercial patterns of cost and profit. Though no one doubts the vigor with which it addresses itself to travel within the United States, General Motors has little interest in travel through space.

As matters now stand, we have almost no institutions that are by central design and purpose directed to participation in modern scientific and technological progress and its large-scale application. We have no organization capable, for example, of taking on the large-scale development of atomic power generators or radically new departures in passenger-carrying aircraft in advance of knowledge that these will be commercially feasible. Much has been accomplished by research and development, not immediately subject to commercial criteria, under the inspiration of military need. This has done more to save us from the partial technological stagnation that is inherent in a consumers' goods economy than we imagine. But it is also a narrow and perilous prop, and it has the further effect of associating great and exciting scientific advances with an atmosphere of fear and even terror.

Nor is this all. The day will not soon come when the problems of either the world or our own polity are solved. Since we do not know the shape of the problems we do not know the requirements for solution. But one thing is tolerably certain. Whether the problem be that of a burgeoning population and of space in which to live with peace and grace, or whether it be the depletion of the materials which nature has stocked in the earth's crust and which have been drawn upon more heavily in this century than in all previous time together, or whether it be that of occupying minds no longer committed to the stockpiling of consumer goods, the basic demand on America will be on its resources of ability, intelligence, and education. The test will be less the effectiveness of our material investment than the effectiveness of our investment in men. We live in a day of grandiose generalization. This one can be made with confidence.

Education, no less than national defense or foreign assistance, is in the public domain. It is subject to the impediments to resource allocation between private and public use. So, once again, our hope for survival, security, and contentment returns us to the problem of guiding resources to the most urgent ends.

To furnish a barren room is one thing. To continue to crowd in furniture until the foundation buckles is quite another. To have failed to solve the problem of producing goods would have been to continue man in his oldest and most grievous misfortune. But to fail to see that we have solved it and to fail to proceed thence to the next task, would be fully as tragic.

NOTE

[1] Advertising is not a simple phenomenon. It is also important in competitive strategy and want creation is, ordinarily, a complementary result of efforts to shift the demand curve of the individual firm at the expense of others or (less importantly, I think) to change its shape by increasing the degree of product differentiation. Some of the failure of economists to identify advertising with want creation may be attributed to the undue attention that its use in purely competitive strategy has attracted. It should be noted, however, that the competitive manipulation of consumer desire is only possible, at least on any appreciable scale, when such need is not strongly felt.

SOME SUGGESTIONS FOR FURTHER READING

Boddewyn, Jean (1961), "Galbraith's Wicked Wants," *Journal of Marketing*, (October), 14–18.

Friedman, Milton and Rose Friedman (1962), *Capitalism and Freedom*, Chicago, IL: The University of Chicago Press.

———— (1980), *Free to Choose*, New York: Harcourt, Brace and Jovanovich.

Galbraith, J. K. (1973), *Economics and the Public Purpose*, Boston, MA: Houghton-Mifflin.

———— (1977), *The Age of Uncertainty*, Boston, MA: Houghton-Mifflin.

Von Hayek, F. A. (1961), "The Non Sequitur of the Dependence Effect," *Southern Economic Journal* (April), 346–348.

11 / A THEORY OF BUYER BEHAVIOR / John A. Howard and Jagdish N. Sheth

In the last fifteen years, considerable research on consumer behavior both at the conceptual and empirical levels has accumulated. This can be gauged by reviews of the research.[1] As a consequence we believe that sufficient research exists in both the behavioral sciences and consumer behavior to attempt a comprehensive theory of buyer behavior. Furthermore, broadly speaking, there are two major reasons at the basic research level which seem to have created the need to take advantage of this opportunity. The first reason is that a great variety exists in today's effort to understand the consumer, and unfortunately there is no integration of this variety. The situation resembles the seven blind men touching different parts of the elephant and making inferences about the animal which differ, and occasionally contradict one another. A comprehensive theory of buyer behavior would hopefully not only provide a framework for integrating the existing variety but also would prepare the researcher to adopt appropriate research designs which would control sources of influences other than those he is immediately interested in. The difficulty of replicating a study and the possibility of getting contradictory findings will be minimized accordingly.

The second major basic research reason for a comprehensive theory is the potential application of research in buying behavior to human behavior in general. In asserting the need to validate psychological propositions in a real world context Sherif has repeatedly and eloquently argued for applied research.[2] Also, McGuire argues that social psychology is moving toward theory-oriented research in *natural settings* because a number of forces are encouraging the movement away from laboratory research, and he cites the current work in buyer behavior as one of these forces.[3]

Again, one way that we can contribute to "pure" areas of behavioral science is by attempting a comprehensive theory which would help to identify and to iron out our own inconsistencies and contradictions. Such an attempt looks ambitious

Reprinted from Reed Moyer, (ed.) *Changing Marketing Systems . . . Consumer, Corporate and Government Interfaces: Proceedings of the 1967 Winter Conference of the American Marketing Association*, 1967, published by the American Marketing Association.

John A. Howard is George E. Warren Professor of Business in the Graduate School of Business, Columbia University. He is a distinguished marketing scholar who has directed studies of consumer behavior for both company and public policy purposes. In addition to *The Theory of Consumer Behavior*, his books include *Marketing Management: Analysis and Control* and *Marketing Theory*.

Jagdish N. Sheth is Walter H. Stellner Distinguished Professor of Business Administration at the University of Illinois. He received his Ph.D. from Columbia University and has served on the faculties of Columbia University and the Sloan School of Management, M.I.T. He is a prolific author in areas of consumer psychology, multivariate methods, and international marketing.

on the surface, but after several years of work and drawing upon earlier work,[4] we are confident that it can be achieved.

A BRIEF SUMMARY OF THE THEORY

Before we describe each component of the theory in detail, it will be helpful to discuss briefly the essentials of our view of the consumer choice process.

Much of buying behavior is more or less repetitive brand choice decisions. During his life cycle, the buyer establishes purchase cycles for various products which determine how often he will buy a given product. For some products, this cycle is very lengthy, as for example in buying durable appliances, and, therefore, he buys the product quite infrequently. For many other products, however, the purchase cycle is short and he buys the product frequently as is the case for many grocery and personal care items. Since there is usually the element of repeat buying, we must present a theory which incorporates the dynamics of purchase behavior over a period of time if we wish to capture the central elements of the empirical process.

In the face of repetitive brand choice decisions, the consumer simplifies his decision process by storing relevant information and routinizing his decision process. What is crucial, therefore, is to identify the elements of decision making, to observe the structural or substantive changes that occur in them over time due to the repetitive nature, and show how a combination of the decision elements affect search processes and the incorporation of information from the buyer's commercial and social environment.

The buyer, having been motivated to buy a product class, is faced with a brand choice decision. The elements of his decision are: (1) a set of motives, (2) several courses of action, and (3) decision mediators by which the motives are matched with the alternatives. Motives are specific to a product class, and they reflect the underlying needs of the buyer. The alternative courses of actions are the purchase of one of the various brands with their potential to satisfy the buyer's motives. There are two important notions involved in the definition of alternatives as brands. First, the brands which are alternatives of the buyer's choice decision at any given time are generally a small number, collectively called his "evoked set." The size of the evoked set is only two or three, a fraction of the brands he is aware of and still smaller fraction of the total number of brands actually available in the market. Second, any two consumers may have quite different alternatives in their evoked sets.

The decision mediators are a set of rules that the buyer employs to match his motives and his means of satisfying those motives. They serve the function of ordering and structuring the buyer's motives and then ordering and structuring the various brands based on their potential to satisfy these ordered motives. The decision mediators develop by the process of learning about the buying situation. They are, therefore, influenced by information from the buyer's environment and even more importantly by the actual experience of purchasing and consuming the brand.

When the buyer is just beginning to purchase a product class such as when a purchase is precipitated by a change in his life cycle, he lacks experience. In order, therefore, to develop the decision mediators, he *actively seeks information* from his commercial and social environments. The information that he either actively seeks or accidentally receives is subject to perceptual processes which not only limits the intake of information (magnitude of information is affected) but modifies it to suit his own frame of reference (quality of information is affected). These modifications are significant since they distort the neat "marketing stimulus-consumer response" relation.

Along with active search for information, the buyer may, to some extent, generalize from past similar experiences. Such generalization can be due to physical similarity of the new product class to the old product class. For example, in the initial purchases of Scotch whisky, the buyer may generalize his experiences in buying of gin. Generalization can also occur even when the two product classes are physically dissimilar but have a common meaning such as deriving from a company-wide brand name. For example, the buyer could generalize his experiences in buying a refrigerator or range to his first purchase of a dishwasher of the same brand.

Whatever the source, the buyer develops sufficient decision mediators to enable him to choose a brand which seems to have the best potential for satisfying his motives. If the brand proves satisfactory, the potential of that brand to satisfy his motives is increased. The result is that the probability of buying that brand is likewise increased. With repeated satisfactory purchases of one or more brands, the buyer is likely to manifest a routinized decision process whereby the sequential steps in buying are well structured so that some event which triggers the process may actually complete the choice decision. Routinized purchasing implies that his decision mediators are well established and that the buyer has strong brand preferences.

The phase of repetitive decision making, in which the buyer reduces the complexity of a buying situation with the help of information and experience, is called the *psychology of simplification*. Decision making can be divided into three stages and used to illustrate the psychology of simplification: Extensive Problem Solving, Limited Problem Solving and Routinized Response Behavior. The further he is along in simplifying his environment, the less is the tendency toward active search behavior. The environmental stimuli related to the purchase situation become more meaningful and less ambiguous. Furthermore, the buyer establishes more cognitive consistency among the brands as he moves toward routinization and the incoming information is then screened both with regard to its magnitude and quality. He becomes less attentive to stimuli which do not fit his cognitive structure and he distorts those stimuli which are forced upon him.

A surprising phenomenon, we believe, occurs in many instances of frequently purchased products such as in grocery and personal care items. The buyer, after attaining routinization of his decision process, may find himself in too simple a situation. He is likely to feel the monotony or boredom associated with such repetitive decision making. It is also very likely that he is dissatisfied with even the most preferred brand. In both cases, he may feel that all existing alternatives including the preferred brand are unacceptable. He therefore feels a need to *complicate* his buying situation by considering new brands, and this process can be called the *psychology of complication*. The new situation causes him to identify a new brand, and so he begins again to simplify in the manner described earlier. Thus with a frequently-purchased item buying is a continuing process with its ups and downs in terms of information seeking analogous to the familiar cyclical fluctuations in economic activity.

ELEMENTS OF THEORY

Any theory of human behavior needs some means for explaining individual differences. The marketing manager also is interested in differentiated masses of buyers. He wants to understand and separate individual differences so that he can classify or segment the total market based upon individual differences. By understanding the psychology of the individual buyer we may achieve this classification. Depending on the internal state of the buyer, a given stimulus may result in a given response. For example, one buyer who urgently needs a product may respond to the ad of a brand in that product class by buying it whereas another buyer who does not need the product may simply notice the ad and store the information or ignore the ad. A construct such as "level of motivation" will then explain the divergent reactions to the same stimulus. Alternatively, two buyers may both urgently need a product, but they buy two different brands. This can be explained by another construct: predisposition toward a brand.

Figure 1 represents the theory of buyer behavior. The central rectangular box isolates the various internal state variables and processes which combined together show the state of the buyer. The inputs to the rectangular box are the stimuli from the marketing and social environments. The outputs are a variety of responses that the buyer is likely to manifest based on the interaction between the stimuli and his internal state. Besides the inputs and outputs, there are a set of seven influences which affect the variables in the rectangular box.[5] These variables appear at the top of the diagram and are labelled "exogenous variables." Their function is to provide a means of adjusting for the interpersonal differences discussed above. The variables within the rectangular box serve the role of endogenous variables in the sense that changes in them are explained but they are something less than endogenous variables. They are not well defined and hence are not measurable. They are hypothetical constructs. Their values are inferred from relations among the output intervening variables. Several of the exogenous variables such as personality, social class and culture have traditionally been treated as part of the endogenous variables. We believe that they affect more specific variables, and by conceptualizing their effect as via the hypothetical constructs, we can better understand their role.

Thus it will be seen that the theory of buyer behavior has four major components; the stimulus variables, the response variable, the hypothetical constructs and the exogenous variables. We will elaborate on each of the components below both in terms of their substance and their interrelationships.

Figure 1. A theory of buyer behavior

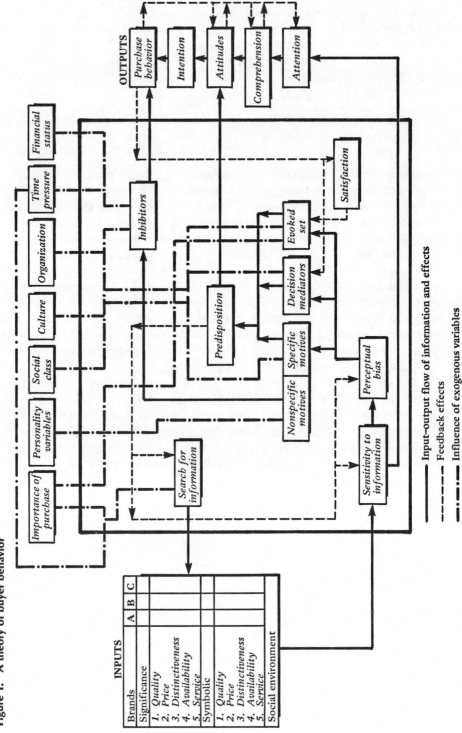

Stimulus Variables

At any point in time, the hypothetical constructs which reflect the buyer's internal state are affected by numerous stimuli from the environment. The environment is classified as Commercial or Social. The commercial environment is the marketing activities of various firms by which they attempt to communicate to the buyer. From the buyer's point of view, these communications basically come either via the physical brands themselves or some linguistic or pictorial representations of the attributes of the brands. If the elements of the brands such as price, quality, service, distinctiveness or availability are communicated through the physical brands (significates) then the stimuli are defined and classified as significative stimuli. If, on the other hand, the attributes are communicated in linguistic or pictorial symbols such as in mass media, billboards, catalogs, salesmen, etc., then the stimuli from commercial sources are classified as symbolic stimuli. We view the marketing mix as the optimum allocation of funds between the two major channels of communication—significative or symbolic—to the buyer.

Each commercial input variable is hypothesized to be multivariate. Probably the five major dimensions of a brand—price, quality, distinctiveness, availability and service—summarize the various attributes. The same dimensions are present in both significative or symbolic communication which become the input stimuli for the buyer. However, certain dimensions may be more appropriately conveyed by significative rather than symbolic communication and vice versa. For example, price is easily communicated by both channels; shape may best be communicated by two-dimensional pictures rather than verbal communication. Finally, size may not be easily communicated by any symbolic representation: the physical product (significate) may be necessary.

The third stimulus input variable is social stimuli. It refers to the information that the buyer's social environment provides regarding a purchase decision. The most obvious is word of mouth communication.

The inputs to the buyer's mental state from the three major sources are then processed and stored by their interaction with a series of hypothetical constructs, and the buyer may react immediately or later.

Hypothetical Constructs

The hypothetical constructs and their interrelationships are the result of an integration of Hull's learning theory,[6] Osgood's cognitive theory,[7] and Berlyne's theory of exploratory behavior[8] along with other ideas.

We may classify the constructs into two classes: (i) those that have to do with perception, and (ii) those having to do with learning. Perceptual constructs serve the function of information processing while the learning constructs serve the function of concept formation. It is interesting that, after years of experience in advertising, Reeves has a very similar classification:[9] his "penetration" is analogous to perceptual variables and his "unique selling propositions" is analogous to learning variables. We will at first describe the learning constructs since they are the major components of decision making; the perceptual constructs which serve the important role of obtaining and processing information are more complex and will be described later.

Learning constructs. The learning constructs are labeled as: (1) Motives—Specific and Nonspecific, (2) Brand Potential of Evoked Set, (3) Decision Mediators, (4) Predisposition toward the brands, (5) Inhibitors, and (6) Satisfaction with the purchase of the brand.

Motive is the impetus to action. Motives or goals may be thought of as constituting a means-end chain and hence, as being general or specific depending upon their position in the chain. Motives can refer to the buyer's specific goals in purchasing a product class. The buyer is motivated by the expectation or anticipation due to past learning of outcome from the purchase of each of the brands in his evoked set.

The specific motives—lower level motives in the means-end chain—are very closely anchored to the attributes of a product class and in this way they become purchase criteria. Examples of specific motives for buying a dietary product such as Metrecal or Sego are low calories, nutrition, taste, and value.

Very often, several specific motives are nothing more than indicators of some underlying more general motive, that is, some motive that is higher in the means-end chain. In the above example, the specific motives of nutrition and low calories might be merely indicators of the common motive of good health.

Motives also serve the important function of raising the buyer's general motivational state or arousal and thereby tuning up the buyer, causing him to pay attention to environmental stimuli. Examples of nonspecific motives are probably anxiety, fear, many of the personality variables such as authoritarianism, exhibitionism, aggressiveness, etc., and social motives of power, status, prestige, etc. Although they are nonspecific, they are not innate, but rather learned, mostly due to acculturation. The nonspecific motives also possess a hierarchy within themselves. For example, anxiety is considered to be the source of another motive, that of the need of money.[10]

Brand Potential of Evoked Set is the second learning construct. A buyer who is familiar with a product class has an evoked set of alternatives to satisfy his motives. The elements of his evoked set are some of the brands that make up the product class. The concept is important because for this buyer the brands in his evoked set constitute competition for the seller.

A brand is, of course, a class concept like many other objects or things. The buyer attaches a *word* to this concept—a label—which is the brand name such as "Campbell's Tomato Soup." Whenever he sees a can of Campbell's Tomato Soup or hears the phrase, the image conveys to him certain satisfactions, procedures for preparation, etc. In short, it conveys certain meaning including its potential to satisfy his motives.

Various brands in the buyer's evoked set will generally satisfy the goal structure differently. One brand may possess potential to the extent that it is an ideal brand for the buyer. Another brand, on the other hand, may satisfy motives just enough to be part of his evoked set. By the process of learning the buyer obtains and stores knowledge regarding each brand's potential and then rank orders them in terms of their want-satisfying potential. The evoked set, in short, is a set of alternatives with each alternative's payoff. Predisposition mentioned below enables the buyer to choose one among them.

Decision Mediator is the third learning construct and it brings together motives and alternatives. The brand potential of each of the brands in his evoked set are the decision alternatives with their payoffs. Decision mediators are the buyer's mental rules for matching the alternatives with his motives, for rank-ordering them in terms of their want-satisfying capacity. As mental rules, they exhibit reasons wherein the cognitive elements related to the alternatives and the motives are structured. The words that he uses to describe these attributes are also the words that he thinks with and that he finds are easy to remember. The criterial attributes are important to the manufacturer because if he knows them he can deliberately build into his brand and promotion those characteristics which will differentiate his brand from competing brands.

The decision mediators thus represent enduring cognitive rules established by the process of learning, and their function is to obtain meaningful and congruent relations among brands so that the buyer can manifest goal-directed behavior. The aim of the theory of buyer behavior is not just the identification of motives and the respective brands but to show their structure as well. It is the decision mediators which provide this structure.

In view of the fact that decision mediators are learned, principles of learning become crucial in their development and change over time. There are two broad sources of learning: (1) actual experiences, and (2) information. Actual experience can be either with the *same* buying situation in the past or with a *similar* buying situation. The latter is generally labelled as generalization as discussed earlier. Similarly, information as a source of learning can be from: (1) the buyer's commercial environment, or (2) his social environment. Later, we will elaborate on each of the sources of learning.

Predisposition, the fourth construct, is the summary effect of the previous three constructs. It refers to the buyer's preference toward brands in his evoked set. It is, in fact, an aggregate index which is reflected in attitude which, in turn, is measured by attitude scales. It might be visualized as the "place" where brands in Evoked Set are compared with Mediator's choice criteria to yield a judgment on the relative contribution of the brands to the buyer's motives. This judgment includes not only an estimate of the value of the brand to him but also an estimate of the confidence with which he holds that position. This uncertainty aspect of Predisposition can be called "brand ambiguity," in that, the more confident he holds it, the less ambiguous is the connotative meaning of the brand to the buyer and the more likely he is to buy it.[11]

Inhibitors, the fifth learning construct, are forces in the environment which create important disruptive influences in the actual purchase of a brand even when the buyer has reasoned out that that brand will best satisfy his motives. In other words, when the buyer is both predisposed to buy a brand and has the motivation to buy some brand in the product class, he may not buy it because several environmental forces inhibit its purchase and prevent him from satisfying his preferences.

We postulate at least four types of inhibitors. They are: (1) high price of the brand, (2) lack of availability of the brand, (3) time pressure on the buyer, and

(4) the buyer's financial status. The first two are part of the environmental stimuli, and therefore, they are part of the input system. The last two come from the two exogenous variables of the same name. It should be pointed out that social constraints emanating from other exogenous variables may also create temporary barriers to the purchase of a brand.

An essential feature of all inhibitors is that they are *not internalized* by the buyer because their occurrence is random and strictly situational. However, some of the inhibitors may persist systematically over time as they concern a given buyer. If they persist long enough, the buyer is likely to incorporate them as part of his decision mediators and thus to internalize them. The consequence is that they may affect even the structure of alternatives and motives.

Satisfaction, the last of the learning constructs, refers to the degree of congruence between the actual consequences from purchase and consumption of a brand and what was expected from it by the buyer at the time of purchase. If the actual outcome is adjudged by the buyer as *at least* equal to the expected, the buyer will feel satisfied. If, on the other hand, the actual outcome is adjudged as less than what he expected, the buyer will feel dissatisfied and his attitude will be less favorable. Satisfaction or dissatisfaction with a brand can exist with respect to any one of the different attributes. If the brand proves more satisfactory than he expected, the buyer has a tendency to enhance the attractiveness of the brand. Satisfaction will, therefore, affect the reordering of the brands in the evoked set for the next buying decision.

Relations among learning constructs. Underlying Predisposition toward the brands and related variables, several important notions are present. The simplest way to describe them is to state that we may classify a decision process as either Extensive Problem Solving, Limited Problem Solving or Routinized Response Behavior depending on the strength of Predisposition toward the brands. In the early phases of buying, the buyer has not yet developed decision mediators well enough; specifically his product class concept is not well formed and predisposition is low. As he acquires information and gains experience in buying and consuming the brand, Decision Mediators become firm and Predisposition toward a brand is generally high.

In Extensive Problem Solving, Predisposition toward the brands is low. None of the brands is discriminated enough based on their criterial attributes for the buyer to show greater brand preference toward any one brand. At this state of decision making, brand ambiguity is high with the result that the buyer actively seeks information from his environment. Due to greater search for information, there exists a greater *latency of response*—the time interval from the initiation of a decision to its completion. Similarly, deliberation or reasoning will be high since he lacks a well-defined product class concept which is the denotative aspect of mediator. He is also likely to consider many brands as part of Evoked Set, and stimuli coming from the commercial environment are less likely to trigger any immediate purchase reaction.

When Predisposition toward the brands is moderate, the buyer's decision process can be called Limited Problem Solving. There still exists brand ambiguity since the buyer is not able to discriminate and compare brands so that he may prefer one brand over others. He is likely to seek information but not to the extent that he seeks it in Extensive Problem Solving. More importantly, he seeks information more on a relative basis to compare and discriminate various brands rather than to compare them absolutely on each of the brands. His deliberation or thinking is much less since Decision Mediators are tentatively well defined. Evoked Set will consist of a small number of brands, each having about the same degree of preference.

In Routinized Response Behavior, the buyer will have a high level of Predisposition toward brands in his evoked set. Furthermore, he has now accumulated sufficient experience and information to have little brand ambiguity. He will in fact discriminate among brands enough to show a strong preference toward one or two brands in the evoked set. He is unlikely to actively seek any information from his environment since such information is not needed. Also, whatever information he passively or accidentally receives, he will subject it to selective perceptual processes so that only congruent information is allowed. Very often, the congruent information will act as "triggering cues" to motivate him to manifest purchase behavior. Much of impulse purchase, we believe, is really the outcome of a strong predisposition and such a facilitating commercial stimulus as store display. The buyer's evoked set will consist of a few brands toward which he is highly predisposed. However, he will have greater preference toward one or two brands in his evoked set and less toward others.

As mentioned earlier, Predisposition is an aggregate index of decision components. Thus, any changes in the components due to learning from experience or information imply some change in Predisposition. The greater the learning, the more the predisposition toward the brands in the evoked set. The exact nature of learning will be described later when we discuss the dynamics of buying behavior.

Perceptual constructs.   Another set of constructs serves the function of information procurement and processing relevant to a purchase decision. As mentioned earlier, information can come from any one of the three stimulus inputs—significative commercial stimuli, symbolic commercial stimuli, and social stimuli. Once again we will here only describe the constructs; their utilization by the buyer will be explained when we discuss the dynamics of buying behavior. The perceptual constructs in Figure 1 are: (1) Sensitivity to Information, (b) Perceptual Bias, and (c) Search for Information.

A perceptual phenomenon implies either ignoring a physical event which could be a stimulus, seeing it attentively or sometimes imagining what is not present in reality. All perceptual phenomena essentially create some change in quantity or quality of objective information.

Sensitivity to Information refers to the opening and closing of sensory receptors which control the intake of information. The manifestation of this phenomenon is generally called perceptual vigilance (paying attention) or perceptual defense (ignoring the information). Sensitivity to Information, therefore, primarily serves as a gatekeeper to information entering into the buyer's mental state. It thus controls the quantity of information input.

Sensitivity to Information, according to Berlyne,[12] is a function of the degree of ambiguity of the stimuli to which the buyer is exposed. If the stimulus is very familiar or too simple, the ambiguity is low and the buyer will not pay attention unless he is predisposed to such information from past learning. Furthermore, if ambiguity of the stimulus continues to be low, the buyer feels a sense of monotony and actually seeks other information, and this act can be said to *complicate* his environment. If the stimulus is very complex and ambiguous, the buyer finds it hard to comprehend and, therefore, he ignores it by resorting to perceptual defense. Only if the stimulus is in the moderate range of ambiguity is the buyer motivated to pay attention and to freely absorb the objective information.

In a single communication, the buyer may at first find the communication complex and ambiguous and so he will resort to perceptual defense and tend to ignore it. As some information enters, however, he finds that it is really at the medium level of ambiguity and so pays attention. On the other hand, it might be that the more he pays attention to it, the more he finds the communication too simple and, therefore, ignores it as the process of communication progresses.

A second variable which governs Sensitivity to Information is the buyer's predisposition toward the brand about which the information is concerned. The more interesting the information, the more likely the buyer is to open up his receptors and therefore to pay attention to the information. Hess has recently measured this by obtaining the strength of pupil dilation.

Perceptual Bias is the second perceptual construct. The buyer not only selectively attends to information, but he may actually distort it once it enters his mental state. In other words, quality of information can be altered by the buyer. This aspect of the perceptual process is summarized in Perceptual Bias. The buyer may distort the cognitive elements contained in information to make them congruent with his own frame of reference as determined by the amount of information he already has stored. A series of cognitive consistency theories have been recently developed to explain how this congruency is established and what the consequences are in terms of the distortion of information we might expect.[13] Most of the qualitative change in information arises because of feedback from various decision components such as Motives, Evoked Set and Decision Mediators. These relations are too complex, however, to describe in the summary.

The perceptual phenomena described above are likely to be less operative if the information is received from the buyer's social environment. This is because: (i) the source of social information, such as a friend, is likely to be favorably regarded by the buyer and therefore proper, undistorted reception of information will occur, and (ii) the information itself is modified by the social environment (the friend) so that it conforms to the needs of the buyer and, therefore, further modification is less essential.

Search for Information is the third perceptual construct. During the total buying phase which extends over time and involves several repeat purchases of a product class, there are stages when the buyer *actively* seeks information. It is very important to distinguish the times when he passively receives information from the situations where he actively seeks it. We believe that perceptual distortion is less operative in the latter instances and that a commercial communication, therefore, at that stage has a high probability of influencing the buyer.

The active seeking of information occurs when the buyer senses ambiguity of the brands in his evoked set. As we saw earlier, this happens in the Extensive

Problem Solving and Limited Problem Solving phases of the decision process. The ambiguity of brand exists because the buyer is not certain of the outcomes from each brand. In other words, he has not yet learned enough about the alternatives to establish an expectancy of potential of the brands to satisfy his motives. This type of brand ambiguity is essentially confined to initial buyer behavior which we have called Extensive Problem Solving. However, ambiguity may still exist despite knowledge of the potential of alternative brands. This ambiguity is with respect to his inability to discriminate because his motives are not well structured: he does not know how to order them. He may then seek information which will resolve the conflict among goals, a resolution that is implied in his learning of the appropriate product class aspect of decision mediators that we discussed earlier.

There is yet another stage of total buying behavior in which the buyer is likely to seek information. It is when the buyer has not only routinized his decision process but he is so familiar and satiated with repeat buying that he feels bored. Then, all the existing alternatives in his evoked set including the most preferred brand become unacceptable to him. He seeks change or variety in that buying situation. In order to obtain this change, he actively searches for information on other alternatives (brands) that he never considered before. At this stage, he is particularly receptive to any information about new brands. Incidentally, here is an explanation for advertising in a highly stable industry. This phenomenon has long baffled both the critics and defenders of the institution of advertising. Newcomers to the market and forgetting do not provide a plausible explanation.

We have so far described the stimulus input variables and the hypothetical constructs. Now we proceed to describe the output of the system—the responses of the buyer.

Response Variables

The complexity of buyer behavior does not stop with the hypothetical constructs. Just as there is a variety of inputs, there exists a variety of buyer responses which becomes relevant for different areas of marketing strategy. This variety of consumer responses can be easily appreciated from the diversity of measures to evaluate advertising effectiveness. We have attempted to classify and order this diversity of buyer responses in the output variables. Most of the output variables are directly related to some and not other constructs. Each output variable serves different purposes both in marketing practice and fundamental research. Let us at first describe each variable and then provide a rationale for their interrelationships.

Attention. Attention is related to Sensitivity to Information. It is a response of the buyer which indicates the magnitude of his information intake. Attention is measured continuously during the time interval when the buyer receives information. There are several psychophysical methods of quantifying the degree of attention that the buyer pays to a message. The pupil dilation is one.

Comprehension. Comprehension refers to the store of knowledge about the brand that the buyer possesses at any point in time. This knowledge could vary from his simply being aware of a single brand's existence to a complete description of the attributes of the product class of which the brand is an element. It reflects the denotative meaning of the brand and in that sense it is strictly in the cognitive realm. It lacks the motivational aspects of behavior. Some of the standard measures of advertising effectiveness such as awareness, aided or unaided recall, and recognition may capture different aspects of the buyer's comprehension of the brand.

Attitude toward a brand.   Attitude toward a brand is the buyer's evaluation of the brand's potential to satisfy his motives. It, therefore, includes the connotative aspects of the brand concept: it contains those aspects of the brand which are relevant to the buyer's goals. Attitude is directly related to Predisposition and so it consists of both the evaluation of a brand in terms of the criteria of choice from Mediator and the confidence with which that evaluation is held.

Intention to buy.   Intention to buy is the buyer's forecast of his brand choice some time in the future. Like any forecast, it involves assumptions about future events including the likelihood of any perceived inhibitors creating barriers over the buyer's planning horizon. Intention to buy has been extensively used in the purchases of durable goods with some recent refinements in terms of the buyer's confidence in his own forecast; these studies are in terms of broadly defined product classes.[14] We may summarize this response of the buyer as something short of actual purchase behavior.

Purchase behavior.   Purchase Behavior refers to the overt act of purchasing a brand. What becomes a part of company's sales or what the consumer records in a diary as a panel member, however, is only the terminal act in the sequence of shopping and buying. Very often, it is useful to observe the complete movement of the buyer from his home to the store and his purchase in the store. Yoell, for example, shows several case histories where a time and motion study of consumer's purchase behavior have useful marketing implications.[15] We think that at times it may be helpful to go so far as to incorporate the act of consumption into the definition of Purchase Behavior. We have, for example, developed and used the technique of sequential decision making where the buyer verbally describes the sequential pattern of his purchase behavior in a given buying situation. Out of this description a "flow chart" of decision making is obtained which reveals the number and the structure of the decision rules that the buyer employs.

Purchase Behavior is the overt manifestation of the buyer's Predisposition in conjunction with any Inhibitors that may be present. It differs from Attitude to the extent that Inhibitors are taken into consideration. It differs from Intention to the extent that it is the actual manifestation of behavior which the buyer only forecasted in his intention.

Several characteristics of Purchase Behavior become useful if we observe the buyer in a repetitive buying situation. These include the incidence of buying a brand, the quantity bought, and the purchase cycle. Several stochastic models of brand loyalty, for example, have been developed in recent years.[16] Similarly, we could take the magnitude purchased and compare light buyers with heavy buyers to determine if heavy buyers are more loyal buyers.

Interrelationship of response variables. In Figure 1, it will be seen that we have ordered the five response variables to create a hierarchy. The hierarchy is similar to the variety of hierarchies used in practice such as AIDA (Attention, Interest, Desire and Action), to the Lavidge and Steiner hierarchy of advertising effectiveness,[17] as well as to the different mental states that a person is alleged by the anthropologists and sociologists to pass through when he adopts an innovation.[18] There are, however, some important differences which we believe will clarify certain conceptual and methodological issues raised by Palda and others.[19]

First, we have added a response variable called Attention which is crucial since it reflects whether a communication is received by the buyer. Secondly, several different aspects of the cognitive realm of behavior such as awareness, recall, recognition, etc., are lumped into one category called Comprehension to suggest that they all are varying indicators of the buyer's storage of information about a brand which can be extended to *product class*, and in this way we obtain leverage toward understanding buyer innovation. Third, we have defined Attitude to include both affective and conative aspects since anyone who wants to establish causal relations between attitude and behavior must bring the motivational aspects into attitude. Furthermore, we separate the perceptual and the preference maps of the buyer into Comprehension and Attitude respectively. Fourth, we add another variable, Intention to Buy, because there are several product classes in both durable and semi-durable goods where properly defined and measured intentions have already proved useful. To the extent that Intention incorporates the buyer's forecast of his inhibitors, it might serve the useful function of informing the firm how to remove the inhibitors before the actual purchase behavior is manifested.

Finally, and most importantly, we have incorporated several feedback effects which were described when we discussed the hypothetical constructs. We will now show the relations as direct connections among response variables but the reader should bear in mind that these "outside" relations are merely the reflection of relations among the hypothetical constructs. For example, Purchase Behavior via Satisfaction entails some consequences which affect Decision Mediators and brand potential in Evoked Set; any change in them can produce change in Predisposition. Attitude is related to Predisposition and, therefore, it can also be changed in the period from pre-purchase to post-purchase. In incorporating this feedback, we are opening the way to resolving the controversy whether Attitude causes Purchase Behavior or Purchase Behavior causes Attitude. Over a period of time, the relation is interdependent, each affecting the other. Similarly, we have a feedback from Attitude to Comprehension and Attention, the rationale for which was given when we described the perceptual constructs.

DYNAMICS OF BUYING BEHAVIOR

Let us now explain the changes in the hypothetical constructs which occur due to learning.

The learning constructs are, of course, directly involved in the change that we label "learning." Since some of the learning constructs indirectly govern the perceptual constructs by way of feedbacks, there is also an indirect effect back upon the learning constructs themselves. As mentioned earlier, learning of Decision Mediators which structure Motives and Evoked Set of Brands which contain brand potentials can occur from two broad sources: (i) past experience and (ii) information. Experience can be further classified as having been derived from buying a specified product or buying some similar product. Similarly, information can come from the buyer's commercial environment or his social environment, and if commercial, it can be significative or symbolic.

We will look at the development and change in learning constructs as due to: (i) generalization from similar buying situations, (ii) repeat buying of the same product class, and (iii) information.

Generalization from Similar Purchase Situations

Some decision mediators are common across several product classes because many motives are common to a wide variety of purchasing activity. For example, a buyer may satisfy his health motive from many product classes by looking for nutrition. Similarly, many product classes are all bought at the same place which very often leads to spatial or contiguous generalization. The capacity to generalize provides the buyer with a truly enormous range of flexibility in adapting his purchase behavior to the myriad of varying market conditions he faces.

Generalization refers to the transfer of responses and of the relevance of stimuli from past situations to new situations which are similar. It saves the buyer time and effort in seeking information in the face of uncertainty that is inevitable in a new situation. Generalization can occur at any one of the several levels of purchase activity, but we are primarily interested in generalization of those decision mediators which only involve brand choice behavior in contrast to store choice or choice of shopping time and day. In other words, we are concerned with brand generalization.

Repeat Purchase Experiences

Another source of change in the learning constructs is the repeated purchase of the same product class over a period of time.

In Figure 1 the purchase of a brand entails two types of feedbacks, one affecting the decision mediators and the other affecting the brand potential of the evoked set. First, the experience of buying with all its cognitive aspects of memory, reasoning, etc., has a learning effect on the decision mediators. This occurs irrespective of which specific brand the buyer chooses in any one purchase decision because the decision mediators like the motives are product-specific and not limited to any one brand. Hence every purchase has an incremental effect in firmly establishing the decision mediators. This is easy to visualize if we remember that buying behavior is a series of mental and motor steps while the actual choice is only its terminal act.

Purchase of a brand creates certain satisfactions for the buyer which the consumer compares with his expectations of the brand's potential and this expectation is the basis on which he made his decision in the first place. This comparison of expected and actual consequences causes him to be satisfied or dissatisfied with his purchase of the brand. Hence, the second feedback from Purchase Behavior to Satisfaction changes the attractiveness of the brand purchased. If the buyer is satisfied with his consumption, he enhances the potential of the brand and this is likely to result in greater probability of its repeat purchase. If he is dissatisfied, the potential of the brand is diminished, and its probability of repeat purchase is also similarly reduced.

If there are no inhibitory forces which influence him, the buyer will continue to buy a brand which proves satisfactory. In the initial stages of decision making he may show some tendency to oscillate between brands in order to formulate his decision mediators. In other words, he may learn by trial-and-error at first and then settle on a brand and thereafter he may buy the brand with such regularity to suggest that he is brand loyal. Unless a product is of very high risk, however, there is a limit as to how long this brand loyalty will continue: he may become bored with his preferred brand and look for something new.

Information as a Source of Learning

The third major source by which the learning constructs are changed is information from the buyer's (i) commercial environment consisting of advertising, promotion, salesmanship and retail shelf display of the competing companies, and (ii) his social environment consisting of his family, friends, reference group and social class.

We will describe the influence of information at first as if the perceptual constructs were absent. In other words, we assume that the buyer receives information with perfect fidelity as it exists in the environment. Also, we will discuss separately the information from the commercial and social environments.

Commercial environment. The company communicates about its offerings to the buyers either by the physical brand (significates) or by symbols (pictorial or linguistic) which represent the brand. In other words, significative and symbolic communication are the two major ways of interaction between the sellers and the buyers.

In Figure 1, the influence of information is shown on Motives, Decision Mediators, Evoked Set, and Inhibitors. We believe that the influence of commercial information on motives (specific and nonspecific) is limited. The main effect is primarily to *intensify* whatever motives the buyer has rather than to create new ones. For example, physical display of the brand may intensify his motives above the threshold level which combined with strong predisposition can result in impulse (unplanned) purchase. A similar reaction is possible when an ad creates sufficient intensity of motives to provide an impetus for the buyer to go to the store. A second way to influence motives is to show the *perceived instrumentality* of the brand and thereby make it a part of the buyer's defined set of alternatives. Finally, to a very limited extent, marketing stimuli may change the *content of the motives*. The general conception both among marketing men and laymen is that marketing stimuli change the buyer's motives. However, on a closer examination it would appear that what is changed is the *intensity* of buyer's motives already provided by the social environment. Many dormant or latent motives may become stimulated. The secret of success very often lies in identifying the change in motives created by social change and intensifying them as seems to be the case in the recent projection of youthfulness in many buying situations.

Marketing stimuli are also important in determining and changing the buyer's evoked set. Commercial information tells him of the existence of the brands (awareness), their identifying characteristics (Comprehension plus brand name) and their relevance to the satisfaction of the buyer's needs (Attitude).

Marketing stimuli are also important in creating and changing the buyer's decision mediators. They become important sources for learning decision mediators when the buyer has no prior experience to rely upon. In other words, when he is in the extensive problem-solving (EPS) stage, it is marketing and social stimuli which are the important sources of learning. Similarly, when the buyer actively seeks information because all the existing alternatives are unacceptable to him, marketing stimuli become important in *changing* his decision mediators.

Finally, marketing stimuli can unwittingly create inhibitors. For example, a company feels the need to emphasize price-quality association, but it may result in high-price inhibition in the mind of the buyer. Similarly, in emphasizing the details of usage and consumption of a product, the communication may create the inhibition related to time pressure.

Social environment. The social environment of the buyer—family, friends, reference groups—is another major source of information in his buying behavior. Most of the inputs are likely to be symbolic (linguistic) although at times the physical product may be shown to the buyer.

Information from his social environment also affects the four learning constructs: Motives, Decision Mediators, Evoked Set and Inhibitors. However, the effect on these constructs is different from that of the commercial environment. First, the information about the brands will be considerably modified by the social environment before it reaches the buyer. Most of the modifications are likely to be in the nature of adding connotative meanings to brand descriptions, and of the biasing effects of the communication's perceptual variables like Sensitivity to Information and Perceptual Bias. Second, the buyer's social environment will probably have a very strong influence on the content of his motives and their ordering to establish a goal structure. Several research studies have concentrated on such influences.[20] Third, the social environment may also affect his evoked set. This will be particularly true when the buyer lacks experience. Furthermore, if the product class is important to the buyer and he is technically incompetent or uncertain in evaluating the consequences of the brand for his needs, he may rely more on the social than on the marketing environment for information. This is well documented by several studies using the perceived risk hypothesis.[21]

Exogenous Variables

Earlier we mentioned that there are several influences operating on the buyer's decisions which we treat as exogenous, that is, we do not explain their formation and change. Many of these influences come from the buyer's social environment and we wish to separate the effects of his environment which have occurred in the past and are not related to a specific decision from those which are current and directly affect the decisions that occur during the period the buyer is being observed. The inputs during the observation period provide information to the buyer to help his current decision making. The past influences are already imbedded in the values of the perceptual and learning constructs. Strictly speaking, therefore, there is no need for some of the exogenous variables which have influenced the buyer in the past. We bring them out explicitly, however, for the sake of research design where the research may control or take into account individual differences among buyers due to such past influences. Incorporating the effects of these exogenous variables will reduce the size of the unexplained variance or error in estimation which it is particularly essential to control under field conditions. Figure 1 presents a set of exogenous variables which we believe provide the control essential to obtaining satisfactory predictive relations between the inputs and the outputs of the system. Let us briefly discuss each of the exogenous variables.

Importance of Purchase refers to differential degrees of ego-involvement or commitment in different product classes. It, therefore, provides a mechanism which must be carefully examined in interproduct studies. Importance of Purchase will influence the size of the Evoked Set and the magnitude of Search for Information. The more important the product class, the larger the Evoked Set.

Time Pressure is a current exogenous variable and, therefore, specific to a decision situation. It refers to the situation when a buyer feels pressed for time due to any of several environmental influences and so must allocate his time among alternative uses. In this process a re-allocation unfavorable to the purchasing activity can occur. Time pressure will create Inhibition as mentioned earlier. It will also unfavorably affect Search for Information .

Financial Status refers to the constraint the buyer may feel because of lack of financial resources. This affects his purchase behavior to the extent that it creates a barrier to purchasing the most preferred brand. For example, a buyer may want to purchase a Mercedes-Benz but lacks sufficient financial resources and, therefore, he will settle for some low-priced American automobile such as a Ford or Chevrolet. Its effect is via Inhibitor.

Personality Traits take into consideration many of the variables such as self-confidence, self-esteem, authoritarianism and anxiety which have been researched to identify individual differences. It will be noted that these individual differences are "topic free" and, therefore, are supposed to exert their effect across product classes. We believe their effect is felt on: (i) nonspecific Motives and (ii) Evoked Set. For example, the more anxious a person, the greater the motivational arousal; dominant personalities are more likely by a small margin to buy a Ford instead of a Chevrolet; the more authoritarian a person, the narrower the category width of his evoked set.

Social and Organizational Setting (Organization) takes us to the group, to a higher level of social organization than the individual. It includes both the informal social organization such as family and reference groups which are relevant for *consumer behavior* and the formal organization which constitutes much of the environment for *industrial purchasing*. Organizational variables are those of small group interaction such as power, status and authority. We believe that the underlying process of intergroup conflicts in both industrial and consumer buying behavior are in principle very similar and that the differences are largely due to the formalization of industrial activity. Organization, both formal and social, is a crucial variable because it influences all the learning constructs.

Social Class refers to a still higher level of social organization, the social aggregate. Several indices are available to classify people into various classes. The most common perhaps is the Warner classification of people into upper-upper, lower-upper, upper-middle, lower-middle, upper-lower, and lower-lower classes. Social class mediates the relation between the input and the output by influencing: (i) specific Motives, (ii) Decision Mediators, (iii) Evoked Set, and (iv) Inhibitors. The latter influence is important particularly in the adoption of innovations.

Culture provides an even more comprehensive social framework than social class. Culture consists of patterns of behavior, symbols, ideas and their attached values. Culture will influence Motives, Decision Mediators, and Inhibitors.

CONCLUSIONS

In the preceding pages we have summarized a theory of buyer brand choice. It is complex. We strongly believe that complexity is essential to adequately describe buying behavior, from the point of view of both marketing practice and public policy.

We hope that the theory can provide new insights into past empirical data and guide future research so as to instill with coherence and unity current research which now tends to be atomistic and unrelated. We are vigorously pursuing a large research program aimed at testing the validity of the theory. The research was designed in terms of the variables specified by the theory and our most preliminary results cause us to believe that it was fruitful to use the theory in this way. Because it specifies a number of relationships, it has clearly been useful in interpreting the preliminary findings. Above all, it is an aid in communication among the researchers and with the companies involved.

Finally, a number of new ideas are set forth in the theory, but we would like to call attention to three in particular. The concept of evoked set provides a means of reducing the noise in many analyses of buying behavior. The product class concept offers a new dimension for incorporating many of the complexities of innovations and especially for integrating systematically the idea of innovation into a framework of psychological constructs. Anthropologists and sociologists have been pretty much content to deal with peripheral variables in their investigations of innovation. The habit-perception cycle in which perception and habit respond inversely offers hope for explaining a large proportion of the phenomenon that has long baffled both the critics and defenders of advertising: large advertising expenditures in a stable market where, on the surface, it would seem that people are already sated with information.

NOTES

[1] Jagdish N. Sheth, "A Review of Buyer Behavior," *Management Science*, Vol. 13 (August, 1967), pp. B718–B756; John A. Howard, *Marketing Theory* (Boston, Mass.: Allyn and Bacon, 1965).

[2] Musafer Sherif and Carolyn Sherif, "Interdisciplinary Coordination as a Validity Check: Retrospect and Prospects," in M. Sherif (ed.), *Problems of Interdisciplinary Relationships in the Social Sciences* (Chicago: Aldine Publishing Company, 1968).

[3] William J. McGuire, "Some Impending Reorientations in Social Psychology," *Journal of Experimental Social Psychology*, Vol. 3 (1967), pp. 124–139.

[4] Patrick Suppes, *Information Processing and Choice Behavior* (Technical Paper No. 9: Institute for Mathematical Studies in the Social Sciences, Stanford University, January 31, 1966), p. 27; John A. Howard, *op. cit.*

[5] Terminology in a problem area that cuts across both economics and psychology is different because each discipline has often defined its terms differently from the other. We find the economists definitions of exogenous versus endogenous, and theory versus model more useful than those of the psychologist. The psychologists' distinction of hypothetical constructs and intervening variables, however, provides a helpful breakdown of endogenous variables. Finally, for the sake of exposition we have often here not clearly distinguished between the theory and its empirical counterparts. Although this practice encourages certain ambiguities, and we lay ourselves open to the charge of reifying our theory, we believe that for most readers it will simplify the task of comprehending the material.

[6] Clark C. Hull, *Principles of Behavior* (New York: Appleton-Century-Crofts, Inc., 1943); Clark C. Hull, *A Behavior System* (New Haven: Yale University Press, 1952).

[7] Charles E. Osgood, "A Behavioristic Analysis of Perception and Meaning as Cognitive Phenomena," *Symposium on Cognition, University of Colorado, 1955* (Cambridge, Harvard University Press, 1957), pp. 75–119; Charles E. Osgood, "Motivational Dynamics of Language Behavior," in J. R. Jones (ed.), *Nebraska Symposium on Motivation, 1957* (Lincoln: University of Nebraska Press, 1957), pp. 348–423.

[8] D. E. Berlyne, "Motivational Problems Raised by Exploratory and Epistemic Behavior," in Sigmund Koch (ed.), *Psychology: A Study of a Science*, Vol. 5 (New York: McGraw-Hill Book Company, 1963).

[9] Rosser Reeves, *Reality in Advertising* (New York: Alfred A. Knopf, Inc., 1961).

[10] J. S. Brown, *The Motivation of Behavior* (New York: McGraw-Hill Book Company, 1961).

[11] George S. Day, "Buyer Attitudes and Brand Choice Behavior." Unpublished Ph.D. Dissertation, Graduate School of Business, Columbia University, 1967.

[12] Berlyne, *op. cit.*

[13] S. Feldman (ed.), *Cognitive Consistency: Motivational Antecedents and Behavioral Consequents* (Academic Press, 1966); Martin Fishbein (ed.), *Readings in Attitude Theory and Measurement* (New York: John Wiley & Sons, 1967).

[14] Thomas F. Juster, *Anticipations and Purchases: An Analysis of Consumer Behavior* (Princeton University Press, 1964 .

[15] William Yoell, *A Science of Advertising through Behaviorism.* Unpublished manuscript, December, 1965.

[16] Sheth, *op. cit.*

[17] R. J. Lavidge and G. A. Steiner, "A Model for Predictive Measurements of Advertising Effectiveness," *Journal of Marketing* (October, 1961), pp. 50–68.

[18] Everett M. Rogers, *The Diffusion of Innovations* (New York: Free Press, 1962).

[19] Kristian S. Palda, "The Hypothesis of a Hierarchy of Effects: A Partial Evaluation," *Journal of Marketing Research* (February, 1966), pp. 13–24.

[20] Sheth, *op. cit.*

[21] Donald F. Cox, *Risk Taking and Information Handling in Consumer Behavior* (Boston, Mass.: Graduate School of Business Administration, Harvard University, 1967).

SOME SUGGESTIONS FOR FURTHER READING

Engel, J. F., D. T. Kollat, and R. D. Blackwell, (1978), *Consumer Behavior*, 3rd edition, New York: Holt, Rinehart, and Winston.

Farley, J. V., J. A. Howard, and L. W. Ring, (1974), *Consumer Behavior Theory and Application*, Boston, MA: Allyn & Bacon, Inc.

———— and L. W. Ring (1970), "An Empirical Test of the Howard-Sheth Model of Buyer Behavior," *Journal of Marketing Research* (November), 427–438.

Holbrook, M. B. (1970), "A Synthesis of the Empirical Studies," in Farley, J. V., J. A. Howard, and L. W. Ring, *Consumer Behavior Theory and Application*, chapter 11, Boston, MA: Allyn & Bacon, Inc.

12 / A GENERAL MODEL FOR UNDERSTANDING ORGANIZATIONAL BUYING BEHAVIOR / Frederick E. Webster, Jr. and Yoram Wind

Industrial and institutional marketers have often been urged to base their strategies on careful appraisal of buying behavior within key accounts and in principal market segments. When they search the available literature on buyer behavior, however, they find virtually exclusive emphasis on consumers, not industrial buyers. Research findings and theoretical discussions about consumer behavior often have little relevance for the industrial marketer. This is due to several important differences between the two purchase processes. Industrial buying takes place in the context of a formal organization influenced by budget, cost, and profit considerations. Furthermore, organizational (i.e., industrial and institutional) buying usually involves many people in the decision process with complex interactions among people and among individual and organizational goals.

Similar to his consumer goods counterpart, the industrial marketer could find a model of buyer behavior useful in identifying those key factors influencing response to marketing effort. A buyer behavior model can help the marketer to analyze available information about the market and to identify the need for additional information. It can help to specify targets for marketing effort, the kinds of information needed by various purchasing decision makers, and the criteria that they will use to make these decisions. A framework for analyzing organizational buying behavior could aid in the design of marketing strategy.

The model to be presented here is a *general* model. It can be applied to all organizational buying and suffers all the weaknesses of general models. It does not describe a specific buying situation in the richness of detail required to make a model operational, and it cannot be quantified. However, generality offers a compensating set of benefits. The model presents a comprehensive view of organizational buying that enables one to evaluate the relevance of specific variables and thereby permits greater insight into the basic processes of industrial buying be-

"A General Model for Understanding Organizational Buying Behavior," Frederick E. Webster, Jr., and Yoram Wind, Vol. 36 (April 1972), pp. 12–19. Reprinted from the *Journal of Marketing*, published by the American Marketing Association.
Frederick Webster is professor of marketing at Dartmouth College. He received his Ph.D. from Stanford University and has taught at Columbia University and Stanford University. He is an expert in the area of industrial marketing.
Yoram Wind is professor of marketing at the Wharton School, University of Pennsylvania. He received his Ph.D. from Stanford University. A prolific author, Wind's latest book is *Product Policy*.

havior. It identifies the *classes* of variables that must be examined by any student of organizational buying, practitioner, or academician. Although major scientific progress in the study of organizational buying will come only from a careful study of specific relationships among a few variables within a given class, this general model can help to identify those variables that should be studied. It can be useful in generating hypotheses and provides a framework for careful interpretation of research results that makes the researcher more sensitive to the complexities of the processes he is studying.

TRADITIONAL VIEWS

Traditional views of organizational buying have lacked comprehensiveness. The literature of economics, purchasing, and, to a limited degree, marketing has emphasized variables related to the buying task itself and has emphasized "rational," economic factors. In these economic views, the objective of purchasing is to obtain the minimum price or the lowest total cost-in-use (as in the materials management model [1]). Some of the models focussing on the buying task have emphasized factors that are not strictly economic such as reciprocal buying agreements[2] and other constraints on the buyer such as source loyalty.[3]

Other traditional views of organizational buying err in the opposite direction, emphasizing variables such as emotion, personal goals, and internal politics that are involved in the buying decision process but not related to the goals of the buying task. This "nontask" emphasis is seen in models which emphasize the purchasing agent's interest in obtaining personal favors,[4] in enhancing his own ego,[5] or in reducing perceived risk.[6] Other nontask models have emphasized buyer-salesman interpersonal interaction[7] and the multiple relationships among individuals involved in the buying process over time.[8] The ways in which purchasing agents attempt to expand their influence over the buying decision have also received careful study.[9] These views have contributed to an understanding of the buying process, but none of them is complete. To the extent that these models leave out task or nontask variables they offer incomplete guidelines for the industrial market strategist and researcher. The tendency in interpreting research results based on these simple models is to overemphasize the importance of some variables and to understate or ignore the importance of others.

AN OVERVIEW OF A GENERAL MODEL

The fundamental assertion of the more comprehensive model to be presented here is that organizational buying is a decision-making process carried out by individuals, in interaction with other people, in the context of a formal organization.[10] The organization, in turn, is influenced by a variety of forces in the environment. Thus, the four classes of variables determining organizational buying behavior are *individual*, *social*, *organizational*, and *environmental*. Within each class, there are two broad categories of variables: Those directly related to the buying problem, called *task* variables; and those that extend beyond the buying problem, called *nontask* variables. This classification of variables is summarized and illustrated in Table 1.

Table 1. Classification and Examples of Variables Influencing Organizational Buying Decisions

	Task	Nontask
Individual	Desire to obtain lowest price	Personal values and needs
Social	Meetings to set specifications	Informal, off-the-job·interactions
Organizational	Policy regarding local supplier preference	Methods of personnel evaluation
		Political climate in an election
Environmental	Anticipated changes in prices	year

The distinction between task and nontask variables applies to all of the classes of variables, and subclasses, to be discussed below. It is seldom possible to identify a given set of variables as exclusively task or nontask; rather, any given set of variables will have both task and nontask dimensions although one dimension may be predominant. For example, motives will inevitably have both dimensions—those relating directly to the buying problem to be solved and those primarily concerned with personal goals. These motives overlap in many important respects and need not conflict; a strong sense of personal involvement can create more effective buying decisions from an organizational standpoint.

Organizational buying behavior is a complex *process* (rather than a single, instantaneous act (and involves many persons, multiple goals, and potentially conflicting decision criteria. It often takes place over an extended period of time, requires information from many sources, and encompasses many interorganizational relationships.

The organizational buying process is a form of problem-solving, and a *buying situation* is created when someone in the organization perceives a problem—a discrepancy between a desired outcome and the present situation—that can potentially be solved through some buying action. Organizational buying behavior includes all activities of organizational members as they define a buying situation and identify, evaluate, and choose among alternative brands and suppliers. The *buying center* includes all members of the organization who are involved in that process. The roles involved are those of user, influencer, decider, buyer, and gatekeeper (who controls the flow of information into the buying center). Members of the buying center are motivated by a complex interaction of individual and organizational goals. Their relationships with one another involve all the complexities of interpersonal interactions. The formal organization exerts its influence on the buying center through the subsystems of tasks, structure (communication, authority, status, rewards, and work flow), technology, and people. Finally, the entire organization is embedded in a set of environmental influences including economic, technological, physical, political, legal, and cultural forces. An overview of the model and a diagrammatic presentation of the relationships among these variables are given in Figure 1.

Figure 1.   A model of organizational buying behavior

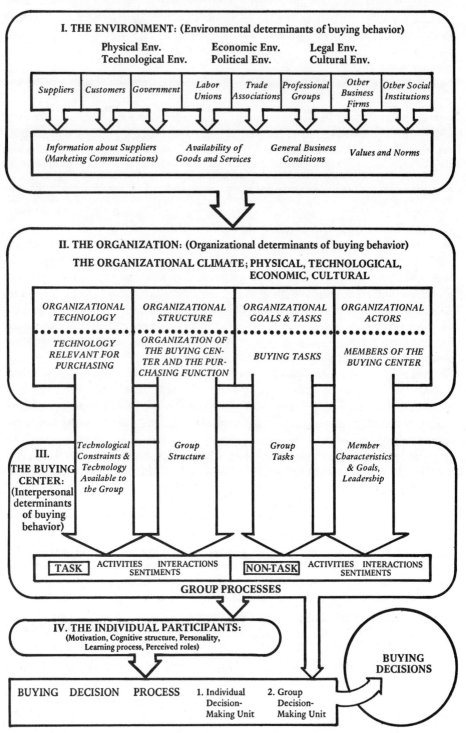

ENVIRONMENTAL INFLUENCES

Environmental influences are subtle and pervasive as well as difficult to identify and to measure. They influence the buying process by providing information as well as constraints and opportunities. Environmental influences include physical (geographic, climate, or ecological), technological, economic, political, legal, and cultural factors. These influences are exerted through a variety of institutions including business firms (suppliers, competitors, and customers), governments, trade unions, political parties, educational and medical institutions, trade associations, and professional groups. The nature of these institutional forms will vary significantly from one country to another, and such differences are critical to the planning of multinational marketing strategies.

As Figure 1 illustrates, environmental influences have their impact in four distinct ways. First, they define the availability of goods and services. This function reflects especially the influence of physical, technological, and economic factors. Second, they define the general business conditions facing the buying organization including the rate of economic growth, the level of national income, interest rates, and unemployment. Economic and political forces are the dominant influences on general business conditions. Some of these forces, such as economic factors, are predominantly (but not exclusively) task variables whereas others such as political variables may be more heavily nontask in nature. Third, environmental factors determine the values and norms guiding interorganizational and interpersonal relationships between buyers and sellers as well as among competitors, and between buying organizations and other institutions such as governments and trade associations. Such values and norms may be codified into laws, or they may be implicit. Cultural, social, legal, and political forces are the dominant sources of values and norms. Finally, environmental forces influence the information flow into the buying organization. Most important here is the flow of marketing communications from potential suppliers, through the mass media and through other personal and impersonal channels. Information flows reflect a variety of physical, technological, economic, and cultural factors.

The marketing strategist, whose customers are organizations, must carefully appraise each set of environmental factors and identify and analyze the institutions that exert those influences in each of the market segments served. This kind of analysis is especially important in entering new markets. For example, economic factors as revealed in measures of general business conditions must be continually assessed where market prices fluctuate and buyers make decisions to build or reduce inventories based on price expectations. Similarly, the impact of technological change in markets served must be considered as the basis for strategic decisions in the areas of product policy and promotion. The necessity of analyzing institutional forms is most readily apparent when markets are multinational in scope and require specific consideration of government policies and trade union influences. Environmental factors are important determinants of organizational buying behavior, but they can be so basic and pervasive that it is easy, and dangerous, to overlook them in analyzing the market.

ORGANIZATIONAL INFLUENCES

Organizational factors cause individual decision makers to act differently than they would if they were functioning alone or in a different organization. Organizational buying behavior is motivated and directed by the organization's goals and is constrained by its financial, technological, and human resources. This class of variables is primarily task-related. For understanding the influence of the formal organization on the buying process, Leavitt's classification of variables is most helpful.[11] According to Leavitt's scheme, organizations are multivariate systems composed of four sets of interacting variables:

Tasks—the work to be performed in accomplishing the objectives of the organization.
Structure—subsystems of communication, authority, status, rewards, and work flow.
Technology—problem-solving inventions used by the firm including plant and equipment and programs for organizing and managing work.
People—the actors in the system.

Each of these subsystems interacts with, and is dependent upon, the others for its functioning. Together, these four interacting sets of factors define the information, expectations, goals, attitudes, and assumptions used by each of the individual actors in their decision making. This general model defines four distinct but interrelated sets of variables that must be carefully considered in the development of marketing strategies designed to influence that process: buying tasks, organization structure, buying technology, and the buying center.

Buying Tasks

Buying tasks are a subset of organizational tasks and goals that evolves from the definition of a buying situation. These are pure task variables by definition. The specific tasks that must be performed to solve the buying problem can be defined as five stages in the buying decision process. (1) Identification of need; (2) establishment of specifications; (3) identification of alternatives; (4) evaluation of alternatives; and (5) selection of suppliers.[12] Buying tasks can be further defined according to four dimensions:

1. The *organizational purpose* served—e.g., whether the reason for buying is to facilitate production, or for resale, or to be consumed in the performance of other organizational functions.
2. The *nature of demand,* especially whether demand for the product is generated within the buying organization or by forces outside of the organization (i.e., "derived" demand) as well as other characteristics of the demand pattern such as seasonal and cyclical fluctuations.
3. The *extent of programming;* i.e., the degree of routinization at the five stages of the decision process.
4. The *degree of decentralization* and the extent to which buying authority has been delegated to operating levels in the organization.

Each of these four dimensions influences the nature of the organizational buying process and must be considered in appraising market opportunities. At each of the five stages of the decision process, different members of the buying center may be involved, different decision criteria are employed, and different information sources may become more or less relevant. Marketing strategies must be adjusted accordingly. There are rich research opportunities in defining the influence of different members of the buying center at various stages of the buying process.[18]

Organizational Structure

The formal organizational structure consists of subsystems of communication, authority, status, rewards, and work flow, all of which have important task and nontask dimensions. Each of these subsystems deserves careful study by researchers interested in organizational buying. The marketing literature does not include studies in this area. A beginning might be several rigorous observational or case studies.

The *communication* subsystem performs four essential functions: (1) Information; (2) command and instruction; (3) influence and persuasion; and (4) integration.[14] The marketer must understand how the communication system in customer organizations *informs* the members of the buying center about buying problems, evaluation criteria (both task and nontask related), and alternative sources of supply. He must appraise how *commands and instructions* (mostly task-related) flow through the hierarchy defining the discretion and latitude of individual actors. The pattern of *influence and persuasion* (heavily nontask in nature) defines the nature of interpersonal interactions within the buying center. Organizational members may differ in the extent to which they prefer either commands and instructions or more subtle influence and persuasion to guide the actions of subordinates. The *integrative* functions of communication become critical in coordinating the functioning of the buying center and may be one of the primary roles of the purchasing manager.

The *authority* subsystem defines the power of organizational actors to judge, command, or otherwise act to influence the behavior of others along both task and nontask dimensions. No factor is more critical in understanding the organizational buying process because the authority structure determines who sets goals and who evaluates (and therefore determines rewards for) organizational performance. The authority structure interacts with the communication structure to determine the degree of decentralization in the decision process.

The *status* system is reflected in the organization chart and defines the hierarchical structure of the formal organization. It also expresses itself in an informal structure. Both the formal and the informal organization define each individual's position in a hierarchy with respect to other individuals. Job descriptions define positions within the organization and the associated dimensions of responsibility and authority. Knowing the responsibility, authority, and the position in the internal status hierarchy of each member of the buying center is a necessary basis for developing an account strategy for the organizational customer. A complete theory of organizational buying will permit accurate predictions of an organizational actor's influence based upon his position and role.

The *rewards* system defines the payoffs to the individual decision maker. It is intimately related to the authority system which determines the responsibilities of organizational actors for evaluating other individuals. Here is the mechanism for relating organizational task accomplishment to individual nontask objectives. Persons join organizations in anticipation of the rewards given by the organization and agree to work toward organizational objectives in return for those rewards. A careful analysis of the formal and social reward structure of the organization as it affects and is perceived by the members of the buying center can be most helpful in predicting their response to marketing effort. The key fact is that people work for organizations in order to earn rewards related to personal goals, both economic and noneconomic.[15]

Every buying organization develops task-related procedures for managing the *work flow* of paperwork, samples, and other items involved in the buying decision process. The flow of paperwork also has nontask aspects which reflect the composition of the buying center as well as the authority and communication subsystems of an organizational structure. Needless to say, marketers must understand the mechanical details of buying procedures. Such procedures also provide documentation of the buying process that can provide useful data for the academic researcher.

Buying Technology

Technology influences both what is bought and the nature of the organizational buying process itself. In the latter respect, technology defines the management and information systems that are involved in the buying decision process, such as computers and management science approaches to such aspects of buying as "make or buy" analysis. More obviously, technology defines the plant and equipment of the organization, and these, in turn, place significant constraints upon the alternative buying actions available to the organization. It is a common failing of industrial marketing strategy, especially for new product introductions, to underestimate the demands that will be placed upon existing technology in customer organizations.[16] A new material, for example, may require new dies and mixing equipment, new skills of production personnel, and substantial changes in methods of production.

Buying Center

The buying center is a subset of the organizational actors, the last of the four sets of variables in the Leavitt scheme. The buying center was earlier defined as consisting of five roles: users, influencers, deciders, buyers, and gatekeepers. Since people operate as part of the total organization, the behavior of members of the buying center reflects the influence of others as well as the effect of the buying task, the organizational structure, and technology.

This interaction leads to unique buying behavior in each customer organization. The marketing strategist who wishes to influence the organizational buying process must, therefore, define and understand the operation of these four sets of organizational variables—tasks, structure, technology, and actors—in each organization he is trying to influence. The foregoing comments provide only the skeleton of an analytical structure for considering each of these factors and its implications for marketing action in a specific buying situation. The marketer's problem is to define the locus of buying responsibility within the customer organization, to define the composition of the buying center, and to understand the structure of roles and authority within the buying center.

SOCIAL (INTERPERSONAL) INFLUENCES

The framework for understanding the buying decision process must identify and relate three classes of variables involved in group functioning in the buying center. First, the various roles in the buying center must be identified. Second, the variables relating to interpersonal (dyadic) interaction between persons in the buying center and between members of the buying center and "outsiders" such as vendors' salesmen must be identified. Third, the dimensions of the functioning of the group as a whole must be considered. Each of these three sets of factors is discussed briefly in the following paragraphs.

Within the organization as a whole only a subset of organizational actors is actually involved in a buying situation. The buying center includes five roles:

Users—those members of the organization who use the purchased products and services.

Buyers—those with formal responsibility and authority for contracting with suppliers.

Influencers—those who influence the decision process directly or indirectly by providing information and criteria for evaluating alternative buying actions.

Deciders—those with authority to choose among alternative buying actions.

Gatekeepers—those who control the flow of information (and materials) into the buying center.

Several individuals may occupy the same role; e.g., there may be several influencers. Also, one individual may occupy more than one role; e.g., the purchasing agent is often both buyer and gatekeeper.

To understand interpersonal interaction within the buying center, it is useful to consider three aspects of role performance: (1) Role *expectations* (prescriptions and prohibitions for the behavior of the person occupying the role and for the behavior of other persons toward a given role); (2) role *behavior* (actual behavior in the role); and (3) role *relationships* (the multiple and reciprocal relationships among members of the group). Together, these three variables define the individual's *role set*. An awareness of each of these dimensions is necessary for the salesman responsible for contacting the various members of the buying center. It is especially important to understand how each member expects the salesman to behave toward him and the important ongoing relationships among roles in the buying center.

As illustrated in Figure 1, the nature of group functioning is influenced by five classes of variables—the individual members' goals and personal characteristics, the nature of leadership within the group, the structure of the group, the tasks performed by the group, and external (organizational and environmental) influences. Group processes involve not only activities but also interactions and sentiments among members, which have both task and nontask dimensions. Finally, the output of the group is not only a task-oriented problem solution (a buying action) but also nontask satisfaction and growth for the group and its members.

In analyzing the functioning of the buying center, it helps to focus attention on the buyer role, primarily because a member of the purchasing department is most often the marketer's primary contact point with the organization. Buyers often have authority for managing the contacts of suppliers with other organizational actors, and thus also perform the "gatekeeper" function. While the buyer's authority for selection of suppliers may be seriously constrained by decisions at earlier stages of the decision process (especially the development of specifications), he has responsibility for the terminal stages of the process. In other words, the buyer (or purchasing agent) is in most cases the final decision maker and the target of influence attempts by other members of the buying center.

In performing their task, purchasing agents use a variety of tactics to enhance their power which vary with the specific problems, the conditions of the organization, and the purchasing agent's personality. The tactics used by purchasing agents to influence their relationships with other departments can be viewed as a special case of the more general phenomenon of "lateral" relationships in formal organizations—those among members of approximately equal status in the formal organizational hierarchy.[17] These include *rule-oriented* tactics (e.g., appealing to the boss for the enforcement of organizational policy; appealing to rules and formal statements of authority); *rule-evading* tactics (e.g., compliance with requests from users that violate organizational policies); *personal-political* tactics (e.g., reliance on informal relationships and friendships to get decisions made and an exchange of favors with other members of the buying center); *educational* tactics (e.g., persuading other members of the organization to think in purchasing terms and to recognize the importance and potential contribution of the purchasing function); and finally, *organizational-interactional* tactics (e.g., change the formal organizational structure and the pattern of reporting relationships and information flows).

Buyers who are ambitious and wish to extend the scope of their influence will adopt certain tactics and engage in bargaining activities in an attempt to become more influential at earlier stages of the buying process. These tactics or bargaining strategies define the nature of the buyer's relationships with others of equal organizational status and structure the social situation that the potential supplier must face in dealing with the buying organization. An understanding of the nature of interpersonal relationships in the buying organization is an important basis for the development of marketing strategy.

THE INFLUENCE OF THE INDIVIDUAL

In the final analysis, all organizational buying behavior is individual behavior. Only the individual as an individual or a member of a group can define and analyze buying situations, decide, and act. In this behavior, the individual is motivated by a complex combination of personal and organizational objectives, constrained by policies and information filtered through the formal organization, and influenced by other members of the buying center. The individual is at the center of the buying process, operating within the buying center that is in turn bounded by the formal organization which is likewise embedded in the influences of the broader environment. It is the specific individual who is the target for marketing effort, not the abstract organization.

The organizational buyer's personality, perceived role set, motivation, cognition, and learning are the basic psychological processes which affect his response to the buying situation and marketing stimuli provided by potential vendors. Similar to consumer markets, it is important to understand the organizational buyer's psychological characteristics and especially his predispositions, preference structure, and decision model as the basis for marketing strategy decisions. Some initial attempts to develop categories of buying decision makers according to characteristic decision styles ("normative" and "conservative") have been reported.[18] Cultural, organizational, and social factors are important influences on the individual and are reflected in his previous experiences, awareness of, attitudes and preference toward particular vendors and products and his particular buying decision models.

The organizational buyer can, therefore, be viewed as a constrained decision maker. Although the basic mental processes of motivation, cognition, and learning as well as the buyer's personality, perceived role set, preference structure, and decision model are uniquely individual; they are influenced by the context of interpersonal and organizational influences within which the individual is embedded. The organizational buyer is motivated by a complex combination of individual and organizational objectives and is dependent upon others for the satisfaction of these needs in several ways. These other people define the role expectations for the individual, they determine the payoffs he is to receive for his performance, they influence the definition of the goals to be pursued in the buying decision, and they provide information with which the individual attempts to evaluate risks and come to a decision.

Task and Nontask Motives

Only rarely can the organizational buyer let purely personal considerations influence his buying decisions: In a situation where "all other things are equal," the individual may be able to apply strictly personal (nontask) criteria when making his final decision. In the unlikely event that two or more potential vendors offer products of comparable quality and service at a comparable price, then the organizational buyer may be motivated by purely personal, nontask variables such as his personal preferences for dealing with a particular salesman, or some special favor or gift available from the supplier.

The organizational buyer's motivation has both task and nontask dimensions. Task-related motives relate to the specific buying problem to be solved and involve the general criteria of buying "the right quality in the right quantity at the right price for delivery at the right time from the right source." Of course, what is "right" is a difficult question, especially to the extent that important buying influencers have conflicting needs and criteria for evaluating the buyer's performance.

Nontask-related motives may often be more important, although there is frequently a rather direct relationship between task and nontask motives. For example, the buyer's desire for promotion (a nontask motive) can significantly influence his task performance. In other words, there is no necessary conflict between task and nontask motives and, in fact, the pursuit of nontask objectives can enhance the attainment of task objectives.

Broadly speaking, nontask motives can be placed into two categories; achievement motives and risk-reduction motives. Achievement motives are those related to personal advancement and recognition. Risk-reduction motives are related, but somewhat less obvious, and provide a critical link between the individual and the organizational decision-making process. This is also a key component of the behavioral theory of the firm[19] where uncertainty avoidance is a key motivator of organizational actors.

The individual's perception of risk in a decision situation is a function of uncertainty (in the sense of a probabilistic assessment) and of the value of various outcomes. Three kinds of uncertainty are significant: Uncertainty about available alternatives; uncertainty about the outcomes associated with various alternatives; and uncertainty about the way relevant other persons will react to various outcomes.[20] This uncertainty about the reaction of other persons may be due to incomplete information about their goals or about how an outcome will be evaluated and rewarded.

Information gathering is the most obvious tactic for reducing uncertainty, while decision avoidance and lowering of goals are means of reducing the value of outcomes. A preference for the status quo is perhaps the most common mode of risk reduction, since it removes uncertainty and minimizes the possibility of negative outcomes. This is one explanation for the large amount of source loyalty found in organizational buying and is consistent with the "satisficing" postulate of the behavioral theory of the firm.

The individual determinants of organizational buyer behavior and the tactics which buyers are likely to use in their dealings with potential vendors must be clearly understood by those who want to affect their behavior.

SUMMARY

This article has suggested the major dimensions and mechanisms involved in the complex organizational buying process. The framework presented here is reasonably complete although the details clearly are lacking. It is hoped that these comments have been sufficient to suggest a general model of the organizational buying process with important implications for the development of effective marketing and selling strategies as well as some implicit suggestions for scholarly research. The model is offered as a skeleton identifying the major variables that must be appraised in developing the information required for planning strategies. Hopefully, the model has also suggested some new insights into an important area of buying behavior presently receiving inadequate attention in the marketing literature.

NOTES

[1] Dean S. Ammer, *Materials Management* (Homewood, Illinois: Richard D. Irwin, Inc., 1962), pp. 12 and 15.

[2] Dean S. Ammer, "Realistic Reciprocity," *Harvard Business Review*, Vol. 40 (January–February, 1962), pp. 116–124.

[3] Yoram Wind, "Industrial Source Loyalty," *Journal of Marketing Research*, Vol. 7 (November, 1970), pp. 450–457.

[4] For a statement of this view, see J. B. Matthews, Jr., R. D. Buzzell, T. Levitt, and R. Frank, *Marketing: An Introductory Analysis* (New York: McGraw-Hill Book Company, Inc., 1964), p. 149.

[5] For an example, see William J. Stanton, *Fundamentals of Marketing*, Second Ed. (New York: McGraw-Hill Book Company, Inc., 1967), p. 150.

[6] Theodore Levitt, *Industrial Purchasing Behavior: A Study of Communications Effects* (Boston: Division of Research, Graduate School of Business Administration, Harvard University, 1965).

[7] Henry L. Tosi, "The Effects of Expectation Levels and Role Consensus on the Buyer-Seller Dyad," *Journal of Business*, Vol. 39 (October, 1966), pp. 516–529.

[8] Robert E. Weigand, "Why Studying the Purchasing Agent is Not Enough," *Journal of Marketing*, Vol. 32 (January, 1968), pp. 41–45.

[9] George Strauss, "Tactics of Lateral Relationship," *Administrative Science Quarterly*, Vol. 7 (September, 1962) pp. 161–186.

[10] The complete model is presented and discussed in detail in Frederick E. Webster, Jr. and Yoram Wind, *Organizational Buying Behavior* (Englewood Cliffs, New Jersey: Prentice-Hall, Inc., in press).

[11] Harold J. Leavitt, "Applied Organization Change in Industry: Structural, Technical, and Human Approaches," in *New Perspectives in Organization Research*, W. W. Cooper, H. J. Leavitt, and M. W. Shelly, II, eds. (New York: John Wiley and Sons, Inc., 1964), pp. 55–71.

[12] A modified version of this model is presented in P. J. Robinson, C. W. Faris, and Y. Wind, *Industrial Buying and Creative Marketing* (Boston: Allyn & Bacon, Inc., 1967), p. 14.

[13] For research on the influence of organizational actors and information sources at various stages of the decision process, see Urban B. Ozanne and Gilbert A. Churchill, "Adoption Research: Information Sources in the Industrial Purchasing Decision," in *Marketing and the New Science of Planning*, Robert L. King, ed. (Chicago, Ill.: American Marketing Association, Fall, 1968), pp. 352–359; and Frederick E. Webster, Jr., "Informal Communication in Industrial Markets," *Journal of Marketing Research*, Vol. 7 (May, 1970), pp. 186–189.

[14] Lee Thayer, *Communication and Communication Systems* (Homewood, Ill.: Richard D. Irwin, Inc., 1968), pp. 187–250.

[15] Yoram Wind, "A Reward-Balance Model of Buying Behavior in Organizations," in *New Essays in Marketing Theory*, G. Fisk ed. (Boston: Allyn & Bacon, 1971).

[16] Frederick E. Webster, Jr., "New Product Adoption in Industrial Markets: A Framework for Analysis," *Journal of Marketing*, Vol. 33 (July, 1969), pp. 35–39.

[17] Same reference as footnote 9.

[18] David T. Wilson, H. Lee Mathews, and Timothy W. Sweeney, "Industrial Buyer Segmentation: A Psychographic Approach," paper presented at the Fall, 1971 Conference of the

American Marketing Association. See also Richard N. Cardozo, "Segmenting the Industrial Market," in *Marketing and the New Science of Planning*, Robert L. King ed. (Chicago: American Marketing Association, 1969), pp. 433–440.

[19] Richard M. Cyert and James G. March, *A Behavioral Theory of the Firm* (Englewood Cliffs, N.J.: Prentice-Hall, 1963).

[20] Donald F. Cox, ed., *Risk Taking and Information Handling in Consumer Behavior* (Boston: Division of Research, Graduate School of Business Administration, Harvard University, 1967).

SOME SUGGESTIONS FOR FURTHER READING

Robinson, P., C. Faris, and Y. Wind (1967), *Industrial Buying and Creative Marketing*, Boston, MA: Allyn & Bacon, Inc.

Sheth, J. N. (1973), "A Model of Industrial Buying Behavior," *Journal of Marketing*, 50–56.

Webster, F. E. Jr. (1978), "Is Industrial Marketing Coming of Age?" *Review of Marketing*, G. Zaltman and T. V. Bonoma, eds., Chicago: American Marketing Association, 138–159.

———— and Y. Wind (1972), *Organizational Buying Behavior*, Englewood Cliffs, N.J.: Prentice-Hall.

Wind, Y. (1978), "Organizational Buying Center: A Research Agenda," *Organizational Buying Behavior*, T. V. Bonoma and G. Zaltman, eds., Chicago: American Marketing Association, 67–76.

13 / PROJECTIVE TECHNIQUES IN MARKETING RESEARCH /
Mason Haire

It is a well accepted maxim in merchandizing that, in many areas, we are selling the sizzle rather than the steak. Our market research techniques ,however, in many of these same areas, are directed toward the steak. The sizzle is the subjective reaction of the consumer; the steak the objective characteristics of the product. The consumer's behavior will be based on the former rather than the latter set of characteristics. How can we come to know them better?

When we approach a consumer directly with questions about his reaction to a product we often get false and misleading answers to our questions. Very often this is because the question which we heard ourselves ask was not the one (or not the only one) that the respondent heard. For example: A brewery made two kinds of beer. To guide their merchandizing techniques they wanted to know what kind of people drank each kind, and particularly, what differences there were between the two groups of consumers. A survey was conducted which led up to the questions "Do you drink —— beer?" (If yes) "Do you drink the *Light* or *Regular*?" (These were the two trade names under which the company marketed.) (After identifying the consumers of each product it was possible to find out about the characteristics of each group so that appropriate appeals could be used, media chosen, etc.

An interesting anomaly appeared in the survey data, however. The interviewing showed (on a reliable sample) that consumers drank *Light* over *Regular* in ratio of 3 to 1. The company had been producing and selling Regular over Light for some time in a ratio of 9 to 1. Clearly, the attempt to identify characteristics of the two kinds was a failure. What made them miss so far?

When we say "Do you drink *Light* or *Regular?*" we are at once asking which brand is used, but also, to some extent, saying "Do you drink the regular run-of-the-mill product or do you drink the one that is more refined and shows more discrimination and taste?" The preponderance of "Light" undoubtedly flows from this kind of distortion.

When we ask questions of this sort about the product we are very often asking also about the respondent. Not only do we say "What is —— product like?" but, indirectly "What are *you* like?" Our responses are often made up of both elements inextricably interwoven. The answers to the second question will carry

Reprinted from the *Journal of Marketing,* published by the American Marketing Association (April, 1950), pp. 649–656.
Mason Haire is a professor of organizational psychology and management at the Massachusetts Institute of Technology, in the Alfred P. Sloan School of Management. A much-published writer on psychology in management and social science research applications in business, his M.A. and Ph.D. in psychology are from Harvard University. Among his many books is *Psychology in Management.*

clichés and stereotypes, blocks, inhibitions, and distortions, whenever we approach an area that challenges the person's idea of himself.

There are many things that we need to know about a consumer's reaction to a product that he can not tell us because they are to some extent socially unacceptable. For instance, the snob appeal of a product vitally influences its sale, but it is a thing that the consumer will not like to discuss explicitly. In other cases the consumer is influenced by motives of which he is, perhaps, vaguely aware, but which he finds difficult to put into words. The interviewer-respondent relationship puts a good deal of pressure on him to reply and to make sense in his reply. Consequently, he gives us stereotypical responses that use clichés which are commonly acceptable but do not necessarily represent the true motives. Many of our motives do not, in fact, "make sense," and are not logical. The question-answer relation demands sense above all. If the response does not represent the true state of affairs the interviewer will never know it. He will go away. If it does not make sense it may represent the truth, but the respondent will feel like a fool and the interviewer will not go away. Much better produce a cliché and be rid of him.

THE NATURE OF PROJECTIVE TESTS

Still other kinds of motives exist of which the respondent may not be explicitly conscious himself. The product may be seen by him as related to things or people or values in his life, or as having a certain role in the scheme of things, and yet he may be quite unable, in response to a direct question, to describe these aspects of the object. Nevertheless, these characteristics may be of great importance as motives. How can we get at them?

Clinical psychologists have long been faced with a parallel set of problems. It is quite usual for a patient to be unable or unwilling to tell the therapist directly what kinds of things are stirring in his motivational pattern. Information about these drives is of vital importance to the process of cure, so a good deal of research has been directed towards the development of techniques to identify and define them. The development of projective techniques as diagnostic tools has provided one of the most useful means to uncover such motivations, and the market-researcher can well afford to borrow their essentials from the therapist.

Basically, a projective test involves presenting the subject with an ambiguous stimulus—one that does not quite make sense in itself—and asking him to make sense of it. The theory is that in order to make it make sense he will have to add to it—to fill out the picture—and in so doing he projects part of himself into it. Since we know what was in the original stimulus we can quite easily identify the parts that were added, and, in this way, painlessly obtain information about the person.

Examples of these tests come readily to hand. Nearly everyone is familiar with the Rorschach Test, in which a subject is shown a series of ink-blots and asked to tell what they look like. Here the stimulus is incomplete in itself, and the interpretation supplied by the patient provides useful information. This test yields fairly general answers about the personality, however, and often we would like to narrow down the area in which the patient is supplying information.

The Thematic Apperception Test offers a good example of this function. Let us suppose that with a particular patient we have reason to suppose that his relation to figures of authority is crucial to his therapeutic problem. We can give him a series of pictures where people are shown, but where the relationship of authority or the characteristics of the authoritarian figure are not complete. He is asked to tell a story about each picture. If in each story the subordinate finally kills the figure of authority we have certain kinds of knowledge; if, on the other hand, he always builds the story so the subordinate figure achieves a secure and comfortable dependence, we have quite different information. It is often quite impossible to get the subject to tell us these things directly. Either he cannot or will not do so. Indirectly, however, he will tell us how he sees authority. Can we get him, similarly, to tell us how a product looks to him in his private view of the world?

APPLICATION OF PROJECTIVE TEST IN MARKET RESEARCH

Let us look at an example of this kind of thing in market research. For the purposes of experiment a conventional survey was made of attitudes toward Nescafé, an instant coffee. The questionnaire included the questions "Do you use instant coffee?" (If *No*) "What do you dislike about it?" The bulk of the unfavorable responses fell into the general area "I don't like the flavor." This is such an easy answer to a complex question that one may suspect it is a stereotype, which at once gives a sensible response to get rid of the interviewer and conceals other motives. How can we get behind this facade?

In this case an indirect approach was used. Two shopping lists were prepared. They were identical in all respects, except that one list specified Nescafé and one Maxwell House Coffee. They were administered to alternate subjects, with no subject knowing of the existence of the other list. The instructions were "Read the shopping list below. Try to project yourself into the situation as far as possible until you can more or less characterize the woman who bought the groceries. Then write a brief description of her personality and character. Wherever possible indicate what factors influenced your judgment."

Shopping List 1
Pound and a half of hamburger
2 loaves Wonder bread
bunch of carrots
1 can Rumford's Baking Powder
Nescafé instant coffee
2 cans Del Monte peaches
5 lbs. potatoes
Shopping List II
Pound and a half of hamburger
2 loaves Wonder bread
bunch of carrots

1 can Rumford's Baking Powder
1 lb. Maxwell House Coffee (Drip Ground)
2 cans Del Monte peaches
5 lbs. potatoes

Fifty people responded to each of the two shopping lists given above. The responses to these shopping lists provided some very interesting material. The following main characteristics of their descriptions can be given:

1. 48 per cent of the people described the woman who bought Nescafé as lazy; 4 per cent described the woman who bought Maxwell House as lazy.
2. 48 per cent of the people described the woman who bought Nescafé as failing to plan household purchases and schedules well; 12 per cent described the woman who bought Maxwell House this way.
3. 4 per cent described the Nescafé woman as thrifty; 16 per cent described the Maxwell House woman as thrifty. 12 per cent described the Nescafé woman as spendthrift; 0 per cent described the Maxwell House woman this way.
4. 16 per cent described the Nescafé woman as not a good wife; 0 per cent described the Maxwell House woman this way. 4 per cent described the Nescafé woman as a good wife; 16 per cent described the Maxwell House woman as a good wife.

A clear picture begins to form here. Instant coffee represents a departure from "home-made" coffee, and the traditions with respect to caring for one's family. Coffee-making is taken seriously, with vigorous proponents for laborious drip and filter-paper methods, firm believers in coffee boiled in a battered sauce pan, and the like. Coffee drinking is a form of intimacy and relaxation that gives it a special character.

On the one hand, coffee making is an art. It is quite common to hear a woman say, "I can't seem to make good coffee," in the same way that one might say, "I can't learn to play the violin." It is acceptable to confess this inadequacy, for making coffee well is a mysterious touch that belongs, in a shadowy tradition, to the plump, aproned figure who is a little lost outside her kitchen but who has a sure sense in it and among its tools.

On the other hand, coffee has a peculiar role in relation to the household and the home-and-family character. We may well have a picture, in the shadowy past, of a big black range that is always hot with baking and cooking, and has a big enamelled pot of coffee warming at the back. When a neighbor drops in during the morning, a cup of coffee is a medium of hospitality that does somewhat the same thing as cocktails in the late afternoon, but does it in a broader sphere.

These are real and important aspects of coffee. They are not physical characteristics of the product, but they are real values in the consumer's life, and they influence his purchasing. We need to know and assess them. The "labor-saving" aspect of instant coffee, far from being an asset, may be a liability in that it violates these traditions. How often have we heard a wife respond to "This cake is delicious!" with a pretty blush and "Thank you—I made it with such and such a prepared cake mix." This response is so invariable as to seem almost compulsive. It is almost unthinkable to anticipate a reply "Thank you, I made it with Pillsbury's flour, Fleischman's yeast, and Borden's milk." Here the specifications are unnecessary. All that is relevant is the implied "I made it"—the art and the credit are carried directly by the verb that covers the process of mixing and processing the ingredients. In ready-mixed foods there seems to be a compulsive drive to refuse credit for the product, because the accomplishment is not the housewife's but the company s.

In this experiment, as a penalty for using "synthetics" the woman who buys Nescaté pays the price of being seen as lazy, spendthrift, a poor wife, and as failing to plan well for her family. The people who rejected instant coffee in the original direct question blamed its flavor. We may well wonder if their dislike of instant coffee was not to a large extent occasioned by a fear of being seen by one's self and others in the role they projected onto the Nescafé woman in the description. When asked directly, however, it is difficult to respond with this. One can not say, "I don't use Nescafé because people will think I am lazy and not a good wife." Yet we know from these data that the feeling regarding laziness and shiftlessness was there. Later studies (reported below) showed that it determined buying habits, and that something could be done about it.

ANALYSIS OF RESPONSES

Some examples of the type of response received will show the kind of material obtained and how it may be analyzed. Three examples of each group are given below.

Descriptions of a Woman Who Bought, Among Other Things, Maxwell House Coffee

"I'd say she was a practical, frugal woman. She bought too many potatoes. She must like to cook and bake as she included baking powder. She must not care much about her figure as she does not discriminate about the food she buys."

"The woman is quite influenced by advertising as signified by the specific name brands on her shopping list. She probably is quite set in her ways and accepts no substitutes."

"I have been able to observe several hundred women shoppers who have made very similar purchases to that listed above, and the only clue that I can detect that may have some bearing on her personality is the Del Monte peaches. This item when purchased singly along with the other more staple foods indicates that she may be anxious to please either herself or members of her family with a 'treat.' She is probably a thrifty, sensible housewife."

Descriptions of a Woman Who Bought, Among Other Things, Nescafé Instant Coffee

"This woman appears to be either single or living alone. I would guess that she had an office job. Apparently, she likes to sleep late in the morning, basing my assumption on what she bought such as Instant Coffee which can be made in a hurry. She probably also has can [sic] peaches for breakfast, cans being easy to open. Assuming that she is just average, as opposed to those dazzling natural beauties who do not need much time to make up, she must appear rather sloppy, taking little time to make up in the morning. She is also used to eating supper out, too. Perhaps alone rather than with an escort. An old maid probably."

"She seems to be lazy, because of her purchases of canned peaches and instant coffee. She doesn't seem to think, because she bought two loaves of bread, and then baking powder, unless she's thinking of making cake. She probably just got married."

"I think the woman is the type who never thinks ahead very far—the type who always sends Junior to the store to buy one item at a time. Also she is fundamentally lazy. All the items, with possible exception of the Rumford's, are easily prepared items. The girl may be an office girl who is just living from one day to the next in a sort of haphazard sort of life."

As we read these complete responses we begin to get a feeling for the picture that is created by Nescafé. It is particularly interesting to notice that the Nescafé woman is protected, to some extent, from the opprobrium of being lazy and haphazard by being seen as a single "office girl"—a role that relieves one from guilt for not being interested in the home and food preparation.

The references to peaches are significant. In one case (Maxwell House) they are singled out as a sign that the woman is thoughtfully preparing a "treat" for her family. On the other hand, when the Nescafé woman buys them it is evidence that she is lazy, since their "canned" character is seen as central.

In terms of the sort of results presented above, it may be useful to demonstrate the way these stories are coded. The following items are extracted from the six stories quoted:

Maxwell House	Nescafé
1. practical frugal likes to cook	1. single office girl sloppy old maid
2. influenced by advertising set in her ways	2. lazy does not plan newlywed
3. interested in family thrifty sensible	3. lazy does not plan office girl

Items such as these are culled from each of the stories. Little by little categories are shaped by the content of the stories themselves. In this way the respondent furnishes the dimensions of analysis as well as the scale values on these dimensions.

Second Test

It is possible to wonder whether it is true that the opprobrium that is heaped on the Nescafé woman comes from her use of a device that represents a short-cut and labor-saver in an area where she is expected to embrace painstaking time-consuming work in a ritualistic way. To test this a variation was introduced into the shopping lists. In a second experiment one hundred and fifty housewives were tested with the form given above, but a sample was added to this group which responded to a slightly different form. If we assume that the rejection in the first experiment came from the presence of a feeling about synthetic shortcuts we might assume also that the addition of one more shortcut to both lists would bring the Maxwell House woman more into line with the Nescafé woman, since the former would now have the same guilt that the Nescafé woman originally had, while the Nescafé woman, already convicted of evading her duties, would be little further injured.

In order to accomplish this a second prepared food was added to both lists. Immediately after the coffee in both lists the fictitious item, "Blueberry Fill Pie Mix" was added. The results are shown in the accompanying table.

It will be seen immediately, in the first two columns, that the group to whom the original form of the list were given showed the same kind of difference as reported above in their estimates of the two women. The group with an additional prepared food, however, brought the Maxwell Coffee woman down until she is virtually undistinguishable from the Nescafé. There seems to be little doubt but that the prepared-food-character, and the stigma of avoiding house-wifely duties is responsible for the projected personality characteristics.

Relation to Purchasing

It is still relevant to ask whether the existence of these feelings in a potential consumer is related to purchasing. It is hypothesized that these personality descriptions provide an opportunity for the consumer to project hopes and fears and anxieties that are relevant to the way the product is seen, and that they represent important parts of her motivation in buying or not buying. To test this hypothesis, a small sample of fifty housewives, comparable in every way to the group just referred to, was given the original form of the shopping list (Nescafé only). In addition to obtaining the personality description, the interviewer, on a pretext, obtained permission to look at her pantry shelves and determine personally whether or not she had instant coffee of any brand. The results of this investigation are shown in the accompanying table.

Table 1. Personality Characteristics Ascribed to Users of Prepared Foods

If They Use	No Prepared Food (Maxwell House alone)		Nescafé (alone)		Maxwell House (plus Pie Mix)		Nescafé (plus Pie Mix)	
They are seen as:	Number	Per Cent	Number	Per Cent	Number	Per Cent	Number	Per Cent
Not Economical	12	17	24	32	6	30	7	35
Lazy	8	11	46	62	5	25	8	40
Poor Personality and Appearance	28	39	39	53	7	35	8	40
N =	72		74		20		20	

The trend of these data shows conclusively that if a respondent sees the woman who buys Nescafé as having undesirable traits, she is not likely to buy instant coffee herself. The projected unacceptable characteristics go with failure to buy, and it does not seem unwarranted to assume that the association is causal.

Furthermore, these projected traits are, to some extent, additive. For instance, if a respondent describes the woman as having one bad trait only, she is about twice as likely not to have instant coffee. However, if she sees her as having two bad traits, and no good ones (e.g., lazy, cannot cook), she is about three times as likely not to have instant coffee as she is to have it. On the other hand, if she sees her as having two good traits (e.g., economical, cares for family), she is about six times as likely to have it as not.

It was pointed out earlier that some women felt it necessary to "excuse" the woman who bought Nescafé by suggesting that she lived alone and hence could not be expected to be interested in cooking, or that she had a job and did not have time to shop better. Women who had instant coffee in the house found excuses almost twice as often as those who did not use instant coffee (12 out of 32, or 42 per cent, against 4 out of 18, or 22 per cent). These "excuses" are vitally important for merchandizing. The need for an excuse shows there is a barrier to buying in the consumer's mind. The presence of excuses shows that there is a way around the barrier. The content of the excuses themselves provides valuable clues for directing appeals toward reducing buying resistance.

CONCLUSIONS

There seems to be no question that in the experimental situation described here:

1. Motives exist which are below the level of verbalization because they are socially unacceptable, difficult to verbalize cogently, or unrecognized.

Table II.

The woman who buys Nescafé is seen as:	By Women Who Had Instant Coffee in the House (N = 32)		By Women Who Did Not Have Instant Coffee in the House (N = 18)	
	Number	Per Cent	Number	Per Cent
Economical**	22	70	5	28
Not economical	0	0	2	11
Cannot cook or does not like to**	5	16	10	55
Plans balanced meals*	9	29	2	11
Good housewife, plans well, cares about family**	9	29	0	0
Poor housewife, does not plan well, does not care about family*	5	16	7	39
Lazy*	6	19	7	39

* A single asterisk indicates that differences this great would be observed only 5 times out of 100 in repeated samplings of a population whose true difference is zero.
** A double asterisk indicates that the chances are 1 in 100. We are justified in rejecting the hypothesis that there is no difference between the groups.

2. These motives are intimately related to the decision to purchase or not to purchase, and
3. It is possible to identify and assess such motives by approaching them indirectly.

Two important general points come out of the work reported. The first is in the statement of the problem. It is necessary for us to see a product in terms of a set of characteristics and attributes which are part of the consumer's "private world," and as such may have no simple relationship to characteristics of the object in the "real" world. Each of us lives in a world which is composed of more than physical things and people. It is made up of goals, paths to goals, barriers, threats, and the like, and an individual's behavior is oriented with respect to these characteristics as much as to the "objective" ones. In the area of merchandizing, a product's character of being seen as a path to a goal is usually very much more important as a determinant of purchasing than its physical dimensions. We have taken advantage of these qualities in advertising and merchandizing for a long time by an intuitive sort of "playing-by-ear" on the subjective aspects of products. It is time for a systematic attack on the problem of the phenomenological description of objects. What kinds of dimensions are relevant to this world of goals and paths and barriers? What kind of terms will fit the phenomenological characteristics of an object in the same sense that the centimetre-gram-second system fits its physical dimensions? We need to know the answers to such questions, and the psychological definitions of valued objects.

The second general point is the methodological one that it is possible, by using appropriate techniques, to find out from the respondent what the phenomenological characteristics of various objects may be. By and large, a direct approach to this problem in terms of straight-forward questions will not yield satisfactory answers. It is possible, however, by the use of indirect techniques, to get the consumer to provide, quite unselfconsciously, a description of the value-character of objects in his environment.

SOME SUGGESTIONS FOR FURTHER READING

Ferber, R. and H. G. Wales (1958), *Motivation and Market Behavior*, Chicago, IL: Richard D. Irwin.

Hill, Conrad R. (1968), "Haire's Classic Instant Coffee Study—18 Years Later," *Journalism Quarterly* (Volume 45), 466–472.

Webster, F. E., Jr. and F. Von Pechman (1970), "A Replication of the 'Shopping List' Study," *Journal of Marketing* (April), 61–63.

Westfield, R. L., H. W. Boyd, Jr. and D. T. Campbell (1957), "The Use of Structured Techniques in Motivation Research," *Journal of Marketing* (October), 134–139.

14 / ISSUES IN MARKETING'S USE OF MULTI-ATTRIBUTE ATTITUDE MODELS / William L. Wilkie and Edgar A. Pessemier

INTRODUCTION

The pointed debates [3, 12, 63, 67] in recent issues of this journal highlight the involvement of marketing researchers in summative attitude models of the type originally proposed by Rosenberg [55] and Fishbein [21]. Interest in the area is increasing; over forty marketing studies have been reported in the past three years.[1] Although it is now clear that marketing applications have substantially altered the formulations originally employed in social psychology, it is less apparent that marketing studies have themselves differed significantly. In the absence of commonly agreed-upon theory, investigations frequently differed in model conceptualizations, semantics, measurement and analysis methods, criteria, and conclusions. A number of significant issues remain for future research. This article will raise these issues, summarize results and perspectives from recent marketing research, and suggest areas for future consideration of a cumulative nature.

Because of the specialized research focus of the article, it is assumed that the reader is familiar with the fundamental rationale for the compensatory multi-attribute attitude model. The model at issue is compositional in approach; an excellent comparison with *decompositional* attitude models is presented by Day [17, 18]. Arguments favoring decomposition models are provided by Green and Wind [25]. Comprehensive theoretical ties and proposals for managerial relevance of composition models have been discussed by Cohen [10], Hughes [32], Ginter and Pessemier [24], and Lunn [41].

THE BASIC MODEL

Unidimensional attitude scales (e.g., "overall like-dislike") offer measurement efficiencies in that instruments can be short, structured, and provide a summary measure of brand affect. A multi-attribute object (e.g., product or brand) is viewed as a bundle of attributes leading to costs and benefits of differential desirability to individuals or segments of the market. Overall affect is posited to reflect the net

"Issues in Marketing's Use of Multi-Attribute Attitude Models," *Journal of Marketing,* Vol. 10 (November 1973), pp. 428–441. Published by the American Marketing Association. Reprinted by permission of the publisher.
William Wilkie is professor of marketing at the University of Florida. He received his Ph.D. from Stanford University and has previously taught at the Purdue University and Harvard University.
Edgar Pessemier is a professor at Purdue University. He received his Ph.D. from Harvard University and has previously taught at the Washington State University. He has published extensively in the product marketing area.

resolution of an individual's cognitions (beliefs) as to the degree to which given objects possess certain attributes weighted by the salience (importance) of each attribute to the individual. Given that the marketing manager can control to some extent the physical characteristics and associated images of his brand, careful assessment of cognitive structures offers a natural approach to formulating important aspects of a marketing strategy.

The potential advantage of multi-attribute models over the simpler "overall affect" approach is in gaining understanding of attitudinal structure. *Diagnosis* of brand strengths and weaknesses on relevant product attributes can then be used to suggest specific changes in a brand and its marketing support. The extent to which this potential advantage is realized, however, depends on the strength of the model and the measurements used by the marketing researcher. As noted above, there are a number of operational issues currently in dispute. Discussion of these issues is provided within the framework of a basic model. Since this terminology is chosen merely to facilitate communication, differences in concepts and semantics will appear as specific issues are discussed.

The basic linear compensatory model is seen to be:

$$A_{jk} = \sum_{i=1}^{n} I_{ik} B_{ijk}$$

where:

i = attribute or product characteristic,
j = brand,
k = consumer or respondent,

such that:

A_{jk} = consumer k's *attitude* score for brand j,
I_{ik} = the *importance* weight given attribute i by consumer k, and
B_{ijk} = Consumer k's *belief* as to the extent to which attribute i is offered by brand j.

In the following section, research issues are categorized by each component of the basic model. Some more general, fundamental questions are also raised within the context of this format.

MARKETING USE OF THE MULTI-ATTRIBUTE MODEL

Recent marketing work with the model has tended to move beyond simple tests of the relationship of A_{jk} with external criteria in order to examine issues related to model inputs, structure, and functioning for situations involving two or more competitive attitude objects. Objects studied include grocery stores, restaurants, personalized rapid transit, hair dryers, television shows, analgesics, soft drinks, instant breakfast, automobiles, detergents, toothpaste, mouthwash, and other frequently purchased consumer goods. In general, results have been consistent across products; the multi-attribute model yields attitude scores which are significantly related to measures of purchase or purchase predisposition. While one might be able to choose better predictors of these dependent variables (e.g., last period purchases), diagnostic benefits often are not offered by the better predictors (M42), [37].[2] The basic purpose of the multi-attribute model is to gain understanding of purchase predisposition. Assessment of its performance in this respect requires a closer look at research issues.

This section deals specifically with marketing applications of the basic model. Forty-two empirical studies plus insights from a number of commentary articles are analyzed with respect to selected issues; see the figure. Variations in conceptualizations, operationalizations, and results are discussed and evaluated to summarize progress and focus attention on key questions for future research. Issue areas derived from the basic model are listed vertically, and include specific problems for each area. The 42 empirical studies are arranged horizontally in approximate chronological order such that temporal tracking of progress is possible. Cell entries reflect representative positions taken on an issue, or that discussions (*) and/or empirical tests (**) are undertaken in the article. Blank cells indicate no substantial mention of an issue, while question marks indicate that no data on an issue are reported, although one would infer that a position was taken. A more detailed key is available at the end of the figure to clarify abbreviations.

Discussion of the matrix is row-wise, reflecting our primary interest in issue analysis rather than article summarization. Because of the complex relationships between model components, much of the summarization is nonevaluative. A critical review and proposals appear in closing statements. "Attribute" issues are discussed first, followed by Importance Weights, Beliefs, Model Structure, and Model Tests. Within each section the rows of the figure provide issues for discussion.

I. Attributes (*i*)

Attributes provide the basic dimensionality of the model and are clearly of crucial theoretical importance. Little guidance from Rosenberg [55] or Fishbein [21] in selection of attributes is available for marketing studies. Issues in this area are concerned with desired characteristics of attributes, generation of attribute lists, inclusion of attributes in the model, and the number and communality of those included.

A primary distinguishing characteristic of the composition model is the assumption that dimensional inputs are known and measured by the researcher. The restrictive nature of this assumption is especially apparent when the model is compared to decomposition approaches. In a research sense, however, the attribute generation problem operates at two levels: *initial specification* of attributes in data gathering and *inclusion* of attributes in the model, which can reflect either direct use of raw data or the results of reworking the raw data in some manner.

A. Initial specification. Research decisions on attribute specification to respondents effectively bound subsequent model analyses in terms of maximum structure dimensionality. Basic criteria for specification of attribute lists require that they be exhaustive, semantically meaningful, subject to unidimensional interpretation, and reflect possible variations in choice or use contexts (M25), [25, 50]. Methods for attribute generation include expert judgment and unstructured group or depth interviews in combination with procedures such as Kelly's repertory grid [57].

Few marketing articles discuss desired characteristics of attributes. Sheth (M4), [61], Hansen (M5), [28], and Pessemier (M17, M25), [49, 50] agree that attributes must reflect consumer perceptual dimensions rather than product characteristics directly measurable and controllable by the marketing manager. In contrast, Heeler et al. (M38), [30] utilize objective product characteristics in a study of new product selections by supermarkets.

As evidenced in row IA of the figure, most marketing studies have used informal interviews to generate attribute lists; no utilization of repertory techniques is reported. All instruments presented a common attribute list to all respondents; the number of attributes presented is shown as the first entry in each cell of row IC. In general, marketing studies have initially specified few attributes and thus generated restricted ranges of data available for model analyses.

B. Attribute inclusion. As shown by single cell entries in row IC, most marketing studies have directly entered all attributes from the measuring instrument into the model. A number of studies have, however, showed effects of utilizing subsets of original attribute lists for inclusion; subset size is reported as the second cell entry in the row. These studies have concerned three basic issues: attribute independence, "salience versus importance" of attributes, and the minimum number of attributes descriptive of attitudinal structures.

1. *Independence assumptions* are desired in the basic model in order to avoid double-counting biases in score summation and confounded interpretations of dimensionality. The original proposals of Rosenberg [55] and Fishbein [21] fail to discuss independence; row IB3 reflects the extent to which the issue is neglected in most marketing studies. Researchers comparing the composition model with multidimensional scaling approaches do raise the issue in providing 3-space or less MDS solutions (M9, M15, M21), [29, 68, 72]. Prior factor analyses reducing attribute lists to three attributes for model inclusion are reported by Hughes and Guerrero (M19), [35] and Lutz (M35), [42]; a factor analytic-type procedure reducing seven attributes to two and one dimensions is presented by Sheth (M4, M7), [61, 62]. Moinpour and Wiley (M36), [46] select three attributes by brand from factor analysis and demonstrate approximately equal model performance compared with use of a ten-attribute list. Pessemier (M17, M25), [49, 50] presents strong arguments for independence requirements in suggesting that prior MDS analysis as well as factor analysis may be appropriate.

2. The *salience versus importance* issue concerns the performance of measured importance ratings in reflecting salient attributes—those which are actually utilized by consumers in evaluating alternative choice objects. All researchers agree that only salient attributes should be included in the model; most then proceed with the assumption that their original list is sufficiently and exhaustively "salient" for all respondents. Operational definitions of salience are rarely undertaken.

This issue is noted by Day [18], who presents five reasons why importance ratings may not represent salience. Sampson and Harris (M6), [58] and Wilkie and Weinreich (M33), [76] report empirical model results supportive of this contention.

$$A_{jk} = \sum_{i=1}^{n} I_{ik} B_{ijk}$$

ISSUES: MATRIX NUMBER	Tigert (1/66) 1	Myers & Alpert (10/68) 2	Bass & Talarzyk (7/69) 3	Sheth (8/69) 4	Hansen (11/69) 5	Sampson & Harris (3/70) 6	Sheth (4/70) 7
I. Attributes (i)							
A. Initial Specification[a]	INT	INT	INT	INT	?	INT	INT
B. Characteristics:		*			*	*	
1. Controllable by Marketer					NO		
2. Common to All Respondents	YES	YES	YES	YES	**	YES	YES
3. Independence				YES			YES
C. Number (n)[b]	11/6		5	7/2	v/3	14	7/1
D. Salience vs. Importance		*				**	
II. Importance Weight (I_ik)				N/A			N/A
A. Stability					NO		
B. Measurement:							
1. Product or Brand Specific	P	P	P		P	P	
2. Instrument	**		RNK		−,+	−,+	
C. Normalization			YES		NO	NO	
III. Beliefs (B_ijk)	N/A						
A. Measurement:							
1. Scale			1-6	1-7	V	**	1-7
2. Ideal Point Used			NO	NO	NO	NO	NO
3. Pre- or Post-I_ik			POST	N/A	V	**	N/A
4. Within i or j			i	i	?	N/A	i
B. Halo Effects Found							
IV. Model Structure	N/A	N/A					
A. Summation (Σ)			YES	NO	YES	YES	NO
B. Use of I_ik			YES	NO	**	YES	NO
C. Minkowski Metric			NO	NO	NO	NO	NO
V. Model Testing	N/A	N/A	**	**	**	**	**
A. Prediction of Behavior[c]			NO	ACT	SIM	NO	ACT
B. Prediction of Preference[d]			PREF	ATT	NO	ATT	ATT
C. Diagnosis of Structure			NO	*	NO	NO	*
D. Comparison With MDS			NO	NO	NO	NO	NO
E. Analysis Model:							
1. Within Indiv. or Cross section			IND	CS	IND	CS	CS
2. Primary Test[e]			CM	REG	H/M	CORR	REG
F. Summary Conclusion[f]			+	+	+	+	+

[a] INT = Group interviews.
[b] Number used in instrument /Minimum number found useful.
[c] ACT = Actual choice; SIM = Simulated choice; RPT = Self report of behavior.
[d] PREF = Preference; ATT = Undimensional attitude or affect.
[e] CM = Confusion matrix; REG = Multiple regression; H/M = Hit-Miss; CORR = Pearson r; r_s = Spearman rho; MDA = Discriminant analysis;

Hughes (12/70)c	Talarzyk & Moinpour (12/70)	Cohen & Houston (1/71)	Lehmann (2/71)	Bass, Pessemier, & Lehmann (4/71)	Alpert (5/71)	Bass & Talarzyk (5/71)	Weinreich (5/71)	Sheth & Talarzyk (6/71)	Pessemier (7/71)	Schendel, Wilkie, & McCann (8/71)	Hughes & Guerrero (8/71)	Cohen & Ahtola (8/71)	Hansen & Bolland (8/71)
8	9	10	11	12	13	14	15	16	17	18	19	20	21
INT	INT	INT	INT	INT	INT	INT	?	INT	N/A	INT	?	INT	?
					*					*			
										NO			
YES	YES	YES	YES	YES	YES	YES	YES	YES	YES	YES	YES	YES	YES
YES	MDS						MDS			*			MDS
3	9	5	6	7	37/6	5	7	5	N/A	20/11	12/3	5	9/3
					**					*	**		
										N/A			
											NO		
P	P	P	P	P	P	P	P	P		P	P	P	P
**	1-6	1-9	**	1-6	1-5	RNK	1-10	1-6		**	V	1-9	1-10
V	NO	NO	NO	NO	NO	YES	NO	NO		V	V	NO	NO
										N/A			
**	1-6	1-9	1-6	1-6	1-7	1-6	1-7	1-6	*		V	1-9	1-10
NO	MDS	NO	**	**	NO	NO	MDS	NO	YES		NO	NO	NO
POST	PRE	?	?	POST	POST	POST	PRE	POST	POST		POST	?	POST
?	?	i	i	i	i	i	i	i	i		i	i	i
		YES	YES			YES					YES		
					N/A				N/A	N/A			
YES	YES	**	YES	YES	NO		YES	YES			V	**	YES
*	YES	**	**	**	**		YES	**			**	**	**
NO	MDS	NO	**	**	NO		MDS	NO			NO	NO	MDS
N/A	**	**	**	**	N/A	N/A	**	**	N/A	N/A	**	**	**
	NO	RPT	RPT	ACT			NO	NO			RPT	RPT	RPT
	PREF	NO	PREF	PREF			PREF	PREF			NO	NO	PREF
	*	*	NO	NO			NO	NO			*	*	*
	**	NO	NO	NO			**	NO			NO	NO	**
	IND	CS	IND	IND			IND	CS			CS	CS	IND
	r_s	REG	r_s	r_s			r_s	REG			REG	MDA	H/M
	+	+	+	+			−	−			+	+	+

CC = Canonical correlation.
f += Basic model supported; − = Basic model
questioned.
* = Issue discussion
= Issue tested.

N/A = Issue not applicable to article.
? = Information not in article.
V = Varies (usually >1 study in article).
MDS = Issue specific to multidimensional scaling.

$$A_{jk} = \sum_{i=1}^{n} I_{ik} B_{ijk}$$

ISSUES: MATRIX NUMBER	Scott & Bennett (9/71) 22	Moinpour & MacLachlan (9/71) 23	Lutz & Howard (9/71) 24	Pessemier (1/72) 25	Ginter (1/72) 26	Winter (1/72) 27	Bass & Talarzyk (2/72) 28
I. Attributes (i)							
A. Initial Specification[a]	?	INT	INT	N/A	INT	INT	INT
B. Characteristics:				*			
1. Controllable by Marketer				NO			
2. Common to All Respondents	**	YES	YES	YES	YES	YES	YES
3. Independence				*			
C. Number (n)[b]	21/5	9	12/3	*	5	6	5
D. Salience vs. Importance				*			
II. Importance Weight (I_ik)				N/A			
A. Stability							
B. Measurement:							
1. Product or Brand Specific	P	P	P		P	P	P
2. Instrument	1-7	1-6	1-3		1-6	1-6	RNK
C. Normalization	NO	NO	NO		**	**	YES
III. Beliefs (B_ijk)							
A. Measurement:							
1. Scale	1-7	1-6	1-7	−, +	1-6	1-6	1-6
2. Ideal Point Used	NO	NO	NO	*	**	**	NO
3. Pre- or Post-I_ik	PRE	PRE	POST	POST	POST	POST	POST
4. Within i or j	?	i	i	i	i	i	i
B. Halo Effects Found							
IV. Model Structure				N/A			
A. Summation (Σ)	NO	YES	NO		YES	YES	YES
B. Use of I_ik	**	**	**		**	**	**
C. Minkowski Metric	NO	NO	NO	*	**	**	NO
V. Model Testing	**	**	**	N/A	**	**	**
A. Prediction of Behavior[c]	NO	NO	ACT		ACT	ACT	NO
B. Prediction of Preference[d]	ATT	PREF	V		PREF	PREF	PREF
C. Diagnosis of Structure	*	NO	*		NO	NO	NO
D. Comparison With MDS	NO	NO	NO		NO	NO	NO
E. Analysis Model:							
1. Within Indiv. or Cross section	CS	BOTH	CS		IND	IND	BOTH
2. Primary Test[e]	REG	V	CC		REG	REG	V
F. Summary Conclusion[f]	+	−	−		+	+	+

[a] INT ▬ Group interviews.
[b] Number used in instrument /Minimum number found useful.
[c] ACT ▬ Actual choice; SIM ▬ Simulated choice; RPT ▬ Self report of behavior.

[d] PREF ▬ Preference; ATT ▬ Undimensional attitude or affect.
[e] CM ▬ Confusion matrix; REG ▬ Multiple regression; H/M ▬ Hit-Miss; CORR ▬ Pearson r; r_s ▬ Spearman rho; MDA ▬ Discriminant analysis;

Cohen & Houston (2/72) 29	Sheth & Talarzyk (2/72) 30	Wilkie & McCann (3/72) 31	Russ (4/72) 32	Wilkie & Weinreich (6/72) 33	Moinpour & Wiley (8/72) 34	Lutz (11/72) 35	Moinpour & Wiley (11/72) 36	Churchill (11/72) 37	Heeler, Kearney, & Mehaffey (2/73) 38	Wright (3/73) 39	Beckwith & Lehmann (5/73) 40	Bass & Wilkie (8/73) 41	Kraft, Granbois, & Summers (8/73) 42
INT	INT	INT	?	?	INT	INT	?	?	*	INT	INT	INT	INT
									YES				
YES	YES	YES	N/A	**	**	YES	YES	**	YES	YES	YES	YES	YES
5	5	6	4	**	**	13	10/3	**	13/4	5	6	5	4
				**									
									N/A	N/A			
P	P	P	P	P	P	P	P	P			P	P	P
1-9	1-6	1-5	?	1-10	1-6	**	1-6	1-4			V	1-6	1-5
NO	NO	NO	?	NO	NO	NO	NO	NO			NO	**	NO
1-9	1-6	1-7	?	1-7	1-6	1-7	1-6	1-7	*	1-7	1-6	1-6	1-5
NO	NO	NO	NO	NO	NO	NO	NO	NO	NO	NO	YES	NO	NO
?	POST	POST	?	PRE	PRE	?	?	POST	N/A	N/A	?	POST	?
i	i	**	?	i	i	N/A	?	N/A	N/A	N/A	i	i	?
YES		**					*				YES		
N/A													
	YES	YES	YES	YES	YES	V	NO	YES	NO	NO	V	V	YES
	**	**	?	**	**	V	NO	**	*	*	**	**	YES
	NO	NO	NO	NO	NO	NO	NO	NO	NO	NO	**	NO	NO
N/A	**	**	**	**	**	**	**	**	**	**	**	**	**
	NO	NO	SIM	NO	NO	NO	NO	NO	ACT	NO	NO	NO	ACT
	PREF	PREF	PREF	PREF	PREF	ATT	PREF	PREF	NO	PREF	PREF	PREF	NO
	NO	NO	N/A	*	NO	*	*	NO	*	*	NO	*	NO
	NO	NO	NO	NO	NO	NO	NO	NO	NO	NO	NO	NO	NO
	CS	IND	IND	IND	IND	CS	CS	CS	CS	IND	IND	**	BOTH
	REG	r_s	H/M	r_s	r_s	V	REG	CORR	REG	REG	V	V	H/M
	−	+	−	−	−	+	−	−	+	−	−	−	−

CC = Canonical correlation.
† + = Basic model supported; − = Basic model questioned.
* = Issue discussion.
** = Issue tested.

N/A = Issue not applicable to article.
? = Information not in article.
V = Varies (usually >1 study in article).
MDS = Issue specific to multidimensional scaling.

The latter study compared stated importance weights with other criteria for successively entering attributes to the model and found importance to perform relatively poorly. Sampson and Harris tested the rank order of 14 attributes' actual correlations with affect against stated importance ranks and report a Spearman rho correlation of −.06. This evidence is sufficient to call closer attention to the loose conceptualization of "salience" and its representation by importance ratings.

3. The question of *number of attributes* to be included in the model is significant in terms of parsimony, diagnosis of attitudinal structure, predictive efficiency, and perhaps for assessment of saliency. Analysis of this issue has been conducted both cross-sectionally and within individuals. Disaggregated (i.e., models in which attribute ratings are not summed) multiple regressions have been most utilized (M4, M13, M21, M22, M38, M41), [1, 8, 29, 30, 60, 61] with analysis usually made for each brand separately using cross-sectional inputs. The number of attributes with significant coefficients is sought and considerable shrinkage is typically experienced with this approach. Results range from only 2 significant attributes of 9 original (M21), [29] to 8 of 37 (M13), [1]. As demonstrated by Bass and Wilkie (M41), [8], however, cross-sectional methods are highly susceptible to data assumptions; the number of significant variables in this study moved from 3 to all 5 of 5 with only minor analytical improvements.

Within-individual analysis is a preferable approach to this issue (M23, M40, M41), [8, 9, 44], as are provisions for allowing individuals to differ in the number and nature of attributes included. Four articles offer varying methodologies and results. Evidence on the former point is provided by Scott and Bennett (M22), [60]. Regression estimates for two hypothesized industrial segments are shown to differ significantly; estimates for the total sample do *not* adequately express key attributes for one of the two segments. With respect to the latter, Hansen (M5), [28] demonstrates that including only the 3 most important attributes to each respondent in the model yields predictions as strong as those with all 24 values. Wilkie and Weinreich (M33), [76] reinforce this notion in reporting that individual differences clearly exist in the number of attributes needed to maximize preference prediction of the model; many respondents peaked at only 1 or 2 attributes entered by a "determinism" (M2), [48] criterion, while others required all 7. On average, 3.6 of 7 attributes were utilized and inclusion of all 7—as in typical model tests—yielded *lower* predictability. Moinpour and Wiley, in contrast, (M34), [45] report weaker predictions using only "important" attributes than those resulting from inclusion of all attributes.

C. Discussion—attributes (i).   Hughes [34] has noted that attribute specification is the weakest part of composition models. The brief summary of issues above demonstrates that this area is underconceptualized. Wright [80] has pointed out that it is not yet clear whether attributes are understood to be dimensions or specific point estimates. It is not likely that answers are available from other disciplines; psychologists are in similar disagreement.

There does seem to be agreement that attributes are perceptual rather than objective product constructs, that reasonable candidate lists can be generated by combining unstructured interviews with techniques such as the repertory grid, and that structured lists can be presented to respondents. A systematic approach to identification and presentation of attributes which accounts for use contexts has been developed by Pessemier (M25), [50]. Independence should be tested before attributes are included to the model, and it is reasonable to expect that only few attributes will dominate a model's predictive/explanatory power.

Complex problems remain, however, in the sense that hard theory on attributes in the consumer context is incomplete. Empirical potential is limited because of a necessity of trading off theoretical gains (e.g., allowing for individual differences through removal of structure in measuring instruments and/or allowing differing number and types of attribute inclusion in the model) against practical losses (e.g., difficulties in coding and assembling data and/or summarizing results). In addition, all results and conclusions with the model are interdependent. Empirical study of issues such as "salience" or number of attributes are forced to rely upon predictive tests which assume control of all other issues of the model. As these other issues are discussed it should become apparent that theoretical development is preferable.

II. Importance (I_{ik})

Importance weights—also termed "value importance," "evaluative aspect," or "saliencies"—provide for individual respondent differences in stress placed on various attributes. As measures of an attribute's contribution to satisfaction, these measures can be useful in market segmentation research [73, 74]. Four model issues related to importance weights are summarized in this section: conceptualization, generality, measurement, and normalization. The question of whether or not importance weights should be included in the basic model is discussed in detail under "model structure" issues.

A. Conceptualization.   In contrast to the lack of theoretical concepts for attributes, several thoughtful articles have provided insights on alternative views of the importance variable. Cohen, Fishbein, and Ahtola [12] and, in a more recent article, Cohen [10] clarify distinctions between the "V" (value) term of a proposed "expectancy-value" model and the importance term of the basic model used in most marketing studies. The essential point appears to be that "importance" can be an ambiguous term which might reflect either prominence *or* value. Misleading results may appear if, for example, prominence of a dimension is used to indicate measured value on that dimension. Whether this potential difficulty is realized, however, depends significantly on methods of attribute specification and presentation as well as measurements used to gather brand beliefs (expectancies). Although further comments on this issue are deferred to the concluding section of the article, note that only 1 of the 42 empirical marketing studies (M6), [58] has operationalized the "value" concept in any form resembling its description.

B. Generality.   This issue refers to the extent to which measured importance or value weights can be considered invariant. Three aspects of invariance arise: test-retest reliability, differences over use or choice contexts, and the likelihood of true change in reaction to exogenous stimuli. None of the 42 papers report tests of reliability such that no evidence is available on this issue. One study measured changes in I_{ik} associated with the provision of additional stimuli. Hughes and Guerrero (M19), [35] found significant changes at attribute levels but not for the summed score after a balanced set of 27 messages were presented to respondents. Hansen (M5), [28] reports data from three studies which show 10 of 22 I_{ik} to change significantly after presentation of situational choice environment descriptions.

Although little evidence is available on generality issues, it does appear that future research should begin with the recognition that I_{ik} may vary by context and also consider importance weights as an alternative candidate to brand belief for marketing actions designed to change brand attitudes. Krugman [38] posits that this strategy is *more* realistic due to low respondent involvements in typical marketing areas. This approach is also discussed by Howard and Sheth [31] and Cohen and Ahtola (M20), [11].

C. Measurement. Measurements of importance are aimed at providing meaningful variations both within and between respondents. All papers reviewed measured importance weights as applied to an entire product class. As seen in IIB2 of the figure, only two studies utilized scales with positive and negative poles as proposed by both Rosenberg and Fishbein; most obtain I_{ik} on bipolar rating scales which range from 1 to 5, 6, or 7.

Four studies have compared alternative measuring instruments. Tigert (M1), [69] tested importance rankings on 11 attributes of toddler tops obtained via paired comparisons ("which of these two attributes is more important?") against rankings derived from respondents' ordering preferences for envelopes containing product information on each attribute. The two methods yielded substantial agreement (Spearman rho = .82) for aggregate importance rank indicating substantial agreement between instruments. Lehmann (M11), [39] reports very little difference between inclusion of rank orders of I_{ik} versus measures obtained on a 1 to 6 bipolar scale in terms of model performance in predicting television show preference. Hughes (M8), [33] studied a 1 to 7 semantic differential versus a constant sum scale in which the respondent allocated 100 importance points to 3 automobile attributes; his analysis of correlations between the I_{ik} and B_{ijk} as measured by each scale leads to the conclusion that the constant sum is superior to the semantic differential in that it forces tradeoff variations among attributes.

Schendel, Wilkie, and McCann (M18), [59] support this conclusion in a study investigating 5 possible instruments for measuring I_{ik}. A comparison of yes/no, rank order, 1 to 6 rating, and 100-point constant sum scales indicated high agreement in aggregated rank orders of importance for shampoo and deodorant. The coefficients of concordance were .88 and .96, respectively. Although the different measurement properties of the scales hampered comparison, significant differences were found in the number of attributes termed important (yes/no $<$ constant sum $<$ 1 to 6 bipolar). The multiplicative and summative data manipulations of the model call for ratio- or interval-scaled data. Given the difficulty of making constant sum judgments, the researcher may wish to have subjects perform simple warm-up tasks or substitute direct magnitude estimation (M18), [52, 59].

D. Normalization. Once importance weights have been obtained, the important issue becomes how to include them in the model. The normalization issue (figure, IIC) refers to the problem of defining the set of I_{ik} weights which enter the model. Stated in simple concrete terms, can one consumer bring "more" importance to the model than another consumer or are attribute importance weights solely a within-consumer relative weighting of attributes? When different respondents operate at different importance levels, idiosyncratic response biases may be present so the researcher may need to normalize the importance weights. If true differences in product class involvement exist which can be captured by the model, and subject responses to importance weights reflect this property of consumers, then no steps need to be taken. Most model tests in the marketing setting, however, have constrained the dependent variable by comparing several competing brands.

It should be noted that importance weight normalization is *not* an issue common to all research on the model but depends upon I_{ik} instruments and model comparisons undertaken. Constant sum scales provide normalized data, as do importance ranks, whatever the validity of their measurement assumptions. Regardless of importance scale used, normalization is not a problem when *static comparisons* of the model are made at the *individual* level. It need be seriously considered only when comparisons are made *across individuals* as in typical applications of correlational analyses at the attribute or brand level *and* when the rating scale does not provide already normalized data.

Ginter (M26), [23] and Winter (M27), [77] compared normalized and non-normalized model adaptations in longitudinal individual-level regressions and found significantly higher r^2 with normalized data in all four product classes studied. Bass and Wilkie (M41), [8] report substantial increases in r^2 associated with normalization of brand-level, cross-sectional regressions across six product categories. While it is not possible to conclude that r^2 will always increase, it is concluded that normalization is always appropriate and possibly essential when cross-sectional analysis is used.

III. Beliefs (B_{ijk})

Brand beliefs (also termed "expectancy," "perceived instrumentality," or "valence") effect the entry of brand-specific judgments and differences into the model. Three model issues of the belief component are summarized in this section: conceptualization, measurement, and halo effects.

A. Conceptualization. Considerable attention has been paid to the question of what belief measures are and are not intended to represent. There is general agreement that the purpose of this variable is to reflect a respondent's perceptions of the association between a particular attribute and a given brand. Controversy has arisen over the nature of "association" elicited in marketing studies—whether the association should represent pure cognition or combine affective and cognitive aspects. The former view is espoused by Cohen and associates [10, 12] in suggesting that "expectancy" should measure only the probability that a brand is associated with or possesses an attribute. The latter approach, in contrast, can include measures of the amount of attribute possession and/or the degree of satisfaction associated with this amount. "Taste," for example, can presumably be measured in terms of the probability of its relationship with brand x, the categories of relationship (e.g., "brand x is sweet-sour, spicy-bland, etc."), or the satisfaction provided through relationship (e.g. "brand x tastes good-bad").

The question of the nature and measurement of attribute beliefs is significant in terms of its impact on other model issues, particularly when the model is applied in the brand-competitive consumer environment. If it is clear the subject is playing the role of a consumer, judgments will likely be biased by the desired levels of the attribute in some context or mix of contexts. As noted in a following section, the desired or ideal level has been formally recognized in model research. Subjects were asked to judge how a brand deviated from the ideal level or where the ideal lies along the attribute continuum.

The nature of attributes (i) specified is also likely to differ among approaches. Importance weights (I_{ik}) are more likely to improve explanatory power when only cognition is measured in B_{ijk}, while it is yet unclear whether the cognitive method will yield variance in B_{ijk} across individuals or brands for highly similar consumer products. Only 1 of the 42 marketing studies has utilized an expectancy measure of B_{ijk} (M6), [58]; almost all have operationalized the third approach which incorporates satisfaction in the B_{ijk} rating.

B. Measurement. Summary characteristics of belief measurement approaches are given in section IIIA of the figure. Bipolar rating scales have typically been used, ideal points have been infrequently included, beliefs have been measured after importance weights, and brands have been competitively rated within each attribute rather than rating all attributes within brand.

Probabilistic scales, as suggested in "expectancy" proposals, have not typically been utilized in marketing studies. Sampson and Harris (M6), [58] test "true-false" versus "probable-improbable" operationalizations of probabilistic measures and find no significant differences. They note, however, that "true-false" may tend to produce polarity in B_{ijk}, that "probable-improbable" poses comprehension problems for older, less educated consumers, and that Fishbein's proposal of "likely, unlikely" is preferable to either alternative.

Another investigation of belief scales is provided by Hughes (M8), [33] who concludes that a 1 to 7 rating scale confounds I_{ik} and B_{ijk} by allowing or encouraging incorporation of importance into the belief measure such that B_{ijk} is more extreme for more important attributes. Supporting evidence on this point is provided by Beckwith and Lehmann (M40), [9]. Thus the constant-sum scale appears preferable for B_{ijk} measurement as well as for importance weights. However the use of within-attribute normalization or standardization may be an appropriate data reduction strategy.

A third approach to belief measurement is the use of "ideal" points for those attributes defined such that "more" is not necessarily better (e.g., sudsiness, sweetness, price, humor). Ideal points offer the additional advantage of fixing a base for measurement of brand differences, and are widely employed in multidimensional scaling approaches which infer their position. In the present context, ideal levels of each attribute are elicited from respondents, as are perceived brand levels. Deviations are entered to the model as B_{ijk}. Typical use of bipolar rating scales, on the other hand, assumes that "more is better" and effectively calculates distance from the end points of the scale.

Four papers report six tests of the model using stated ideal points versus typical belief measures assuming that more is better. Lehmann (M11), [39] (television show preference), Bass, Pessemier, and Lehmann (M12), [4] (soft drink preference), Ginter (M26), [23] (spray disinfectants and detergents), and Winter (M27), [77] (scouring pads and facial tissues) all found the typical approach to perform slightly better than the use of ideal points. They do *not* conclude, however, that ideal points are not useful; considerable difficulty was experienced with respondent comprehension of ideal point questions and is believed to have led to the disappointing results. Pessemier (M25), [50] discusses these problems and presents an alternative methodology for obtaining belief measures based upon resource constrained, purchase ideal points controlled for use context.

C. Halo effects. This potential problem for the inclusion of B_{ijk} in the model is concerned with the extent to which belief ratings vary across attributes for a given brand. Halo effects have long been recognized in personality and psychological testing as potential suppressors of important variation. The presence of halo effects in the marketing model, while not necessarily affecting predictive tests, will confound investigations as to the dimensionality of attitude structure and impair diagnostic analyses of brand strengths and weaknesses. Since halo effects are presumed to reflect a spread of brand affect across dimensions, B_{ijk} measures incorporating satisfactions are most susceptible.

As shown in row IIIB of the figure, every marketing study investigating this issue has found clear evidence of halo effects in B_{ijk} measures. Lehmann (M11), [39] reports highly significant correlations between attribute beliefs for television shows. Bass, Pessemier, and Lehmann (M12), [4] observe a "slight halo effect" across soft drink attributes. Bass and Talarzyk (M14), [6] report a "completely consistent pattern of more favorable belief ratings given by respondents who prefer a particular brand" in their study of 50 such measurements for toothpaste and mouthwash. Cohen and Ahtola likewise report a "thirty for thirty" pattern on toothpaste brands and attributes from a different data bank (M20), [11]. Most researchers have explained these findings as reflectors of cognitive consistency operators in the brand evaluation process. Cohen and Houston (M29), [14] extend this explanation by positing a "cognitive reevaluation" process for brand-loyal consumers.

The magnitude of observed halo effects might also, however, depend in part upon measuring instruments. Wilkie and McCann (M31), [75] studied this possibiliy by varying the order and instructions in measurement instruments to encourage or discourage halo effects. Because halo is inferred from data, and may be presumed to operate only under conditions of polar affect, a measure of B_{ijk} dispersion is preferable in operationalization. Their results show significant differences in dispersion by instrument, indicating that the researcher can control, to some extent, the variation in B_{ijk} as reported by respondents. Dispersions were *higher* for polar brands, indicating that marketers should pay particular attention to handling of mid-rated brands for which respondents may have less interest and information.

A comparison with typical instruments indicates that B_{ijk} measures can be improved by including warm-up instructions which discourage yea-saying, by rating all brands within attribute, and by reducing opportunities for comparison of responses with prior ratings.

IV. Model Structure

The multiplicative, summative, and implicit linear manipulations of the basic model characterize it as a *linear compensatory* attitude model. Both belief ratings and importance weights are presumed to add explanatory power; belief ratings contribute brand differences while importance weights provide differential stress on attributes. Within attribute each unit is assumed to provide equal marginal utility; brands can achieve given attitude scores by compensating for low ratings on one attribute with high ratings on another.

Model structure issues are seen to be essentially internal or external in nature. Internal issues accept the basic assumptions of composition and compensatory models but question the specific manipulations of multiplication of two components, summation over all attributes, and the linear Minkowski metric. External issues concern the value of the present model as compared to alternative approaches exemplified by conjunctive, disjunctive, lexicographic, or decomposition models. The three internal issues of summation, inclusion of I_{ik}, and alternative Minkowski metrics are discussed prior to consideration of alternative models.

A. Summation.   Row IVA of the figure shows that most studies have utilized the summed score approach suggested in the basic model. Note, however, that summing logarithmic or other transformations of the elements of the model may be appropriate. Some version of "disaggregation" in which attributes retain their separate metrics are possible, and conceptual discussions favoring this latter approach have appeared in several articles. Sheth (M7), [62] makes four major points for disaggregation: (1) summation is not theoretically explained by its advocates, (2) summation of ratings obtained on bipolar scales leads to a compromise (average) value, (3) summation of positive and negative ratings assumes that one cancels out another, and (4) his previous empirical studies regressing affect on beliefs have shown summation to consistently lower predictive power as compared to keeping beliefs separate in multiple regression. Cohen and Houston (M10), [13] agree with Sheth's position and add that the disaggregated approach is especially appealing in terms of diagnosis of bases of consumer attitudes and in analysis of attitude change. Lutz and Howard (M24), [43] concur in pointing out that summation results in considerably less utilization of the very information which had such intuitive appeal for marketers in the first place.

Empirical analyses of disaggregation versus summation are few. Cohen and Ahtola (M20), [11] report higher classification rates in disaggregated multiple discriminant analysis, while Cohen and Houston (M10), [13] and Bass and Wilkie (M41), [8] found little difference in r^2 between summated and disaggregated multiple regressions. Related work by Green, Carmone, and Wind using conjoint measures yielded similar conclusions [27].

The essence of this issue should be recognized to include requirements of analysis. The proponents of disaggregation correctly point out that the identity of individual attributes is preserved such that diagnosis of attitude structure is enhanced. While it is possible to perform disaggregated analysis at the individual level, most disaggregated analyses have utilized cross-sectional techniques. These techniques can be used only at the cost of assuming respondent homogeneity in scale measurement, in attitude dimensionality, and in functional relationships of attitudes to brand preference or choice behavior. It should therefore be noted that cross-sectional disaggregation *gives up* an intrinsically appealing aspect of the basic model—that of a unidimensional measure of affect which is idiosyncratic to the individual.

B. Inclusion of I_{ik}. The question of whether or not importance weights belong in the basic model has received more attention in marketing studies than any other issue. As seen in row IVB of the figure, 25 of the 42 empirical articles explicitly discuss or test this issue.

Two related questions have occurred with respect to contributions from importance weights: whether or not explanatory power is reduced (i.e., "suppression" effects of I_{ik}) and why it is not raised. Empirical evidence and conceptual discussions of these questions are summarized in a recent JMR article by Bass and Wilkie (M41), [8] and therefore are not reviewed here.

The weight of evidence on suppression results indicates that importance weights are not likely to reduce explanatory power of the model (M41), [8]. Neither, however, do they add strikingly to prediction. Measurement explanations for this lack of power center on the variance of I_{ik} weights and their relationship with belief measures. Sheth and Talarzyk (M16, M30), [64, 65] and Hughes (M8), [33] hypothesized that respondents might implicitly incorporate importance into belief ratings; Beckwith and Lehmann (M40), [9] demonstrate that respondents do tend to spread belief ratings more on attributes rated as important. Cohen and Ahtola (M20), [11] point out that I_{ik} often yield high mean values with little variation available for explanatory power. Wilkie and McCann (M31), [75] and Beckwith and Lehmann (M40), [9] discuss the impact of halo effects in belief ratings; highly correlated B_{ijk} would allow little additional explanation by importance weights. Given these positions it appears that the importance or value component should continue to be included in the model. Arguments favoring these measures include some aspects of model theory (M20), [11], selected diagnostic objectives (M41), [8], and the requirements of future studies utilizing cognitive-type beliefs (i.e., expectancy studies which may require importance components). Pessemier, however, favors cognitive/affective attribute data that include judged or implied ideal points and importance weights (if used) that are specific to selected purchase use contexts [54].

C. Minkowski metric. A third internal model structure issue concerns the question of how the model converts belief importance ratings into a resulting attitude score. More specifically, we are concerned with how belief distinctions made between attributes and brands should be represented in appropriate psychological metrics describing affect and/or preference. In economic theory terms we are interested in the behavior of marginal utility as more or less of an attribute is offered.

Since the basic model implicitly assumes a Minkowski metric = 1 (i.e., a linear system), it is useful to rewrite our basic formula to explicate this assumption:

$$A_{jk} = \left[\sum_{i=1}^{n} |I_{ik} B_{ijk}|^r \right]^{1/r},$$

where r = Minkowski metric = 1.

The judgment that $r = 1$ assumes that the marginal utility of an attribute deviation or level remains unchanged across all product classes, attributes, and consumers (before adjusting for idiosyncratic importance weights). This simplifying assumption of the model is not based on strong theoretical arguments nor have alternative formulations been fully developed and tested. The issue remains open to further development and empirical examination. Other metrics or different values of the Minkowski content may be preferred; $r < 1$ will give lower B_{ijk} proportionately greater weights, while $r > 1$ gives higher B_{ijk} proportionately more influence on A_{jk}. Multidimensional joint-space models, for example, require that a distance measure be calculated to represent the proximities of B_{ijk} to the subjects' ideal points. Here, typically $r = 1$ or $r = 2$ (city-block or Euclidean distance) measures are used. The more widely used Euclidean model gives larger deviations proportionately greater weight for A_{jk}. Other distance functions have been suggested by Pessemier which have some appealing theoretical properties (M25), [50].

Returning to the basic model, weights apply typically to beliefs recorded as deviations from the lower end of bipolar scales which assume a "more the better" attribute scale. A clearer instance of the need for deviation weights occurs with use of "ideal" points for attributes whose preferred levels might lie anywhere on the scale (e.g., sudsiness). Does attractiveness decrease linearly as brands move away from the ideal level, or at some faster or slower rate? Exponential and power models reflecting these assumptions are discussed in Einhorn and Gonedes [19], Schönemann and Wang [66], and Pessemier (M25), [50].

Four articles have compared city-block to Euclidean distance for within-individual analyses in studies that used an ideal point formulation of the traditional additive model. Lehmann (M11), [39] found average Spearman rank correlations of .72 versus .68 (for $r = 1$ and $r = 2$ respectively), while Bass, Pessemier, and Lehmann (M12), [4] report averages of .70 against .68 for a beliefs-only version of the model. In both cases other measures of performance also favored $r = 1$, but it is not likely that statistical significance was reached. Separate analysis of variance studies by Ginter (M26), [23] and Winter (M27), [77], however, found $r = 1$ provided significantly better preference predictions.

In the case of the simple model and the more widely used types of attribute measurements, the available evidence supports the implicit city-block distance function. The narrow base of investigations, however, indicates that more researchers should explicitly recognize and investigate this issue.

D. Alternative models. The purpose of Minkowski metrics is to provide for differential *intra-attribute* weights in a manner similar to the inter-attribute stresses provided by importance weights (M39), [79]. Several significant alternative models extend this notion by positing that not all attributes need be considered; that perceptions of a brand's position on an attribute are used as criteria to narrow the dimensionality of choice [18]. *Conjunctive* models reflect extreme stress on the negative end of attribute scales; brands are rated high only if minimum levels on *all* attributes are exceeded. *Disjunctive* models place stress on the positive pole; brands are rated high only when seen as superior on one or more relevant attributes. *Lexicographic* models posit sequential attention to the order of salience of attributes; preference for a brand is established through consideration of only the most salient attribute. Equivalence of two or more brands on this dimension introduces them to the next most salient attribute and so on until the choice is clear.

Several studies have compared these alternatives with the basic (linear compensatory) model. Russ (M32), [56] reports tests of several formulations of the lexicographic model which outperform the basic model in information processing tasks. Heeler, Kearney, and Mehaffey (M38), [30], in contrast, found the compensatory model superior to both conjunctive and disjunctive models in predictions of new product acceptances and rejections by supermarket buyers. Wright (M39), [79] also found the linear model better than either conjunctive or disjunctive forms in tasks "reconstructing" brand belief systems, while nonlinear models performed better for active information processing tasks.

The distinction between models of information processing and models of processed information is an important one, since post-decision cognitive structure might vary from that utilized in active decision making as a function of time pressure (M39), [79], risk variables [22], cognitive consistency operators (M29), [14], and experimental factors. The basic linear compensatory model was developed in social psychology as a static approach for describing an existing attitudinal structure. Most marketing studies have adopted this perspective of the model. The difference in purpose between this model and dynamic utility or decision models suggests that results from the basic model must be carefully evaluated before translations to information processing tasks are made.

V. Model Comparisons

A. Purpose. Model comparison issues involve the manner in which the researcher utilizes data and model structure in order to reach conclusions regarding the multi-attribute attitude model. Four basic questions have been investigated in marketing studies: (1) comparisons of model performance against non-attitudinal predictive models (e.g., chance, market share, demographic predictions), (2) comparisons of the basic model against purely affective measures, (3) comparisons of the model against predictions generated by the alternative methodology of nonmetric multi-dimensional scaling (MDS), and (4) comparisons of model structures within the basic model framework.

Section V of the figure summarizes approaches taken in the testing process. Row VF reports the summary conclusion of each article on the viability of the traditional model on the major question tested in each study. Most articles have studied the model's performance against non-attitudinal predictions and without fail report positive results. There is little question that brand attitudes will predict brand preferences or controlled choice behavior significantly better than chance assignments of preference or choice. All authors implicitly or explicitly express approval of the general nature of the approach; this is *not* an issue in these articles.

The negative signs in row VF of the figure represent arguments that the basic model can be improved through alteration. Three studies test the traditional composition model against MDS (decompositional) predictions; results are mixed, with Talarzyk and Moinpour (M9), [68] finding the traditional model superior, Hansen and Bolland (M21), [29] reporting conflicting results for two product classes, and Weinreich (M15), [72] obtaining better predictions with MDS.

The nature of dependent variables used in analysis is indicated in VA and VB of the figure. An encouraging number of studies have moved toward choice behavior through panel data, laboratory simulated choices, or self-reports of past purchasing behavior. A recent article by Kraft, Granbois, and Summers (M-42), [37], for example, compares the predictive ability of the basic model against several alternative predictors of actual choice behavior. Many studies employed more than one criterion variable and testing approach; in these cases the approach closest to the traditional format is noted.

It is evident that predictive comparisons are advantageous criteria in empirical work with the model. "Diagnosis" of the underlying attitude structure is commonly cited as another advantage of the basic model. Entries in row VC indicate relatively few studies present a diagnosis of structure, and none use this as a central element in appraising results. Not much attention has been devoted to the difficulties which might arise when diagnostic criteria are used to judge the value of a model. A distinct and important connection exists between diagnostic discussions and model structures utilized in the test process.

B. Analysis model. As mentioned earlier in discussion of model structure, proponents of the disaggregate model typically utilize cross-sectional test methodologies. As shown in section VE of the figure, the disaggregative model structure typically leads to multiple regression, multiple discriminant analysis, and canonical correlation models and the associated test statistics.

The original operationalizations of Rosenberg [55] and Anderson and Fishbein [2] also utilized cross-sectional analyses, but in these cases only one attitude object was tested. Most marketing studies, however, obtain data on several (5–8) *competing* brands as attitude objects and therefore need not resort to cross-sectional analysis (M3, M28), [5, 7].

Evidence from several studies points out potential difficulties with cross-sectional assumptions. Scott and Bennett (M22), [60] show significant differences in regression functions for two segments of an industrial sample; assumptions of homogeneity in the entire sample lead to considerably poorer predictions with the disaggregative model. Bass and Wilkie (M41), [8] present a comparison of cross-sectional and within-individual analyses which shows the individual level methodology to provide a much higher rate of correct preference predictions. These results add some support to arguments against the use of cross-sectional analyses in marketing studies. In the absence of natural homogeneity or prior clustering of respondents, three arguments are convincing:

1. The underlying theories of attitude are obviously theories of idiosyncratic cognitions and affects (M23), [44].
2. Interpersonal utility comparisons cannot be given rigorous meaning [3].
3. Marketing strategies derived from cross-sectional results may be misdirected toward an artificial "average" (M39), [79].

It is important to recall, however, that homogenous behavior of subgroups of consumers (market segments) have always been of central concern to marketing scholars and practitioners. Therefore, finding groups that are "homogeneous enough" for cross-sectional analyses may be as important as improving the ways in which individual behavior may be more accurately modeled.

Diagnostic analysis of brand/attribute relationships is possible with individual level techniques. Disaggregated individual level regressions can be run with temporal measures (M26, M27), [23, 77] or when a number of alternative objects are available (M11, M39), [39, 79] to estimate idiosyncratic attribute weights. When fewer brands are under study, sequential attribute introduction techniques as proposed by Wilkie and Weinreich (M33), [76] can yield individual differences in the number and nature of attributes. When differential attribute stresses are suspected for both individuals and brands, clustering followed by multi-staged estimation procedures described by Pessemier (M25), [50] are appropriate. Also, single subject reduced-space configurations based on discriminant methods can yield detailed attribute analyses of brand perceptions and/or preferences at the individual level [51].

A final point on model comparisons concerns theory and hypothesis testing. The multi-attribute attitude model as presently constituted is not a falsifiable theory, hence the theory is not testable. The direction of cumulative research and thought on this model is, however, moving toward the sort of construct specifications characteristic of mature theoretical disciplines.

SUMMARY CONCLUSIONS

This article has presented an analysis of significant issues facing application of an important type of multi-attribute attitude model to the brand competitive marketing environment. The model is directed toward one subset of marketing considerations—providing valid measures of purchase predispositions within the consumer context. Forerunners of marketing applications of this model are found in social psychological studies of attitude, but it is clear that marketing adaptations have significantly departed from the original proposals of Rosenberg [55] and Fishbein [21].

A systematic review of empirical studies and discussions on marketing's use of this model is useful in providing an additional perspective on research issues. This review demonstrates the rapid advance from uncritical model application to a present atmosphere of controversy and cumulative analyses on specific issues. The significance and difficulty of model formulation is apparent. Reactions to published applications of the model have underlined this conclusion and contributed useful new findings.

The position one takes about the potential long-run value of this particular compensatory multi-attribute model heavily depends upon each investigator's beliefs about how the issues covered in this article will be resolved. At least three related areas need further research and development: model conceptualization, component measurement, and testing methodologies.

Criterion for Future Development of Multi-Attribute Choice Theory and Related Models

To evaluate properly the research presented here, a broad view is needed of the purpose for developing multi-attribute models. Since many unidimensional models will efficiently measure affect and/or predict choice behavior, the principal justification for multi-attribute models must be found elsewhere. Kernan has succinctly stated the problem as it relates to much of the multi-attribute research reported in this article: "Affect = f (affect) isn't much of a model" [36].

The unique contributions which multi-attribute theories of preference and choice can make are found in the area of *design*. A model which cannot help analysts and decision-makers improve the characteristics of choice objects and/or their delivery systems is prone to be theoretically vacuous. On the other hand, a model that links the characteristics of choice objects and/or their associated delivery program to manifest preferences increases understanding and the capacity for favorable action. Control is also enhanced if the model encourages the development of natural taxonomies of individuals which admit efficient action. For example, it is much more useful to have homogeneous consumer segments with common model coefficients when these segments also have other common properties which make them accessible to feasible design decisions. Finding a small group of consumers who would prefer a redesigned product may be of little value if the individual members of the group do not share other properties such as media exposure, geographic location, or shopping habits since it may be impractical to efficiently deliver the product.

Therefore, scholars and practitioners should prize models that yield understanding and suggest feasible procedures for favorable control. Several composition models which have not been discussed here may offer more promise than the one which has been discussed. Analysis of variance models, especially conjoint measurement models that develop part worth functions by using monotone methods such as Kruskal's MONANOVA Algorithm, may prove to be highly useful approaches [16, 20, 26, 27]. The Discriminant/PREFMAP procedures discussed by Pessemier [24, 40, 53] and the hierarchical threshold model proposed by Montgomery and others also appear promising [47, 71]. These models yield richer functional and/or spatial representations of multi-attribute judgments. They also lend themselves naturally to applied design and segmentation studies. Whether these or other directions, e.g., [34, 78], being actively explored by other investigators will prove to be theoretically satisfying and fully effective in applied work must await considerable additional model development and testing.

NOTES

[1] A number of similar studies conducted in England are not reviewed in this article, see Tuck [70].

[2] The designation (M42) refers to the matrix number in the figure.

REFERENCES

1. Alpert, Mark I. "Identification of Determinant Attributes: A Comparison of Methods," *Journal of Marketing Research,* 8 (May 1971), 184–91.

2. Anderson, Lynn R. and Martin Fishbein. "Prediction of Attitude from the Number, Strength, and Evaluative Aspect of Beliefs about the Attitude Object: A Comparison of Summation and Congruity Theories," in M. Fishbein, ed., *Readings in Attitude Theory and Measurement.* New York: Wiley, 1967, 437–43.

3. Bass, Frank M. "Fishbein and Brand Preference: A Reply," *Journal of Marketing Research,* 9 (November 1972), 461.

4. ———, Edgar A. Pessemier, and Donald R. Lehmann. "An Experimental Study of Relationships Between Attitudes, Brand Preference, and Choice," *Behavioral Science,* 17 (November 1972), 532–41.

5. Bass, Frank M. and W. Wayne Talarzyk. "A Study of Attitude Theory and Brand Preference," Institute Paper No. 252, Institute for Research in the Behavioral, Economic and Management Sciences, Krannert Graduate School of Industrial Administration, Purdue University, 1969.

6. ———. "Using Attitude to Predict Individual Brand Preference," *Occasional Papers in Advertising,* 4 (May 1971), 63–72.

7. ———. "An Attitude Model for the Study of Brand Preference," *Journal of Marketing Research,* 9 (February 1972), 93–6.

8. Bass, Frank M. and William L. Wilkie. "A Comparative Analysis of Attitudinal Predictions of Brand Preference," *Journal of Marketing Research,* 10 (August 1973), 262–9.

9. Beckwith, Neil E. and Donald R. Lehmann. "The Importance of Differential Weights in Multiple Attribute Models of Consumer Attitude," *Journal of Marketing Research,* 10 (May 1973), 141–5.

10. Cohen, Joel B. "Toward an Integrated Use of Expectancy-Value Attitude Models," paper presented at the ACR/AMA Workshop on Buyer/Consumer Information Processing, Chicago, 1972.

11. ——— and Olli T. Ahtola. "An Expectancy X Value Analysis of the Relationship Between Consumer Attitudes and Behavior," *Proceedings.* Second Annual Conference, Association for Consumer Research, 1971, 344–64.

12. Cohen, Joel B., Martin Fishbein, and Olli T. Ahtola. "The Nature and Uses of Expectancy-Value Models in Consumer Attitude Research," *Journal of Marketing Research,* 9 (November 1972), 456–60.

13. Cohen, Joel B. and Michael Houston. "The Structure of Consumer Attitudes: The Use of Attribute Possession and Importance Scores," Faculty Working Paper No. 2, College of Commerce and Business Administration, University of Illinois, 1971.

14. ———. "Cognitive Consequences of Brand Loyalty," *Journal of Marketing Research,* 9 (February 1972), 97–9.

15. Churchill, Gilbert A. "Linear Attitude Models: A Study of Predictive Ability," *Journal of Marketing Research,* 9 (November 1972), 423–6.

16. Davidson, J. D. "Forecasting Demand for a New Mode of Transportation," *Proceedings.* Third Annual Conference, Association for Consumer Research, Chicago, 1972, 294–303.

17. Day, George S. "Theories of Attitude Structure and Change," in S. Ward and T. Robertson, eds., *Consumer Behavior: Theoretical Sources.* Englewood Cliffs, N.J.: Prentice-Hall, 1973.

18. ———. "Evaluating Models of Attitude Structure," *Journal of Marketing Research,* 9 (August 1972), 279–86.

19. Einhorn, Hillel J. and Nicholas Gonedes. "An Exponential Discrepancy Model for Attitude Evaluation," *Behavioral Science*, 16 (March 1971), 152–7.

20. Fiedler, John A. "Condominium Design and Pricing: A Case Study in Consumer Trade-off Analysis," *Proceedings*. Third Annual Conference, Association for Consumer Research, Chicago, 1972, 279–93.

21. Fishbein, Martin. "A Behavior Theory Approach to the Relations between Beliefs about an Object and the Attitude toward the Object," in M. Fishbein, ed., *Readings in Attitude Theory and Measurement*. New York: Wiley, 1967, 389–99.

22. Fischer, Gregory W. "Four Methods for Assessing Multi-Attribute Utilities: An Experimental Validation," technical report, Engineering Psychology Laboratory, University of Michigan, 1972.

23. Ginter, James L. "Attitude Change and Choice Behavior in New Product Introduction," unpublished doctoral dissertation, Purdue University, 1972.

24. ———— and Edgar A. Pessemier. "Profiles of Market Segments and Product Competitive Structures," Institute Paper No. 409, Institute for Research in the Behavioral, Economic and Management Sciences, Krannert Graduate School of Industrial Administration, Purdue University, 1973.

25. Green, Paul E. and Yoram Wind. "Recent Approaches to the Modeling of Individuals' Subjective Evaluations," paper presented at the Attitude Research Conference, American Marketing Association, Madrid, 1972.

26. ———— and Arun K. Jain. "Consumer Menu Preference: An Application of Additive Conjoint Measurement," *Proceedings*. Third Annual Conference, Association for Consumer Research, Chicago, 1972, 304–15.

27. Green, Paul E., Frank J. Carmone, and Yoram Wind. "Subjective Evaluation Models and Conjoint Measurement," *Behavioral Science*, 17 (May 1972), 288–99.

28. Hansen, Flemming. "Consumer Choice Behavior: An Experimental Approach," *Journal of Marketing Research*, 6 (November 1969), 436–43.

29. ———— and Thomas Bolland. "Relationship Between Cognitive Models of Choice and Non-Metric Multi-dimensional Scaling," *Proceedings*. Second Annual Conference, Association for Consumer Research, 1971, 376–88.

30. Heeler, Roger M., Michael J. Kearney, and Bruce J. Mehaffey. "Modeling Supermarket Product Selection," *Journal of Marketing Research*, 10 (February 1973), 34–7.

31. Howard, John A. and Jagdish N. Sheth. *The Theory of Buyer Behavior*. New York: Wiley, 1969.

32. Hughes, G. David. *Attitude Measurement for Marketing Strategies*. Glenview, Ill.: Scott-Foresman, 1971.

33. ————. "Distinguishing Salience and Valence," paper presented at the Attitude Research Worshop, University of Illinois, 1970.

34. ————. "Trends in the Development of Multi-Attribute Models," paper presented at the ACR/AMA Workshop on Buyer/Consumer Information Processing, Chicago, 1972.

35. ———— and Jose L. Guerrero. "Testing Cognitive Models Through Computer-Controlled Experiments," *Journal of Marketing Research*, 8 (August 1971), 291–7.

36. Kernan, Jerome B. "Comments on the Role of Summated Attribute Models in the Central Processing of Information," paper presented at the ACR/AMA Workshop on Buyer/Consumer Information Processing, Chicago, 1972.

37. Kraft, Frederic B., Donald H. Granbois, and John O. Summers. "Brand Evaluation and Brand Choice: A Longitudinal Study," *Journal of Marketing Research*, 10 (August 1973), 235–41.

38. Krugman, Herbert F. "The Impact of Television Advertising: Learning Without Involvement," *Public Opinion Quarterly*, 29 (Fall 1965), 349–56.

39. Lehmann, Donald R. "Television Show Preference: Application of a Choice Model," *Journal of Marketing Research*, 8 (February 1971), 47–55.

40. ———— and Edgar A. Pessemier. "Market Structure Modeling Via Clustering and Discriminant Analysis," Institute Paper No. 407, Institute for Research in the Behavioral, Economic and Management Sciences, Krannert Graduate School of Industrial Administration, Purdue University, 1973.

41. Lunn, J. A. "Perspectives in Attitude Research: Methods and Applications," *Journal of the Market Research Society*, 11 (July 1969), 201–13.

42. Lutz, Richard J. "Investigating the Feasibility of Personalized Rapid Transit: An Experimental Approach," *Proceedings*. Third Annual Conference, Association for Consumer Research, Chicago, 1972, 800–6.

43. ———— and John A. Howard. "Toward a Comprehensive View of the Attitude-Behavior Relationship: The Use of Multiple-Set Canonical Analysis," *Proceedings*. Social Statistics Section, American Statistical Association, 1971, 215–24.

44. Moinpour, Reza and Douglas L. MacLachlan. "The Relations Among Attribute and Importance Components of Rosenberg-Fishbein Type Attitude Models: An Empirical Investigation," *Proceedings*. Second Annual Conference, Association for Consumer Re-Research, 1971, 365–75.

45. Moinpour, Reza and James B. Wiley. "An Empirical Investigation of Expectancy-Like Models in Marketing," paper presented at the Fall Conference, American Marketing Association, 1972.

46. ————. "An Approach to the Resolution of Multicollinearity in the Attribute Structure of Attitudes," *Proceedings*. Third Annual Conference, Association for Consumer Research, Chicago, 1972, 341–8.

47. Montgomery, David B. "New Product Distribution: An Analysis of Supermarket Buyer Decisions," Marketing Science Institute Research Program, Cambridge, Mass., 1973, 63.

48. Myers, James H. and Mark I. Alpert. "Determinant Buying Attitudes: Meaning and Measurement," *Journal of Marketing*, 32 (October 1968), 13–20.

49. Pessemier, Edgar A. "Measuring Stimulus Attributes to Predict Individual Preference and Choice," Institute Paper No. 318, Institute for Research in the Behavioral, Economic and Management Sciences, Krannert Graduate School of Industrial Administration, Purdue University, 1972.

50. ————. "Multi-Attribute Models for Predicting Individual Preference and Choice," Institute Paper No. 346, Institute for Research in the Behavioral, Economic and Management Sciences, Krannert Graduate School of Industrial Administration, Purdue University, 1972.

51. ————. "Single Subject Discriminant Configurations," Institute Paper No. 406, Institute for Research in the Behavioral, Economic and Management Sciences, Krannert Graduate School of Industrial Administration, Purdue University, 1973.

52. ———— and Norman R. Baker. "Project and Program Decisions in Research and Development," *R & D Management*, 2 (October 1971), 3–14.

53. Pessemier, Edgar A. and Paul H. Root. "The Dimensions of New Product Planning," *Journal of Marketing*, 37 (January 1973), 10–8.

54. Pessemier, Edgar A. and William L. Wilkie. "Multi-Attribute Choice Theory—A Review and Analysis," paper presented at the ACR/AMA Workshop on Buyer/Consumer Information Processing, Chicago, 1972.

55. Rosenberg, Milton J. "Cognitive Structure and Attitudinal Affect," *Journal of Abnormal and Social Psychology*, 53 (November 1956), 367–72.

56. Russ, Frederick A. "Evaluation Process Models: Objective and Subjective Comparisons," paper presented to the Nineteenth International Meetings, The Institute of Management Sciences, 1972.

57. Sampson, Peter. "Using the Repertory Grid Test," *Journal of Marketing Research*, 9 (February 1972), 78–81.

58. ———— and Paul Harris. "A User's Guide to Fishbein," *Journal of the Market Research Society*, 12 (July 1970), 145–66.

59. Schendel, Dan E., William L. Wilkie, and John M. McCann. "An Experimental Investigation of Attribute Importance," *Proceedings*. Second Annual Conference, Association for Consumer Research, 1971, 404–16.

60. Scott, Jerome E. and Peter D. Bennett. "Cognitive Models of Attitude Structure: Value Importance *is* Important," *Proceedings*. Fall Conference, American Marketing Association, 1971, 346–50.

61. Sheth, Jagdish N. "Attitude as a Function of Evaluative Beliefs," paper presented at the AMA Conference Workshop, Columbus, 1969.

62. ————. "An Investigation of Relationships Among Evaluative Beliefs, Affect, Behavioral Intention and Behavior," working paper, College of Commerce and Business Administration, University of Illinois, 1970.

63. ———. "Reply to Comments on the Nature and Uses of Expectancy-Value Models in Consumer Attitude Research," *Journal of Marketing Research,* 9 (November 1972), 462–5.

64. ——— and W. Wayne Talarzyk. "Relative Contribution of Perceived Instrumentality and Value Importance Components in Determining Attitudes," Faculty Working Paper No. 15, College of Commerce and Business Administration, University of Illinois, 1971.

65. ———. "Perceived Instrumentality and Value Importance as Determinants of Attitudes," *Journal of Marketing Research,* 9 (February 1972), 6–9.

66. Schönemann, Peter J. and Ming Mei Wang. "An Individual Difference Model for the Multidimensional Analysis of Preference Data," *Psychometrika,* 37 (September 1972), 275–309.

67. Talarzyk, W. Wayne. "A Reply to the Response to Bass, Talarzyk, and Sheth," *Journal of Marketing Research,* 9 (November 1972), 465–7.

68. ——— and Reza Moinpour. "Comparison of an Attitude Model and Coombsian Unfolding Analysis for the Prediction of Individual Brand Preference," paper presented at the Attitude Research Workshop, University of Illinois, 1970.

69. Tigert, Douglas J. "An Investigation of Experimental Techniques to Determine the Relative Importance of Various Product Attributes in the Consumer Decision-Making Process," Institute Paper No. 126, Institute for Research in the Behavioral, Economic and Management Sciences, Krannert Graduate School of Industrial Administration, Purdue University, 1966.

70. Tuck, Mary. "Fishbein Theory and the Bass-Talarzyk Problem," *Journal of Marketing Research,* 10 (August 1973), 345–8.

71. Tversky, Amos. "Elimination by Aspects: A Theory of Choice," *Psychological Review,* 79 (July 1972), 281–99.

72. Weinreich, Rolf P. "Analysis of Store Preference: The Fishbein Formulation versus the Multidimensional Scaling Approach," unpublished honors paper, Cornell University, 1971.

73. Wilkie, William L. "Extension and Tests of Alternative Approaches to Market Segmentation," Institute Paper No. 323, Institute for Research in the Behavioral, Economic and Management Sciences, Krannert Graduate School of Industrial Administration, Purdue University, 1971.

74. ———. "The Product Stream of Market Segmentation: A Research Approach," *Proceedings.* Fall Conference, American Marketing Association, 1971, 317–21.

75. ——— and John M. McCann. "The Halo Effect and Related Issues in Multi-Attribute Models—An Experiment," Institute Paper No. 377, Institute for Research in the Behavioral, Economic and Management Sciences, Krannert Graduate School of Industrial Administration, Purdue University, 1972.

76. Wilkie, William L. and Rolf P. Weinreich. "Effects of the Number and Type of Attributes Included in an Attitude Model: More is *not* Better," *Proceedings.* Third Annual Conference, Association for Consumer Research, 1972, 325–40.

77. Winter, Frederick W. "A Laboratory Experimental Study of the Dynamics of Attitude and Choice Behavior," unpublished doctoral dissertation, Purdue University, 1972.

78. Winters, Lewis C. "A Discussion of Unresolved Issues in Belief-Attitude Models," paper presented at the ACR/AMA Workshop on Buyer/Consumer Information Processing, Chicago, 1972.

79. Wright, Peter L. "Analyzing Consumer Judgment Strategies: Paradigm, Pressures and Priorities," Faculty Working Paper No. 94, University of Illinois, 1973.

80. ———. "A Consumer Vocabulary for Research on Cognitive Structure," Faculty Working Paper No. 93, University of Illinois, 1973.

SOME SUGGESTIONS FOR FURTHER READING

Cohen, J. B. (1974), "Toward an Integrated Use of Expectancy-Value Attitude Models," in G. D. Hughes and M. L. Ray (eds.), *Buyer/Consumer Information Processing,* Chapel Hill: University of North Carolina Press, 331–346.

Fishbein, M. (1967), "Attitude and the Prediction of Behavior," in M. Fishbein (ed.), *Readings in Attitude Theory and Measurement*, New York: Wiley.

—————— and I. Ajzen (1975), *Belief, Attitude, Intention and Behavior*, Reading, MA: Addison-Wesley.

Lutz, R. J. and J. R. Bettman (1977), "Multiattribute Models in Marketing: A Bicentennial Review," in A. Woodside, J. Sheth, and P. Bennett, (eds.), *Consumer and Industrial Buying Behavior*, chapter 10, New York: North-Holland.

Rosenberg, M. J. (1956), "Cognitive Structure and Attitudinal Affect," *Journal of Abnormal and Social Psychology*, Vol. 63, 367–72.

15 / GROUP INFLUENCE IN MARKETING / Foundation for Research on Human Behavior

On the common sense level the (reference group) concept says in effect that man's behavior is influenced in different ways and in varying degrees by other people. Comparing one's own success with that of others is a frequent source of satisfaction or disappointment. Similarly, before making a decision one often considers what such and such a person or such and such a group (whose opinion one has *some* reason to follow) would do in these circumstances, or what they would think of one for making a certain decision rather than another. Put in these ways, of course, reference group influence represents an unanalyzed truism which has long been recognized. The problem to which social scientists have been addressing themselves intensively only for the last two decades, however, concerns the refinement of this common sense notion to the end that it might be applied meaningfully to concrete situations.

The real problems are to determine which kinds of groups are likely to be referred to by which kinds of individuals under which kinds of circumstances in the process of making which decisions, and to measure the extent of this reference group influence. Towards this end empirical researches have been conducted in recent years which have at least made a start in the process of refining the reference group concept.

Reference group theory as it has developed has become broad enough to cover a wide range of social phenomena, both with respect to the relation of the individual to the group and with respect to the type of influence exerted upon the individual by the group in question.

KINDS OF REFERENCE GROUPS

Reference groups against which an individual evaluates his own status and behavior may be of several kinds.

They may be *membership* groups to which a person actually belongs. There can be small face-to-face groups in which actual association is the rule, such as families or organizations, whether business, social, religious, or political. On the

Reprinted from *Group Influence in Marketing and Public Relations* (Ann Arbor: Foundation for Research on Human Behavior, 1956), pp. 1–12.
The Foundation for Research on Human Behavior is a nonprofit organization with headquarters at Ann Arbor, Michigan. The Foundation exists for the purpose of making grants for scientifically worthy and potentially practical research at institutions across the nation. Grants are made in consultation with a Research Advisory Committee drawn largely from contributing companies.

other hand, there can be groups in which actual membership is held but in which personal association is absent. (For example, membership in a political party, none of whose meetings are personally attended.)

Reference groups may be *categories* to which a person automatically belongs by virtue of age, sex, education, marital status and so on. This sort of reference group relationship involves the concept of role. For example, before taking a certain action an individual might consider whether this action would be regarded as appropriate in his role as a man or husband or educated person or older person or a combination of all of these roles. What is involved here is an individual's perception of what society, in general or that part of it with which he has any contact, expects people of his age, or sex, or education or marital status to do under given circumstances.

They may be *anticipatory* rather than actual membership groups. Thus a person who aspires to membership in a group to which he does *not* belong may be more likely to refer to it or compare himself with its standards when making a decision than he is to refer to the standards of the group in which he actually belongs but would like to leave. This involves the concept of upward mobility. When such upward mobility is sought in the social or business world it is ordinarily accompanied by a sensitivity to the attitudes of those in the groups to which one aspires, whether it involves the attitudes of country club members in the eyes of the aspiring non-member or the attitudes of management in the eyes of the ambitious wage earner or junior executive.

There are also negative, *dissociative* reference groups. These constitute the opposite side of the coin from the anticipatory membership groups. Thus an individual sometimes avoids a certain action because it is associated with a group (to which the individual may or may not in fact belong) from which he would like to dissociate himself.

INFLUENCE ON INDIVIDUAL BEHAVIOR

Reference groups influence behavior in two major ways. First, they influence *aspiration levels* and thus play a part in producing satisfaction or frustration. If the other members of one's reference group (for example, the neighbors) are wealthier, more famous, better gardeners, etc., one may be dissatisfied with one's own achievements and may strive to do as well as the other.

Second, reference groups influence *kinds* of behavior. They establish approved patterns of using one's wealth, of wearing one's fame, of designing one's garden. They set tabus too, and may have the power to apply actual sanctions (for example, exclusion from the group). They thus produce *conformity* as well as *contentment* (or discontentment).

These two kinds of influence have, however, a good deal in common. Both imply certain perceptions on the part of the individual, who attributes characteristics to the reference group which it may or may not actually have. Both involve psychological rewards and punishment.

RELATIVE DEPRIVATION—AN EXAMPLE OF
REFERENCE GROUP INFLUENCE

As already indicated, one of the chief problems in the field of reference group theory is to identify which of several groups that might serve as a frame of reference under given circumstances actually invoked by an individual.

This is sometimes difficult to get at directly, as individuals are not always *aware* of which reference groups they are evaluating their behavior against, or may not be anxious to reveal them where they are conscious of such groups.

During World War II the Research Branch of the United States Army was concerned with morale of troops under different circumstances, and the morale often seemed not to reflect objective conditions. Thus, for example, soldiers in the Military Police who had received fewer promotions than their opposite numbers in the Air Force were nevertheless more satisfied with their rank than were the average Air Force men. Many similar phenomena were noted in which the men who were apparently suffering greater hardship on an absolute basis were more satisfied than others apparently suffering less hardship on an absolute basis. In an effort to explain these *apparent* inconsistencies the concept of "relative deprivation" was introduced. It was found that in each case there existed a reference group with which the individual soldier tended to compare his own lot. Only if he felt deprived *relative to this group* did his morale suffer. Two examples should suffice.

Army promotions. The fact that Military Police were often more satisfied with their progress than were the more rapidly promoted Air Force Men was explained as follows: Absolute achieved status evidently was not the key to their feelings but rather the relation of the soldier's status to that of others he regarded as his standard of comparison. Thus the Private First Class in the Military Police may have been more satisfied than the Corporal in the Air Force, because in the Military Police virtually no enlisted man expected to get higher than Private First Class, while in the Air Force soldiers saw sergeants and better all around them.

Negro troops. It was found that the morale of Northern Negroes in southern army camps was higher than that of Northern Negroes in northern camps located in the areas where presumably Negroes in general were accorded better treatment. This apparent incongruity was again explained by identifying the reference group against which the Northern Negro compared himself in each instance. The reference group which turned this apparent inconsistency into a plausible reaction in this case was the Negro civilians whom the soldiers encountered while on pass in neighboring towns. The Negro soldier's pay was the same in the North as it was in the South, but in the North he found Negro civilians making so much money in defense plants that his pay appeared small by comparison. On the other hand, relative to most Negro civilians he saw in southern towns, the Negro soldier had a position of comparative wealth and dignity. Thus the psychological values of Army life to the Negro soldier in the South relative to the Southern Negro civilian greatly exceeded the psychological values of Army life to the Negro soldier in the north relative to the Northern Negro civilian.

THE PRACTICAL VALUE OF THE REFERENCE GROUP CONCEPT IN MARKETING AND PUBLIC RELATIONS

In applying the reference group concept to practical problems in marketing and public relations three basic questions arise:

1. *Reference Group Relevance*—How do you determine whether and to what extent reference group influence is operating in a given situation? The reference group is after all just one of many influences in decision making, varying greatly in prominence from situation to situation.
2. *Reference Group Identification*—How do you identify the particular reference group or groups or individuals who are most relevant in influencing decisions under given circumstances? This is perhaps the most difficult question to answer in many cases, particularly where multiple reference groups are involved.
3. *Reference Group Identification and Effective Communication*—Once having identified the nature of the group influence operating in a given situation, how do you then make use of this knowledge in achieving the most effective *communication* with the groups or individuals?

The payoff is of course in this area, since the answers to the first two questions are of value only to the extent that they can be translated into more pertinent and effective communications, designed to influence purchasing behavior or the attitudes of various publics towards an organization.

Experimental evidence is now available which sheds light on each of these three questions. From this evidence as well as from the general advancement in the methodology of social research in recent years there have emerged some generalizations, very tentative in nature. These can be applied only with the most careful attention to the special circumstances operating in individual instances, and serve more as guides to fruitful ways of examining problems as they arise than as simple answers to problems.

Whether or not reference group influence is likely to come into play in the decisions of individuals depends on many interrelated factors. For descriptive purposes, however, it is convenient to consider some of these factors under two major headings:

1. *Influence determinants which vary primarily according to the individual making the decision,* such as the feeling of security or insecurity with respect to potential reference groups, the perception of the positions of these groups concerning kinds of behavior expected or stands on specific issues, and the extent of knowledge about the matter on which a decision must be made.
2. *Influence determinants which vary primarily according to the matter to be decided,* such as the attributes of the product, in a marketing situation, or the nature of the organization and issue at stake, in a public relations situation.

In marketing, it is rarely practical to utilize information about individual differences (the first class above), because products must be designed and advertised with large groups in mind.[1] In public relations, on the other hand, individual differences may be very important. In this area the *general* attention level with respect to a particular issue is often low. Under these circumstances the relevant public may be largely confined to a few individuals, and in such cases knowledge of the relation between these individuals and potential reference groups would certainly be to the point.

A. INDIVIDUAL DIFFERENCES AND REFERENCE GROUP INFLUENCE

1. The Relation of Security Level and Conformity to Reference Group Influence

A tentative generalization which has emerged in this area and which has been supported by some experimental evidence is this:

Individuals enjoying the greatest amount of security by virtue of their prestige and status within a group will generally conform (both publicly and privately) to the standards of that group, but are also freest to deviate from the group norms on occasions when, to their minds, particular circumstances seem to justify such deviations. On the other hand those with lowest feelings of security and least status in a group are most likely *publicly* to conform to its norms on all occasions even though harboring private opposition and resentment. The latter holds, of course, only if there are penalties associated with loss of membership in the particular group. Conformity then serves the purpose of maintaining membership in that group.

The following experiment conducted under laboratory conditions at Yale University lent support to this hypothesis.[2]

Eighteen groups, each composed of six Yale freshmen, were formed for the experiment. They were motivated to cooperate by being told that they would meet for several sessions to work on certain problems and that the best group would win a prize. To promote group cohesion without sacrificing cooperation, each group was told that it would stop from time to time to evaluate its own members and expel any who were seriously interfering with the progress of the group. It was pointed out, however, that such expulsion was not to be taken lightly, as it would carry a considerable stigma and hence was only to be considered under very serious circumstances. The groups were given several problems on which they were asked to come to some agreement. One of these problems was in the area of juvenile delinquency. Each of the 18 groups was presented with some information about two gangs of juvenile delinquents, and asked to decide which of these gangs most deserved help from a social worker. The information was structured in such a way as to make Gang A appear to be the logical candidate for aid from the social worker. As planned by the researchers, the various units deliberated and came to the jointly-arrived-at decision that Gang A most deserved aid. After these group decisions were made, artificial images were set up in the mind of each individual as to how highly he was regarded by the group to which he belonged. This was accomplished by having the group members rate each other, in writing; however, the experiment leader did not use this information but gave each student fictitious information on how he was regarded by other members of his six-man group. One person in each group was told that he was very highly regarded, two were told that they had been given an average rating, another two that the group's regard for them was quite low, and finally one member of each group was told that he was on the verge of rejection.

After these varying images of esteem by the particular group had been established (designed to set up feelings ranging all the way from very high to very low sense of security) a new item of information about the juvenile gangs was introduced. This item introduced some counter evidence pointing rather clearly in favor of Gang B as being the logical choice for aid.

After the new evidence was introduced, private and public expressions of conformity to the originally announced judgments of the group were obtained from those of very low, average and high prestige (as artificially manipulated for experimental purposes) with the following results:

1. Men with the lowest prestige and security in relation to their group—those who believed they were on the verge of expulsion—were, when queried privately, most willing to deviate from the originally established norm of their group. However, when placed in the position of having to take a public stand these same people were most likely to conform to the originally announced norms of the groups, and least likely to deviate even though their own private inclination on the basis of the facts at hand was to do so.
2. Men with average status and security exhibited considerable conformity, even in their private opinions.
3. Men with highest status and security were found, when queried privately, to be quite willing to differ from the original group decision and felt the greatest freedom to express their non-conformity publicly.

These relationships may be expressed graphically as follows:

Figure 1.   Status determines the consistency between public and private conformity

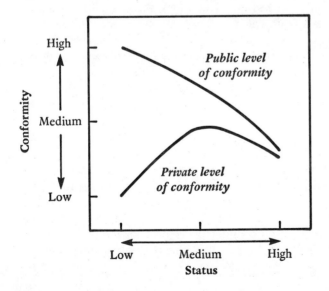

Practical Implications

If a person has high status and feels very secure relative to a group, he can be appealed to directly on the merits of the case and is in the best position to take the lead in deviating should he so desire, with least risk of losing status with the group he prizes. Seeking to influence such people through reference group appeals, when the merits of the case are inconsistent with the appeals, may have little success.

On the other hand, as suggested by the data just reviewed, those with lesser status in their group and less feeling of security are most likely to be influenced in public or visible actions by appeals involving their reference group. They are more likely to observe the norms of the group than others, even if they privately disagree with its specific position, since they require acceptance from the group for their own security. However, if the reference group influence conflicts with their own judgment or works against their own best interests, they are likely to develop an underlying resistance to the idea. Such resistance may find expression in other ways.

A practical example of the operation of this principle in the field of public relations and specifically in the area of influencing legislation may be drawn from experience in Washington. Particularly on issues where mass public attention and interest is low, considerable effort is concentrated on the most crucial of all publics, Congress itself. A Congressman of course has several reference groups, prominent among which are his constituents and the remainder of Congress. Naturally he greatly values the esteem of both of these groups. His very existence in Congress depends on the former and his self-esteem as well as the degree of cooperation he can depend upon getting for his own projects depends upon the high regard of the latter. The Congressman's status and security with regard to his constituents may be measured by such items as the size of his pluralities and the length of his service. Within Congress his status may be measured by, among other things, such items as seniority and cooperation by other members in the past.

Suppose a group was interested in changing a long standing piece of legislation which appeared to have represented the majority views of Congress for a considerable period of time. Suppose also that there was considerable merit in the proposed change, but that the public was relatively little concerned with this legislation. The Congressman's primary reference group with respect to this issue is likely, therefore, to be his colleagues in the House. A freshman Congressman with little security and status would not, even though he privately favored this new legislation, be likely to oppose publicly the prevailing reference group position, by introducing the legislation or placing his name on an initial list of sponsors, while a Congressman with security and status might be more willing to do so.

For those outside of Congress interested in seeing the measure passed, winning the support of so-called bellwethers within Congress for this would be a primary objective. Such Congressmen, by virtue of their secure position in Congress, are most free to deviate and take the lead on occasions, where the case merits it. Though they generally show considerable respect for the norms of their "club" they are also in the best position to ignore this reference group when the right occasion arises.

2. The Individual's Perception of Norms of Potential Reference Group

Perhaps one of the more obvious limitations on the relevance of a potential reference group in influencing a decision is an individual's lack of knowledge or incorrect perception of the group's actual position on an issue, even where he values the group's views or at least its acceptance of him. Thus, for example, the American Legion may be an effective reference group for a substantial number of veterans with respect to veterans' legislation. It may be much less so, however, in connection with views on international affairs. The Legion has a position on such matters, but the average veteran is much less likely to know just what that position is. Along this line, a study[3] conducted for a Church Council found issues on which the Church's national policy was not followed by a considerable portion of the Church's members. The study revealed that these differences between Church policy and the opinions of its individual members were not necessarily conscious nonconformity with group norms, but rather in many cases reflected ignorance of what those norms were.

One practical implication from these studies is that the effective influence of a reference group, even one known to command a substantial following, may be increased by giving special publicity to the position of the group on a specific issue.

3. Independent Knowledge About the Matter to Be Decided

Experimental evidence has indicated that reference group influence is particularly potent in an informational vacuum. Where the individual has little if any knowledge about the attributes of a product or the issues involved in a public relations campaign, reference group influence is maximized. On the other hand, where the individual has personal knowledge and experience, the reference group influence is likely to be *less* relevant, other things being equal. Thus, for example, in the same study of a Church and its parishioners alluded to above, it was found that uninformed parishioners tended to have the same attitudes on secular issues as did their clergymen, but among those parishioners who were politically informed and had other sources of information on these issues there was a tendency more often to ignore the positions taken by their clergymen.

B. DIFFERENT KINDS OF DECISIONS AND REFERENCE GROUP INFLUENCE

1. Marketing and Reference Group Relevance

As has already been suggested, the reference group constitutes just one of the many influences in buying decisions, and this influence varies from product to product. How then does one determine whether reference group influence is likely to be a factor in buying behavior in connection with a given product or brand? Research has been conducted on the various factors that influence buying behavior with reference to several products, and out of this have emerged some general ideas about how reference group influences may enter into purchasing.

Buying may be a completely individualistic kind of activity or it may be very much socially conditioned. Consumers are often influenced by what others buy, especially those persons with whom they compare themselves, or use as reference groups.

The conspicuousness of a product is perhaps the most general attribute bearing on its susceptibility to reference group influence. There are two aspects to conspicuousness in this particular context that help to determine reference group influence. First the article must be conspicuous in the most obvious sense that it can be seen and identified by others. Secondly it must be conspicuous in the sense of standing out and being noticed. In other words, no matter how visible a product is, if virtually everyone owns it, it is not conspicuous in the second sense of the word. This leads to a further distinction: reference groups may influence either (a) the purchase of a product, or (b) the choice of a particular brand of type, or (c) both.

The possible susceptibility of various product and brand buying to reference group influence is suggested in the following figure.

According to this classification a particular item might be susceptible to reference group influence in its purchase in three different ways, corresponding to three of the four cells in the figure below. Reference group influence may operate with

Figure 2. Products and brands of consumer goods may be classified by extent to which reference groups influence their purchase

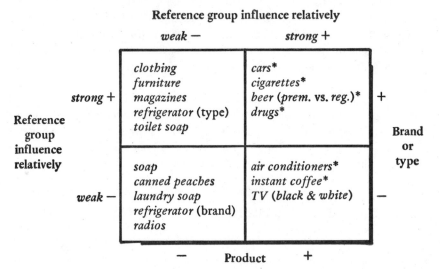

| | Reference group influence relatively | |
	weak −	*strong* +
strong +	*clothing* *furniture* *magazines* *refrigerator* (type) *toilet soap*	*cars** *cigarettes** *beer (prem. vs. reg.)** *drugs**	**+**
weak −	*soap* *canned peaches* *laundry soap* *refrigerator* (brand) *radios*	*air conditioners** *instant coffee** *TV (black & white)*	**−**

Reference group influence relatively (strong +, weak −) · Brand or type (+, −) · − Product +

* The classification of all starred products is based on actual experimental evidence. Other products in this table are classified speculatively on the basis of generalizations derived from the sum of research in this area and confirmed by the judgment of seminar participants.

respect to product alone (Brand + Product −) as in the upper left cell, or it may operate both with respect to brand and product (Brand + Product +) as in the upper right cell, or it may operate with respect to product but not brand (Brand − Product +) as in the lower right cell.

Only the "minus-minus" items of the kind illustrated (Brand − Product −) in the lower left cell are not likely to involve any significant reference group influence in their purchase *at the present time.*

What are some of the characteristics that place an item in a given category, and what significance do such placements have for marketing and advertising policy?

a. "Product plus, brand plus" items.   Autos constitute an article where both the product and the brand are socially conspicuous. Whether or not a person buys a car, and also what particular brand he buys, is likely to be influenced by what others do. This also holds true for cigarettes, for drugs (decisions made by M.D.'s as to what to prescribe) and for beer with respect to type (premium vs. regular) as opposed to brand. Cigarettes and drugs, however, qualify as "plus-plus" items in a manner different from cars.

For example, while the car belongs to a class of products where brand differentiation is based at least substantially on real differences in attributes, the cigarette belongs to a class of product in which it is difficult to differentiate one brand from another by attributes: hence attributes are ascribed largely through reference group appeal built up by advertising. Popular images of the kinds of people who smoke various brands have been created at great cost, and in some cases additional images are being created to broaden a particular brand's market. In the case of drugs, it was found that the reference group influencing *whether* the product was used was different from that influencing the particular *brand* selected. Reference group influence was found to be prominent in determining whether or not beer was purchased at all, and also in determining whether regular or premium beer was selected. It did not appear to influence strongly choice of a particular brand.

b. "Product plus, brand minus" items.   Instant coffee is one of the best examples of this class of items. Whether it is served in a household depends in considerable part on whether the housewife, in view of her own reference groups and the image she has of their attitudes towards this product, considers it appropriate to serve it. The brand itself in this instance is not conspicuous or socially important and is a matter largely for individual choice. In the case of air conditioners, it was found that little prestige attached to the particular brand used, and reference group influence related largely to the idea of purchasing the product itself. Analysis in one city revealed that the purchase of this often "visible from the outside" product was concentrated in small neighborhood areas. Clusters of conditioners were frequently located in certain rows and blocks. In many cases clusters did not even cross streets. Immediate neighbors apparently served as a powerfully influential group in the purchase of these appliances. In this general class may also be found the black and white TV set, with its antenna often visible on the outside of the house. As the saturation point in black and white TV set ownership rapidly approaches, however, the influence of reference groups may soon become minor, and the product can then be put in the "brand minus, product minus" quadrant, along with refrigerators. Color TV may remain in the "brand plus, product minus" quadrant, with type (color) rather than brand per se the element which is strongly related to reference groups.

c. "Product minus, brand plus" items.   This group is made up essentially of products that all people or at least a very high proportion of people use, although differing as to type or brand.

Perhaps the leading example in this field is clothing. There could hardly be a more socially visible product than this, but the fact that everyone in our society wears clothing takes the *product* out of the area of reference group influence. The *type* of clothing purchased is, however, very heavily influenced by reference groups, with each subculture in the population (teenagers, zootsuiters, Ivy League collegians, western collegians, workers, bankers, advertising men, etc.) setting its own standards and often prescribing within fairly narrow limits what those who feel related to these groups can wear. Similarly, though not quite as dramatically, articles like furniture, magazines, refrigerators and toilet soap are seen in almost all homes, causing their purchase in general to fall outside of the orbit of reference group influence. The visibility of these items, however, coupled with the wide variety of styles and types among them make the selection of particular kinds highly susceptible to reference group influence.

d. "Product minus, brand minus" items.   Purchasing behavior in this class of items is governed largely by product attributes rather than by the nature of the presumed users. In this group neither the products nor the brands tend to be socially conspicuous. This is not to say that personal influence cannot operate with respect to purchasing the kind of items included in this group. As with all products some people tend to exert personal influence and others tend to be influenced by individual persons. Reference groups as such, however, exert relatively little influence on buying behavior in this class of items. Examples of items in this category are salt, canned peaches, laundry soap and radios. It is apparent that placement in this category is not *necessarily* inherent in the product itself and hence is not a static placement. Items can move in and out of this category.

While it is true that items which are essential socially inconspicuous, like salt and laundry soap, are natural candidates for this category, it is not entirely out of the realm of possibility that through considerable large scale advertising and other promotional efforts images of the kind of people who use certain brands of salt or laundry soap could be built up so as to bring reference group influence into play on such items, much as has been the case with cigarettes. The task here would be more difficult, however, since the cigarette is already socially visible. On the other hand, items such as radios and refrigerators which are conspicuously visible and whose purchase was once subject to considerable reference group influence have now slipped into this category through near saturation in ownership.

Implications of Strong and Weak Reference Group Influence for Advertising and Marketing

It should be stressed again that this scheme of analysis is introduced to show how reference group influence might enter into purchasing behavior in certain cases. It cannot be regarded as generally applicable to marketing problems on all levels. There is still a need to know more precisely where many different products or brands fit into this scheme. Attempts to fit products and brands into the classification above suggest research that needs to be done to obtain more relevant information about each product.

Assuming, however, that a product or brand has been correctly placed with respect to the part played by reference groups in influencing its purchase, how can this help in marketing the product in question?

Where neither product nor brand appear to be associated strongly with reference group influence, advertising should emphasize the product's attributes, intrinsic qualities, price, and advantages over competing products.

Where reference group influence is operative, the advertiser should stress the kinds of people who buy the product, reinforcing and broadening where possible the existing stereotypes of users. This involves learning what the stereotypes are and what specific reference groups enter into the picture, so that appeals can be "tailored" to each major group reached by the different media employed.

Although it is important to see that the "right" kind of people use a product, a crucial problem is to make sure that the popular image of the product's users is as broad as possible without alienating any important part of the product's present or potential market in the process. Creating or reinforcing a stereotype of consumers which is too small and exclusive for a mass-produced item may exclude a significant portion of the potential market. On the other hand, some attempts to appeal to new groups through advertising in mass media have resulted in the loss of existing groups of purchasers whose previous (favorable) image of the product-user was adversely affected. One possible means for increasing the base of the market for a product by enlarging the image of its users is to use separate advertising media through which a new group can be reached without reducing the product's appeal to the original group of users. Another method might be to appeal to a new group through cooperative advertising by a number of companies producing the product, possibly through a trade association. This would minimize the risk to an individual producer who, trying to reach a new group of users through his own advertising (women as opposed to men or wealthy as opposed to average people, for example), might antagonize people who had a strong need to identify with the *original* image of the product's kind of user.

Product Attributes Versus Reference Group Influence

A technique which could serve to assess the relative influence of reference groups, as compared with product attributes, on the purchase of any given product was employed in research on a food product which will be referred to as product "X."

A cross-section of "X" users was asked several questions relating to particular attributes of "X," such as whether it was more harmful or beneficial for one's health, whether or not it was considered fattening, whether it was considered extravagant or economical, whether or not it tasted good, and so on. These same people were also asked a reference group-oriented question about "X," to determine whether or not "X" was popular with most of their friends. It was found that there was usually more "X" eating among people who reacted negatively to "X" 's attributes but admitted to its popularity among most of their friends, than among those who reacted positively to "X" 's attributes but indicated that it was not popular with their friends.

These relationships are shown in Table 1 on the next page.

In this table, the scores in parentheses are those of people whose replies showed both attribute influence and reference group influence exerting pressure in the same direction.

Special attention should be directed towards the other scores. These represent situations in which people are under cross-pressures. For each of the four attributes considered, the reference group influence is stronger than the attribute influence, in the use of "X." This is brought out by the arrows, which point toward the cross-pressure situations where the reference group influence is adverse. In all of these, consumption frequency is less than where attribute influence alone is negative. Or, put another way, positive perception of reference group behavior with respect to the food product ("X" is very popular) coupled with negative perception of its actual attribute value ("X" does more harm than good, is fattening, etc.) leads to more consumption than negative perception of reference group behavior ("X" not very popular) coupled with positive perception of actual attribute value ("X" does more good than harm, not fattening, economical).

As can be seen from the comparisons indicated by the arrows, reference group influence is markedly stronger than attribute influence for three of the four attributes. Only for "taste" does the attribute influence come close to competing with reference group influence in determining consumption of "X."

One implication of this finding would be that advertising by the "X" industry might stress the variables that are related to the products' *social* utility for its consumers, rather than base its advertising solely on the *physical* attributes of the product.

In a study of a beverage, it was found that, of those who drank the beverage in question, 95% claimed that their friends also drank it, while of those who did not drink this beverage 85% also claimed that their friends did *not* drink it.

Some products, then, must be sold to whole social groups rather than primarily to individuals.

NOTES

[1] An exception to this generalization may be found in the case of personal selling, where knowledge of the individuals specific relation to and perception of certain groups would be highly relevant.

[2] J. E. Dittes and H. H. Kelley, "Effects of Different Conditions of Acceptance upon Conformity to Group Norms," *Journal of Abnormal and Social Psychology* (1956).

[3] Bureau of Applied Social Research, Columbia University.

Table 1. Relation Between Reference Group and Attribute Influence in Use of Food Product "X"

Product Attribute	+ Reference Group — With most of respondent's friends "X" is:	
	Very Popular	Not Very Popular
Effects of "X" on health	Index of Frequency of Eating "X" *	
+ more good than harm	(.41)	—.10
— more harm than good	.08	(—.51)
+ do not avoid fattening food and/or feel "X" is not really or a little fattening	(.30)	—.21
— try to avoid fattening food and feel "X" is really or a little fattening	.14	(—.29)
Economic Value Judgment		
+ fairly economical	(.29)	—.20
— sort of an extravagance	.11	(—.33)
Taste Judgment		
+ tastes good	(.42)	.05
— no reference to good taste**	.09	(—.38)

* All scores in the above table constitute an index of the frequency of "X" eating among respondents falling into the given cell. The scoring procedure used was:
 Frequent "X" users—score + 1
 Medium "X" users—score 0
 Occasional "X" users—score —1
The final score is derived by subtracting the number of occasional "X" users in a given cell from the number of frequent users and dividing the remainder by the total number of respondents in the cell.
For example, the index score .41 was obtained as follows:
329 respondents felt that a moderate amount of "X" does more good than harm AND report that "X" is very popular with most of their friends.
Of these 329 respondents 178 are frequent "X" users, 97 are medium "X" users, and 43 are occasional "X" users.
 The score: 178 — 43 = 135   The Index value: 135/329 = 41
** "Tastes good" represents the selection of this phrase from a word list of various attributes that might be applied to "X". "No Reference to Good Taste" refers to those respondents who did not select "Tastes Good" from the word list.
Source: Bureau of Applied Social Research, Columbia University. Reprinted with permission.

SOME SUGGESTIONS FOR FURTHER READING

Ostlund, L. E. (1973), "Role Theory and Group Dynamics," *Consumer Behavior: Theoretical Sources*, S. Ward and T. S. Robertson (eds.), Englewood Cliffs, N.J.: Prentice-Hall.

Stafford, J. E. (1966), "Effects of Group Influence on Consumer Brand Preferences," *Journal of Marketing* (February), 68–75.

———— and Cocanougher, A. B. (1977), "Reference Group Theory," *Project on Synthesis of Knowledge of Consumer Behavior*, RANN Program, National Science Foundation, R. Ferber (ed.), 361–380.

Wind, Y. (1977), "Retrospective Comment" in L. E. Boone (ed.), *Classics in Consumer Behavior*, 225–235.

16 / NEW PRODUCT ADOPTION AND DIFFUSION / Everett M. Rogers

The studies of the diffusion of innovations, including the part played by mass communication, promise to provide an empirical and quantitative basis for developing more rigorous approaches to theories of social change.

Melvin L. De Fleur (1966, p. 138)

Diffusion of innovations has the status of a bastard child with respect to the parent interests in social and cultural change: too big to ignore but unlikely to be given full recognition.

Frederick C. Fliegel and Joseph E. Kivlin (1966, p. 235n)

Diffusion research is thus emerging as a single, integrated body of concepts and generalizations, even though the investigations are conducted by researchers in several scientific disciplines.

Everett M. Rogers (1971, p. 47)

The purposes of this paper are (1) to summarize what we have learned from research on the diffusion of innovations that contributes to our understanding of new product adoption and diffusion, (2) to discuss how the academic history and the intellectual structuring of the diffusion field have affected its contributions and its shortcomings, and (3) to indicate future research priorities on the diffusion of innovations.

Our focus here is especially on the last 10-year period and on the diffusion of a particular type of innovation (new products), but for historical and comparative purposes, we also must briefly deal with the origins of diffusion research.

Since about the mid-1960s, there has been considerable interest in diffusion research on the part of consumer researchers and a certain degree of integration of diffusion frameworks and research findings into the literature on consumer behavior. For example, the leading textbook on consumer behavior today features a chapter on the diffusion and adoption of innovations. Many marketing texts these days have a chapter on diffusion, or at least give considerable coverage to such topics as the innovation-decision process, adopter categories, opinion leadership, and the S-shaped diffusion curve.

Further, about 8 percent of the 1,800 publications dealing with empirical research on the diffusion of innovations, available to date, were authored by researchers associated with the field of marketing. These studies, mostly conducted

Everett M. Rogers, "New Product Adoption and Diffusion." Reprinted from *Journal of Consumer Research* (March 1976), pp. 290–301, published by The Journal of Consumer Research, Inc.
Everett Rogers is a professor in the Institute for Communication Research at Stanford University. His landmark book, *Diffusion of Innovations,* helped him win the Paul D. Converse award for contribution to the theory and science of marketing.

since the mid-1960s, focus on new products as innovations. The present paper deals not only with these 8 percent of all diffusion publications but also with the other 92 percent, since I believe that the findings, methodologies, and theoretic frameworks from research on various types of innovations has applicability to consumers' adoption of new products. The adoption of most innovations entails the purchase of a new product, although this fact has often not been recognized by diffusion scholars.

THE RISE OF DIFFUSION RESEARCH AS AN INVISIBLE COLLEGE

From Revolutionary Paradigm to Classical Model

The origins of research on the diffusion of innovations trace from (1) the German-Austrian and the British schools of diffusionism in anthropology (whose members claimed that most changes in a society resulted from the introduction of innovations from other societies) and (2) the French sociologist Gabriel Tarde (1903), who pioneered in proposing the S-shaped diffusion curve and the role of opinion leaders in the process of "imitation." But the "revolutionary paradigm" for diffusion research occurred in the early 1940s when two sociologists, Bryce Ryan and Neal Gross (1943), published their seminal study of the diffusion of hybrid seed corn among Iowa farmers.

Any given field of scientific research begins with a major breakthrough or reconceptualization that provides a new way of looking at some phenomenon (Kuhn, 1962). This revolutionary paradigm typically sets off a furious amount of intellectual effort as promising young scientists are attracted to the field, either to advance the new conceptualization with their research or to disprove certain of its aspects. Gradually, a scientific consensus about the field is developed, and perhaps after several generations of academic scholars, the "invisible college" (composed of researchers on a common topic who are linked by communication ties) declines in scientific interest as fewer findings of an exciting nature are turned up. These are the usual stages in the normal growth of science, Kuhn (1962) claims.

Research on the diffusion of innovations has followed these rise-and-fall stages rather closely, although the final stage of demise has not yet begun (Crane, 1972). The hybrid corn study set forth a new approach to the study of communication and change that was soon followed up by an increasing number of scholars in a wide variety of scientific fields. Within 10 years (by 1952), over 100 diffusion researches were completed; during the next decade (by 1962), another 450; and by the end of 1974, another 1,250. So today there are over 2,700 publications about the diffusion of innovations, including about 1,800 empirical research reports and 900 other writings (Figure 1).[1] The amount of scientific activity in investigating the diffusion of innovations has increased at an exponential rate (doubling almost every two years) since the revolutionary paradigm appeared 32 years ago, as Kuhn's (1962) theory of the growth of science would predict.

The main elements in the "classical model" of the diffusion of new ideas that emerged are (1) the *innovation*, defined as an idea, practice, or object per-

Figure 1. Cumulative Number of Empirical Diffusion Research Publications, by Year of Publication

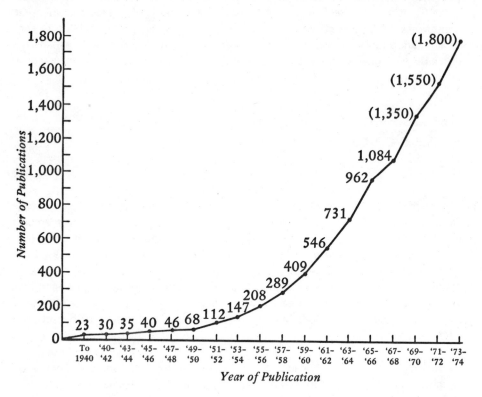

ceived as new by an individual or other relevant unit of adoption, (2) which is *communicated* through certain *channels* (3) over *time* (4) among the members of a *social system*. The Ryan and Gross (1943) study focused on hybrid corn, one of the most important innovations in midwestern agriculture. Data were gathered by personal interviews with all the Iowa farmers in two communities. The rate of adoption of the agricultural innovation followed an S-shaped, normal curve when plotted on a cumulative basis over time. The first farmers to adopt (the innovators) were more cosmopolite (indicated by traveling more frequently to Des Moines) and of higher socioeconomic status than later adopters. The typical Iowa farmer first heard about the innovation from a seed corn salesman, but interpersonal communication with peers was the most frequent channel leading to persuasion. The innovation process from awareness/knowledge to final adoption averaged about nine years, indicating that considerable time was required for adoption to occur.

Diffusion research is a particular type of communication research, but it began outside the academic field of communication. This was mostly a matter of timing, since the Ryan and Gross (1943) study preceded the first university centers or departments of communication by a good dozen years. Research on persuasion and attitude change, on nonverbal communication, and on most of the other important topics for communication research also began in psychology, anthropology, sociology, or other social sciences and then came to flower in the hands of communication scholars. The diffusion research approach was taken up in a variety of fields: education, anthropology, medical sociology, marketing, geography, and, most of all, rural sociology. Each of these disciplines pursued diffusion research in its specialized way and, for some time, without much interchange with the other diffusion research traditions.

The Intellectual Watershed of 1960

The year 1960 was in several respects a turning point for research on the diffusion of innovations. For one thing, the old disciplinary boundaries began to break down, and diffusion research began to emerge as "a single, integrated body of concepts and generalizations" (Rogers, 1971, p. 47). This emergence did not necessarily mean that all diffusion scholars completely agreed on definitions of concepts or on the most appropriate methods of inquiry, but at least the scholars generally recognized that they were investigating the same basic type of human behavior. Evidence of this recognition is shown in the works cited in their publications, as well as in the methods and models that they followed.

Second, researchers in the academic field of mass communication began to engage in diffusion research, at first by investigating the diffusion of major news events carried by the mass media: Alaskan statehood, the launching of Sputnik, and President Kennedy's assassination. The most noted news-event diffusion study, itself representing a "mini-revolutionary paradigm," was by Deutschmann and Danielson (1960). Today there are over 100 such news-event diffusion studies. Communication scholars soon began to study many types of other innovations, including technological innovations in agriculture, health, and family planning, especially in the developing nations of Latin America, Africa, and Asia.[2]

The early 1960s marked the beginning of a sharp takeoff in the number of diffusion studies in developing countries. Pioneering ventures in this direction by S.A. Rahim (1961) in Bangladesh and by Paul J. Deutschmann and Orlando Fals Borda (1962a, b) in Colombia suggested that new ideas spread among peasants in villages in a generally similar pattern to their diffusion in more media-saturated settings like the United States and Europe. The diffusion process, and the concepts and models utilized to analyze it, seemed to be cross-culturally valid, at least in the sense that comparable results were found in the new settings.

There were compelling reasons for the fast growth of diffusion studies in developing countries after 1960. Technology was assumed to be at the heart of development, at least in the dominant paradigm of development popular until very recent years.[3] In fact, innovativeness was thought to be the best single indicant of the multifaceted dimension called "modernization," the individual-level equivalent of development at the societal or system level (Rogers, 1969). Therefore, microlevel investigations of the diffusion of technological innovations among villagers were of direct relevance to development planners and other government officials in developing nations. These research results, and the general framework of diffusion, provided development agencies with both a kind of theoretical approach and an evaluation procedure.

The number of diffusion researches in developing nations totaled only about 54 in 1960 (13 percent of all diffusion studies), but rose steeply to over 800 or so by 1975, when about half of all diffusion studies were conducted in Latin America, Africa, and Asia. The major developing country of study is India, with over 450 of the 800 diffusion researches in developing countries.

An important boost to the internationalization of the diffusion field was the rise of KAP surveys in developing countries during the 1960s. KAP studies are sample surveys of knowledge (K), attitudes (A), and practice (P)—that is, adoption —of family planning innovations. K, A, and P are the logical dependent variables in evaluations of family planning communication campaigns, and, as national family planning programs arose after 1960 in many developing nations (especially in Asia) to cope with the population problem, KAP-type diffusion researches blossomed on all sides. Over 500 such KAP surveys were conducted in 72 nations by 1973 (Rogers, 1973, p. 377); India alone was the location for over half these investigations.

With the exception of the Taichung experiment in Taiwan (Freedman and Takeshita, 1969), the intellectual contribution of these KAP surveys "to scientific understanding of human behavior change has been dismal" (Rogers, 1973, p. 378). However, the KAP studies have provided a useful function by generally showing that most parents in developing countries want fewer children than they actually have, and that the majority desire a government family planning program. Even the harshest critic of KAP studies, Professor Philip M. Hauser (1967, p. 405), stated: "KAP survey results, erroneous or not, have helped to persuade prime ministers, parliaments, and the general population to move in a desirable direction and have provided family planning program administrators with 'justification' for budgets and programs."

Intellectually speaking, the family planning diffusion studies were generally disappointing, although several modifications in the "classical diffusion model" (such as the payment of incentives to promote diffusion and the use of nonprofessional change agent aides to help overcome the taboo nature of family planning communication) did emerge when family planning programs found the model wanting (Rogers, 1973). Also, the family planning diffusion studies gave a boost to field experimental research designs,[4] for over a dozen such experiments in various nations followed the Taichung study (Rogers and Agarwala-Rogers, 1975).

The rise of these field experiments, in place of one-shot survey designs, helped to overcome some of the methodological difficulties of diffusion studies in coming to grips with the "over-time" aspects of the communication of new ideas.

MARKETING RESEARCH ON DIFFUSION

While many of the field experimental designs in the diffusion field were conducted in developing nations and were concerned with family planning innovations, a number of other field experiments were carried out in the United States by marketing researchers.

The marketing tradition of diffusion research has come on strong since the early 1960s. Marketing managers of firms have long been concerned with how to launch new products more efficiently. One reason for this interest is the high failure rate of new consumer products, estimated at 92 percent of the approximately 6,000 new consumer items introduced each year (Conner, 1964).

The adoption of most innovations involves sale of a new product, of course, and it was easy for commercial firms to conceive of their new products as innovations and to adapt the theoretical and methodological framework of diffusion research to marketing problems. University faculty members in graduate schools of business led the way into diffusion research (Zaltman, 1965), to be followed soon after by marketing researchers in the employ of commercial firms. Unfortunately, a large proportion of these research reports lie only in the secret files of the sponsoring companies because of competitive threat, and they are thus unavailable to attempts at academic synthesis and the progress of scientific understanding of the diffusion process.

Much of the diffusion research in the marketing field was conducted either by the commercial manufacturers of the new product or by university professors with the sponsorship, or at least the cooperation, of the manufacturers. One advantage of this close relationship was that the diffusion researchers in the field of marketing often had some degree of control over the diffusion strategies that were used to promote the new products. This is a particularly important ingredient in the conduct of field experiments on diffusion. In fields other than marketing, diffusion scholars have seldom been able to manipulate the "treatment" variables, and it has therefore been impossible to conduct field experiments.

Perhaps a somewhat typical illustration of the field experimental approach by marketing researchers is provided by Arndt's (1967) study of the diffusion of a new food product. A letter about this innovation, enclosing a coupon allowing its purchase at one-third price, was sent to 495 housewives living in a married-student apartment complex. Personal interviews were carried out with these consumers 16 days after the diffusion campaign was launched. Arndt found that interpersonal communication about the new product frequently led to its initial purchase. Housewives who perceived the innovation as risky were more likely to seek the advice of their neighborhood opinion leaders about it. Naturally, this type of field experiment allowed determination of the impact of the reduced-price sample offer; the measure of impact was the rate of adoption (that is, purchase) of the new food product.

The diffusion research tradition of marketing has displayed an especially strong bias toward producing research results of use to the innovation's source (that is, the manufacturer of the new product) rather than to the consumers. This pro-innovation and pro-source orientation is also characteristic of other branches of diffusion research (a point to which we shall return), but less so than in the field of marketing.

One cannot help but wonder how the research approach (and the understandings that were obtained) might have been different if the Ryan and Gross (1943) hybrid corn study had been sponsored by the Iowa Farm Bureau Federation rather than by the Iowa Agricultural Extension Service and if the Coleman, Katz, and Menzel (1966) investigation of a new medical drug had been conducted under the auspices of the American Medical Association rather than Pfizer Drug Company. Perhaps "diffusion" research would have been called something like "innovation-seeking" or the "evaluation of innovations" had the receivers been in control (Rogers, 1971, p. 79).

The source-bias in marketing research on diffusion is especially surprising since this scientific specialty is often called "*consumer* research" in graduate schools of marketing, and it is often inspired by the "marketing concept," an approach that puts the customer in control of the marketing process, at least in principle (Kotler and Zaltman, 1971). In diffusion researches following the marketing concept, the customer has often been studied, but usually to the advantage of the seller of the new product or service.

Even though the studies were usually commissioned by the selling agencies, consumers have often benefited from the diffusion researches in which they were respondents if their needs were met by the new products that emerged from such diffusion researches. These investigations *can* put the consumer in the driver's seat regarding new products, especially through a variant of diffusion inquiry called "acceptability research," in which the consumers' desires are determined and then a new product is designed to meet these previously unmet needs. Acceptability research began at the hands of marketing researchers and is now also followed in wider contexts. For example, the World Health Organization is currently involved in a research program in which the desired qualities of contraceptives are determined for the fertile audience in Latin America, Africa, and Asia to guide WHO biomedical researchers in the invention and development of future methods of family planning. This acceptability approach puts the potential consuming couples in the position, via survey research, of helping design more acceptable contraceptives.

Nevertheless, certain basic consumer-oriented research questions have not been asked in diffusion research, such as, How can the consumer be protected against the influence of advertising (or other promotional) messages? What information does the consumer need to know in order to make intelligent innovation decisions?

LACK OF A PROCESS ORIENTATION

We shall now consider the first of three important conceptual/methodological biases in diffusion research, which also characterize other types of communication research:

1. Lack of a process orientation.
2. A pro-innovation bias (and an associated ignoring of causality).
3. A psychological orientation, leading to shortchanging structure.

Every textbook definition of the concept of communication either states or directly implies that it is a *process*.[5] Thus, one might expect an overwhelming emphasis in research and theory on the conceptualization of communication as process. However, a recent analysis by Arundale (1971) shows that the research designs and measurements of communication almost never allow analysis of the over-time aspects of communication that would be necessary to explore process adequately. Very little communication research includes data at more than one observation point, and almost none at more than two such points in time. Therefore, almost all communication research is unable to trace the change in a variable over time; it deals only with the present tense of behavior. Communication thus becomes, in the actuality of communication research, an artificially halted snapshot.

Why has communication research not dealt more adequately with the change-over-time aspects of process?

1. We lack concepts and propositions that reflect a process orientation.
2. Time-series data are expensive to gather, unless one depends on respondent recall, a procedure that is often less than satisfactory.
3. Data gathering repeated over time leads to problems of respondent sensitization (unless one uses unobtrusive and nonreactive measurement methods), since communication research itself is a communication process.
4. Communication researchers are often pressured by research sponsors, doctoral requirements, and other logistic forces to produce immediate results; this is a strong discouragement to over-time research designs.

Thus, unfortunately, we define communication as process, but then proceed in communication research to treat communication as a one-shot affair.

Diffusion research is only slightly "less bad" in this respect than other types of communication research. Because *time* is one of the four essential elements in the diffusion process, and thus receives more explicit attention than in other types of communication research, it should be stressed in the research designs utilized in diffusion research.

These designs consist mainly of correlational analyses of cross-sectional data gathered in one-shot surveys of the respondents, thus following exactly the method pioneered by Ryan and Gross (1943). By 1968 (the last time a tabulation was made of the methodologies used in diffusion studies), only 65 of the then 1,084 empirical diffusion publications (about 6 percent) reported results from field experiments, and most of these field experiments had been done since 1960 (our turning-point year in the diffusion field, as mentioned earlier). Even allowing for the 67 diffusion publications (another 6 percent) that reported longitudinal panel studies at two or more points in time, the vast majority (about 88 percent) of all diffusion researches are one-shot surveys permitting only cross-sectional data analysis. Such research designs cannot tell us very much about the *process* of diffusion over time other than what can be reconstructed from recall data.

Diffusion studies are particularly able to rely on "moving pictures" of behavior rather than on "snapshots" because of their unique capacity to trace the sequential flow of an innovation through a social system. However, diffusion researchers mainly have relied on their respondents' ability to recall their date of awareness or adoption of a new idea. Essentially, the respondent is asked to look back over his shoulder and mentally reconstruct his past history of innovation experiences. This hindsight ability is not very accurate and undoubtedly varies on the basis of (1) the innovations' salience to the respondents; (2) the length of time over which recall is requested; and (3) individual differences in education, mental ability, etc.

Future diffusion research ought to develop improved methods for tracer studies, in which alternative sources of data are used to provide validity checks on recall data over time.[6] Much greater use should be made of field experiments and longitudinal panel studies, which, by their research designs, are able to take "moving pictures" of the diffusion process.

THE PRO-INNOVATION BIAS AND CAUSALITY

The second important bias found in most diffusion research is an inherent pro-change bias, which assumes that the innovations studied are "good" and should be adopted by everyone. Undoubtedly hybrid corn *was* profitable for each of the Iowa farmers in the Ryan and Gross (1943) study, but most other innovations that have been studied do not have this high degree of relative advantage. Many individuals, for their own good, should *not* adopt them.

The pro-innovation bias, coupled with the unfortunate and overwhelming dependence on survey research designs, means that diffusion research has mostly studied "what is" instead of "what could be" about diffusion processes. Therefore, method has followed the assumption that innovation is good, that the present process of diffusion is satisfactory and needs only minor tune-up rather than a major overhaul. Röling, Ascroft, and Chege (1974) have heavily scored diffusion research on this count, arguing that it has often led to increased inequity; field experimental designs are needed to test alternatives to current practice instead of replicating more surveys of "what is."

The pro-innovation bias in diffusion research, and its overwhelming reliance on correlational analysis of survey data, often led in the past to avoiding or ignoring the issue of causality. We often speak of "independent" and "dependent" variables in diffusion research, having taken these terms from experimental designs and then used them rather loosely with correlational analysis. A dependent variable thus means little more than the main variable in which the investigator is interested. In about 60 percent of all diffusion researches, the dependent variable is *innovativeness,* defined as the degree to which a responding unit is relatively earlier in adopting an innovation than other units in the system. It is implied that the independent variables "lead to" innovativeness, although it is often unstated or uncertain whether this really means that an independent variable *causes* innovativeness.

In order for variable X to be the cause of variable Y, (1) X must precede Y in time order, (2) they must be related or covary, and (3) X must have a "forcing quality" on Y. Most diffusion researches have only determined that various independent variables covary with innovativeness; correlational analysis of one-shot survey data does not allow the determination of time order. Diffusion research has tarried too long at step 3 in Table 1 and should move on to step 4.

Correlational studies face a particular problem of time order that might be called "yesterday's innovativeness": In most diffusion surveys, innovativeness is measured "today" with recall data about past adoption behavior, while the independent variables are measured in the present tense. It is obviously impossible for an individual's attitudes, formed and measured now, to cause his adoption of an innovation three years previously (this would amount to X following Y in time order, thus making it impossible for X to cause Y).

Table 1.   A classification of stages in social science research

Research Stages	Research Purpose	Research Method
1. Problem delineation	To define what we are looking for, and the extent to which it is a social problem	Qualitative analysis, such as case studies, observation, unstructured interviews, and literature review
2. Variable identification	To identify variables which might be linked to the problem, and to describe possible interconnections between these variables	Exploratory case studies, and other qualitative methods that are low on structure
3. Determination of relationships among the variables	To determine the clusters of relevant variables required for prediction, and to analyze their patterns of relationships	Cross-sectional, correlational analysis of quantitative survey data
4. Establishment of causality among the variables	To determine which factors are critical in promoting or inhibiting the problem	Longitudinal studies, and small-scale experiments with (1) over-time data, (2) in which at least one variable changes prior to the others, so as to determine time order
5. Manipulation of causal variables for policy-formation purposes	To determine the correspondence between a theoretical problem solution and the manipulable factors	Field experiments
6. Evaluation of alternative polices/programs	To assess the expected, as well as the unanticipated consequences of various programs/policies before and after they are applied on a large scale, and to determine the effectiveness of such programs in overall problem solution	Controlled field comparisons, such as the interrupted time-series field experiment

Source: Based on Gordon, MacEachron, and Fisher, "A Contingency Model for the Design of Problem-Solving Research Problems," *Millbank Memorial Fund Quarterly*, Spring 1974, p. 193. Permission for use granted by the Millbank Memorial Fund.

So again we see the importance of research designs that allow us to learn the over-time aspects of diffusion. Field experiments are ideally suited to the purpose of assessing the effect of various independent variables (the treatments) on the dependent variable of innovativeness.

In order for X to cause Y, they must covary. If such covariance is very low, X is probably not a cause of Y. If their common variance is high, X *may* be a cause of Y. Diffusion research has specialized in determining the correlates of innovativeness.

Forcing quality, the way in which X acts on Y, is a theoretical rather than an empirical issue. The theoretical reasoning why certain variables might have a forcing quality on others needs to be given much greater attention in diffusion research. Theoretical approaches from other fields of communication study may have application to conceptualizing the forcing quality of certain independent variables on innovativeness and other dependent variables.

THE PSYCHOLOGICAL BIAS THAT SHORT-CHANGES STRUCTURE

The psychological bias in diffusion research stems from (1) its historical roots in academe and (2) the researchers' acceptance of how social problems are defined. Several early communication scholars came from psychological backgrounds, and it was only natural that their models of communication (and diffusion) largely ignored social-structural variables that affect communication. The transactional and relational nature of human communication tended to be overlooked, and this shortcoming was also characteristic of diffusion research, at least until fairly recently.

The Individual as the Unit of Analysis

The overwhelming focus on the *individual* as the unit of analysis in communication research (while largely ignoring the importance of communication *relationships* between sources and receivers) is often due to the assumption that the individual, as the unit of response, must consequently be the unit of analysis (Coleman, 1958–59). The monadic view of human behavior determined that "the kinds of substantive problems on which such research focused tended to be problems of 'aggregate psychology,' that is, *within*-individual problems, and never problems concerned with relations between people" (Coleman, 1958–59, p. 28). The use of survey methods in communication research has "de-structured" behavior:

Using random sampling of individuals, the survey is a sociological meat-grinder, tearing the individual from his social context and guaranteeing that nobody in the study interacts with anyone else in it. It is a little like a biologist putting his experimental animals through a hamburger machine and looking at every hundredth cell through a microscope; anatomy and physiology get lost; structure and function disappear and one is left with cell biology. [Barton, 1968, p. 1]

The main focus in diffusion research on the individual as the unit of analysis has only recently shifted to the dyad, clique, network, or system of individuals, centering on the communication relationships between individuals rather than on the individuals themselves. Encouraging attempts to overcome the psychological bias in diffusion research are provided by network analysis and by the open-systems approach.

These conceptual/methodological approaches suggest that even when the individual is the unit of response, the communication relationship (even though *it* can't "speak") can be the unit of analysis via some type of sociometric measurement. Sampling and data analysis procedures for relational analysis are being worked out,[7] but we still lack relational concepts and theories linking these concepts. Until diffusion scholars begin to think in relational terms, there will not be much relational analysis.

Person-Blame

The second reason for the artificially "de-structured" psychological bias in communication research is the acceptance of a *person-blame–causal-attribution* definition of the social problems that we study: Individual-blame is the tendency to hold an individual responsible for his problems. Obviously, what is done about a social problem, including research, depends on how it is defined. Since communication scientists seldom participate in the identification and definition of social problems, they borrow or accept these definitions from alarmists, government officials, and other scientists.

Many illustrations of individual-blame can be cited in behavioral research. Caplan and Nelson (1973) found a high degree of individual-blame in psychological research on such problems as highway safety and race relations. They asked, "Why do we constantly study the poor rather than the nonpoor in order to understand the origins of poverty?"

An example of individual-blame is the poster produced by a pharmaceutical manufacturer: "LEAD PAINT CAN KILL!" The poster blamed mothers for allowing their children to eat paint. In New Haven, Connecticut, with the highest reported rates of lead paint poisoning of children in the U.S., landlords are legally prohibited from using lead paint on the inside of residences (W. Ryan, 1971). But the poster blames the mother, not the paint manufacturers or the landlords. And this tendency toward stressing individual-blame rather than system-blame is very common in communication research.

Diffusion research was originally (and for many years) as guilty as other types of communication research in following an individual-blame approach:

We note an assumption in diffusion writings that the rate of adoption should be speeded up, that the innovation should be adopted by receivers, etc. [This is a consequence of the pro-innovation bias of diffusion research.] Seldom is it implied in diffusion documents that the source or the channels may be at fault for not providing more adequate information, for promoting inadequate or inappropriate innovations, etc. [Rogers, 1971, p. 79]

This psychological bias in diffusion research began with the hybrid seed corn study. Strangely, Ryan and Gross (1943) did not gather sociometric data about the interpersonal diffusion of the innovation within their two Iowa communities of study even though (1) they found that interpersonal communication from neighbors was essential in clinching adoption decisions and (2) their sampling design of a complete census of farmers in the two communities was ideal for gathering relational data for network-analysis purposes.

RESTORING SOCIAL STRUCTURE TO DIFFUSION RESEARCH

The refocusing of diffusion researches had to wait until later investigations, especially the drug study among medical doctors by Coleman et al. (1966). Then it became a common procedure for diffusion scholars to ask their respondents sociometric questions of the general form, "From whom in this system did you obtain information that led you to adopt this innovation?" The sociometric dyad represented by each answer to this question could consequently be punched on an IBM card (including data on the characteristics of the seeker *and* the sought), which then became the unit of analysis.

The relational data thus obtained were utilized to provide deeper insight into the role of opinion leaders in the two-step flow of communication, a conceptualization that was originated by Lazarsfeld, Berelson, and Gaudet (1944) prior to most diffusion research. Later research showed that the two-step flow hypothesis was mainly a gross oversimplification, since the flow of communication may actually have any number of steps, but the concept of opinion leadership has much theoretical and practical utility. Diffusion researches were able to advance understandings of opinion leadership because of their unique capacity to focus on the *flow* of innovations, new messages (to the receiver) that seem to leave deeper (and hence more recallable) scratches on men's minds. The tracer quality of an innovation's diffusion pathways aids the investigation of the flow of communication messages, and especially the role of certain individuals such as opinion leaders in this flow. For instance, the complicated relationship of leadership and group norms, first raised theoretically by George Homans (1961, p. 339), has received rather definite empirical elucidation by diffusion scholars, resulting in the proposition: *"When the system's norms favor change, opinion leaders are more innovative, but when the norms are traditional, opinion leaders are not especially innovative"* (Rogers, 1971, p. 219).

Network Analysis of Diffusion

Most communication research has largely ignored the effect of social structure on communication behavior, as we pointed out earlier, and diffusion research to date has only partly realized its full potential in this regard. *Network analysis* is a method of research for identifying the communication structure of a system in which sociometric data about communication flows or patterns are analyzed by using interpersonal relationships as the units of analysis (Rogers and Agarwala-Rogers, 1976). This tool promises to capitalize on the unique ability of diffusion inquiry to reconstruct specific message flows in a system and then to overlay the social structure of the system on these flows. The innovation's diffusion brings life to the otherwise static nature of the structural variables; network analysis permits understanding the social structure as it channels the process of diffusion. About the only other place in communication research where network analysis has been used to restore social structure to the communication process is in a few recent investigations of organizational communication.

The first, and very partial, attempts toward network analysis of the diffusion process simply identified opinion leaders in a system and determined their mass media and interpersonal communication behavior. This approach was only a slight extension of the usual monadic analysis, moving toward a relation type of analysis.

Next, diffusion scholars began to plot sequential–over-time sociograms of the diffusion of an innovation among the members of a system. Tentative steps were taken toward using communication relationships (such as sociometric dyads) as the units of analysis. This advance allowed data analysis of a "who-to-whom" communication matrix and facilitated inquiry into the identification (1) of cliques within the total system[8] and how such structural subgroupings affected the diffusion of an innovation and (2) of specialized communication roles such as liaisons, bridges, and isolates,[9] thus allowing communication research to proceed far beyond the relatively simpler issue of studying just opinion leadership. Further, the measurement of various structural indexes (such as system connectedness and system openness[10]) for individuals, cliques, or entire systems (such as organizations or communities) now became possible. Generally, system innovativeness is positively related to connectedness and to system openness.

These network analyses necessitated a new kind of sampling, as well as a shift to relational units of analysis. Instead of random samples of scattered individuals in a large population, the network studies usually depended on gathering data from *all* the eligible respondents in a system (such as a village) or a sample of such systems (Table 2). Usually these sample designs meant less emphasis on the ability to generalize the research results, which was traded off for a greater focus on understanding the role of social structures on diffusion flows. If such research were to study social structure, it had to sample intact social structures, or at least the relevant parts of them.

The Strength of Weak Ties

Out of the network analyses of interpersonal diffusion grew a research issue that came to be called "the strength of weak ties" (Granovetter, 1973; Liu and Duff,

Table 2. Comparison of monadic and relational analysis in research on the diffusion of innovations

Characteristics of the Research Approach	Type of Diffusion Research Approach	
	Monadic Analysis	*Relational Analysis*
1. Unit of analysis	The individual	The communication relationship between two (or more) individuals
2. Most frequent sample design	Random samples of scattered individuals in a large sample (in order to maximize the generalizability of the research results)	Complete census of all eligible respondents in a system (such as a village), or a sample of such intact systems
3. Types of data utilized	Personal and social characteristics of individuals, and their communication behavior	Same as for monadic analysis, plus sociometric data about communication relationships
4. Main type of data analysis methods	Correlational analysis of cross-sectional survey data	Various types of network analysis of cross-sectional survey data
5. Main purpose of the research	To determine the variables (usually characteristics of individuals) related to innovativeness	To determine how social-structural variables affect diffusion flows in a system

1972).[11] The proposition summarizing this research is, *The informational strength of dyadic communication relationships is inversely related to the degree of homophily (and the strength of the attraction) between the source and the receiver.* Or, in other words, an innovation is diffused to a larger number of individuals and traverses a greater social distance when passed through weak ties rather than strong ones (Granovetter, 1973).

For any given topic, each individual operates in his/her particular communication environment consisting of a number of friends and acquaintances with whom the topic is discussed most frequently. These friends are usually highly homophilous (or similar) with the individual and with each other, and most of the individual's friends are friends of each other, thus constituting an "interlacking network" (Laumann, 1973; Rogers, 1973). This homophily and close attraction facilitate effective communication, but they act as a barrier preventing new ideas from entering the network. There is thus not much informational strength in the interlocking network; some heterophilous ties into the network are needed to give it more openness. These "weak ties" enable innovations to flow from clique to clique via liaisons and bridges. There is a cohesive power to the weak ties.

Laumann (1973) found important differences in political behavior, organizational participation, and consumer behavior between Detroit men with interlocking networks and those with radial networks. Thus the nature of these personal communication networks is perhaps one important way to distinguish consumers, at least in their receptivity to innovations. Innovators have more radial personal networks, and interlocking networks are more likely centered on later adopters.

Network analysis of the diffusion of the IUD in the Philippines demonstrated this strength of weak ties: The innovation spread most easily within interlocking cliques among housewives of very similar social status (Liu and Duff, 1972). But heterophilous flows were necessary to link these cliques; usually these "weak ties" connected two women who were not close friends and allowed the IUD to travel from a higher-status to a somewhat lower-status housewife. Therefore, at least occasional heterophilous dyadic communication in a network was a structural prerequisite for effective diffusion.

The case of network analysis on the strength of weak ties illustrates an important recent trend in diffusion research: The concepts used in this analysis are *relational* constructs. Perhaps we are seeing the real beginning of relational thinking in communication research.

CONCLUSIONS

Our quick tour of the past 32 years of diffusion research provides many examples of Thorstein Veblen's concept of "trained incapacity": By being taught to "see" innovativeness, opinion leadership, and other aspects of the classical model of diffusion, we failed to "see" much else. Acceptance of a revolutionary paradigm by scholars in a field enables them to cope with uncertainty and information overload through the simplification of reality that the paradigm represents. It also imposes and standardizes a set of assumptions and conceptual biases that, once begun, are difficult to recognize and overcome.

In my opinion the research designs, concepts, and measurement procedures of diffusion research have been very stereotyped. This similarity has facilitated the synthesis of diffusion findings, a task to which I have contributed; in fact, all diffusion studies look a good deal alike. But such standardization of research approaches has also greatly limited the contribution of diffusion research to more effective social programs and to furthering the scientific understanding of communication and human behavior change. Presumably this indictment is what one dean of a U.S. school of communication had in mind when he characterized the diffusion field as "a mile wide and an inch deep."

Nevertheless, I believe that *research on the diffusion of innovations has played an important role in helping put social structure back in the communication process.* Focus on structural variables has increasingly characterized diffusion research in the past decade, and the techniques of network analysis promise exciting further steps in this direction. Eventually this trend may help communication research shed its psychological bias and person-blame orientation.

For network analysis to fulfill its potential, however, I feel we must improve the methods of data gathering and measurement. Sociometric questions about communication behavior leave much to be desired; adequate evidence of their accuracy and stability over time are presently lacking. Unobtrusive, nonreactive measures are needed to provide validity checks on sociometry, leading to a multiple-measurement approach. At present, I believe our data-analysis techniques for relational analysis of communication behavior have far outrun the quality of our measurement.

Longitudinal panel designs for network analysis of diffusion processes are also needed; along with field experiments, they help secure the necessary data to illuminate the over-time process aspects of diffusion (and communication) and to facilitate exploration of the causal relationships involved in communication behavior.

Time is an explicit element in all diffusion research. But the measurement of time is one of the most egregious methodological weaknesses of past diffusion inquiry through its overwhelming dependence on recall data.

Thus, network analysis of over-time data and field experiments are robust tools offering promise for research on the diffusion of innovations in the years ahead.

Consumer researchers have already made important contributions to understanding the diffusion of innovations, and the diffusion model has extended the scope of investigations of the consumption of new products.

NOTES

[1] All of these 1,800 empirical research publications, plus another 900 nonempirical, publications (bibliographies, theoretical works, etc.), are held in the Diffusion Documents Center in the Department of Population Planning at the University of Michigan. A bibliography of these 2,700 items (Rogers and Thomas, 1975) is available from the Department at no cost.

[2] Detail on the convergence of diffusion research with communication research is provided by Katz (1960) and Rogers (1967).

[3] In addition to assuming that capital-intensive technology was the vital ingredient in development, the dominant paradigm assumed that a nation had to pass through an industrial revolution en route to development, and that economic growth (guided by central planning agencies and quantified in aggregate terms like GNP) largely constituted the nature of development. After the paradigm shift, the newer conceptions of development stressed (1) the *equality* of distribution, (2) popular *participation* in decentralized development planning

and execution, (3) *self-reliance* and independence in development, and (4) *integration* of traditional with modern systems (Rogers, 1975a).

[4] A *field experiment* is an active intervention by an experimenter who administers a treatment (in the form of a program, project, or activity) to randomly selected respondents arranged in groups that are equivalent in the way they are chosen, with at least one treatment group and one control group (who do not receive the treatment).

[5] A common definition of *communication* is the process by which an idea is transferred from a source to a receiver with the intent to change his/her behavior.

[6] For example, in a study of the diffusion of a new drug among medical doctors, the physicians' recall data were checked against pharmacists' sales records for each doctor (Coleman et al., 1966).

[7] *Relational analysis* is a research approach in which the unit of analysis is a relationship between two or more individuals (Rogers and Bhowmik, 1970–71).

[8] A *clique* is a subsystem whose elements interact with each other relatively more frequently than with other members of the communication system.

[9] A *liaison* is an individual who interpersonally connects two or more cliques within a system, without belonging to any clique. A *bridge* is an individual who is a member of a communication clique and has a link to an individual who is a member of a different communication clique. An *isolate* is an individual who has few communication contacts with the rest of the system.

[10] *System connectedness* is the degree to which the members of a system as a whole are linked with each other in communication flows. *System openness* is the degree to which a system exchanges information with its environment.

[11] These two sets of authors independently discovered the diffusion strength of weak sociometric ties, and although approaching the issue in somewhat different ways, they published articles with virtually identical titles within a few months of each other in 1972–73. Professors Liu, Duff, and Granovetter were well read in the diffusion literature but had not previously published on this topic, and their articles showed a relatively fresh approach to analyzing diffusion networks. Perhaps this relative newness in working with the classical diffusion model was one requisite for the originality of their contribution.

REFERENCES

Arndt, J. "Role of Product-Related Conversations in the Diffusion of a New Product," *Journal of Marketing Research*, 4 (August 1967), 291–95.

Arundale, R. B. *The Concept of Process in Human Communication Research*. Unpublished doctoral dissertation, Michigan State University, 1971.

Barton, A. H. "Bringing Society Back In: Survey Research and Macro-Methodology," *American Behavioral Scientist*, 12 (November–December 1968), 1–9.

Caplan, N. and S. D. Nelson. "On Being Useful: The Nature and Consequences of Psychological Research on Social Problems," *American Psychologist*, 28 (March 1973), 199–211.

Coleman, J. S. "Relational Analysis: The Study of Social Organization with Survey Methods," *Human Organization*, 17 (Winter 1958–59), 28–36.

Coleman, J. S., E. Katz, and H. Menzel. *Medical Innovation: A Diffusion Study*. Indianapolis: Bobbs-Merrill, 1966.

Conner, J. T. "Needed: New Economics for a New Era," *Printers' Ink*, 287 (May 29, 1964), 35–37.

Crane, D. *Invisible Colleges: Diffusion of Knowledge in Scientific Communities*. Chicago: University of Chicago Press, 1972.

De Fleur, M. L. *Theories of Mass Communication*. New York: McKay, 1966.

Deutschmann, P. J. and O. F. Borda. *Communication and Adoption Patterns in an Andean Village*. San José, Costa Rica: Programa Interamericano de Información Popular and Facultad de Sociologia, Universidad Nacional de Colombia, 1962a.

Deutschmann, P. J. and O. F. Borda. *La Comunicación de las Ideas entre los Campesinos Colombianos: Un Análisis Socio-Estadístico. Monografias Sociologicas* 14. Bogota: Universidad Nacional de Colombia, 1962b.

Deutschmann, P. J. and W. A. Danielson. "Diffusion of Knowledge of the Major News Story," *Journalism Quarterly,* 37 (Summer 1960), 345–55.

Fliegel, F. C. and J. E. Kivlin. "Attributes of Innovations as Factors in Diffusion," *American Journal of Sociology,* 72 (November 1966), 235–48.

Freedman, R. and J. Y. Takeshita. *Family Planning in Taiwan: An Experiment in Social Change.* Princeton: Princeton University Press, 1969.

Gordon, G., A. E. MacEachron, and G. L. Fisher. "A Contingency Model for the Design of Problem-Solving Research Problems: A Perspective on Diffusion Research," *Milbank Memorial Fund Quarterly/Health and Society,* 52 (Spring 1974), 185–220.

Granovetter, M. "The Strength of Weak Ties," *American Journal of Sociology,* 78 (May 1973), 1360–80.

Hauser, P. M. " 'Family Planning and Population Programs': A Book Review Article," *Demography,* 4 (no. 1, 1967), 397–414.

Homans, G. C. *Social Behavior: Its Elementary Forms.* New York: Harcourt, Brace and World, 1961.

Katz, E. "Communication Research and the Image of Society: Convergence of two Traditions," *American Journal of Sociology,* 65 (March 1960), 435–40.

Kotler, P., and G. Zaltman. "Social Marketing: An Approach to Planned Social Change," *Journal of Marketing,* 35 (July 1971), 3–12.

Kuhn, T. K. *The Structure of Scientific Revolutions.* Chicago: University of Chicago Press, 1962.

Laumann, E. O. *Bonds of Pluralism: The Form and Substance of Urban Social Networks.* New York: Wiley, 1973.

Lazarsfeld, P. F., B. Berelson, and H. Gaudet. *The People's Choice.* New York: Duell, Sloan, and Pearce, 1944.

Liu, W. T. and R. W. Duff. "The Strength in Weak Ties," *Public Opinion Quarterly,* 36 (Fall 1972), 361–66.

Rahim, S. A. *Diffusion and Adoption of Agricultural Practices: A Study of Pattern of Communication, Diffusion and Adoption of Improved Agricultural Practice in a Village in East Pakistan.* Technical publication no. 7. Comilla, Pakistan: (Bangladesh) Academy for Village Development, 1961.

Robertson, T. S. *Innovative Behavior and Communication.* New York: Holt, Rinehart & Winston, 1971.

Rogers, E. M. "Mass Communication and the Diffusion of Innovations: Conceptual Convergence of Two Research Traditions." Paper presented at the Association for Education in Journalism, Boulder, Colorado, 1967.

————. *Modernization among Peasants: The Impact of Communication.* New York: Holt, Rinehart & Winston, 1969.

————. *Communication of Innovations: A Cross-Cultural Approach.* (2nd ed.) New York: Free Press, 1971.

————. *Communication Strategies for Family Planning.* New York: Free Press, 1973.

SOME SUGGESTIONS FOR FURTHER READING

Arndt, J. (1977), "New Product Diffusion: The Interplay of Innovativeness, Opinion Leadership, Learning, Perceived Risk, and Product Attributes," in Sheth, J. N., *Models of Buyer Behavior,* New York: Harper & Row, 327–335.

Rogers, E. M. (1976), "A Personal History of Research on the Diffusion of Innovations," in A. R. Andreason and S. Sudman, (eds.), *Public Policy, and Marketing Thought,* Chicago, IL: American Marketing Association, 43–63.

———— and P. C. Thomas (1975), *Bibliography on the Diffusion of Innovations,* Ann Arbor: Department of Population Planning, University of Michigan.

Roberston, T. S. (1974), "A Critical Examination of 'Adoption Process' Models of Consumer Behavior," in J. Sheth (ed.), *Models of Buyer Behavior,* New York: Harper & Row, 271–295.

17 / PSYCHOGRAPHICS: A CRITICAL REVIEW / William D. Wells

Among the standard fixtures in marketing research, the demographic profile is probably the most familiar. Age, income, education, and other indications of position in life space have so much influence on so many kinds of consumer behavior that users of a product or a brand, viewers of a TV program, or readers of a magazine are virtually certain to differ from the rest of the population on one or more of the common demographic dimensions. Marketing researchers collect demographics as a matter of routine, and marketers feel comfortable using them.

But demographic profiles, essential though they may be, have not been deemed sufficient. Especially since the end of World War II researchers have engaged in a continuous search for new, more comprehensive, and more exciting descriptions. It is as though demographics provided only a nodding acquaintance, and marketers wanted to know their customers much better.

Until recently this search has followed two somewhat different directions. Starting with the classic study by Koponen [74], investigators have repeatedly tried to correlate consumer behavior with scores obtained from standardized personality inventories. And, starting with Dichter's innovative studies of consumers' motivations [31], students of the consumer's mind have tried to apply the concepts and methods of clinical psychology to virtually every aspect of marketing.

From Koponen's study on, the work with personality inventories has been judged "equivocal" [65]. The correlations have almost invariably been low, and the relationships uncovered have often been so abstract that they could not be used with confidence in making real-world marketing decisions.

Motivation research has fared much better. In spite of severe criticisms on both ethical and methodological grounds, motivation research enjoyed a tremendous vogue; in its current form—the small scale "qualitative study"—it still has many busy practitioners. It is somewhat ironic that the more rigorous of these two approaches has proved relatively sterile, while the sloppier methodology continues to produce results that intelligent people judge to be of great value.

Sometime during the 1960s a blend of these two traditions began to take shape. Variously called "life style" [102, 104], "psychographic" [29, 89, 90, 91, 95, 109], or "activity and attitude" [54, 55] research, this blend combines the objectivity of the personality inventory with the rich, consumer-oriented, descriptive detail of the qualitative motivation research investigation. This new blend has attracted considerable attention, both among "academics" and among "real-world"

William D. Wells, "Psychographics: A Critical Review," Vol. 12 (May 1975), pp. 196–213. Published by the American Marketing Association. Reprinted by permission of the publisher. William Wells is Senior Vice President for Needham Harper and Steers advertising agency. He previously taught at the University of Chicago and has pioneered studies in the area of psychographics. He received his Ph.D. in psychology from Stanford University.

marketers. It has also attracted its share of criticism, and its share of skeptical questions as to its true usefulness and value [26, 33, 45, 86, 110, 120, 124, 142].

This review attempts to take stock of the present status and future prospects of psychographic research, including consumer-oriented research with standardized personality inventories. It begins with a definition of the field. It continues with examples of five somewhat different approaches to psychographic analysis. And it concludes with a critical discussion of the reliability, validity, and usefulness of psychographic measurements.

DEFINITIONS

Although the need for a common definition of psychographics is obvious, no single definition has met with general approval. Twenty-four articles on psychographics contain no less than 32 definitions, all somewhat different [29, 30, 33, 45, 53, 68, 79, 83, 89, 92, 95, 100, 105, 108, 109, 110, 111, 119, 120, 134, 140, 142, 143, 146], and each new publication seems to produce still another verson of what psychographic research is or is not. Within this diversity, however, certain common elements are clearly visible.

Something More Than Demographics

All psychographic researchers have attempted to move beyond demographics into areas that are relatively untried and unfamiliar. Depending upon the investigator's objectives and to some extent upon his taste, the added dimensions have run from one or two [11, 23, 44, 67, 80] to several hundred [1, 102, 125, 136, 145] and have embraced a wide range of content, including activities, interests, opinions, needs, values, attitudes, and personality traits. In some cases the variables have been "homemade," and in others they have been borrowed from standardized attitude scales or personality inventories. In all cases, however, the common theme has been that demographic attributes alone are not enough.

Quantitative, Not Qualitative

Second, most psychographic researchers have employed precoded, objective questionnaires that can be self-administered or administered by ordinary survey interviewers. Precoding makes the data amenable to complex multivariate statistical analysis; ease of administration encourages—or at least permits—use of large, representative samples. Both practices distinguish psychographic studies from studies in the qualitative motivation research tradition.

Operationally, then, psychographic research can be defined as quantitative research intended to place consumers on psychological—as distinguished from demographic—dimensions. Because it goes beyond the standard and the accepted, it offers the possibility of new insights and unusual conclusions. Because it is quantitative rather than discursive, it opens the way to large, representative samples of respondents, and to multivariate statistical analysis of findings.

FIVE EXAMPLES

A Psychographic Profile Based on General "Life-Style" Dimensions

The need for good descriptions of consumers is well expressed in the following comment by an advertising copy writer:

> ... Imagine that I've got to write an ad on a Sunday afternoon, and I want to feel sure I'm on the right track. I want to double check myself that people will understand it/react to it/remember it, plus a few subtleties like will they like it, dislike it, etc.
>
> So, I trudge all the way around the block, talking to the neighbors, and forty houses later I have a slight idea of what will happen to my ad when it reaches the world. That's what I understand Research does, only a lot more intelligently and a lot more thoroughly and in a lot more neighborhoods.
>
> A writer writes out of his personal collection of life experiences and his knowledge of people, and he imagines and projects them and he tries to translate them into his viewer's or his reader's terms. But he's feeding off himself. He's just one person. He can't afford to trust just his own experience. Research extends the writer. Information is his life blood. He can't write out of thin air. Anything that adds to his storehouse of information is necessary and vital [75].

Similar needs are felt by all others who must create products, services, or messages for customers they cannot meet in person. Just as the writer knows that he cannot feed only off himself, so also the product designer and the marketing manager know that they run grave risks when they rely solely on their own assumptions. Almost all of marketing is communication; marketers are most effective when they know their audiences.

As an example of the descriptive value of psychographic dimensions, consider the somewhat esoteric problem of communicating with consumers who are heavy users of shotgun ammunition. Persons of this sort would be of special interest to anyone who manufactures, markets, or advertises shotguns, ammunition, or associated hunting paraphenalia; to operators of hunting lodges and private hunting areas; to publishers of hunting magazines; and to government officials who promote or regulate this form of recreation.

A demographic profile of the heavy user of shotgun ammunition appears in Table 1. The man who spends at least $11 per year on shotgun shells differs from the nonbuyer in that he tends to be younger, lower in income and education, and more concentrated in blue collar occupations. He is also more apt to be living in rural areas, especially in the South.

Now reflect upon the implication of this pattern. Hunting is a risky sport. Is the hunter a risk taker? Is he likely to follow rules on his own, or does he re-

Table 1. Demographic profile of the heavy user of shotgun ammunition

	Percent who spend $11+ per year on shotgun ammunition (141)	Percent who don't buy (395)
Age		
Under 25	9	5
25–34	33	15
35–44	27	22
45–54	18	22
55+	13	36
Occupation		
Professional	6	15
Managerial	23	23
Clerical-Sales	9	17
Craftsman	50	35
Income		
Under $6,000	26	19
$6,000–$10,000	39	36
$10,000–$15,000	24	27
$15,000+	11	18
Population Density		
Rural	34	12
2,500–50,000	11	11
50,000–500,000	16	15
500,000–2 million	21	27
2 million+	13	19
Geographic Division		
New England—Mid-Atlantic	21	33
Central (N, W)	22	30
South Atlantic	23	12
E. South Central	10	3
W. South Central	10	5
Mountain	6	3
Pacific	9	15

Source: [107].

quire external control? Hunting is a violent sport. Is the hunter attracted by violence in general? What other products would make good tie-in sales with hunting equipment? Is the hunter also a fisherman or a camper? Is he especially interested in food? Is he a regular newspaper reader? Is he a regular patron of discount stores? From the demographic profile alone, a marketer with a thorough knowledge of young, blue-collar, nonurban life styles might be able to guess the answers to at least some of these questions, but few would guess them all.

The data in Table 2 show how psychographic information can put flesh on demographic bones. These data came from a general life-style study that happened to contain a question about shotgun ammunition along with questions about approximately 100 other products and services. The questionnaire also contained questions about a wide range of activities, interests, and opinions; about reading of major magazines; and viewing of a large number of television programs. The study was not designed around shotgun users, or around the users of any other single product.

Table 2. Psychographic profile of the heavy user of shotgun ammunition

Base	Percent who spend $11+ per year on shotgun ammunition (141)	Percent who don't buy (395)
I like hunting	88	7
I like fishing	68	26
I like to go camping	57	21
I love the out-of-doors	90	65
A cabin by a quiet lake is a great place to spend the summer	49	34
I like to work outdoors	67	40
I am good at fixing mechanical things	47	27
I often do a lot of repair work on my own car	36	12
I like war stories	50	32
I would do better than average in a fist fight	38	16
I would like to be a professional football player	28	18
I would like to be a policeman	22	8
There is too much violence on television	35	45
There should be a gun in every home	56	10
I like danger	19	8
I would like to own my own airplane	35	13
I like to play poker	50	26
I smoke too much	39	24
I love to eat	49	34
I spend money on myself that I should spend on the family	44	26
If given a chance, most men would cheat on their wives	33	14
I read the newspaper every day	51	72

Source: [107].

In spite of this lack of focus, the data in Table 2 show some interesting patterns. First, it is obvious that hunting is not an isolated phenomenon but rather is associated with other rugged outdoor endeavors. Shotgun shell buyers not only like to hunt, they also like to fish and to go camping. They even like to work outdoors. These relationships are interesting and useful because they suggest activities and settings, other than hunting scenes, that might be appropriate for shotgun ammunition advertising. They suggest products that might be especially appropriate for joint promotions or other cooperative marketing ventures, such as displaying shotgun ammunition near camping or fishing equipment in retail outlets. Table 2 also shows that ammunition buyers are apt to be do-it-yourselfers, which suggests that hunters are apt to be buyers of hardware and tools.

Items in the third group in Table 2 suggest some hypotheses about the psychological makeup of the shotgun ammunition buyer. Compared with the non-buyer he is definitely more attracted by violence, suggesting that detective, war, and violent Western TV programs ought to draw audiences with disproportionate numbers of shotgun users, and that action and adventure magazines ought to be considered when placing advertising associated with hunting. Relationships between product use and media exposure are always best documented by direct cross-tabulation, but when these data are not available (and they often are not) relationships suggested by life-style patterns can provide helpful direction.

The relatively high levels of agreement with the fourth section of Table 2 suggest that the hunter is generally less risk-averse than is his nonhunting counterpart. To policy makers charged with keeping hunters from shooting themselves and each other, this willingness to accept risk would suggest that sober warnings about the dangers of firearms may well be ineffective. Lest this conclusion seem hopelessly naive, let it be noted that sober warnings about the dangers of firearms are exactly what some policy makers have attempted.

The relatively high levels of agreement with the fifth section suggest a combination of self-indulgence and lack of internal control that seems congruent with the attitude toward risk just noted. If the hunter is in fact self-indulgent and relatively conscienceless, it would seem unwise to rely on appeals to fair play and conservation to regulate his activities. Again, such appeals have been tried with less success than expected.

The level of agreement with "I love to eat" and the hunter's professed willingness to spend money on himself suggest markets for premium foods designed to be taken along on hunting expeditions. These two findings also suggest the suitability of game-preparation recipes for hunting magazines, and they indicate that quantity and quality of food should get particular attention from proprietors of hunting lodges. Hunters don't mind roughing it, but they want it to be a well-fed roughness.

Finally, the relatively low level of agreement with "I read the newspaper every day" should serve as a warning to shotgun ammunition advertisers. This is not to assert that media decisions, positive or negative, should ever be based on responses to a single survey item. Rather, it suggests that any shotgun ammunition advertiser who is spending his budget in newspapers should think twice about alternatives.

This brief example shows how a psychographic profile obtained almost incidentally in the context of a large, general life-style survey can provide suggestions and hypotheses that bear on a wide range of marketing and policy decisions. A demographic profile alone would perhaps have provided some of these inferences, but surely not all of them.

This example also shows how a psychographic profile can help the marketer avoid some traps a demographic profile would have set for him. Knowing that heavy users of shotgun ammunition tend to be younger, more in blue collar occupations, and less urban than nonusers might suggest that they would be heavier users of beer, more interested in television, more interested in spectator sports, more prone to use credit, and more apt to shop at discount stores. Yet buyers of shotgun ammunition do not differ significantly from nonbuyers on any of these dimensions.

Other psychographic life-style profiles that have appeared in the literature include carryout foods [130]; eye makeup, shortening, oranges, and lemons [133, 136]; beer [103, 127]; mouthwash [127]; heavy duty hand soap [103]; bank charge cards [102]; department stores [83]; and air travel [11]. They also include profiles of the readers of magazines [117, 128] and of viewers of various television programs [104, 128]. In all these cases the psychographic data have provided rich, descriptive detail that could not have been inferred from demographics. See also [1, 47, 50, 58, 77, 118, 132, 136, 138].

A Product-Specific Psychographic Profile

In the previous example, the psychographic profile was drawn from a large set of general life-style items. Because the item list was large and diverse, some of the items happened to be related to consumption of shotgun ammunition. When a psychographic study is devoted to a single product category, it is not necessary to depend on item diversity to get useful relationships. Rather, the investigator can focus upon a limited set of relevant, product-related dimensions.

An excellent example of this use of psychographics is provided in a report by Young [144] on the "positioning" of the Ford Pinto. According to Young, the introductory Pinto advertising portrayed the car as "carefree, small (and) romantic." The strategy was "to sell to small car prospects; to compete against imported small cars; to say that the car was carefree, trouble free, beautifully styled, and economical" [144, p. 15].

As the introduction of the Pinto proceeded, psychographic research disclosed that potential Pinto buyers had a less romantic orientation toward cars and driving. They endorsed statements like "I wish I could depend on my car more," "I am more practical in car selection," "A car offers me a chance to tinker with machinery," "I like to feel how powerful my car is" and "The only function for a car is transportation." They rejected statements like "The kind of car you have is important as to how people see you" and "Taking care of a car is too much trouble."

As a result of this research, the Pinto was repositioned (in advertising, by its new agency) as "The epitomy of function, exemplifying basic economical transportation, trading on Ford's heritage of the Model A." Consequently, "Today Pinto is the largest selling subcompact, outselling Volkswagen by a sizeable margin" [144, p. 15].

Now it is admittedly farfetched to assume that all (or maybe even most) of Pinto's success was due to this change in position. But it does seem reasonable to believe that emphasis on economic and practicality appealed to the salient needs of potential subcompact buyers, and that the revised message communicated ideas that potential customers would find most persuasive.

Personality Traits as Descriptors

A report on 'Ecologically Concerned Consumers: Who Are They?" [72] provides a third example of psychographic analysis. In this report the dependent variable was an "index of ecological concern" that included both attitudes toward ecological issues and conservationist behavior. The independent variables were 7 demographic characteristics, 12 personality traits taken from standardized personality inventories, and a variable called "perceived consumer effectiveness." This attribute was measured by degree of disagreement with "It is futile for the individual consumer to try to do anything about pollution."

The 20 independent variables were first screened by analysis of variance to determine which of them discriminated between respondents who were high and respondents who were low in ecological concern. The 10 variables that survived the screening were then input to Multiple Classification Analysis to "predict" the degree of ecological concern expressed by each respondent. To avoid confusion it should be noted that in this study, as in most psychographic studies, the term "predict" cannot be taken literally. Since the data were all collected at the same point in time, "prediction" really means correlation.

The MCA coefficients for the "factors that were found to be most significant" in "predicting" ecological concern are shown in Table 3. The coefficients show how much the members of each category differ in ecological concern from the total sample. Thus, respondents who were low in perceived consumer effectiveness were 2.49 points below average in ecological concern, respondents who were medium were 4.04 points below average, and so on.

This study differs from the ammunition study and the Pinto study in two important ways. First, in the ammunition and Pinto studies the descriptions of the target groups were developed by considering *all* the psychographic items that discriminated between the target group and the remainder of the population. In this study, on the other hand, the answers that respondents gave to the personality scale questions were summed to produce higher level, more abstract scores on

Table 3. MCA profile of the ecologically concerned consumer

Factor	Level	Regression coefficient
Perceived consumer effectiveness	Very low	—
	Low	−2.49
	Medium	−4.04
	High	−1.04
	Very high	2.54
Tolerance	Very low	.15
	Low	− .79
	Medium	− .39
	High	− .04
	Very high	1.00
Understanding	Very low	− .92
	Low	− .81
	Medium	.22
	High	.27
	Very high	1.25
Harm avoidance	Very low	− .59
	Low	.13
	Medium	.27
	High	.73
	Very high	−1.22
Annual family income	Under $5,000	− .39
	$5,000 to $6,999	− .24
	$7,000 to $9,999	.10
	$10,000 to $14,999	− .15
	$15,000 and over	.74

Mean = 11.31.
R^2 = .28.

"tolerance," "understanding," and "harm avoidance." This procedure had the effect of eliminating much of the rich descriptive detail that might have been provided by the individual questions. We do not know what answers produced high scores or low scores on the personality dimensions.

Second, in the ammunition and Pinto studies the profiles were developed by cross-tabulating *all* of the psychographic items with the dependent variable. In this study, the independent variables were linked to the dependent variable by a type of multiple regression. Like all other forms of multiple regression, MCA suppresses variables that are closely related to variables that are allowed to enter the equation. As a result, variables closely related to each other could not all have entered the description of the ecologically concerned consumer, even though they might have discriminated sharply in a cross-tabulation.

Many other examples of this general approach are to be found in the literature. In one of the earliest psychographic studies, Koponen regressed Edwards Personal Preference Schedule scores on consumption of cigarettes and readership of several magazines [74]. A group of investigators from the Advertising Research Foundation regressed the same set of independent variables against consumption of toilet paper, with predictable and poetically just results [5]. Frank, Massy, and Lodahl did the same for coffee, tea, and beer [41]. Wilson [139] factor analyzed an activity, interest, and opinion inventory and regressed various AIO factors against consumption of a list of products that included soft drinks, lipstick, and stomach remedies. And Darden and Reynolds [27] used scales representing fashion interest, fashion venturesomeness, cognitive style, information seeking, relative popularity and relative self-confidence to "predict" fashion opinion leadership. See also [21, 25, 39, 46, 69, 85, 87, 100, 123].

In all these cases a large set of descriptive items was reduced to a smaller number of more abstract scores, and this reduced set of independent variables was then linked to the dependent variable by means of some form of multiple regression. The descriptions thus provided were therefore more abstract and less redundant than the descriptions that would have been provided by simple cross-tabulation of the uncondensed raw data.

A General Life-Style Segmentation Study

A report of a major study by the Newspaper Advertising Bureau [109] provides an example of still another approach to psychographics. In this study a national sample of approximately 4,000 respondents completed questionnaires containing 300 psychographic questions, several dozen questions about product use, and questions about exposure to various media. The psychographic questions were reduced to a smaller set of scales by R-type factor analysis, and the resulting factor scores were input to Q-type factor analysis to place the respondents into relatively homogeneous groups. Condensed descriptions of the eight male groups are given in Figure 1.

This study differs from the first three in that it did not assume that members of any target group are all very similar. Instead of attempting to discover what hunters, Pinto buyers, or ecologically concerned consumers have in common, this

Figure 1. Eight male psychographic segments

Group I. *"The Quiet Family Man"* (8% of total males)

He is a self-sufficient man who wants to be left alone and is basically shy. Tries to be as little involved with community life as possible. His life revolves around the family, simple work and television viewing. Has a marked fantasy life. As a shopper he is practical, less drawn to consumer goods and pleasures than other men.

Low education and low economic status, he tends to be older than average.

Group II. *"The Traditionalist"* (16% of total males)

A man who feels secure, has self-esteem, follows conventional rules. He is proper and respectable, regards himself as altruistic and interested in the welfare of others. As a shopper he is conservative, likes popular brands and well-known manufacturers.

Low education and low or middle socio-economic status; the oldest age group.

Group III. *"The Discontented Man"* (13% of total males)

He is a man who is likely to be dissatisfied with his work. He feels bypassed by life, dreams of better jobs, more money and more security. He tends to be distrustful and socially aloof. As a buyer, he is quite price conscious.

Lowest education and lowest socio-economic group, mostly older than average.

Group IV. *"The Ethical Highbrow"* (14% of total males)

This is a very concerned man, sensitive to people's needs. Basically a puritan, content with family life, friends, and work. Interested in culture, religion and social reform. As a consumer he is interested in quality, which may at times justify greater expenditure.

Well educated, middle or upper socio-economic status, mainly middle aged or older.

Group V. *"The Pleasure Oriented Man"* (9% of total males)

He tends to emphasize his masculinity and rejects whatever appears to be soft or feminine. He views himself a leader among men. Self-centered, dislikes his work or job. Seeks immediate gratification for his needs. He is an impulsive buyer, likely to buy products with a masculine image.

Low education, lower socio-economic class, middle aged or younger.

Group VI. *"The Achiever"* (11% of total males)

This is likely to be a hardworking man, dedicated to success and all that it implies, social prestige, power and money. Is in favor of diversity, is adventurous about leisure time pursuits. Is stylish, likes good food, music, etc. As a consumer he is status conscious, a thoughtful and discriminating buyer.

Good education, high socio-economic status, young.

Group VIII. *"The He-Man"* (19% of total males)

He is gregarious, likes action, seeks an exciting and dramatic life. Thinks of himself as capable and dominant. Tends to be more of a bachelor than a family man, even after marriage. Products he buys and brands preferred are likely to have "self-expressive value," especially a "Man of Action" dimension.

Well educated, mainly middle socio-economic status, the youngest of the male groups.

Group VIII. *"The Sophisticated Man"* (10% of total males)

He is likely to be an intellectual, concerned about social issues, admires men with artistic and intellectual achievements. Socially cosmopolitan, broad interests. Wants to be dominant, and a leader. As a consumer he is attracted to the unique and fashionable.

Best educated and highest economic status of all groups, younger than average.

study admitted the possibility that users of a product might fall into several quite different segments.

The wisdom of this approach is illustrated in Table 4. There it can be seen that the heavy users of several products and several brands, the readers of some magazines and the viewers of some TV programs tend to be concentrated in two or more segments that differ quite significantly from each other. When that is the case, any attempt to discover the characteristics of an undifferentiated target

Table 4. Product and media use by psychographic group

	Psychographic group[a] *percentages*							
	I	*II*	*III*	*IV*	*V*	*VI*	*VII*	*VIII*
Drink Beer	45	56	57	51	75	59	80	72
Smoke cigarettes	32	40	40	29	54	42	51	38
Air travel outside U.S.	4	4	6	7	5	8	12	19
Air travel, domestic	14	15	14	26	19	32	20	42
Use Brand X deodorant	7	7	6	8	14	10	9	12
Used headache remedy in past four weeks	53	60	66	61	61	64	65	67
Read current issue of:								
Playboy	8	11	8	13	25	27	36	30
National Geographic	21	13	11	30	13	28	16	27
Time	17	8	7	16	9	26	17	29
Newsweek	17	14	8	20	11	18	13	22
Field & Stream	10	12	14	8	12	9	13	3
Popular Mechanics	11	6	9	9	9	9	8	6
Viewed in past week:								
Sanford & Son	32	35	29	19	26	25	27	23
Sonny & Cher	17	24	22	19	14	24	30	22
Marcus Welby	26	25	26	23	20	16	20	18
Rowen & Martin	21	23	17	15	22	20	23	21
New Dick Van Dyke	19	15	16	13	11	8	10	12

[a] Described in Figure 1.

group—e.g., "the heavy beer drinker," "the user of Brand X deodorant," "the *Playboy* reader," or "the TV news viewer"—whether by simple cross-tabulation or by multiple regression—will be sure to underestimate the importance of the attributes upon which the segments differ. In extreme cases, when one segment of the target group is above average on a particular attribute and another segment is below average, merging the two segments into one target group can make the target group appear to be not different from the remainder of the population. (See [54, 55] for a neat example of this phenomena.)

A Product-Specified Segmentation

In the preceding example, the segmentation was based on general—as opposed to product related—psychographic items. When the investigation is devoted to one product, the investigator can focus upon product-related material. An example of the latter approach is given in a report by Pernica [95] of a stomach remedy segmentation. Pernica developed a list of 80 items that included symptom frequency, end benefits provided by different brands, attitudes toward treatment, and beliefs about ailments. Items tapping general personality traits were recast so as to be product specific. For instance, "I worry too much" was translated into "I seem to get stomach problems if I worry too much."

The 80 product-specific items were reduced to 13 factors by R factor analysis, and scores on the 13 factors were input into Q factor analysis to assign the respondents to homogeneous groups. The segments were described both in terms of the variables that went into the segmentation and in terms of personality traits, life-style attributes, and demographic characteristics (Figure 2). The ability of this procedure to discriminate among the brands in this product category is shown in Table 5.

Note that the discrimination produced by the product-specific approach is somewhat sharper than the discrimination produced by the more general segmentation. This outcome is common. When the segmentation is based upon the dimensions upon which brands differ, it is almost certain to discriminate more sharply among brands than when it is based upon more general considerations [54, 55, 143, 146]. Other examples of the product-specific approach can be found in [12, 30, 42, 52, 145–8].

This case history, and the four that precede it, provide five different examples of psychographic analysis. Collectively they show how psychographics can supplement demographics in interesting and useful ways. Individually they show the range of capabilities of these techniques, and they provide previews of some problems and ambiguities. We now turn to critical discussion of the problems that have arisen in the application of psychographic methods.

Figure 2.   Segmentation of Stomach Remedy Users

The Severe Sufferers. The Severe Sufferers are the extreme group on the potency side of the market. They tend to be young, have children, and be well educated. They are irritable and anxious people, and believe that they suffer more severely than others. They take the ailment seriously, fuss about it, pamper themselves, and keep trying new and different products in search of greater potency. A most advanced product with new ingredients best satisfies their need for potency and fast relief, and ties in with their psychosomatic beliefs.

The Active Medicators. The Active Medicators are on the same side of the motivational spectrum. They are typically modern suburbanites with average income and education. They are emotionally well adjusted to the demands of their active lives. They have learnt to cope by adopting the contemporary beliefs of seeking help for every ill, and use remedies to relieve even minor signs of ailments and every ache and pain. In a modern product, they seek restoration of their condition and energy, mental recovery, and a lift for their active lives. They are influenced by a brand's reputation and by how well it is advertised. They tend to develop strong brand loyalties.

The Hypochondriacs. The Hypochondriacs are on the opposite side of the motivational spectrum. They tend to be older, not as well educated, and women. They have conservative attitudes toward medication and a deep concern over health. They see possible dangers in frequent use of remedies, are concerned over side effects, and afraid of remedies with new ingredients and extra potency. To cope with these concerns, they are strongly oriented toward medical authority, seeking guidance in treatment, and what products they should use. They hold rigid beliefs about the ailment and are disciplined in the products they use, and how frequently. They want a simple, single-purpose remedy, which is safe and free from side effects, and backed by doctors or a reputable company.

The Practicalists. The Practicalists are in the extreme position on this side of the motivational spectrum. They tend to be older, well educated, emotionally the most stable, and least concerned over their ailment or the dangers of remedies. They accept the ailment and its discomforts as a part of life, without fuss and pampering. They use a remedy as a last resort, and just to relieve the particular symptom. They seek simple products whose efficacy is well proven, and are skeptical of complicated modern remedies with new ingredients and multiple functions.

Table 5. Brand Use of Stomach Remedy Segments (Percent Use Brand Most Often)

Brand	Severe sufferers	Active medicators	Hypochondriacs	Practicalists
A	6	3	1	1
B	32	23	10	8
C	16	17	12	5
D	16	19	24	8
E	5	29	37	51

CRITICAL DISCUSSION

Questions about psychographics can be classified under four major headings: reliability, validity, applications to real-world marketing problems, and contributions to the study of consumer behavior. These topics will be discussed in turn, with special reference to the five case histories just given.

Reliability of Individual Terms and Scales

Here the term *reliability* is used in the restricted technical sense—i.e., freedom from *random* error [84, 93]. Although reliability of this sort is quite important, it is far from being the sole determinant of what a marketer is likely to be thinking about when he asks, "Can I rely on this study to guide my actions?" The other factors involved in that difficult and much more general question will be discussed in subsequent sections of this article.

When assessing reliability, it is important to distinguish between two major uses for psychographic measurements. One use is as a public opinion poll. An investigator might want to know, for example, how many people agree with "There should be a gun in every home," "Television commercials put too much emphasis on sex," or "I consider myself to be a member of the silent majority." In this use, when samples are of the size typically found in marketing surveys, *random* errors tend to cancel, and overall averages and percentages tend to be quite stable.

The other use of psychographics is in relationships, either in cross-tabulations—as in the shotgun and Pinto examples—or in "predictions" of dependent variables like ecological concern. Reliability is particularly important in studies of relationships because unreliable measurements can, in and of themselves, make strong relationships appear to be weak [84, 93].

Very little has been published on the reliability of "homemade" psychographic items and scales. In a review of the evidence available in 1971, Pessemier and Bruno [16, 98] reported a range of six-month test-retest reliability coefficients for individual items from "under .30" to "over .80" with a median between .60 and .69. And they reported reliability coefficients for multi-item scales ranging from .64 to .90, with a median of about .80. More recently, Darden and Reynolds [28] reported split-half reliabilities for 13 psychographic dimensions ranging from .60 to .89, with a median of .80.

Authors of standardized personality scales, like the scales used to identify the ecologically concerned consumer, normally provide evidence on scale reliability in their test manuals. Additional reliability data can often be found in *The Mental Measurements Yearbook* [18] and in literature reviews in such journals as *Psychological Bulletin*. These sources show that the standardized scales most often used by psychographic researchers have reliabilities that run from about .70 to about .90—somewhat higher than the reported reliabilities of homemade variables.

What all this says is that both homemade and standardized psychographic measurements *can* have reliability high enough to support fairly strong relationships. However, it also says that the reliability of some psychographic measurements—especially some individual homemade items—may well be low enough to put a rather severe limitation on accuracy of "prediction."

Reliability of Dependent Variables

The maximum possible correlation between two variables is fully as dependent upon the reliability of what is being predicted as it is upon the reliability of the predictor [84, 93]. In psychographic studies, where the dependent variable is normally some form of consumer behavior, this means that strong relationships cannot be obtained unless the consumer behavior itself is measured accurately, no matter how reliable the psychographic measurements may be. This limitation is compounded by the fact that some kinds of consumer behavior—such as choice of a specific brand on a given occasion or exposure to a particular television program—may be so unstable that accurate prediction is virtually impossible, quite apart from any random measurement errors. Indeed, Bass [9] has gone so far as to assert that individual brand choice is so unstable that it can *never* be accurately predicted, by psychographics or by anything else.

With a few exceptions, psychographic researchers have not investigated the reliability of dependent variables. Successful prediction implies (but does not certify) adequate reliability. But unsuccessful prediction leaves the researcher in a quandary. Unsuccessful prediction can be due to unreliability in the psychographic measurements, to unreliability in the dependent variables, to lack of any "real" relationships between the psychographics and the behavior in question, or to some combination of all three. In the absence of reliability data it is impossible to determine which is the case.

Reliability of Relationships

In psychographic studies, as in other forms of marketing research, it is normal to find painstaking analysis of relationships that may be due at least in part to chance. In the shotgun ammunition study, for example, it is not possible to be sure that the same differences between buyers and nonbuyers would be found in a new sample drawn from the same population of respondents. Similarly, one cannot be sure that the same attitudes would identify subcompact car buyers if the Pinto study were repeated; or that, on replication, ecologically concerned consumers would differ from people in general as indicated by the data in Table 3. In the ecology study, some of the findings are particularly suspect. It does not seem at all likely that ecological concern really increases with income up to $10,000, drops between $10,000 and $14,999 and then resumes its upward climb. A much more probable explanation for that particular irregular relationship is some chance quirk in the data.

The only sure safeguard against being deceived by chance relationships is replication. When replication is impossible, the best procedure is to divide the sample into random parts, complete the analysis on one part, and then determine whether the same conclusions would have been reached via an identical analysis of the holdout group [6, 7, 14, 22, 34, 94, 141]. It is indeed unfortunate that this procedure has been the exception rather than the rule.

Reliability of Structure

Closely related to the question of reliability of relationships is the question of reliability of structure: do psychographic variables relate to each other in much the same way from study to study? In their reliability review Pessemier and Bruno compared factor analysis results from five large scale studies, including one conducted in Canada. They concluded that "the wide range of variables employed and the constructs to which they relate appear to be sufficiently reliable for both practical and theoretical purposes" [98, p. 397]. This conclusion is encouraging because it asserts that items tend to hang together in much the same way when studies are repeated. If that were not the case, it would be hard to put much credence in their relationship to anything else.

A further and more difficult question concerns the stability of the segments produced by various clustering procedures. If the Newspaper Advertising Bureau's general life-style segmentation or Pernica's segmentation of stomach remedy users were repeated on new samples of consumers, would the same conclusions be reached as to segment content and segment size? The answer to that question is of the utmost practical importance. If segments vary greatly in size, or disappear altogether, from one analysis to another, it makes no sense at all to develop products, messages, or media schedules on the assumption that the segments are real.

In a caveat that has gone largely unheeded, Appel and Warwick noted in 1969 that: "Although Q-analysis is capable of reliably classifying people into relatively homogenous groups based on psychographic data, there is a real question as to how many such groups can be reliably specified. . . . Unless the analyst is able to certify the reliability of the Q-group designations, the study findings are in serious question" [4, p. 25].

In the same vein, Johnson has more recently stated, "It has been the sad experience of many researchers that cluster analysis has produced interpretable groups differing dramatically in meaningful ways—and then subsequent analysis of new data has obtained equally convincing but entirely unrelated results. There are some uses of cluster analysis with which this would not be troublesome; but more frequently it would be an indication that neither solution is to be trusted" [62, p. 8].

The reliability of segments produced by empirical clustering procedures depends on several factors. First, and probably most important, reliability depends upon whether sharply differing, relatively homogeneous groups of consumers actually exist in the respondent population. The more segmented the population really is, the more the segmentation will be influenced by real structure, and not by adventitious bleeps [57]. Second, reliability will be influenced by the number of variables used, the size of the respondent sample, the accuracy with which the respondents answered the questions, and anything else that influences the stability of the correlations upon which the segmentation is based. Reliability will be influenced by the number of segments extracted. The larger the number of segments, the less likely they are to be reproducible [4]. And finally, reliability will depend upon the segmentation technique employed. Hierarchical clustering [61], a technique that has been used in a number of proprietary studies, may be much less reliable than alternative methods.

At this point in the developement of psychographics, techniques for deriving segments are still primitive. We need to know much more about the conditions under which they succeed and the conditions under which they fail. We know for sure, however, that cluster solutions can be quite unstable, especially when the number of clusters is large. For this reason, it is especially important to compute the analysis on randomly selected halves of the sample and to reject solutions that do not match. This minimum requirement has often not been met. (See, for example [3, 12, 25, 39, 42, 76, 100].)

Reliability Summary

The available data indicate that psychographic measurements and analytic procedures can have satisfactory reliability. But, generally satisfactory reliability does not imply adequate reliability in all cases, and it may well be that some of the failures to find useful relationships between psychographics and consumer behavior have been due to instability in the measurements themselves. This may be especially true of the dependent variables, which can be unreliable both in the sense that they contain substantial amounts of random error, and in the sense that the behavior being measured is intrinsically unstable.

Unreliability also reduces the confidence one can place in relationships revealed by cross-tabulations or regressions, and the confidence one can place in clusters, both as to content and as to size. When important decisions are to be made on the basis of psychographics, it is essential that cross-tabulations, regressions, or clusters be cross-validated against holdout samples. It is all too easy to overanalyze findings that may be partially due to chance.

Validity

The term *validity* is used here in the traditional way. That is, a measurement is "valid" to the degree that it really does measure what it was intended to measure.

Like other measurements, psychographic measurements can be reliable without being valid. They can be relatively free of random error but so full of irrelevancies and biases that conclusions based on them are partly (or even completely) false.

The question of the validity of psychographics is difficult and complex and cannot be answered simply. Here it is pursued under four headings: (1) construct validity of "homemade" psychographic variables, (2) construct validity of standardized scales, (3) construct validity of segments, and (4) predictive validity.

Construct Validity of Homemade Psychographic Variables

The construct validity of a measurement is established by showing that it relates to other variables to which it should be related, and does not relate to other variables to which it should not be related [19, 48, 93]. The process of establishing construct validity is normally spread out over time. It involves gradual accumulation of evidence, often by independent investigators, rather than a single finding of valid or not.

Pessemier and Bruno's review of the stability of certain psychographic constructs [16, 98] provides some evidence that bears upon the construct validity question. The fact that similar factors did indeed emerge when similar sets of items were answered by independent samples of respondents provides some assurance that individual psychographic items tend to relate to each other in internally consistent ways. While that finding is far from conclusive evidence of construct validity, it is a beginning. It shows that items which should go together do go together, while items that should not do not.

Further evidence of internal consistency can be found in the relationships between psychographics and demographics. Frequently one finds that the relationship between demographic and psychographic variables makes perfectly good sense. The evidence is not always conclusive, but when young people differ from old people in expected ways, or when more college graduates than nongraduates agree with "most of my friends have had a college education," the responses to the psychographic items seem right.

Beyond internal consistency, evidence for the construct validity of homemade items and scales is hard to find. The most general practice is to assume, unless there is evidence to the contrary, that the respondent is reporting accurately. Stated this baldly, the assumption sounds naive, but it is common in marketing research. When respondents are asked about brand preferences, exposure to media, or consumption of products, the general practice is to take answers at face value, even though it is known that such answers are sometimes wrong.

Much stronger evidence on construct validity would come from painstaking item-by-item and scale-by-scale convergent and discriminant validation [19]. That process has scarcely even begun, and it is so vastly complex that it will surely never be completed. In the meantime, users of homemade variables must be content with the assumption that respondents' answers contain a useful amount of valid information.

The Construct Validity of Standardized Scales

The psychographic researcher who uses standardized scales is less dependent upon face validity than is the researcher who assembles his own set of independent variables. Almost all published attitude scales and personality inventories are accompanied by at least some validity data, and some instruments are accompanied by quite a lot. If the scale has been widely used, the results of construct validity studies can be found in the *Mental Measurements Yearbook* and in reviews in psychological journals.

It is virtually impossible to make a valid generalization about the construct validity of standardized personality and attitude scales. Indeed, it often seems that the more a scale is investigated the less agreement there is as to its true meaning. (See for example [36, 38].)

It is safe to say, however, that the information that is available has frequently been ignored. In a recent review of personality inventories in consumer research, Kassarjian observed, "Typically a convenient, available, easily scored, and easy-to-administer personality inventory is selected and administered along with questionnaires on purchase data and preferences. The lack of proper scientific method and hypothesis generation is supposedly justified by the often-used disclaimer that the study is exploratory" [65, p. 416]. He followed that observation with a quote from Jacoby that also bears repeating: "... in most cases, no a *priori* thought is directed to *how*, or especially *why*, personality should or should not be related to that aspect of consumer behavior being studied. Moreover, the few studies which do report statistically significant findings usually do so on the basis of post-hoc 'picking and choosing' out of large data arrays" [60, p. 244].

Failure to make sensible use of construct validity data has been all too common. Its implications will be discussed in the next to the last section of this review.

The Construct Validity of Segments

Anyone who makes policy decisions on the basis of segmentations like those shown in Figures 1 and 2 must necessarily assume that relatively homogeneous groups of consumers fitting those descriptions actually exist. As noted in the reliability discussion, one way to check on this assumption is to determine whether the segments hold up under cross-validation with a held out sample of respondents. If segments disappear or change dramatically in size from one sample to another, the notion that the segments are "real" would appear to be tenuous indeed.

But even when segments hold up under cross-validation, there is still the question of how accurately the descriptions fit each member of each group. The "Traditionalist" described in Figure 1 is said to represent 16% of the adult male population—about 10 million people. How many of these 10 million really do differ from other consumers in all of those ways?

At present, questions about the reality of psychographic segments have no good answers, and with rare exceptions [40, 61, 62, 63, 81, 82, 86], such questions have scarcely even been approached. Few aspects of psychographics are more in need of basic research.

Predictive Validity

In econometrics, the validity of a model is established by its ability to predict the summed or averaged behavior of large numbers of individuals. In psychometrics, the validity of a test is established by its ability to predict the behavior of separate individuals. This distinction is important because the degree of accuracy that can be expected of predictions at the aggregate level is much higher than the degree of accuracy that can be expected of predictions at the individual level. One can predict with virtual certainty that there will be a traffic jam on the George Washington Bridge on a pleasant summer Friday afternoon; but one cannot be sure Arbuthnot will be in it.

The results of individual level predictions with psychographic instruments have paralleled the experience in research on personality. In the absence of good reason to believe that the psychographic construct would be closely related to the specific consumer behavior being studied, correlations have usually run between +.20 and −.20, with many close to zero [5, 15, 41, 49, 51, 70, 73, 76, 87, 88, 99, 100, 101, 131, 137]. When the psychographic constructs have been clearly relevant to the behavior being studied, individual correlations have been in the .20s and .30s [13, 20, 27, 102, 128]. And when relevant dimensions have been linked together in multiple regression, multiple correlations have been in the .50s and .60s [2, 43, 69, 96, 139].

Whether this record is good or bad depends greatly upon one's point of view. Many critics have declared that low correlations are of no practical value and have dismissed them out of hand [5, 7, 35, 64, 66]. But, as Bass, Tigert, and Lonsdale [10] have cogently argued, accounting for differences among groups of consumers, rather than explaining the variance in individual behavior, is often the real object of psychographic analysis. From that standpoint, the record looks much better.

The data in Table 2 are typical of the group differences that can be produced by psychographic items. Some of the differences are quite large, and many of them are larger than the differences produced by the demographic variables in Table 1. The data in Table 3 are typical of the discriminating power of more abstract general personality traits. The differences produced by the personality traits are rather small; but, as in the shotgun example, the differences produced by psychographics are larger than the differences produced by demographics.

Other comparisons of psychographics and demographics can be found in reports by Wilson [139], Good and Suchland [46], King and Sproles [69], Nelson [89], Pessemier and Tigert [96], and Berger and Schott [17]. These reports all show that the predictive validity of psychographic variables is likely to be substantially higher than the predictive validity of the demographic attributes that have long been accepted as good, true, and beautiful in marketing research.

Validity Summary

It is difficult to give a concise answer to the question: "Are psychographic measurements valid?" The answer would depend greatly upon exactly what type of validity the questioner had in mind. Even within a single type of validity the answer would vary greatly from study to study. The evidence does show that psychographic variables generally relate to each other, to demographics, and to use of products and media in ways that make perfectly good sense. That is not a very strong statement, but at least it says that the patterns in the data are consistent with what we believe to be true about consumer behavior.

The evidence on predictive validity shows that psychographic variables seldom account for large portions of the variance of individual behavior. However, this evidence also shows that psychographic variables are capable of producing substantial differences between groups of consumers, and that these differences are often larger than the differences produced by the standard demographic profile.

From a policy point of view, the most immediately pressing question concerns the reality of psychographic segments. Marketers who make important decisions on the basis of segmentation studies urgently need ways to determine when the products of cluster analysis or Q factor analysis represent real groups of real consumers, and when they represent figments of the computer's imagination.

APPLICATIONS TO MARKETING PROBLEMS

The last two sections of this review bear upon usefulness—first in the context of real-world marketing problems, then in the context of present and potential contributions to a more general understanding of consumer behavior. The real-world discussion will argue that reliability and validity are neither necessary nor sufficient to insure that psychographic data can be used. The remainder of the discussion will argue that psychographic methods have already made significant contributions to the understanding of consumer behavior, and these contributions are likely to become more important as time goes on.

How to Get Valid, Useless Results

The results of psychographic research can be reliable and valid, and still not useful, when relationships that should not have been expected fail to appear. This may seem like a perfectly obvious observation, yet—as Kassarjian and Jacoby have already indicated—the literature is full of attempts to predict consumer behavior from personality test scores in the absence of any good reason to believe that the two should be related [59]. Perhaps the classic example of this shot-in-the-dark approach is an early psychographic effort in which scales from The Edwards Personal Preference Schedule—scales intended to measure such needs as autonomy, dominance, order, and endurance—were correlated with purchases of single- and double-ply toilet tissue [5]. Even if it were true that all of the measurements in this study were perfectly reliable and perfectly valid, the failure to find a significant correlation between need for dominance, for example, and purchase of toilet paper, could hardly come as much of a surprise. The same general comment applies to Evans's finding that the Edwards scales cannot separate Ford owners from Chevrolet owners [37]; to Robertson and Myers's finding that California Psychological Inventory scores do not account for much of the variance in innovativeness or opinion leadership [116]; to Kollat and Willett's finding that a set of general personality traits including optimism, belief in fate, and belief in multiple causation of events did not predict impulse purchasing [73]; and to many other negative findings that have not been published. The general proposition is: when one has no reason to believe that the psychographic constructs should be related to the consumer behavior in question, a negative finding—even though all the measurements may be highly reliable and highly valid—is not worth much.

Another way to circumvent usefulness is to be too abstract. A grand example of abstraction carried to extremes is provided in a study by Sparks and Tucker [122]. This study found that a latent canonical root with heavy positive loadings on sociability and emotional stability, and a heavy negative loading on responsibility, accounted for much of the variance of a dimension that represents heavy consumption of alcoholic beverages, cigarettes, and shampoo. The study also found that a second latent dimension represented by a heavy positive loading on emotional stability and a heavy negative loading on cautiousness accounted for much of the variance of a dimension that represents heavy consumption of after-shave lotion, light consumption of headache remedies, light consumption of mouthwash and coffee, and disinclinication to adopt new fashions. Assuming for the moment that this finding is both reliable and valid, just what does one do with it?

Third, psychographic measurements may be reliable and valid but so close to the behavior being studied that the relationship is essentially redundant. In Table 2, the best predictor of shotgun ammunition use is "I like to hunt." In Table 3, the best predictor of low ecological concern is agreement with "It is futile for the individual consumer to try to do anything about pollution." In Darden and Reynolds's study of men's fashions [27], the best predictors of fashion opinion leadership were two scales measuring "fashion interest" and "fashion venturesomeness." Findings of this sort are useful in the very restricted sense that they point to the construct validity of the psychographic items, but they are hardly likely to be greeted by marketing managers as world-shaking revelations.

To be useful in making real-world marketing decisions, psychographic data must be in some middle range between being almost totally redundant and being entirely unrelated to the behavior being studied. They must contain just the right amount of surprise. When that is the case, they can be very useful indeed, even when correlations are not high and even when questions about reliability and validity cannot be completely answered. This principle applies to profiles and to segmentations, for the same basic reason.

Why Psychographic Profiles Are Useful

To see why psychographic profiles are useful even in the absence of assured reliability and validity, it is necessary to consider the alternatives. Consider, for example, the copy writer quoted toward the beginning of this review. Confronted with a deadline for creating an advertisement, he could sit in his office and imagine his audience. But he might be wrong. As he said, he can't afford to trust just his own experience. He might do his own informal psychographic study—trudge all the way around the block talking to the neighbors. But to the degree that his neighbors are different from his customers, this informal research might easily be misleading.

The copy writer might depend upon a qualitative motivation study. If he did, he would be looking at findings from a small unrepresentative sample, and he would be depending upon the subjective judgment of the motivation research analyst. He might examine a demographic profile obtained from a large scale quantitative market survey. But, as the shotgun study illustrates, he would almost surely miss some valid relationships, and he would almost surely make some false inferences. Given these alternatives, it is easy to see why psychographic profiles have seen wide use in spite of legitimate questions as to reliability and validity. The copy writer cannot wait for convergent and discriminant validation. He must produce an advertisement, and to do that, he must use whatever information he can get.

The same basic problem confronts product designers, package designers, product managers, and media analysts. What product features will fit the life style of the potential customer? To what sort of person should the package be designed to appeal? Is the customer for this product or service unusually price conscious? Fashion conscious? Concerned about pollution? Concerned about his health? What are consumers' attitudes and opinions about what appears in magazines, newspapers, radio, and TV? All of these questions are regularly answered by some combination of intuition and quantitative and qualitative research. In many cases psychographic profiles add information that would not otherwise be available.

Why Psychographic Segmentations Are Useful

General segmentations like the Newspaper Advertising Bureau study offer the opportunity to tailor new products and services to the needs of different groups within the consumer population. It is easy to see that the "Quiet Family Man," the "Traditionalist," the "Ethical Highbrow," and the "Pleasure Oriented Man" (Figure 1) ought to have quite different requirements in automobiles, entertainment, vacations, insurance policies, food, and clothing. The life-style descriptions show those need patterns in considerable detail, and the media data normally collected in such studies show how to reach each group [121].

Product-specific segmentations like the stomach remedy study offer the opportunity to position and reposition existing brands. They show what needs the product meets within each group, and which brands are best at meeting them. With this information the marketer can appeal directly and efficiently to those groups most apt to find his brand appealing, and he can create new brands to fit need patterns his brand cannot satisfy. Parallel values accrue to marketers of services.

But the question remains—are the descriptions of the segments reliable and valid? Do real groups of real consumers fitting these descriptions actually exist?

If the answer is yes, the user of a psychographic segmentation has at his disposal a new and superior way of understanding his customers. If the answer is no, the marketer who takes a segmentation study seriously is marketing to a family of fictions.

In view of the reservations already expressed as to the reliability and validity of segmentation procedures it might seem that the wisest course would be to ignore psychographics until the procedures have been thoroughly validated. But again, one must consider the alternatives. Marketers know that the customers for a product or a service are frequently not much alike. They know that empirical segmentation procedures hold out the possibility of new insights into how consumers may be divided into groups. And they know that the reliability and validity of segmentation procedures have not been established beyond all doubt. Given that dilemma, many marketers have elected to conduct and to use segmentation studies even when fully aware of the art's imperfections.

UNDERSTANDING CONSUMER BEHAVIOR

Finally, psychographic methods have contributed to more general knowledge of consumer behavior in at least three ways. Psychographic profiles have shed new light on some of the familiar and recurring topics in consumer research. Trend data now becoming available have shown how consumers are changing and how they are not. And general segmentations of the consumer population have created new typologies within which consumer behavior might be more efficiently described and better understood. This review concludes with brief descriptions of studies in each of these fields.

Profiles

Psychographic profiles have already contributed to our understanding of opinion leadership [69, 113, 126], innovativeness [23, 32, 60, 97, 126], retail out-shopping [114], private brand buying [17], social class [129], consumerist activitism [56], catalog buying behavior [112], store loyalty [115], differences between Canada and the United States [8], differences between French-speaking and English-speaking Canadians [125], and concern for the environment [71, 72]. In all these cases the value added by the psychographic profile was much the same as the value added to the description of the shotgun ammunition buyer. Sometimes psychographics confirmed the existence of attributes that might have been inferred from demographic profiles. Sometimes they revealed the existence of attributes that a demographic profile did show. And sometimes they disconfirmed inferences that would have been incorrect. It seems certain that the trend toward psychographic descriptions of interesting groups of consumers will continue, and that such descriptions will become accepted as necessary components of studies of this kind.

Trend Data

As studies are repeated, it becomes possible to accumulate trend data that show how consumers are changing and how they are not changing. Such data are particularly valuable in an era when every other observer is prepared to describe "the changing consumer" and to make predictions about the effects of these changes upon markets for goods and services. In monitoring trends, the task of empirical psychographic analysis is to separate the changes that are actually happening from the changes that are not [24, 106].

New Typologies

The third application of psychographics to the study of consumer behavior is just now beginning to take shape. General segmentations, like the Newspaper Advertising Bureau study and the series of life-style studies conducted by the Leo Burnett Company [24, 92, 105, 106], have begun to produce the outlines of a new consumer typology. As groupings like those shown in Figure 1 are identified and confirmed by independent sets of investigators, it is at least possible that marketers will begin to think routinely in terms of segments marked off by common sets of activities, interests, needs, and values, and to develop products, services, and media schedules specifically to meet them.

At present, agreement among general segmentation studies is pretty far from complete. Differences in item content, sampling procedure and analytic technique have produced different sets of findings, each claiming to be real. Yet, even though the segments produced by various general segmentation studies differ in a number of ways, there is enough similarity among them to suggest that eventual consensus is not a vain hope. If consensus eventually is reached, there will be a new way of thinking about consumers as like-style groups.

Summary of Uses

To the marketing practitioner, psychographic methods have offered a way of describing consumers that has many advantages over alternative methods, even though much work on reliability and validity remains to be done. To researchers with more general interests, psychographic methods have offered new ways of looking at old problems, new dimensions for charting trends, and a new vocabulary in which consumer typologies may be described.

From the speed with which psychographics have diffused through the marketing community, it seems obvious that they are perceived as meeting a keenly felt need. The problem now is not so much one of pioneering as it is one of sorting out the techniques that work best. As that process proceeds, it seems extremely likely that psychographic methods will gradually become more familiar and less controversial, and eventually will merge into the mainstream of marketing research.

REFERENCES

1. *A Psychographic View of the Los Angeles Marketing Area.* Los Angeles, Calif.: Los Angeles Times, 1972.
2. Ahmed, Sadrudin A. "Prediction of Cigarette Consumption Level With Personality and Socioeconomic Variables," *Journal of Applied Psychology,* 56 (October 1972), 437–8.
3. Alpert, Mark I. "Personality and the Determinants of Product Choice," *Journal of Marketing Research,* 9 (February 1972), 89–92.
4. Appel, Valentine and Kenneth Warwick. *Procedures for Defining Consumer Market Targets.* New York: Grudin/Appel Research Corporation, 1969.
5. *Are There Consumer Types?* New York: Advertising Research Foundation, 1964.
6. Armstrong, J. Scott. "Derivation of Theory by Means of Factor Analysis, or Tom Swift and His Electric Factor Analysis Machine," *American Statistician,* 21 (December 1967), 17–21.
7. Arndt, Johan. *Market Segmentation.* Bergen, Norway: Universitetsforlaget, 1974.
8. Arnold, Stephen J. and Douglas J. Tigert. "Canadians and Americans: A Comparative Analysis," paper delivered at the Annual Convention of the American Psychological Association, Montreal, Canada, 1973.
9. Bass, Frank M. "The Theory of Stochastic Preference and Brand Switching," *Journal of Marketing Research,* 11 (February 1974), 1–20.
10. ———, Douglas J. Tigert, and Ronald F. Lonsdale. "Market Segmentation: Group Versus Individual Behavior," *Journal of Marketing Research,* 5 (August 1968), 264–70.
11. Behavior Science Corporation. *Developing the Family Travel Market.* Des Moines, Iowa: Better Homes and Gardens, 1972.
12. Bernay, Elayn K. "Life Style Analysis as a Basis for Media Selection," in Charles King and Douglas Tigert, eds., *Attitude Research Reaches New Heights.* Chicago: American Marketing Association, 1971, 189–95.
13. Birdwell, Al B. "A study of the Influence of Image Congruence on Consumer Choice," *Journal of Business,* 41 (January 1968), 76–88.
14. Bither, Steward W. and Ira J. Dolich. "Personality as a Determinant Factor in Store Choice," *Proceedings.* Third Annual Conference, Association for Consumer Research, 1972, 9–19.
15. Brody, Robert P. and Scott M. Cunningham. "Personality Variables and the Consumer Decision Process," *Journal of Marketing Research,* 5 (February 1968), 50–7.
16. Bruno, Albert V. and Edgar A. Pessemier. "An Empirical Investigation of the Validity of Selected Attitude and Activity Measures," *Proceedings.* Third Annual Conference, Association for Consumer Research, 1972, 456–74.
17. Burger, Philip C. and Barbara Schott. "Can Private Brand Buyers Be Identified?" *Journal of Marketing Research,* 9 (May 1972), 219–22.
18. Buros, Oscar K. *The Seventh Mental Measurements Yearbook.* Highland Park, N.J.: The Gryphon Press, 1972.
19. Campbell, Donald T. and Donald W. Fiske. "Convergant and Discriminant Validation by the Multitrait-Multimethod Matrix," *Psychological Bulletin,* 56 (March 1959), 81–105.
20. Carman, James M. "Correlates of Brand Loyalty: Some Positive Results," *Journal of Marketing Research,* 7 (February 1970), 67–76.
21. Claycamp, Henry J. "Characteristics of Owners of Thrift Deposits in Commercial Banks and Savings and Loan Associations," *Journal of Marketing Research,* 2 (May 1965), 163–70.
22. Cooley, W. W. and P. R. Lohnes. *Multivariate Procedures in the Behavioral Sciences.* New York: John Wiley, 1962.
23. Coney, Kenneth A. "Dogmatism and Innovation; A Replication," *Journal of Marketing Research,* 9 (November 1972), 453–5.
24. Coulson, John S. "How Much Has The Consumer Changed?" paper presented at the Meeting of the American Association for Public Opinion Research, 1974.

25. Cunningham, William H. and William J. E. Crissy. "Market Segmentation by Motivation and Attitude," *Journal of Marketing Research,* 9 (February 1972), 100–2.

26. Danzig, Fred. "Int'l Marketing Congress Hears Psychographics Criticized, Defended," *Advertising Age,* 3 (June 1969), 104–5.

27. Darden, William R. and Fred D. Reynolds. "Predicting Opinion Leadership for Men's Apparel Fashions," *Journal of Marketing Research,* 9 (August 1972), 324–8.

28. ———. "Backward Profiling of Male Innovators," *Journal of Marketing Research,* 11 (February 1974), 79–85.

29. Demby, Emanuel. "Psychographics: Who, What, Why, When, Where and How," in Charles King and Douglas Tigert, eds., *Attitude Research Reaches New Heights.* Chicago: American Marketing Association, 1971, 196–9.

30. ———. "Psychographics and From Whence It Came," in William D. Wells, ed., *Life Style and Psychographics.* Chicago: American Marketing Association, 1974, 9–30.

31. Dichter, Ernest. *Handbook of Consumer Motivations.* New York: McGraw-Hill, 1964.

32. Donnelly, James H., Jr. "Social Character and Acceptance of New Products," *Journal of Marketing Research,* 7 (February 1970), 111–3.

33. Dorny, Lester R. "Observations on Psychographics," in Charles King and Douglas Tigert, eds., *Attitude Research Reaches New Heights.* Chicago: American Marketing Association, 1971, 200–1.

34. Einhorn, Hillel J. "Alchemy in the Behavioral Sciences," *Public Opinion Quarterly,* 36 (Fall 1972), 367–78.

35. Engel, James F., David T. Kollat, and Roger D. Blackwell. "Personality Measures and Market Segmentation," *Business Horizons,* 12 (June 1969), 61–70.

36. Entwisle, Doris R. "To Dispel Fantasies about Fantasy-Based Measures of Achievement Motivation," *Psychological Bulletin,* 77 (June 1972), 377–91.

37. Evans, Franklin B. "Psychological and Objective Factors in the Prediction of Brand Choice: Ford vs. Chevrolet," *Journal of Business,* 32 (October 1959), 340–69.

38. Fiske, Donald W. "Can A Personality Construct Be Validated?" *Psychological Bulletin,* 80 (August 1973), 89–92.

39. Frank, Ronald E. "Predicting New Product Segments," *Journal of Advertising Research,* 12 (June 1972), 9–13.

40. Frank, Ronald E. and Paul E. Green. "Numerical Taxonomy in Marketing Analysis: A Review Article," *Journal of Marketing Research,* 5 (February 1968), 83–94.

41. Frank, Ronald E., William F. Massy, and Thomas M. Lodahl. "Purchasing Behavior and Personal Attributes," *Journal of Advertising Research,* 9 (December 1969), 15–24.

42. Frank, Ronald E. and Charles E. Strain. "A Segmentation Research Design Using Consumer Panel Data," *Journal of Marketing Research,* 9 (November 1972), 385–90.

43. Fry, Joseph N. "Personality Variables and Cigarette Brand Choice," *Journal of Marketing Research,* 8 (August 1971), 298–304.

44. Gardner, David M. "An Exploratory Investigation of Achievement Motivation Effects on Consumer Behavior," *Proceedings.* Third Annual Conference, Association for Consumer Research, 1972, 20–33.

45. Garfinkle, Norton. "The Value and Use of Psychographic Information in Decision Making," in Charles W. King and Douglas Tigert, ed., *Attitude Research Reaches New Heights.* Chicago: American Marketing Association, 1971, 206–10.

46. Good, Walter S. and Otto Suchsland. *Consumer Life Styles and Their Relationship to Market Behavior Regarding Household Furniture.* East Lansing, Mich.: Michigan State University Research Bulletin, No. 26, 1970.

47. Gottlieb, Morris J. "Segmentation by Personality Types," in Lynne H. Stockman, ed., *Advancing Marketing Efficiency.* Chicago: American Marketing Association, 1959, 148–58.

48. Green, Paul E. and Donald S. Tull. *Research for Marketing Decisions,* second edition. Englewood Cliffs, N.J.: Prentice-Hall, 1970.

49. Greeno, Daniel W., Montrose S. Sommers, and Jerome B. Kernan. "Personality and Implicit Behavior Patterns," *Journal of Marketing Research,* 10 (February 1973), 63–9.

50. Grubb, Edward L. and Gregg Hupp. "Perception of Self, Generalized Stereotypes and Brand Selection," *Journal of Marketing Research,* 5 (February 1968), 58–63.

51. Gruen, Walter. "Preference for New Products and Its Relationship to Different Measures of Conformity," *Journal of Applied Psychology*, 44 (December 1960), 361–4.

52. Heller, Harry E. "Defining Target Markets by Their Attitude Profiles," in Lee Adler and Irving Crespi, eds., *Attitude Research on the Rocks*. Chicago: American Marketing Association, 1968, 45–57.

53. "How Nestle Uses Psychographics," *Media Decisions*, (July 1973), 68–71.

54. Hustad, Thomas P. and Edgar A. Pessemier. "Segmenting Consumer Markets with Activity and Attitude Measures," Institute Paper No. 298, Krannert Graduate School of Industrial Administration, Purdue University, 1971.

55. ———. "The Development and Application of Psychographic, Life-Style and Associated Activity and Attitude Measures," in W. D. Wells, ed., *Life Style and Psychographics*. Chicago: American Marketing Association, 1974, 31–70.

56. ———. "Will the Real Consumer Activist Please Stand Up: An Examination of Consumers' Opinions About Marketing Practices," *Journal of Marketing Research*, 10 (August 1973), 319–24.

57. Inglis, Jim and Douglas Johnson. "Some Observations on, and Developments in, the Analysis of Multivariate Survey Data," *Journal of the Market Research Society*, 12 (April 1970), 75–98.

58. Jacobson, Eugene and Jerome Kossoff. "Self-Percept and Consumer Attitudes Toward Small Cars," *Journal of Applied Psychology*, 47 (August 1963), 242–5.

59. Jacoby, Jacob. "Personality and Consumer Behavior: How Not to Find Relationships," Purdue Papers in Consumer Psychology, No. 102, 1969.

60. ———. "Personality and Innovation Proneness," *Journal of Marketing Research*, 8 (May 1971), 244–7.

61. Johnson, Richard M. "How Can You Tell if Things are 'Really' Clustered?" Paper read at a joint meeting of the New York chapters of the American Statistical Association and American Marketing Association, New York, 1972.

62. ———. *Using Q Analysis in Marketing Research*. Chicago: Market Facts, Inc., 1974.

63. Joyce, Timothy and C. Channon. "Classifying Market Survey Respondents," *Applied Statistics*, 5 (November 1966), 191–215.

64. Kassarjian, Harold H. "Social Character and Differential Preference for Mass Communication," *Journal of Marketing Research*, 2 (May 1965), 146–53.

65. ———. "Personality and Consumer Behavior: A Review," *Journal of Marketing Research*, 8 (November 1971), 409–18.

66. ———. "Personality and Consumer Behavior: A Way Out of the Morass," paper presented at the 1973 meeting of the American Psychological Association.

67. Kay, Herbert. *Important News About Prime-Prospect Service*. Montclair, N.J.: Herbert Kay Research, Inc., 1969.

68. King, Charles W. "Social Science, Pragmatic Marketing Research and Psychographics," in Charles W. King and Douglas J. Tigert, eds., *Attitude Research Reaches New Heights*. Chicago: American Marketing Association, 1971, 228–31.

69. ——— and George B. Sproles. "The Explanatory Efficacy of Selected Types of Consumer Profile Variables in Fashion Change Agent Identification," Institute Paper No. 425, Krannert Graduate School of Industrial Administration, Purdue University, 1973.

70. King, Charles W. and John O. Summers. "Attitudes and Media Exposure," *Journal of Advertising Research*, 11 (February 1971), 26–32.

71. Kinnear, Thomas C., James R. Taylor, and Sadrudin A. Ahmed. "Socioeconomic and Personality Characteristics as They Relate to Ecologically-Constructive Purchasing Behavior," *Proceedings*. Third Annual Conference, Association for Consumer Research, 1972, 34–60.

72. ———. "Ecologically Concerned Consumers: Who Are They?" *Journal of Marketing Research*, 38 (April 1974), 20–4.

73. Kollat, David T. and Ronald P. Willett. "Customer Impulse Purchasing Behavior," *Journal of Marketing Research*, 1 (September 1960), 6–12.

74. Koponen, Arthur. "Personality Characteristics of Purchasers," *Journal of Advertising Research*, 1 (September 1960), 6–12.

75. Kuelper, Robert. "The Pit and the Pendulum," internal memo, Chicago: Leo Burnett Company, 1970.

76. Lessig, V. Parker and John O. Tollefson. "Market Segmentation Through Numerical Taxonomy," *Journal of Marketing Research*, 8 (November 1971), 480–7.

77. *Life Style of the WWD Subscriber.* New York: Women's Wear Daily, 1971.

78. "Life Style Portrait of the Hunter," *Journal of Leisure Research*, in press.

79. Lovell, M. R. C. "European Developments in Psychographics," in W. D. Wells, ed., *Life Style and Psychographics.* Chicago: American Marketing Association, 1974, 257–76.

80. Lunn, J. A. "Psychological Classification," *Commentary*, 8 (July 1966), 161–73.

81. ———. "Empirical Techniques in Consumer Research," in D. Pym, ed., *Industrial Society: Social Sciences in Management.* Baltimore: Penguin Books, 1968, .401–25.

82. Massy, William F., Ronald E. Frank, and Yoram Wind. *Market Segmentation.* Englewood Cliffs, N.J.: Prentice-Hall, 1972.

83. May, Eleanor G. "Psychographics in Department Store Imagery," Working Paper P-65. Cambridge, Mass.: Marketing Science Institute, 1971.

84. McNemar, Quinn. *Psychological Statistics*, second edition. New York: John Wiley & Sons, 1955.

85. Michaels, Peter W. "Life Style and Magazine Exposure," in Boris W. Becker and Helmut Becker, ed., *Combined Proceedings: Marketing Education and the Real World and Dynamic Marketing in a Changing World.* Chicago: American Marketing Association, 1973, 324–31.

86. Monk, Donald. "Burnett Life Style Research," *European Research: Marketing Opinion Advertising*, 1 (January 1973), 14–9.

87. Montgomery, David B. "Consumer Characteristics Associated With Dealing: An Empirical Example," *Journal of Marketing Research*, 8 (February 1971), 118–20.

88. Myers, John G. "Determinants of Private Brand Attitude," *Journal of Marketing Research*, 4 (February 1967), 73–81.

89. Nelson, Alan R. "A National Study of Psychographics," paper delivered at the International Marketing Congress, American Marketing Association, June 1969.

90. ———. "New Psychographics: Action-Creating Ideas, Not Lifeless Statistics," *Advertising Age*, 1 (June 28, 1971), 34.

91. ———. "Psyching Psychographics: A Look at Why People Buy," in Charles W. King and Douglas J. Tigert, eds., *Attitude Research Reaches New Heights.* Chicago: American Marketing Association, 1971, 181–8.

92. *New Information on Sugar User Psychographics.* Chicago: Leo Burnett, 1972.

93. Nunnally, Jim C. *Psychometric Theory.* New York: McGraw-Hill, 1967.

94. Overall, J. E. and C. J. Klett. *Applied Multivariate Analysis.* New York: McGraw-Hill, 1971.

95. Pernica, Joseph. "The Second Generation of Market Segmentation Studies: An Audit of Buying Motivation," in W. D. Wells, ed., *Life Style and Psychographics.* Chicago: American Marketing Association, 1974, 277–313.

96. Pessemier, Edgar A. and Douglas J. Tigert. "A Taxonomy of Magazine Readership Applied to Problems in Marketing Strategy and Media Selection," Institute Paper No. 195, Krannert Graduate School of Industrial Administration, Purdue University, 1967.

97. Pessemier, Edgar A., Philip C. Burger, and Douglas J. Tigert. "Can New Product Buyers Be Identified?" *Journal of Marketing Research*, 4 (November 1967), 349–54.

98. Pessemier, Edgar A. and Albert Bruno. "An Empirical Investigation of the Reliability and Stability of Activity and Attitude Measures," Reprint Series No. 391, Krannert Graduate School of Industrial Administration, 1971.

99. Peters, William H. and Neil M. Ford. "A Profile of Urban In-Home Shoppers: The Other Half," *Journal of Marketing*, 36 (January 1972), 62–4.

100. Peterson, Robert A. "Psychographics and Media Exposure," *Journal of Advertising Research*, 12 (June 1972), 17–20.

101. ———— and Allan L. Pennington. "SVIB Interests and Product Preferences," *Journal of Applied Psychology*, 53 (August 1969), 304–8.

102. Plummer, Joseph T. "Life Style Patterns and Commercial Bank Credit Card Usage," *Journal of Marketing*, 35 (April 1971), 35–41.

103. ————. "Learning About Consumers as Real People: The Application of Psychographic Data," paper presented to the Montreal Chapter, American Marketing Association, November 1971.

104. ————. "Life Style Patterns: A New Constraint for Mass Communications Research," *Journal of Broadcasting*, 16 (Winter 1971–72), 79–89.

105. ————. "The Theory and Uses of Life Style Segmentation," *Journal of Marketing*, 38 (January 1974), 33–7.

106. ————. "Life Style and Social Change: Evolutionary—Not Revolutionary," paper read at the 20th Annual AMA Management Seminar, Toronto, 1973.

107. ————. "Life Style Portrait of the Hunter," *Journal of Leisure Research* (in press).

108. ————. "Applications of Life Style Research to the Creation of Advertising Campaigns," in W. D. Wells, ed., *Life Style and Psychographics*. Chicago: American Marketing Association, 1974, 157–69.

109. *Psychographics: A Study of Personality, Life Style, and Consumption Patterns*. New York: Newspaper Advertising Bureau, 1973.

110. Reiser, Richard J. "Psychographics: Marketing Tool or Research Toy?" *Chicago Marketing Scene*, (October 1972), 8–9.

111. Reynolds, Fred D. *Psychographics: A Conceptual Orientation*. Research Monograph No. 6. Athens, Ga.: Division of Research, University of Georgia, College of Business Administration, 1973.

112. ————. "An Analysis of Catalog Buying Behavior," *Journal of Marketing*, 38 (July 1974), 47–51.

113. ———— and William R. Darden. "Mutually Adaptive Effects of Interpersonal Communication," *Journal of Marketing Research*, 8 (November 1971), 449–54.

114. ————. "Intermarket Patronage: A Psychographic Study of Consumer Outshoppers," *Journal of Marketing*, 36 (October 1972), 50–4.

115. ———— and Warren S. Martin. "The Store Loyal Consumer: A Life Style Analysis," *Journal of Retailing*, in press.

116. Robertson, Thomas S. and James H. Myers. "Personality Correlates of Opinion Leadership and Innovative Buying Behavior," *Journal of Marketing Research*, 6 (May 1969), 164–8.

117. Roper, Elmo and associates. *Movers and Shakers*. New York: Harper-Atlantic Sales, 1970.

118. Ross, Ivan. "Self-Concept and Brand Preference," *The Journal of Business*, 44 (January 1971), 38–50.

119. Segnit, Susanna and Simon Broadbent. "Life Style Research," *European Research: Marketing Opinion Advertising*, 1 (January 1973), 6–13.

120. Simmons, W. R. "Overall Impressions of Psychographics," in Charles A. King and Douglas J. Tigert, eds., *Attitude Research Reaches New Heights*. Chicago: American Marketing Association, 1971, 215–9.

121. Skelly, Florence and Elizabeth Nelson. "Market Segmentation and New Product Development," *Scientific Business*, 4 (Summer 1966), 13–22.

122. Sparks, David L. and W. T. Tucker. "A Multivariate Analysis of Personality and Product Use," *Journal of Marketing Research*, 8 (February 1971), 67–70.

123. Summers, John O. "The Identity of Women's Clothing Fashion Opinion Leaders," *Journal of Marketing Research*, 7 (May 1970), 178–85.

124. Teleki, Margot. "The Research Go-Round," *Media-Scope*, (March 1970), 27–32, 38–40.

125. *The Lifestyles of English and French Canadian Women*. Toronto: Vickers and Benson Ltd., Marketing Services Department, 1972.

126. Tigert, Douglas J. "Psychometric Correlates of Opinion Leadership and Innovation," unpublished working paper, University of Chicago, 1969.

127. ————. "A Research Project in Creative Advertising Through Life Style Analysis,"

in Charles W. King and Douglas J. Tigert, eds., *Attitude Research Reaches New Heights*. Chicago: American Marketing Association, 1971, 223–7.

128. ———. "Life Style Analysis as a Basis for Media Selection," in W. D. Wells, ed., *Life Style and Psychographics*. Chicago: American Marketing Association, 1974, 171–201.

129. ——— and William D. Wells. "Life Style Correlates of Age and Social Class," paper presented at the First Annual Meeting, Association for Consumer Research, Amherst, 1970.

130. Tigert, Douglas J., Richard Lathrope, and Michael Bleeg. "The Fast Food Franchise: Psychographic and Demographic Segmentation Analysis," *Journal of Retailing*, 47 (Spring 1971), 81–90.

131. Tucker, W. T. and John J. Painter. "Personality and Product Use," *Journal of Applied Psychology*, 45 (October 1961), 325–9.

132. Vitz, Paul C. and Donald Johnston. "Masculinity of Smokers and the Masculinity of Cigarette Images," *Journal of Applied Psychology*, 49 (June 1965), 155–9.

133. Wells, William D. "Segmentation by Attitude Types," in Robert L. King, ed., *Marketing and the New Science of Planning*. Chicago: American Marketing Association, 124–6.

134. ———. "Life Style and Psychographics: Definitions, Uses and Problems," in W. D. Wells, ed., *Life Style and Psychographics*. Chicago: American Marketing Association, 1974, 315–63.

135. ——— and Arthur D. Beard. "Personality and Consumer Behavior," in Scott Ward and Thomas S. Robertson, eds., *Consumer Behavior: Theoretical Sources*. Englewood Cliffs, N.J.: Prentice-Hall, 1973, 141–99.

136. Wells, William D. and Douglas J. Tigert. "Activities, Interests, and Opinions," *Journal of Advertising Research*, 11 (August 1971), 27–35.

137. Westfall, Ralph. "Psychological Factors in Predicting Product Choice," *Journal of Marketing*, 26 (April 1962), 34–40.

138. "What's Their Life Style?" *Media Decisions*, (September 1969), 34–35, 70, 72.

139. Wilson, Clark L. "Homemaker Living Patterns and Marketplace Behavior—A Psychometric Approach," in J. S. Wright and J. L. Goldstucker, eds., *New Ideas for Successful Marketing*. Chicago: American Marketing Association, 1966, 305–47.

140. Wind, Yoram and Paul E. Green. "Some Conceptual, Measurement, and Analytical Problems in Life Style Research," in W. D. Wells, ed., *Life Style and Psychographics*. Chicago: American Marketing Association, 1974, 97–126.

141. Wind, Yoram, Paul E. Green, and Arun K. Jain. "Higher Order Factor Analysis in the Classification of Psychographic Variables," *Journal of the Market Research Society*, 15 (October 1973), 224–32.

142. Yoell, William. "Causes of Buying Behavior: Mythology or Fact?" in Mernard A. Morin, ed., *Marketing in a Changing World*. Chicago: American Marketing Association, 1969, 241–8.

143. Young, Shirley. "Psychographics Research and Marketing Relevancy," in Charles A. King and Douglas J. Tigert, eds., *Attitude Research Reaches New Heights*. Chicago: American Marketing Association, 1971, 220–2.

144. ———. "Research Both for Strategic Planning and for Tactical Testing," *Proceedings*. 19th Annual Conference, Advertising Research Foundation, New York, 1973, 13–6.

145. ———. "The Dynamics of Measuring Unchange," in Russell Haley, ed., *Attitude Research in Transition*. Chicago: American Marketing Association, 1972, 49–82.

146. Ziff, Ruth. "Psychographics for Market Segmentation," *Journal of Advertising Research*, 11 (April 1971), 3–10.

147. ———. "Closing the Consumer-Advertising Gap Through Psychographics," *Combined Proceedings: Marketing Education and the Real World and Dynamic Marketing in a Changing World*. Chicago: American Marketing Association, 1973, 457–61.

148. ———. "The Role of Psychographics in The Development of Advertising Strategy," in W. D. Wells, ed., *Life Style and Psychographics*. Chicago: American Marketing Association, 1974, 127–55.

SOME SUGGESTIONS FOR FURTHER READING

Mehrotra, S. and W. D. Wells (1977), "Psychographics and Buyer Behavior: Theory and Recent Empirical Findings," in A. Woodside, J. N. Sheth, and P. D. Bennett, (eds.) *Consumer and Industrial Buying Behavior*, chapter 4, 49–65.

Plummer, J. T. (1974), "The Concept and Application of Life Style Segmentation" *Journal of Marketing* (January), 33–37.

Villani, K. E. A. and Y. Wind (1975), "On The Usage of 'Modified' Personality Trait Measures in Consumer Research," *Journal of Consumer Research* (December), 223–228.

Wells, W. D. (1974), *Life Style and Psychographics*, Chicago, IL: American Marketing Association.

III / MARKETING ANALYSIS

In addition to understanding buyer behavior, the marketing manager must be cognizant of factors that influence such behavior in particular markets. Purchasing patterns in a given market are shaped by the dynamic interactions of demand conditions, the institutional arrangement of firms, and the marketing strategies adopted by the firms. Systematic research is necessary to assess the effect of these three forces on consumers so that the firm then can take advantage of these opportunities in the market.

The Buzzell, Gale, and Sultan article keynotes Part III. Using a large empirical data base, it demonstrates the significant and enduring relationships among marketing strategy, market share, and return on investment. The Day paper amplifies these relationships by focusing on the factors involved in strategic product portfolio planning. This paper summarizes much of the important work on marketing planning contributed to the literature in the '70s by marketing practitioners.

The concept on which strategic planning is founded is market segmentation. Two of the best expositions of this concept are Haley's benefit segmentation and Johnson's product space. The Haley paper describes the combination of demographic, personality, lifestyle, and behavior characteristics of buyers to identify the specific benefits they are seeking Johnson's work employs multidimensional scaling procedures to construct the product space, which is a geometric representation of buyers' perceptions of products or brands.

Aspinwall's thinking predates the empirical work of Haley and Johnson but is in effect an illustration of the relationships between market segments and the characteristics of products. Even though a number of product taxonomies have been proposed in the literature, Aspinwall's characteristics of goods stands as the most imaginative attempt to integrate product properties and buyers' wants and desires. The power of this schema is illustrated in Aspinwall's subsequent paper, in which he links his characteristics of goods to the ways various kinds of products are promoted and distributed. Hollander examines the dynamic nature of the distribution function. He discusses the institutional structure of retailing, using examples from various kinds of countries.

Part III concludes with two papers that explore aspects of the marketing mix often ignored in the theoretical literature. Davis and Silk focus the concepts and techniques in behavioral science on the complex interactions involved in behavioral selling. Finally, Burck offers a masterful review of the literature in pricing; it is not often that an article from the popular press attains the status of a classic.

18 / MARKET SHARE—A KEY TO PROFITABILITY / Robert D. Buzzell, Bradley T. Gale, and Ralph G.M. Sultan

It is now widely recognized that one of the main determinants of business profitability is market share. Under most circumstances, enterprises that have achieved a high share of the markets they serve are considerably more profitable than their smaller-share rivals. This connection between market share and profitability has been recognized by corporate executives and consultants, and it is clearly demonstrated in the results of a project undertaken by the Marketing Science Institute on the Profit Impact of Market Strategies (PIMS). The PIMS project, on which we have been working since late 1971,[1] is aimed at identifying and measuring the major determinants of return on investment (ROI) in individual businesses. Phase II of the PIMS project, completed in late 1973, reveals 37 key profit influences, of which one of the most important is market share.

There is no doubt that market share and return on investment are strongly related. *Exhibit I* shows average pretax ROI figures for groups of businesses in the PIMS project that have successively increasing shares of their markets. (For an explanation of how businesses, markets, and ROI results are defined and measured in the PIMS project, see the ruled insert on pp. 282–283.) On the average, a difference of 10 percentage points in market share is accompanied by a difference of about 5 points in pretax ROI.

While the PIMS data base is the most extensive and detailed source of information on the profit/market-share relationship, there is additional confirming evidence of its existence. For instance, companies enjoying strong competitive positions in their primary product markets tend to be highly profitable. Consider, for example, such major companies as IBM, Gillette, Eastman Kodak, and Xerox, as

Authors' note: We wish to acknowledge the contributions of our associates in the PIMS project to the results reported in this paper. Sidney Schoeffler, Donald F. Heany, and James Conlin made valuable suggestions, and Paula Nichols carried out numerous analyses very efficiently and cheerfully. The authors are, of course, solely responsible for any errors or misinterpretations that remain.

Robert Buzzell, professor of Business Administration at Harvard University, received his Ph.D. at Ohio State University. He is a former executive director of the Marketing Science Institute.
Bradley Gale is a professor of Economics at the University of Massachusetts. He directed the economic analysis of the PIMS project.
Ralph Sultan is chief economist of the Royal Bank of Canada in Montreal. He is a former faculty member at Harvard University.

Exhibit I.   Relationship between market share and pretax ROI

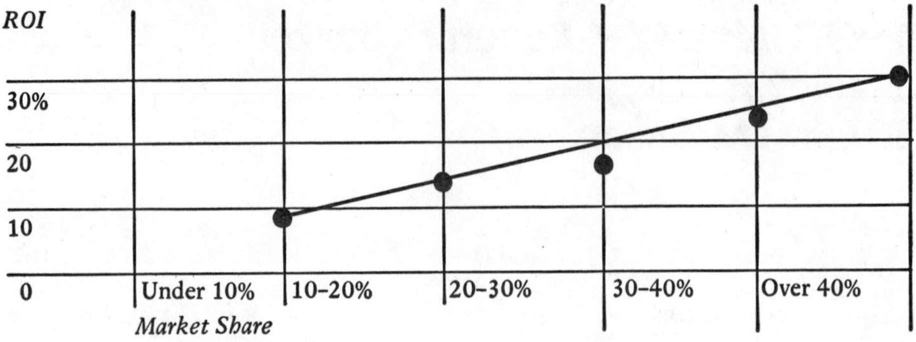

well as smaller, more specialized corporations like Dr. Scholl (foot care products) and Hartz Mountain (pet foods and accessories).

Granted that high rates of return usually accompany high market share, it is useful to explore the relationship further. Why is market share profitable? What are the observed differences between low- and high-share businesses? Does the notion vary from industry to industry? And, what does the profitability/market-share relationship imply for strategic planning? In this article we shall attempt to provide partial answers to these questions by presenting evidence on the nature, importance, and implications of the links between market share and profit performance.

WHY MARKET SHARE IS PROFITABLE

The data shown in *Exhibit I* demonstrate the differences in ROI between high- and low-market-share businesses. This convincing evidence of the relationship itself, however, does not tell us why there is a link between market share and profitability. There are at least three possible explanations:

Economies of scale. The most obvious rationale for the high rate of return enjoyed by large-share businesses is that they have achieved economies of scale in procurement, manufacturing, marketing, and other cost components. A business with a 40% share of a given market is simply twice as big as one with 20% of the same market, and it will attain, to a much greater degree, more efficient methods of operation within a particular type of technology.

Closely related to this explanation is the so-called "experience curve" phenomenon widely publicized by the Boston Consulting Group.[2] According to BCG, total unit costs of producing and distributing a product tend to decline by a more or less constant percentage with each doubling of a company's cumulative output. Since, in a given time period, businesses with large market shares generally also have larger cumulative sales than their smaller competitors, they would be expected to have lower costs and correspondingly higher profits.

Market power. Many economists, especially among those involved in antitrust work, believe that economies of scale are of relatively little importance in most industries. These economists argue that if large-scale businesses earn higher profits than their smaller competitors, it is a result of their greater market power: their size permits them to bargain more effectively, "administer" prices, and, in the end, realize significantly higher prices for a particular product.[3]

Quality of management. The simplest of all explanations for the market-share/ profitability relationship is that both share and ROI reflect a common underlying factor: the quality of management. Good managers (including, perhaps, lucky ones!) are successful in achieving high shares of their respective markets; they are also skillful in controlling costs, getting maximum productivity from employees, and so on. Moreover, once a business achieves a leadership position—possibly by developing a new field—it is much easier for it to retain its lead than for others to catch up.

These explanations of why the market-share/profitability relationship exists are not mutually exclusive. To some degree, a large-share business may benefit from all three kinds of relative advantages. It is important, however, to understand from the available information how much of the increased profitability that accompanies high market share comes from each of these or other sources.

HOW MARKET SHARE RELATES TO ROI

Analysis of the PIMS data base sheds some light on the reasons for the observed relationship between market share and ROI. Businesses with different market-share levels are compared as to financial and operating ratios and measures of relative prices and product quality in *Exhibit II*. In examining these figures, remember that the PIMS sample of businesses includes a wide variety of products and industries. Consequently, when we compare businesses with market shares under 10%, say, with those having shares over 40%, we are not observing differences in costs and profits within a single industry. Each subgroup contains a diversity of industries, types of products, kinds of customers, and so on.

Differences Between High-and-Low-Share Businesses

The data in *Exhibit II* reveal four important differences between high-share businesses and those with smaller shares. The samples used are sufficiently large and balanced to ensure that the differences between them are associated primarily with variations in market share, and not with other factors. These differences are:

1. *As market share rises, turnover on investment rises only somewhat, but profit margin on sales increases sharply.* ROI is, of course, dependent on both the rate of net profit on sales and the amount of investment required to support a given volume of sales. *Exhibit II* reveals that the ratio of investment to sales declines only slightly, and irregularly, with increased market share. The data show too that capacity utilization is not systematically related to market share.

On the surface then, higher investment turnover does not appear to be a major

Exhibit II.　**Relationships of market share to key financial and operating ratios for overall PIMS sample of businesses**

Financial and operating ratios	Market share Under 10%	10%–20%	20%–30%	30%–40%	Over 40%
Capital structure:					
Investment/sales	68.66	67.74	61.08	64.66	63.98
Receivables/sales	15.52	14.08	13.96	15.18	14.48
Inventory/sales	9.30	8.97	8.68	8.68	8.16
Operating results:					
Pretax profit/sales	−0.16	3.42	4.84	7.60	13.16
Purchases/sales	45.40	39.90	39.40	32.60	33.00
Manufacturing/sales	29.64	32.61	32.11	32.95	31.76
Marketing/sales	10.60	9.88	9.06	10.45	8.57
R&D/sales	2.60	2.40	2.83	3.18	3.55
Capacity/utilization	74.70	77.10	78.10	75.40	78.00
Product quality: average of percents superior minus inferior	14.50	20.40	20.40	20.10	43.00
Relative price*	2.72	2.73	2.65	2.66	2.39
Number of businesses	156	179	105	67	87

* Average value on 5-point scale:
5 = 10% or more lower than leading competitors' average;
3 = within 3% of competition;
1 = 10% or more higher than competition.

factor contributing to higher rates of return. However, this observation is subject to some qualification. Our analysis of the PIMS data base shows that investment intensity (investment relative to sales) tends to vary directly with a business's degree of vertical integration.

(The degree of vertical integration is measured as the ratio of the total value added by the business to its sales. Both the numerator and denominator of the ratio are adjusted by subtracting the pretax income and adding the PIMS average ROI, multiplied by the investment.)

Vertical integration thus has a strong negative relation to the ratio of purchases to sales. Since high market-share businesses are on the average somewhat more vertically integrated than those with smaller shares, it is likely that investment turnover increases somewhat more with market share than the figures in *Exhibit II* suggest. In other words, as shown in *Exhibit III,* for a given degree of vertical integration, the investment-to-sales ratio declines significantly, even though overall averages do not.

Nevertheless, *Exhibit II* shows that the major reason for the ROI/market-share relationship is the dramatic difference in pretax profit margins on sales. Businesses with market shares under 10% had average pretax losses of 0.16%. The average ROI for businesses with under 10% market share was about 9%. Obviously, no individual business can have a negative profit-to-sales ratio and still earn a positive

Exhibit III.   Effect of vertical integration on investment/sales ratio

Vertical Integration	Market share Under 10%	10%–20%	20%–30%	30%–40%	Over 40%
Low	65	61	46	58	55
High	77	76	75	70	69

ROI. The apparent inconsistency between the averages reflects the fact that some businesses in the sample incurred losses that were very high in relation to sales but that were much smaller in relation to investment. In the PIMS sample, the average return on sales exhibits a strong, smooth, upward trend as market share increases.

Why do profit margins on sales increase so sharply with market share? To answer this, it is necessary to look in more detail at differences in prices and operating expenses.

2. *The biggest single difference in costs, as related to market share, is in the purchases-to-sales ratio.* As shown in *Exhibit II*, for large-share businesses—those with shares over 40%—purchases represent only 33% of sales, compared with 45% for businesses with shares under 10%.

How can we explain the decline in the ratio of purchases to sales as share goes up? One possibility, as mentioned earlier, is that high-share businesses tend to be more vertically integrated—they "make" rather than "buy," and often they own their own distribution facilities. The decline in the purchases-to-sales ratio is quite a bit less (see *Exhibit IV*) if we control for the level of vertical integration. A low purchases-to-sales ratio goes hand in hand with a high level of vertical integration.

Other things being equal, a greater extent of vertical integration ought to result in a rising level of manufacturing costs. (For the nonmanufacturing businesses in the PIMS sample, "manufacturing" was defined as the primary value-creating activity of the business. For example, processing transactions is the equivalent of manufacturing in a bank.) But the data in *Exhibit II* show little or no connection between manufacturing expense, as a percentage of sales, and market share. This could be because, despite the increase in vertical integration, costs are offset by increased efficiency.

This explanation is probably valid for some of the businesses in the sample, but we believe that, in the majority of cases, the decline in costs of purchased materials also reflects a combination of economies of scale in buying and, perhaps, bargaining power in dealing with suppliers. Economies of scale in procurement arise from lower costs of manufacturing, marketing, and distributing when suppliers sell in large quantities. For very large-scale buyers, custom-designed com-

Exhibit IV.   Purchase-to-sales ratio corrected for vertical integration

Vertical Integration	Market share Under 10%	10%–20%	20%–30%	30%–40%	Over 40%
Low	54	51	53	52	46
High	32	27	29	24	23

ponents and special formulations of materials that are purchased on long-term con- tracts may offer "order of magnitude" economies.

Still another possible explanation of the declining purchases-to-sales ratio for large-share businesses might be that they charge higher prices, thus increasing the base on which the percentage is figured. This does not, however, appear to be the case.

In *Exhibit II* we give measures of price relative to competition for each group of businesses that indicate otherwise. Because of the great difficulty of computing meaningful relative price-index numbers, the measure we used here is rather crude. We asked the PIMS participants to indicate on a five-point scale whether their prices were "about the same" as major competitors, "somewhat" higher or lower, or "substantially" higher or lower for each business. The average values of this scale measure are virtually identical for each market-share group, except for those with shares over 40%.

Despite the similarity of relative prices for the first four share groups, the purchases-to-sales ratios decline in a regular, substantial fashion as share increases. In light of this, we do not believe that the decline in purchase costs is a reflection of higher price levels imposed by "market power."

3. *As market share increases, there is some tendency for marketing costs, as a percentage of sales, to decline.* The difference in marketing costs between the smallest and largest market-share groups amounts on the average to about 2% of sales. We believe that this reflects true scale economies, including the spreading of fixed marketing costs and the ability of large-share businesses to utilize more effi- cient media and marketing methods. In the case of industrial products, large scale permits a manufacturer to use his own sales force rather than commissioned agents and, at some point, to utilize specialized sales forces for specific product lines or markets. For consumer goods, large-scale businesses may derive an important cost advantage from their ability to utilize the most efficient mass-advertising media.

In addition, leading brands of consumer products appear to benefit to some extent from a "bandwagon effect" that results from the brand's greater visibility in retail stores or greater support from retail store sales personnel. For example, Anheuser-Busch has for some time enjoyed lower advertising costs per case of beer than its smaller rivals—just as the advertising expense per car of General Motors is significantly lower than that of other competing auto manufacturers.

4. *Market leaders develop unique competitive strategies and have higher prices for their higher-quality products than do smaller-share businesses.* The figures in *Exhibit II* do not show smooth, continuous relationships between market share and the various components of price, cost, and investment. Indeed, it appears that one pattern operates as share increases up to 40%, but a somewhat different pattern above that figure.

Particularly, there are substantial differences in relative price and product qual- ity between market leaders and the rest of the sample. Market leaders obtain higher prices than do businesses with smaller market shares. A principal reason for this may be that market leaders also tend to produce and sell significantly higher- quality products and services than those of their lower-share competitors.

We measured quality as follows: We asked the participating companies to judge for each business the proportions of total sales comprised of products and services that were "superior," "equivalent," and "inferior" to those of leading competitors. The figures shown in *Exhibit II* are averages of the differences between the superior quality and the inferior quality percentages.

The measures we used for relative price and relative quality are not, of course, directly comparable. Thus it is impossible to determine which is greater—the price premiums earned by market leaders, or the differential in the quality of their products. But it is clear that the combination of significantly higher prices and quality represents a unique competitive position for market leaders.

Market leaders, in contrast to their smaller competitors, spend significantly higher amounts on research and development, relative to sales. As shown in *Exhibit II*, the average ratio of R&D to sales for the highest-share group of businesses was 3.55%—nearly 40% greater than the ratio for the under-10% share group. This, combined with the quality advantage enjoyed by market leaders, suggests that they typically pursue a strategy of product leadership. Certainly this is consistent with what is known about innovative leaders such as Eastman Kodak, IBM, and Procter & Gamble.

Given that market leaders have a high market share and thus the profitability that goes with it, it is natural to question whether the share and profitability ratio shifts from industry to industry. In other words, do businesses in some kinds of industries need a higher share than others to be profitable?

Variations Among Industries

While our analyses of the PIMS data base clearly demonstrate a strong general relationship between ROI and market share, they also indicate that the importance of share varies considerably from one type of industry or market situation to another. Two of the more striking variations are summarized in *Exhibit IV*. These figures show that:

1. *Market share is more important for infrequently purchased products than for frequently purchased ones.* For infrequently purchased products, the ROI of the average market leader is about 28 percentage points greater than the ROI of the average small-share business. For frequently purchased products (those typically bought at least once a month), the correspondingly ROI differential is approximately 10 points.

Why? Infrequently purchased products tend to be durable, higher unit-cost items such as capital goods, equipment, and consumer durables, which are often complex and difficult for buyers to evaluate. Since there is a bigger risk inherent in a wrong choice, the purchaser is often willing to pay a premium for assured quality.

Frequently purchased products are generally low unit-value items such as foods or industrial supplies. The risk in buying from a lesser-known, small-share supplier is lower in most cases, so a purchaser can feel free to shop around.

2. *Market share is more important to businesses when buyers are "fragmented" rather than concentrated.* As *Exhibit V* shows, when buyers are fragmented (i.e., no small group of consumers accounts for a significant proportion of total sales), the ROI differential is 27 percentage points for the average market leader. However, when buyers are concentrated, the leaders' average advantage in ROI is reduced to only 19 percentage points greater than that of the average small-share business.

A likely explanation for this is that when buyers are fragmented, they cannot bargain for the unit cost advantage that concentrated buyers receive, thus allowing higher profits for the large-share business. Obviously, then, the ROI differential is smaller when buyers are somewhat concentrated. In this case, powerful buyers tend to bargain away some of the seller's cost differential by holding out for low prices.

Clearly, the strategic implications of the market-share/profitability relationship vary according to the circumstances of the individual business. But there is no doubt that the relationship can be translated into dynamic strategies for all companies trying to set market goals.

Exhibit V.   Industry variations in the share/ROI relationship

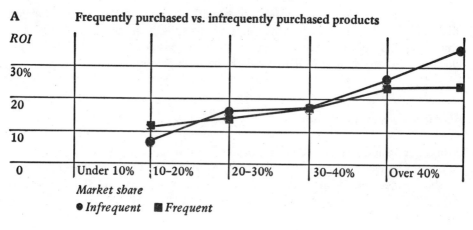

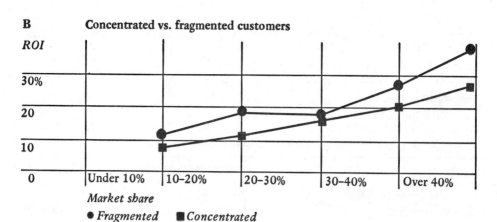

WHAT THE ROI/MARKET SHARE LINK MEANS FOR STRATEGY

Because market share is so strongly related to profitability, a basic strategic issue for top management is to establish market-share objectives. These objectives have much to do with the rate of return that can reasonably be budgeted in the short and long runs, as well as the capital requirements and cash flow of a business.

Setting Market-Share Goals

What market-share goals are feasible, or even desirable, obviously depends on many things, including the strength of competitors, the resources available to support a strategy, and the willingness of management to forgo present earnings for future results. At the risk of oversimplification, we can classify market-share strategies into three rather broad groups:

1. Building strategies are based on active efforts to increase market share by means of new product introductions, added marketing programs, and so on.
2. Holding strategies are aimed at maintaining the existing level of market share.
3. Harvesting strategies are designed to achieve high short-term earnings and cash flow by permitting market share to decline.

When does each of these market-share strategies seem most appropriate? How should each be implemented? The experiences documented in the PIMS data base provide some clues.

Building strategies. The data presented in *Exhibit I* imply that, in many cases, even a marginally acceptable rate of return can be earned only by attaining some minimum level of market share. If the market share of a business falls below this minimum, its strategic choices usually boil down to two: increase share or withdraw. Of course there are exceptions to this rule.

But we are convinced that in most markets there is a minimum share that is required for viability. RCA and General Electric apparently concluded that they were below this minimum in the computer business, and they pulled out. Similarly, Motorola, with an estimated 6% to 7% share of U.S. TV-set sales, and a rumored loss of $20 million in the period from 1970 to 1973, announced its intention early in 1974 to sell the business to Matsushita.

On the other hand, when share is not so low as to dictate withdrawal, but is still not high enough to yield satisfactory returns, managers can consider aggressive share-building strategies. They should recognize, however, that (a) big increases in share are seldom achieved quickly; and (b) expanding share is almost always expensive in the short run.

Among the 600 businesses in the PIMS sample, only about 20% enjoyed market share gains of 2 points or more from 1970 to 1972. As might be expected, successful building strategies were most common among relatively new businesses. Of those that have begun operations since 1965, over 40% achieved share increases of 2 points or more—compared with only 17% of the businesses established before 1950.

Generally speaking, businesses that are building share pay a short-run penalty for doing so. *Exhibit VI* compares ROI results for businesses with different beginning market shares and for businesses with decreasing, steady, and increasing shares over the period 1970 to 1972. Generally, the businesses that were "building" (i.e., had share increases of at least 2 points) had ROI results of 1 to 2 points lower than those that maintained more or less steady ("holding") positions. The short-term cost of building was greatest for small-share businesses, but even for market leaders, ROI was significantly lower when share was rising than it was when share was stable.

Schick's campaign to build sales of the "Flexamatic" electric shaver during 1972 and 1973 dramatically illustrates the cost of increasing market share. In late 1972 Schick introduced the Flexamatic by means of a controversial national advertising campaign in which direct performance comparisons were made with its leading competitors. Trade sources have estimated that Schick spent $4.5 million in 1972 and $5.2 million in 1973 on advertising, whereas the company's advertising expenditures in 1970 and 1971 had been under $1 million annually.

In one sense the effort was successful: by late 1972 Schick's market share had doubled from 8% to 16%. But the impact on company profits was drastic. Schick's operating losses for the fiscal year ending February 28, 1974 amounted to $14.5 million on sales of $93.8 million, and it appears that although it was not the only cause, the high promotional cost of the Flexamatic campaign was a major contributing factor. Only time can tell whether Schick's short-term losses will prove to be justified by increased future cash flows.

The Schick example is, no doubt, an extreme one. Nevertheless, a realistic assessment of any share-building strategy should take into account the strong likelihood that a significant price will have to be paid—at least in the short run. Depending on how great the gains are and how long it takes to achieve them, this cost may or may not be offset by the longer-term gains.

In a recent article, William Fruhan demonstrated that there was a positive re-

Exhibit VI. How ROI is affected by market-share changes

Market share 1970	Market-share strategies		
	Building: up 2 points or more	Holding: less than 2 points up or down	Harvesting: down 2 points or more
	Average ROI, 1970–1972		
Under 10%	7.5%	10.4%	10.0%
10%–20%	13.3	12.6	14.5
20%–30%	20.5	21.6	9.5
30%–40%	24.1	24.6	7.3
40% or over	29.6	31.9	32.6

lation between market share and rate of return for automobile manufacturers and for retail food chains.[4] Yet he also cited examples of disasters stemming from over-ambition in the market-share dimension from the computer industry, the retail food business, and the airline companies.

The main thrust of Fruhan's article was to encourage business strategists to consider certain questions before launching an aggressive market-share expansion strategy: (1) Does the company have the necessary financial resources? (2) Will the company find itself in a viable position if its drive for expanded market share is thwarted before it reaches its market share targets? (3) Will regulatory authorities permit the company to achieve its objective with the strategy it has chosen to follow? Negative responses to these questions would obviously indicate that a company should forgo market-share expansion until the right conditions are created.

It is fairly safe for us to say, therefore, that whenever the market position of a business is reasonably satisfactory, or when further building of share seems excessively costly, managers ought to follow holding strategies.

Holding strategies.   By definition, a holding strategy is designed to preserve the status quo. For established businesses in relatively mature markets—which is to say, for the majority of businesses in advanced economies—holding is undoubtedly the most common strategic goal with respect to market share.

A key question for businesses that are pursuing holding strategies is, "What is the most profitable way to maintain market position?" The answer to this question depends on many things, including the possibilities and costs of significant technological change and the strength and alertness of competitors. Because competitive conditions vary so much, few reliable generalizations can be made about profit-maximizing methods of maintaining market share.

Nevertheless, our analyses of the PIMS data base do suggest some broad relationships between ROI and competitive behavior. For example, our data indicate that large-share businesses usually earn higher rates of return when they charge premium prices. (Recall that this pricing policy is usually accompanied by premium quality.) Also, ROI is usually greater for large-share businesses when they spend more than their major competitors, in relation to sales, on sales force effort, advertising and promotion, and research and development.

For small-share businesses, however, the most profitable holding strategy is just the opposite: on the average, ROI is highest for these businesses when their prices are somewhat below the average of leading competitors and then their rates of spending on marketing and R&D are relatively low.

Harvesting strategies.   Opposed to a share-building strategy is one of "harvesting" —deliberately permitting share to fall so that higher short-run earnings and cash flow may be secured. Harvesting is more often a matter of necessity than of strategic choice. Cash may be urgently needed to support another activity—dividends, for example, or management's earnings record. Whatever the motivation, corporate management sometimes does elect to "sell off" part of a market-share position.

The experience of the businesses in the PIMS data pool, summarized in *Exhibit VI*, indicates that only large-share businesses are generally able to harvest successfully. Market leaders enjoyed rates of return about three quarters of a point higher when they allowed market share to decline than when they maintained it over the period 1970–1972. For the other groups of businesses shown in *Exhibit VI*, differences in ROI between "holding" and "harvesting" are irregular. Of course, these comparisons also reflect the influence of factors other than strategic choice. Market share was lost by many businesses because of intensified competition, rising costs, or other changes which hurt both their profitability and their competitive positions. For this reason, it is impossible to derive a true measure of the profitability of harvesting. Nevertheless, the PIMS data support our contention that, under proper conditions, current profits can be increased by allowing share to slide.

When does harvesting make sense, assuming it is a matter of choice? A reduction in share typically affects profits in a way directly opposite to that of building: ROI is increased in the short run but reduced in the longer term. Here again, a trade-off must be made. The net balance will depend on management's assessment of the direction and timing of future developments such as technological changes, as well as on its preference for immediate rather than deferred profits.

Balancing Costs and Benefits

Evidence from the PIMS study strongly supports the proposition that market share is positively related to the rate of return on investment earned by a business. Recognition of this relationship will affect how managers decide whether to make or buy to decrease purchasing costs, whether to advertise in certain media, or whether to alter the price or quality of a product. Also, recognizing that emphasis on market share varies considerably among industries and types of market situations, decisions concerning product and customer are likely to be influenced. For instance, a small competitor selling frequently purchased, differentiated consumer products can achieve satisfactory results with a small share of the market. Under other conditions, it would be virtually impossible to earn satisfactory profits with a small share (e.g., infrequently purchased products sold to large, powerful buyers).

Finally, choices among the three basic market share strategies also involve a careful analysis of the importance of market share in a given situation. Beyond this, strategic choice requires a balancing of short-term and long-term costs and benefits. Neither the PIMS study nor any other empirical research can lead to a "formula" for these strategic choices. But we hope that the findings presented here will at least provide some useful insights into the probable consequences of managers' choices.

THE PIMS DATA BASE

The data on which this article is based come from the unique pool of operating experience assembled in the PIMS project, now in its third year of operations at the Marketing Science Institute. During 1973, 57 major North American corporations supplied financial and other information on 620 individual "businesses" for the three-year period 1970–1972.

Each business is a division, product line, or other profit center within its

parent company, selling a distinct set of **products** or **services** to an identifiable group or groups of **customers,** in competition with a well-defined
set of competitors. Examples of businesses include manufacturers of TV sets;
man-made fibers; and nondestructive industrial testing apparatus.

Data were compiled for individual businesses by means of special allocations of existing company data and, for some items, judgmental estimates
supplied by operating managers of the companies.

For each business, the companies also provided estimates of the total
sales in the market served by the business. Markets were defined, for purposes
of the PIMS study, in much narrower terms than the "industries" for which
sales and other figures are published by the Bureau of the Census. Thus the
data used to measure market size and growth rates cover only the specific
products or services, customer types, and geographic areas in which each
business actually operates.

The **market share** of each business is simply its dollar sales in a given
time period, expressed as a percentage of the total market sales volume. The
figures shown are average market shares for the three-year period 1970–1972.
(The average market share for the businesses in the PIMS sample was 22.1%.)

Return on investment was measured by relating **pretax operating profits**
to the **sum of equity and long-term debt.** Operating income in a business
is after deduction of allocated corporate overhead costs, but **prior** to any
capital charges assigned by corporate offices. As in the case of market share
data, the ROI figures shown in **Exhibits I, V,** and **VI** are averages for 1970–
1972.

As explained in the earlier HBR article, the focus of the PIMS project has
been primarily on ROI because this is the performance measure most often
used in strategic planning. We recognize, however, that ROI results are often
not entirely comparable between businesses. When the plant and equipment
used in a business have been almost fully depreciated, for example, its ROI
will be inflated. Also, ROI results are affected by patents, trade secrets, and
other proprietary aspects of the products or methods of operation employed
in a business. These and other differences among businesses should naturally
be kept in mind in evaluating the reasons for variations in ROI performance.

NOTES

[1] See the earlier article on Phases I and II of the project by Sidney Schoeffler, Robert D.
Buzzell, and Donald F. Heany, "Impact of Strategic Planning on Profit Performance," HBR
March–April 1974.

[2] Boston Consulting Group, Inc., *Perspectives on Experience* (Boston, 1968 and 1970).

[3] This general argument has been made in numerous books, articles, and speeches dealing
with antitrust economics, see, for example, Joe S. Bain, *Industrial Organization,* 2nd edition
(New York, John Wiley & Sons, 1968), especially Chapter 6.

[4] "Pyrrhic Victories in Fights for Market Share," HBR September–October 1972.

SOME SUGGESTIONS FOR FURTHER READING

Abell, D. F. and J. S. Hammond (1979), *Strategic Marketing Planning, Englewood Cliffs,*
NJ: Prentice-Hall.

Fruhan, W. E. (1972), "Pyrrhic Victories in Fights for Market Share," *Harvard Business
Review* (September–October), 100–107.

Hammermesh, R. G., M. J. Anderson, Jr., and J. E. Harris (1978), "Strategies for Low Market Share Businesses," *Harvard Business Review* (May–June), 95–102.

Kotler, P. and P. N. Bloom (1975), "Strategies for High Market-Share Companies," *Harvard Business Review* (January–February), 63–72.

Schoeffler, S., R. D. Buzzell, and D. F. Heany (1974), "Impact of Strategic Planning on Profit Performance," *Harvard Business Review* (March–April), 137–145.

19 / A STRATEGIC PERSPECTIVE ON PRODUCT PLANNING / George S. Day

INTRODUCTION

The past decade has seen growing recognition that the product planning function within diversified companies of all sizes involves tradeoffs among competing opportunities and strategies. During this period the combination of more complex markets, shorter product life cycles and social, legal and governmental trends put a premium on minimizing the degree of risk in the product mix. More recently, managers have had to cope with severe resource constraints, stemming partly from weaknesses in the capital markets and a general cash shortage, and the triple traumas of the energy crisis, materials shortages and inflation.

Some of the manifestations of the new climate for product planning are skepticism toward the value of full product lines, unwillingness to accept the risks of completely new products, an emphasis on profit growth rather than volume growth and active product elimination and divestment programs.[1] Yet managements cannot afford to turn their backs on all opportunities for change and attempt to survive simply by doing a better job with the established products and services. Eventually all product categories become saturated or threatened by substitutes and diversification becomes essential to survival. Consumer goods companies are especially feeling this pressure as the productivity of line extensions or product adaptations directed at narrow market segments declines. Also the likelihood of regulatory actions directed at products, such as aerosols and cyclamates, points up the risks of having a closely grouped product line.[2] More than ever, long-run corporate health is going to depend on the ability of product planners to juggle those conflicting pressures of diversification and consolidation.

The pervasive nature of the resource allocation problem in product planning is the focus of this article. The emphasis is on the basic issues of the role of new and established products and markets and the choice of areas of new product development to pursue. The first issue is addressed in the context of the product portfolio, which describes the mixture of products that generate cash and in which the company can invest cash. A detailed examination of the product portfolio begins with its component parts, the product life cycle and the notion of market dominance, and then turns to the implications for strategic planning and resource allocation.

Once the role of new products has been established, the issue of where to

Reprinted with permission from *Journal of Contemporary Business*. Copyright © 1975, pp. 1–34.
George Day is a professor of Marketing at the University of Toronto. He received his Ph.D. from Columbia University and has taught at Stanford University and Western Ontario.

look is addressed with an explicit statement of a search strategy. This statement defines the characteristics of desirable opportunities in terms that are meaningful to product planners.

STRATEGIC PLANNING AND PRODUCT PLANNING

There are as many concepts of strategy as writers on the subject.[3] Several of the more useful definitions for our immediate purposes are:

- Decisions today which affect the future (not future decisions)
- Major questions of resource allocation that determine a company's long-run results
- The calculated means by which the firm deploys its resources—i.e., personnel, machines and money—to accomplish its purpose under the most advantageous circumstances
- A competitive edge that allows a company to serve the customers better than its competitors
- The broad principles by which a company hopes to secure an advantage over competitors, an attractiveness to buyers and a full exploitation of company resources.

Following these definitions, the desired output of the strategic planning process is a long-run plan "that will produce an attractive growth rate and a high rate of return on investment by achieving a market position so advantageous that competitors can retaliate only over an extended time period at a prohibitive cost." [4]

Most strategic planning processes and the resulting plans show a distinct family resemblance, although the specifics obviously vary greatly. These specifics usually include[5]: (1) a statement of the mission of the strategic business unit (SBU),[6] (2) the desired future position the SBU and the corporation wants to attain, comprising measurable profitability, sales, market share, efficiency and flexibility objectives, (3) the key environmental assumptions and the opportunities and threats, (4) a statement of the strengths, weaknesses and problems of the SBU and its major competitors, (5) the strategic gap between the desired and forecasted position of the SBU, (6) actions to be taken to close the gap—the strategy and (7) the required resources and where they can be obtained, including financial resources such as net cash flow, the equity base and debt capacity and management capabilities. These are the main elements of the planning process that are relevant to product planning, leaving aside the issues of detailed implementation plans, contingency plans, which state in advance what modifications will be made if key environmental or competitor assumptions turn out to be false, and the monitoring procedures.

What is lacking in the planning process just described is a systematic procedure for generating and choosing strategic alternatives. One of the greatest weaknesses of current strategic plans is the lack of viable strategy alternatives which present very different approaches and outcomes. Too frequently top management sees only one strategy which the SBU has decided is best in terms of its own and the managers' personal needs and objectives. This ignores the interdependency among products (the portfolio aspect)[7] and the possibility that what is best for each SBU is not necessarily best for the entire company.[8] In recognition of this problem, the planning process shown in Figure I incorporates an analysis of the product portfolio. The remainder of this paper is devoted to the uses and limitations of the product portfolio and the implications for developing strategy alternates that optimize the long-run position of the firm.

THE COMPONENTS OF THE PRODUCT PORTFOLIO

Market share and stage in the product life cycle have long been regarded as important determinants of profitability. The contribution of the product portfolio concept is that it permits the planner to consider these two measures simultaneously in evaluating the products of an entire company or a division or SBU.

The Value of Market Share Dominance

The belief in the benefits of a dominant market share is rooted deeply in the experience of executives. It is reinforced by the facts of life in most markets:

- The market leader is usually the most profitable
- During economic downturns, customers are likely to concentrate their purchases in suppliers with large shares, and distributors and retailers will try to cut inventories by eliminating the marginal supplier

Figure I. Highlighting product planning activities in the strategic planning process

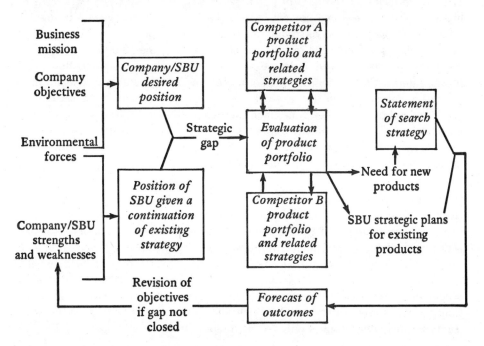

- During periods of economic growth, there is often a bandwagon effect with a large share presenting a positive image to customers and retailers.[9]

Of course, market domination has its own pitfalls, beyond antitrust problems, "... monopolists flounder on their own complacency rather than on public opposition. Market domination produces tremendous internal resistance against any innovation and makes adaptation to change dangerously difficult. Also, it usually means that the enterprise has too many of its eggs in one basket and is too vulnerable to economic fluctuations." [10] The leader is also highly vulnerable to competitive actions, especially in the pricing area, since the leader establishes the basic industry price from which smaller competitors can discount.

The clearest evidence of the value of market share comes from a study of The Profit Impact of Market Strategies (PIMS) of 620 separate businesses by the Marketing Science Institute which, in turn, draws on earlier work by General Electric. Early results indicated that market share, investment intensity (ratio of total investment to sales) and product quality were the most important determinants of pretax return on investment, among a total of 37 distinct factors incorporated into the profit model.[11] On average it was found that a difference of 10 points in market share was accompanied by a difference of about 5 points in pretax ROI. As share declined from more than 40 percent to less than 10 percent, the average pretax ROI dropped from 30 percent to 9.1 percent.

The PIMS study also provided some interesting insights into the reasons for the link between market share and profitability.[12] The results point to economies of scale and, especially, the opportunities for vertical integration as the most important explanations. Thus high-share businesses (more than 40 percent) tend to have low ratios of purchases to sales because they make rather than buy and own their distribution facilities. The ratio of purchases to sales increases from 33 percent for high-share businesses to 45 percent for low-share (less than 10 percent) businesses. But because of economies of scale in manufacturing and purchasing there is no significant relationship between manufacturing expenses or the ratio of sales to investment and the market share. To some degree these results also support the market power argument of economists; market leaders evidently are able to bargain more effectively (either through the exercise of reciprocity or greater technical marketing skills) and obtain higher prices than their competition (but largely because they produce and sell higher-quality goods and services). The fact that market leaders spend a significantly higher percentage of their sales on R and D suggests that they pursue a conscious strategy of product leadership.

Experience curve analysis. The importance of economies of scale in the relationship of market share and profitability is verified by the experience curve concept. Research, largely reported by the Boston Consulting Group, has found that in a wide range of businesses (including plastics, semiconductors, gas ranges and life insurance policies), the total unit costs, in constant dollars, decline by a constant percentage (usually 20 to 30 percent) with each doubling of accumulated units of output or experience.[13] Since the experience effect applies to all value added, it subsumes economies of scale and specialization effects along with the well-known learning curve which applies only to direct labor costs.

An experience curve, when plotted on a log-log scale as in Figure II, appears as a straight line. The locations of the competitors on this curve are determined approximately by their respective accumulated experience, for which relative market share is a good surrogate (this may not be true if some competitors recently have entered the market by buying experience through licenses or acquisitions). Then it follows that the competitor with the greatest accumulated experience will have the lowest relative costs and, if prices are similar between competitors, also will have the greatest profits. Of course, companies that fail to reduce costs along the product category experience curve and who are not dominant will be at an even greater competitive disadvantage.

Figure II shows a price prevailing at one point in time. Over the long run, prices also will decline at roughly the same rate as costs decline. The major exception to this rule occurs during the introduction and growth state of the life cycle, when the innovator and/or dominant competitor, is tempted to maintain prices at a high level to recoup the development costs. The high price umbrella usually achieves this immediate end because unit profits are high. The drawback is the incentive to higher cost competitors to enter the market and attempt to increase their market shares. In effect, the dominant competitor is trading future market share for current profits. This may be sensible if the early leader: (1) has a number of attractive new product opportunities requiring cash, (2) there are potential competitors whose basic business position will enable them eventually to enter the product category regardless of the pricing strategy[14] or (3) significant barriers to entry can be erected.

Product Life Cycle

That products pass through various stages between life and death (introduction → growth → maturity → decline) is hard to deny. Equally accepted is the notion that

Figure II. Cost experience curve showing relative profit levels of competitors

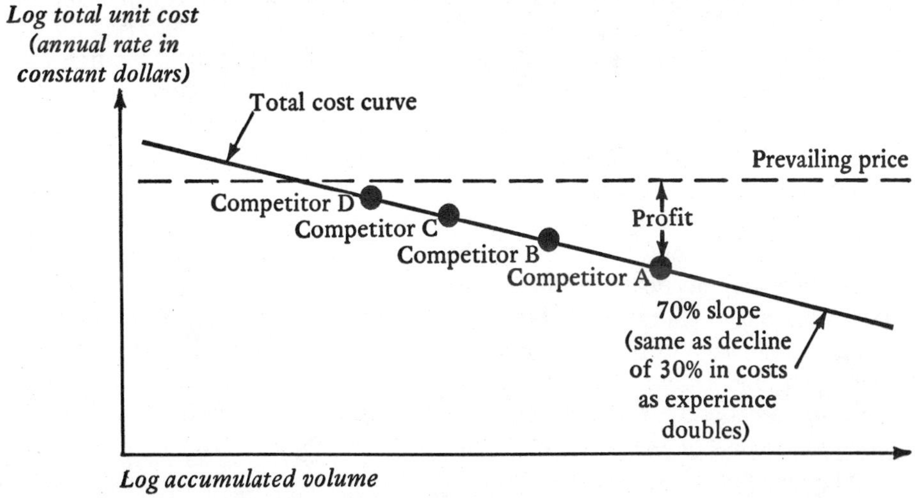

Log total unit cost (annual rate in constant dollars)

Total cost curve

Prevailing price

Competitor D
Competitor C
Competitor B
Competitor A

Profit

70% slope
(same as decline
of 30% in costs
as experience
doubles)

Log accumulated volume

a company should have a mix of products with representation in each of these stages.

Thus the concept of a product life cycle would appear to be an essential tool for understanding product strategies.[15] Indeed this is true, but only *if* the position of the product and the duration of the cycle can be determined. This caveat should be kept in mind when considering the following summary of the important aspects of the product life cycle:

- Volume and profit growth attract competition during the early *growth* (or takeoff) stage of the life cycle. The product market is even more attractive if the innovator lacks the capacity to satisfy demand. However, these competitors may contribute to the growth of sales by their market development expenditures and product improvements.
- Purchase patterns and distribution channels are still fluid during the rapid *growth* stage. For this reason, market shares can be increased at relatively low cost over short periods of time by capturing a disproportionate share of incremental sales (especially where these sales come from new users rather than heavier usage by existing users).
- As a product reaches *maturity* there is evidence of saturation, finer distinctions in benefits surrounding the product and appeals to special segments.
- There is often an industry shake-out to signal the *end* of the rapid growth stage. The trigger might be an excessive number of competitors who have to resort to price cutting to survive; a dominant producer who seeks to regain share; or a large competitor buying into the market (and all these effects will be accentuated by an economic slow down). The result is a period of consolidation during which marginal competitors either drop out, merge with other small competitors or sell out to larger competitors.
- During the *maturity* stage, market-share relationships tend to stabilize; distribution patterns have been established and are difficult to change. This, in turn, contributes to inertia in purchasing relationships and selling oriented toward maintaining relationships. Any substantial increase in share of market will require a reduction in a competitor's capacity utilization which will be resisted vigorously. As a result, gains in share are both time-consuming and costly. This is not necessarily the case if the attempt to gain shares is spearheaded by a significant improvement in product value or performance which the competitor cannot easily match. A case in point is the growth in private labels, or distributor-controlled labels, in both food and general merchandising categories.
- As substitutes appear and/or sales begin to decline, the core product behaves like a commodity and is subject to intense and continuing price pressure. The result is further competitors dropping out of the market, since only those with extensive accumulated experience and cost-cutting capability are able to generate reasonable profits and ROI's.
- The *decline* stage can be forestalled by vigorous promotion (plus, a new creative platform) and product improvement designed to generate more frequent usage or new users and applications.[16] Of course, if these extensions are sufficiently different, a new product life cycle is launched.

Measurement and Interpretation Problems

The concepts underlying the product portfolio are much easier to articulate than to implement.

What is the product-market? The crux of the problem is well stated by Moran:

In our complex service society there are no more product classes—not in any meaningful sense, only as a figment of file clerk imagination. There are only use classes—users which are more central to some products and peripheral to others—on a vast overlapping continuum. To some degree, in some circumstances almost anything can be a partial substitute for almost anything else. An eight-cent stamp substitutes to some extent for an airline ticket.[17]

Where does this leave the manager who relies on share of some (possibly ill-defined) market as a guide to performance evaluation and resource allocation. First he or she must recognize that most markets do not have neat boundaries. For example, patterns of substitution in industrial markets often look like continuua, i.e., zinc, brass, aluminum and engineered plastics such as nylon and polycarbonates can be arrayed rather uniformly along dimensions of price and performance. A related complication, more pertinent to consumer product markets, is the possibility of segment differences in perceptions of product substitutability. For example, there is a timid, risk-averse segment that uses a different product for each kind of surface cleaning (i.e., surface detergents, scouring powders, floor cleaners, bleaches, lavatory cleaners and general-purpose wall cleaners). At the other extreme is the segment that uses detergent for every cleaning problem. Thirdly, product/markets may have to be defined in terms of distribution patterns. Thus, tire companies treat the OEM and replacement tire markets as separate and distinct, even though the products going through these two channels are perfect substitutes so far as the end customer is concerned.

Perhaps the most important consideration is the time frame. A long-run view, reflecting strategic planning concerns, invariably will reveal a larger product-market to account for: (1) changes in technology, price relationships and availability which may remove or reduce cost and performance limitations, e.g., the boundaries between minicomputers, programmable computers and time-sharing systems in many use situations are becoming very fuzzy; (2) the time required by present and prospective buyers to react to these changes, which includes modifying behavior patterns, production systems, etc. and (3) considerable switching among products over long periods of time to satisfy desires for variety and change, as is encountered in consumer goods with snacks, for example.

Despite these complexities, the boundaries of product markets usually are established by four-digit Standard Industrial Classification (SIC) categories and/or expert judgment. The limitations of the SIC are well known[18] but often do not outweigh the benefits of data availability in a convenient form that can be broken down further to geographic markets. In short, the measure is attractive on tactical grounds (for sales force, promotional budget, etc., allocation) but potentially misleading for strategic planning purposes.

What is market dominance?   A measure of market share, per se, is not a good in-dicator of the extent to which a firm dominates a market. The value of a 30 percent share is very different in a market where the next largest competitor has 40 percent than in one where the next largest has only 20 percent. Two alternative measures which incorporate information on the structure of the competition are:

• Company share ÷ share of largest competitor
• Company share ÷ share of largest three largest competitors.

The former measure is more consistent with the implications of the experience curve, while the latter is perhaps better suited to highly concentrated markets (where the four-firm concentration ratio is greater than 80 percent, for example). Regardless of which measure is used it is often the case that the dominant firm has to be at least 1.5 times as large as the next biggest competitor in order to ensure profitability. When there are two large firms of roughly equal shares, espe-cially in a growth business such as nuclear power generators, the competition is likely to be severe. In this instance, both General Electric and Westinghouse have about 40 percent shares and don't expect to be profitable on new installations until after 1977. Conversely, when the two largest firms have small shares, say less than 5 percent, neither measure of market dominance is meaningful.

Evidence of market share dominance, no matter how it is measured, will not be equally meaningful in all product markets. Results from the PIMS study[19] suggest that importance of market share is influenced most strongly by the frequency of purchases.

While the full reasons for this difference in profitability are obscure they prob-ably relate to differences in unit costs and prior buyer experience with the available alternatives which, in turn, determine willingness to reduce risk by buying the market leader and/or paying a premium price. Also, the frequently purchased category is dominated by consumer goods where there is considerable proliferation of brand names through spin offs, flankers, fighting brands, etc. in highly segmented markets. Each of these brands, no matter how small, shares production facilities and will have low production and distribution costs, although they may be treated as separate businesses.[20] It is hardly surprising that the experience curve concept is difficult to apply to consumer goods. Most of the successful applications have been with infrequently purchased industrial products; relatively undifferentiated, with high value added compared to raw material costs and fairly stable rates of capacity utilization.

A further caveat regarding the experience curve concerns the extent to which

Return on investment

Share market	Infrequently purchased (<once/mon)	Frequently purchased (>once/mon)
Under 10%	6.9%	12.4%
10–19	14.4	13.7
20–29	17.8	17.4
30–39	24.3	23.1
Over 40	34.6	22.9

costs ultimately can be reduced. The experience curve clearly does not happen according to some immutable law; it requires careful management and some degree of long-run product stability (and, ideally, standardization). These conditions cannot be taken for granted and will be threatened directly by the customer demand for product change and competitive efforts to segment the market. In effect, product innovation and cost efficiency are not compatible in the long-run.[21]

A related question concerns the relevance of the experience curve to a new competitor in an established market. It is doubtful that a new entrant with reasonable access to the relevant technology would incur the same level of initial costs as the developers of the market.

What is the stage in the product life cycle?   It is not sufficient to simply know the current rate of growth of the product category. The strategic implications of the product life cycle often hinge on forecasting changes in the growth rate and, in particular, on establishing the end of the growth and maturity stages.

The first step in utilizing the life cycle is to ensure that the product class is identified properly. This may require a distinction between a broad product type (cigarettes) and a more specific product form (plain filter cigarettes). Secondly, the graph of product (type or form) sales needs to be adjusted for factors that might obscure the underlying life cycle, i.e., price changes, economic fluctuations and population changes. The third and most difficult step is to forecast when the product will move from one stage to another. The specific problems are beyond the scope of this article. However, the range of possibilities is illustrated by these various leading indicators of the "top-out" point.[22]

- Evidence of saturation; declining proportion of new trier versus replacement sales
- Declining prices and profits
- Increased product life
- Industry over capacity
- Appearance of new replacement product or technology
- Changes in export/import ratio
- Decline in elasticity of advertising and promotion, coupled with increasing price elasticity
- Changes in consumer preferences

These measures generally will indicate only the *timing* of the top-out point, and each is sufficiently imprecise that it is strongly advisable to use as many as possible in combination. Forecasts of the product sales *level* to be achieved at the top-out point may be obtained by astute incorporation of the leading indicators into: (1) technological forecasts, (2) similar product analysis (where sales patterns of products with analogous characteristics are used to estimate the sales pattern of the new product) or (3) epidemiological models whose parameters include initial sales rates and market saturation levels estimated with marketing research methods.[23]

ANALYZING THE PRODUCT PORTFOLIO

The product life cycle highlights the desirability of a variety of products/services with different present and prospective growth rates. However, this is not a sufficient condition for a well balanced portfolio of products that will ensure profitable long-run growth. Two other factors are market share position and the need to balance cash flows within the corporation. Some products should *generate* cash (and provide acceptable reported profits) and others should *use* cash to support growth; otherwise, the company will build up unproductive cash reserves or go bankrupt.[24] These issues are clarified by jointly considering share position and market growth rate, as in the matrix of Figure III. The conceptualization used here is largely attributable to the Boston Consulting Group.[25]

It must be stressed that the growth-share matrix discussed here is simply one way of conceptualizing the product portfolio. It has been useful as a device for synthesizing the analyses and judgments of the earlier steps in the planning process, especially in facilitating an approach to strategic decision making that considers the firm to be a whole that is more than the sum of its separate parts. For these purposes, the arbitrary classifications of products in the growth-share matrix are adequate to differentiate the strategy possibilities.[26]

Figure III. Describing the product portfolio in the market share growth matrix. (Arrows indicate principal cash flows.)

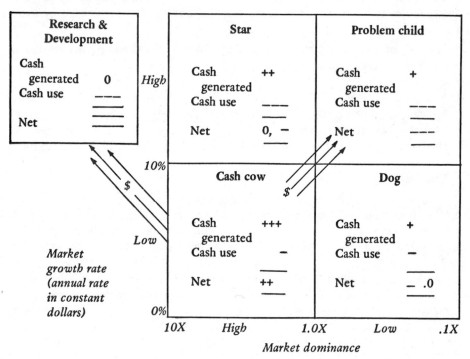

Market growth rate (annual rate in constant dollars)

Market dominance

(Ratio of company share of next largest competitor)

Product Portfolio Strategies

Each of the four basic categories in the growth-share matrix implies a set of strategy alternatives that generally are applicable to the portfolio entries in that category.[27]

Stars. Products that are market leaders, but also growing fast, will have substantial reported profits but need a lot of cash to finance the rate of growth. The appropriate strategies are designed primarily to protect the existing share level by reinvesting earnings in the form of price reductions, product improvement, better market coverage, production efficiency increases, etc. Particular attention must be given to obtaining a large share of the new users or new applications that are the source of growth in the market. Management may elect, instead, to maximize short-run profits and cash flow at the expense of long-run market share. This is highly risky because it usually is predicated on a continuing stream of product innovations and deprives the company of a cash cow which may be needed in the future.

Cash cows. The combination of a slow market growth and market dominance usually spells substantial net cash flows. The amount of cash generated is far in excess of the amount required to maintain share. All strategies should be directed toward maintaining market dominance—including investments in technological leadership. Pricing decisions should be made cautiously with an eye to maintaining price leadership. Pressure to overinvest through product proliferation and market expansion should be resisted unless prospects for expanding primary demand are unusually attractive. Instead, excess cash should be used to support research activities and growth areas elsewhere in the company.

Dogs. Since there usually can be only one market leader and because most markets are mature, the greatest number of products fall in this category.[28] Such products are usually at a cost disadvantage and have few opportunities for growth at a reasonable cost. Their markets are not growing, so there is little new business to compete for, and market share gains will be resisted strenuously by the dominant competition.

The product remains in the portfolio because it shows (or promises) a modest book profit. This accounting result is misleading because most of the cash flow must be reinvested to maintain competitive position and finance inflation.[29] Another characteristic of a dog is that individual investment projects (especially those designed to reduce production costs) show a high ROI. However, the competitive situation is such that these returns cannot be realised in surplus cash flow that can be used to fund more promising projects. In addition there are the potential hidden costs of unproductive demands on management time (and consequent missed opportunities) and low personnel morale because of a lack of achievement.

The pejorative label of dog becomes increasingly appropriate the closer the product is to the lower-right corner of the growth/share matrix.[30] The need for positive action becomes correspondingly urgent. The search for action alternatives should begin with attempts to alleviate the problem without divesting. If these possibilities are unproductive, attention then can shift to finding ways of making the product to be divested as attractive as possible; then to liquidation and, finally if need be, to abandonment:

- Corrective action. Naturally all reasonable cost-cutting possibilities should be examined, but, as noted above, these are not likely to be productive in the long-run. A related alternative is to find a market segment that can be dominated. The attractiveness of this alternative will depend on the extent to which the segment can be protected from competition—perhaps because of technology or distribution requirements.[31] What must be avoided is the natural tendency of operating managers to arbitrarily redefine their markets in order to improve their share position and thus change the classification of the product when, in fact, the economics of the business are unchanged. This is highly probable when the product-market boundaries are ambiguous.
- Harvest. This is a conscious cutback of all support costs to the minimum level to maximize the product's profitability over a foreseeable lifetime, which is usually short. This cutback could include reducing advertising and sales effort, increasing delivery time, increasing the acceptable order size and eliminating all staff support activities such as marketing research.
- Value added. Opportunities may exist for reparceling a product or business that is to be divested. This may involve dividing the assets into smaller units or participating in forming a "kennel of dogs" in which the weak products of several companies are combined into a healthy package. This latter alternative is especially attractive when the market is very fractionated.
- Liquidation. This is the most prevalent solution usually involving a sale as a going concern but, perhaps, including a licensing agreement. If the business/product is to be sold as a unit, the problem is to maximize the selling price—a function of the prospective buyers need for the acquisition (which will depend on search strategy) and their overhead rate. For example, a small company may find the product attractive and be able to make money because of low overhead.
- Abandonment. The possibilities here include giveaways and bankruptcy.

Problem children.   The combination of rapid growth rate and poor profit margins creates an enormous demand for cash. If the cash is not forthcoming, the product will become a dog as growth inevitably slows. The basic strategy options are fairly clear-cut; either invest heavily to get a disproportionate share of the new sales or buy existing share by acquiring competitors and thus move the product toward the star category or get out of the business using some of the methods just described.

Consideration also should be given to a market segmentation strategy, but only if a defensible niche can be identified and resources are available to gain dominance. This strategy is even more attractive if the segment can provide an entree and experience base from which to push for dominance of the whole market.

Further Strategic Implications

While the product portfolio is helpful in suggesting strategies for specific products, it is equally useful for portraying the overall health of a multiproduct company. The issue is the extent to which the portfolio departs from the balanced display of Figure IV, both for the present and in 3 to 5 years.

Among the indicators of overall health are size and vulnerability of the cash cows (and the prospects for the stars, if any) and the number of problem children and dogs. Particular attention must be paid to those products with large cash appetites. Unless the company has abundant cash flow, it cannot afford to sponsor many such products at one time. If resources (including debt capacity) are spread too thin, the company simply will wind up with too many marginal products and suffer a reduced capacity to finance promising new product entries or acquisitions in the future. Some indication of this type of resource misallocation can be obtained from a comparison of the growth rates of the product class and the company's entrant (as illustrated in Figure V). Ideally, nothing should be in the upper sector where market growth exceeds company growth—unless the product is being harvested.

Competitive analysis.   Product portfolios should be constructed for each of the major competitors. Assuming competitive management follows the logic just described, they eventually will realize that they can't do everything. The key question is which problem children will be supported aggressively and which will be eliminated. The answer obviously will be difficult to obtain, but has an important bearing on the approach the company takes to its own problem children.

Of course, a competitive position analysis has many additional dimensions which must be explored in depth before specific competitive actions and reactions within each product category can be forecast.[32] This analysis, coupled with an

Figure IV.   A balanced product portfolio

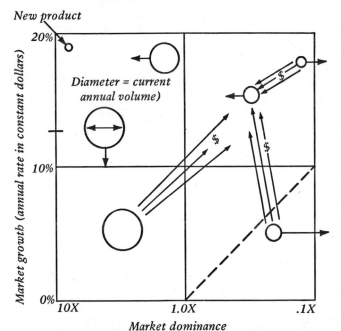

Figure V. Market industry versus company growth rates. (Illustrative diversified company —diameters are proportional to current annual sales volume.)

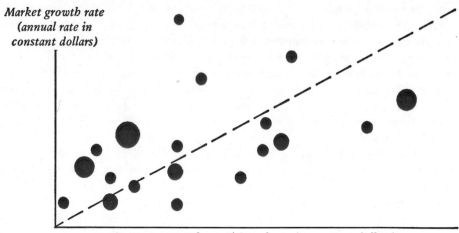

Market growth rate (annual rate in constant dollars)

Company growth rate (annual rate in constant dollars)

understanding of competitive portfolios, becomes the basis for any fundamental strategy employing the military concept of concentration which essentially means to concentrate strength against weakness.[38]

Dangers in the pursuit of market share. Tilles has suggested a number of criteria for evaluating strategy alternatives.[34] The product portfolio is a useful concept for addressing the first three: (1) environmental consistency, (2) internal consistency and (3) adequacy of resources. A fourth criteria considers whether the degree of risk is acceptable, given the overall level of risk in the portfolio.

The experience of a number of companies, such as G.E. and RCA, in the mainframe computer business, points to the particular risks inherent in the pursuit of market share. An analysis of these "pyrrhic victories"[35] suggests that greatest risks can be avoided if the following questions can be answered affirmatively: (1) Are company financial resources adequate? (2) If the fight is stopped short for some reason, will the corporation's position be competitively viable? and (3) Will government regulations permit the corporation to follow the strategy it has chosen? The last question includes antitrust policies which now virtually preclude acquisitions made by large companies in related fields[36] and regulatory policies designed to proliferate competition, as in the airline industry.

Organizational implications. Although this discussion has focused on the financial and market position aspects of the product portfolio, the implications encompass the deployment of all corporate resources—tangible assets as well as crucial intangibles of management skills and time.

One policy that clearly must be avoided is to apply uniform performance objectives to all products, or SBU's, as is frequently attempted in highly decentralized profit-center management approaches. The use of flexible standards, tailored to the realities of the business, logically should lead to the recognition that different kinds of businesses require very different management styles. For example, stars and problem children demand an entrepreneurial orientation, while cash cows emphasize skills in fine tuning marketing tactics and ensuring effective allocation of resources. The nature of specialist support also will differ; e.g., R and D support being important for growth products and financial personnel becoming increasingly important as growth slows.[37] Finally, since good managers, regardless of their styles are always in short supply, the portfolio notion suggests that they not be expended in potentially futile efforts to turn dogs into profitable performers. Instead they should be deployed into situations where the likelihood of achievement and, hence, of reinforcement, is high.

Other methods of portraying the portfolio.   The growth-share matrix is far from a complete synthesis of the underlying analyses and judgments as to the position of the firm in each of its product-markets. The main problem of the matrix concerns the growth rate dimension. While this is an extremely useful measure in that it can have direct implications for cash flows, it is only one of many possible determinants of the attractiveness of the market. A list of other possible factors is summarized in Table I. (Not all these factors will be relevant to all markets.) The importance of each factor depends on the company's capabilities, but careful consideration will help to identify unusual threats, such as impending government regulations, that might significantly reduce future attractiveness. Similarly, market share may not provide a comprehensive indication of the company's position in each market; as in the case of a leader in a market that is rapidly fragmenting.

Table I.   Factors determining market and industry attractiveness

Market	• Size (present and potential)
	• Growth/stage in life cycle
	• Diversity of user segments
	• Foreign opportunities
	• Cyclicality
Competition	• Concentration ratio
	• Capacity utilization
	• Structural changes (e.g., entries and exits)
	• Position changes
	• Vertical threats/opportunities
	• Sensitivity of shares and market size to price, service, etc.
	• Extent of "captive" business
Profitability	• Level and trend of leaders
	• Contribution rates
	• Changes/threats on key leverage factors (e.g., scale economies and pricing)
	• Barriers to entry
Technology	• Maturity/volatility
	• Complexity
	• Patent protection
	• Product/process opportunities
Other	• Social/environmental
	• Government/political
	• Unions
	• Human factors

The qualitative aspects of overall attractiveness and position also can be incorporated into a matrix which portrays the product portfolio [see below]. This matrix does not have the immediate cash flow implication of the growth-share matrix, thus, it should be used as a complementary, rather than a replacement approach.

NEW PRODUCT PLANNING

A product portfolio analysis identifies the need for new products or new markets and the probable level of available resources but does not indicate where to look. This presents management with a number of difficult questions:

• What degree of relationship to the present business is necessary and desirable?
• What are the possibilities for internal development versus acquisition?
• When is an innovation preferred to an imitation and vice versa?
• What are the characteristics of desirable new products?

These and innumerable other questions have to be answered before personnel in the product planning, corporate development or other responsible functions can pursue their tasks efficiently. In short, top management must decide how much growth is desired and feasible, the contribution of new versus established products and the broad direction as to how the growth will be achieved.

What is needed is a strategy statement that specifies those areas where development is to proceed and identifies (perhaps by exclusion) those areas that are off-limits. As Crawford notes, "the idea of putting definitive restrictions on new product activity is not novel, but use of it, especially sophisticated use, is still not widespread." [38] The major criticisms of a comprehensive statement of new product development strategy are that it will inhibit or restrict creativity and that ideas with great potential will be rejected. Experience suggests that clear guidance improves creativity by focusing energy on those areas where the payoff is likely to be greatest. Also, experience shows that significant breakthroughs outside the bounds of the

Industry or market attractiveness. (Arrow represents forecast of change in position. Diameter [of circles] is proportional to share of company sales contributed by product.)

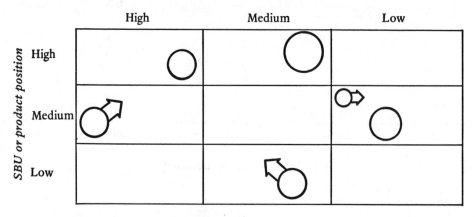

product development strategy statement can be accommodated readily in an on-going project evaluation and screening process.

The New Product Development Strategy Statement

The essential elements of this statement are the specification of the product-market scope, the basic strategies to be used for growing within that scope and the characteristics of desirable alternatives. These elements guide the search for new product ideas, acquisitions, licenses, etc., and form the basis for a formal screening procedure.

Product-market scope. This is an attempt to answer the basic question, "what business(es) do we want to be in" and is a specific manifestation of the mission of the SBU or company. There is no ready-made formula for developing the definition of the future business. One approach is to learn from definitions that have been useful in guiding successful strategies. For example, the General Electric Housewares SBU defines their present (circa 1973) business as "providing consumers with functional aids to increase the enjoyment or psychic fulfillment of selected lifestyles"—specifically those dealing with preparation of food, care of the person, care of personal surroundings and planning assistance. In the future their business will expand to include recreation, enhancement of security and convenient care of the home.

This statement of the future business satisfied one important criteria [sic]: that it be linked to the present product-market scope by a clearly definable common thread. In the case of G.E. Housewares, the common thread is with generic needs being satisfied (or problems being solved, as the case may be). Ansoff argues that the linkage also can be with product characteristics, distribution capability or underlying technology—as long as the firm has distinctive competency in these areas.[39]

Other criteria for appraising the usefulness of a description of the future business opportunities are: (1) specificity—if the definition of product-market scope is too general, it won't have an impact on the organization (e.g., consider the vagueness of being in the business of supplying products with a plug on the end); (2) flexibility—the definition should be adapted constantly to recognize changing environmental conditions (e.g., Gerber no longer can say that babies are their only business), (3) attainability—can be undertaken within the firm's resources and competencies and (4) competitive advantage—it always is preferable to protect and build on these strengths and competencies that are not possessed as fully by the competition.[40]

Basic strategies for growth. At the broad level of a new product development strategy, the basic issues are the *growth vector,* or the direction the firm is moving within the chosen product-market scope, and the emphasis on *innovation* versus *imitation.*

There are almost an infinite number of possibilities for growth vectors. The basic alternatives are summarized in Figure VI.[41] There is no intention here to suggest that these strategies are mutually exclusive; indeed, various combinations can be pursued simultaneously in order to close the strategic gaps identified in the overall planning process. Furthermore, most of the strategies can be pursued either by internal development or acquisition and coupled with vertical diversification (either forward toward a business that is a customer or backward toward a business that is a supplier).

The choice of growth vector will be influenced by all the factors discussed earlier as part of the overall corporate planning process. Underlying any choice is, by necessity, an appraisal of the risks compared with the payoffs. The essence of past experience is that growth vectors within the existing market (or, at least, closely related markets) are much more likely to be successful than ventures into new markets.[42] Therefore, diversification is the riskiest vector to follow—especially if it is attempted by means of internal development. The attractiveness of acquisitions for diversification is the chance to reduce the risks of failure by buying a known entity with (reasonably) predictable performance.

An equally crucial basic strategy choice is the degree of emphasis on innovation versus imitation. The risks of being an innovator are well known so few, if any, diversified corporations can afford to be innovators in each product-market. There are compelling advantages to being first in the market if barriers to entry (because of patent protections, capital requirements, control over distributions, etc.) can be erected, the product is difficult to copy or improve on and the introductory period is short. The imitator, by contrast, is always put at a cost disadvantage by a successful innovator and must be prepared to invest heavily to build a strong market position. While profits over the life of the product may be lower for an imitator, the risks are much lower because the innovator has provided a full-scale market test which can be monitored to determine the probable growth in future sales. Also, the innovator may provide significant opportunities by not serving all segments or, more likely, by not implementing the introduction properly.

The conscious decision to lead or follow pervades all aspects of the firm. Some

Figure VI. Growth vector alternatives

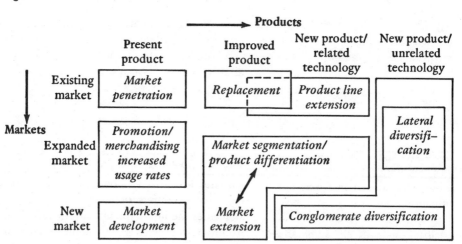

of the important differences that result can be seen from the various strategic orientations to high technology markets discussed by Ansoff and Steward:

- First to market ... based on strong R and D, technical leadership and risk taking
- Follow the leader ... based on strong development resources and the ability to act quickly as the market starts its growth phase
- Applications engineering ... based on product modifications to fit needs of particular customers in mature markets
- Me-too ... based on superior manufacturing efficiency and cost control.[43]

Characteristics of desirable alternatives. Three fundamental questions have to be asked of each new product or service being sought or considered: (1) How will a strong competitive advantage be obtained? The possibilities range from superiority in underlying technology or product quality, to patent protection, to marketing requirements. Another dimension of this question is the specification of markets or competitors to be avoided on the grounds that these situations would blunt the pursuit of a competitive advantage. (2) What is the potential for synergy? This asks about joint effects, or "the mutually reinforcing impact a product-market entry has on a firm's efficiency and effectiveness." [44] Synergy can be sought for defensive reasons, in order to supply a competence that the firm lacks or to spread the risks of a highly cyclical industry, as has motivated a number of mergers in the machine tool industry. Alternatively, synergy can utilize an existing competence such as a distribution system (notable examples here are Gillette and Coca Cola), a production capability, promotional skills, etc. In addition, "financial reinforcement may occur either because of the relative pattern of funds generation and demand ... or because the combination is more attractive to the financial community than the pieces would be separately." [45] (3) What specific operating results are required? The possibilities here usually are expressed in terms of threshold or minimum desirable levels:

- Rate of market growth
- Payback period (despite its deficiencies it is a reflection of the risk level)
- Minimum sales level. (This is a function of fixed costs and scale of operations: the danger is that a product with good long-run potential will be rejected because of modest short-run sales possibilities.)
- Profit levels, cash flow and return on assets. (Each of these financial requirements must be developed in light of the firm's product portfolio.)

SUMMARY

Too often product planning is conducted as though each established product or service, and new product opportunity being sought or evaluated were independent of the other products of the firm. The implication is that corporate performance is the sum of the contributions of individual profit centers or product strategies.[46]

This article emphasizes the need to consider the interdependencies of products as parts of a portfolio described by market share dominance and market growth rate before overall corporate performance can be optimized. Only then can decisions as to resource allocation, growth and financial objectives and specific strategies be developed for established products and the need for new products identified.

There is little doubt that the future will see increasing acceptance of a broad systems approach to overall corporate strategy, in general, and to product planning, in particular. There are already a number of successful practitioners to emulate (who have gained a competitive edge that cannot be ignored).[47] More importantly, as the business environment becomes increasingly resource-constrained there may be no other choice for most firms.

NOTES

[1] "The Squeeze on Product Mix," *Business Week* (5 January 1974), pp. 50–55, "Toward Higher Margins and Less Variety," *Business Week* (14 September 1974), pp. 98–99; E. B. Weiss, "We'll See Fewer New Products in 1975—Culprit Is Shortage of Capital, Resources," *Advertising Age* (2 December 1974); "Corrective Surgery," *Newsweek* (27 January 1975), p. 50; and Jack Springer, "1975: Bad Year for New Products; Good Year for Segmentation," *Advertising Age* (10 February 1975), pp. 30–39.

[2] Barry R. Linsky, "Which Way to Move with New Products," *Advertising Age* (22 July 1974), pp. 45–46.

[3] George A. Steiner, *Top Management Planning* (London: Macmillan, 1969); H. Igor Ansoff, *Corporate Strategy* (New York: McGraw-Hill, 1965).

[4] David T. Kollat, Roger D. Blackwell and James F. Robeson, *Strategic Marketing* (New York: Holt, Rinehart and Winston, 1972), p. 12.

[5] This description of the planning process has been adapted from Kollat, et al, *Strategic Marketing*; Louis V. Gerstner, "The Practice of Business: Can Strategic Planning Pay Off?" *Business Horizons* (December 1972); Herschner Cross, "New Directions in Corporate Planning," An address to Operations Research Society of America (Milwaukee, Wisconsin: 10 May 1973).

[6] The identification of "strategic business units" is a critical first step in any analysis of corporate strategy. Various definitions have been used. Their flavor is captured by the following guidelines for defining a business: (1) no more than 60 percent of the expenses should represent arbitrary allocations of joint costs, (2) no more than 60 percent of the sales should be made to a vertically integrated (downstream) subsidiary and (3) the served market should be homogeneous; i.e., segments are treated as distinct if they represent markedly different shares, competitors and growth rates.

[7] E. Eugene Carter and Kalman J. Cohen, "Portfolio Aspects of Strategic Planning," *Journal of Business Policy*, 2 (1972), pp. 8–30.

[8] C. H. Springer, "Strategic Management in General Electric," *Operations Research* (November–December 1973), pp. 1177–1182.

[9] Bernard Catry and Michel Chevalier, "Market Share Strategy and the Product Life Cycle," *Journal of Marketing*, 38 (October 1974), pp. 29–34.

[10] Peter F. Drucker, *Management: Tasks, Responsibilities, Practices* (New York: Harper and Row, 1973), p. 106.

[11] Sidney Schoeffler, Robert D. Buzzell and Donald F. Heany, "Impact of Strategic Planning on Profit Performance," *Harvard Business Review* (March–April 1974), pp. 137–145.

[12] Robert D. Buzzell, Bradley T. Gale and Ralph G. M. Sultan, "Market Share, Profitability and Business Strategy," unpublished working paper (Marketing Science Institute, August 1974).

[13] For more extended treatments and a variety of examples, see Patrick Conley, "Experience Curves as a Planning Tool," *IEEE Transactions* (June 1970); *Perspectives on Experience* (Boston: Boston Consulting Group, 1970); and "Selling Business a Theory of Economics," *Business Week* (8 September 1974).

[14] "An example of this situation was DuPont's production of cyclohexane. DuPont was the first producer of the product but the manufacture of cyclohexane is so integrated with the operations of an oil refinery that oil refiners have an inherent cost advantage over companies, such as DuPont, without an oil refinery." Robert B. Stobaugh and Philip L. Townsend, "Price Forecasting and Strategic Planning: The Case of Petrochemicals," *Journal of Marketing Research*, 12 (February 1975), pp. 19–29.

[15] Theodore Levitt, "Exploit the Product Life Cycle," *Harvard Business Review* (November– December 1965), pp. 81–94.

[16] Harry W. McMahan, "Like Sinatra, Old Products Can, Too, Get a New Lease on Life," *Advertising Age* (25 November 1974), p. 32.

[17] Harry T. Moran, "Why New Products Fail," *Journal of Advertising Research* (April 1973).

[18] See Douglas Needham, *Economic Analysis and Industrial Structure* (New York: Holt, Rinehart and Winston); Sanford Rose, "Bigness Is a Numbers Game," *Fortune* (November 1969).

[19] Buzzell, Gale and Sultan, "Market Share, Profitability."

[20] An extreme example is Unilever in the UK with 20 detergent brands all sharing joint costs to some degree.

[21] William J. Abernathy and Kenneth Wayne, "Limit of the Learning Curve," *Harvard Business Review*, 52 (September–October 1974), pp. 109–119.

[22] Aubrey Wilson, "Industrial Marketing Research in Britain," *Journal of Marketing Research*, 6 (February 1969), pp. 15–28.

[23] John C. Chambers, Satinder K. Mullick and Donald D. Smith, *An Executives' Guide to Forecasting* (New York: John Wiley and Sons, 1974); Frank M. Bass, "A New Product Growth Model for Consumer Durables," *Management Science*, 15 (January 1969), pp. 215– 227.

[24] Of course the cash flow pattern also may be altered by changing debt and/or dividend policies. (For most companies, the likelihood of new equity funding is limited). Limits on growth are imposed when the additional business ventures to be supported have too high a business risk for the potential reward and/or the increase in debt has too high a (financial) risk for the potential rewards.

[25] Among the publications of the Boston Consulting Group that describe the portfolio are: Perspectives on Experience (1970) and the following pamphlets authored by Bruce D. Henderson in the general perspectives series; "The Product Portfolio" (1970); "The Experience Curve Reviewed: The Growth Share Matrix or the Product Portfolio" (1973); and "Cash Traps" (1972).

[26] A similar matrix reportedly is used by the Mead Corporation; see John Thackray, "The Mod Matrix of Mead," *Management Today* (January 1972), pp. 50–53, 112. This application has been criticized on the grounds of oversimplification, narrow applicability and the unwarranted emphasis on investment versus new investment. Indeed the growth-share matrix is regarded by Thackray as primarily a device for achieving social control.

[27] William E. Cox, Jr., "Product Portfolio Strategy: An Analysis of the Boston Consulting Group Approach to Marketing Strategies," *Proceedings of the American Marketing Association*, 1974.

[28] It is also typical that the weighted ratio of average market share versus the largest competitor is greater than 1.0. This reflects the contribution of the cash cows to both sales and profits. It also accounts for the familiar pattern whereby 20 percent of the products account for 80 percent of the dollar margin (a phenomena generally described as Pareto's Law).

[29] The Boston Consulting Group defines such products as cash traps when the required reinvestment, including increased working capital, exceeds reported profit plus increase in permanent debt capacity: Bruce D. Henderson, "Cash Traps," *Perspectives*, Number 102 (Boston Consulting Group, 1972).

[30] The label may be meaningless if the product is part of a product line, an integral component of a system or where most of the sales are internal.

[31] It should be noted that full line/full service competitors may be vulnerable to this strategy if there are customer segments which do not need all the services, etc. Thus, Digital Equipment Corp. has prospered in competition with IBM by simply selling basic hardware and depending on others to do the applications programming. By contrast, IBM provides,

for a price, a great deal of service backup and software for customers who are not self-sufficient. "A Minicomputer Tempest," *Business Week* (27 January 1975), pp. 79–80.

[82] Dimensions such as product and pricing policy, geographic and distributor strength, delivery patterns, penetration by account size and probable reaction to our company initiatives need to be considered. See C. Davis Fogg, "Planning Gains in Market Share," *Journal of Marketing*, 38 (July 1974), pp. 30–38.

[83] This concept is developed by Harper Boyd, "Strategy Concepts" unpublished manuscript, 1974, and is based on B. H. Liddel Hart, *Strategy: The Indirect Approach* (London: Faber and Faber, 1951).

[84] Seymour Tilles, "How to Evaluate Corporate Strategy," *Harvard Business Review*, 41 (July–August 1963).

[85] William E. Fruhan, "Pyrrhic Victories in Fights for Market Share," *Harvard Business Review*, 50 (September–October 1972).

[86] "Is John Sherman's Antitrust Obsolete?" *Business Week* (23 March 1974).

[87] Stephen Dietz, "Get More Out of Your Brand Management," *Harvard Business Review* (July–August 1973).

[88] C. Merle Crawford, "Strategies for New Product Development: Guidelines for a Critical Company Problem," *Business Horizons* (December 1972), pp. 49–58.

[89] H. Igor Ansoff, *Corporate Strategy*.

[40] Kenneth Simmonds, "Removing the Chains from Product Policy," *Journal of Management Studies* (February 1968).

[41] This strategy matrix was influenced strongly by the work of David T. Kollat, Roger D. Blackwell and James F. Robeson, *Strategic Marketing* (New York: Holt, Rinehart and Winston, 1972), pp. 21–23 which, in turn, was adapted from Samuel C. Johnson and Conrad Jones, "How to Organize for New Products," *Harvard Business Review*, 35 (May–June 1957), pp. 49–62.

[42] According to the experience of A. T. Kearney, Inc., the chances of success are a direct function of how far from home the new venture is aimed. Specifically, the likelihood of success for an improved product into the present market is assessed as 0.75, declines to 0.50 for a new product with unrelated technology into the present market and to 0.25 for an existing product into a new market. The odds of success for external diversification are as low as 0.05. These numbers are mainly provocative because of the difficulties of defining what constitutes a failure (is it a product that failed in test or after national introduction, for example). See "Analyzing New Product Risk," *Marketing for Sales Executives* (The Research Institute of America, January 1974).

[43] H. Igor Ansoff and John Steward, "Strategies for a Technology-Based Business," *Harvard Business Review*, 45 (November–December 1967), pp. 71–83.

[44] Kollat, Blackwell and Robeson, *Strategic Marketing*, p. 24.

[45] Seymour Tilles, "Making Strategy Explicit," in H. Igor Ansoff (ed.) *Business Strategy* (London: Penguin Books, 1969), p. 203.

[46] Bruce D. Henderson, "Intuitive Strategy," *Perspectives*, No. 96 (The Boston Consulting Group, 1972).

[47] See "Selling Business a Theory of Economics," *Business Week* (8 September 1973), "G. E.'s New Strategy for Faster Growth," *Business Week* (8 July 1972), "First Quarter and Stockholders Meeting Report (Texas Instruments, Inc., 8 April 1973); "The Winning Strategy at Sperry Rand," *Business Week* (24 February 1973), "How American Standard Cured Its Conglomeritis," *Business Week* (28 September 1974); "G. E. Revamps Strategy: Growth through Efficiency," *Advertising Age* (3 June 1974).

SOME SUGGESTIONS FOR FURTHER READING

Abell, D. F. (1978), "Strategic Windows," *Journal of Marketing* (July), 21–26.
——— (1980), *Defining the Business: The Starting Point of Strategic Planning*, Englewood Cliffs, NJ: Prentice-Hall.

Day, G. S., A. D. Shocker, and R. Srivantava (1979), "Customer-Oriented Approaches to Identifying Product Markets," *Journal of Marketing* (Fall), 8–19.

Enis, B. M. (1980), "GE, PIMS, BCG and the PLC", *BUSINESS* (May–June), 10–18.

————, R. LaGarce, and A. E. Prell (1977), "Extending the Product Life Cycle, *Business Horizons* (June), 46–56.

20 / BENEFIT SEGMENTATION: A DECISION-ORIENTED RESEARCH TOOL / Russell I. Haley

Market segmentation has been steadily moving toward center stage as a topic of discussion in marketing and research circles. Hardly a conference passes without at least one session devoted to it. Moreover, in March the American Management Association held a three-day conference entirely concerned with various aspects of the segmentation problem.

According to Wendell Smith, "segmentation is based upon developments on the demand side of the market and represents a rational and more precise adjustment of product and marketing effort to consumer or user requirements."[1] The idea that all markets can be profitably segmented has now received almost as widespread acceptance as the marketing concept itself. However, problems remain. In the extreme, a marketer can divide up his market in as many ways as he can describe his prospects. If he wishes, he can define a left-handed segment, or a blue-eyed segment, or a German-speaking segment. Consequently, current discussion revolves largely around which of the virtually limitless alternatives is likely to be most productive.

SEGMENTATION METHODS

Several varieties of market segmentation have been popular in the recent past. At least three kinds have achieved some degree of prominence. Historically, perhaps the first type to exist was geographic segmentation. Small manufacturers who wished to limit their investments, or whose distribution channels were not large enough to cover the entire country, segmented the U.S. market, in effect, by selling their products only in certain areas.

However, as more and more brands became national, the second major system of segmentation—demographic segmentation—became popular. Under this philosophy targets were defined as younger people, men, or families with children. Unfortunately, a number of recent studies have shown that demographic variables

Reprinted from the *Journal of Marketing*, published by the American Marketing Association. Russell I. Haley, "Benefit Segmentation: A Decision-Oriented Research Tool," *Journal of Marketing*, Vol. 32, pp. 30–35, July 1968.
Russell I. Haley is president of Haley, Oberholtser and Associates, specialists in marketing research and advertising. He has long been associated with attitude research and market segmentation studies. Mr. Haley received his M.B.A. from Columbia University in statistics.

such as age, sex, income, occupation and race are, in general, poor predictors of behavior and consequently, less than optimum bases for segmentation strategies.[2]

More recently, a third type of segmentation has come into increasing favor—volume segmentation. The so-called "heavy half" theory, popularized by Dik Twedt of the Oscar Mayer Company,[3] points out that in most product categories one-half of the consumers account for around 80% of the consumption. If this is true, the argument goes, shouldn't knowledgeable marketers concentrate their efforts on these high-volume consumers? Certainly they are the most *valuable* consumers.

The trouble with this line of reasoning is that not all heavy consumers are usually available to the same brand—because they are not all seeking the same kinds of benefits from a product. For example, heavy coffee drinkers consist of two types of consumers—those who drink chain store brands and those who drink premium brands. The chain store customers feel that all coffees are basically alike and, because they drink so much coffee, they feel it is sensible to buy a relatively inexpensive brand. The premium brand buyers, on the other hand, feel that the few added pennies which coffees like Yuban, Martinson's Chock Full O'Nuts, and Savarin cost are more than justified by their fuller taste. Obviously, these two groups of people, although they are both members of the "heavy half" segment, are not equally good prospects for any one brand, nor can they be expected to respond to the same advertising claims.

These three systems of segmentation have been used because they provide helpful guidance in the use of certain marketing tools. For example, geographic segmentation, because it describes the market in a discrete way, provides definite direction in media purchases. Spot TV, spot radio, and newspapers can be bought for the geographical segment selected for concentrated effort. Similarly, demographic segmentation allows media to be bought more efficiently since demographic data on readers, viewers, and listeners are readily available for most media vehicles. Also, in some product categories demographic variables are extremely helpful in differentiating users from non-users, although they are typically less helpful in distinguishing between the users of various brands. The heavy-half philosophy is especially effective in directing dollars toward the most important parts of the market.

However, each of these three systems of segmentation is handicapped by an underlying disadvantage inherent in its nature. All are based on an ex post facto analysis of the kinds of people who make up various segments of a market. They rely on *descriptive* factors rather than *causal* factors. For this reason they are not efficient predictors of future buying behavior, and it is future buying behavior that is of central interest to marketers.

BENEFIT SEGMENTATION

An approach to market segmentation whereby it is possible to identify market segments by causal factors rather than descriptive factors, might be called "benefit segmentation." The belief underlying this segmentation strategy is that the benefits which people are seeking in consuming a given product are the basic reasons for the existence of true market segments. Experience with this approach has shown that benefits sought by consumers determine their behavior much more accurately than do demographic characteristics or volume of consumption.

This does not mean that the kinds of data gathered in more traditional types of segmentation are not useful. Once people have been classified into segments in accordance with the benefits they are seeking, each segment is contrasted with all of the other segments in terms of its demography, its volume of consumption, its brand perceptions, its media habits, its personality and life-style, and so forth. In this way, a reasonably deep understanding of the people who make up each segment can be obtained. And by capitalizing on this understanding, it is possible to reach them, to talk to them in their own terms, and to present a product in the most favorable light possible.

The benefit segmentation approach is not new. It has been employed by a number of America's largest corporations since it was introduced in 1961.[4] However, case histories have been notably absent from the literature because most studies have been contracted for privately, and have been treated confidentially.

The benefit segmentation approach is based upon being able to measure consumer value systems in detail, together with what the consumer thinks about various brands in the product category of interest. While this concept seems simple enough, operationally it is very complex. There is no simple straightforward way of handling the volumes of data that have to be generated. Computers and sophisticated multivariate attitude measurement techniques are a necessity.

Several alternative statistical approaches can be employed, among them the so-called "Q" technique of factor analysis, multi-dimensional scaling, and other distance measures.[5] All of these methods relate the ratings of each respondent to those of every other respondent and then seek clusters of individuals with similar rating patterns. If the items rated are potential consumer benefits, the clusters that emerge will be groups of people who attach similar degrees of importance to the various benefits. Whatever the statistical approach selected, the end result of the analysis is likely to be between three and seven consumer segments, each representing a potentially productive focal point for marketing efforts.

Each segment is identified by the benefits it is seeking. However, it is the *total configuration* of the benefits sought which differentiates one segment from another, rather than the fact that one segment is seeking one particular benefit and another a quite different benefit. Individual benefits are likely to have appeal for several segments. In fact, the research that has been done thus far suggests that most people would like as many benefits as possible. However, the *relative* importance they attach to individual benefits can differ importantly and, accordingly, can be used as an effective lever in segmenting markets.

Of course, it is possible to determine benefit segments intuitively as well as with computers and sophisticated research methods. The kinds of brilliant insights which produced the Mustang and the first 100-millimeter cigarette have a good chance of succeeding whenever marketers are able to tap an existing benefit segment.

However, intuition can be very expensive when it is mistaken. Marketing history is replete with examples of products which someone felt could not miss. Over the longer term, systematic benefit segmentation research is likely to have a higher proportion of successes.

But is benefit segmentation practical? And is it truly operational? The answer to both of these questions is "yes." In effect, the crux of the problem of choosing the best segmentation system is to determine which has the greatest number of practical marketing implications. An example should show that benefit segmentation has a much wider range of implications than alternative forms of segmentation.

An Example of Benefit Segmentation

While the material presented here is purely illustrative to protect the competitive edge of companies who have invested in studies of this kind, it is based on actual segmentation studies. Consequently, it is quite typical of the kinds of things which are normally learned in the course of a benefit segmentation study.

The toothpaste market has been chosen as an example because it is one with which everyone is familiar. Let us assume that a benefit segmentation study has been done and four major segments have been identified—one particularly concerned with decay prevention, one with brightness of teeth, one with the flavor and appearance of the product, and one with price. A relatively large amount of supplementary information has also been gathered (Table 1) about the people in each of these segments.

The decay prevention segment, it has been found, contains a disproportionately large number of families with children. They are seriously concerned about the possibility of cavities and show a definite preference for fluoride toothpaste. This is reinforced by their personalities. They tend to be a little hypochondriacal and, in their life-styles, they are less socially-oriented than some of the other groups. This segment has been named The Worriers.

The second segment, comprised of people who show concern for the bright-

Table 1. Toothpaste market segment description

Segment name:	The sensory segment	The sociables	The worriers	The independent segment
Principal benefit sought:	Flavor, product appearance	Brightness of teeth	Decay prevention	Price
Demographic strengths:	Children	Teens, young people	Large families	Men
Special behavioral characteristics:	Users of spearmint-flavored toothpaste	Smokers	Heavy users	Heavy users
Brands disproportionately favored:	Colgate, Stripe	Macleans, Plus White, Ultra Brite	Crest	Brands on sale
Personality characteristics:	High self-involvement	High sociability	High hypochondriasis	High autonomy
Life-style characteristics:	Hedonistic	Active	Conservative	Value-oriented

ness of their teeth, is quite different. It includes a relatively large group of young marrieds. They smoke more than average. This is where the swingers are. They are strongly social and their life-style patterns are very active. This is probably the group to which toothpastes such as Macleans or Plus White or Ultra Brite would appeal. This segment has been named the Sociables.

In the third segment, the one which is particularly concerned with the flavor and appearance of the product, a large portion of the brand deciders are children. Their use of spearmint toothpaste is well above average. Stripe has done relatively well in this segment. They are more ego-centered than other segments, and their life-style is outgoing but not to the extent of the swingers. They will be called The Sensory Segment.

The fourth segment, the price-oriented segment, shows a predominance of men. It tends to be above average in terms of toothpaste usage. People in this segment see very few meaningful differences between brands. They switch more frequently than people in other segments and tend to buy a brand on sale. In terms of personality, they are cognitive and they are independent. They like to think for themselves and make brand choices on the basis of their judgment. They will be called The Independent Segment.

Marketing Implications of Benefit Segmentation Studies

Both copy directions and media choices will show sharp differences depending upon which of these segments is chosen as the target—The Worriers, The Sociables, The Sensory Segment, or The Independent Segment. For example, the tonality of the copy will be light if The Sociable Segment or The Sensory Segment is to be addressed. It will be more serious if the copy is aimed at The Worriers. And if The Independent Segment is selected, it will probably be desirable to use rational, two-sided arguments. Of course, to talk to this group at all it will be necessary to have either a price edge or some kind of demonstrable product superiority.

The depth-of-sell reflected by the copy will also vary, depending upon the segment which is of interest. It will be fairly intensive for The Worrier Segment and for The Independent Segment, but much more superficial and mood-oriented for The Sociable and Sensory Segments.

Likewise, the setting will vary. It will focus on the product for The Sensory Group, on socially-oriented situations for The Sociable Group, and perhaps on demonstration or on competitive comparisons for The Independent Group.

Media environments will also be tailored to the segments chosen as targets. Those with serious environments will be used for The Worrier and Independent Segments, and those with youthful, modern and active environments for The Sociable and The Sensory Groups. For example, it might be logical to use a larger proportion of television for The Sociable and Sensory Groups, while The Worriers and Independents might have heavier print schedules.

The depth-of-sell needed will also be reflected in the media choices. For The Worrier and Rational Segments longer commercials—perhaps 60-second commercials—would be indicated, while for the other two groups shorter commercials and higher frequency would be desirable.

Of course, in media selection the facts that have been gathered about the demographic characteristics of the segment chosen as the target would also be taken into consideration.

The information in Table 1 also has packaging implications. For example, it might be appropriate to have colorful packages for The Sensory Segment, perhaps aqua (to indicate fluoride) for The Worrier Group, and gleaming white for The Sociable Segment because of their interest in bright white teeth.

It should be readily apparent that the kinds of information normally obtained in the course of a benefit segmentation study have a wide range of marketing implications. Sometimes they are useful in suggesting physical changes in a product. For example, one manufacturer discovered that his product was well suited to the needs of his chosen target with a single exception in the area of flavor. He was able to make a relatively inexpensive modification in his product and thereby strengthen his market position.

The new product implications of benefit segmentation studies are equally apparent. Once a marketer understands the kinds of segments that exist in his market, he is often able to see new product opportunities or particularly effective ways of positioning the products emerging from his research and development operation.

Similarly, benefit segmentation information has been found helpful in providing direction in the choice of compatible point-of-purchase materials and in the selection of the kinds of sales promotions which are most likely to be effective for any given market target.

Generalizations from Benefit Segmentation Studies

A number of generalizations are possible on the basis of the major benefit segmentation studies which have been conducted thus far. For example, the following general rules of thumb have become apparent:

- It is easier to take advantage of market segments that already exist than to attempt to create new ones. Some time ago the strategy of product differentiation was heavily emphasized in marketing textbooks. Under this philosophy it was believed that a manufacturer was more or less able to create new market segments at will by making his product somewhat·different from those of his competitors. Now it is generally recognized that fewer costly errors will be made if money is first invested in consumer research aimed at determining the present contours of the market. Once this knowledge is available, it is usually most efficient to tailor marketing strategies to existing consumer-need patterns.
- No brand can expect to appeal to all consumers. The very act of attracting one segment may automatically alienate others. A corollary to this principle is that any marketer who wishes to cover a market fully must offer consumers more than a single brand. The flood of new brands which have recently appeared on the market is concrete recognition of this principle.
- A company's brands can sometimes cannibalize each other but need not necessarily do so. It depends on whether or not they are positioned against the same

segment of the market. Ivory Snow sharply reduced Ivory Flakes' share of market, and the Ford Falcon cut deeply into the sales of the standard size Ford because, in each case, the products were competing in the same segments. Later on, for the same companies, the Mustang was successfully introduced with comparatively little damage to Ford; and the success of Crest did not have a disproportionately adverse effect on Gleem's market position because, in these cases, the segments to which the products appealed were different.

- New and old products alike should be designed to fit *exactly* the needs of some segment of the market. In other words, they should be aimed at people seeking a specific combination of benefits. It is a marketing truism that you sell people one at a time—that you have to get *someone* to buy your product before you get *anyone* to buy it. A substantial group of people must be interested in your specific set of benefits before you can make progress in a market. Yet, many products attempt to aim at two or more segments simultaneously. As a result, they are not able to maximize their appeal to any segment of the market, and they run the risk of ending up with a dangerously fuzzy brand image.

- Marketers who adopt a benefit segmentation strategy have a distinct competitive edge. If a benefit segment can be located which is seeking exactly the kinds of satisfactions that one marketer's brand can offer better than any other brand, the marketer can almost certainly dominate the purchases of that segment. Furthermore, if his competitors are looking at the market in terms of traditional types of segments, they may not even be aware of the existence of the benefit segment which he has chosen as his market target. If they are ignorant in this sense, they will be at a loss to explain the success of his brand. And it naturally follows that if they do not understand the reasons for his success, the kinds of people buying his brand, and the benefits they are obtaining from it, his competitors will find it very difficult to successfully attack the marketer's position.

- An understanding of the benefit segments which exist within a market can be used to advantage when competitors introduce new products. Once the way in which consumers are positioning the new product has been determined, the likelihood that it will make major inroads into segments of interest can be assessed, and a decision can be made on whether or not counteractions of any kind are required. If the new product appears to be assuming an ambiguous position, no money need be invested in defensive measures. However, if it appears that the new product is ideally suited to the needs of an important segment of the market, the manufacturer in question can introduce a new competitive product of his own, modify the physical properties of existing brands, change his advertising strategy, or take whatever steps appear appropriate.

Types of Segments Uncovered Through Benefit Segmentation Studies

It is difficult to generalize about the types of segments which are apt to be discovered in the course of a benefit segmentation study. To a large extent, the segments which have been found have been unique to the product categories being analyzed. However, a few types of segments have appeared in two or more private studies. Among them are the following:

The Status Seeker	. . . a group which is very much concerned with the prestige of the brands purchased.
The Swinger	. . . a group which tries to be modern and up to date in all of its activities. Brand choices reflect this orientation.
The Conservative	. . . a group which prefers to stick to large successful companies and popular brands.
The Rational Man	. . . a group which looks for benefits such as economy, value, durability, etc.
The Inner-Directed Man	. . . a group which is especially concerned with self-concept. Members consider themselves to have a sense of humor, to be independent and/or honest.
The Hedonist	. . . a group which is concerned primarily with sensory benefits.

Some of these segments appear among the customers of almost all products and services. However, there is no guarantee that a majority of them or, for that matter, any of them exist in any given product category. Finding out whether they do and, if so, what should be done about them is the purpose of benefit segmentation research.

CONCLUSION

The benefit segmentation approach is of particular interest because it never fails to provide fresh insight into markets. As was indicated in the toothpaste example cited earlier, the marketing implications of this analytical research tool are limited only by the imagination of the person using the information a segmentation study provides. In effect, when segmentation studies are conducted, a number of smaller markets emerge instead of one large one. Moreover, each of these smaller markets can be subjected to the same kinds of thorough analyses to which total markets have been subjected in the past. The only difference—a crucial one—is that the total market was a heterogeneous conglomeration of sub-groups. The so-called average consumer existed only in the minds of some marketing people. When benefit segmentation is used, a number of relatively homogeneous segments are uncovered. And, because they are homogeneous, descriptions of them in terms of averages are much more appropriate and meaningful as marketing guides.

NOTES

[1] Wendell R. Smith, "Product Differentiation and Market Segmentation as Alternative Product Strategies," *Journal of Marketing*, Vol. XXI (July, 1956), pp. 3–8.

[2] Ronald E. Frank, "Correlates of Buying Behavior for Grocery Products," *Journal of Marketing*, Vol. 31 (October, 1967), pp. 48–53; Ronald E. Frank, William Massey, and Harper W. Boyd, Jr., "Correlates of Grocery Product Consumption Rates," *Journal of Marketing Re-*

search, Vol. 4 (May, 1968), pp. 184–190; and Clark Wilson, "Homemaker Living Patterns and Marketplace Behavior—A psychometric Approach," in John S. Wright and Jac L. Goldstucker, Editors, *New Ideas for Successful Marketing,* Proceedings of 1966 World Congress (Chicago: American Marketing Association, June, 1966), pp. 305–331.

[3] Dik Warren Twedt, "Some Practical Applications of the 'Heavy Half' Theory" (New York: Advertising Research Foundation 10th Annual Conference, October 6, 1964).

[4] Russell I. Haley, "Experimental Research on Attitudes Toward Shampoos," an unpublished paper (February, 1961).

[5] Ronald E. Frank and Paul E. Green, "Numerical Taxonomy in Marketing Analysis: A Review Article," *Journal of Marketing Research,* Vol. V (February, 1968), pp. 83–98.

SOME SUGGESTIONS FOR FURTHER READING

Green, P. E., and Y. Wind (1975), "New Way to Measure Consumers' Judgments," *Harvard Business Review* (July–August), 107–117.

Haley, R. I. (1971), "Beyond Benefit Segmentation," *Journal of Advertising Research* (August), 3–8.

Johnson, R. M. (1974), "Trade-Off Analysis of Consumer Values," *Journal of Marketing Research* (May), 121–127.

Wind, Y. (ed.), (1978), "Special Section on Marketing Segmentation Research," *Journal of Marketing Research* (August), 315–412.

——— and R. Cardozo (1974), "Industrial Marketing Segmentation," *Industrial Marketing Management* (June), 153–166.

21 / MARKET SEGMENTATION: A STRATEGIC MANAGEMENT TOOL / Richard M. Johnson

Like motivation research in the late 1950's, market segmentation is receiving much attention in research circles. Although this term evokes the idea of cutting up a market into little pieces, the real role of such research is more basic and potentially more valuable. In this discussion *market segmentation analysis* refers to examination of the structure of a market as perceived by consumers, preferably using a geometric spatial model, and to forecasting the intensity of demand for a potential product positioned anywhere in the space.

The purpose of such a study, as seen by a marketing manager, might be:

1. To learn how the brands or products in a class are perceived with respect to strengths, weaknesses, similarities, etc.
2. To learn about consumers' desires, and how these are satisfied or unsatisfied by the current market.
3. To integrate these findings strategically, determining the greatest opportunities for new brands or products and how a product or its image should be modified to produce the greatest sales gain.

From the position of a marketing research technician, each of these three goals translates into a separate technical problem:

1. To construct a product space, a geometric representation of consumers' perceptions of products or brands in a category.
2. To obtain a density distribution by positioning consumers' ideal points in the same space.
3. To construct a model which predicts preferences of groups of consumers toward new or modified products.

This discussion will focus on each of these three problems in turn, suggesting solutions now available. Solutions to the first two problems can be illustrated with actual data, although currently solutions for the third problem are more tentative. This will not be an exhaustive catalog of techniques, nor is this the only way of structuring the general problem of forecasting consumer demand for new or modified products.

Richard M. Johnson, "Market Segmentation: A Strategic Management Tool" (February 1975), pp. 13–18. Published by the American Marketing Association. Reprinted by permission of the publisher.
Richard Johnson is Vice President of Market Facts. He has published a number of articles in the area of multivaritate methods.

CONSTRUCTING THE PRODUCT SPACE

A spatial representation or map of a product category provides the foundation on which other aspects of the solution are built. Many equally useful techniques are available for constructing product spaces which require different assumptions and possess different properties. The following is a list of useful properties of product spaces which may be used to evaluate alternative techniques:

1. *Metric:* distances between products in space should relate to perceived similarity between them.
2. *Identification:* directions in the space should correspond to identified product attributes.
3. *Uniqueness/reliability:* similar procedures applied to similar data should yield similar answers.
4. *Robustness/foolproofness:* procedures should work every time. It should not be necessary to switch techniques or make basic changes in order to cope with each new set of data.
5. *Freedom from improper assumptions:* other things being equal, a procedure that requires fewer assumptions is preferred.

One basic distinction has to do with the kinds of data to be analyzed. Three kinds of data are frequently used.

Similarity/Dissimilarity Data

Here a respondent is not concerned in any obvious way with dimensions or attributes which describe the products judged. He makes global judgments of relative similarity among products, with the theoretical advantage that there is no burden on the researcher to determine in advance the important attributes or dimensions within a product category. Examples of such data might be: (1) to present triples of products and ask which two are most or least similar, (2) to present pairs of products and ask which pair is most similar, or (3) to rank order *k*-1 products in terms of similarity with the *k*th.

Preference Data

Preference data can be used to construct a product space, given assumptions relating preference to distances. For instance, a frequent assumption is that an individual has ideal points in the same space and that product preference is related in some systematic way to distances from his ideal points to his perception of products' locations. As with similarity/dissimilarity data, preference data place no burden on the researcher to determine salient product attributes in advance. Examples of preference data which might lead to a product space are: (1) paired comparison data, (2) rank orders of preference, or (3) generalized overall ratings (as on a 1 to 9 scale).

Attribute Data

If the researcher knows in advance important product attributes by which consumers discriminate among products, or with which they form preferences, then he may ask respondents to describe products on scales relating to each attribute. For instance, they may use rating scales describing brands of beer with respect to price vs. quality, heaviness vs. lightness, or smoothness vs. bitterness.

In addition to these three kinds of data, *procedures* can be *metric* or *nonmetric*. Metric procedures make assumptions about the properties of data, as when in computing a mean one assumes that the difference between ratings of values one and two is the same as that between two and three, etc. Nonmetric procedures make fewer assumptions about the nature of the data; these are usually techniques in which the only operations on data are comparisons such as "greater than" or "less than." Nonmetric procedures are typically used with data from rank order or paired comparison methods.

Another issue is whether or not a *single product space* will adequately represent all respondents' perceptions. At the extreme, each respondent might require a unique product space to account for aspects of his perceptions. However, one of the main reasons for product spaces' utility is that they summarize a large amount of information in unusually tangible and compact form. Allowing a totally different product space for each respondent would certainly destroy much of the illustrative value of the result. A compromise would be to recognize that respondents might fall naturally into a relatively small number of subgroups with different product

Figure 1. The Chicago beer market

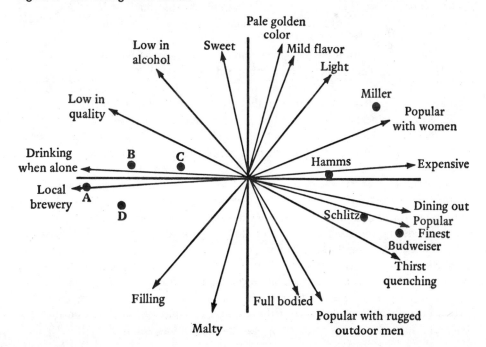

perceptions. In this case, a separate product space could be constructed for each subgroup.

Frequently a single product space is assumed to be adequate to account for important aspects of all respondents' *perceptions*. Differences in *preference* are then taken into account by considering each respondent's ideal product to have a unique location in the common product space, and by recognizing that different respondents may weight dimensions uniquely. This was the approach taken in the examples to follow.

Techniques which have received a great deal of use in constructing product spaces include nonmetric multidimensional scaling [3, 7, 8, 12], factor analysis [11], and multiple discriminant analysis [4]. Factor analysis has been available for this purpose for many years, and multidimensional scaling was discussed as early as 1938 [13]. *Nonmetric* multidimensional scaling, a comparatively recent development, has achieved great popularity because of the invention of ingenious computing methods requiring only the most minimal assumptions regarding the nature of the data. Discriminant analysis requires assumptions about the metric properties of data, but it appears to be particularly robust and foolproof in application.

These techniques produce similar results in most practical applications. *The* technique of multiple discriminant analysis will be illustrated here.

EXAMPLES OF PRODUCT SPACES

Imagine settling on a number of attributes which together account for all of the important ways in which products in a set are seen to differ from each other. Suppose that each product has been rated on each attribute by several people, although each person has not necessarily described more than one product.

Given such data, multiple discriminant analysis is a powerful technique for constructing a spatial model of the product category. First, it finds the weighted combination of attributes which discriminates most among products, maximizing an *F*-ratio of between-product to within-product variance. Then second and subsequent weighted combinations are found which discriminate maximally among products, within the constraint that they all be uncorrelated with one another. Having determined as many discriminating dimensions as possible, average scores can be used to plot products on each dimension. Distances between pairs of products in this space reflect the amount of discrimination between them.[1]

Figure 1 shows such a space for the Chicago beer market as perceived by members of Market Facts' Consumer Mail Panels in a pilot study, September 1968. Approximately 500 male beer drinkers described 8 brands of beer on each of 35 attributes. The data indicated that a third sizable dimension also existed, but the two dimensions pictured here account for approximately 90% of discrimination among images of these 8 products.

The location of each brand is indicated on these two major dimensions. The horizontal dimension contrasts premium quality on the right with popular price on the left. The vertical dimension reflects relative lightness. In addition, the mean rating of each product on each of the attributes is shown by relative position on each attribute vector. For instance, Miller is perceived as being most popular with women, followed by Budweiser, Schlitz, Hamms, and four unnamed, popularly priced beers.

As a second example, the same technique was applied to political data. During the weeks immediately preceding the 1968 presidential election, a questionnaire was sent to 1,000 Consumer Mail Panels households. Respondents were asked to agree or disagree with each of 35 political statements on a four-point scale. Topics were Vietnam, law and order, welfare, and other issues felt to be germane to current politics. Respondents also described two preselected political figures, according to their perceptions of each figure's stand on each issue. Discriminant analysis indicated two major dimensions accounting for 86% of the discrimination among 14 political figures.

The liberal vs. conservative dimension is apparent in the data, as shown in Figure 2. The remaining dimension apparently reflects perceived favorability of attitude toward government involvement in domestic and international matters. As in the beer space, it is only necessary to erect perpendiculars to each vector to observe each political figure's relative position on each of the 35 issues. Additional details are in [5].

Multiple discriminant analysis is a major competitor of nonmetric multidimensional scaling in constructing product spaces. The principal assumptions which the former requires are that: (1) perceptions be homogeneous across respondents, (2) attribute data be scaled at the interval level (equal intervals on rating scales),

Figure 2.   The political space, 1968

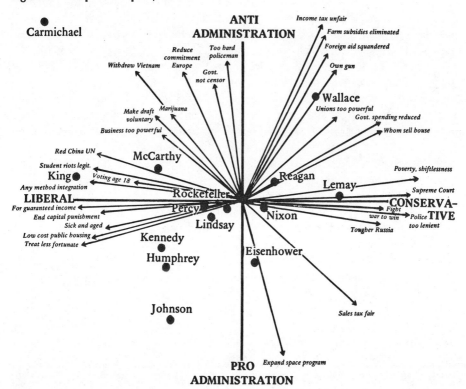

(3) attributes be linearly related to one another, and (4) amount of disagreement (error covariance matrix) be the same for each product.

Only the first of these assumptions is required by most nonmetric methods, and some even relax that assumption. However, the space provided by multiple discriminant analysis has the following useful properties:

1. Given customary assumptions of multivariate normality, there is a test of significance for distance (dissimilarity) between any two products.
2. Unlike nonmetric procedures, distances estimated among a collection of products do not depend upon whether or not additional products are included in the analysis. Any of the brands of beer or political figures could have been deleted from the examples and the remaining object locations would have had the same relationships to one another and to the attribute vectors.
3. The technique is reliable and well known, and solutions are unique, since the technique cannot be misled by any local optimum.

OBTAINING THE DISTRIBUTION OF CONSUMERS' IDEAL POINTS

After constructing a product space, the next concern is estimating consumer demand for a product located at any particular point. The demand function over such a space is desired and can be approximated by one of several general approaches.

The first is to locate each person's ideal point in the region of the space implied by his rank ordered preferences. His ideal point would be closest to the product he likes best, second closest to the product he likes second best, etc. There are several procedures which show promise using this approach [2, 3, 7, 8, 12], although difficulties remain in practical execution. This approach has trouble dealing with individuals who behave in a manner contrary to the basic assumptions of the model, as when one chooses products first on the far left side of the space, second on the far right side, and third in the center. Most individuals giving rank orders of preference do display such nonmonotonicity to some extent, understandably producing problems for the application of these techniques.

The second approach involves deducing the number of ideal points at each region in space by using data on whether a product has too much or too little of each attribute. This procedure has not yet been fully explored, but at present seems to be appropriate to the multidimensional case only when strong assumptions about the shape of the ideal point distribution are given.

The third approach is to have each person describe his ideal product, with the same attributes and rating scales as for existing products. If multiple discriminant analysis has been used to obtain a product space, each person's ideal product can then be inserted in the same space.

There are considerable differences between an ideal point location inferred from a rank order of preference and one obtained directly from an attribute rating. To clarify matters, consider a single dimension, heaviness vs. lightness in beer. If a previous mapping has shown that Brands, A, B, C, and D are equally spaced on this one dimension, and if a respondent ranks his preferences as B, C, A, and D, then his ideal must lie closer to B than to A or C and closer to C than to A. This narrows the feasible region for his ideal point down to the area indicated in Figure 3. Had he stated a preference for A, with D second, there would be no logically corresponding position for his ideal point in the space.

However, suppose these products have already been given the following scale positions on a heavy/light dimension: A = 1.0, B = 2.0, C = 3.0, and D = 4.0. If a respondent unambiguously specifies his ideal on this scale at 2.25, his ideal can be put directly on the scale, with no complexities. Of course, it does not follow *necessarily* that his stated rank order of preference will be predictable from the location of his ideal point.

There is no logical reason why individuals must be clustered into market segments. Mathematically, one can cope with the case where hundreds or thousands of individual ideal points are each located in the space. However, it is much easier to approximate such distributions by clustering respondents into groups. Cluster analysis [6] has been used with the present data to put individuals into a few groups with relatively similar product desires (beer) or points of view (politics).

Figure 4 shows an approximation to the density distribution of consumers' ideal points in the Chicago beer market, a "poor man's contour map." Ideal points tended somewhat to group themselves (circles) into clusters. It is not implied that all ideal points lie within the circles, since they are really distributed to some extent throughout the entire space. Circle sizes indicate the relative sizes of clusters, and the center of each is located at the center of its circle.

A representation such as this contains much potentially useful marketing information. For instance, if people can be assumed to prefer products closer to their ideal points, there may be a ready market for a new brand on the lower or "heavy" side of the space, approximately neutral in price/quality. Likewise, there may be opportunities for new brands in the upper middle region, decidedly light and neutral in price/quality. Perhaps popularly priced Brand A will have marketing problems, since this brand is closest to no cluster.

Figure 5 shows a similar representation for the political space, where circles represent concentrations of voters' points. These are not ideal points, but rather personally held positions on political issues. Clusters on the left side of the space intended to vote mostly for Humphrey and those on the right for Nixon in the 1968 election. Throughout the space, the percentage voting Republican increases generally from left to right.

It may be surprising that the center of the ideal points lies considerably to the right of that of the political figures. One possible explanation is that this study dealt

Figure 3. A one-dimensional product space

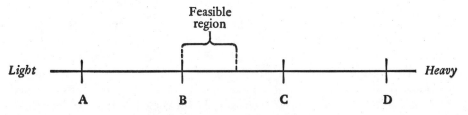

Figure 4.   Distribution of ideal points in product space

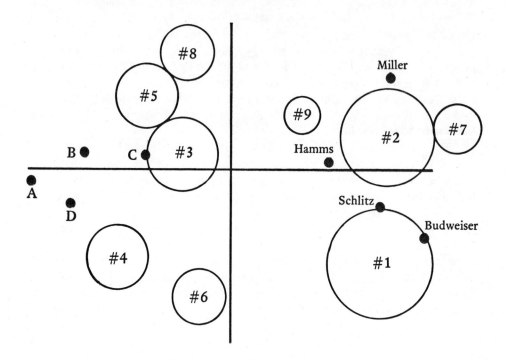

solely with positions on *issues,* so matters of style or personality did not enter the definition of the space. It is entirely possible that members of clusters one and eight, the most liberal, found Nixon's position on issues approximately as attractive as Humphrey's, but they voted for Humphrey on the basis of preference for style, personality, or political party. Likewise, members of cluster two might have voted strongly for Wallace, given his position, but he received only 14% of this cluster's vote. He may have been rejected on the basis of other qualities. The clusters are described in more detail in [5].

A small experiment was undertaken to test the validity of this model. Responses from a class of sociology students in a western state university showed them to be more liberal and more for decreasing government involvement internationally than any of the eight voter clusters. Their position is close to McCarthy's, indicated by an "S."

STRATEGIC INTEGRATION OF FINDINGS

Having determined the position of products in a space and seen where consumer ideal points are located, how can such findings be integrated to determine appropriate product strategy? A product's market share should be increased by repositioning: (1) closer to ideal points of sizable segments of the market, (2) farther from other products with which it must compete, and (3) on dimensions weighted heavily in consumers' preferences. Even these broad guidelines provide some basis

Figure 5. **Voter segment positions relative to political figures**

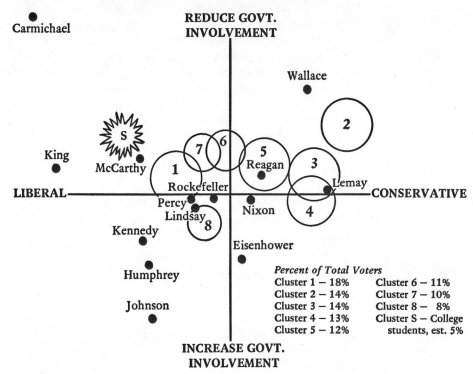

for marketing strategy. For instance, in Figure 4, Brand A is clearly farthest from all clusters and should be repositioned.

In Figure 5, Humphrey, Kennedy, and Johnson could have increased their acceptance with this respondent sample by moving upwards and to the right, modifying their perceived position. Presumably, endorsement of any issue in the upper right quadrant or a negative position on any issue in the lower left quadrant of Figure 2 would have helped move Humphrey closer to the concentration of voters' ideal points.

Although the broad outlines of marketing strategy are suggested by spaces such as these, it would be desirable to make more precise quantitative forecasts of the effect of modifying a product's position. Unfortunately, the problem of constructing a model to explain product choice behavior based on locations of ideal points and products in a multidimensional space has not yet been completely solved, although some useful approaches are currently available.

As the first step, it is useful to concentrate on the behavior of clusters of respondents rather than that of individuals, especially if clusters are truly homogeneous. Data predicting behavior of groups are much smoother and results for a few groups are far more communicable to marketing management than findings stated in terms of large numbers of individual respondents.

If preference data are available for a collection of products, one can analyze the extent to which respondents' preferences are related to distances in the space. Using regression analysis, one can estimate a set of importance weights for each cluster or, if desired, for each respondent, to be applied to the dimensions of the product space. Weights would be chosen providing the best explanation of cluster or individual respondent preferences in terms of weighted distances between ideal points and each product's perceived location. If clusters, rather than individuals, are used, it may be desirable to first calculate perference scale values or utilities for each cluster [1, 9]. Importance weights can then be obtained using multiple regression to predict these values from distances. If explanations of product preference can be made for *existing products*, which depend only on locations in space, then the same approach should permit *predictions* of preference levels for new or modified products to be positioned at specific locations in the space.

Models of choice behavior clearly deserve more attention. Although the problem of constructing the product space has received much attention, we are denied the full potential of these powerful solutions unless we are able to quantify relationships between distances in such a space and consumer choice behavior.

SUMMARY

Market segmentation studies can produce results which indicate desirable marketing action. Techniques which are presently available can: (1) construct a product space, (2) discover the shape of the distribution of consumers' ideal points throughout such a space, and (3) identify likely opportunities for new or modified products.

In the past, marketing research has often been restricted to *tactical* questions such as package design or pricing levels. However, with the advent of new techniques, marketing research can contribute directly to the development of *strategic* alternatives to current product marketing plans. There remains a need for improved technology, particularly in the development of models for explaining and predicting preferential choice behavior. The general problem has great practical significance, and provides a wealth of opportunity for development of new techniques and models.

NOTE

[1] McKeon [10] has shown that multiple discriminant analysis produces the same results as classic (metric) multidimensional scaling of Mahalanobis' distances based on the same data.

REFERENCES

1. Bradley, M. E. and R. A. Terry. "Rank Analysis of Incomplete Block Designs: The Method of Paired Comparisons," *Biometrika*, 39 (1952), 324–45.
2. Carroll, J. D. "Individual Differences and Multidimensional Scaling," Murray Hill, N.J.: Bell Telephone Laboratories, 1969.
3. Guttman, Louis. "A General Nonmetric Technique for Finding the Smallest Space for a Configuration of Points," *Psychometrika*, 33 (December 1968), 469–506.

4. Johnson, Richard M. "Multiple Discriminant Analysis," unpublished paper, Workshop on Multivariate Methods in Marketing, University of Chicago, 1970.

5. ———. "Political Segmentation," paper presented at Spring Conference on Research Methodology, American Marketing Association, New York, 1969.

6. Johnson, Stephen C. "Hierarchial Clustering Schemes," *Psychometrika*, 32 (September 1967), 241–54.

7. Kruskal, Joseph B. "Multidimensional Scaling by Optimizing Goodness of Fit to a Nonmetric Hypothesis," *Psychometrika*, 29 (March 1964), 1–27.

8. ———. "Nonmetric Multidimensional Scaling: A Numerical Method," *Psychometrika*, 29 (June 1964), 115–29.

9. Luce, R. D. "A Choice Theory Analysis of Similarity Judgments," *Psychometrika*, 26 (September 1961), 325–32.

10. McKeon, James J. "Canonical Analysis," *Psychometric Monographs*, 13.

11. Tucker, Ledyard. "Dimensions of Preference," Research Memorandum RM–60–7, Princeton, N.J.: Educational Testing Service, 1960.

12. Young, F. W. "TORSCA, An IBM Program for Nonmetric Multidimensional Scaling," *Journal of Marketing Research*, 5 (August 1968), 319–21.

13. Young, G. and A. S. Householder. "Discussion of a Set of Points in Terms of Their Mutual Distances," *Psychometrika*, 3 (March 1938), 19–22.

SOME SUGGESTIONS FOR FURTHER READING

Assael, H. and A. M. Roscoe (1976), "Approaches to Market Segmentation Analysis," *Journal of Marketing* (October), 67–76.

Blattberg, R. S. and S. K. Sen (1974), "Market Segmentation Using Models of Multi-dimensional Purchasing Behavior," *Journal of Marketing* (October), 17–28.

Green, P. E. and Y. Wind (1973), *Multiattribute Decisions in Marketing: A Measurement Approach*, Hinsdale, IL: Dryden Press.

Myers, J. H. (1976), "Benefit Structure Analysis: A New Tool for Product Planning," *Journal of Marketing* (October), 23–32.

Wind, Y. (1978), "Issues and Advances in Segmentation Research," *Journal of Marketing Research* (August), 317–337.

Young, S., L. Ott, and B. Feigen, (1978), "Some Practical Considerations in Market Segmentation, *Journal of Marketing Research* (August), 405–412.

22 / THE MARKETING CHARACTERISTICS OF GOODS / Leo V. Aspinwall

The characteristics of goods theory attempts to arrange all marketable goods in systematic and useful fashion. It has been tested both in the classroom and in application to business problems. It provides a perspective and frame of reference for organizing marketing facts and for weighing marketing decisions. Previous efforts included the three-way classification of products as convenience goods, shopping goods, and specialty goods. The characteristics of goods theory sets up a continuous scale rather than discrete classes and defines the criteria by which any product can be assigned to an appropriate place on the scale. All of these criteria lend themselves to objective measurement, at least potentially. By contrast, it would be rather difficult to distinguish a shopping good from a convenience good in positive, quantitative terms.

The marketing characteristics of a product determine the most appropriate and economical method for distributing it. To fix its position on the scale, representing the variation in these characteristics, is to take the first major step toward understanding its marketing requirements. To know these characteristics is to be able to predict with a high degree of reliability how a product will be distributed, since most products conform to the pattern. Serious departure from the theoretical expectations will almost certainly indicate the need for change and improvement in distribution methods. These considerations apply both to physical distribution and to the parallel problem of communications including the choice of promotional media and appeals. It follows also that goods having similar characteristics call for similar handling. Finally, if precise weights or values could be assigned to each characteristic, their combination would determine the unique position of a product on the marketing scale.

CHARACTERISTICS OF GOODS THEORY

The problem-solving process often leads into totally unfamiliar areas which sometimes bring us to a dead end. Only occasionally do these probing excursions uncover new combinations of old ideas that have some relevance to the problem in hand. When such combinations prove to be useful the mind is quick to employ

Reprinted from Leo V. Aspinwall, *Four Marketing Theories* (Boulder, Colorado: University of Colorado, 1961), by permission of the author.
The late Leo V. Aspinwall was professor emeritus at the University of Colorado, having headed the marketing and real estate division for 27 years. Before teaching, he served in the Bureau of Business Research at that university. Professor Aspinwall received his B.A. degree from the University of South Dakota and his M.B.A. at the University of Colorado. He was noted for his perceptive analyses of marketing phenomena.

such combinations again for problems of the same general type, so that repeated use tends to formulate a framework of reference which can be readily used for problem solving. Into the framework thus formulated the problem can be fitted so that the relationship of the integral parts can be observed. This may well be a mental sorting operation which seeks to classify problems into similar groups for greater efficiency in the unending task of problem solving.

The characteristics of goods theory is the result of one of these mental excursions, and its repeated use has had the effect of crystalizing the combination of old ideas into a fairly stabilized form. The theory has been revised from time to time through the constructive criticism of my colleagues, but whether it will ever be in final form is doubtful, since the dynamic character of all marketing activity is such that changes are more likely than anything else. Somehow the thought of achieving a final state of equilibrium is rather frightening.

CHARACTERISTICS OF GOODS

The problem of weights or values being assigned to these individual characteristics has been one of the real difficulties in giving the theory a mathematical setting. So far that objective has not been fully achieved. We have been obliged to deal with relative values which might be considered as an intermediary stage in the theory's development. The analogy of an electric circuit may eventually prove useful in formulating a mathematical approach. Getting goods distributed is not unlike moving an electric current through resistance factors, each of which takes a part of the gross margin. When the good finally reaches the consumer's hands, ready for consumption, all of the gross margin has been used. Looking at this idea from the consumer end, the amount of the gross margin the consumer has given up in order to enjoy the utilities the good provides is, in fact, the voltage that the electric current must have in order to pass through the resistance factors and finally reach the consumer.

The decision as to the number and kinds of characteristics to be used was approached by setting up tests which these characteristics should meet. These criteria are:

1. Every characteristic selected must be applicable to every good.
2. Every characteristic selected must be relatively measurable in terms of its relationship to every good.
3. Every characteristic must be logically related to all the other characteristics.

This brings us to the point of defining a characteristic. A characteristic is a distinguishing quality of a good relative to its stable performance in a market and its relationship to the consumers for whom it has want-satisfying capacity. Under this definition five characteristics have been selected, each of which must in turn be defined. These are:

1. Replacement rate.—This characteristic is defined as *the rate at which a good is purchased and consumed by users in order to provide the satisfaction a consumer expects from the product.* The replacement rate is associated with the

concept of a flow or movement of units of a good from producer to ultimate consumer. The idea is somewhat akin to a turnover rate, except that our understanding of turnover is related to the number of times per year that an average stock of goods is bought and sold. Replacement rate as used here is consumer-oriented. It asks how often the consumer buys shoes—once each month, once each six months, or once each year? It does not ask whether or not the shoes have been consumed, but only how often the market must be ready to make shoes available for consumers. This characteristic differentiates the rate or flow of different goods and attempts to envision the market mechanism that will meet the aggregate needs of consumers. This is marketing in motion as dictated by consumer purchasing power.

It may be helpful to introduce a few illustrative cases and at the same time show how the idea of relative measurement is used. Loaves of bread, cigarettes, packets of matches all have high replacement rates in terms of relative measurement. Some people consume bread more often than others, yet the average frequency of all bread eaters in a consumption area determines the replacement rate for bread. In comparison with grand pianos, bread has a high replacement rate and grand pianos have a low replacement rate. Men's shirts and ready-to-wear have medium replacement rates when compared to bread and grand pianos. Here we can visualize fast moving streams, slow moving streams and moderately moving streams of different kinds of goods, each with its characteristically different rate of replacement.

2. Gross margin.—The definition of gross margin as used here is not different from its use in marketing generally. *The money sum which is the difference between the laid in cost and the final realized sales price* is the gross margin. It is brought to mind at once that there are several gross margins involved in moving goods from factory gates to final consumer. What is meant here is the summation of all the gross margins involved. It is that total money sum necessary to move a good from point of origin to final consumer. It might be thought of as channel costs or as the fare a good must pay to reach its destination. If the amount of gross margin is less than the fare needed, the good will not reach destination. The calculation of the gross margin is a market-oriented function which is based, in the final analysis, on the amount of money a consumer will exchange for a particular good. If the consumer elects to pay a money fund which is less than the production cost and the necessary marketing costs, the good will not be marketed because the gross margin is too low in relation with the other characteristics. The availability of gross margin is the force that operates our marketing system. Suppose a consumer

Chart I.   Characteristics of goods theory

| | | Color Classification | |
Characteristics	Red Goods	Orange Goods	Yellow Goods
Replacement Rate	High	Medium	Low
Gross Margin	Low	Medium	High
Adjustment	Low	Medium	High
Time of Consumption	Low	Medium	High
Searching Time	Low	Medium	High

wishes to procure a pack of cigarettes from a vending machine and the machine is set to operate when a twenty-five cent piece is inserted in the slot. Nothing would happen if a ten-cent piece were dropped into the slot, except that the ten-cent piece would be returned to the customer. The gross margin contained in the twenty-five-cent piece was large enough to bring the consumer the cigarettes he needed.

This may be the appropriate place to call attention to the fact that whenever the flow of goods is arrested for whatever reason, costs begin to take a larger share of the planned gross margin and may actually prevent a good from reaching the final market. Such losses as may have been incurred in the stoppage must be borne by someone, and the calculations made by marketing men are such that loss situations cannot be tolerated, and the flow of goods will be stopped. The secondary action in such a case is that a money flow back to the producer also stops, which in turn closes down production. While this may be oversimplified, it does emphasize the importance of gross margin to the whole economic process.

Chart II. Schematic array of a few selected goods (plotted in terms of yellow goods)

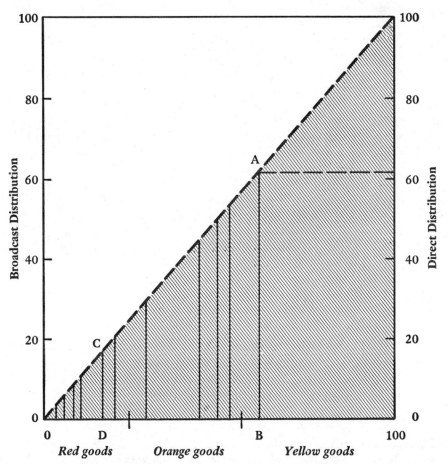

Certain types of goods are necessarily involved in storage by reason of their seasonal production. Storage assumes the availability of the needed amount of gross margin to pay these costs, otherwise such goods would not be stored. Whatever takes place during the movement of goods from producer to consumer affects gross margin.

This is the first opportunity to test these characteristics against the criteria set up for their selection. It has been shown that the replacement rate is applicable to all goods and that the replacement rate is relatively measurable. Lastly the question must be asked: Is the replacement rate related to gross margin? This is without doubt the most important relationship of all those needing demonstration in this theory. The relationship is inverse. Whenever replacement rate is high gross margin is low and, conversely, when replacement rate is low then gross margin is high. Thus, when goods move along at a lively clip the costs of moving them are decreased. This relationship brings to mind some economic laws which bear on the situation. The theory of decreasing costs seems to apply here to show that marketing is a decreasing-cost industry. This might be stated as follows: As the number of units distributed increases, the cost per unit distributed tends to decrease up to the optimum point. Mass distribution insofar as marketing is concerned has important possibilities. This is amply demonstrated in modern marketing operations. Goods handling in modern warehouses has been studied in this light and warehousing costs have been decreased, which in turn has expedited the flow of goods into consumer's hands. Here again, economic laws operate to induce the seller to pass on savings in marketing costs. Small decreases in gross margin tend to bring forth a disproportionately larger market response.

The relationship of replacement rate and gross margin has thus far been concerned with the increasing side of the relationship. When replacement rate is low and gross margin is relatively higher, it is not difficult to envision higher marketing costs. Almost at once it can be seen that selling costs will be relatively higher per unit. The gross margin on the individual sale of a grand piano or major appliance must bear the cost of direct sales, including salaries and commissions for salesmen who negotiate with prospective buyers and very often make home demonstrations. The fact that shipping costs are higher in moving pianos is well known. If car-lot shipments are used there are likely to be some storage costs involved, and this additional cost must come out of gross margin. It can be shown that high-value goods such as jewelry and silverware reflect this relationship in much the same way. This inverse relationship between replacement rate and gross margin strikes a balance when goods with a medium rate of replacement are involved.

3. Adjustment.—An important characteristic which pertains to all goods and which has been named "adjustment" is defined as *services applied to goods in order to meet the exact needs of the consumer.* These services may be performed as the goods are being produced or at any intermediate point in the channel of distribution or at the point of sale. Adjustment as a characteristic of all goods reflects the meticulous demands of consumers that must be met in the market. Even in such goods as quarts of milk there is evidence of adjustment. Some consumers demand milk with low fat content, others require milk with high fat content, to

name but one of the items of adjustment which pertains to milk. The matter of size of package, homogenized or regular, and even the matter of added vitamins come under adjustment. The services applied to milk are performed in the processing plant in anticipation of the adjustments the consumer may require. Here slight changes in the form or in size of package are adjustments performed in advance of the sale of the product. This type of adjustment imposes additional costs involving somewhat larger inventories and the use of a greater amount of space, with all that this implies. It can be easily understood that costs are involved whenever adjustments are performed, so that additional amounts of gross margin are necessary. Adjustments made at the point of production become manufacturing costs which only mildly affect the marketing operation, so that the measured amount of adjustment in the marketing channel is relatively low.

Goods with a high replacement rate have low adjustment, but the reverse is true when goods have low replacement rates. Goods with a medium replacement rate have a medium amount of adjustment. Here the inverse relationship between replacement rate and adjustment has been demonstrated, as well as the direct relationship between gross margin and adjustment.

4. Time of consumption.—Time of consumption as a characteristic of goods can be defined as *the measured time of consumption during which the good gives up the utility desired*. This characteristic is related to the replacement rate to a considerable degree, since goods with a low time of consumption are likely to have a high rate of replacement. The inverse relationship is true, but a low time of consumption does not mean that a repetitive purchasing program is maintained by the same consumer. Aspirin gives up its utility in the short period of time during which it is being consumed, but a purchase replacement may not occur until another headache needs attention. The idea of consumption time is more closely related to non-durable goods both in the consumer and industrial classes.

The time of consumption characteristic pertains to all goods, and the amount of this time is relatively measurable, which satisfies the criterion of relationship to all goods and the criterion of relative measurability. The final criterion of relationship to all other characteristics is also met in that low time of consumption is directly related to adjustment and gross margin and inversely related to the rate of replacement.

5. Searching time.—The characteristic of searching time can be defined as *the measure of average time and distance from the retail store* and hence convenience the consumer is afforded by market facilities. Suppose the need to purchase a package of cigarettes comes up for immediate attention for a consumer. The amount of effort exerted on his part to procure the needed cigarettes is correlated with the amount of searching time. In this case the amount of inconvenience suffered is usually very low since the market has reacted to the fact that there is a wide and insistent demand for cigarettes. To meet this demand, points of purchase are established wherever large numbers of potential customers are to be found. The result of such market action is that cigarettes can be purchased at many different places and in many different institutions, and the searching time is low. The old idea expressed in another way: consumers are motivated by a drive for con-

venience. Out of these relationships we have come to recognize "the span of convenience" for each product. Consumers cannot easily be forced to expend an amount of time and energy that is disproportionate to the satisfaction they expect to receive from the goods in question.

It can easily be seen that for certain goods the searching time will be low, while for certain other goods the searching time will be much larger. The amount of time and energy expended by a customer in the process of furnishing a new home would be very great and therefore, searching time would be correspondingly high. There is the need for examining the offerings of many stores, and even though these stores may be located fairly close to each other, in all probability, they will be located at some distance from the consumer's home. The reality of this situation is expressed in the characteristics of the goods. Searching time can be readily envisioned by the fact that we have many more market outlets for cigarettes than we do for grand pianos or furniture and, therefore, market availability for cigarettes is low and for pianos it is high.

Searching time is directly related to gross margin, adjustment, and time of consumption, and is inversely related to replacement rate. Searching time as a characteristic of goods pertains to all goods and for each and every good it is relatively measurable.

This information can now be fitted into a chart which will keep the relationships of the characteristics of goods in position as they pertain to all goods. This chart will show that goods with the same relative amounts of these five characteristics fall into the same broad classifications. Arbitrary names can be fitted to these broad classifications for greater convenience in conveying ideas about goods and the various ways in which they are distributed.

COLOR CONCEPT

This chart introduces an additional element into the characteristics of good theory: the color classification. The idea that goods with similar characteristics are similar to each other lends itself to the establishment of three large classes of goods that can be named in such a manner as to convey the idea of an array of goods. The choice of color names may be inept in some respects, but the idea of an array of goods, based upon the sum of the relative values of characteristics of goods, is important. The length of light rays for red, orange, and yellow, in that order, is an array of light rays representing a portion of the spectrum. For our present purpose it is more convenient to use the three colors only, rather than the seven of the full spectrum. The idea of an infinite gradation of values can be envisioned by blending these colors from red to yellow with orange in between. This is the idea we wish to convey as concerning all goods.

The sum of the characteristics for each and every good is different, and the sum of characteristics for red goods is lower than the sum of the characteristics for yellow goods. The chart shows red goods to have four low values and one of a high value, while yellow goods have four high values and one low.

It is useful to stress this tension between replacement rate and the other four marketing characteristics, since they all tend to decrease as replacement rate increases. That is equivalent to saying that as demand for a product increases, marketing methods tend to develop which reflect economies in the various aspects of marketing costs. It is easily possible, of course, to transform replacement rate into its inverse for use in arriving at a weighted index of the five characteristics. If replacement rate were expressed as the average number of purchases in a year, the inverse measure would be the average number of days between purchases. This measure would be low for red goods and high for yellow, like all of the other characteristics.

A schematic diagram can now be set up which represents all possible gradations in goods from red through orange to yellow. As shown in Chart II, page 331, a simple percentage scale from 0 to 100 is laid out on both coordinates. It is true that the weighted value for any product could be laid out on a single line. Yet there is an advantage in the two-dimensional chart for the purpose of visualizing an array of goods. The scale of values thus really consists of all the points on the diagonal line in the accompanying chart. Since there is an infinite number of points on any line segment, the scale provides for an infinite array of goods. If the chart were large enough, vertical lines could be drawn with each line representing a product now on the market. Even after these lines were drawn there would still remain an infinite number of positions in between. Many of these positions might serve to identify goods which have been withdrawn from the market or others which might be introduced in the future.

Line AB represents a good having an ordinate value of 63, indicating the sum of the characteristics of this good. In the general classification it has 63 percent yellow characteristics and 37 percent red characteristics. Translated into marketing terms, this good might be ladies' ready-to-wear dresses sold through department stores and shipped directly from the factory to these stores in the larger cities. The smaller cities are served by wholesalers who carry small stocks of these goods along with other dry goods items. Thus the marketing channels utilized for distributing this good would be direct to large department store accounts and semi-broadcast through specialty wholesalers serving smaller city accounts.

Line CD in its position near the red end of the scale has a yellow characteristics value of 15 and a red value of 85, which puts this good in the large classification as a red good. The sum of the characteristics value in the scale 0 to 100 is 85 percent red. This might well be a soap product which is sold mainly by broadcast distribution using a broker, wholesaler, retailer channel. The 15 percent yellow characteristic might indicate specialty salesmen's activity involving factory drop shipments. The latter type of distribution is more direct and might account for the 15 percent of direct distribution from the factory to the retailer.

The position of a good on the color scale is not static. Most products fall in the yellow classification when they are first introduced. As they become better known and come to satisfy a wider segment of consumer demand, the replacement rate increases and the good shifts toward the red end of the scale. Thus there is a red shift in marketing which offers a rather far-fetched analogy to the red shift in astronomy which is associated with the increasing speed of movement of heavenly bodies. There is also an opposing tendency in marketing, however, resulting from the constant shrinking of gross margin as a good moves toward the red end of the scale. Marketing organizations, in the effort to maintain their gross margin, may improve or differentiate a good which has moved into the red category, so that some of these new varieties swing all the way back into yellow. Thereafter the competitive drive for volume serves to accelerate the movement toward the red end of the scale again.

CONCLUSION

The characteristics of goods theory provides a basis for making marketing policy decisions concerning goods of all kinds and gives an insight into the way in which marketing channels can be used. The use of the broad color classification provides a basis for more exact communication in dealing with marketing problems.

SOME SUGGESTIONS FOR FURTHER READING

Bucklin, L. P. (1963), "Retail Strategy and the Classification of Consumer Goods," *Journal of Marketing* (January), 51–56.

Copeland, M. T. (1932), "Relation of Consumer's Buying Habits to Marketing Methods," *Harvard Business Review* (April), 282–289.

Enis, B. M. (1979), "Countering the Goods/Services Dichotomy: An Alternative Taxonomy for Product Strategy," *Proceedings*, Sixth, International Research Seminar in Marketing, Gordes, France.

———— and K. J. Roering (1980), "Product Classification Taxonomies: Synthesis and Consumer Implications," in Charles W. Lamb, Jr. (ed.) *Theoretical Developments in Marketing*, Chicago: American Marketing Association, 186–189.

Holbrook, M. B. and J. Howard (1977), "Consumer Research on Frequently Purchased Non-Durable Goods and Services: A Review," *Synthesis of Knowledge in Consumer Behavior*, R. Ferber, ed., Washington, D.C.: National Science Foundation.

23 / PARALLEL SYSTEMS OF PROMOTION AND DISTRIBUTION / Leo V. Aspinwall

The sponsor of a product must decide how it is to be promoted and what channels to use for its physical distribution. He is confronted with a variety of possibilities both for stimulating demand and for moving his product to the consumer. It turns out that there is a parallel relationship between these two aspects of the marketing problem with a distribution system and its appropriate counterpart in promotion usually occurring together. This pairing of systems occurs because the promotion and distribution requirements of a product are both dependent on the marketing characteristics of the goods. [Article 22 in this book] explained how goods might be arrayed according to their marketing characteristics into groups designated as red, orange, and yellow. It was further shown that this array could be translated into a numerical scale and presented in simple graphic form. The purpose of the present article is to indicate how the position of a product on this scale can be used to identify the parallel systems of promotion and distribution which should be used in marketing the product.

THE PARALLEL SYSTEMS THEORY

This set of ideas has come to be designated as the parallel systems theory. It is the kind of theory which is intended to be helpful in resolving fundamental practical issues in marketing. Theory alone cannot settle all the details of a marketing plan. It may save much time and effort by indicating the starting point for planning and the appropriate matching of systems of promotion and distribution. The gross margin earned on a product provides the fund which must cover the costs of marketing distribution and marketing promotion. The management of this fund involves many of the most critical decisions with which marketing executives have to deal. Even slight errors of judgment in this regard may spell the difference between profit and loss.

   The parallel systems theory begins with a simple thesis which may be stated as follows: The characteristics of goods indicate the manner of their physical distribution and the manner of promotion must parallel that physical distribution. Thus, we have parallel systems, one for physical distribution and one for promotion.

Reprinted from Leo V. Aspinwall, *Four Marketing Theories* (Boulder, Colorado: University of Colorado, 1961) by permission of the author.
The late Leo V. Aspinwall was professor emeritus at the University of Colorado, having headed the marketing and real estate division for 27 years. Before teaching, he served in the Bureau of Business Research at that university. Professor Aspinwall received his B.A. degree from the University of South Dakota and his M.B.A. at the University of Colorado. He was noted for his perceptive analyses of marketing phenomena.

The movement of goods and the movement of information are obviously quite different processes. It was to be expected that specialized facilities would be developed for each function. The fact that these developments take place along parallel lines is fundamental to an understanding of marketing. A few special terms must be introduced at this point for use in discussing parallel systems.

A channel for the physical distribution of goods may be either a short channel or a long channel. The shortest channel, of course, is represented by the transaction in which the producer delivers the product directly to its ultimate user. A long channel is one in which the product moves through several stages of location and ownership as from the factory to a regional warehouse, to the wholesaler's warehouse, to a retail store, and finally to the consumer. The parallel concepts in promotion may be compared to contrasting situations in electronic communication. On the one hand there is the closed circuit through which two people can carry on a direct and exclusive conversation with each other. On the other hand there is broadcast communication such as radio and television whereby the same message can be communicated to many people simultaneously.

In general, long channels and broadcast promotion are found together in marketing while short channels and closed circuit or direct promotion are found together. The parallel systems theory attempts to show how these relationships arise naturally out of the marketing characteristics of the goods.

CHARACTERISTICS OF GOODS AND MARKETING SYSTEMS

It will be remembered from the preceding article that goods were arrayed according to their marketing characteristics as red, orange, and yellow. Marketing systems can be arrayed in similar and parallel fashion. Red goods call for long channels and broadcast promotion. Yellow goods call for short channels and closed circuit promotion. Orange goods are intermediate as to their marketing characteristics and, hence, are intermediate as to the kind of distribution and promotion systems which they require. There is a continuous gradation from red to yellow and from broadcast to direct methods of marketing.

One of the fundamental marketing characteristics of goods is replacement rate. That is the frequency with which the average consumer in the market buys the product or replenishes the supply of it carried in his household inventory. Red goods are goods with a high replacement rate. A market transaction which occurs with high frequency lends itself to standardization and specialization of function. The movement of goods and the movement of information each becomes clearly marked and separate. Opportunity arises for a number of specialized marketing agencies to participate in distribution, and the result is what has been called the "long channel." Messages to the ultimate user become as standardized as the product itself. This type of information and persuasion does not need to follow the long distribution channel from step to step in its transmission from producer to consumer. Such messages are broadcast to consumers through both electronic and printed advertising media which provide a more appropriate channel.

Yellow goods are low in replacement rate and high in other marketing characteristics such as adjustment. Requirements for this class of goods tend to vary from one user to another. Adjustment embraces a variety of means by which goods are fitted to individual requirements. The marketing process remains relatively costly and a large percentage of gross margin necessarily goes along with high adjustment. The opportunity for standardization and specialization is slight compared to that of red goods. Physical movement and promotion remain more closely associated, with a two-way communication concerning what is available and what is needed finally resulting in the delivery of the custom-made product. A transaction between a man and his tailor would illustrate this type of marketing. Many kinds of industrial equipment are specially designed for the given user and would also be at the extreme yellow end of the scale. The short channel is prevalent in such situations and all promotion or related communication moves ·through a closed circuit.

Many products lie in the middle range which has been designated as orange goods. They have been produced to standard specifications but with the knowledge that they will have to be adapted in greater or less degree in each individual installation. The replacement rate is high enough to offer moderate opportunity for standardization and specialization. At least one intermediary is likely to enter the picture, such as an automobile dealer buying from the manufacturer and selling to the consumer or an industrial distributor serving as a channel between two manufacturers. The car sold to customers may be of the same model and yet be substantially differentiated to meet individual preferences as to color and accessories. Broadcast media are used in promotion but not on the same scale relatively as for soaps or cigarettes. The industrial distributor is often supported in his efforts by specialty salesmen or sales engineers employed by the manufacturer. Advertising of a semi-broadcast character is likely to be used. That is to say that messages are specially prepared for various segments of the market for which the appeal of the product is expected to be somewhat different. This approach lies between the standardized message to all users on the one hand and the individualized closed circuit negotiation on the other.

One qualification which may properly be suggested at this point is that marketing systems are not quite so flexible as this discussion suggests, but must conform to one type or another. Thus a channel for physical distribution could have two steps or three steps but not two and a half. Nevertheless the picture of continuous variation along a scale is generally valid because of the combinations which are possible. A producer may sell part of his output through wholesalers who service retailers and sell the remainder direct to retailers. The proportions may vary over time so that one channel presently becomes dominant rather than the other. Similarly broadcast promotion may gradually assume greater importance in the marketing mix even though a large but declining amount of adjustment is involved in some individual sales.

MOVEMENT OF GOODS AND MOVEMENT OF INFORMATION

The schematic relationship between goods and marketing systems is shown in Chart I. This simple diagram depicts the parallels which have been discussed. It will be noted that the segment of the line allowed is greater for orange goods than for red goods and greater for yellow than for orange. It is a readily observable fact that the number of separate and distinct items in any stock of goods increases as replacement rate decreases. A drug store, for example, has to sell more separate items to achieve the same volume of sales as a grocery store. An exclusive dress shop will need more variation in styles and models than a store operating in the popular price range. Paint brushes, files, or grinding wheels will be made up in a great multiplicity of specifications to serve the industrial market as compared to the few numbers which suffice for the household user. Red goods by their very nature are those in which a single item is bought frequently because it meets the requirements of many occasions for use while in the yellow goods more numerous items with less frequent sales are required for a more accurate matching of diverse and differentiated use situations.

The second chart is intended to demonstrate the relationship between goods and the methods of distribution and promotion. It is not intended to show an accurate mathematical relationship since the data from which it is constructed are not mathematically accurate, but it does implement understanding of the problems with which marketing executives must deal. The reasoning is deductive, moving from the general to the specific and provides a quick basis for reaching an answer which can readily be adjusted to a specific case. The readings from the diagram are in complementary percentages that must be accepted as rough measurements of the kinds and amounts of distribution and promotion. Long channel distribution and broadcast promotion are grouped together as related elements of the marketing mix and designated as "broadcast" for the sake of simplicity. The line representing these two elements in combination slopes downward to the right since this type of expenditure can be expected to be relatively high for red goods and relatively low for yellow goods. Similarly short channel distribution and closed circuit communication are thrown together under the designation of "direct." The line representing direct promotion and distribution slopes upward from left to right.

Chart I.   Relationship between goods and marketing systems

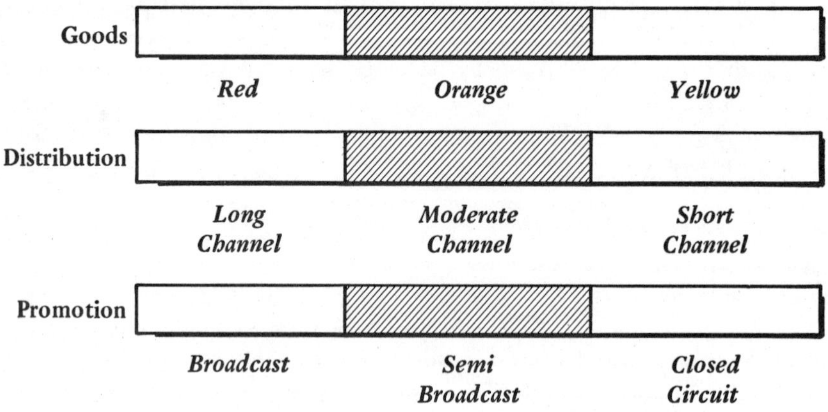

Goods		
Red	*Orange*	*Yellow*

Distribution		
Long Channel	*Moderate Channel*	*Short Channel*

Promotion		
Broadcast	*Semi Broadcast*	*Closed Circuit*

Chart II. Parallel systems theory

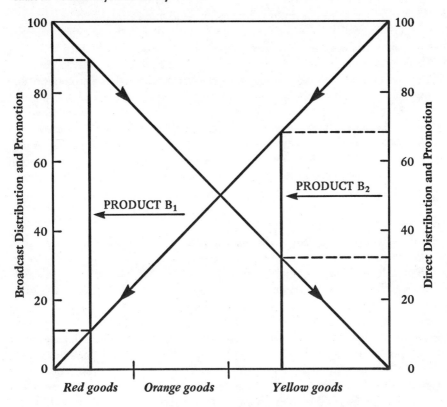

APPLICATION TO A MANAGEMENT PROBLEM

A short time ago a project was undertaken for a well-known manufacturer whose operation is such that the range of products his company manufactures covers the scale from red goods to yellow goods. In following the reasoning of the characteristics of goods theory and the parallel systems theory he was able to locate a certain product in its position on the base line. He drew the ordinate representing this product and found from the diagram that the distribution indicated was a modified direct distribution and that accordingly a considerable amount of direct promotion should be used. In reviewing what actually was being done with this product he knew that promotion was mostly broadcast while the distribution was a modified direct. Thus, promotion and distribution were not running parallel and such a finding for this product provided a substantial explanation of the poor performance this product was making. Research had confirmed that it was an excellent product and that it was priced correctly so that a reasonable volume of sales should have been expected. The planned sales for the product were not realized and to correct this situation a more extensive broadcast promotion program was launched, but from this program little or no increase in sales was realized. At this point the manufacturer decided that it would be worth a try to follow out the indicated promotional and distributional plan shown in the parallel systems theory analysis. A program of direct promotion was initiated and results were immediately forthcoming. The full sales expectations were realized and the manufacturer decided to establish a special division to handle the product which since that time has produced even more sales at costs considerably below the estimated costs.

A somewhat closer look at this case revealed that broadcast promotion was reaching thousands of people who were in no way qualified users of the product and that the type of advertising message was such that qualified users were unable to specify the product even if they wished to do so. A careful study of the problem showed that the direct promotion had produced all of the sales results. Thus the cost of the broadcast promotion had to be borne by qualified users and the result was a higher price than would have been needed if direct promotional means had been employed. The final result of this operation was that prices were lowered and the profit position for the manufacturer and all institutions in the distribution channel was improved.

Product B_2 in the diagram represents the product discussed in the case above located in its correct position. Reading the ordinate value in the vertical scale shows that the product it represents should be distributed 69 percent direct and that promotion should also be 69 percent direct. The complementary 31 percent reading shown indicates that 31 percent of the distribution should be broadcast and 31 percent of the promotion should be of the broadcast type. Product B_1 shown on the diagram is product B_2 as it was incorrectly located on the base line array of goods. The incorrect location was based on a measurement of the method of promotion that was being used. Actually this product was being distributed correctly by a modified direct method, and consequently consumers who might have been influenced to use the product had no means by which to exercise their wishes; the product was not available in retail stores in such a way as to make it readily available to qualified customers.

By making analyses of products and their distribution and promotional programs, it will be found that many products are not in conformity with the parallel systems theory, and yet seem to be successful products. This would not of itself disprove the theory. Such results might indicate that better results might be had if the programs were modified in the direction indicated by the theory. This can often be done at a comparatively small cost by using test sales areas in which the adjustment can be made without affecting the national system in which the product may be operating. The results from such experimentation should confirm the analysis made under the parallel systems·theory. A large amount of case material has been collected on the parallel systems theory but there seems to be an almost endless variety of cases and there is a need for constantly studying the problem in the light of the improvements in communications and distribution.

CONCLUSION

A further definition for broadcast promotion seems to be needed as well as for direct promotion. Whenever promotional means are used, without knowledge in advance of the identity of prospective users, the promotional means is considered to be broadcast. The firm employing broadcast promotional means relies upon the chance contact with potential customers for the product or service. The broadcast distributional means for such a product are so arranged that the customer for the product who has been reached by this type of promotion can exercise his choice conveniently and quickly. Retail stores are available within a short radius of the consumer who may wish to purchase the product. Thus, the sales gap is shortened both as to time and distance and the effectiveness of the broadcast means of promotion is enhanced. The key fact that makes this type of marketing economical is that while the prospective users are unidentified, they represent a large proportion of the general public which will be exposed to the broadcast message. The opposite of broadcast promotion is direct promotion. The definition of direct promotion turns on the fact that the recipient of the direct communication is known in advance, so that the message reaches the intended purchaser by name and address or by advance qualification of the prospect as to his need and ability to purchase the product. The most direct means would be a salesman who calls upon a selected prospect whose address and name is known in advance, and where judgment has been passed upon his need for the product, and whose ability to pay for the product has been ascertained. The next in order might be a direct first-class letter or telegram sent to a prospect. Then perhaps door-to-door selling or mailing to persons found on selected mailing lists. These selected means of direct promotion used show a widening sales gap between the customer and the product. It is readily seen that broadcast promotion creates the widest sales gap. At the same time it can readily be seen that the marketing radius over which the customer may have to search for the product is increased. Compensating for this increased radius are the more intensive means of promotion that result from direct promotion, which will induce the customer willingly to undertake greater inconveniences of time and distance in order to procure the product.

These definitions relate directly back to the characteristics of goods theory. Whenever a high replacement is involved it becomes physically impossible to effect distribution by direct means. Such a situation calls for mass selling and mass movement of goods wherein all economies of volume selling and goods handling are brought into play. The low gross margin on the individual transaction requires that the aggregate gross margin resulting from mass selling be ample to get the job done. It seems ludicrous to think of fashioning cigarettes to the consumers' needs at the point of sale, putting on filters and adjusting lengths to king size. The gross margin required to do such a job would put cigarettes in the price class of silverware and the number of people who could purchase on that basis would be very small. But mounting a diamond in a special setting is not at all ludicrous, because the gross margin available is large enough to undertake such adjustment. It would be redundant to go through the whole list of characteristics since it is perfectly clear what the relationships would be.

These two theories are excellent marketing tools and aid materially in understanding the marketing processes and their interactions. At the same time they may become dangerous tools in the hands of those who are not skilled in marketing. Even the experienced practitioners need to be fully cognizant of the technological advances as they occur and how these advances affect marketing processes. Skill in use of these tools should increase with experience in applying them to actual marketing situations.

SOME SUGGESTIONS FOR FURTHER READING

Davis, H. L., and A. J. Silk (1972), "Interaction and Influence Processes in Industrial Selling," *Sloan Management Review* (Winter), 56–76.

Enis, Ben M. and M. P. Mokwa (1979), "The Marketing Management Matrix: A Taxonomy for Strategy Comprehension," in *Conceptual and Theoretical Developments in Marketing*, O. C. Ferrell, S. W. Brown, and C. M. Lamb, eds., Chicago: American Marketing Association.

Heskett, J. L. (1973), "Sweeping Changes in Distribution," *Harvard Business Review* (March–April), 123–132.

McCammon, B. C. Jr., and W. L. Hammer (1974), "A Frame of Reference for Improving Productivity in Distribution," *Atlanta Economic Review* (September–October), 9–13.

Perrault, W. D. Jr., and F. A. Russ (1974), "Physical Distribution's Service: A Neglected Aspect of Marketing Management," *MSU Business Topics* (Summer), 37–45.

24 / THE WHEEL OF RETAILING /
Stanley C. Hollander

"The wheel of retailing" is the name Professor Malcolm P. McNair has suggested for a major hypothesis concerning patterns of retail development. This hypothesis holds that new types of retailers usually enter the market as low-status, low-margin, low-price operators. Gradually they acquire more elaborate establishments and facilities, with both increased investments and higher operating costs. Finally they mature as high-cost, high-price merchants, vulnerable to newer types who, in turn, go through the same pattern. Department-store merchants, who originally appeared as vigorous competitors to the smaller retailers and who have now become vulnerable to discount house and supermarket competition, are often cited as prime examples of the wheel pattern.[1]

Many examples of conformity to this pattern can be found. Nevertheless, we may ask: (1) Is this hypothesis valid for all retailing under all conditions? (2) How accurately does it describe total American retail development? (3) What factors cause wheel-pattern changes in retail institutions?

The following discussion assembles some of the slender empirical evidence available that might shed some light on these three questions: In attempting to answer the third question, a number of hypotheses should be considered that marketing students have advanced concerning the forces that have shaped retail development.

TENTATIVE EXPLANATIONS OF THE WHEEL

(A) Retail personalities. New types of retail institutions are often established by highly aggressive, cost-conscious entrepreneurs who make every penny count and who have no interest in unprofitable frills. But, as P. D. Converse has suggested, these men may relax their vigilance and control over costs as they acquire age and wealth. Their successors may be less competent. Either the innovators or their successors may be unwilling, or unable, to adjust to changing conditions. Consequently, according to this view, deterioration in management causes movement along the wheel.[2]

(B) Misguidance. Hermann Levy has advanced the ingenious, if implausible, explanation that retail trade journals, seduced by profitable advertising from the store

Reprinted from the *Journal of Marketing*, published by the American Marketing Association (July, 1960), pp. 37–42.
Stanley C. Hollander is professor of marketing at Michigan State University. He has been an analyst for a chain of retail stores and has taught at the Universities of Buffalo, Pennsylvania, and Minnesota. His published work is in the field of retailing, and he holds a B.S. from New York University, an M.A. from the American University, and a Ph.D. in economics from the University of Pennsylvania. *Explorations in Retailing,* which Professor Hollander edited, is a milestone in the academic progress of the retailing field.

equipment and supply industry, coax merchants into superfluous "modernization" and into the installation of overly elaborate facilities.[3]

(C) Imperfect competition. Although retail trade is often cited as the one type of business that approaches the Adam Smith concept of perfect competition, some economists have argued that retailing actually is a good example of imperfect competition. These economists believe that most retailers avoid direct price competition because of several forces, including resale price maintenance, trade association rules in some countries, and, most important, the fear of immediate retaliation. Contrariwise, the same retailers feel that service improvements, including improvements in location, are not susceptible to direct retaliation by competitors. Hence, through a ratchet process, merchants in any established branch of trade tend to provide increasingly elaborate services at increasingly higher margins.[4]

(D) Excess capacity. McNair attributes much of the wheel effect to the development of excess capacity, as more and more dealers enter any branch of retail trade.[5] This hypothesis rests upon an imperfect competition assumption, since, under perfect competition excess capacity would simply reduce margins until the excess vendors were eliminated.

(E) Secular trend. J. B. Jefferys has pointed out that a general, but uneven, long-run increase in the British standard of living provided established merchants with profitable opportunities for trading up. Jefferys thus credits adjustments to changing and wealthier market segments as causing some movement along the wheel. At the same time, pockets of opportunity have remained for new, low-margin operations because of the uneven distribution of living-standard increases.[6]

(F) Illusion. Professor B. Holdren has suggested in a recent letter that present tendencies toward scrambled merchandising may create totally illusory impressions of the wheel phenomenon. Store-wide average margins may increase as new, high-markup lines are added to the product mix, even though the margins charged on the original components of that mix remain unchanged.

DIFFICULTIES OF ANALYSIS

An examination of the actual development of retail institutions here and abroad does shed some light on both the wheel hypothesis and its various explanations. However, a number of significant difficulties hinder the process.

1. Statements concerning changes in retail margins and expenses are the central core of the wheel hypothesis. Yet valid information on historical retail expense rates is very scarce. Long-run changes in percentage margins probably do furnish fairly reliable clues to expense changes, but this is not true over short or intermediate periods. For example, 1957 furniture-store expense rates were about 5 percentage points higher than their 1949–1951 average, yet gross margins actually declined slightly over the same period.[7]

2. Historical margin data are somewhat more plentiful, but these also have to be dredged up from fragmentary sources.[8]
3. Available series on both expenses and margins merely note changes in retailers' outlays and receipts. They do not indicate what caused those changes and they do not report changes in the costs borne by suppliers, consumers, or the community at large.
4. Margin data are usually published as averages that may, and frequently do, mask highly divergent tendencies.
5. A conceptual difficulty presents an even more serious problem than the paucity of statistics. When we talk about "types" of retailers, we think of classifications based upon ways of doing business and upon differences in price policy. Yet census categories and other systems for reporting retail statistics are usually based upon major differences in commodity lines. For example, the "pineboard" druggists who appeared in the 1930s are a "type" of retailing for our purposes. Those dealers had cruder fixtures, charged lower prices, carried smaller assortments, gave more attention to turnover, and had less interest in prescriptions than did conventional druggists. Yet census reports for drugstores necessarily included all of the pineboards that maintained any sort of prescription department.

Discount houses provide another example of an important, but amorphous, category not reflected in census classifications. The label "discount house" covers a variety of retailers. Some carry stocks, others do not. Some have conventional store facilities, whereas others operate in office buildings, lofts, and warehouses. Some feature electrical appliances and hard goods, while others emphasize soft goods. Some pose as wholesalers, and others are practically indistinguishable from all other popular priced retailers in their fields. Consequently discount dealers' operating figures are likely to be merged into the statistics reported for other appliance, hardware, or apparel merchants.

EXAMPLES OF CONFORMITY

British

British retailing provides several examples of conformity to the wheel pattern. The grocery trade has gone through several wheel-like evolutions, according to a detailed analysis made by F. G. Pennance and B. S. Yamey.[9] Established firms did initiate some changes and some margin reductions, so that the pattern is obscured by many cross currents. But the major changes seem to have been due to the appearance and then the maturation, first, of department-store food counters; then of chain stores; and finally, of cut-price and cash-and-carry stores. Now supermarkets seem to be carrying the pattern through another evolution.[10]

Jefferys also has noted a general long-run upgrading in both British department stores and chains.[11] Vague complaints in the co-operative press and a decline in consumer dividend rates suggest that wheel-like changes may have occurred in the British co-operative movement.[12]

American

Very little is known about retail margins in this country before the Civil War. Our early retail history seems to have involved the appearance, first, of hawkers, walkers, and peddlers; then, of general stores; next, of specialty stores; and finally, of department stores. Each of these types apparently came in as a lower-margin, lower-price competitor to the established outlets, and thus was consistent with the wheel pattern. We do not know, however, whether there was simply a long-run decline in retail margins through successive improvements in retail efficiency from one type to another (contrary to the wheel pattern), or whether each of the early types was started on a low-margin basis, gradually "up-graded," and so provided room for the next entrant (in accordance with the pattern).

The trends toward increasing margins can be more easily discerned in many branches of retailing after the Civil War. Barger has described increases over the years 1869–1947 among important retail segments, including department stores, mail-order firms, variety stores, and jewelry dealers. He attributes much of the pre-World War I rise in department-store margins to the absorption of wholesaling functions. Changes in merchandise mix, such as the addition of soda fountains and cafeterias to variety stores and the upgrading of mail-order merchandise, seem to have caused some of the other increases. Finally, he believes changes in customer services have been a major force in raising margins.[13] Fabian Linden has extended Barger's observations to note similar 1949–1957 margin increases for department stores, variety chains, and appliance dealers.[14]

Some other examples of at least partial conformity to the wheel pattern may be cited. Many observers feel that both discount-house services and margins have increased substantially in recent years.[15] One major discount-house operator has stated that he has been able to keep his average markup below 12%, in spite of considerable expansion in his facilities and commodity mix.[16] However, the consensus seems to be that this probably is an exception to the general rule.

A study of gasoline pricing has pointed out how many of the so-called "off-brand" outlets have changed from the "trackside" stations of pre-war days. The trackside dealers typically maintained unattractive and poorly equipped installations, at out-of-the-way locations where unbranded gasoline was sold on a price basis. Today many of them sell well-promoted regional and local brands, maintain attractive, efficient stations, and provide prompt and courteous service. Some still offer cut prices, but many have raised their prices and margins up to or above national brand levels.[17] Over time, many of the pine-board druggists also seem to have become converted to fairly conventional operations.[18]

NON-CONFORMING EXAMPLES

Foreign

In underdeveloped countries, the relatively small middle- and upper-income groups have formed the major markets for "modern" types of retailing. Supermarkets and other modern stores have been introduced in those countries largely at the top of the social and price scales, contrary to the wheel pattern.[19] Some non-conforming examples may also be found in somewhat more industrialized environments. The vigorous price competition that developed among Japanese department stores during the first three decades of this century seems directly contrary to the wheel hypothesis.[20] B. S. Yamey's history of resale price maintenance also reports some price-cutting by traditional, well-established British merchants who departed from the wheel pattern in the 1880s and 1890s.[21] Unfortunately, our ignorance of foreign retail history hinders any judgment of the representatives of these examples.

American

Automatic merchandising, perhaps the most "modern" of all American retail institutions, departed from the wheel pattern by starting as a high-cost, high-margin, high-convenience type of retailing.[22] The department-store branch movement and the concomitant rise of planned shopping centers also has progressed directly contrary to the wheel pattern. The early department-store branches consisted of a few stores in exclusive suburbs and some equally high-fashion college and resort shops.

Only in relatively recent years have the branches been adjusted to the changing and more democratic characteristics of the contemporary dormitory suburbs. Suburban shopping centers, too, seem to have appeared first as "Manhasset Miracle Miles" and "Ardmores" before reaching out to the popular price customers. In fact, complaints are still heard that the regional shopping centers have displayed excessive resistance to the entry of really aggressive, low-margin outlets.[23] E. R. A. Seligman and R. A. Love's study of retail pricing in the 1930s suggests that pressures on prices and margins were generated by all types of retailers. The mass retailing institutions, such as the department and chain stores, that had existed as types for many decades were responsible for a goodly portion of the price cutting.[24] As McNair has pointed out, the wheel operated very slowly in the case of department stores.

Finally, Harold Barger has described the remarkable stability of overall distributive margins during the years 1919–1947.[25] Some shifting of distributive work from wholesalers to retailers apparently affected their relative shares of the total margins during this period, but this is not the type of change contemplated by the wheel pattern. Of course, the stability Barger notes conceivably could have been the result of a perfectly smooth functioning of the pattern, with the entrance of low-margin innovators providing exactly the right balance for the upcreep of margins in the longer established types. But economic changes do not come in smooth and synchronized fashion, and Barger's data probably should indicate considerably wider oscillations if the wheel really set the mold for all retailing in the post-war period.

CONCLUSIONS

The number of non-conforming examples suggests that the wheel hypothesis is not valid for all retailing. The hypothesis, however, does seem to describe a fairly common pattern in industrialized, expanding economies. Moreover, the wheel is not simply an illusion created by scrambled merchandising, as Holdren suggests. Undoubtedly some of the recent "upcreep" in supermarket average margins is due to the addition of nonfood and other high margin lines. But in recent years the wheel pattern has also been characteristic of department-store retailing, a field that has been relatively unreceptive to new commodity groups.[26]

In some ways, Jefferys' secular trend explanation appears most reasonable. The tendency of many established retailers to reduce prices and margins during depressions suggests also that increases may be a result of generally prospering environments. This explanation helps to resolve an apparent paradox inherent in the wheel concept. Why should reasonably skilled businessmen make decisions that consistently lead their firms along seemingly profitable routes to positions of vulnerability? Jefferys sees movement along the wheel as the result of sensible, business-like decisions to change with prospering market segments and to leave the poorer customers to low-margin innovators. His explanation is supported by the fact that the vulnerability contemplated by the wheel hypothesis usually means only a loss of market share, not a loss of absolute volume. At least in the United States, though, this explanation is partially contradicted by studies showing that prosperous consumers are especially prone to patronize discount houses. Also they are equally as likely to shop in supermarkets as are poorer consumers.[27]

The imperfect competition and excess capacity hypotheses also appear highly plausible. Considerably more investigation is needed before their validity can be appraised properly. The wheel pattern developed very slowly, and very recently in the department-store field. Yet market imperfections in that field probably were greater before the automobile gave the consumer shopping mobility. Major portions of the supermarket growth in food retailing and discount-house growth in appliance distribution occurred during periods of vastly expanding consumption, when excess capacity probably was at relatively low levels. At the moment there is little evidence to suggest any clear-cut correlation between the degree of market imperfection and the appearance of the wheel pattern. However, this lack may well be the result of the scarcity of empirical studies of retail competition.

Managerial deterioration certainly must explain some manifestations of the wheel, but not all. Empires rise and fall with changes in the quality of their leadership, and the same thing seems true in business. But the wheel hypothesis is a hypothesis concerning types of retailing and not merely individual firms. Consequently, the managerial-deterioration explanation holds true only if it is assumed that new people entering any established type of retailing as the heads of both old and new companies are consistently less competent than the first generation. Again, the fact that the wheel has operated very slowly in some fields suggests that several successive managerial generations can avoid wheel-like maturation and decay.

NOTES

[1] M. P. McNair, "Significant Trends and Developments in the Postwar Period," in A. B. Smith (editor), *Competitive Distribution in a Free, High-Level Economy and Its Implications for the University* (Pittsburgh: University of Pittsburgh Press, 1958), pp. 1–25, at pp. 17–18.

[2] P. D. Converse, "Mediocrity in Retailing," *Journal of Marketing* (April, 1959), pp. 419–420.

[3] Hermann Levy, *The Shops of Britain* (London: Kegan Paul, Trench, Trubner & Co., 1947), pp. 210–211.

[4] D. L. Shawver, *The Development of Theories of Retail Price Determination* (Urbana: University of Illinois Press, 1956), p. 92.

[5] Same reference as footnote 1.

[6] J. B. Jefferys, *Retail Trading in Great Britain, 1850–1950* (Cambridge: Cambridge University Press, 1954), various pages, especially p. 96.

[7] Cited in Fabian Linden, "Department Store Operations," *Conference Board Business Record* (October, 1958), pp. 410–414, at p. 411.

[8] See Harold Barger, *Distribution's Place in the American Economy Since 1869* (Princeton: Princeton University Press, 1955).

[9] F. G. Pennance and B. S. Yamey, "Competition in the Retail Grocery Trade, 1850–1939," *Economica* (March, 1955), pp. 303–317.

[10] "La Methode Americaine," *Time* (November 16, 1959), pp. 105–106.

[11] Same reference as footnote 6.

[12] "Battle of the Dividend," *Co-operative Review* (August, 1956), p. 183; "Independent Commission's Report," *Co-operative Review* (April, 1958), pp. 84–89; £52 Million Dividend in 1957," *Co-operative Review* (August 1958), pp. 171-172.

[13] Same reference as footnote 8, p. 82.

[14] See footnote 7.

[15] D. A. Loehwing, "Resourceful Merchants," *Barron's* (November 17, 1958), p. 3.

[16] S. Masters, quoted in "Three Concepts of Retail Service," *Stores* (July–August, 1959), pp. 18–21.

[17] S. M. Livingston and T. Levitt, "Competition and Retail Gasoline Prices," *The Review of Economics and Statistics* (May, 1959), pp. 119–132, at p. 132.

[18] Paul C. Olsen, *The Marketing of Drug Products* (New Brunswick: Rutgers University Press, 1948), pp. 130–132.

[19] H. S. Hettinger, "Marketing in Persia," *Journal of Marketing* (January, 1951), pp. 289–297; H. W. Boyd, Jr., R. M. Clewett, & R. L. Westfall, "The Marketing Structure of Venezuela," *Journal of Marketing* (April, 1958), pp. 391–397; D. A. Taylor, "Retailing in Brazil," *Journal of Marketing* (July, 1959), pp. 54–58; J. K. Galbraith and R. Holton, *Marketing Efficiency in Puerto Rico* (Cambridge: Harvard University Press, 1955), p. 35.

[20] G. Fukami, "Japanese Department Stores," *Journal of Marketing* (July, 1953), pp. 41–49, at p. 42.

[21] "The Origins of Resale Price Maintenance," *The Economic Journal* (September, 1952), pp. 522–545.

[22] W. S. Fishman, "Sense Makes Dollars," *1959 Directory of Automatic Merchandising* (Chicago: National Automatic Merchandising Association, 1959), p. 52; M. V. Marshall, *Automatic Merchandising* (Boston: Graduate School of Business Administration, Harvard University, 1954), pp. 108–109, 122.

[23] P. E. Smith, *Shopping Centers* (New York: National Retail Merchants' Association, 1956), pp. 11–12; M. L. Sweet, "Tenant-Selection Policies of Regional Shopping Centers," *Journal of Marketing* (April, 1959), pp. 399–404.

[24] E. R. A. Seligman and R. A. Love, *Price Cutting and Price Maintenance* (New York: Harper & Brothers, 1932).

[25] Same reference as footnote 8, pp. ix, x.

[26] R. D. Entenberg, *The Changing Competitive Position of Department Stores in the United States by Merchandise Lines* (Pittsburgh: University of Pittsburgh Press, 1957), p. 52.

[27] R. Holton, *The Supply and Demand Structure of Food Retailing Services, A Case Study* (Cambridge: Harvard University Press, 1954).

SOME SUGGESTIONS FOR FURTHER READING

Bates, A. D. (1976), "The Troubled Future of Retailing," *Business Horizons* (August), 22–28.

Bucklin, L. T. (1973), "A Theory of Channel Control," *Journal of Marketing* (January), 30–47.

Davidson, W. R. (1976), "The Retail Life Cycle," *Harvard Business Review* (November–December), 89–96.

Goldman, Arieh (1975), "The Role of Trading Up in the Development of the Retail System," *Journal of Marketing* (January), 54–62.

Langeard, E. and R. Peterson (1975), "Diffusion of Large Scale Food Retailing in France: Supermarche et Hypermarche," *Journal of Retailing* (Fall), 43–63ff.

Walker, B. J. and M. J. Etzel (1973), "The Internationalization of U.S. Franchise Systems: Progress and Procedures," *Journal of Marketing* (April), 38–46.

25 / INTERACTION AND INFLUENCE PROCESSES IN PERSONAL SELLING / Harry L. Davis and Alvin J. Silk

INTRODUCTION

When stock is being taken of the current state of marketing knowledge, one frequently hears it said that personal selling is a neglected area of study. The point is usually made that despite its generally greater significance as a marketing expense than media advertising, personal selling has been the object of much less model-building and empirical study. There are, however, indications that the situation is changing. The amount of attention being paid to sales force management problems in the management science/operations research literature appears to be increasing.[1] Sales operations are also the focal point of much of the work going on in the area of marketing information systems.[2]

This paper reviews some relevant developments of yet another sort—behavioral research of yet another sort—behavioral research on personal selling. A great deal of research on the behavior of salesmen has been conducted in the past, but most of it has dealt with psychological testing and the prediction of salesmen's performance. A quite different point of view is reflected in the material examined here. Our interest centers on efforts to apply social psychological knowledge about interaction and influence processes to selling problems.

The paper is organized as follows: We first consider investigations of customer-salesman interaction. We then consider their implications for sales force management. Work that treats selling as interpersonal influence is then discussed. Finally, findings are summarized and further applications of behavioral research are suggested.

SELLING AS INTERPERSONAL INTERACTION

A criticism sometimes made of behavioral science research is that after cutting through the specialized lingo and complex methodology, one finds in barely recognizable form, little more than an affirmation of what was already "obvious" to

Reprinted from *Sloan Management Review*, Vol. 12, (Winter 1972), pp. 59–76, by permission of Sloan Management Review.
Harry Davis is a professor of marketing at the University of Chicago. He received his Ph.D. from Northwestern University and has published considerable research in the area of marital roles in decision process.
Alvin Silk is a professor of marketing at the Massachusetts Institute of Technology. He received his Ph.D. from Northwestern University and has taught at UCLA and the University of Chicago.

everyone—mere "truisms, platitudes, and tautologies." [8] Thus, the observation that the most fundamental aspect of personal selling is the "interaction" that goes on between a prospect and a salesman may well appear as yet another example of befuddling the commonplace with fancy verbiage. While it may seem self-evident that selling involves interaction, such a description implies a somewhat different view of the selling process than that which is generally stressed in the vast literature of this field. More important, some empirical studies of personal selling as inter-action have begun to appear which offer fresh insights of practical significance into a number of thorny issues of long standing.

The Customer-Salesman Dyad

The person primarily responsible for stimulating the current interest in salesman-prospect interaction is Franklin B. Evans. Examining a sample of the abundant and diverse writings of practitioners on the subject of selling, Evans points out that "invariably these deal with only the salesman's point of view." [4] The customer is certainly not ignored in these conventional writings but the emphasis is, under-standably, on how to sell. The typical discussion places the customer, at least im-plicitly, in a somewhat passive role. In prescribing such things as the personal characteristics required of the "successful" salesman, means of diagnosing and adapting to customer's needs, persuasive techniques, etc., salesmanship authorities naturally focus on how the salesman's behavior affects the outcome of a sales contact. As a consequence, analysis of the influence of the prospect on the process tends to be neglected.

A similar imbalance characterizes most part empirical research on personal selling which is also voluminous—as Miner has observed, "there is little question but that the salesman is one of the most extensively studied men in the business world." [5] The focus of attention in most empirical research has been on the pre-diction of some measure of salesman performance from information about the salesman's background characteristics and a variety of personality, interest, and ability factors measured by psychological testing instruments.[6] The results of these attempts to discover criteria useful for recruiting and selecting salesmen have been quite mixed—sizeable correlations have been reported for certain sales occupations while in numerous other studies, few of which are ever published, no meaningful relationships have been found.[7] Even for its limited intended purpose (*i.e.*, to aid in making personnel decisions), the value of this work remains highly controversial and, as has been noted by others, it has contributed very little to our understanding of why or how a salesman becomes effective.[8] In attempting to predict sales per-formance, this research has concentrated almost entirely on the characteristics of salesmen and has failed to take explicit account of who the salesman interacts with in attempting to make a sale.[9] The assumption tacitly made is that differences among salesmen with respect to the types of prospects they contact are minimal, and hence variations in performance must be due to differences among the sales-men themselves. As we shall discuss below, such an assumption seems tenuous for many if not most types of selling. In contrast, Evans argues that the unit of analyses in personal selling research should not be the salesman alone but rather the *interaction dyad*—the salesman-prospect pair involved in a sales encounter.

Evans summarizes his position as follows:

... the sale (or no sale) is the result of the particular interaction situation, the face-to-face contact of the given salesman and his prospect. The result of the contact depends not on the characteristics of either party alone but how the two parties view and react to each other.[10]

Interpersonal Attraction

Given such an orientation, what can behavioral science suggest about the nature of a prospect-salesman interaction and the chance of a sale being made? One source of relevant ideas is research on "interpersonal attraction."[11] The general question motivating work by social psychologists and sociologists in this area is: why is a person attracted to certain individuals and repelled by others? There is a considerable body of evidence to suggest that the answer lies in how similar the two individuals are. It has been repeatedly demonstrated in a long list of both experimental and correlational studies of such phenomena as friendship formation, mate selection, and survey interviewing that a strong positive relationship exists between interpersonal similarity and liking.[12] Various dimensions of similarity have been investigated including background characteristics (e.g., race, age, status, ethnicity, etc.), attitudes, interests, values, and personality. The proposition that similarity leads to liking can be derived from several theoretical positions such as those involving models of cognitive consistency[13] and social exchange[14] but most emphasize the notion that interacting with others who are similar to, or agree with oneself provides rewards or need satisfaction.

Salesman-Customer Similarity

Drawing on these ideas, Evans hypothesized that "the more similar the parties in the dyad are, the more likely a favorable outcome, a sale."[15] Evans tested this hypothesis in a field study of life insurance selling.[16] The latter was chosen because it represented an area where the salesman (rather than the product offering and/or other promotion) appeared to be the critical factor determining whether or not a sale was made. A group of 86 experienced male agents were selected from three insurance firms. From records of all the face-to-face contacts they made during a four-week period, a random sample of 168 sold and 183 unsold prospects was chosen. On the average, personal interviews were conducted with the sample eleven weeks after the date of the salesman's visit. Care was taken to minimize the chance of respondents' making a connection between the sales call and the interview. Sold and unsold prospects responded to a questionnaire covering the following classes of variables: attitudes and knowledge of life insurance and life insurance salesmen in general; attitudes and perceptions of the "last" insurance agent who had called on them; management of personal finances; demographics, background, and physical characteristics; and personality needs. Essentially the same instruments were administered to the salesmen; however, they rated themselves on scales similar to those the prospects had used to describe the salesmen who had contacted them.

In general, the results supported the similarity hypothesis; the insurance agents were found to be more like the sold than the unsold prospects. Evans demonstrated that whether or not a prospect would buy insurance from a particular agent could *not* be predicted in any straightforward manner solely on the basis of knowledge of the prospect's attitudinal, personality, and demographic characteristics. As groups, the sold and unsold prospects were essentially similar in all the above respects.

However, when the three groups were compared to one another, the salesmen appeared to be more like the sold prospects than the unsolds. To illustrate, the difference in mean ages between the salesmen and sold prospects was 1.2 years while that for the salesmen and unsold prospects was 2.5 years. The same pattern manifested itself when similar comparisons were made with respect to numerous variables ranging from background and physical characteristics through personality needs. Furthermore, not only did objective measures of the variables indicate that the salesmen were more similar to the sold than the unsold prospects, but the sold prospects tended to *perceive* the salesmen as more like themselves than the unsolds did.

The basic notion underlying Evans' work is that the more similar a salesman and prospect are, the greater will be their mutual attraction which, in turn, enhances the likelihood of a sale being made—i.e., the more a prospect likes a salesman, the greater the chance that the latter will be able to influence the former. The findings summarized above indicated that the probability of a sale occurring was related to salesman-prospect similarity.

In addition, Evans investigated the intervening variable, liking. As expected, sold prospects evaluated the salesman more favorably than did the unsolds. Evans describes the differences between the sold and unsold prospects' reactions to the salesmen as follows: The successful salesman is seen by sold prospects as (1) an expert in insurance, (2) similar to themselves in outlook and situation, (3) as a person they'd like to know better, and (4) interested in them personally, not just as a source of revenue.[17]

The sold and unsold prospects held a common and quite negative stereotype of the "typical" insurance salesman as an aggressive, fast-talking, untrustworthy type. However, the two groups did not share the same view of the particular agents who had contacted them. Compared to the unsolds, the ratings of the particular salesmen given by sold prospects were more positive and closer to the salesmen's own evaluations of themselves. This would suggest that salesman-prospect similarity facilitated the development of a friendly relaxed interaction. Since Evans' study was basically a correlational one utilizing data obtained *after* the salesman-prospect contact had taken place, whether the sold prospects' greater liking of the salesmen preceded or followed the sale cannot be determined. Clearly, the similarity-attraction hypothesis would suggest that liking was the antecedent condition and the occurrence of the sale, the consequence. On the other hand, for a variety of reasons one would expect prospects to evaluate a salesman from whom they had bought an insurance policy more positively than one from whom they had declined to buy. For example, there is evidence that individuals tend to like persons who have influenced them.[18]

A similar question about causal priorities might also be raised concerning the relationship Evans observed between perceived prospect-salesman similarity and the occurrence of a sale. Although it has been frequently demonstrated experimentally that similarity leads to interpersonal liking, there is also a large body of evidence which indicates that persons tend to perceive others whom they like as similar to themselves.[19] Thus, an association between perceived similarity and purchasing could reflect causation in either direction. However, Evans found that not only did the sold prospects *perceive* the salesmen to be more similar to themselves than the unsolds but in fact they actually were when compared in terms of objective measures, such as physical and personality characteristics, which would remain unchanged before and after the sales transaction.

If one accepts the basic notion that salesman-prospect similarity affects the likelihood of a sale being made, then the practical question that naturally comes to mind is: with respect to what attributes is similarity critical? Two additional studies have been reported which provide some further support for Evans' views and are relevant to this question. Another study of life insurance selling carried out by Gadel [20] suggests that age may be a key factor. An analysis of some 22,000 policies revealed that agents' sales tended to be concentrated among persons who were in the same age group as themselves. This concentration was greatest for young agents and tended to decrease with years of experience. If salesman-prospect similarity affects sales success, salesmen are likely to develop an awareness of this condition. To the extent that insurance agents have some latitude in choosing prospects, one would expect them to seek out prospects similar to themselves. Clearly, their ability to do so is limited by what they can ascertain about a prospect before making a sales contact. Given the ways agents learn about prospects initially, it is probably easier to obtain a rough indication of the prospect's age and to use that as a screening criterion; rather than attempt to assess other personal characteristics. Of course, agents may well use more than one criterion.

A quite different aspect of customer-salesman similarity was investigated by Tosi in a study of middleman selling.[21] Here attention was focused on the extent to which customer and salesman share the same conception of the salesman's role. A group of 40 wholesale drug salesmen and 103 retail pharmacists whom the former contacted regularly were asked to indicate their perceptions of the "ideal" and "actual" behavior of salesmen on a set of predetermined scales. Differences between the salesman's and customer's responses on the "ideal" scales were taken as a measure of *role consensus*—the extent to which the salesman and customer agreed as to what the salesman's behavior should be. Discrepancies between the ideal and actual ratings given by either the salesman or the customer were used as indicators of *expectation level*—the degree to which the salesman's actual behavior was perceived to differ from that which was considered desirable.

Tosi hypothesized that both role consensus and expectation level would be related to sales performance. Two indices of the latter variable were employed: the share of a given customer's business placed with the salesman's firm, and the number of *other* suppliers also serving the customer. Contrary to the first hypothesis, no statistically significant relationship was found between role consensus and either measure of sales success. However, the buyers' expectation levels were shown to be related to the number of suppliers they purchased from but not to the share of business the salesmen obtained.[22]

That is, the less the discrepancy between buyer's conception of the "ideal" behavior of a salesman and his perception of how the particular salesman actually conducted himself, the fewer other suppliers the customer tended to deal with. Thus it appeared that agreement between the customer and salesman as to how the salesman *ought* to behave did not have any bearing on the latter's effectiveness; but the closer the salesman came to meeting the customer's expectations regarding how he should function, the smaller the number of competitors he would have to contend with.

Selling Strategies

The studies of Evans, Gadel, and Tosi described above dealt primarily with the relationship between salesman-prospect similarity and sales performance. All three were correlational investigations based on data obtained after the sales contacts had been made. As such, they were not well suited to uncovering exactly what transpires between the salesman and prospect in the course of their encounters. The interpersonal attraction theory referred to above would suggest that salesman-prospect similarity is conducive to the occurrence of an amicable exchange between the two parties, thereby making it more likely that the salesman will be able to influence the prospect to buy.

Willett and Pennington made a detailed study of the content of customer-salesman interactions occurring in retail stores in connection with the purchase of certain appliances.[23] The interactions were tape-recorded in a seemingly unobtrusive way and content-analyzed using the scheme developed by Bales which distinguishes between task or instrumental behavior on the one hand, and socioemotional or affective behavior on the other.[24] Comparisons were drawn between "successful" and "unsuccessful" transactions involving 132 customers and 14 salesmen. The interactions that resulted in immediate purchases appeared to be characterized by more suggestion-seeking and giving and fewer displays of negative feelings than those interactions that were not culminated by a purchase. Although salesman-customer similarity was not examined, these data constitute evidence that interactions preceding a sale tend to be friendlier, more free-flowing exchanges than those which do not produce a purchase.

From a managerial standpoint, the important question about sales interactions is, of course, how the salesman's behavior affects the outcome. What can the salesman do to shape the course along which an interaction proceeds? Are certain selling strategies and techniques more effective than others in this regard? Consider the following problem. In selling paint to consumers, who will be more successful: the salesman who appears to customers to be more knowledgeable about using paint than they are, or one whom customers perceive as having about the same amount of experience (or lack thereof) as themselves? At first glance, most would probably opt for the prediction favoring the salesman who appeared more knowledgeable than his customers—i.e., the more experienced a salesman is perceived as being with respect to his product, the more likely it is that he can influence a customer to buy. Besides its common sense appeal, this proposition finds support in numerous experimental studies of communications source credibility which have been demonstrated that the effectiveness of a given message in changing attitudes varies according to the amount of expertise attributed to the source of the message.[25] However, application of the salesman-customer similarity hypothesis to this situation leads to just the opposite prediction. The amount of experience a salesman claims to have had with the product could affect the customer's perception of their similarity. For the typical consumer who is only an occasional painter, the more painting the salesman indicates he personally has done, the less similar he will appear to the novice buyer and hence, the less influence the salesman will have with the buyer.

The efficacy of these two competing factors, salesman expertise and customer-salesman similarity, was investigated in a field experiment conducted by Brock.[26] Over a five-month period, two part-time salesmen in the paint department of a retail store attempted to influence customers to purchase paint at a different price level from that which they initially selected. After a consumer indicated that he wished to buy a given amount of some variety of paint at a particular price, the salesman tried to alter his choice by delivering one of two predetermined appeals. Half the time the salesman represented himself as being similar to customers by emphasizing that the magnitude of his own recent paint consumption was the same as the amount being purchased by the customer. For the other half of the cases, the dissimilar or "expert" condition was applied by having the salesman portray himself as having just used twenty times the quantity of paint the consumer planned to buy. Attempts were made to influence some customers to buy at higher prices and others at lower prices than they originally intended. The results indicated that similarity was more important than expertise. While the dissimilar salesman was presumably perceived as more knowledgeable about paint, he was less effective than the salesman who identified his own paint consumption as similar to that of his customers. The differential effectiveness of the two approaches held up over attempts to persuade consumers to buy higher as well as lower priced paints.

Central to the view of selling as interpersonal interaction is the proposition that the more a prospect likes a salesman, the greater the influence the salesman will have on the prospect. This would imply that ingratiating consumers should be an effective selling tactic. Farley and Swinth performed an experiment bearing on this matter.[27] The main purpose of the study was to compare the impact of two different sales messages for a roll-up yardstick. One message, dubbed the "product pitch," emphasized a description and demonstration of the product's features. The other, a "personal pitch," featured a favorable personal discussion of the customer's role and stressed how the product was compatible with it. A group of 87 females served as subjects—about a third were undergraduates and the remainder were housewives. After hearing one of the presentations, subjects chose between the product and an equivalent sum of money ($0.75) and then rated the product and the salesman on a number of scales. The percentage choosing the yardstick over the money was slightly greater for the group hearing the personal rather than the product pitch. However, the difference was not statistically significant.

Paradoxically, subjects exposed to the product pitch evaluated both the product and the salesman more positively than those receiving the personal pitch. Regardless of which sales presentation they heard, those selecting the product had more favorable attitudes toward the product and the salesman than those who chose to take the money. Here again, the design of the study did not permit the direction of causal relations between attitudes and choice to be untangled. As Farley and Swinth note, the results suggest that an effective sales appeal alters the buyer's perception of the attractiveness of the product and the salesman and hence, *both* considerations require attention in designing sales messages.

IMPLICATIONS FOR SALES FORCE MANAGEMENT

We began the last section by suggesting that personal selling might be fruitfully viewed as salesman-prospect interaction. One stream of research from the small groups field was identified as being especially relevant to the problem of understanding the determinants of effective salesman performance—that dealing with the subject of interpersonal attraction. Applying the core idea of this work to personal selling suggests that the greater the similarity between a salesman and a prospect, the more the prospect will like the salesman and, therefore, the greater the salesman's influence. We then reviewed a handful of empirical studies that embrace the interactionist view of selling within the framework of this proposition. While the number of investigations available is limited and various kinds of methodological questions can be raised about them, significant relationships between several aspects of customer-salesman similarity and buying have been reported with considerable, but by no means total, regularity. Much remains to be learned about why and under what conditions this relationship occurs. For example, it would be useful to consider how not only similarity but also complementarity between salesmen and customers is related to sales success. While the old adage that "birds of a feather flock together" seems plausible enough, is there not also something in that other oft-repeated maxim about "opposites attracting?" In pursuing such questions the available behavioral literature should prove useful as a source of ideas for conditional propositions which can be tested so as to refine our knowledge about where a certain relationship does or does not hold. A theory of interpersonal *congruency* has been proposed which suggests that under certain circumstances attraction will be facilitated by dissimilarities as well as similarities.[28]

Research has scarcely begun on the question of how and to what extent the salesman can influence and/or control the direction a sales interaction takes by modifying his own behavior in appropriate ways. Nonetheless, Brock's provocative experiment dealing with customer-salesman similarity with respect to product experience is indicative of how a non-obvious relationship involving an important control variable suggested by the similarity-attraction hypothesis can be studied in a natural sales setting. An intriguing question raised by Brock's study is: in what types of selling situations will it be more effective to stress salesman-customer differences rather than similarities with respect to product expertise? Here again, the behavioral literature can offer some relevant insights. Recently a review has appeared which attempts to integrate research on interpersonal similarity and attraction with that bearing on source credibility and attitude change.[29]

Having discussed research on sales interactions at some length, we may now consider what practical implications it may have. This work is relevant to several aspects of sales force management.

Recruitment, Selection, and Manpower Planning

The notion that the outcome of a sales contact depends on customer-prospect similarity casts doubt on the usefulness of much research and practice in the area of salesman recruitment and selection, which is aimed at identifying a successful "sales type."[30] If a firm's potential customers are appreciably more heterogeneous than its sales force, it may be effectively excluding itself from penetrating certain market segments. Simple models of the size and composition of a sales force can be structured for manpower planning purposes to assure that sales forces will be matched to the markets they serve with respect to key characteristics.[31]

Sales training. Training for salesmen should focus on helping them develop the special skills they require to be effective in interacting with prospects.[32] For example, a familiarity with existing knowledge about how perceptions of others are developed might enable salesmen to discriminate better among prospects.[33] There is much room for improvement in this area. One study showed that salesmen *failed* to perceive as ready to buy 69 percent of appliance shoppers who had previously indicated that they had definite purchasing plans.[34] Salesmen might be taught more reliable procedures for identifying the prospect status of shoppers.

Allocating Salesmen to Customers

A number of suggestions as to how a closer match between the characteristics of salesmen and prospects might be effected in the life insurance field have been made.[35] For example, a salesman who uncovers a prospect quite unlike himself could turn over the lead to another salesman who is more similar to the prospect and who, therefore, would have a better chance of making the sale. The notion that salesmen should be "compatible" with the customers they serve is certainly not new, but knowledge of what dimensions of similarity and differences are critical in a particular type of selling might lead to improved matchings.[36]

SELLING AS INTERPERSONAL INFLUENCE

In this section we shall consider some work in which selling is viewed as a *process* of influence and an attempt is made to apply behavioral knowledge about this phenomenon to problems of personal selling.

Influencing others via verbal communications is the salesman's basic stock and trade. At the same time, the study of communication and persuasion has long represented one of the major areas of interest to social psychologists.[37] In light of this, one might expect to find that the large body of behavioral science theory and research findings on this subject would have considerable use in dealing with problems of personal selling. While general discussions of "selling as communication" are readily available[38] and so-called "principles of persuasion" are sometimes presented in sales training programs,[39] the diligent reader of the marketing literature would be hard pressed to come up with a very extensive list of systematic applications of behavioral science knowledge about influence to issues of real concern to practitioners in the field of personal selling. Fortunately, examples of the productive utilization of behavioral science research on influence processes are available, and an examination of some of this work will serve to illustrate what behavioral scientists have to say about persuasion and how these ideas might be brought to bear on selling problems.

Using Group Pressure to Overcome Buyer Resistance

The most sophisticated and creative application of behavioral research on influence processes to personal selling that has come to our attention is a program developed by Jacoba Varela, a consultant in Uruguay.[40] The selling problem tackled was that faced by an upholstery firm in marketing fabrics to retailers. The firm's sales objectives conflicted with the established buying habits of both consumers and retailers. The product being promoted was ready-made curtains. Traditionally, however, Uruguayan housewives had their curtains custom-made. The firm's effort to sell retailers in the fall also ran contrary to the latter's customary practice of selecting new fabrics only in the spring. Furthermore, economic conditions were extremely adverse. Severe inflation had led to stringent government policies to curb consumer spending. To deal with this difficult set of circumstances, Varela designed a most elaborate and extensive selling program based on a number of concepts and propositions borrowed from social psychological research on influence. A few aspects of this work can be described here.

One phase of Varela's program made use of the results of Asch's classic experiments on group pressure and conformity.[41] Briefly, the typical Asch experiment is run as follows.

An unsuspecting person enters a laboratory with seven other persons who are confederates of the experimenter. The experimental task requires that each subject match a standard line with one of three other lines of varying lengths. All subjects report their judgments orally and in a particular order so that six of the seven confederates give their answers before the naive subject does. The correct answer is easily determined since the sizes of the lines are clearly presented. However, by pre-arrangement, the experimenter's confederates unanimously begin to give incorrect answers. Suddenly the subject finds that the judgments of all those around him completely contradict what he perceives to be the obviously correct answer. In this way, group pressure is exerted on the subject to modify his judgment in the direction of the majority. The experiment consists of several trials and on each the subject may either respond correctly or agree with the group of confederates and give the incorrect answer. Replications of this experiment, varying such things as the stimulus conditions and the size of the majority, have been made many times. The results show that about one third of the naive subjects yield to group pressure and alter their answers to be in accord with the majority.

Such an experimental finding would surely seem to be a prime candidate for the "interesting but irrelevant" category as far as suggesting anything applicable to personal selling. The subjects (college undergraduates), setting (artificial and highly controlled), and task (judging line length) bear little resemblance to selling curtains to retailers in South America. The dissimilarity between the real and laboratory worlds has led some to question the generalizability and hence the usefulness of marketing of this type of research.[42]

Varela largely circumvented this issue by skillfully manipulating the sales situation so that it essentially became a simulation of Asch's laboratory setting. Rather than have the company's salesmen sell the retailers in the stores, prospective buyers were invited to the company's offices. Buyers came in small groups. In the firm's own showroom, various facilities could be used which enabled the product line to be presented far more effectively than would have been possible in the retailers' stores. As an item was being presented, the salesmen made an assessment of how favorably impressed each of the prospective buyers was with the product. The salesmen had been trained to scan buyers' facial expressions and look for other cues that might reflect evaluations of the product. The buyer appearing most favorable was then asked for his opinion of the product and encouraged to explain why his reaction was positive. By this process the buyer was led to commit himself gradually and finally asked to place an order. In the meantime, the salesmen had been on the alert for indications of how the other buyers were reacting. The buyer identified as being next most positive was asked to express his views and the whole process was repeated. Thus the salesmen proceeded from the most to the least positive buyer and thereby took advantage of the opportunity of bringing to bear on those initially unfavorable the pressure of their peers who held more positive attitudes. In line with Asch's experimental results, a large percentage of resistant buyers are reported to have been successfully converted by this approach.

What has been described above represents only one phase of a much larger program developed by Varela which involved the ingenious use of numerous facets of social psychological knowledge about influence. For example, attention was given to the difficult persuasive task of convincing the retailer to come to the firm's showroom in the first place. To reduce their opposition, an approach referred to as the "foot in the door technique" was used. It has been demonstrated that once a person has carried out a small request, he is more likely to comply with a larger one.[43] Hence, before inviting the retailers to the showroom, Varela had the salesmen ask the retailers to display a small sign in their stores. If they agreed to this small favor, when the salesman returned a week later he asked them to come to the showroom. Having once made a small commitment to the salesman, the retailer was more likely to take the next, larger step on the path leading to a sale that had been carefully laid by Varela. The last phase of the selling strategy was aimed at developing their long-run loyalty. Techniques suggested by research on "immunizing" persons against counterpersuasion were employed in an effort to reduce the retailers' susceptibility to the promotion of competitors.[44] From all indications, the total campaign developed by Varela was highly successful. Large sales increases were realized despite unfavorable economic conditions.

The Influence of Company Reputation on Salesman Effectiveness

An example of a somewhat different use of research on communication and influence processes may be found in Levitt's experimental study of the role of company reputation in industrial selling.[45] The basic issue studied by Levitt was whether the evaluations of a new product made by those involved in the purchase decision process of industrial organizations are influenced by the general attitudes they hold toward the producing firm. Industrial marketers have long debated the value of expenditures on such activities as media campaigns undertaken for purposes of building a favorable corporate image. One rationale sometimes put forth in support of such programs is that they make buyers more receptive to the firm's salesmen. Implementing the elaborate kind of experimental design needed to measure such an effect would be extremely difficult in an industrial market— especially in the absence of a model of the process to help guide the research in deciding what effects to look for. Levitt developed a framework for analyzing this problem using concepts suggested by communications research on the influence of source credibility on communications effectiveness.[46] He then carried out a laboratory experiment which enabled him to achieve the degree of control required to study the problem.

As we noted in the earlier discussion of salesman-customer similarity, it has been shown in a number of experiments that the same message will produce attitude change when it is ascribed to a source of high rather than low credibility. Competence and trustworthiness are the components of credibility that have been manipulated in these studies.[47] Levitt suggests that the effectiveness of an industrial salesman will be influenced by the general reputation, among buyers, of the firm he represents much in the same way that source credibility affects the impact of an impersonal communication. In the parlance of communications research, the salesman is the communicator, the material he presents constitutes the message, and the firm for which he sells is the source.

A second factor considered by Levitt was the quality of the salesman's presentation. He was interested, for example, in the question of whether a high quality sales presentation made by a salesman from a lesser known firm could be as effective as a lesser quality sales presentation made by a salesman from a better known firm. The final factor examined was the recipient of the sales effort. Levitt reasoned that persons in various management roles who became involved in the purchase decision process (purchasing agents and technical personnel) would evaluate a new product from different frames of reference and hence might be differentially affected by a given message from a given source. Thus, the overall impact of the salesman was hypothesized to be dependent upon the source he represents (company reputation), the quality of his sales presentation, and the type of audience he is dealing with (technical vs. purchasing personnel).

The experimental test of these ideas involved exposing subjects to one of four versions of a ten minute filmed sales presentation for a fictitious but plausible new product (a paint ingredient). In one version the salesman gave a careful, professional ("good") presentation while in the other the same salesman delivered a less polished ("poor") presentation. Company reputation was manipulated by varying the name of the firm which the salesman was identified as representing. A significant feature of the study was that experienced business personnel were used as subjects. A group of 113 practicing purchasing agents and 130 engineers and scientists participated in the experiment. Immediately after viewing the film and again five weeks later, subjects filled out a questionnaire which asked, among other things, (1) whether they would recommend that the product be given further consideration by others in their organization, and (2) would they favor adoption of the product if such a decision were theirs to make. Levitt suggests that the decision implied in the second question involves more risk than that connected with the first. The expected effects of company reputation and quality of the sales presentation were observed with regard to the willingness of both the purchasing agents and the technical personnel to recommend the product to others. However, for the riskier choice of whether or not to adopt the product, the pattern of results was more complex. The intriguing finding that emerged was that company reputation influenced the propensity of technical personnel to adopt the product, but *not* that of the purchasing agents. Levitt offers two explanations for this unexpected result. It is possible that as a result of being frequently exposed to salesmen, purchasing agents become sophisticated in judging products from sales presentations and learn to discount the effect of company reputation. Alternatively, it may simply be that the purchasing agent wishes to encourage competition among his suppliers and, in so doing, may tend to favor less well-known companies. The principal implication would seem to be that a seller's reputation makes a difference to a salesman in getting a favorable first hearing for a new product with both purchasing and technical personnel but when it comes to making an actual purchase decision, the advantage of a good reputation only obtains with technical personnel.

Discussion

The above examples serve to illustrate two of the ways in which behavioral research on influence processes can be useful in dealing with selling problems. Levitt's study represents the kind of application which results in a better understanding of a previously ill-structured problem. The findings bearing on the differential responsiveness of the purchasing and technical personnel are examples of the kind of suggestive new insights which such efforts may produce. Follow-up research is needed to test and refine these ideas further.

In Varela's work, we saw an application of a different order. There, behavioral concepts were used to develop specific, operational selling procedures that apparently worked. This type of immediate and direct application rarely occurs. In assessing the applicability of behavioral science research findings to practical problems, a question frequently asked is whether the results produced in the comfort and control of a psychological laboratory can be extrapolated to the complexity of the real world. Perhaps the lesson worth remembering from Varela's work is that we should also consider what opportunities there may be to arrange our real world problem situation so that it begins to resemble the laboratory setting where our knowledge is more certain.

SUMMARY AND CONCLUSIONS

The studies reviewed above serve to illustrate the possibility of bringing knowledge about interaction and influence processes to bear on specific operating problems associated with personal selling. Research on interpersonal similarity and attraction suggests a set of variables and relationships that not only appear relevant to understanding variability in salesmen's performance but also have some immediate implications for policy issues surrounding the selection, training, and allocation of salesmen. Examples were also given where concepts borrowed from psychological research on influence processes had been used both to analyze problems pertaining to selling strategies and techniques, and to develop operational methods for solving them.

While behavioral research offers marketers a great deal of material that is potentially useful to them, the utilization of such knowledge in dealing with practical marketing problems is not a simple task. Successful applications would appear to require two critical ingredients. The first is the skills and knowledge of what Guetzkow refers to as a "social engineer or middleman"—"someone who knows how to transform basic knowledge into useable forms." [48] An unusual combination of talents is needed to perform this role effectively. On the one hand, such a person must have the training and background that gives him a firm grasp of a broad range of behavioral science subject matter. On the other hand, he must also be of both a creative and practical bent if he is to be able to interact with management personnel and identify their problems.

The other element needed is the kind of problem-oriented, programmatic approach to applying behavioral science notions to real world problems which Ray has proposed with reference to advertising.[49] To assure relevance, the starting point is a careful definition of the practitioner's problem. The next step is a search for applicable behavioral science knowledge. The key variables of the problem must be identified in theoretical terms and a model selected which interrelates them. Ideally, the latter should take the form of conditional propositions (or "micro-theoretical notions" to use Ray's terminology)—statements which not only describe relationships between variables but also specify qualifying or limiting conditions. Following that comes empirical testing and estimation and this involves a gradual movement from highly controlled (e.g., laboratory) to more natural (i.e., field) research settings. The final stops are production, implementation, and monitoring of results. Difficulties encountered at any stage require a re-cycling of activities. By such a systematic approach one hopes to avoid the failures and disappointments which plague efforts to transfer knowledge from the realm of behavioral science to the real world.

Most of the applications described in this paper essentially represent work at the beginning or middle stages of Ray's scheme. The task ahead is to carry forward through the subsequent stages those promising ideas that appear to have some practical payoff.

NOTES

[1] The December 1971 issue of *Management Science*, which is devoted entirely to marketing models, contains four papers dealing with sales force problems.

[2] See Smith *et al.* [35].

[3] See, for example, Henry [22]. For an opposing view on this issue see Lazarsfeld [25].

[4] See Evans [12], p. 76.

[5] See Miner [31], p. 6.

[6] For a recent review of some of this work see Cotham [11].

[7] See, for example, Stevens [36].

[8] See Willett and Pennington [41].

[9] One of the methods for evaluating salesmen, reported by Chapple [10] some years ago, was a mechanical device which recorded the time pattern of responses of a subject as he interacted with an observer in a standardized interview.

[10] See Evans [13], p. 25.

[11] See Berscheid and Walster [6].

[12] Extensive reviews of various aspects of this literature are available. See Bramel [7], Byrne [9], Lindzey and Byrne [27], esp. pp. 496–509; Lott and Lott [28], and Marlow and Gergen [29], esp. pp. 621–637.

[13] See Heider [21] and Newcomb [32].

[14] See Homans [23] and Thibaut and Kelley [38].

[15] See Evans [12], p. 78.

[16] Only a brief, preliminary account of this work, by Evans [12], has appeared in the literature. We have relied here on a more extensive, but unpublished, report by Evans [13].

[17] See Evans [13], p. xii.

[18] See Lott and Lott [28], p. 276.

[19] See Lott and Lott [28], p. 290.

[20] See Gadel [17].

[21] See Tosi [39].

[22] The salesmen's expectation level was also significantly related to the number of suppliers but in a nonlinear manner.

[23] See Willett and Pennington [41].

[24] See Bales [4].

[25] See McGuire [30], pp. 182–187.

[26] See Brock [8].

[27] See Farley and Swinth [14].

[28] See Marlow and Gergen [29], pp. 629–631.

[29] See Simons *et al.* [34].

[30] See Evans [13].

[31] See Gadel [17].

[32] See Webster [40].

[33] See Taguiri [37].

[34] See Granbois and Willett [19].

[35] See Evans [13].

[36] See Stevens [36].

[37] A number of short, highly readable accounts of this research are available. See Karlins and Abelson [24] and Zimbardo and Ebbesen [42]. Undoubtedly, the best and most complete review of the field is McGuire [30].

[38] See, for example, Webster [40].

[39] See, for example, Andelson [1].

[40] This discussion is based on descriptions of Varela's work given in Festinger [15] and Zimbardo and Ebbesen [42], pp. 114–122.

[41] See Asch [3].

[42] See, for example, Greenberg [18].

[43] See Freedman and Fraser [16].

[44] See McGuire [30], pp. 258–265.

[45] See Levitt [26].

[46] See Bauer [5].

[47] See McGuire [30], pp. 182–187.

[48] See Guetzkow [20], p. 77.

[49] See Ray [33].

REFERENCES

1. Andelson, R. P. "Harnessing Engineers and Scientists to the Sales Effort." In J. S. Wright and J. L. Goldstucker (eds.), *New Ideas for Successful Marketing,* pp. 204–215, Proceedings of the June 1966 Conference of the American Marketing Association, Chicago.

2. Aronson, Elliot, and Lindzey, Gardner (eds.), *Handbook of Social Psychology,* 2nd ed. Reading, Mass., Addison-Wesley, 1968–69.

3. Asch, S. E., "Effects of Group Pressure Upon the Modification and Distortion of Judgements," In E. E. Maccoby, T. M. Newcomb, and E. Hartley (eds.), *Readings in Social Psychology,* 3rd ed. Holt, Rinehart, and Winston, 1958, pp. 174–183.

4. Bales, R. F. "A Set of Categories for the Analysis of Small Group Interactions," *American Sociological Review,* Vol. 15 (April 1950), pp. 257–263.

5. Bauer, R. A. "Source Effect and Persuasibility: A New Look." In D. F. Cox (ed.), *Risk Taking and Information Handling in Consumer Behavior,* pp. 559–578. Boston, Mass., Division of Research, Graduate School of Business Administration, Harvard University, 1967.

6. Berscheid, E., and Walster, E. H. *Interpersonal Attraction.* Reading, Mass., Addison-Wesley, 1969.

7. Bramel, D. "Interpersonal Attraction, Hostility, and Perception," In Judson Mills (ed.), *Experimental Social Psychology,* pp. 1–120. New York, MacMillan, 1969.

8. Brock, T. C. "Communicator-Recipient Similarity and Decision Change," *Journal of Personality and Social Psychology,* Vol. I, no. 6 (June 1965), pp. 650–654.

9. Byrne, D. "Attitudes and Attraction." In Leonard Berkowitz (ed.), *Advances in Experimental Social Psychology,* Vol. 4, pp. 35–89. New York, Academic Press, 1969.

10. Chapple, E. D. "The Interaction Chronograph: Its Evolution and Present Applications," *Personnel,* Vol. 25 (January 1949), pp. 295–307.

11. Cotham, J. C. III. "Selecting Salesmen: Approaches and Problems," *MSU Business Topics,* Vol. 18, no. 1 (Winter 1970), pp. 64–72.

12. Evans, F. B. "Selling as a Dyadic Relationship," *American Behavioral Scientist,* Vol. 6, no. 9 (May 1963), pp. 76–79.

13. Evans, F. B. "Dyadic Interaction in Selling: A New Approach." Unpublished monograph, Graduate School of Business, University of Chicago, 1964.

14. Farley, J. U., and Swinth, R. L. "Effects of Choice and Sales Message on Customer-Salesman Interaction," *Journal of Applied Psychology,* Vol. 51, no. 2 (April 1967), pp. 107–110.

15. Festinger, L. "The Application of Behavioral Science Knowledge." Paper presented at the Sloan School of Management, Massachusetts Institute of Technology, Cambridge, Mass., Fall 1968.

16. Freedman, J. L., and Fraser, S. C. "Compliance Without Pressure: The Foot-in-the-Door Technique." *Journal of Personality and Social Psychology*, Vol. 4, no. 2 (August 1966), pp. 195–202.

17. Gadel, M. S. "Concentration by Salesmen on Congenial Prospects." *Journal of Marketing*, Vol. 28, no. 2 (April 1964) pp. 64–66.

18. Greenberg, A. "Is Communications Research Worthwhile?" *Journal of Marketing*, Vol. 31, no. 1 (January 1967), pp. 48–50.

19. Granbois, D. H., and Willett, R. P. "Patterns of Conflicting Perceptions Among Channel Members." In L. G. Smith (ed.), *Reflections on Progress in Marketing*, pp. 86–100. Proceedings of the Winter 1964 Conference of the American Marketing Association, Chicago, 1965.

20. Guetzkow, H. "Conversion Barriers in Using the Social Sciences," *Administrative Science Quarterly*, Vol. 4, no. 1 (June 1959), pp. 68–81.

21. Heider, F. *The Psychology of Interpersonal Relations*, New York, Wiley, 1958.

22. Henry, J. Review of "Human Behavior: An Inventory of Scientific Findings," by B. Berelson and G. A. Steiner, *Scientific American*, Vol. 211, no. 1 (July 1964), pp. 129ff.

23. Homans, G. C. *Social Behavior: Its Elementary Forms.* New York, Harcourt, Brace & World, 1961.

24. Karlins, M., and Abelson, H. I. *Persuasion*, 2nd ed. New York, Springer, 1970.

25. Lazarsfeld, P. F. "The American Soldier—An Expository Review," *Public Opinion Quarterly*, Vol. 13, no. 3 (Fall 1949), pp. 377–404.

26. Levitt, T. *Industrial Purchasing Behavior*. Boston, Mass., Division of Research, Graduate School of Business Administration, Harvard University, 1965.

27. Lindzey, Gardner, and Byrne, D. "Measurement of Social Choice and Interpersonal Attractiveness." In [2], Vol. 2, pp. 452–525.

28. Lott, A. J., and Lott, B. E. "Group Cohesiveness as Interpersonal Attractiveness: A Review of Relationships with Antecedent and Consequent Variables." *Psychological Bulletin*, Vol. 64, no. 4 (October 1965), pp. 259–309.

29. Marlow, D., and Gergen, K. J. "Personality and Social Interaction." In [2], Vol. 3, pp. 590–665.

30. McGuire, W. J. "The Nature of Attitudes and Attitude Change." In [2], Vol. 3, Chapter 21, pp. 136–314.

31. Miner, J. B. "Personality and Ability Factors in Sales Performance," *Journal of Applied Psychology*, Vol. 46, no. 1 (February 1962), pp. 6–13.

32. Newcomb, T. M. "An Approach to the Study of Communicative Acts," *Psychological Review*, Vol. 60, no. 6 (November 1953), pp. 393–404.

33. Ray, M. L. "The Present and Potential Linkages Between the Microtheoretical Notions of Behavioral Science and the Problems of Advertising: A Proposal for a Research System." In H. L. Davis and A. J. Silk (eds.), *Behavioral and Management Science in Marketing*, New York, Ronald (forthcoming).

34. Simons, H. W., Berkowitz, N. N., and Moyer, R. J. "Similarity, Credibility, and Attitude Change: A Review and A Theory," *Psychological Bulletin*, Vol. 73, no. 1 (January 1970), pp. 1–16.

35. Smith, S. V., Brien, R. H., and Stafford, J. E. (eds.), *Readings in Marketing Information Systems*. Boston, Houghton Mifflin, 1968.

36. Stevens, S. N. "The Application of Social Science Findings to Selling and the Salesman." In *Aspects of Modern Management*, Management Report No. 15, pp. 85–94. New York, American Management Association, 1958.

37. Taguiri, R. "Person Perception." In [2], Vol. 3, pp. 395–449.

38. Thibaut, J. W., and Kelley, H. H. *The Social Psychology of Groups*, New York, Wiley, 1959.

39. Tosi, H. L. "The Effects of Expectation Levels and Role Consensus on the Buyer-Seller Dyad," *Journal of Business*, Vol 39, no. 4 (October 1966), pp. 516–529.

40. Webster, F. E., Jr. "Interpersonal Communication and Salesman Effectiveness," *Journal of Marketing,* Vol. 32, no. 3 (July 1968), pp. 7–13.
41. Willett, R. P., and Pennington, A. L. "Customer and Salesman: The Anatomy of Choice and Influence in a Retail Setting." In R. M. Haas (ed.), *Science, Technology, and Marketing,* pp. 598–616. Proceedings of the Fall 1966 Conference of the American Marketing Association, Chicago.
42. Zimbardo, P., and Ebbesen, E. B. *Influencing Attitudes and Changing Behavior.* Reading, Mass., Addison-Wesley, 1969.

SOME SUGGESTIONS FOR FURTHER READINGS

Donnelly, J. H. and J. N. Ivancevich (1975), "Role Clarity and the Salesmen," *Journal of Marketing* (January), 71–74.

Enis, B. M. and L. D. Chonko (1978), "A Review of Personal Selling: Implications for Managers and Researchers," in *Review of Marketing 1978,* G. Zaltman, and T.V. Bonoma (eds.), Chicago: American Marketing Association, 276–302.

Lutz, R. J. and P. Kakkar (1975), "Situational Influence in Interpersonal Persuasion," *Proceedings of the Association for Consumer Research* (November), 370–378.

Sheth, J. N. (1975), "Buyer-Seller Interaction: A Framework," *Proceedings of the Association for Consumer Research* (Winter), 382–386.

Walker, O. C. Jr., G. A. Churchill, Jr., and N. N. Ford (1977), "Motivation and Performance in Industrial Selling: Present Knowledge and Needed Research," *Journal of Marketing Research* (May), 156–168.

26 / THE MYTHS AND REALITIES OF CORPORATE PRICING / Gilbert Burck

Corporate profits may be recovering briskly this year, but resentment and suspicion of profits are rising briskly too. It is by now an article of faith in some sophisticated circles that the U.S. has become a corporate state, in which giant companies increasingly dominate markets and write their own price tickets regardless of demand by practicing "administered" and "target return" pricing. Ask ten campus economists whether prices will fall with demand in industries that are concentrated—that is, dominated by a few *large firms*—and nine of them will tell you that prices won't fall as much as they would if the industry were competitive. And almost everywhere the putative pricing power of big business is equated with the well-known monopoly power that organized labor exercises over wages.

So the pressure is mounting to police pricing practices and other "abuses" in concentrated industries. Senator George McGovern, for example, is denouncing oligopolies as responsible for most of the nation's inflation, and is sponsoring measures to break up big companies. Meanwhile, the notion that price controls should become a permanent American institution is certainly taken seriously by more and more people. The Price Commission itself, which has adopted the practice of regulating prices by relating them to profit margins of the past three years, seems to be leaning toward a theory of managed prices.

Yet all these passionately cherished attitudes and opinions are based at best on half truths, and perhaps on no truth at all. The portentous fact is that the theory of administered prices is totally unproven, and is growing less and less plausible as more evidence comes in. Always very controversial, it has lately been subjected to an extended counterattack of highly critical analysis.

Some of the best work on the subject is being done by the privately funded Research Program in Competition and Business Policy at the University of California (Los Angeles) Graduate School of Management, under Professor J. Fred Weston. For nearly two years now, Weston and his group have been taking a fresh, empirical approach to subjects like industrial concentration, profits, competition, and prices. Their techniques include asking businessmen themselves how they set prices, and trying to find out why businessmen's formal statements about their price policies are usually so different from their actual practices.

The program, among other things, hopes to come up with a new theory of corporate profitability. "So far," Weston says, "we find that profit rates are not significantly higher in concentrated than in nonconcentrated industries. What we

Gilbert Burck, "The Myths and Realities of Corporate Pricing." Reprinted from the April 1972 issue of FORTUNE magazine by special permission; © 1972 Time Inc.
Gilbert Burck is Associate Editor for *Fortune* Magazine and has written extensively in the business area for *Fortune*.

do find is that there is a relationship between efficiency and profits and nothing else." But a vast amount of work, Weston admits, needs to be done. As happens so often in the dismal science, the more economists find out about a subject, the more they realize (if they are honest) how much they still have to learn.

MR. MEANS SHOWS THE WAY

The argument about administered prices is now nearly 40 years old; one philoprogenitive professor who took sides at the start is preparing to instruct his grandson on the subject. Few controversies in all economic history, indeed, have used up so many eminent brain-hours or so much space in learned journals. Much if not most of the argument has been conducted on a macroeconomic level; that is, it has been concerned with analyzing overall statistics on industrial concentration and comparing them with figures on prices. And that is exactly what was done by the man who started the argument by coining the phrase "administered price" in the first place. He is Gardiner Means, 75, author (with the late Adolph Berle) of the celebrated book *The Modern Corporation and Private Property*, published in 1932.

Like a lot of economists in that day, Means was looking for reasons why the great depression occurred. He noticed that many prices remained stable or at least sticky, even when demand was falling. Thus demand was depressed still further, and with it production and employment. Means's figures showed that wholesale prices fluctuated less in highly concentrated industries than in others; so to distinguish these prices from classic free-market prices, which are assumed to fluctuate with demand, he called them "administered" prices, or prices set by fiat and held constant "for a period of time and a series of transactions."

As an explanation for depression, Means's theory got some devastatingly critical attention over the next few years, but it did not fade away. In the middle 1950s it was revived as a major explanation for cost-push inflation, which Means calls administrative inflation; i.e., the supposed power of big business to raise prices arbitrarily. In 1957 the theory was taken up by Senator Estes Kefauver's antitrust and monopoly subcommittee, whose chief economist was John M. Blair, one of the nation's most energetic and passionate foes of industrial concentration. Ere long, dozens of the nation's eminent economists got into the argument, and many confected novel and often persuasive arguments in behalf of the theory of administered prices. Besides Blair, the advocates included the Johnson Administration's "new economists," such as James Duesenberry, Otto Eckstein, Gardner Ackley, and Charles Schultze, with "independent" savants like Adolph Berle and J. K. Galbraith helping out from time to time.

WHY DID THEY WAIT SO LONG?

The burden of proof, of course, is on the advocates of administered-price theory. They must do more than merely nourish a prejudice, particularly if their thesis is to provide a reliable guide for antitrust and other public policy (to say nothing of serving as a base for a new interpretation of the American economy, such as

Galbraith vouchsafed to the world in his book, *The New Industrial State*). In other words, they must offer very convincing evidence they are right. That, it is fair to say, they have not done. In 1941 economists Willard Thorp and Walter Crowder, in a study for the Temporary National Economic Committee, used a sophisticated analysis of price, volume, and concentration to conclude that there was no significant relationship between the level of seller concentration and price behavior and volume. Shortly afterward, Alfred Neal, now president of the Committee for Economic Development, argued that any measure of price inflexibility must consider cost changes, "a matter over which industries have little if any discretion." These and other attacks on Means's theory seemed to dispose of it as a proven cause of depression.

As a major explanation of cost-push inflation, the theory was also subjected to severe criticism. Murray N. Rothbard of the Polytechnic Institute of Brooklyn, for one, simply laughs at the theory of administered prices, and terms it a bogey. "If Big Business is causing inflation by suddenly and wickedly deciding to raise prices," he says, "one wonders why it hadn't done so many years before. Why the wait? If the answer is that now monetary and consumer demand have been increasing, then we find that we are back in a state of affairs determined by demand, and that the law of supply and demand hasn't been repealed after all."

Just two years ago the National Bureau of Economic Research printed a little book calculated to put an end to the argument. It was called *The Behavior of Industrial Prices*, and was written by George J. Stigler, a distinguished economist at the University of Chicago, and James K. Kindahl, of the University of Massachusetts. Stigler and Kindahl correctly observed that, owing to hidden discounts and concessions, a company's quoted prices are often very different from the prices it actually gets. So instead of using official figures compiled by the Bureau of Labor Statistics on sellers' quotations, as Means and others had done, Stigler and Kindahl used prices at which their surveys told them sales were made. These were then matched with figures on industry concentration. The Stigler-Kindahl findings for the period 1957–61 did not differ much from findings made with B.L.S. figures. But the findings for 1961–66 differed considerably, and Stigler and Kindahl at least showed that prices in concentrated industries were not as inflexible as some people thought. What is very important is that Stigler and Kindahl probably understated their case because their surveys did not manage to get at true selling prices. As most business journalists are well aware, companies neither record nor generally talk about all the "under the table" prices and other valuable concessions they make when the market is sluggish.

"NORMAL" PROFIT ISN'T SO NORMAL

While this macroeconomic analysis of price and concentration was going on, a few economists were beginning to take a microeconomic or closeup view of pricing. Why not ask businessmen themselves just how they really price their products? This bright idea, however, proved not so easy to apply as to state. Classic economic theory says business should set prices to balance supply and demand—i.e., "to clear the market." But in 1939 two economists at Oxford University published a survey

"OLIGOPOLIES" AND INFLATION:
A THEORY DEBUNKED

A popular belief among economists is that companies in concentrated industries (those dominated by a few big firms) have the market power to write their own price tickets, while those in unconcentrated industries do not. Household durables and automobiles are supposed to provide the worst examples of oligopolistic pricing. These charts suggest just the opposite. Between 1953 and 1958, when the consumer price index rose 8.1 per cent, the price of services rose twice as much, while the price of household durables actually declined 3.4 per cent. The price of new cars, it is true, rose 5.9 per cent, but probably because Regulation W, which limited time payments, was suspended in 1952, enabling people to buy more expensive cars. In the period 1958–66, the consumer price index rose 12.2 per cent. While the price of services soared, the price of both household durables and new cars actually dropped. In 1966–71, years of great inflation, the price index rose about 25 per cent. And while the price of services rose 37 per cent, that of household durables rose only 15 per cent and that of new cars only 13 per cent.

of 38 British companies that found most of them tended to price their output pretty much on a stodgy cost-plus basis, almost as if they were accountants, or trying to behave like Gardiner Means's oligopolists.

It remained for Professor I. F. Pearce of the University of Nottingham to clear up the paradox. Pearce had been trained as a cost accountant, and understood why prices are not always what they seem. He pointed out that business almost universally bases prices on a cost figure, which in turn is based on both past cost data and future cost estimates; an economist would call this figure the long-term average cost. In most firms, moreover, a recognized profit margin remains stable over periods long enough to be significant, and is therefore considered normal. "What is less generally known, except to those who practice the art of price fixing," Pearce says, "is how often and for what a variety of reasons 'normal' profit is not in fact charged against any particular sale. . . . The informal adjustment of margins, since it is both informal and *ad hoc*, tends to be left out of any general discussion of price fixing routine, *and yet the issue really turns upon it.* Margins charged are highly sensitive to the market under normally competitive conditions, and the 'norm' is simply that figure around which they fluctuate."

To demonstrate what he meant, Pearce made an elaborate study of one medium-sized British manufacturing firm. He sent out questionnaires and conducted formal interviews, and made a record of quoted prices and actual selling prices. He found that a wide variation existed between the margins talked about in interviews and surveys and the margins actually achieved. "Normal" profit margins, in other words, were mere checkpoints in the company's planning process.

Of course, a significant minority of U.S. businesses actually do price on a cost-plus basis—the regulated monopolies like utilities, pipelines, and transportation companies, as well as a lot of military contractors. At first glance, many unregulated companies also seem to price on a cost-plus basis. This is only natural. Since

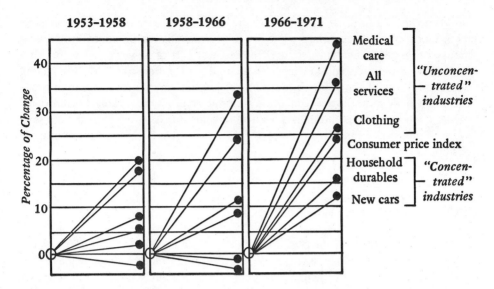

they obviously cannot survive unless they take in more than they spend, the easiest way to think about a price is first to think like an accountant: price equals costs plus overhead plus a fair profit. Cost-plus, furthermore, is a useful ritual, with great public-relations advantages. A smart, prudent businessman would no more publicly brag about charging all the traffic will bear than he would publicly discourse on his wife's intimate charms. Recoiling from branding himself a "profiteer," he admits only to wanting a "fair" return. Ironically, this had made him a sitting duck for economists who accuse him of not striving to maximize his profits because he controls the market, and of changing his prices only when his planned return is threatened.

WHEN IT'S RIGHT TO CHARGE ALL YOU CAN GET

But no mechanical formula can guarantee a profit. Both cost and profit estimates depend on volume estimates; and volume, among many other things, depends on the right price, whether that price maximizes unit profit right away or not. A company with unused capacity and a growing market may well take the classical course of cutting prices and temporarily earning a smaller return on investment than it considers normal. But it may have equally cogent reasons for not cutting prices. The theories of administered prices have pointed accusing fingers at business' behavior in the recession of 1957–1958, when it raised prices somewhat in the face of falling demand. What happened was that costs were increasing faster than demand was falling. According to the theory of pure competition, they should have raised prices. That they did, both small firms and large.

On the other hand, many companies, particularly those with new products, do charge all the traffic will bear, and so they should. It is not going too far to attribute the innovativeness and technical progress of the Western world to this kind of profit maximizing, and the innovative backwardness of the Soviet Union and East

Europe to the absence of it. The hope of realizing extraordinary profits on their innovations, at least temporarily, is what drives capitalist corporations into risking money on research. DuPont's strategy for the best part of 50 years was to develop "proprietary" products and to charge all it could get for them as long as the getting was good. So with the giants in data processing, pharmaceuticals, machine tools, and other high technologies. But these proprietary profits inevitably fire up competition, which invades the market with innovations of its own. Thus the story of Western industrial progress is the story of the progressive liquidation of proprietary positions.

THE RAZOR BLADES WERE TOO CHEAP

This is not to say that all or even most businesses are skillful practitioners of the art of pricing. Daniel Nimer, a vice president of a large Chicago company, has made an avocation of studying pricing, and lectures and conducts surveys and seminars on the subject both here and abroad. Nimer believes that business in general is still far too inflexible in its pricing techniques, and too prone to take a merely satisfactory return. The most frequent error, Nimer says, is to fail to charge what the traffic will bear, particularly when marketing a novel product. In 1961, Wilkinson Sword Ltd. brought out its new stainless-steel razor blades at 15.8 cents apiece. Overnight Wilkinson accumulated a staggering backlog of orders, the sort of thing that usually results in delivery delays and an expensive crash expansion program. Had Wilkinson started at 20 cents a blade, Nimer believes, it would have been much better able to fortify its position. Among Nimer's pearls of wisdom:

1. A big backlog is a nearly infallible indication of an underpriced product.
2. Always make decisions today that will help you tomorrow, and remember that it is easier to cut prices tomorrow than to raise them.
3. The key to pricing is to build value into the product and price it accordingly.
4. Above all, pricing is both analytical and intuitive, a scientific art.

SETTING A TARGET

The major if not the first case study of U.S. pricing was published in 1958 by the Brookings Institution, in its book *Pricing in Big Business*. The authors were A.D.H. Kaplan (who was then a senior staff economist at Brookings and is now retired), Joel B. Dirlam of Rhode Island University, and Robert F. Lanzillotti of the University of Florida. Using questionnaires, interviews, and memos, the trio analyzed the pricing policies of 20 of the largest U.S. companies, including G.E., G.M., Alcoa, A&P, Sears, Robuck, and U.S. Steel. Although the actual practices of the companies were predictably hard to describe and even harder to generalize about, the authors did manage to narrow the corporations' *goals* to five. The most typical pricing objectives, the authors decided, were to achieve (1) a target return on investment, (2) stable prices and markups over costs, (3) a specified market share, (4) a competitive position. Another objective, not so frequently cited, was to compete by taking advantage of product differences. The study's conclusion, written by Kaplan, was that many big, powerful companies seem not to be overwhelmingly controlled by the market, yet even they do not dominate the market. They do not have things their own way, with steady prices and rates of return, but are constantly forced to examine and change their policies.

Manifestly this study gives scant comfort to the administered-price theorists. Professor Lanzillotti apparently felt it was too easy on big business. Granted money to do further work on the data, he came up with a more critical interpretation of them in an article in the *American Economic Review* of December, 1958. Since Lanzillotti is now a member of the Price Commission and has been described as knowing "more about prices" than anyone else on that body, his thoughts are worth attending to. Lanzillotti devoted much of his thesis to the prevalence of so-called target-return pricing, which at that time was an almost esoteric concept.

When companies use target-return pricing, he explained, they do not try to maximize short-term profits. Instead they start with a rate of return they consider satisfactory, and then set a price that will allow them to earn that return when their plant utilization is at some "standard" rate—say 80 per cent. In other words, they determine standard costs at standard volume and add the margin necessary to return the target rate of profit over the long run.

More and more companies, Lanzillotti argued, are adopting target-return pricing, either for specific products or across the board. He also concluded that the companies have the size to give them market power. Partly because of this power and partly because the companies are vulnerable to criticism and potential antitrust action, all tend to behave more and more like public utilities. Target-return pricing, with some exceptions in specific product lines, implies a policy of stable or rigid pricing.

Many of Lanzillotti's conclusions have already proved vulnerable to micro-economic analysis, most particularly at the hands of J. Fred Weston, who launched U.C.L.A.'s Research Program in Competition and Business Policy about two years ago. Prior to that, Weston studied finance and economics at the University of Chicago and wrote the three most popular (and profitable) textbooks on business finance. He got into pricing by a side door, having steeped himself in the literature on corporate resource allocation. He spent a considerable part of three years talking about that subject with executives—at first formally, then informally and postprandially. But he soon began to realize that he was also talking about the way prices were made. So he shifted his emphasis from financial to economic questions, and broadened considerably the scope of his work. Like others before him, he discovered that what businessmen formally say about their pricing and what they do about it are often very different. And their action is more consistent with classical theory than their talk.

In a major paper not yet published, Weston proceeds to apply his investigations to the three "popular" and related theories that were at the heart of the administered-price concept:

1. that large corporations generally try to realize a target markup or target return on investment;

2. that their prices tend to be inflexible, uncompetitive, and unresponsive to changes in demand;
3. that contrary to a fundamental postulate of classic economic theory, large, oligopolistic corporations do not maximize profits, but use their market power to achieve planned or target profit levels.

THE CONSTRAINTS OF THE MARKET

The concept of target pricing, Weston's research showed, was an arrant oversimplification of what actually happens in large companies. "The Brookings study," he explains, "focused on talking to top sales and marketing men, who take a target as given. If you talk to top executives, you find they use the target as a screening device, a reference point." Pricing decisions, he found out, cannot be (and are not) made apart from other business decisions; price lists are based on long-run demand curves. In fact, all the considerations that go to make investment and other policies also go into pricing, either deliberately or intuitively.

Neither large nor small businesses have price "policies," Weston adds; pricing is too much interwoven with other factors to be formulated independently of them. And most of the people Weston talked to kept emphasizing the constraints of the market. In short, target-return pricing is not what the critics of business think it to be. If anything, it is an interim checkpoint set up by management to specify tentatively the company's potential.

Often, Weston argues, critics of corporate pricing condemn behavior as oligopolistic that does nothing more than follow modern accounting practices. Firms of all sizes use accounting budgets, plans, and controls to formulate performance objectives. Standard volume represents the firms' best judgment of the expected volume of operations, and standard cost is the unit cost at standard volume. And a technique called variance analysis compares management's actual performance with standard performance in order to evaluate and improve the former.

Economic textbooks, says Weston, have failed to keep up with such developments in the art of management, with the result that economists often fail to understand the nature and implications of business planning. In *The New Industrial State*, for example, Galbraith argues that planning by firms, aided by government, is eliminating the market mechanism. Nonsense, says Weston. Planning and control as management uses them do not eliminate the market or its uncertainties. Planning and control are what the market forces you to do. Since they provide a way of judging performance and spotting defects, a device to shorten the reaction time to uncertainty and change, they really increase the market's efficiency.

HOW DETROIT REACTS

The administered-price theorists have pointed to the auto industry as the archetype of a disciplined oligopoly whose prices are very rigid. This characterization is largely based on the industry's practice of setting dealers' recommended prices at the beginning of a model year. Actually, the auto companies change those prices, sometimes frequently and substantially, as the year rolls on and specific models demonstrate their popularity or lack of it. The price changes take a wide variety of forms: bonuses for sales exceeding quotas, bonuses for models not doing well, and so on. As Professor Yale Brozen of the University of Chicago analyzes the industry: "Competition in the auto market actually *makes* the retail price. If the retail price is low relative to wholesale prices, the dealers can't live, and the company must give them better margins; if the retail price is high, the dealers tend to get rich, and the company raises wholesale prices and steps up production."

Now that foreign competition has become so powerful, the auto companies find it harder than ever to price arbitrarily. "Take our Vega," a G.M. man says with some feeling. "If anything is the reverse of target-return pricing, that Vega is. We did not *make* its price. We had to *take* a price that was set by our competitors. Then the only way we could make a profit was to bring our costs down."

Summing up the alleged reluctance of large corporations to compete, Weston quotes Professor Martin Bailey of Brookings, who describes the idea as "a theory in search of a phenomenon."

The third allegation dealt with by Weston—i.e., that the large corporation, in formulating its price policies, does not seek to maximize profits—is a tough one to prove either way. "Management's approach to pricing is based upon planned profits," Lanzillotti has contended. "If we are to speak of 'administered' decisions in the large firm, it is perhaps more accurate to speak of administered *prices*." To support his contention, Lanzillotti reexamined profit data on the 20 companies covered in the Brookings book. The data seemed to verify his belief that large firms are able to achieve their target returns on investment.

Weston noticed two major defects in the argument. One was that targets were specified for only 7 of the 20 firms. The other was that Lanzillotti defined return on investment as the ratio of income before preferred-stock dividends to stockholders' net worth, including preferred stock, which makes the return look artificially large. But return on investment is normally and more realistically defined as the ratio of income (before interest payments) to total operating assets. On this basis, the figures show a big discrepancy between target and actual returns. And the Lanzillotti table included results for only the years 1947–55. When the figures were extended through 1967, there was an even larger discrepancy.

"WE JUST DON'T KNOW"

Moreover, the returns above target were consistent with a lot of contradictory theses—with target pricing, with random behavior, and with profit maximization; the returns below target were also consistent with a number of alternative theses. Weston's final conclusion: Studies by Lanzillotti and by others have established neither that large firms are able to "control" or plan profits, nor that they do not want to maximize or optimize profits. Case not proved: additional evidence and analysis needed.

"The third proposition probably cannot be answered anyway," Weston adds.

"How do you know if firms are maximizing their profits? In an early draft I made the mistake of thinking that a company earning more than target was maximizing its profits. This isn't necessarily so. We just don't know. We are, however, finding out a lot of positive facts about other related things. It has always been assumed, for example, that there will be collusion in an industry with few firms. But the fact is that we are beginning to get solid evidence that competitive efficiency is an important characteristic of such industries."

This finding, Weston points out, is consistent with the work of Professor Brozen, who has analyzed in detail the profitability of hundreds of companies. "Concentrated industries are concentrated because that, apparently, is the efficient way to organize those industries," says Brozen. "Unconcentrated industries are unconcentrated because that, apparently, is the efficient way to organize them."

THE BIG COMPANY AS COST LEADER

Standard textbook theory assumes that only "atomistic" industries—i.e., those with many companies and dominated by none—are perfectly competitive in price and highly responsive to changing tastes and technologies. But Weston contends that companies in concentrated industries can and do serve the consumer just as effectively. This view, incidentally, is persuasively set forth in a new book, *In Defense of Industrial Concentration*, by Professor John S. McGee, on leave from the University of Washington. The notion that concentration leads to the end of capitalism, McGee argues, springs from indefensibly narrow definitions of both competition and the aims of the economic system. Economic competition is best understood as an evolutionary process and not as a rigid structure or set of goals. But there is no necessary conflict between concentration and "competitiveness," even when the latter word is used in its narrow sense.

You can't explain the new competition with narrow textbook theory, Weston says. Big companies may be price leaders, but they are also cost leaders. Continually subjected to the efforts of rivals to steal business away, they deal with this uncertainty by reducing costs wherever they can. As Weston sees it, this kind of price leadership does not result in high prices and restricted output, as textbook theory says it should. What it does is to compel companies to try to strike a balance between growing as fast as possible and raising earnings per share as fast as possible.

ARE OLIGOPOLISTS MORE PROFITABLE?

Among the other provocative papers financed by the U.C.L.A. program is an unpublished dissertation on the relationship between industrial concentration and prices, by Steven H. Lustgarten, 28, who now teaches economics at the Baruch College of the City University of New York. His investigations show that during the period 1954–58, prices rose faster in concentrated industries. But the reason seems logical. Firms expanded plant and equipment at an abnormal rate. As production costs increased, prices did too. So Lustgarten could neither confirm nor reject the theory that 1954–58 was a period of profit-push-inflation. For the years 1958–63, however, there was no relationship between concentration and price changes. The theory of administered prices, in other words, remained unproved.

A study of concentration and profits was done by Dr. Stanley Ornstein, 33, a consultant to the program. He examined the traditional hypothesis that, as concentration increases, the likelihood of collusion or "weak competitive pressures" also increases, and leads to higher profits in concentrated industries than in others. Not so, says Ornstein. Because stock market prices represent the discounted value of expected future earnings, Ornstein used stock market values to represent profitability over the long run. To eliminate false correlations, he also examined individual profit rates of the largest corporations in each industry, 131 companies in all, and subjected them to multiple regression analysis, a mathematical technique that is used to determine the relative influences of several variables.

"From 1947 through 1960," Ornstein observes, "the return on equity dropped from around 15 per cent to 8 or 9 per cent, and in a continuous trend. Long-term fluctuations like this shouldn't occur if there is collusion or administered bias." Like Brozen, Ornstein finds no connection between high profits and concentration. On the contrary, he finds there is vigorous competition among so-called oligopolists. His conclusion, made after much analysis, was somewhat more cautious: "This study does not disprove the traditional hypothesis [that oligopoly is characterized by high profitability], any more than previous studies proved it. It does show, however, that prior conclusions have gone far beyond those warranted by economic theory."

REMEMBER THE NEW YORK YANKEES

One of the U.C.L.A. program's most distinguished participants is Professor Harold Demsetz, 41, on leave from the University of Chicago, where he taught for eight years. Demsetz' interests at present lie mainly in identifying the true sources of corporate efficiency. He maintains that when there is no real barrier to the entry of new competitors, concentration is not an index of monopoly power. Therefore, if a concentrated industry has a high rate of return, monopoly power is not the cause of it. Concentration results from the operation of normal market forces, and from a company's ability to produce a better or cheaper product or both, and to market it efficiently. Some companies are downright lucky, and some outperform others, while some are both lucky and superior performers.

Confirming Demsetz' belief, Professor Michael Granfield, 28, has tentatively concluded that differences in efficiency may account for most differences in profit levels, and that high profits do not necessarily imply high prices but often quite the opposite—high volume and low prices. One way he accounts for efficiency is by what he calls Team Theory. "The old saw holds that the team outperforms its individual members; it may be right," says Granfield. "Although other companies are constantly hiring executives away from I.B.M., these companies never seem to do as well as I.B.M."

"Many managerial economies are not always evident," Ornstein adds.

"The only way to get them is to get the whole team. The New York Yankees were a winning team for years; the technical skills responsible for their record accounted for only about 10 to 20 percent of the answer. What is really involved is managerial skills, and they can't be duplicated. To some extent a successful management is synergistic. By this I mean that there seem to be managerial economies of scale just as there are multiplant economies of scale. If so, the argument that you can break up big business and not hurt the consumer is wrong."

It may not be long before the program staff develops a formal theory about what really makes enterprises excel, and why the country is better off handling them with a certain amount of care instead of busting them up like freight trains in a classification yard, or subjecting them to permanent price controls.

STORED IN THE MINDS OF MILLIONS

The theory of administered prices, however, is not yet done for. Its new critics will doubtless find the going slow. Before their credo can hope to gain "popular" acceptance, it must first achieve standing in professional economic journals. And it has, for the moment, absolutely no political appeal. Thanks in large part to Ralph Nader, the big corporation is the whipping boy of the day. Indeed, George Stigler glumly predicts that the controversy will continue for another generation or more. "Administered-price theory," he says, "is like the Sacco-Vanzetti case. Whatever the jury's verdict, the defendants' innocence is stored in the minds of millions. So is the 'guilt' of administered prices, and the businessmen who practice them."

The administered-price theorists are not resting on their oars, either. Gardiner Means, who started it all nearly 40 years ago, now argues that the recent combination of inflation and recession can be explained *only* by his administered-price thesis. In the June, 1972, issue of the *American Economic Review*, he defines his theory and then tears into the Stigler-Kindahl book, which he says misrepresents his position.

What may be more important in its effect on public opinion, John Blair, he of the Kefauver committee, is publishing a monumental 832-page volume entitled *Economic Concentration—Structure, Behavior and Public Policy*. This opus contains something from almost everybody who has written about concentration, and is complete with dozens of charts, as well as an introduction by Means. The fruit of more than 30 years of fighting big business, the work is larded with quotations and chuck-full of footnotes. Blair's mind is made up, and his book is passionately partisan; but that will probably not prevent it from being given glowing reviews in the popular press.

For all this, there seems no doubt that the case against the theory of administered prices will grow stronger. Groups like Weston's are being organized elsewhere. The University of Rochester, for example, has set up the Center for Research in Government Policy and Business in its Graduate School of Management, and is looking around for private donations.

No matter what such groups find, it will be salutary. For the controversy about administered prices proves, among other things, how little Americans know about the inner workings of the big corporation, the country's most characteristic institution. And if present trends in research are any indication, the more that can be learned, the stronger will be the case for revising wrong notions about corporate behavior.

SOME SUGGESTIONS FOR FURTHER READING

Dean, J. (1976), "Pricing Policies for New Products," *Harvard Business Review* (November–December), 141–153.

Guiltinan, J. P. (1976), "Risk-Aversive Pricing Policies: Problems and Alternatives," *Journal of Marketing* (January), 10–15.

Monroe, K. B. (1979), *Pricing: Making Profitable Decisions,* New York: McGraw-Hill.

——— and A. J. Della Bitta (1978), "Models for Pricing Decisions," *Journal of Marketing Research* (August), 413–428.

Weston, J. F. (1972), "Pricing Behavior of Large Firms," *Western Economic Journal* (March), 1–18.

IV / MARKETING MANAGEMENT

Once the marketing manager has analyzed consumers and markets, he or she must manage the elements of the marketing mix so as to take advantage of the opportunities revealed by these analyses. Marketing management should be approached systematically and comprehensively. Thus, Part IV begins with Adler's vivid exposition of the systems concept. This article is closely complemented by Borden's concept of the marketing mix. Borden enumerates the major factors about which marketing managers must make decisions. The remaining articles in this part focus on the classic expositions of those factors.

In 1972, Trout and Ries articulated a controversial concept that they termed *product positioning*. Ensuing years have found this concept increasingly accepted by marketing practitioners and scholars. The authors therefore can perhaps be forgiven for "tooting their own horns" a bit in the retrospective commentary. The '70s also saw considerable changes in the venerable product manager concept. This evolution is discussed in the paper by Buell.

In advertising, the concept of the hierarchy of effects continues to receive considerable attention. The classic exposition is by Lavidge and Steiner. This concept was empirically tested by Ackoff and Emshoff in a large-scale experiment extending over a number of years. The results are somewhat surprising.

In contrast to many of the concepts in marketing, the idea of the marketing channel is unique to this discipline. The classic exposition of conflict and cooperation in market channels is provided by Mallen. Bucklin then attempts to relate the product taxonomies exemplified by the work of Aspinwall presented earlier in this volume to channel strategy. The pricing aspects of marketing management are represented by the pioneering work of Green in Bayesian decision theory. This conceptualization has never become widely accepted by marketing practitioners, but some marketing scholars expect that the advent of the fourth generation computers and the increasing need for efficiency in marketing decision-making in the '80s will lead to a resurgence of interest in Bayesian techniques.

Finally, this edition of *Marketing Classics* closes with the thoughtful article by Bauer and Greyser. Although written a number of years ago, this paper continues to illustrate one of the major difficulties faced by marketing managers—the increasing need to understand, and to communicate with, those who make and influence public policy toward marketing. The editors hope that such dialogues will happen in the '80s.

27 / SYSTEMS APPROACH
TO MARKETING / Lee Adler

More and more businessmen today recognize that corporate success is, in most cases, synonymous with marketing success and with the coming of age of a new breed of professional managers. They find it increasingly important not only to pay lip service to the marketing concept but to do something about it in terms of (a) customer orientation, rather than navel-gazing in the factory, (b) organizational revisions to implement the marketing concept, and (c) a more orderly approach to problem solving.

In an increasing number of companies we see more conscious and formal efforts to apply rational, fact-based methods for solving marketing problems, and greater recognition of the benefits these methods offer. While these benefits may be newly realized, there is nothing new about the underlying philosophy; in the parlance of military men and engineers, it is the systems approach. For, whether we like it or not, marketing is, by definition, a system, if we accept Webster's definition of systems as "an assemblage of objects united by some form of regular interaction or interdependence." Certainly, the interaction of such "objects" as product, pricing, promotion, sales calls, distribution, and so on fits the definition.

There is an expanding list of sophisticated applications of systems theory—and not in one but in many sectors of the marketing front. The construction of mathematical and/or logical models to describe, quantify, and evaluate alternate marketing strategies and mixes is an obvious case in point. So, too, is the formulation of management information systems[1] and of marketing plans with built-in performance measurements of predetermined goals. But no less vital is the role of the systems approach in the design and sale of products and services. When J. P. Stevens Company color-harmonizes lines and bedspreads, and towels and bath mats, it is creating a product system. And when Avco Corporation sells systems management to the space exploration field, involving the marriage of many scientific disciplines as well as adherence to budgetary constraints, on-time performance, and quality control, it is creating a *service* system.

In this article I shall discuss the utilization of the systems concept in marketing in both quantitative and qualitative ways with case histories drawn from various industries. In doing so, my focus will be more managerial and philosophical than technical, and I will seek to dissipate some of the hocus-pocus, glamour, mystery, and fear which pervade the field. The systems concept is not esoteric or "science fiction" in nature (although it sometimes *sounds* that way in promotional descrip-

Reprinted from *Harvard Business Review*, Vol. 45 (May–June, 1967), pp. 105–118. Copyright © 1967 by the President and Fellows of Harvard College; all rights reserved.
Lee Adler, professor of marketing at Farleigh Dickinson University, holds an M.B.A. from New York University. He has extensive experience in marketing research and management positions, and he is a frequent contributor of provocative articles to the marketing literature. Formerly, he was director of marketing research for RCA Corporation and is also a sculptor of some renown.

tions). Its advantages are not subtle or indirect; as we shall see, they are as real and immediate as decision making itself. The limitations are also real, and these, too, will be discussed.

(Readers interested in a brief summary of the background and the conceptual development of the systems approach may wish to turn to the box on pages 389 and 390.)

PROMISING APPLICATIONS

Now let us look at some examples of corporate application of the systems approach. Here we will deal with specific parts or "subsystems" of the total marketing system. Exhibit I is a schematic portrayal of these relationships.

Products and Services

The objective of the systems approach in product management is to provide a complete "offering" to the market rather than merely a product. If the purpose of busi-

Exhibit 1. Marketing subsystems and the total system

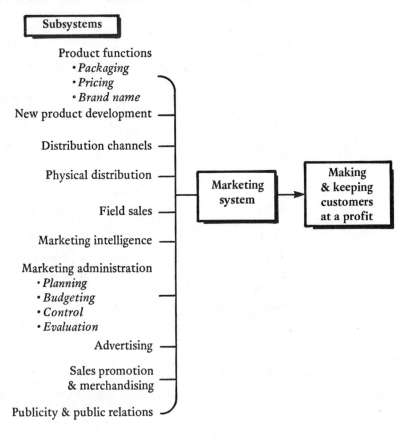

ness is to create a customer at a profit, then the needs of the customer must be carefully attended to; we must, in short, study what the customer is buying or wants to buy, rather than what we are trying to sell.

In the consumer products field we have forged ahead in understanding that the customer buys nutrition (not bread), beauty (not cosmetics), warmth (not fuel oil). But in industrial products this concept has been slower in gaining a foothold. Where it has gained a foothold, it expresses itself in two ways: the creation of a complete product system sold (1) as a unit, or (2) as a component or components which are part of a larger consumption system.

Perhaps the most eloquent testimony to the workability and value of the systems approach comes from companies that have actually used it. For a good example let us turn to the case of The Carborundum Company. This experience is especially noteworthy because it comes from industrial marketing, where, as just indicated, progress with the systems concept has generally been slow.

WHAT IS THE SYSTEMS APPROACH?

There seems to be agreement that the systems approach sprang to life as a semantically identifiable term sometime during World War II. It was associated with the problem of how to bomb targets deep in Germany more effectively from British bases, with the Manhattan Project, and with studies of optimum search patterns for destroyers to use in locating U-boats during the Battle of the North Atlantic.[1] Subsequently, it was utilized in the defeat of the Berlin blockade. It has reached its present culmination in the success of great military systems such as Polaris and Minuteman.

Not surprisingly, the parallels between military and marketing strategies being what they are, the definition of the systems approach propounded by The RAND Corporation for the U.S. Air Force is perfectly apt for marketers:

An inquiry to aid a decision-maker choose a course of action by systematically investigating his proper objectives, comparing quantitatively where possible the costs, effectiveness, and risks associated with the alternative policies or strategies for achieving them and *formulating additional alternatives if those examined are found wanting.*[2]

The systems approach is thus an orderly, "architectural" discipline for dealing with complex problems of choice under uncertainty.

Typically, in such problems, multiple and possibly conflicting objectives exist. The task of the systems analyst is to specify a closed operating network in which the components will work together so as to yield the optimum balance of economy, efficiency, and risk minimization. Put more broadly, the systems approach attempts to apply the "scientific method" to complex marketing problems studied *as a whole*; it seeks to discipline marketing.

But disciplining marketing is no easy matter. Marketing must be perceived as a *process* rather than as a series of isolated discrete actions; competitors must be viewed as components of each marketer's own system. The process must also be comprehended as involving a flow and counterflow of information and behavior between marketers and customers. Some years ago, Marion Harper, Jr., now chairman of The Interpublic Group of Companies, Inc., referred to the flow of information in marketing communications as the cycle of "listen (i.e., marketing research), publish (messages, media), listen (more marketing research), revise, publish, listen...." More recently, Raymond A. Bauer referred to the "transactional" nature of communications as a factor in the motivations, frames of reference, needs, and so forth of recipients of messages. The desires of the communicator alone are but part of the picture.[3]

Pushing this new awareness of the intricacies of marketing communications still further, Theodore Levitt identified the interactions between five different forces—sources effect (i.e., the reputation or credibility of the sponsor of the message), sleeper effect (the declining influence of source credibility with the passage of time), message effect (the character and quality of the message), communicator effect (the impact of the transmitter—e.g., a salesman), and audience effect (the competence and responsibility of the audience).[4] Casting a still broader net are efforts to model the entire purchasing process, and perhaps the ultimate application of the systems concept is attempts to make mathematical models of the entire marketing process.

Mounting recognition of the almost countless elements involved in marketing and of the mind-boggling complexity of their interactions is a wholesome (though painful) experience. Nevertheless, I believe we must not ignore other ramifications of the systems approach which are qualitative in nature. For the world of marketing offers a vast panorama of non- or part-mathematical systems and opportunities to apply systems thinking. We must not become so bedazzled by the brouhaha of the operations research experts as to lose sight of the larger picture.

[1] See Glen McDaniel, "The Meaning of The Systems Movement to the Acceleration and Direction of the American Economy," in *Proceedings of the 1964 Systems Engineering Conference* (New York, Clapp & Poliak, Inc., 1964), p. 1; see also E. S. Quade, editor, *Analysis for Military Decisions* (Santa Monica, California, The RAND Corporation, 1964), p. 6.
[2] Quade, *op. cit.*, p. 4.
[3] "Communications as a Transaction," *Public Opinion Quarterly*, Spring 1963, p. 83.
[4] See Theodore Levitt, *Industrial Purchasing Behavior* (Boston, Division of Research, Harvard Business School ,1965), p. 25ff.

Birth of the concept. Founded in 1894, the company was content for many years to sell abrasives. It offered an extremely broad line of grinding wheels, coated abrasives, and abrasive grain, with a reputed capacity for 200,000 different products of varying type, grade, and formulation. But the focus was on the product.

In the mid-1950s, Carborundum perceived that the market for abrasives could be broadened considerably if—looking at abrasives through customers' eyes—it would see the product as fitting into *metal polishing, cleaning,* or *removal systems*. Now Carborundum is concerned with all aspects of abrading—the machine, the contact wheel, the workpiece, the labor cost, the overhead rate, the abrasive, and, above all, the customer's objective. In the words of Carborundum's president, W. H. Wendel:

That objective is never the abrasive per se, but rather the creation of a certain dimension, a type of finish, or a required shape, always related to a minimum cost. Since there are many variables to consider, just one can be misleading. To render maximum service, Carborundum (must offer) a complete system.[2]

Organizational overhaul. To offer such a system, management had to overhaul important parts of the organization:

(1) The company needed to enhance its knowledge of the total system. As Wendel explains:

We felt we had excellent knowledge of coated abrasive products, but that we didn't have the application and machine know-how in depth. To be really successful in the business, we had to know as much about the machine tools as we did the abrasives.[3]

To fill this need, Carborundum made three acquisitions—The Tysaman Machine Company, which builds heavy-duty snagging, billet grinding, and abrasive cut-off machines; Curtis Machine Company, a maker of belt sanders; and Pangborn Corporation, which supplied systems capability in abrasive blast cleaning and finishing.

(2) The company's abrasive divisions were reorganized, and the management of them was realigned to accommodate the new philosophy and its application. The company found that *centering responsibility for the full system in one profit center* proved to be the most effective method of coordinating approaches in application engineering, choice of distribution channels, brand identification, field sales operations, and so forth. This method was particularly valuable for integrating the acquisitions into the new program.

(3) An Abrasives Systems Center was established to handle development work and to solve customer problems.

(4) Technical conferences and seminars were held to educate customers on the new developments.

(5) Salesmen were trained in machine and application knowledge.

Planning. A key tool in the systems approach is planning—in particular, the use of what I like to call "total business plans." (This term emphasizes the contrast with company plans that cover only limited functions.) At Carborundum, total business plans are developed with extreme care by the operating companies and divisions. Very specific objectives are established, and then detailed action programs are outlined to achieve these objectives. The action programs extend throughout the organization, including the manufacturing and development branches of the operating unit. Management sets specific dates for the completion of action steps and defines who is responsible for them. Also, it carefully measures results against established objectives. This is done both in the financial reporting system and in various marketing committees.

Quantitative methods. Carborundum has utilized various operations research techniques, like decision tree analysis and PERT, to aid in molding plans and strategies. For example, one analysis, which concerned itself with determining the necessity for plant expansion, was based on different possible levels of success for the marketing plan. In addition, the computer has been used for inventory management, evaluation of alternate pricing strategies for systems selling, and the measurement of marketing achievements against goals.

It should be noted, though, that these quantitative techniques are management tools only and that much of the application of systems thinking to the re-deployment of Carborundum's business is qualitative in nature.

Gains achieved. As a consequence of these developments, the company has opened up vast new markets. To quote Carborundum's president again:

Customers don't want a grinding wheel, they want metal removed. . . . The U.S. and Canadian market for abrasives amounts to $700 million a year. But what companies spend on stock removal—to bore, grind, cut, shape, and finish metal—amounts to $30 billion a year." [4]

Illustrating this market expansion in the steel industry is Carborundum's commercial success with three new developments—hot grinding, an arborless wheel to speed metal removal and cut grinding costs, and high-speed conditioning of carbon steel billets. All represent conversions from non-abrasive methods. Carborundum now also finds that the close relationship with customers gives it a competitive edge, opens top customer management doors, gains entree for salesmen with prospects they had never been able to "crack" before. Perhaps the ultimate accolade is the company's report that customers even come to the organization itself, regarding it as a consultant as well as a supplier.

Profitable Innovation

The intense pressure to originate successful new products cannot be met without methodologies calculated to enhance the probabilities of profitable innovation. The systems approach has a bearing here, too. Exhibit II shows a model for "tracking" products through the many stages of ideation, development, and testing to ultimate full-scale commercialization. This diagram is in effect a larger version of the "New Product Development" box in Exhibit I.

Observe that this is a logical (specifically, sequential), rather than numerical, model. While some elements of the total system (e.g., alternate distribution channels and various media mixes) can be analyzed by means of operations research techniques, the model has not been cast in mathematical terms. Rather, the flow diagram as a whole is used as a checklist to make sure "all bases are covered" and to help organize the chronological sequence of steps in new product development. It also serves as a conceptual foundation for formal PERT application, should management desire such a step, and for the gradual development of a series of equations linking together elements in the diagrams, should it seem useful to experiment with mathematical models.

Marketing Intelligence

The traditional notion of marketing research is fast becoming antiquated. For it leads to dreary chronicles of the past rather than focusing on the present and shedding light on the future. It is particularistic, tending to concentrate on the study of tiny fractions of a marketing problem rather than on the problem as a whole. It lends itself to assuaging the curiosity of the moment, to fire-fighting, to resolving internecine disputes. It is a slave to technique. I shall not, therefore, relate the term *marketing research* to the systems approach—although I recognize, of course, that some leading businessmen and writers are breathing new life and scope into the ideas referred to by that term.

The role of the systems approach is to help evolve a *marketing intelligence* system tailored to the needs of each marketer. Such a system would serve as the ever-alert nerve center of the marketing operation. It would have these major characteristics:

Continuous surveillance of the market.
A team of research techniques used in tandem.
A network of data sources.
Integrated analysis of data from the various sources.
Effective utilization of automatic data-processing equipment to distill mountains of raw information speedily.
Strong concentration not just on reporting findings but also on practical, action-oriented recommendations.

Concept in use.   A practical instance of the use of such an intelligence system is supplied by Mead Johnson Nutritionals (division of Mead Johnson & Company), manufacturers of Metrecal, Pablum, Bib, Nutrament, and other nutritional specialties. As Exhibit III shows, the company's Marketing Intelligence Department has provided information from these sources:

A continuing large-scale consumer market study covering attitudinal and behavioral data dealing with weight control.
Nielsen store audit data, on a bimonthly basis.
A monthly sales audit conducted among a panel of 100 high-volume food stores in 20 markets to provide advance indications of brand share shifts.
Supermarket warehouse withdrawal figures from Time, Inc.'s new service, Selling Areas-Marketing, Inc.
Salesmen's weekly reports (which, in addition to serving the purposes of sales management control, call for reconnaissance on competitive promotions, new product launches, price changes, and so forth).
Advertising expenditure data, by media class, from the company's accounting department.
Figures on sales and related topics from company factories.
Competitive advertising expenditure and exposure data supplied by the division's advertising agencies at periodic intervals.
A panel of weight-conscious women.

To exemplify the type of outputs possible from this system, Mead Johnson will be able, with the help of analyses of factory sales data, warehouse withdrawal information, and consumer purchases from Nielsen, to monitor transactions at each stage of the flow of goods through the distribution channel and to detect accumulations or developing shortages. Management will also be able to spot sources of potential problems in time to deal with them effectively. For example, if factory sales exceed consumer purchases, more promotional pressure is required. By con-

Exhibit II. Work flow and systems chart for management of new products (continues through page 397)

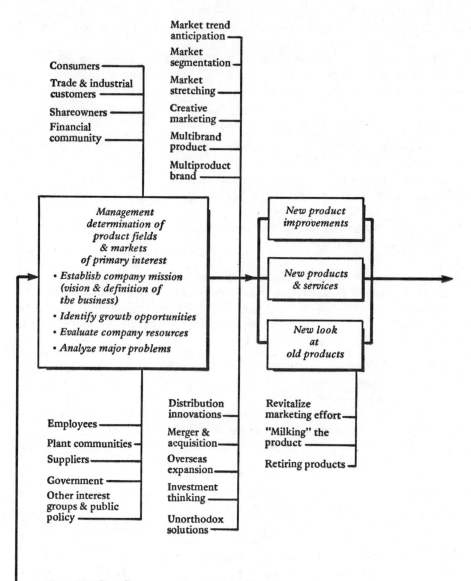

Note: This flow diagram was developed by Paul E. Funk, President, and the staff of McCann/ITSM, Inc.

trast, if factory sales lag behind consumer purchases, sales effort must be further stimulated.

Similarly, the company has been able to devise a practical measurement of advertising's effectiveness in stimulating sales—a measurement that is particularly appropriate to fast-moving packaged goods. By relating advertising outlays and exposure data to the number of prospects trying out a product during a campaign

Exhibit II.   Part 2

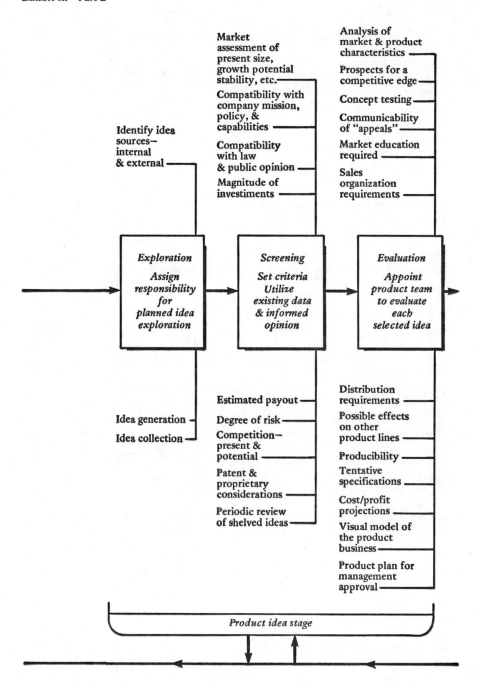

Exhibit II.   Part 3

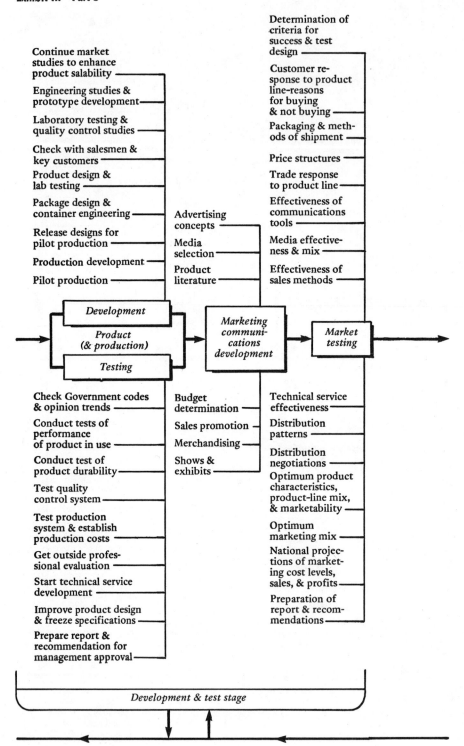

Continue market studies to enhance product salability

Engineering studies & prototype development

Laboratory testing & quality control studies

Check with salesmen & key customers

Product design & lab testing

Package design & container engineering

Release designs for pilot production

Production development

Pilot production

Determination of criteria for success & test design

Customer response to product line-reasons for buying & not buying

Packaging & methods of shipment

Price structures

Trade response to product line

Effectiveness of communications tools

Media effectiveness & mix

Effectiveness of sales methods

Advertising concepts

Media selection

Product literature

Development

Product (& production)

Testing

Marketing communications development

Market testing

Check Government codes & opinion trends

Conduct tests of performance of product in use

Conduct test of product durability

Test quality control system

Test production system & establish production costs

Get outside professional evaluation

Start technical service development

Improve product design & freeze specifications

Prepare report & recommendation for management approval

Budget determination

Sales promotion

Merchandising

Shows & exhibits

Technical service effectiveness

Distribution patterns

Distribution negotiations

Optimum product characteristics, product-line mix, & marketability

Optimum marketing mix

National projections of marketing cost levels, sales, & profits

Preparation of report & recommendations

Development & test stage

Exhibit II. Part 4

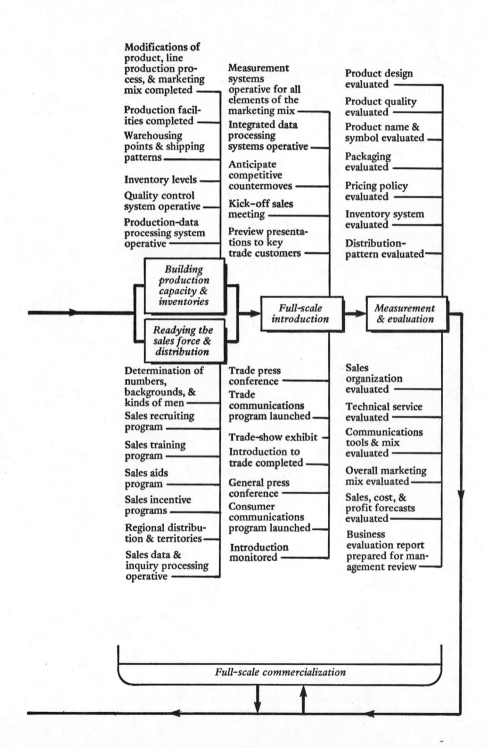

Modifications of product, line production process, & marketing mix completed —

Production facilities completed —

Warehousing points & shipping patterns —

Inventory levels —

Quality control system operative —

Production-data processing system operative —

Measurement systems operative for all elements of the marketing mix —

Integrated data processing systems operative —

Anticipate competitive countermoves —

Kick-off sales meeting —

Preview presentations to key trade customers —

Product design evaluated

Product quality evaluated

Product name & symbol evaluated —

Packaging evaluated —

Pricing policy evaluated —

Inventory system evaluated —

Distribution-pattern evaluated —

Building production capacity & inventories

Readying the sales force & distribution

Full-scale introduction

Measurement & evaluation

Determination of numbers, backgrounds, & kinds of men —

Sales recruiting program —

Sales training program —

Sales aids program —

Sales incentive programs —

Regional distribution & territories —

Sales data & inquiry processing operative —

Trade press conference —

Trade communications program launched —

Trade-show exhibit —

Introduction to trade completed —

General press conference —

Consumer communications program launched —

Introduction monitored —

Sales organization evaluated —

Technical service evaluated —

Communications tools & mix evaluated —

Overall marketing mix evaluated —

Sales, cost, & profit forecasts evaluated —

Business evaluation report prepared for management review —

Full-scale commercialization

Exhibit III.   Mead Johnson's marketing intelligence system

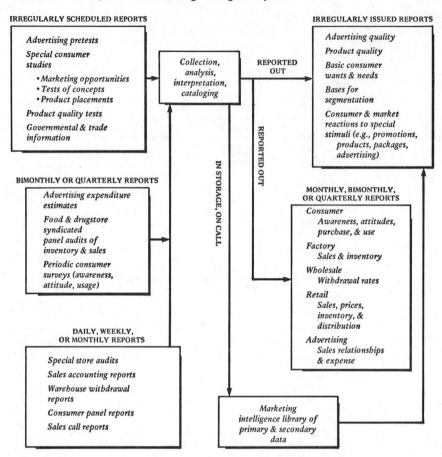

IRREGULARLY SCHEDULED REPORTS

Advertising pretests

Special consumer studies
- *Marketing opportunities*
- *Tests of concepts*
- *Product placements*

Product quality tests

Governmental & trade information

BIMONTHLY OR QUARTERLY REPORTS

Advertising expenditure estimates

Food & drugstore syndicated panel audits of inventory & sales

Periodic consumer surveys (awareness, attitude, usage)

DAILY, WEEKLY, OR MONTHLY REPORTS

Special store audits

Sales accounting reports

Warehouse withdrawal reports

Consumer panel reports

Sales call reports

Collection, analysis, interpretation, cataloging

REPORTED OUT

IN STORAGE, ON CALL

REPORTED OUT

IRREGULARLY ISSUED REPORTS

Advertising quality

Product quality

Basic consumer wants & needs

Bases for segmentation

Consumer & market reactions to special stimuli (e.g., promotions, products, packages, advertising)

MONTHLY, BIMONTHLY, OR QUARTERLY REPORTS

Consumer   Awareness, attitudes, purchase, & use

Factory   Sales & inventory

Wholesale   Withdrawal rates

Retail   Sales, prices, inventory, & distribution

Advertising   Sales relationships & expense

Marketing intelligence library of primary & secondary data

(the number is obtained from the continuing consumer survey), it is possible to calculate the advertising cost of recruiting such a prospect. By persisting in such analyses during several campaigns, the relative value of alternative advertising approaches can be weighed. Since measurement of the sales, as opposed to the communications, effects of promotion is a horrendously difficult, costly, and chancy process, the full significance of this achievement is difficult to exaggerate.

Benefits realized.   Mead Johnson's marketing intelligence system has been helpful to management in a number of ways. In addition to giving executives early warning of new trends and problems, and valuable insights into future conditions, it is leading to a systematic *body* of knowledge about company markets rather than to isolated scraps of information. This knowledge in turn should lead utlimately to a theory of marketing in each field that will explain the mysteries that baffle marketers today. What is more, the company expects that the system will help to free its marketing intelligence people from fire-fighting projects so that they can concentrate on long-term factors and eventually be more consistently creative.

Despite these gains, it is important to note that Mead Johnson feels it has a long road still to travel. More work is needed in linking individual data banks. Conceptual schemes must be proved out in pracitce; ways must still be found to reduce an awesome volume of data, swelled periodically by new information from improved sources, so as to make intelligence more immediately accessible to decision makers. And perhaps the biggest problem of the movement, one underlying some of the others, is the difficulty in finding qualified marketing-oriented programmers.

Physical Distribution

A veritable revolution is now taking place in physical distribution. Total systems are being evolved out of the former hodgepodge of separate responsibilities, which were typically scattered among different departments of the same company. These systems include traffic and transportation, warehousing, materials handling, protective packaging, order processing, production planning, inventory control, customer service, market forecasting, and plant and warehouse site selection. Motivating this revolution are the computer, company drives to reduce distribution costs, and innovations in transportation, such as jet air freight, container ships, the interstate highway network, and larger and more versatile freight cars.

Distribution is one area of marketing where the "bread-and-butter" uses of the computer are relatively easily deployed for such functions as order processing, real-time inventory level reports, and tracking the movements of goods. Further into the future lie mathematical models which will include every factor bearing on distribution. Not only will packaging, materials handling, transportation and warehouse, order processing, and related costs be considered in such models; also included will be sales forecasts by product, production rates by factory, warehouse locations and capacities, speeds of different carriers, etc. In short, a complete picture will be developed for management.

Program in action. The experiences of the Norge Division of Borg-Warner Corporation point up the values of the systems approach in physical distribution. The firm was confronted externally with complaints from its dealers and distributors, who were trying to cope with swollen inventories and the pressures of "loading deals." Internally, because coordination of effort between the six departments involved in distribution was at a minimum, distribution costs and accounts receivable were mounting persistently.

To grapple with this situation, Norge undertook a comprehensive analysis of its distribution system. Out of this grew a new philosophy. A company executive has described the philosophy to me as follows:

An effective system of physical distribution cannot begin at the end of the production line. It must also apply at the very beginning of the production process—at the planning, scheduling, and forecasting stages. Logistics, in short, is part of a larger marketing system, not just an evaluation of freight rates. We must worry not only about finished refrigerators, but also about the motors coming from another manufacturer, and even about where the copper that goes into those motors will come from. We must be concerned with *total* flow.

To implement this philosophy, the appliance manufacturer took the following steps:

1. It reorganized the forecasting, production scheduling, warehousing, order processing, and shipping functions into *one* department headed by a director of physical distribution.
2. The management information system was improved with the help of EDP equipment tied into the communications network. This step made it possible to process and report data more speedily on orders received, inventory levels, and the actual movement of goods.
3. Management used a combination of computer and manual techniques to weigh trade-offs among increased costs of multiple warehousing, reduced long-haul freight and local drayage costs, reduced inventory pipeline, and the sales value of an improved "total" product offering. Also assessed were trade-offs between shorter production runs and higher inventory levels, thereby challenging the traditional "wisdom" of production-oriented managers that the longer the run, the better.
4. The company is setting up new regional warehouses.

As a result of these moves, Norge has been able to lower inventories throughout its sales channels and to reduce accounts receivable. These gains have led, in turn, to a reduction of the company's overall investment and a concomitant increase in profitability.

It is essential to note that even though Norge has used operations research as part of its systems approach, many aspects of the program are qualitative. Thus far, the company has found that the development of an all-encompassing model is not warranted because of (a) the time and cost involved, (b) the probability that the situation will change before the model is completed, (c) a concern that such a model would be so complex as to be unworkable, and (d) the difficulty of testing many of the assumptions used. In addition, management has not tried to quantify the impact of its actions on distributor and retailer attitudes and behavior, possible competitive countermoves, and numerous other factors contributing to results.

Toward Total Integration

The integration of systems developed for product management, product innovation, marketing intelligence, physical distribution, and the other functions or "subsystems" embraced by the term *marketing* creates a total marketing system. Thus, marketing plans composed according to a step-by-step outline, ranging from enunciation of objectives and implementational steps to audit and adjustment to environmental changes, constitute a complete application of systems theory. Further, as the various subsystems of the overall system are linked quantitatively, so that the effect of modifications in one element can be detected in other elements, and as the influences of competitive moves on each element are analyzed numerically, then the total scheme becomes truly sophisticated.

PLUSES AND MINUSES

Two elements underlie the use and benefits of systems theory—order and knowledge. The first is a homely virtue, the second a lofty goal. Marketing is obviously not alone among all human pursuits in needing them; but, compared with its business neighbors, production and finance, marketing's need is acute indeed. The application of the systems concept can bring considerable advantages. It offers:

A methodical problem-solving orientation—with a broader frame of reference so that all aspects of a problem are examined.

Coordinated deployment of all appropriate tools of marketing.

Greater efficiency and economy of marketing operations.

Quicker recognition of impending problems, made possible by better understanding of the complex interplay of many trends and forces.

A stimulus to innovation.

A means of quantitatively verifying results.

These functional benefits in turn yield rich rewards in the marketplace. The most important gains are:

A deeper penetration of existing markets—As an illustration, the Advanced Data Division of Litton Industries has become a leader in the automatic revenue control business by designing systems meshing together "hardware" and "software."

A broadening of markets—For example, the tourist industry has attracted millions of additional travelers by creating packaged tours that are really product-service systems. These systems are far more convenient and economical than anything the consumer could assemble himself.

An extension of product lines—Systems management makes it more feasible to seek out compatibilities among independently developed systems. Evidence of this idea is the work of automatic control system specialists since the early 1950's.[5] Now similar signs are apparent in marketing. For example, Acme Visible Records is currently dovetailing the design and sale of its record-keeping systems with data-processing machines and forms.

A lessening of competition or a strengthened capacity to cope with competition—The systems approach tends to make a company's product line more unique and attractive. Carborundum's innovation in metal-removal systems is a perfect illustration of this.

Problems in Practice

Having just enumerated in glowing terms the benefits of the systems approach, realism demands that I give "equal time" to the awesome difficulties its utilization presents. There is no better evidence of this than the gulf between the elegant and sophisticated models with which recent marketing literature abounds and the actual number of situations in which those models really work. For the truth of the matter is that we are still in the foothills of this development, despite the advances of a few leaders. Let us consider some of the obstacles.

Time and manpower costs.   First of all, the systems approach requires considerable time to implement; it took one company over a year to portray its physical distribution system in a mathematical model before it could even begin to solve its problems. RCA's Electronic Data Processing Division reports models taking three to five years to build after which holes in the data network have to be filled and the model tested against history. Add to this the need for manpower of exceptional intellectual ability, conceptual skills, and specialized education—manpower that is in exceedingly short supply. Because the problems are complex and involve all elements of the business, one man alone cannot solve them. He lacks the knowledge, tools, and controls. And so many people must be involved. It follows that the activation of systems theory can be very costly.

Absence of "canned" solutions.   Unlike other business functions where standardized approaches to problem solving are available, systems must be tailored to the individual situation of each firm. Even the same problem in different companies in the same industry will frequently lead to different solutions because of the impact of other inputs, unique perceptions of the environment, and varying corporate missions. These factors, too, compound time and expense demands.

"Net uncertainties."   Even after exhaustive analysis, full optimization of a total problem cannot be obtained. Some uncertainty will always remain and must be dealt with on the basis of judgment and experience.

Lack of hard data.   In the world of engineering, the systems evolved to date have consisted all or mostly of machines. Systems engineers have been wise enough to avoid the irrationalities of man until they master control of machines. Marketing model-builders, however, have not been able to choose, for the distributor, salesman, customer, and competitor are central to marketing. We must, therefore, incorporate not only quantitative measures of the dimensions of things and processes (e.g., market potential, media outlays, and shipping rates), but also psychological measures of comprehension, attitudes, motivations, intentions, needs—yes, even psychological measures of physical behavior. What is needed is a marriage of the physical and behavioral sciences—and we are about as advanced in this blending of disciplines as astronomy was in the Middle Ages.

Consider the advertising media fields as an instance of the problem:

A number of advertising agencies have evolved linear programming or simulation techniques to assess alternate media schedules. One of the key sets of data used covers the probabilities of exposure to all or part of the audience of a TV program, magazine, or radio station. But what is exposure, and how do you measure it? What is optimum frequency of exposure, and how do you measure it? How does advertising prevail on the predispositions and perceptions of a potential customer? Is it better to judge advertising effects on the basis of exposure opportunity, "impact" (whatever that is), messages retained, message comprehension, or attitude shifts or uptrends in purchase intentions? We do not have these answers yet.

Even assuming precise knowledge of market dimensions, product performance, competitive standing, weights of marketing pressure exerted by direct selling, advertising and promotion, and so on, most marketers do not yet know, except in isolated cases, how one force will affect another. For instance, how does a company "image" affect the setting in which its salesmen work? How does a company's reputation for service affect customer buying behavior?

Nature of marketing men. Man is an actor on this stage in another role. A good many marketing executives, in the deepest recesses of their psyches, are artists, not analysts. For them, marketing is an art form, and, in my opinion, they really do not want it to be any other way. Their temperament is antipathetic to system, order, knowledge. They enjoy flying by the seat of their pants—though you will never get them to admit it. They revel in chaos, abhor facts, and fear research. They hate to be trammeled by written plans. And they love to spend, but are loath to assess the results of their spending.

Obviously, such men cannot be sold readily on the value and practicality of the systems approach! It takes time, experience, and many facts to influence their thinking.

Surmounting the Barriers

All is not gloom, however. The barriers described are being overcome in various ways. While operations research techniques have not yet made much headway in evolving total marketing systems and in areas where man is emotionally engaged, their accomplishments in solving inventory control problems, in sales analysis, in site selection, and in other areas have made many businessmen more sympathetic and open-minded to them.

Also, mathematical models—even the ones that do not work well yet—serve to bolster comprehension of the need for system as well as to clarify the intricacies among subsystems. Many models are in this sense learning models; they teach us how to ask more insightful questions. Moreover, they pinpoint data gaps and invite a more systematized method for reaching judgments where complete information does not exist. Because the computer abhors vague generalities, it forces managers to analyze their roles, objectives, and criteria more concretely. Paradoxically, it demands more, not less, of its human masters.

Of course, resistance to mathematical models by no means makes resistance to the systems approach necessary. There are many cases where no need may ever arise to use mathematics or computers. For the essence of the systems approach is not its techniques, but the enumeration of options and their implications. A simple checklist may be the only tool needed. I would even argue that some hard thinking in a quiet room may be enough. This being the case, the whole trend to more analysis and logic in management thinking, as reflected in business periodicals, business schools, and the practices of many companies, will work in favor of the development of the systems approach.

It is important to note at this juncture that not all marketers need the systems approach in its formal, elaborate sense. The success of some companies is rooted in other than marketing talents; their expertise may lie in finance, technology, administration, or even in personnel—as in the case of holding companies having an almost uncanny ability to hire brilliant operating managers and the self-control to leave them alone. In addition, a very simple marketing operation—for example, a company marketing one product through one distribution channel—may have no use for the systems concept.

Applying the Approach

Not illogically, there is a system for applying the systems approach. It may be outlined as a sequence of steps:

1. *Define the problem and clarify objectives.* Care must be exercised not to accept the view of the propounder of the problem lest the analyst be defeated at the outset.

2. *Test the definition of the problem.* Expand its parameters to the limit. For example, to solve physical distribution problems it is necessary to study the marketplace (customer preferences, usage rates, market size, and so forth), as well as the production process (which plants produce which items most efficiently, what the interplant movements of raw materials are, and so forth). Delineate the extremes of these factors, their changeability, and the limitations on management's ability to work with them.

3. *Build a model.* Portray all factors graphically, indicating logical and chronological sequences—the dynamic flow of information, decisions, and events. "Closed circuits" should be used where there is information feedback or go, no-go and recycle signals (see Exhibit II).

4. *Set concrete objectives.* For example, if a firm wants to make daily deliveries to every customer, prohibitive as the cost may be, manipulation of the model will yield one set of answers. But if the desire is to optimize service at lowest cost, then another set of answers will be needed. The more crisply and precisely targets are stated, the more specific the results will be.

5. *Develop alternative solutions.* It is crucial to be as open-minded as possible at this stage. The analyst must seek to expand the list of options rather than merely assess those given to him, then reduce the list to a smaller number of practical or relevant ones.

6. *Set up criteria or tests of relative value.*

7. *Quantify some or all of the factors or "variables."* The extent to which this is done depends, of course, on management's inclinations and the "state of the art."

8. *Manipulate the model.* That is, weigh the costs, effectiveness, profitability, and risks of each alternative.

9. *Interpret the results, and choose one or more courses of action.*

10. *Verify the results.* Do they make sense when viewed against the world as executives know it? Can their validity be tested by experiments and investigations?

Forethought and Perspective

Successful systems do not blossom overnight. From primitive beginnings, they evolve over a period of time as managers and systems specialists learn to understand each other better, and learn how to structure problems and how to push out the frontiers of the "universe" with which they are dealing. Companies must be prepared to invest time, money, and energy in making systems management feasible. This entails a solid foundation of historical data even before the conceptual framework for the system can be constructed. Accordingly, considerable time should be invested at the outset in *thinking* about the problem, its appropriate scope, options, and criteria of choice before plunging into analysis.

Not only technicians, but most of us have a way of falling in love with techniques. We hail each one that comes along—*deus ex machina*. Historically, commercial research has wallowed in several such passions (e.g., probability sampling, motivation research, and semantic scaling), and now operations research appears to be doing the same thing. Significantly, each technique has come, in the fullness of time, to take its place as one, but only one, instrument in the research tool chest. We must therefore have a broad and dispassionate perspective on the systems approach at this juncture. We must recognize that the computer does not possess greater magical properties than the abacus. It, too, is a tool, albeit a brilliant one.

Put another way, executives must continue to exercise their judgment and experience. Systems analysis is no substitute for common sense. The computer must adapt itself to their styles, personalities, and modes of problem solving. It is an aid to management, not a surrogate. Businessmen may be slow, but the good ones are bright; the electronic monster, by contrast, is a speedy idiot. It demands great acuity of wit from its human managers lest they be deluged in an avalanche of useless paper. (The story is told of a sales manager who had just found out about the impressive capabilities of his company's computer and called for a detailed sales analysis of all products. The report was duly prepared and wheeled into his office on a dolly.)

Systems users must be prepared to revise continually. There are two reasons for this. First, the boundaries of systems keep changing; constraints are modified; competition makes fresh incursions; variables, being what they are, vary, and new ones crop up. Second, the analytical process is iterative. Usually, one "pass" at problem formulation and searches for solutions will not suffice, and it will be necessary to "recycle" as early hypotheses are challenged and new, more fruitful insights are stimulated by the inquiry. Moreover, it is impossible to select objectives without knowledge of their effects and costs. That knowledge can come only from analysis, and it frequently requires review and revision.

Despite all the efforts at quantification, systems analysis is still largely an art. It relies frequently on inputs based on human judgment; even when the inputs are numerical, they are determined, at least in part, by judgment. Similarly, the outputs must pass through the sieve of human interpretation. Hence, there is a positive correlation between the pay-off from a system and the managerial level involved in its design. The higher the level, the more rewarding the results.

Finally, let me observe that marketing people merit their own access to computers as well as programmers who understand marketing. Left in the hands of accountants, the timing, content, and format of output are often out of phase with marketing needs.

CONCLUSION

Nearly 800 years ago a monk wrote the following about St. Godric, a merchant later turned hermit:

He laboured not only as a merchant but also as a shipman . . . to Denmark, Flanders, and Scotland; in which lands he found certain rare, and therefore more precious, wares, which he carried to other parts wherein he knew them to be least familiar, and coveted by the inhabitants beyond the price of gold itself, wherefore he exchanged these wares for others coveted by men of other lands. . . .[6]

How St. Godric "knew" about his markets we are not told, marketing having been in a primitive state in 1170. How some of us marketers today "know" is, in my opinion, sometimes no less mysterious than it was eight centuries ago. But we are trying to change that, and I will hazard the not very venturesome forecast that the era of "by guess and by gosh" marketing is drawing to a close. One evidence of this trend is marketers' intensified search for knowledge that will improve their command over their destinies. This search is being spurred on by a number of powerful developments. To describe them briefly:

The growing complexity of technology and the accelerating pace of tech-nological innovation.

The advent of the computer, inspiring and making possible analysis of the relationships between systems components.

The intensification of competition, lent impetus by the extraordinary velocity of new product development and the tendency of diversification to thrust everybody into everybody else's business.

The preference of buyers for purchasing from as few sources as possible, thereby avoiding the problems of assembling bits and pieces themselves and achieving greater reliability, economy, and administrative convenience. (Mrs. Jones would rather buy a complete vacuum cleaner from one source than the housing from one manufacturer, the hose from another, and the attach-ments from still another. And industrial buyers are not much different from Mrs. Jones. They would rather buy an automated machine tool from one manufacturer than design and assemble the components themselves. Not to be overlooked in this connection, is the tremendous influence of the U.S. government in buying systems for its military and aerospace programs.)

The further development and application of the systems approach to market-ing represents, in my judgment, the leading edge in both marketing theory and practice. At the moment, we are still much closer to St. Godric than to the mil-lenium, and the road will be rocky and tortuous. But if we are ever to convert marketing into a more scientific pursuit, this is the road we must travel. The sys-tems concept can teach us how our businesses really behave in the marketing arena, thereby extending managerial leverage and control. It can help us to con-front more intelligently the awesome complexity of marketing, to deal with the hazards and opportunities of technological change, and to cope with the intensifi-cation of competition. And in the process, the concept will help us to feed the hungry maws of our expensive computers with more satisfying fare.

NOTES

[1] See, for example, Donald F. Cox and Robert E. Good, "How to Build a Marketing Information System," *Harvard Business Review* (May–June 1967); pp. 145–54.

[2] "Abrasive Maker's Systems Approach Opens New Markets," *Steel,* December 27, 1965, p. 38.

[3] *Ibid.*

[4] "Carborundum Grinds at Faster Clip," *Business Week,* July 23, 1966, pp. 58, 60.

[5] See *Automatic and Manual Control: Papers Contributed to the Conference at·Cranford, 1951,* edited by A. Tustin (London, Butterworth's Scientific Publications, 1952).

[6] *Life of St. Godric,* by Reginald, a monk of Durham, c. 1170.

SOME SUGGESTIONS FOR FURTHER READING

Ansoff, H. I. (1977), "The State of Practice in Planning Systems," *Sloan Management Review* (Winter), 1–24.

Bowman, E. H. (1974), "Epistemology, Corporate Strategy and Academia," *Sloan Management Review* (Winter), 35–50.

Kotler, P., W. Gregor, and W. Rogers (1977), "The Marketing Audit Comes of Age," *Sloan Management Review* (Winter), 25–43.

Lorange, P. and R. F. Vancil (1976), "How to Design a Strategic Planning System," *Harvard Business Review* (September–October), 75–81.

Montgomery, D. B., and C. B. Weinberg (1979), "Toward Strategic Intelligence Systems," *Journal of Marketing* (Fall), 41–52.

28 / THE CONCEPT OF THE MARKETING MIX / Neil H. Borden

I have always found it interesting to observe how an apt or colorful term may catch on, gain wide usage, and help to further understanding of a concept that has already been expressed in less appealing and communicative terms. Such has been true of the phrase "marketing mix," which I began to use in my teaching and writing some 15 years ago. In a relatively short time it has come to have wide usage. This note tells of the evolution of the marketing mix concept.

The phrase was suggested to me by a paragraph in a research bulletin on the management of marketing costs, written by my associate, Professor James Culliton.[1] In this study of manufacturers' marketing costs he described the business executive as a

"decider," an "artist"—a "mixer of ingredients," who sometimes follows a recipe as he goes along, sometimes adapts a recipe to the ingredients immediately available, and sometimes experiments with or invents ingredients no one else has tried.

I liked his idea of calling a marketing executive a "mixer of ingredients," one who is constantly engaged in fashioning creatively a mix of marketing procedures and policies in his efforts to produce a profitable enterprise.

For many years previous to Culliton's cost study the wide variations in the procedures and policies employed by managements of manufacturing firms in their marketing programs and the correspondingly wide variation in the costs of these marketing functions, which Culliton aptly ascribed to the varied "mixing of ingredients," had become increasingly evident as we had gathered marketing cases at the Harvard Business School. The marked differences in the patterns or formulae of the marketing programs not only were evident through facts disclosed in case histories, but also were reflected clearly in the figures of a cost study of food manufacturers made by the Harvard Bureau of Business Research in 1929. The primary objective of this study was to determine common figures of expenses for various marketing functions among food manufacturing companies, similar to the common cost figures which had been determined in previous years for various

Reprinted from *Journal of Advertising Research,* © Advertising Research Foundation, Inc. (June, 1964), pp. 2–7.
Neil H. Borden, Professor Emeritus of Harvard, spent a summer lecturing in Australia, served for three years as a consultant in India, and lectured on management in Singapore. His M.B.A. degree is from Harvard, where he has taught since 1922. He is a past president of the American Marketing Association and has published work on many phases of advertising. His 1942 study, *The Economic Effects of Advertising,* is still recognized as a definitive work.

kinds of retail and wholesale businesses. In this manufacturer's study we were unable, however, with the data gathered to determine common expense figures that had much significance as standards by which to guide management, such as had been possible in the studies of retail and wholesale trades, where the methods of operation tended toward uniformity. Instead, among food manufacturers the ratios of sales devoted to the various functions of marketing such as advertising, personal selling, packaging, and so on, were found to be widely divergent, no matter how we grouped our respondents. Each respondent gave data that tended to uniqueness.

Culliton's study of marketing costs in 1947–48 was a second effort to find out, among other objectives, whether a bigger sample and a more careful classification of companies would produce evidence of operating uniformities that would give helpful common expense figures. But the result was the same as in our early study: there was wide diversity in cost ratios among any classifications of firms which were set up, and no common figures were found that had much value. This was true whether companies were grouped according to similarity in product lines, amount of sales, territorial extent of operations, or other bases of classification.

Relatively early in my study of advertising, it had become evident that understanding of advertising usage by manufacturers in any case had to come from an analysis of advertising's place as one element in the total marketing program of the firm. I came to realize that it is essential always to ask: what overall marketing strategy has been or might be employed to bring about a profitable operation in light of the circumstances faced by the management? What combination of marketing procedures and policies has been or might be adopted to bring about desired behavior of trade and consumers at costs that will permit a profit? Specifically, how can advertising, personal selling, pricing, packaging, channels, warehousing, and the other elements of a marketing program be manipulated and fitted together in a way that will give a profitable operation? In short, I saw that every advertising management case called for a consideration of the strategy to be adopted for the total marketing program, with advertising recognized as only one element whose form and extent depended on its careful adjustment to the other parts of the program.

The soundness of this viewpoint was supported by case histories throughout my volume, *The Economic Effects of Advertising.*[2] In the chapters devoted to the utilization of advertising by business, I had pointed out the innumerable combinations of marketing methods and policies that might be adopted by a manager in arriving at a marketing plan. For instance, in the area of branding, he might elect to adopt an individualized brand or a family brand. Or he might decide to sell his product unbranded or under private label. Any decision in the area of brand policy in turn has immediate implications that bear on his selection of channels of distribution, sales force methods, packaging, promotional procedure, and advertising. Throughout the volume the case materials cited show that the way in which any marketing function is designed and the burden placed upon the function are determined largely by the overall marketing strategy adopted by managements to meet the market conditions under which they operate. The forces met by different firms vary widely. Accordingly, the programs fashioned differ widely.

Regarding advertising, which was the function under focus in the economic effects volume, I said at one point:

In all the above illustrative situations it should be recognized that advertising is not an operating method to be considered as something apart, as something whose profit value is to be judged alone. An able management does not ask, "Shall we use or not use advertising," without consideration of the product and of other management procedures to be employed. Rather the question is always one of finding a management formula giving advertising its due place in the combination of manufacturing methods, product form, pricing, promotion and selling methods, and distribution methods. As previously pointed out different formulae, i.e., different combinations of methods, may be profitably employed by competing manufacturers.

From the above it can be seen why Culliton's description of a marketing manager as a "mixer of ingredients" immediately appealed to me as an apt and easily understandable phrase, far better than my previous references to the marketing man as an empiricist seeking in any situation to devise a profitable "pattern" or "formula" of marketing operations from among the many procedures and policies that were open to him. If he was a "mixer of ingredients," what he designed was a "marketing mix."

It was logical to proceed from a realization of the existence of a variety of "marketing mixes" to the development of a concept that would comprehend not only this variety, but also the market forces that cause managements to produce a variety of mixes. It is the problems raised by these forces that lead marketing managers to exercise their wits in devising mixes or programs which they hope will give a profitable business operation.

To portray this broadened concept in a visual presentation requires merely:

1. A list of the important elements or ingredients that make up marketing programs.
2. A list of the forces that bear on the marketing operation of a firm and to which the marketing manager must adjust in his search for a mix or program that can be successful.

The list of elements of the marketing mix in such a visual presentation can be long or short, depending on how far one wishes to go in his classification and sub-classification of the marketing procedures and policies with which marketing managements deal when devising marketing programs. The list of elements which I have employed in my teaching and consulting work covers the principal areas of marketing activities which call for management decisions as revealed by case histories. I realize others might build a different list. Mine is as follows:

Elements of the Marketing Mix of Manufacturers

1. *Product Planning*—policies and procedures relating to:
   a. Product lines to be offered—qualities, design, etc.
   b. Markets to sell—whom, where, when, and in what quantity.
   c. New product policy—research and development program.

2. *Pricing*—policies and procedures relating to:
   a. Price level to adopt.
   b. Specific prices to adopt—odd-even, etc.
   c. Price policy—one-price or varying price, price maintenance, use of list prices, etc.
   d. Margins to adopt—for company, for the trade.
3. *Branding*—policies and procedures relating to:
   a. Selection of trade marks.
   b. Brand policy—individualized or family brand.
   c. Sale under private label or unbranded.
4. *Channels of Distribution*—policies and procedures relating to:
   a. Channels to use between plant and consumer.
   b. Degree of selectivity among wholesalers and retailers.
   c. Efforts to gain cooperation of the trade.
5. *Personal Selling*—policies and procedures relating to:
   a. Burden to be placed on personal selling and the methods to be employed in:
      1. Manufacturer's organization.
      2. Wholesale segment of the trade.
      3. Retail segment of the trade.
6. *Advertising*—policies and procedures relating to:
   a. Amount to spend—i.e., the burden to be placed on advertising.
   b. Copy platform to adopt:
      1. Product image desired.
      2. Corporate image desired.
   c. Mix of advertising–to the trade, through the trade, to consumers.
7. *Promotions*—policies and procedures relating to:
   a. Burden to place on special selling plans or devices directed at or through the trade.
   b. Form of these devices for consumer promotions, for trade promotions.
8. *Packaging*—policies and procedures relating to:
   a. Formulation of package and label.
9. *Display*—policies and procedures relating to:
   a. Burden to be put on display to help effect sale.
   b. Methods to adopt to secure display.
10. *Servicing*—policies and procedures relating to:
    a. Providing service needed.
11. *Physical Handling*—policies and procedures relating to:
    a. Warehousing.
    b. Transportation.
    c. Inventories.
12. *Fact Finding and Analysis*—policies and procedures relating to:
    a. Securing, analysis, and the use of facts in marketing operations.

Also, if one were to make a list of all the forces which managements weigh at one time or another when formulating their marketing mixes, it would be very long indeed, for the behavior of individuals and groups in all spheres of life has a bearing, first, on what goods and services are produced and consumed, and second, on the procedures that may be employed in bringing about exchange of these goods and services. However, the important forces which bear on marketers, all arising from the behavior of individuals or groups, may readily be listed under four heads, namely, the behavior of consumers, the trade, competitors, and government.

The next outline contains these four behavior forces with notations of some of the important behavioral determinants within each force. These must be studied and understood by the marketer, if his marketing mix is to be successful. The great quest of marketing management is to understand the behavior of humans in response to the stimuli to which they are subjected. The skillful marketer is one who is a perceptive and practical psychologist and sociologist, who has keen insight into individual and group behavior, who can foresee changes in behavior that develop in a dynamic world, who has creative ability for building well-knit programs because he has the capacity to visualize the probable response of consumers, trade, and competitors to his moves. His skill in forecasting response to his marketing moves should well be supplemented by a further skill in devising and using tests and measurements to check consumer or trade response to his program or parts thereof, for no marketer has so much prescience that he can proceed without empirical check.

Here, then, is the suggested outline of forces which govern the mixing of marketing elements. This list and that of the elements taken together provide a visual presentation of the concept of the marketing mix.

Market Forces Bearing on the Marketing Mix

1. *Consumers' Buying Behavior*—as determined by their:
   a. Motivation in purchasing.
   b. Buying habits.
   c. Living habits.
   d. Environment (present and future, as revealed by trends, for environment influences consumers' attitudes toward products and their use of them).
   e. Buying power.
   f. Number (i.e., how many).
2. *The Trade's Behavior*—wholesalers' and retailers' behavior, as influenced by:
   a. Their motivations.
   b. Their structure, practices, and attitudes.
   c. Trends in structure and procedures that portend change.
3. *Competitors' Position and Behavior*—as influenced by:
   a. Industry structure and the firm's relation thereto.
      1. Size and strength of competitors.
      2. Number of competitors and degree of industry concentration.
      3. Indirect competition—i.e., from other products.
   b. Relation of supply to demand—oversupply or undersupply.
   c. Product choices offered consumers by the industry—i.e., quality, price, service.
   d. Degree to which competitors compete on price vs. nonprice bases.

e. Competitors' motivations and attitudes—their likely response to the actions of other firms.

f. Trends technological and social, portending change in supply and demand.

4. *Government Behavior*—controls over marketing:

a. Regulations over products.

b. Regulations over pricing.

c. Regulations over competitive practices.

d. Regulations over advertising and promotion.

When building a marketing program to fit the needs of his firm, the marketing manager has to weigh the behavioral forces and then juggle marketing elements in his mix with a keen eye on the resources with which he has to work. His firm is but one small organism in a large universe of complex forces. His firm is only a part of an industry that is competing with many other industries. What does the firm have in terms of money, product line, organization, and reputation with which to work? The manager must devise a mix of procedures that fit these resources. If his firm is small, he must judge the response of consumers, trade, and competition in light of his position and resources and the influence that he can exert in the market. He must look for special opportunities in product or method of operation. The small firm cannot employ the procedures of the big firm. Though he may sell the same kind of product as the big firm, his marketing strategy is likely to be widely different in many respects. Innumerable instances of this fact might be cited. For example, in the industrial goods field, small firms often seek to build sales on a limited and highly specialized line, whereas industry leaders seek patronage for full lines. Small firms often elect to go in for regional sales rather than attempt the national distribution practiced by larger companies. Again, the company of limited resources often elects to limit its production and sales to products whose potential is too small to attract the big fellows. Still again, companies with small resources in the cosmetic field not infrequently have set up introductory marketing programs employing aggressive personal selling and a "push" strategy with distribution limited to leading department stores. Their initially small advertising funds have been directed through these selected retail outlets, with the offering of the products and their story told over the signatures of the stores. The strategy has been to borrow kudos for their products from the leading stores' reputations and to gain a gradual radiation of distribution to smaller stores in all types of channels, such as often comes from the trade's follow-the-leader behavior. Only after resources have grown from mounting sales has a dense retail distribution been aggressively sought and a shift made to place the selling burden more and more on company-signed advertising.

The above strategy was employed for Toni products and Stoppette deodorant in their early marketing stages when the resources of their producers were limited (cf. case of Jules Montenier, Inc. in Borden and Marshall).[3] In contrast, cosmetic manufacturers with large resources have generally followed a "pull" strategy for the introduction of new products, relying on heavy campaigns of advertising in a rapid succession of area introductions to induce a hoped-for, complete retail coverage from the start. (cf. case of Bristol-Myers Company in Borden and Marshall).[4] These introductory campaigns have been undertaken only after careful programs of product development and test marketing have given assurance that product and selling plans had high promise of success.

Many additional instances of the varying strategy employed by small versus large enterprises might be cited. But those given serve to illustrate the point that managements must fashion their mixes to fit their resources. Their objectives must be realistic.

LONG VS. SHORT TERM ASPECTS OF MARKETING MIX

The marketing mix of a firm in a large part is the product of the evolution that comes from day-to-day marketing. At any time the mix represents the program that a management has evolved to meet the problems with which it is constantly faced in an ever-changing, ever-challenging market. There are continuous tactical maneuvers: a new product, aggressive promotion, or price-change initiated by a competitor must be considered and met; the failure of the trade to provide adequate market coverage or display must be remedied; a faltering sales force must be reorganized and stimulated; a decline in sales share must be diagnosed and remedied; an advertising approach that has lost effectiveness must be replaced; a general business decline must be countered. All such problems call for a management's maintaining effective channels of information relative to its own operations and to the day-to-day behavior of consumers, competitors, and the trade. Thus, we may observe that short-range forces play a large part in the fashioning of the mix to be used at any time and in determining the allocation of expenditures among the various functional accounts of the operating statement.

But the overall strategy employed in a marketing mix is the product of longer-range plans and procedures dictated in part by past empiricism and in part, if the management is a good one, by management foresight as to what needs to be done to keep the firm successful in a changing world. As the world has become more and more dynamic, blessed is that corporation which has managers who have foresight, who can study trends of all kinds—natural, economic, social, and technological—and, guided by these, devise long-range plans that give promise of keeping their corporations afloat and successful in the turbulent sea of market change. Accordingly, when we think of the marketing mix, we need to give particular heed today to devising a mix based on long-range planning that promises to fit the world of five or ten or more years hence. Provision for effective long-range planning in corporate organization and procedure has become more and more recognized as the earmark of good management in a world that has become increasingly subject to rapid change.

To cite an instance among American marketing organizations which have shown foresight in adjusting the marketing mix to meet social and economic change, I look upon Sears Roebuck and Company as an outstanding example. After building an unusually successful mail order business to meet the needs of a rural America, Sears management foresaw the need to depart from its marketing pattern as a mail order company catering primarily to farmers. The trend from a rural to an urban United States was going on apace. The automobile and good roads promised to make town and city stores increasingly available to those who continued to be farmers. Relatively early, Sears launched a chain of stores across the land, each easily accessible by highway to both farmer and city resident, and with adequate parking space for customers. In time there followed the remarkable telephone and mail order plan directed at urban residents to make buying easy for Americans when congested city streets and highways made shopping increasingly distasteful. Similarly, in the areas of planning products which would meet the desires of consumers in a fast-changing world, of shaping its servicing to meet the needs of a wide variety of mechanical products, of pricing procedures to meet the challenging competition that came with the advent of discount retailers, the Sears organization has shown a foresight, adaptability, and creative ability worthy of emulation. The amazing growth and profitability of the company attest to the foresight and skill of its managements. Its history shows the wisdom of careful attention to market forces and their impending change in devising marketing mixes that may assure growth.

USE OF THE MARKETING MIX CONCEPT

Like many concepts, the marketing mix concept seems relatively simple, once it has been expressed. I know that before they were ever tagged with the nomenclature of "concept," the ideas involved were widely understood among marketers as a result of the growing knowledge about marketing and marketing procedures that came during the preceding half century. But I have found for myself that once the ideas were reduced to a formal statement with an accompanying visual presentation, the concept of the mix has proved a helpful device in teaching, in business problem solving, and, generally, as an aid to thinking about marketing. First of all, it is helpful in giving an answer to the question often raised as to "what is marketing?" A chart which shows the elements of the mix and the forces that bear on the mix helps to bring understanding of what marketing is. It helps to explain why in our dynamic world the thinking of management in all its functional areas must be oriented to the market.

In recent years I have kept an abbreviated chart showing the elements and the forces of the marketing mix in front of my classes at all times. In case discussion it has proved a handy device by which to raise queries as to whether the student has recognized the implications of any recommendation he might have made in the areas of the several elements of the mix. Or, referring to the forces, we can question whether all the pertinent market forces have been given due consideration. Continual reference to the mix chart leads me to feel that the students' understanding of "what marketing is" is strengthened. The constant presence and use of the chart leaves a deeper understanding that marketing is the devising of programs that successfully meet the forces of the market.

In problem solving the marketing mix chart is a constant reminder of:

1. The fact that a problem seemingly lying in one segment of the mix must be deliberated with constant thought regarding the effect of any change in that

sector on the other areas of marketing operations. The necessity of integration in marketing thinking is ever present.

2. The need of careful study of the market forces as they might bear on problems in hand.

In short, the mix chart provides an ever-ready checklist as to areas into which to guide thinking when considering marketing questions or dealing with marketing problems.

MARKETING: SCIENCE OR ART?

The quest for a "science of marketing" is hard upon us. If science is in part a systematic formulation and arrangement of facts in a way to help understanding, then the concept of the marketing mix may possibly be considered a small contribution in the search for a science of marketing. If we think of a marketing science as involving the observation and classification of facts and the establishment of verifiable laws that can be used by the marketer as a guide to action with assurance that predicted results will ensue, then we cannot be said to have gotten far toward establishing a science. The concept of the mix lays out the areas in which facts should be assembled, these to serve as a guide to management judgment in building marketing mixes. In the last few decades American marketers have made substantial progress in adopting the scientific method in assembling facts. They have sharpened the tools of fact finding—both those arising within the business and those external to it. Aided by these facts and by the skills developed through careful observation and experience, marketers are better fitted to practice the art of designing marketing mixes than would be the case had not the techniques of gathering facts been advanced as they have been in recent decades. Moreover, marketers have made progress in the use of the scientific method in designing tests whereby the results from mixes or parts of mixes can be measured. Thereby marketers have been learning how to subject the hypotheses of their mix artists to empirical check.

With continued improvement in the search for and the recording of facts pertinent to marketing, with further application of the controlled experiment, and with an extension and careful recording of case histories, we may hope for a gradual formulation of clearly defined and helpful marketing laws. Until then, and even then, marketing and the building of marketing mixes will largely lie in the realm of art.

NOTES

[1] James W. Culliton, *The Management of Marketing Costs* (Boston: Division of Research, Graduate School of Business Administration, Harvard University, 1948).

[2] Neil H. Borden, *The Economic Effects of Advertising* (Homewood, Illinois: Richard D. Irwin, 1942).

[3] Neil H. Borden and M. V. Marshall, *Advertising Management: Text and Cases* (Homewood, Illinois: Richard D. Irwin, 1959), pp. 498–518.

[4] *Ibid.*, pp. 518–33.

SOME SUGGESTIONS FOR FURTHER READING

Enis, B. M. and Mokwa, M. P. (1979), "The Marketing Management Matrix: A Taxonomy for Strategy Comprehension," in *Conceptual and Theoretical Developments in Marketing*, O. C. Ferrell, S. W. Brown, and C. M. Lamb, eds., Chicago: American Marketing Association.

Frey, A. W. (1961), *Advertising*, 3rd ed., New York: Ronald Press, 30.

Lazer, W. and Kelley, E. J. (1962), *Managerial Marketing: Perspectives and Viewpoints*, rev. ed., Homewood, Ill.; Richard D. Irwin, 413.

McCarthy, E. J. (1978), *Basic Marketing: A Managerial Approach*, 6th ed., Homewood, Ill.; Richard D. Irwin, 30.

29 / POSITIONING CUTS THROUGH CHAOS IN MARKETPLACE / Jack Trout and Al Ries

As far as advertising is concerned, the good old days are gone forever.

As the president of a large consumer products company said recently, "Count on your fingers the number of successful new national brands introduced in the last two years. You won't get to your pinky."

Not that a lot of companies haven't tried. Every supermarket is filled with shelf after shelf of "half successful" brands. The manufacturers of these me-too products cling to the hope that they can develop a brilliant advertising campaign which will lift their offspring into the winner's circle.

Meanwhile, they hang in there with coupons, deals, point of purchase displays. But profits are hard to come by and that "brilliant" advertising campaign, even if it comes, doesn't ever seem to turn the brand around.

No wonder management people turn skeptical when the subject of advertising comes up. And instead of looking for new ways to put the power of advertising to work, management invents schemes for reducing the cost of what they are currently doing. Witness the rise of the house agency, the media buying service, the barter deal.

ADS DON'T WORK LIKE THEY USED TO

The chaos in the marketplace is a reflection of the fact that advertising just doesn't work like it used to. But old traditional ways of doing things die hard. "There's no reason that advertising can't do the job," say the defenders of the status quo, "as long as the product is good, the plan is sound and the commercials are creative."

But they overlook one big, loud reason. The marketplace itself. The noise level today is far too high. Not only the volume of advertising, but also the volume of products and brands.

To cope with this assault on his or her mind, the average consumer has run out of brain power and mental ability. And with a rising standard of living the average consumer is less and less interested in making the "best" choice. For many of today's more affluent customers, a "satisfactory" brand is good enough.

Reprinted with permission from the May 1, 1972, issue of Advertising Age. Copyright 1972 by Crain Communications, Inc.
Jack Trout is president and Al Ries is chairman of Ries, Cappiello, Colwell, Inc., an advertising agency. Both authors have published pioneering articles in the conceptual area of positioning products. Their concepts have heavily influenced practical marketing strategy.

Advertising prepared in the old, traditional ways has no hope of being successful in today's chaotic marketplace.

In the past, advertising was prepared in isolation. That is, you studied the product and its features and then you prepared advertising which communicated to your customers and prospects the benefits of those features.

It didn't make much difference whether the competition offered those features or not. In the traditional approach, you ignored competition and made every claim seem like a preemptive claim. Mentioning a competitive product, for example, was considered not only bad taste, but poor strategy as well.

In the positioning era, however, the rules are reversed. To establish a position, you must often not only name competitive names, but also ignore most of the old advertising rules as well.

In category after category, the prospect already knows the benefits of using the product. To climb on his product ladder, you must relate your brand to the brands already there.

AVIS TOOK 'AGAINST' POSITION

In today's marketplace, the competitor's image is just as important as your own. Sometimes more important. An early success in the positioning era was the famous Avis campaign.

The Avis campaign will go down in marketing history as a classic example of establishing the "against" position. In the case of Avis, this was a position against the leader.

"Avis is only Number 2 in rent-a-cars, so why go with us? We try harder."

For 13 straight years, Avis lost money. Then they admitted they were No. 2 and have made money every year since. Avis was able to make substantial gains because they recognized the position of Hertz and didn't try to attack them head-on.

VW MADE "UGLY" POSITION WORK

A company can sometimes be successful by accepting a position that no one else wants. For example, virtually all automobile manufacturers want the public to think they make cars that are good looking. As a result, Volkswagen was able to establish a unique position for themselves. By default.

The strength of this position, of course, is that it communicates the idea of reliability in a powerful way. "The 1970 VW will stay ugly longer" was a powerful statement because it is psychologically sound. When an advertiser admits a negative, the reader is inclined to give them the position.

A similar principle is involved in Smucker's jams and jellies. "With a name like Smucker's," says the advertising, "you know it's got to be good."

BATTLE OF THE COLAS

The advantage of owning a position can be seen most clearly in the soft drink field. Three major cola brands compete in what is really not a contest. For every ten bottles of Coke, only four bottles of Pepsi and one bottle of Royal Crown are consumed.

While there may be room in the market for a No. 2 cola, the position of Royal Crown is weak. In 1970, for example, Coca-Cola's sales increase over the previous year (168,000,000 cases) was more than Royal Crown's entire volume (156,000,000 cases).

Obviously, Coke has a strong grip on the cola position. And there's not much room left for the other brands. But, strange as it might seem, there might be a spot for a reverse kind of product. One of the most interesting positioning ideas is the one currently being used by Seven-Up. It's the "Un-Cola" and it seems silly until you take a closer look.

"Wet and Wild" was a good campaign in the image era. But the "Un-Cola" is a great program in the positioning era. Sales jumped something like 10 per cent the first year the product was positioned against the cola field. And the increases have continued.

The brilliance of this idea can only be appreciated when you comprehend the intense share of mind enjoyed by the cola category. Two out of three soft drinks consumed in the U.S. are cola drinks.

By linking the product to what's already in the mind of the prospect, the Un-Cola position establishes Seven-Up as an alternative to a cola drink.

A somewhat similar positioning program is working in the media field. This is the "third newsweekly" concept being used by *Sports Illustrated* to get into the mind of the media buyer.

It obviously is an immensely successful program. But what may not be so obvious, is why it works. The "third newsweekly" certainly doesn't describe *Sports Illustrated*. (As the Un-Cola doesn't describe Seven-Up.)

What it does do, however, is to relate the magazine to a media category that is uppermost in the prospect's mind (as the Un-Cola relates to the soft drink category that is uppermost in the mind).

Both the Seven-Up and the *Sports Illustrated* programs are dramatic reminders that positioning is not something you do with the product. Positioning is something you do with the mind. That is, you position the product in the mind of the prospect.

YOU CAN REPOSITION COMPETITOR

In order to position your own brand, it's sometimes necessary to reposition the competitor.

In the case of Beck's beer, the repositioning is done at the expense of Lowenbrau: "You've tasted the German beer that's the most popular in America. Now taste the German beer that's the most popular in Germany."

This strategy works because the prospect had assumed something about Lowenbrau that wasn't true.

The current program for Raphael aperitif wine also illustrates this point. The ads show a bottle of "made in France" Raphael and a bottle of "made in U.S.A." Dubonnet. "For $1.00 a bottle less," says the headline, "you can enjoy the imported one." The shock, of course, is to find that Dubonnet is a product of the U.S.

PLIGHT OF AIRLINE X

In the positioning era, the name of a company or product is becoming more and more important. The name is the hook that allows the mind to hang the brand on its product ladder. Given a poor name, even the best brand in the world won't be able to hang on.

Take the airline industry. The big four domestic carriers are United, American, TWA and an airline we'll call Airline X.

Like all airlines, Airline X has had its ups and downs. Unfortunately, there have been more downs than ups. But unlike some of its more complacent competitors, Airline X has tried. A number of years ago, it brought in big league marketing people and pushed in the throttle.

Airline X was among the first to "paint the planes," "improve the food" and "dress up the stewardesses" in an effort to improve its reputation.

And Airline X hasn't been bashful when it comes to spending money. Year after year, it has one of the biggest advertising budgets in the industry. Even though it advertises itself as "the second largest passenger carrier of all the airlines in the free world," you may not have guessed that Airline X is Eastern. Right up there spending with the worldwide names.

For all that money, what do you think of Eastern? Where do you think they fly? Up and down the East Coast, to Boston, Washington, Miami, right? Well, Eastern also goes to St. Louis, New Orleans, Atlanta, San Francisco, Acapulco. But Eastern has a regional name and their competitors have broader names which tell the prospect they fly everywhere.

Look at the problem from just one of Eastern's cities, Indianapolis. From Indianapolis, Eastern flies *north* to Chicago, Milwaukee and Minneapolis. And *south* to Birmingham and Mobile. They just don't happen to fly *east*.

And then there is the lush San Juan run which Eastern has been serving for more than 25 years. Eastern used to get the lion's share of this market. Then early last year American Airlines took over Trans Caribbean. So today, who is number one to the San Juan sun? Why American, of course.

No matter how hard you try, you can't hang "The Wings of Man" on a regional name. When the prospect is given a choice, he or she is going to prefer the national airline, not the regional one.

B. F. GOODRICH HAS IDENTITY CRISIS

What does a company do when its name (Goodrich) is similar to the name of a much larger company in the same field (Goodyear)?

Goodrich has problems. They could reinvent the wheel and Goodyear would get most of the credit.

If you watched the Super Bowl last January, you saw both Goodrich and Goodyear advertise their "American-made radial-ply tires." But which company do you think got their money's worth at $200,000 a pop?

We haven't seen the research, but our bet would be on Goodyear, the company that owns the tire position.

BEWARE OF THE NO-NAME TRAP

But even bad names like Eastern and Goodrich are better than no name at all.

In *Fortune's* list of 500 largest industrials, there are now 16 corporate non-entities. That is, 16 major American companies have legally changed their names to meaningless initials.

How many of these companies can you recognize: ACF, AMF, AMP, ATO, CPC, ESB, FMC, GAF, NVF, NL, PPG, RCA, SCM, TRW, USM and VF?

These are not tiny companies either. The smallest of them, AMP, has more than 10,000 employees and sales of over $225,000,000 a year.

What companies like ACF, AMF, AMP and the others fail to realize is that their initials have to stand for something. A prospect must know your name first before he or she can remember your initials.

GE stands for General Electric. IBM stands for International Business Machines. And everyone knows it. But how many people knew that ACF stood for American Car & Foundry?

Furthermore, now that ACF has legally changed its name to initials, there's presumably no way to even expose the prospect to the original name.

An exception seems to be RCA. After all, everyone knows that RCA stands for, or rather used to stand for, Radio Corp. of America.

That may be true today. But what about tomorrow? What will people think 20 years from now when they see those strange initials? Roman Catholic Archdiocese?

And take Corn Products Co. Presumably it changed its name to CPC International because it makes products out of lots of things besides corn, but you can't remember "CPC" without bringing Corn Products Co. to mind. The tragedy is, CPC made the change to "escape" the past. Yet the exact opposite occurred.

LINE EXTENSION CAN BE TRAP, TOO

Names are tricky. Consider the Protein 21/29 shampoo, hair spray, conditioner, concentrate mess.

Back in 1970, the Mennen Co. introduced a combination shampoo conditioner called "Protein 21." By moving rapidly with a $6,000,000 introductory campaign (followed by a $9,000,000 program the next year), Mennen rapidly carved out a 13 per cent share of the $300,000,000 shampoo market.

Then Mennen hit the line extension lure. In rapid succession, the company introduced Protein 21 hair spray, Protein 29 hair spray (for men), Protein 21 conditioner (in two formulas), Protein 21 concentrate. To add to the confusion, the original Protein 21 was available in three different formulas (for dry, oily and regular hair).

Can you imagine how confused the prospect must be trying to figure out what to put on his or her head? No wonder Protein 21's share of the shampoo market has fallen from 13 per cent to 11 per cent. And the decline is bound to continue.

FREE RIDE CAN BE COSTLY

Another similar marketing pitfall recently befell, of all companies, Miles Laboratories.

You can see how it happens. A bunch of the boys are sitting around a conference table trying to name a new cold remedy.

"I have it," says Harry. "Let's call it Alka-Seltzer Plus. That way we can take advantage of the $20,000,000 we're already spending to promote the Alka-Seltzer name."

"Good thinking, Harry," and another money-saving idea is instantly accepted.

But lo and behold, instead of eating into the Dristan and Contac market, the new product turns around and eats into the Alka-Seltzer market.

And you know Miles must be worried. In every TV commercial, the "Alka-Seltzer" gets smaller and smaller and the "Plus" gets bigger and bigger.

Related to the free-ride trap, but not exactly the same, is another common error of judgment called the "well-known name" trap.

Both General Electric and RCA thought they could take their strong positions against IBM in computers. But just because a company is well known in one field doesn't mean it can transfer that recognition to another.

In other words, your brand can be on top of one ladder and nowhere on another. And the further apart the products are conceptually, the greater the difficulty of making the jump.

In the past when there were fewer companies and fewer products, a well-known name was a much greater asset than it is today. Because of the noise level, a "well-known" company has tremendous difficulty trying to establish a position in a different field than the one in which it built its reputation.

YOU CAN'T APPEAL TO EVERYONE

A human emotion called "greed" often leads an advertiser into another error. American Motors' introduction of the Hornet is one of the best examples of the "everybody" trap.

You might remember the ads, "The little rich car. American Motors Hornet: $1,994 to $3,589."

A product that tries to appeal to everyone winds up appealing to no one. People who want to spend $3,500 for a car don't buy the Hornet because they don't want their friends to think they're driving a $1,900 car. People who want to spend $1,900 for a car don't buy the Hornet because they don't want a car with $1,600 worth of accessories taken off of it.

AVOID THE F.W.M.T.S. TRAP

If the current Avis advertising is any indication, the company has "forgotten what made them successful."

The original campaign not only related No. 2 Avis to No. 1 Hertz, but also exploited the love that people have for the underdog. The new campaign (Avis is going to be No. 1) not only is conventional "brag and boast" advertising, but also dares the prospect to make the prediction not come true.

Our prediction: Avis ain't going to be No. 1. Further prediction: Avis will lose ground to Hertz and National.

Another company that seems to have fallen into the forgotten what made them successful trap is Volkswagen.

"Think small" was perhaps the most famous advertisement of the sixties. Yet last year VW ran an ad that said, "Volkswagen introduces a new kind of Volkswagen. Big."

O.K., Volkswagen, should we think small or should we think big?

Confusion is the enemy of successful positioning. Prediction: Rapid erosion of the Beetle's position in the U.S. market.

The world seems to be turning faster.

Years ago, a successful product might live 50 years or more before fading away. Today, a product's life cycle is much shorter. Sometimes it can be measured in months instead of years.

New products, new services, new markets, even new media are constantly being born. They grow up into adulthood and then slide into oblivion. And a new cycle starts again.

Yesterday, beer and hard liquor were campus favorites. Today it's wine.

Yesterday, the well-groomed man had his hair cut every week. Today, it's every month or two.

Yesterday, the way to reach the masses was the mass magazines. Today, it's network TV. Tomorrow, it could be cable.

The only permanent thing in life today is change. And the successful companies of tomorrow will be those companies that have learned to cope with it.

The acceleration of "change" creates enormous pressures on companies to think in terms of tactics rather than strategy. As one respected advertising man commented, "The day seems to be past when long-range strategy can be a winning technique."

But is change the way to keep pace with change? The exact opposite appears to be true.

The landscape is littered with the debris of projects that companies rushed into in attempting to "keep pace." Singer trying to move into the boom in home appliances. RCA moving into the boom in computers. General Foods moving into the boom in fast-food outlets. Not to mention the hundreds of companies that threw away their corporate identities to chase the passing fad to initials.

While the programs of those who kept at what they did best and held their ground have been immensely successful. Maytag selling their reliable appliances. Walt Disney selling his world of fantasy and fun. Avon calling.

And take margarine. Thirty years ago the first successful margarine brands positioned themselves against butter. "Tastes like the high-priced spread," said a typical ad.

And what works today? Why the same strategy. "It isn't nice to fool Mother Nature," says the Chiffon commercial, and sales go up 25 per cent. Chiffon is once again the best selling brand of soft margarine.

LONG-RANGE THINKING IMPORTANT

Change is a wave on the ocean of time. Short-term, the waves cause agitation and confusion, but long-term the underlying currents are much more significant.

To cope with change, it's important to take a long-range point of view. To determine your basic business. Positioning is a concept that is cumulative. Something that takes advantage of advertising's long-range nature.

In the seventies a company must think even more strategically than it did before. Changing the direction of a large company is like trying to turn an aircraft carrier. It takes a mile before anything happens. And if it was a wrong turn, getting back on course takes even longer.

To play the game successfully, you must make decisions on what your company will be doing not next month or next year, but in five years, ten years. In other words, instead of turning the wheel to meet each fresh wave, a company must point itself in the right direction.

You must have vision. There's no sense building a position based on a technology that's too narrow. Or a product that's becoming obsolete. Remember the famous *Harvard Business Review* article entitled "Marketing Myopia"? It still applies.

If a company has positioned itself in the right direction, it will be able to ride the currents of change, ready to take advantage of those opportunities that are right for it. But when an opportunity arrives, a company must be ready to move quickly.

Because of the enormous advantages that accrue to being the leader, most companies are not interested in learning how to *compete* with the leader. They want to be the leader. They want to be Hertz rather than Avis. *Time* rather than *Newsweek*. General Electric rather than Westinghouse.

Historically, however, product leadership is usually the result of an accident, rather than a preconceived plan.

The xerography process, for example, was offered to 32 different companies (including IBM and Kodak) before it wound up at the old Haloid Co. Renamed Haloid Xerox and then finally Xerox, the company has since dominated the copier market. Xerox now owns the copier position.

Were IBM and Kodak stupid to turn down xerography? Of course not. These companies reject thousands of ideas every year.

Perhaps a better description of the situation at the time was that Haloid, a small manufacturer of photographic supplies, was desperate, and the others weren't.

As a result, it took a chance that more prudent companies couldn't be expected to take.

When you trace the history of how leadership positions were established, from Hershey in chocolate to Hertz in rent-a-cars, the common thread is not marketing skill or even product innovation. The common thread is seizing the initiative before the competitor has a chance to get established. In someone's oldtime military terms, the marketing leader "got there firstest with the mostest." The leader usually poured in the marketing money while the situation was still fluid.

IBM, for example, didn't invent the computer. Sperry Rand did. But IBM owns the computer position because they built their computer fortress before competition arrived.

And the position that Hershey established in chocolate was so strong they didn't need to advertise at all, a luxury that competitors like Nestle couldn't afford.

You can see that establishing a leadership position depends not only on luck and timing, but also upon a willingness to "pour it on" when others stand back and wait.

Yet all too often, the product leader makes the fatal mistake of attributing its success to marketing skill. As a result, it thinks it can transfer that skill to other products and other marketing situations.

Witness, for example, the sorry record of Xerox in computers. In May of 1969, Xerox exchanged nearly 10,000,000 shares of stock (worth nearly a billion dollars) for Scientific Data Systems Inc. Since the acquisition, the company (renamed Xerox Data Systems) has lost millions of dollars, and without Xerox's support would have probably gone bankrupt.

And the mecca of marketing knowledge, International Business Machines Corp., hasn't done much better. So far, the IBM plain-paper copier hasn't made much of a dent in Xerox's business. Touché.

The rules of positioning hold for all types of products. In the packaged goods area, for example, Bristol-Myers tried to take on Crest toothpaste with Fact (killed after $5,000,000 was spent on promotion). Then they tried to go after Alka-Seltzer with Resolve (killed after $11,000,000 was spent). And according to a headline in the February 7 [1972] issue of *Advertising Age*, "Bristol-Myers will test Dissolve aspirin in an attempt to unseat Bayer."

The suicidal bent of companies that go head-on against established competition is hard to understand. They know the score, yet they forge ahead anyway. In the marketing war, a "charge of the light brigade" happens every day. With the same predictable result.

ONE STRATEGY FOR LEADER

Successful marketing strategy usually consists of keeping your eyes open to possibilities and then striking before the product leader is firmly fixed.

As a matter of fact, the marketing leader is usually the one who moves the ladder into the mind with his or her brand nailed to the one and only rung. Once there, what can a company do to keep its top-dog position?

There are two basic strategies that should be used hand in hand. They seem contradictory, but aren't. One is to ignore competition, and the other is to cover all bets.

As long as a company owns the position, there's no point in running ads that scream, "We're No. 1." Much better is to enhance the product category in the prospect's mind. Notice the current IBM campaign that ignores competition and sells the value of computers. All computers, not just the company's types.

Although the leader's advertising should ignore the competition, the leader shouldn't. The second rule is to cover all bets.

This means a leader should swallow his or her pride and adopt every new product development as soon as it shows signs of promise. Too often, however, the leader pooh-poohs the development, and doesn't wake up until it's too late.

ANOTHER STRATEGY FOR NON-LEADERS

Most companies are in the No. 2, 3, 4 or even worse category. What then?

Hope springs eternal in the human breast. Nine times out of ten, the also-ran sets out to attack the leader, a la RCA's assault on IBM. Result: Disaster.

Simply stated, the first rule of positioning is this: You can't compete head-on against a company that has a strong, established position. You can go around, under or over, but never head-to-head.

The leader owns the high ground. The No. 1 position in the prospect's mind. The top rung of the product ladder.

The classic example of No. 2 strategy is Avis. But many marketing people misread the Avis story. They assume the company was successful because it tried harder.

Not at all. Avis was successful because it related itself to the position of Hertz. Avis preempted the No. 2 position. (If trying harder were the secret of success, Harold Stassen would be president.)

Most marketplaces have room for a strong No. 2 company provided they position themselves clearly as an alternative to the leader. In the computer field, for example, Honeywell has used this strategy successfully.

"The other computer company vs. Mr. Big," says a typical Honeywell ad. Honeywell is doing what none of the other computer companies seems to be willing to do. Admit that IBM is, in fact, the leader in the computer business. Maybe that's why Honeywell and Mr. Big are the only large companies reported to be making money on computers.

SOME 'STRONG' POSITIONS AREN'T

Yet there are positions that can be taken. These are positions that look strong, but in reality are weak.

Take the position of Scott in paper products. Scott has about 40 per cent of the $1.2 billion market for towels, napkins, toilet tissues and other consumer paper products. But Scott, like Mennen with Protein 21, fell into the line-extension trap.

ScotTowels, ScotTissue, Scotties, Scottkins, even BabyScott. All of these items undermined the Scott foundation. The more products hung on the Scott name, the less meaning the name had to the average consumer.

When Procter & Gamble attacked with Mr. Whipple and his tissue-squeezers, it was no contest. Charmin is now the No. 1 brand in the toilet-tissue market.

In Scott's case, a large "share of market" didn't mean they owned the position. More important is a large "share of mind." The housewife could write "Charmin, Kleenex, Bounty and Pampers" on her shopping list and know exactly what products she was going to get. "Scott" on a shopping list has no meaning. The actual brand names aren't much help either. Which brand, for example, is engineered for the nose, Scotties or ScotTissue?

In positioning terms, the name "Scott" exists in limbo. It isn't firmly ensconced on any product ladder.

ELIMINATE EGOS FROM DECISION MAKING

To repeat, the name is the hook that hangs the brand on the product ladder in the prospect's mind. In the positioning era, the brand name to give a product is probably a company's single, most important marketing decision.

To be successful in the positioning era, advertising and marketing people must be brutally frank. They must try to eliminate all ego from the decision making process. It only clouds the issue.

One of the most critical aspects of "positioning" is being able to evaluate objectively products and how they are viewed by customers and prospects.

As a rule, when it comes to building strong programs, trust no one, especially managers who are all wrapped up in their products. The closer people get to products, the more they defend old decisions or old promises.

Successful companies get their information from the marketplace. That's the place where the program has to succeed, not in the product manager's office.

A company that keeps its eye on Tom, Dick and Harry is going to miss Pierre, Hans and Yoshio.

Marketing is rapidly becoming a worldwide ball game. A company that owns a postion in one country now finds that it can use that position to wedge its way into another.

IBM has 62 per cent of the German computer market. Is this fact surprising? It shouldn't be. IBM earns more than 50 per cent of its profits outside the U.S.

As companies start to operate on a world-wide basis, they often discover they have a name problem.

A typical example is U.S. Rubber, a world-wide company that marketed many products not made of rubber. Changing the name to Uniroyal created a new corporate identity that could be used worldwide.

CREATIVITY TAKES BACK SEAT

In the seventies, creativity will have to take a back seat to strategy.

Advertising Age itself reflects this fact. Today you find fewer stories about individual campaigns and more stories about what's happening in an entire industry. Creativity alone isn't a worthwhile objective in an era where a company can spend millions of dollars on great advertising and still fail miserably in the marketplace.

Consider what Harry McMahan calls the "Curse of Clio." In the past, the American Festival has made special awards to "Hall of Fame Classics." Of the 41 agencies that won these Clio awards, 31 have lost some or all of these particular accounts.

But the cult of creativity dies hard. One agency president said recently, "Oh, we do positioning all the time. But after we develop the position, we turn it over to the creative department." And too often, of course, the creativity does nothing but obscure the positioning.

In the positioning era, the key to success is to run the naked positioning statement, unadorned by so-called creativity.

ASK YOURSELF THESE QUESTIONS

If these examples have moved you to want to apply positioning thinking to your own company's situation, here are some questions to ask yourself:

1. What position, if any, do we already own in the prospect's mind?

Get the answer to this question from the marketplace, not the marketing manager. If this requires a few dollars for research, so be it. Spend the money. It's better to know exactly what you're up against now than to discover it later when nothing can be done about it.

2. What position do we want to own?

Here is where you bring out your crystal ball and try to figure out the best position to own from a long-term point of view.

3. What companies must be out-gunned if we are to establish that position?

If your proposed position calls for a head-to-head approach against a marketing leader, forget it. It's better to go around an obstacle rather than over it. Back up. Try to select a position that on one else has a firm grip on.

4. Do we have enough marketing money to occupy and hold the position?

A big obstacle to successful positioning is attempting to achieve the impossible. It takes money to build a share of mind. It takes money to establish a position. It takes money to hold a position once you've established it.

The noise level today is fierce. There are just too many "me-too" products and too many "me-too" companies vying for the mind of the prospect. Getting noticed is getting tougher.

5. Do we have the guts to stick with one consistent positioning concept?

With the noise level out there, a company has to be bold enough and consistent enough to cut through.

The first step in a positioning program normally entails running fewer programs, but stronger ones. This sounds simple, but actually runs counter to what usually happens as corporations get larger. They normally run more programs, but weaker ones. It's this fragmentation that can make many large advertising budgets just about invisible in today's media storm.

6. Does our creative approach match our positioning strategy?

Creative people often resist positioning thinking because they believe it restricts their creativity. And it does. But creativity isn't the objective in the seventies. Even "communications" itself isn't the objective.

The name of the marketing game in the seventies is "positioning." And only the better players will survive.

RETROSPECTIVE COMMENTARY

THE POSITIONING ERA: A VIEW TEN YEARS LATER

If one word could be said to have marked the course of advertising in the decade of the '70s it is the word "positioning." Positioning has become the buzzword of advertising and marketing people, not only in this country, but around the world.

It was just 10 years ago that the word and the concept were introduced for the first time to the advertising community in the pages of *Industrial Marketing* and *Advertising Age.*

The article, written by Jack Trout, named names and made predictions, all based on the "rules" of a game Jack called positioning.

On positioning's 10th anniversary, it might be interesting to look back at that 1969 article and see what changes have taken place.

Today's marketplace is no longer responsive to strategies that worked in the past. There are just too many products, too many companies and too much marketing noise. We have become an overcommunicated society. (1969)

The question most frequently asked us is "why"? Why do we need a new approach to advertising and marketing?

The answer today is the same as it was then. We have become an overcommunicated society. With only 5% of the world's population, America consumes 57% of the world's advertising output. The per capita consumption of advertising in the U.S. today is about $200 a year.

If you spend $1,000,000 a year on advertising, you are bombarding the average consumer with less than ½¢ of advertising, spread out over 365 days—a consumer who is already exposed to $200 worth of advertising from other companies.

In our overcommunicated society, to talk about the "impact" of advertising is to seriously overstate the potential effectiveness of your messages. It's an egocentric view that bears no relationship to the realities of the marketplace itself.

In the communication jungle out there, the only hope to score big is to be selective, to concentrate on narrow targets, to practice segmentation. In a word, "positioning" is still the name of the game today.

The mind, as a defense against the volume of today's communications, screens and rejects much of the information offered it. In general, the mind accepts only that which matches prior knowledge or experience. (1969)

Millions of dollars have been wasted trying to change minds with advertising. Once a mind is made up, it's almost impossible to change it. Certainly not with a weak force like advertising.

The average person can tolerate being told something about which he or she knows nothing. (This is why "news" is an effective advertising approach.) But the average person can't tolerate being told he or she is "wrong." Mind-changing is the road to advertising disaster.

Back in 1969, Jack used the computer industry as an example of the folly of trying to change minds.

Company after company tried to tell people its computers were "better" than IBM's. Yet that doesn't "compute" in the prospect's mind. "If you're so smart," says the prospect, "how come you're not rich like IBM?"

The computer "position" in the minds of most people is filled with the name of a company called "IBM." For a competitive computer manufacturer to obtain a favorable position in the prospect's mind, he or she must somehow relate the company to IBM's position.

In other words, don't try to change the prospect's mind at all. Accept what's up there and work around it. It's the only hope in today's overcommunicated society.

Positioning is a game where the competitor's image is just as important as your own. Sometimes more important. (1969)

The classic example is the famous Avis campaign.

"Avis is only No. 2 in rent-a-cars. So why go with us? We try harder." This program was extremely successful for Avis until corporate egos got in the way. Then the company launched a campaign which said "Avis is going to be No. 1."

No way.

Be honest. In the last 15 years, Avis has run many different advertising campaigns. "The wizard of Avis." "You don't have to run through airports." Etc. But what is the single theme that leaps into your mind when someone mentions Avis?

Of course, "Avis is only No. 2., etc." Yet Avis in the last few years has consistently ignored this No. 2 concept.

We call this the "F.W.M.T.S." trap. (Forgot What Made Them Successful.)

If you want to be successful today, you can't ignore the competitor's position. Nor can you walk away from your own. In the immortal words of Woody Allen, "Play it where it lies."

Another advertiser that fell into the F.W.M.T.S. trap is Seven-Up. With the "Uncola" campaign, the company successfully positioned its 7UP drink as an alternative to Coke and Pepsi. (Almost two-thirds of all the soft drinks consumed in the U.S. are cola drinks.)

But the current campaign says, "America is turning 7UP." America is doing no such thing. Seven-Up is advertising its aspirations. No different conceptually than the "Avis is going to be No. 1" campaign. And no more effective.

In the positioning era, the name of your company or product is becoming more and more important. (1969)

No aspect of positioning has proved as controversial as the "importance of the name."

Our 1969 example was Eastern Airlines. Among the four largest domestic airlines, Eastern consistently ranks at the bottom on passenger surveys.

Why? Eastern has a "regional" name that puts them in a different category than the big nationwide carriers (American, United, Trans World Airlines). The name Eastern puts the airline in the same category with Southern, North Central, Piedmont, Allegheny. The regional airline category.

After 10 years of effort, Eastern still ranks at the bottom of the big four.

You see what you expect to see. The passenger who has a bad experience on American or United says, "It was just one of those things." An exception to the good service he or she was expecting.

The passenger who has a bad experience on Eastern says, "It's that darn Eastern Airlines again." A continuation of the bad service he or she was expecting.

One prime objective of all advertising is to heighten expectations. To create the illusion that the product or service will perform the miracles you expect. And presto, it does.

Recently, Allegheny Airlines has seen the light. The new name: USAir. Now watch them take off.

Yes, but that's consumer advertising and the industrial customer buys on reason, not emotion. On logic and facts.

As IBM's competitors. Or Xerox's or General Electric's.

Especially for high technology, high visibility products like computers and copiers, the average industrial customer tends to be far more emotional than your average Charmin-squeezing housewife. (Who, more often than not, is downright practical.)

Industrial customers are also cursed by a "play it safe" attitude.

You can't blame them. No housewife ever got fired for buying the wrong brand of coffee. But plenty of industrial buyers have been in deep trouble over a high-technology buy that went sour. (Babcock & Wilcox will have trouble pushing its nuclear power plants in the future no matter how "superior" its specs are.)

The trend in industrial products is toward more sophistication, more use of integrated circuits, fiber optics, lasers, etc. So you can expect the industrial buyer to buy more on feelings, hunches and especially reputation. And less on objective product comparisons.

Which is why "factual expository copy" is getting less important in industrial advertising and "positioning" more important.

Your program has to go beyond just establishing a name. Too many programs start there and end there. To secure a worthwhile position for a corporate name, you need a thought to go with it. (1969)

Ten years ago, the Olin campaign was getting a lot of creative kudos. And the ads were beautifully done. But what is Olin? What is its position?

Even today, these questions have no clear-cut answer in the mind of the prospect.

Line Extension Trap

You can't hang a company on a name. You need an idea. Of all the positioning concepts suggested by the 1969 article, this one has proved to be the most useful. It led directly to what we call "the line extension trap."

When the marketing history of the '70s is written, the single most significant trend will have to be "line extension." Line extension has swept through the marketing community like Sherman through Georgia. And for some very sound reasons.

Logic is on the side of line extension. Arguments of economics. Trade acceptance. Customer acceptance. Lower advertising costs. Increased income. Reduced costs. The corporate image.

As we said, logic is on the side of line extension. Truth, unfortunately, is not. The paradox of marketing is that conventional wisdom is almost always wrong.

Xerox went out and bought a computer company with a perfectly good name. Scientific Data Systems.

And what was the first thing they did? They changed the name to Xerox Data Systems. Then they ran an ad that said, "This Xerox machine can't make a copy."

Any Xerox machine that couldn't make a copy was headed for trouble, believe us.

When Xerox folded their computer operations, it cost another $84,000,000 to sweep up the mess.

Singer went out and did the same thing with the old, respected Friden name. One of their introductory ads said, "Singer Business Machines introduces Touch & Know."

Get it? Touch and know, touch and sew.

This is the ultimate positioning mistake. To try to transfer a generic brand name to a different product sold to a different market. And then, to top it all off, to knock off your own sewing machine slogan.

Touch and Go would have been more appropriate. When they folded this operation, Singer set a record. They recorded one of the largest one quarter write-offs ever reported by any company anywhere in the world—$341,000,000.

If your corporate name is inappropriate for the new product you intend to market, create a new one. And a new position.

One thing that's worse than a 'just a name' program is one without a name. That sounds like it could never happen, doesn't it? Well, it does when companies use initials instead of a name. (1969)

This idea was later developed into what we call "The no-name trap." Of all the positioning concepts outlined back in 1969, this one generated the most instant acceptance. The superiority of a name over a meaningless set of initials could generally be documented by market research.

The initialitus that struck American business in the late '60s and early '70s abated. Some companies even went back to their original names.

A company has no hope to make progress head-on against the position that
IBM has established. (1969)

This is perhaps the most quoted sentence from the original article—as true
today as it was then.

IBM has an overwhelming position in the broad middle range of computers.
So, how do you compete against IBM in computers? The 1969 article had a suggestion on how to do it.

It's almost impossible to dislodge a strongly dug-in leader who owns the high
ground. You're a lot better off to open up a new front or position—that is, unless
you enjoy being shot-up. (1969)

A New Front

The big computer successes in the '70s were the companies that avoided going
head-to-head with IBM—Digital Equipment Corp. and Data General, in particular,
at the low end of the market.

Even Apple and Radio Shack have done profitable computer business, in the
home market.

This "new front" idea has been developed in our marketing warfare seminars
into a concept called "flanking warfare." You avoid the competitor's high ground
by outflanking them.

Another problem that occurs fairly often is represented by the one B.F. Goodrich
faces. What do you do when your name [Goodrich] is similar to the name of a
larger company in the same field [Goodyear]? (1969)

Goodrich has problems. Our research indicates that they could reinvent
the wheel and Goodyear would get most of the credit. If ever a company could
benefit from a name change, they're one. (1969)

In 1968, Goodyear had sales of $2,926,000,000 while B.F. Goodrich's sales
were $1,340,000,000. A ratio of 2.2 to 1.

Ten years later, in 1978, Goodyear had sales of $7,489,000,000 while B.F.
Goodrich had sales of $2,594,000,000. A ratio of 2.9 to 1.

So the rich get richer. Fair enough.

But what is odd is that the loser's advertising continues to get all the publicity.
"We're the other guys" got a lot of favorable attention in the press. But not a
lot of favorable attention from the tire-buying public.

The Real Reckoning

But what really rattled the cages of the Madison Ave. mavens was positioning's
implied attack on "creativity."

Even though creativity was not mentioned in the 1969 article, we didn't hesitate to attack it later on. By 1972, we were saying, "Creativity is dead. The name
of the advertising game in the '70s is positioning."

In truth, the decade of the '70s might well be characterized as a "return to reality." White knights and black eyepatches gave way to such positioning concepts as Lite Beer's "Everything you've always wanted in a great beer. And less."

Poetic? Yes. Artful? Yes. But also a straightforward, clearly defined explanation of the basic positioning premise.

On the occasion of positioning's 10th anniversary, it might be appropriate to ask, where do we go from here?

If creativity belonged to the '60s and positioning to the '70s, where will we be in the '80s?

Would you believe us if we told you in the next decade we will be burying the marketing concept?

Probably not, but we'll tell you anyway.

For at least 50 years now, astute advertising people have preached the marketing gospel. "The customer is king," said the marketing moguls. Over and over again, they used their wondrous presentations to warn top management that to be "production" oriented instead of "customer" oriented was to flirt with disaster.

But it's beginning to look like "King Customer" is dead. And that they're selling a corpse to their management.

Plenty of companies who have dutifully followed their marketing experts have seen millions of dollars disappear in valiant but disastrous customer-oriented efforts.

Who do you suppose masterminded those classic positioning mistakes? Not amateurs, but full-fledged marketing professionals with briefcases full of credentials.

General Electric in computers. Singer in business machines. Sara Lee in frozen dinners.

Of course, these marketing executives had excuses. "Product problems." "Not enough capital." Or the ever popular, "Not enough distribution" were often cited to explain these failures.

Can it be that marketing, itself, is the problem?

Many managers are beginning to realize that something is wrong—that the traditional definition of marketing (to be customer-oriented) is becoming an obsolete concept.

A New Perspective

To get a better perspective of the situation, you have to go back to the '20s, when industry started its dramatic march forward. It was then that business first became production oriented. This was the heyday of Henry Ford and his Model T.

You could have any color you wanted as long as it was black. Mr. Ford was more interested in keeping his production lines rolling (and his prices down) than in keeping his customers satisfied.

You might think that advertising was an unnecessary luxury in a production-oriented economy. Quite the contrary.

Advertising was an important ingredient in the scheme of things. Advertising's first commandment was "Mass advertising creates mass demand which makes mass production possible."

Neat. Except that General Motors tooled up its production lines to please its prospects rather than its production engineers and quickly grabbed the sales leadership from Ford.

Things haven't been the same since.

In the aftermath of World War II, business became customer-oriented with a vengeance.

The marketing man was in charge, no doubt about it, and his prime minister was marketing research.

But today, every company has become marketing oriented. Knowing what the customer wants isn't too helpful if a dozen other companies are already serving his or her wants.

American Motor's problem is not the customer. American Motor's problem is General Motors, Ford and Chrysler.

To be successful today, a company must be "competitor" oriented. It must look for weak points in the positions of its competitors and then launch marketing attacks against those weak points. For example, while others were losing millions in the computer business, DEC was making millions by exploiting IBM's weakness in small computers.

Similarly, Savin established a successful beachhead in small, inexpensive copiers. A weak point in the Xerox lineup.

And from out of nowhere came a product called Bubble Yum to take a big bite out of the bubble gum market. By exploiting the competitions' weakness of being hard to chew, they over-ran some strongly entrenched brands that had been around for years.

There are those who would say that competitors are always considered in a well-thought-out marketing plan. Indeed they are. Usually towards the back of the book under a heading entitled "Competitive Evaluation." Almost as an afterthought.

Upfront with prominence is the major part of the plan. The details of marketplace, the various demographic segments and a myriad of "customer" research statistics carefully gleaned from endless focus groups, test panels, concept and market tests.

The Battle Plan

The future marketing plan won't look like this. In fact, it won't be called a marketing plan at all. But a competitive plan, or a battle plan.

In the battle plan of the future, many more pages will be dedicated to the competition. The plan will carefully dissect each participant in the marketplace. It will develop a list of competitive strengths and weaknesses as well as a plan of action to either exploit or defend against them.

There might even come a day when this plan will contain a dossier on each of the competitors' key management people which will include their favorite tactics and style of operation. (Not unlike those Germans kept on the Allied commanders in World War II.)

And we're not talking about the distant future. Already the first signs of this trend are starting to appear in the professional journals.

In the August, 1978, issue of *Management Review,* is a report entitled, "Customer or competitor: Which guideline for marketing?" In the article, Alfred R. Oxenfeldt and William L. Moore spell out six "weaknesses" that can make a firm vulnerable to an attack from a competitor. The article's basic premise was that switching to a competitor orientation can provide a better payoff.

In the August, 1978, issue of *Business Horizons,* William S. Sachs and George Benson state the issue more directly: "Is it time to discard the marketing concept?"

These articles point out that a small, but growing, number of experts believe that the customer isn't what he or she used to be.

Confusion has set in. In many categories, customers no longer perceive any large differences in products. Thus brand choice will not be based on a rational search of all brands in the category but on a brand that was previously tried. Or the leader. Or the one positioned to the prospect's segment.

Once buying patterns are established, it has become more and more difficult to change them. The customer doesn't really want to accept any more information on a category that he or she has already cataloged in the mind. No matter how dramatically or how creatively this information is presented.

What does all this portend for the marketing people of the '80s? Or whatever they are going to be called.

In simple terms, it means that they have to be prepared to wage marketing warfare. Successful marketing campaigns will have to be planned like military campaigns.

Strategic planning will become more and more important. Companies will have to learn how to attack, defend and flank their competition. And when to resort to guerrilla warfare.

They will need better intelligence on how to anticipate competitive moves.

On the personal level, successful marketing people will have to exhibit many of the same virtues that make a great general—courage, boldness, loyalty and perseverance.

The winners in the marketing battles of the future will be those men and women who have best learned the lessons of military history—the marketing people who have learned to plan like Alexander the Great, maneuver like Napoleon Bonaparte and fight like George S. Patton.

They will also be the marketing people who know their competitors better than they know their own customers.

SOME SUGGESTIONS FOR FURTHER READING

Boyd, H. W. Jr., Ray, M. L. and Strong, E. C. (1972), "An Attitudinal Framework for Advertising Strategy," *Journal of Marketing,* vol. 36, published by the American Marketing Association, 27–33.

Dhalla, N. K. (1978), "Assessing the Long-term Value of Advertising," *Harvard Business Review* (January–February), 87–95.

Ehrenberg, A. S. C. (1974), "Repetitive Advertising in the Consumer," *Journal of Advertising Research* (April), 140–146.

Greenland, L. (1972), "Is This the Era of Positioning?" *Advertising Age* (May 29).

30 / THE CHANGING ROLE OF THE PRODUCT MANAGER IN CONSUMER GOODS COMPANIES / Victor P. Buell

What the proper role of the product or brand manager should be remains a troublesome question for the managements of consumer goods companies. It is particularly a problem for packaged goods producers, who are the most frequent users of this organizational device.

The role of the product manager has undergone several changes since the product management system was first introduced. That these changes have not produced entirely satisfactory results is evident in the continuing public debate on this topic. Titles of selected articles and papers illustrate the situation:

The Product Manager System Is In Trouble[1]
Has the Product Manager Failed? Or the Folly of Imitation[2]
Product Management—Vision Unfulfilled [3]
Brand Manager VS Creative Man: The Clash of Two Cultures[4]
Brand Manager VS Advertising Director—Must One of Them Go? [5]
Product Managers and Advertising—A Study of Conflict, Inexperience and Opportunity.[6]

The purpose of this article is to review the changes that have occurred in the product management form of organization since its introduction, to explore the reasons behind the continuing controversy, and to examine current changes in management thinking and their implications for the future. To this end, the author uses material from his recent study of several leading consumer goods manufacturers and major advertising agencies.

THE STUDY: BACKGROUND AND APPROACH

Much of the controversy has centered on the degree of control the product manager exercises over advertising. Under a grant from the Association of National Advertisers (ANA), the author studied the advertising decision-making process in companies with major advertising expenditures.[7] Although its overall purpose was broader, the study provided the opportunity to explore management attitudes

Victor Buell, "The Changing Role of the Product Manager in Consumer Goods Companies," *Journal of Marketing*, Vol. 39 (July 1975), pp. 3–11. Published by the American Marketing Association. Reprinted by permission of the publisher.
Victor Buell is professor of Marketing at the University of Massachusetts. He previously worked for American Standard, Archer Daniels Midland, and Hoover Company. He is a past president of the American Marketing Association.

toward product management and to gather information on the restructuring this system currently is undergoing.

In-depth interviews were held during the summer and fall of 1972 with 63 executives in 20 leading companies which represented ten consumer industry classifications plus one miscellaneous category. Extensive interviews were also held with 23 executives in ten major advertising agencies.

Sixteen of the companies produced packaged goods primarily and four produced consumer durables primarily. Product management was the predominant form of marketing organization in fifteen of the companies; a functional form predominated in five. Some of the companies used one organizational form in some divisions and the other form in other divisions.

Survey Sample

The combined domestic sales of the 20 companies surveyed exceeded $60 billion, and their combined advertising expenditures were over $1.5 billion. Seventeen were among the 50 largest advertisers and 10 ranked among the top 20. The primary industry classifications of the consumer packaged goods companies included food; drugs and cosmetics; soaps, cleansers, and allied products; soft drinks; tobacco; paper; liquor; and one miscellaneous category. The consumer durable goods companies fell under the industry classifications of electric appliances, automobiles, and building products.

Participant companies were selected with the assistance of the Management Policy Committee of the Association of National Advertisers. Selection criteria included: (1) company commitment to a large advertising budget, (2) recognized leadership position in the company's industry, (3) management willingness to participate, and (4) multiple industry representation. Preference was given to companies that had extensive experience with product managers. Advertising agencies were selected from among leading agencies that served one or more of the 20 manufacturing companies. To encourage participation and frank discussion, participants were assured that neither companies nor individuals would be identified in the report.

Thirty-one corporate executives were interviewed, including chairmen, presidents, executive and group vice-presidents, and staff vice-presidents. Positions occupied by the 32 divisional executives interviewed included presidents, marketing vice-presidents, directors of marketing or advertising, directors of brand management, and group product managers.

The 10 advertising agencies in the study were among the nation's 20 largest and had combined U.S. billings in excess of $2 billion. Agency executives interviewed included chairmen, presidents, executive and senior vice-presidents, and vice-presidents.

Data Collection Method

All interviews were conducted by the author. Interviews were open-ended and ranged in length from one to three hours. Policies, procedures, and files were made freely available. Interviews with agency executives provided cross-checks on information developed with their clients.

The purpose of the study was to gain understanding of the reasons behind advertising and marketing management practices rather than duplicate the quantitative data developed by the more commonly used mail questionnaire. Because of the qualitative nature of the study, findings are reported primarily as the author's interpretations of prevailing management practices, attitudes, and intentions rather than in the form of statistical summaries. The findings have been reported to the participating executives and have been discussed in depth with several of them.

While the study provides the principal data source for this article, conclusions are based also on interviews with executives during other research projects by the author, reviews of product management literature, and recent reports of mail surveys.

Because of the selective sample, the findings are not representative of all companies. The findings are important in that they represent managerial viewpoints in consumer goods companies with leadership positions, most of whom employ large numbers of product managers.

HISTORICAL DEVELOPMENTS

The product management system, although introduced nearly 50 years ago, did not come into general use until the 1950s. The Association of National Advertisers, in a recent study among its members, found that the following percentages of participating companies used product managers: packaged goods—85% (93% of those with annual advertising expenditures exceeding $10 million); other consumer goods —34%; industrial goods—55%.[8]

Product management is a response to the organizational problem of providing sufficient management attention to individual products and brands when there are too many for any one executive to coordinate effectively all of the aspects of the marketing mix. Companies, or divisions of companies, with a limited line of products normally follow a functional plan of organization wherein departments such as sales, advertising and sales promotion, marketing research, product planning, and customer service report to a common marketing executive. When shifting from this purely functional organization, product managers are added to assist the chief marketing executive by assuming the planning and coordination for individual products or product lines.

Although the product manager has made possible greater management concentration by product, the position also has created new problems. Responsibility often has been assigned to the product manager for achievement of goals such as sales volume, share of market, and even profit in some cases; yet the product manager has no line authority over the functional departments that execute his plans.

Shift of Advertising Responsibility to the Product Manager

A key change in the original concept was made when companies shifted the management of advertising from the advertising manager to the product manager. In leading packaged goods companies that currently use product managers, one rarely finds an advertising department on the organization chart. If one is there, it is usually at the group or corporate level, where it provides services common to several divisions, such as media planning and coordinating media purchases.

The reasons for phasing out the separate advertising function were: (a) to reduce costs, which rose as the advertising department expanded to manage the advertising for increasing numbers of products and brands; and (b) to give the product manager more control over execution of a major marketing function. Such a move was possible because the advertising agency was available to develop and place advertising.

Figures 1 and 2 provide examples of typical functional and product management organizations. While details may vary from company to company, these charts reflect the main differences that exist between the two organizational forms in the companies studied by the author.

Companies Assume the Planning Function

Concurrent with the growth of the product management function, companies began to assume the marketing planning and service functions—with the exception of creative and media—that had been performed for them by their advertising agencies.

As marketing grew in sophistication during the 1950s, much of the know-how was centered in the agencies. Gradually, however, companies expanded their own

Figure 1. Functional marketing organization

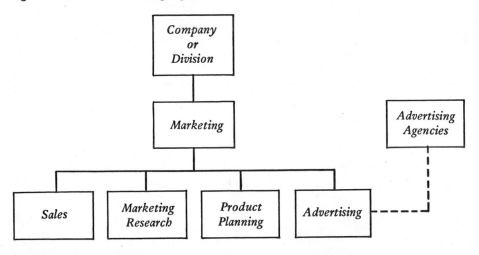

Figure 2. Product management organization

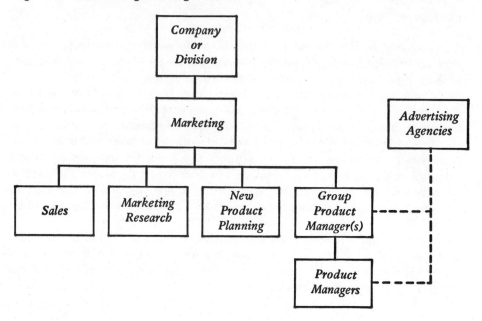

supporting service functions and the responsibility for initiating marketing plans became a key function of the product manager. This change has been made with little criticism. Agencies have accepted the idea that marketing planning should originate within the company, and they are aware of the growing effectiveness of the product manager as a planner.

Increases in Intervening Management Levels

As companies grow, the product manager becomes further removed from the real decision-making levels of management. When products were fewer in number product managers reported directly to higher-level executives, who had the authority to make broad decisions and implement programs. As product lines proliferated, and the numbers of product managers grew correspondingly, intervening levels of supervision became necessary. In large companies today, product managers may be anywhere from two to four levels below the executive who has the real decision-making authority and the clout to see that plans are carried out.

Due to rapid growth, companies also have shifted to filling product manager positions with younger, less experienced people. This relative inexperience, plus separation from the key decision maker, has increased management concern over the degree of authority that should be delegated to the product manager. These concerns are particularly strong with respect to advertising because of the magnitude of advertising costs and the importance of advertising to product success.

Continued Use of Functional Organization

The ANA study of its members found that 34% of the participating larger consumer durable goods companies used product managers, as compared with 85% of the packaged goods companies. Why do some companies stay with the functional form?

Pearson and Wilson believe there may be good reasons why a company should prefer the functional organization.[9] In fact, they think some companies have made a mistake in switching to product management before it was really necessary. They maintain that companies with a line of similar products, with one dominant product line, or with several large product lines (sufficient to support divisionalization) might be better off avoiding product management. It was not long after Pearson left McKinsey & Co. to become president of PepsiCo that the Pepsi-Cola division did away with product managers.[10] This division sells a related line of soft drinks with one dominant product—Pepsi-Cola.

Three of the consumer durable goods companies interviewed by the author had functional marketing setups. The major appliance group of an electrical company and the major division of an automotive manufacturer each had relatively few products although they accounted for large dollar sales. Both companies preferred to use advertising to build the overall brand name in addition to promoting individual products; they felt they could achieve better control through the functional advertising manager. The third company, a manufacturer of building products, organized its product divisions by markets and channels. Historically, the corporate advertising department has supervised the development of advertising and sales promotion for the various market sales managers, who appear to prefer this arrangement.

While there are good reasons why many companies do not use product management, there appears to be no significant defection by current users, as was implied in the article that featured the PepsiCo story.[11] Of the 211 companies surveyed by the ANA, 5% had adopted product management during the preceding three years, as compared with 1% who had abandoned it.[12] Clewett and Stasch, in a survey of 160 product managers and other marketing executives, found less than 1% who felt that product management was likely to be discontinued in their divisions.[13] In the author's study, none of the fifteen companies that used product management planned to change.

No doubt some companies will shift from product management from time to time for sound organizational reasons or out of sheer frustration. But there is no evidence of a trend in this direction. If a trend exists it would appear to be in the direction of continued adoption of product management.

CURRENT MANAGEMENT ATTITUDES

Executives interviewed by the author were concerned about the product management system but were committed to making it work better. Their attitudes appeared to be changing with respect to the question of the product manager's responsibility and authority and his role in advertising. They also expressed concern over the scarcity of advertising specialists within their companies.

Disaffection with the "Little President" Concept

Almost all of the executives interviewed recognized that the earlier concept of the product manager as a "little president" or "little general manager," with profit responsibility, was unrealistic. As the manager of a paper products company said:

We've gotten away from the concept of the guy who runs his own little company. We want our product managers to be profit conscious, but what we're really talking about is sales volume.

Remnants of the concept persist, however, as illustrated by excerpts from two recruiting brochures. The brochure of a household products company states:

The Product Manager has responsibility for his brand. He is not only responsible for its management, he is accountable for its overall performance. . . . The Product Manager is not just a marketing manager, but in many respects a general manager of a good size business.

When this statement was pointed out to an executive of this company the author was told that it no longer represents management opinion; that, in fact, the company's product managers have no decision-making authority.

The brochure of a food company, after explaining the product manager's role in developing objectives and strategies, says: "The Product Manager is responsible for the execution and performance of the brands entrusted to him."

In describing the position, the marketing director of another food company probably came closest to prevailing management attitudes when he avoided mentioning responsibility for execution or performance:

Our product manager's job is planning—objectives and strategy—monitoring progress, coordinating budget development and control, and working with other departments—Home Economics and Manufacturing, for example—on product cost and quality.

Clarifying the Advertising Role

Packaged goods executives pretty much agree that the typical product manager has insufficient training, experience, or skill to be entrusted with important creative decisions. They tend to share the view of the agency vice-president who told the author: "Advertising is too important a decision to be left in the hands of a product manager. His role should be planning and coordination—not advertising approval."

Agency critics complain that because of his inexperience the product manager is too cautious and too meticulous in judging creative work; he delays the development process and causes dilution of creative copy by requiring repeated rework;

and, to compensate for his insecurity, he relies too heavily on copy testing, which normally produces inconclusive data. Company executives agree. All want the product manager involved in advertising decision making, but they are developing procedures that get agency recommendations up the line to the final decision maker as quickly as possible. Agencies, it should be noted, are reassigning responsibility for client contact to higher management levels to correspond with the client management levels making advertising decisions.

Current top management attitudes are reflected in the following comments. The president of a personal products company said:

I want the best people in a profit center working on, and approving, marketing decisions. We try to set the atmosphere and tone so that our brand manager feels important, yet knows that advertising is too important to be decided at the bottom level.

The executive vice-president of a drug products company explained his company's position this way:

We give much authority to the product manager other than the copy side— sales promotion, for example. But we let him know he is not to be the final authority on advertising. We say the person who knows the most about advertising should make the ultimate decision.

Companies, however, do make a distinction between *major* and *minor* advertising decisions. Figure 3 indicates the differences in executive levels that deal with decisions of varying importance. Major decisions may include almost anything to do with an important product or, for less important products, they may involve only significant matters, such as a change in strategy. The author's research showed that advertising decisions considered to be major were made most frequently at the division manager or division marketing manager levels, with some going to the corporate level. None of the companies believed *major* creative-type advertising decisions were made by the product manager. Decisions considered minor, on the other hand, most frequently were made at the product manager and division middle management (group product manager) levels. Understanding this distinction may help to clarify the sometimes confusing results of those mail surveys that indicate that the product manager makes advertising decisions: he does make some decisions, but usually not the major ones.

Considering the past sharp criticisms by agency executives it is worth noting that these complaints have been directed primarily at the product manager's role in the advertising approval process. In contrast, they agree with his role as the authoritative source of information and as marketing planner. An agency vice-president who works with both functional and product management organizations volunteered this comment:

I would rather work with a product manager than with an advertising manager. The product manager has all the information, although he may be unaware of the broader strategies. But in the vertical organization, each person has only a part of the information we require.

Figure 3. Where advertising companies say creative decisions are made

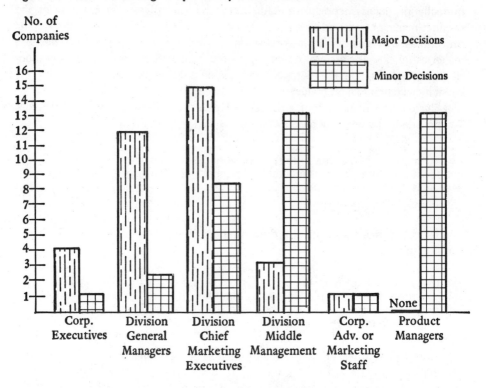

Note: The figures represented by the bars total more than the number of companies because decisions may be made jointly by two or more executives, decisions may be made by one executive in the absence of another, or the decision level may vary by degree of importance within the Major or Minor categories. *Source*: Adapted from Victor P. Buell, *Changing Practices in Advertising Decision-Making and Control* (New York: Association of National Advertisers, 1973), p. 49.

Need for the Advertising Specialist

After several years of operating without advertising departments, many company executives now wonder whether they have any real advertising expertise left in-house. The normal promotion route provides added experience in judging ad' vertising, and one learns from his mistakes and successes. But experience does not necessarily develop the kind of expertise in judging creative work that comes from long and intensive involvement in the development of advertising by talented people. Some marketing executives seem to have better creative judgment than others, but promotion up the line from product manager does not automatically guarantee success in this area.

To replace the skills that were lost with the demise of the advertising department, three companies have created a new position, staff advertising director, to provide creative counsel to product managers and others concerned with advertising decisions. Whereas the former advertising manager made the advertising decision, the new advertising director provides counsel to those charged with the decision-making responsibility.

Where this position has been introduced, it has usually been placed within the division marketing management organization. Executives report that product and other managers exhibit reluctance to avail themselves of staff counsel when it is located in corporate headquarters.

How Much Authority?

The persistent, unresolved question puzzling management is how much and what kind of authority the product manager needs. Luck, in discussing the many functional areas with which the product manager must interact, states: "Product managers are seriously hampered by ambiguity of authority in the execution of their plans and decisions. . . ." [14]

A common management attitude was expressed by the group vice-president of a liquor company, who said: "The brand manager's authority is the authority of his influence and knowledge." While true as far as it goes, this conclusion seems oversimplified. Several studies bear on the issue.

Lucas, in a mail survey of 60 product managers, found that four in five believed their degree of control over the decision areas of advertising, marketing research, and market testing was "adequate for their assigned responsibilities." [15] Smaller proportions reported that they had adequate control over the personal selling, production, and distribution functions and in the areas of legal affairs, advertising expenditures, and pricing. That these product managers did not consider their responsibilities insignificant is evident in the fact that two-thirds felt that they had major, or even 100%, responsibility for product profit.

The mail survey of 160 executives, primarily product managers and group product managers, conducted by Clewett and Stasch found product managers to be "less than major participants" in the decision areas of advertising, product, packaging, pricing, and personal selling. [16] They were reported to be "major participants" in marketing research and promotion. When tasks, as opposed to decision making, were considered this study reported that product managers had a "major role" in planning, budgeting, scheduling, communicating plans and maintaining enthusiasm for them, monitoring progress, revising plans, and reporting performance. The two studies appear to disagree only in the area of advertising decision authority.

Gemmill and Wileman report that in the absence of direct authority, product managers influence action by using reward power, coercive power, expert power, and referent (i.e., personal relationships) power. [17] They found that product managers who primarily employed expert/referent power were the most effective.

Dietz has identified at least two types of product managers: the *brand coordinator*, who has no entrepreneurial responsibility; and the *brand champion*, who has responsibility for making entrepreneurial recommendations. [18] Common to both types, he says, are the responsibilities for planning, securing approval of plans, coordinating the execution of plans by functional departments, and evaluating the results of the actions taken. Dietz suggests that the brand coordinator needs little authority to fulfill his responsibility but that the more aggressive brand champion reaches out for authority in frustration over the slowness with which higher levels of management arrive at decisions.

As mentioned earlier, the author's findings indicate that the product manager's authority varies with the relative importance of the decision and that his influence varies with his experience and competence. As a division president in a food products company said:

The product manager system works well for us, but we don't have a set way of working with every product manager. Some are more experienced and some are more aggressive than others.

Consensus appears to exist with respect to the product manager's responsibility for planning, coordinating, and evaluating. Differences continue with respect to the questions of authority over execution and the authority to make decisions. The present answer for the last two would seem to be "it all depends."

As a result of these changing management attitudes, all companies interviewed indicated that they had made, or were making, changes in their product manager setups with respect to functions, authority, management decision-making levels, staffing, or length of time in the job. Eight indicated that they were acting in all of these areas.

Management accepts the system but believes it needs improvement. The president of a food company expressed the viewpoint of many when he commented: "There is nothing fundamentally wrong with the product manager system, but I don't think we operate it as well as we should."

Emphasizing Position Strengths—Deemphasizing Weaknesses

In redefining the job, management is emphasizing the functions that product managers can perform well and deemphasizing those aspects of the position with inherent weaknesses. Emphasis is being placed on the role of the product manager as the gatherer and synthesizer of all information about the product and its markets, as the developer of plans, as the communicator of approved plans, and as the monitor of performance. Management expects the product manager to have a deep personal commitment to the success of his product, while they recognize that he alone cannot be held responsible for achievement of sales and profits. Ultimate responsibility, they believe, must rest with the executive in a position to control all marketing activities.

The role of the product manager as decision maker is being deemphasized. The current trend is for decision-making authority to be given in accordance with the importance of the decision area and to vary with the experience and competence of the individual product manager. The product manager will remain involved with the decision-making process, but he will be encouraged to bring key decisions to his manager's attention. As one marketing director said, "The brand manager's job is to get good decisions made irrespective of who makes them."

Controlling Resource Allocation at Higher Levels

Management not only wants decisions made where the most competence exists, but it also recognizes the need to control resource allocations among products. The president of a liquor company put it this way: "Our brand managers make many decisions but they don't make the key ones. Someone at a higher level must look at the broad allocation of expenditures."

Obviously, the product manager is not in a position to see the overall picture. The more effective an individual product manager is, the better job he may do in obtaining a disproportionate share of functional resources. It is higher management's job to see that money and other resources are allocated on the basis of profit potential.

The idea that decision making should be moved up the line rather than down the line does not sit well with long-term advocates of decentralized management. However, most executives interviewed seemed to have come to terms with this issue. They recognized that on matters that have a major impact on profit, decisions should be made where all the necessary information is available and where competence exists to make the best judgment. This means that different decisions will be made at different levels, but it does not preclude participation by the product manager, who should have the most information about his product and market. Exceptions to this philosophy were found at the corporate level in three companies. Checks at the division levels in these companies indicate, however, that major advertising decisions were, in fact, being made at the marketing vice-president or division president levels.

Staffing with Marketing Experience

During the 1960s and early 1970s, a number of companies sought out the recent MBA graduate to fill the assistant product manager position. The graduate schools provided a selective recruiting source of people with broad management training. Though not unhappy with the quality of these recruits, managements have found that their limited training in marketing (particularly in advertising) and the usual absence of marketing experience are drawbacks for product management. They complain, also, that higher competitive compensation levels for the MBA tend to upset established wage patterns.

With the exception of two major packaged goods producers, the companies interviewed had reduced their reliance on the graduate business school as a primary recruiting source for product management. Five had eliminated this source entirely. They were recruiting instead from advertising agencies and other companies and were making internal transfers from sales, marketing research, and the like, in order to obtain people with marketing experience. Some of these people may already have their MBA degree, which is considered a plus, but the emphasis is being placed on marketing experience.

Slowing Job Turnover

Simultaneously, eight of the companies were upgrading the position and attempting to hold incumbents in the job for longer periods. This has not been easy, since the job attracts high-potential, well-motivated individuals who consider product management a stepping stone to higher management. To attract and hold good people, companies in the past have advanced them from assistant to associate to product manager to group product manager fairly rapidly. Switching to different product groups often occurred along the way.

This "churning" is felt to be undesirable. Incumbents do not stay with a product long enough to develop the desired product and market expertise. Furthermore, short-term assignments do not encourage the long-range planning that can enhance market position. Through different hiring practices and by providing incentives to remain with a product longer, the eight companies hope to increase product manager effectiveness. Other managements that would like to increase longevity in the job explain that they have been unable to do so because of rapid company growth.

FUTURE IMPLICATIONS

In summary, over the years the product manager system has undergone a number of changes and it is still in the process of change. Because the position corresponds to none of the classic line, staff, or functional positions it has never fit neatly into traditional organizational structure. Yet for companies with many products it affords a better means of product-by-product management concentration than does functional organization. For this reason—and despite its acknowledged problems—most companies that are using the product management system plan to stay with it.

It is too early to tell whether the current trend to emphasize planning and coordination, and deemphasize decision making, will resolve the major problems. The same can be said for attempts to improve staffing and to lengthen incumbent tenure.

In some ways the product manager system appears to be in tune with current organizational behavior theory, with its emphasis on group cooperation and participative decision making and its deemphasis of hierarchical authority patterns. The author found, for example, that those organizations with the longest product management experience appeared to be most happy with it, apparently because people throughout these organizations better understand the system. People seem to recognize the reasons for cooperating with the product manager in the absence of any formal authority on his part. The corporate advertising vice-president of one long-time user of product management emphasized this point:

What makes our system tick is not organization or who makes the decision, but something more intangible—our people are trained in the company system and everyone knows how it works.

No doubt we have not heard the last of the product manager problem nor the last of change. Until a better idea comes along, however, we are likely to see continued use of the system and continued efforts to improve it.. Product management has been, and will continue to be, an intriguing subject for organizational theorists and practicing managers alike.

NOTES

[1] Stephens W. Dietz, *Advertising Age*, June 2, 1969, pp. 43–44.

[2] *Sales Management*, January 1, 1967, pp. 27–29.

[3] David J. Luck and Theodore Nowak, *Harvard Business Review*, Vol. 43 (May–June 1965), p. 143.

[4] Ralph Leezenbaum, *Marketing Communications*, April 1970, pp. 40–43.

[5] *Advertising Age*, January 27, 1969, p. 53.

[6] James F. Pomeroy, paper presented to the Association of National Advertisers Workshop on Development and Approval of Creative Advertising, New York, April 2, 1969.

[7] Victor P. Buell, *Changing Practices in Advertising Decision-Making and Control* (New York: Association of National Advertisers, 1973).

[8] *Current Advertising Practices: Opinions as to Future Trends* (New York: Association of National Advertisers, 1974).

[9] Andrall E. Pearson and Thomas W. Wilson, Jr., *Making Your Marketing Organization Work* (New York: Association of National Advertisers, 1967).

[10] "The Brand Manager: No Longer King," *Business Week*, June 9, 1973, pp. 58–66.

[11] Same reference as footnote 10.

[12] Same reference as footnote 8.

[13] Richard M. Clewett and Stanley F. Stasch, "Product Managers in Consumer Packaged Goods Companies" (Working paper, Northwestern University Graduate School of Management, March 1974).

[14] David J. Luck, "Interfaces of a Product Manager," *Journal of Marketing*, Vol. 33 (October 1969), pp. 32–36.

[15] Darrell B. Lucas, "Point of View: Product Managers in Advertising," *Journal of Advertising Research*, Vol. 12 (June 1972), pp. 41–44.

[16] Same reference as footnote 13.

[17] Gary R. Gemmill and David L. Wileman, "The Product Manager as an Influence Agent," *Journal of Marketing*, Vol. 36 (January 1972), pp. 26–30.

[18] Stephens Dietz "Get More Out of Your Brand Management," *Harvard Business Review*, Vol. 51 (July–August 1973), p. 127.

SOME SUGGESTIONS FOR FURTHER READING

Clewett, R. M. and Stasch, S. F. (1975), "Shifting Role of the Product Manager," *Harvard Business Review* (January–February), 65–73.

Luck, D. J. (1969), "Interfaces of a Product Manager," *Journal of Marketing*, (October), 32–36.

Morein, J. A. (1975), "Shift from Brand to Product Line Marketing," *Harvard Business Review* (September–October), 56–64.

"The Brand Manager: No Longer King," *Business Week* (June 9, 1973).

31 / A MODEL FOR PREDICTIVE MEASUREMENTS OF ADVERTISING EFFECTIVENESS / Robert J. Lavidge and Gary A. Steiner

What are the functions of advertising? Obviously the ultimate function is to help produce sales. But all advertising is not, should not, and cannot be designed to produce immediate purchases on the part of all who are exposed to it. Immediate sales results (even if measurable) are, at best, an incomplete criterion of advertising effectiveness.

In other words, the effects of much advertising are "long-term." This is sometimes taken to imply that all one can really do is wait and see—ultimately the campaign will or will not produce.

However, if something is to happen in the long run, something must be happening in the short run, something that will ultimately lead to eventual sales results. And this process must be measured in order to provide anything approaching a comprehensive evaluation of the effectiveness of the advertising.

Ultimate consumers normally do not switch from disinterested individuals to convinced purchasers in one instantaneous step. Rather, they approach the ultimate purchase through a process or series of steps in which the actual purchase is but the final threshold.

SEVEN STEPS

Advertising may be thought of as a force, which must move people up a series of steps:

1. Near the bottom of the steps stand potential purchasers who are completely *unaware of the existence* of the product or service in question.

Reprinted from the *Journal of Marketing*, published by the American Marketing Association (October, 1961), pp. 59–62.
Robert J. Lavidge is president of Elrick and Lavidge, Chicago-based market research and marketing consulting firm. A faculty member in the Northwestern University Evening Division, he received his B.A. degree from DePauw and his M.B.A. from the University of Chicago. He is a past president of the American Marketing Association. He is co-editor (with R. J. Holloway) of *Marketing and Society: The Challenge.*
Gary A. Steiner was, before his death, professor of business at the University of Chicago, from which he earned an M.A. degree in sociology and a Ph.D. in psychology. He also served as a consultant in applications of psychological techniques. He was co-author with B. L. Berenson) of *Human Behavior: An Inventory of Scientific Findings.*

2. Closer to purchasing, but still a long way from the cash register, are those who are merely *aware of its existence.*
3. Up a step are prospects who *know what the product has to offer.*
4. Still closer to purchasing are those who have favorable attitudes toward the product—those who *like the product.*
5. Those whose favorable attitudes have developed to the point of *preference over all other possibilities are up still another step.*
6. Even closer to purchasing are consumers who couple preference with a desire to buy and the *conviction* that the purchase would be wise.
7. Finally, of course, is the step which translates this attitude into actual *purchase.*

Research to evaluate the effectiveness of advertisements can be designed to provide measures of movement on such a flight of steps.

The various steps are not necessarily equidistant. In some instances the "distance" from awareness to preference may be very slight, while the distance from preference to purchase is extremely large. In other cases, the reverse may be true. Furthermore, a potential purchaser somtimes may move up several steps simultaneously.

Consider the following hypotheses. The greater the psychological and/or economic commitment involved in the purchase of a particular product, the longer it will take to bring consumers up these steps, and the more important the individual steps will be. Contrariwise, the less serious the commitment, the more likely it is that some consumers will go almost "immediately" to the top of the steps.

An impulse purchase might be consummated with no previous awareness, knowledge, liking, or conviction with respect to the product. On the other hand, an industrial good or an important consumer product ordinarily will not be purchased in such a manner.

DIFFERENT OBJECTIVES

Products differ markedly in terms of the role of advertising as related to the various positions on the steps. A great deal of advertising is designed to move people up the final steps toward purchase. At an extreme is the "Buy Now" ad, designed to stimulate immediate overt action. Contrast this with industrial advertising, much of which is not intended to stimulate immediate purchase in and of itself. Instead, it is designed to help pave the way for the salesman by making the prospects aware of his company and products, thus giving them knowledge and favorable attitudes about the ways in which those products or services might be of value. This, of course, involves movement up the lower and intermediate steps.

Even within a particular product category, or with a specific product, different advertisements or campaigns may be aimed primarily at different steps in the purchase process—and rightly so. For example, advertising for new automobiles is likely to place considerable emphasis on the lower steps when new models are first brought out. The advertiser recognizes that his first job is to make the potential customer aware of the new product, and to give him knowledge and favorable attitudes about the product. As the year progresses, advertising emphasis tends to move up the steps. Finally, at the end of the "model year" much emphasis is placed on the final step—the attempt to stimulate immediate purchase among prospects who are assumed, by then, to have information about the car.

The simple model assumes that potential purchasers all "start from scratch." However, some may have developed negative attitudes about the product, which place them even further from purchasing the product than those completely unaware of it. The first job, then, is to get them off the negative steps—before they can move up the additional steps which lead to purchase.

THREE FUNCTIONS OF ADVERTISING

The six steps outlined, beginning with "aware," indicate three major functions of advertising. The first two, awareness and knowledge, relate to *information or ideas.* The second two steps, liking and preference, have to do with favorable *attitudes or feelings* toward the product. The final two steps, conviction and purchase, are to produce *action*—the acquisition of the product.

These three advertising functions are directly related to a classic psychological model which divides behavior into three components or dimensions:

1. The *cognitive* component—the intellectual, mental, or "rational" states.
2. The *affective* component—the "emotional" or "feeling" states.
3. The *conative or motivational* component—the "striving" states, relating to the tendency to treat objects as positive or negative goals.

This is more than a semantic issue, because the actions that need to be taken to stimulate or channel motivation may be quite different from those that produce knowledge. And these, in turn, may differ from actions designed to produce favorable attitudes toward something.

FUNCTIONS OF ADVERTISING RESEARCH

Among the first problems in any advertising evaluation program are to:

1. Determine what steps are most critical in a particular case, that is, what the steps leading to purchase are for most consumers.
2. Determine how many people are, at the moment, on which steps.
3. Determine which people on which steps it is most important to reach.

Advertising research can then be designed to evaluate the extent to which the advertising succeeds in moving the specified "target" audience(s) up the critical purchase steps.

Table 1 summarizes the stair-step model, and illustrates how several common advertising and research approaches may be organized according to their various "functions."

Table 1. Advertising and advertising research related to the model

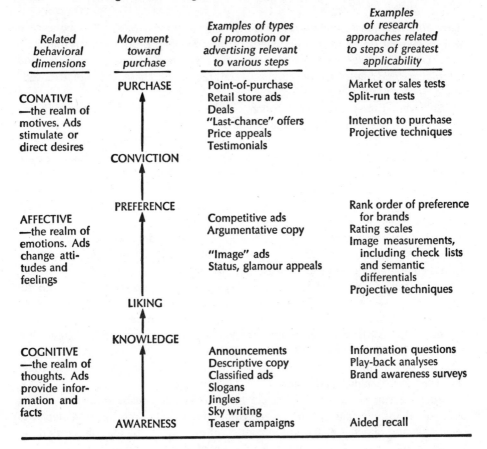

Related behavioral dimensions	Movement toward purchase	Examples of types of promotion or advertising relevant to various steps	Examples of research approaches related to steps of greatest applicability
CONATIVE —the realm of motives. Ads stimulate or direct desires	PURCHASE ↑ ↑ CONVICTION	Point-of-purchase Retail store ads Deals "Last-chance" offers Price appeals Testimonials	Market or sales tests Split-run tests Intention to purchase Projective techniques
AFFECTIVE —the realm of emotions. Ads change attitudes and feelings	↑ PREFERENCE ↑ ↑ LIKING	Competitive ads Argumentative copy "Image" ads Status, glamour appeals	Rank order of preference for brands Rating scales Image measurements, including check lists and semantic differentials Projective techniques
COGNITIVE —the realm of thoughts. Ads provide information and facts	↑ KNOWLEDGE ↑ ↑ AWARENESS	Announcements Descriptive copy Classified ads Slogans Jingles Sky writing Teaser campaigns	Information questions Play-back analyses Brand awareness surveys Aided recall

Over-all and Component Measurements

With regard to most any product there are an infinite number of additional "sub-flights" which can be helpful in moving a prospect up the main steps. For example, awareness, knowledge and development of favorable attitudes toward a specific product feature may be helpful in building a preference for the line of products. This leads to the concept of other steps, subdividing or "feeding" into the purchase steps, but concerned solely with more specific product features or attitudes.

Advertising effectiveness measurements may, then, be categorized into:

1. Over-all or "global" measurements, concerned with measuring the results—the consumers' positions and movement on the purchase steps.
2. Segment or component measurements, concerned with measuring the relative effectiveness of various means of moving people up the purchase steps—the consumers' positions on ancillary flights of steps, and the relative importance of these flights.

Measuring Movement on the Steps

Many common measurements of advertising effectiveness have been concerned with movement up either the first steps or the final step on the primary purchase flight. Examples include surveys to determine the extent of brand awareness and information and measures of purchase and repeat purchase among "exposed" versus "unexposed" groups.

Self-administered instruments, such as adaptations of the "semantic differential" and adjective check lists, are particularly helpful in providing the desired measurements of movement up or down the middle steps. The semantic differential provides a means of scaling attitudes with regard to a number of different issues in a manner which facilitates gathering the information on an efficient quantitative basis. Adjective lists, used in various ways, serve the same general purpose.

Such devices can provide relatively spontaneous, rather than "considered," responses. They are also quickly administered and can contain enough elements to make recall of specific responses by the test participant difficult; especially if the order of items is changed. This helps in minimizing "consistency" biases in various comparative uses of such measurement tools.

Efficiency of these self-administered devices make it practical to obtain responses to large numbers of items. This facilitates measurement of elements or components differing only slightly, though importantly, from each other.

Carefully constructed adjective check lists, for example, have shown remarkable discrimination between terms differing only in subtle shades of meaning. One product may be seen as "rich," "plush," and "expensive," while another one is "plush," "gaudy," and "cheap."

Such instruments make it possible to secure simultaneous measurements of both *global* attitudes and *specific* image components. These can be correlated with each other and directly related to the content of the advertising messages tested.

Does the advertising change the thinking of the respondents with regard to specific product attributes, characteristics or features, including not only physical characteristics but also various image elements such as "status"? Are these changes commercially significant?

The measuring instruments mentioned are helpful in answering these questions. They provide a means for correlating changes in specific attitudes concerning image components with changes in global attitudes or position on the primary purchase steps.

Testing the Model

When groups of consumers are studied over time, do those who show more movement on the measured steps eventually purchase the product in greater proportions or quantities? Accumulation of data utilizing the stair-step model provides an opportunity to test the assumptions underlying the model by measuring this question.

THREE CONCEPTS

This approach to the measurement of advertising has evolved from three concepts:

1. Realistic measurements of advertising effectiveness must be related to an understanding of the functions of advertising. It is helpful to think in terms of a model where advertising is likened to a force which, if successful, moves people up a series of steps toward purchase.
2. Measurements of the effectiveness of the advertising should provide measurements of changes at all levels on these steps—not just at the levels of the development of product or feature awareness and the stimulation of actual purchase.
2. Changes in attitudes as to specific image components can be evaluated together with changes in over-all images, to determine the extent to which changes in the image components are related to movement on the primary purchase steps.

SOME SUGGESTIONS FOR FURTHER READING

Bettman, J. R. (1979), *An Information Processing Theory of Consumer Choice.* Reading, MA: Addison-Wesley.

Colley, R. H. (1961), *Defining Advertising Goals for Measured Advertising Results.* New York: Association of National Advertisers.

Palda, K. S. (1966), "The Hypotheses of a Hierarchy of Effects: A Partial Evaluation," *Journal of Marketing Research* (February), 13–24.

Robinson, P. J., Faris, C. W. and Wind, Y. (1967), *Industrial Buying and Creative Marketing.* *Boston:* Allyn & Bacon.

Rogers, E. M. (1976), "New Product Adoption and Diffusion," *Journal of Marketing Research* (May), 196–301.

Strong, E. K. (1925), *The Psychology of Selling.* New York: McGraw-Hill.

32 / ADVERTISING RESEARCH AT ANHEUSER-BUSCH, INC. (1963–68)* / Russell L. Ackoff and James R. Emshoff

The association with Anheuser-Busch, Inc. (A-B) that is described here began in 1959. Over the last fifteen years research has been carried out on almost every aspect of A-B's operations and planning. The company's view of this association has appeared in several articles.[1] *Business Week* and *Fortune*[2] have described aspects of this work and some of the theoretical output has also appeared.[3] This article, however, is the first case study to be published. It provides an account of a sequence of investigations involving advertising of the company's principal product, BUDWEISER beer.

BACKGROUND

A-B's original contact was made by E. H. Vogel, Jr., then manager of business planning. Work over the first few years was devoted to determining when new breweries would be required, where they should be located, and what size they should be. Facility plans were developed to cover a ten-year period. Capital requirements for these facilities were estimated and a financial model of the firm was developed and used to predict capital availability. The model showed that not quite enough capital would have been available to finance the building program without increasing the company's traditional debt to debt-equity ratio. Research then turned to ways of making more capital available when needed.

Production operations involving scheduling and allocation of demand to breweries already had been studied and modified to yield much of the potential savings. Marketing, which involved a major share of the company's expenditures, had not yet been analyzed. An initial examination into this area revealed that the largest category of marketing cost involved advertising. Therefore, in 1961 we first recommended research into it. The proposal was turned down because of the

* The authors acknowledge the major roles of Drs. Eli S. Marks and Maurice Sasieni in the work reported in this article.

Reprinted from *Sloan Management Review* (Winter 1975), pp. 1–15, by permission of Sloan Management Review.

Russell Ackoff holds an endowed chair at the University of Pennsylvania. He has been a pioneer in the areas of operations research and corporate planning. His Ph.D. is from the University of Pennsylvania, and he has served on the faculty at Case Institute of Technology. James Emshoff is director of the Bureau of Research at the University of Pennsylvania. He has worked for McKinsey and Company as well as his own consulting firm.

widespread satisfaction with the company's advertising. Responsible managers were unwilling to evaluate and modify a successful program. Research turned instead to distribution and inventories.

ADVERTISING EXPENDITURES

Just before mid 1961 August A. Busch, Jr., then president and chairman of the board, asked us if we would evaluate an advertising decision he was about to make. In that year BUDWEISER was budgeted to receive about $15,000,000 worth of advertising. Mr. Busch had been approached by the vice president of marketing with a request for an additional $1,200,000 to be spent on advertising in twelve of the 198 areas into which the company divided its national market. The vice president had defended his proposal on the basis of the projected increase in sales that he believed would result. Mr. Busch explained that he was confronted with such a proposal every year and that he always had accepted it. He intended to do the same again, but he asked, "Is there any way I can find out at the end of the year whether I got what I paid for?" We said we would think about it and make some suggestions.

The proposal we presented to Mr. Busch shortly thereafter consisted of allowing the Marketing Department to select any six of the twelve areas initially proposed and giving it $600,000 for additional advertising. The remaining six areas would not be touched and would be used as controls. This biased selection procedure was intended to overcome some of the opposition that the Marketing Department felt toward any effort to evaluate its proposal.

Earlier we had developed an equation for forecasting monthly sales in each market area. Our plan now was to measure the deviation of actual monthly sales from the forecast for each market area in the test. Using the statistical characteristics of the forecasts we estimated that we had a 95 percent chance of detecting a 4 percent increase in sales in the areas with additional advertising. Since the increase predicted by the Marketing Department was in excess of this amount, Mr. Busch authorized the test and it was initiated.

The test was conducted over the last six months of 1961 yielding 72 (12 × 6) observations. The analysis of these data failed to reveal a significant difference between the test and control areas. Nevertheless, the control areas did better on average than was forecast. Therefore, we assumed that all the sales above those forecasted were attributable to the increased advertising and evaluated the results accordingly. Even under this assumption the increased amount of advertising was *not* justified by the deliberately overestimated increase in sales attributed to it.

Encouraged by these results, Mr. Busch asked us to design research directed at determining what amount should be spent on advertising. However, he wanted to proceed with caution, because he believed that much of the success of BUDWEISER, which was leading the beer market with a share of 8.14 percent in 1962, was due to its quality[3] and the effectiveness with which this was communicated through its advertising. When we suggested research involving experimentation with market areas he authorized use of fifteen such areas provided they did not include any of the company's major markets.

Constrained in this way we sought an experimental design that would maximize learning about advertising expenditures. Our design effort was guided by two methodological principles. First, we knew that the company advertised for only one reason: *to increase sales.* Therefore, we were determined to measure the effect of advertising *on sales* and not on more easily measured intervening variables such as recall of messages or attitudes toward the product. For this reason we decided to continue to use deviations of actual from forecast sales as the variable to be observed. This allowed us to cancel out much of the effect on sales due to factors other than advertising. Accordingly, efforts to improve forecasting of monthly market-area sales were continuous.

Secondly, we were committed to an attempt to *explain* the casual effect of advertising on consumer purchases and not merely to find statistical correlations between them. Our search of the marketing literature for such an explanation was futile; it only revealed correlations and regressions between advertising and sales. These usually showed that increases (or decreases) in the former were associated with increases (or decreases) in the latter. From such associations it was almost universally inferred, and incorrectly, that increases in advertising yield increases in sales almost without limit. We believed that what these analyses really showed was that most companies forecast next year's sales quite accurately and then set their advertising budgets as a fixed percentage of predicted sales. In other words, forecasts of increased sales produce increased advertising.

Our commitment to experimentation derived from a determination to find a causal connection between advertising and sales, not merely an association between them, and to develop an ability to manipulate advertising so as to produce desired effects on sales that could be observed.

Since we knew of no tested theory, we fabricated our own. Our hunch was that advertising could be considered to be a stimulus and sales a response to it. Much is known about the general nature of stimulus-response functions. They usually take the form shown in Figure 1. Therefore, we formulated the following hypotheses:

A small amount of advertising has virtually no effect on sales but as the amount is increased it pushes the response through a *threshold* after which it produces an increasing effect. This effect decreases and flattens out once the respondents are *saturated;* that is, they either turn off further exposure to the stimulus or are consuming up to their capabilities or capacities. Response to further increases in advertising remains relatively unchanged until the respondents reach *supersaturation,* a point beyond which they respond negatively.

In an earlier study conducted for the Lamp Division of the General Electric Company[4] we had found such a relationship between frequency of sales calls (stimulus) and purchases (response). In the sales-call context the idea of supersaturation is not as shocking as it is in advertising. Clearly, there is an amount of a salesman's presence that is intolerable to a buyer. Beyond this one would expect the buyer to try to get rid of the salesman by discontinuing his purchases. Similarly, we felt reasonably sure that, for example, if all television advertising were for only one product, the public would react negatively.

Figure 1. A typical stimulus-response function

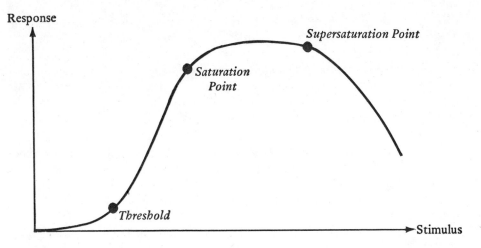

The First Experiment

A minimal experiment would have involved applying the same percentage change in advertising expenditure to each of the fifteen market areas allotted to us and comparing the results obtained from them with those obtained from an equal number of control areas. But we needed only nine areas to obtain the level of accuracy set as our target: to be able to detect a 2 percent difference in sales 95 percent of the time. The introduction of two different treatments, one involving an increase and the other a decrease in advertising expenditures, required eighteen test areas, three more than were available to us. However, even an experiment with two different treatments would yield only three points: the average effect of each treatment and that of the control group. The difficulty this presented derived from the fact that every configuration of three points except one, V-shaped, could be fitted to the relationship (Figure 1) that we wanted to test. Therefore, there was a very low probability that even a three-level experiment would disprove our hypothetical relationship; hence, it was a very poor test of the validity of this relationship.

For these reasons we decided to ask for three different treatments and a control group even though this would require twenty-seven markets plus nine under control. Four experimental points could disprove our theory as easily as it could confirm it and, therefore, would have provided a reasonable test of it.

We had nothing to go on but our intuition in selecting the experimental treatment levels: a 50 percent reduction, and 50 and 100 percent increases in budgeted levels of advertising. We wanted to make changes large enough to produce observable effects on sales, assuming such changes had any such effect, and large enough so that if there were no observable effects this fact could not be dismissed because the changes were believed to be too small. Two increases rather than decreases were selected to make the experiment more palatable to the Marketing Department.

When this four-level design was presented it was rejected because it involved the use of too many market areas. However, Mr. Busch agreed to our use of eighteen rather than fifteen areas provided that we change the reduction in advertising we had proposed from 50 to 25 percent. He felt that a 50 percent reduction might irreparably damage the areas so treated. This left us with a three-level experiment: -25%, 0%, and $+50\%$ changes from budget.

Although we were not completely happy with this outcome because it did not provide an adequate test of our theory, we were pleased that we had the opportunity to conduct even a limited experiment. We were reasonably sure that if it produced interesting results, restrictions on future experiments would be lifted.

A $3 \times 3 \times 3$ factorially designed experiment was prepared in which two other important marketing variables were explicitly controlled: *the amount spent on sales effort* (salesmen) and *the amount spent on point-of-sales displays and signs*. We also would have liked to control pricing but this was precluded. This design is illustrated in Figure 2.

Market areas were selected randomly from the "permissible list" and randomly assigned to the twenty-seven treatments. Use of the "permissible list" could obviously bias our results but again our hope was that the results would justify further experimentation and that it would not be so restricted.

The experiment was carried out over the calendar year 1962 thereby yielding twelve observations of each market area. We were able to reach a conclusion at the end of six months, but the experiment was continued to build up confidence in the results. The results, however, attracted little confidence; they were too much at variance with expectations within the company and its advertising agency. The

Figure 2.   The 3 x 3 x 3 experiment

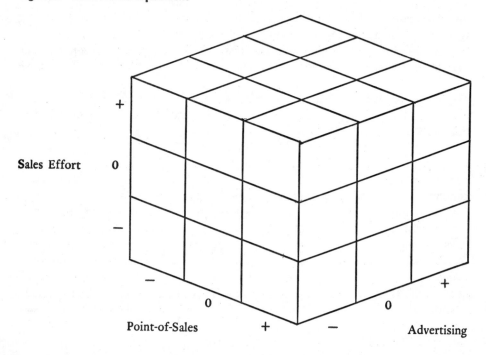

Sales Effort   +   0   −

Point-of-Sales   +   0   −   Advertising

three points shown in Figure 3 fell into the only configuration, V-shaped, that was inconsistent with our theory because the relationship being tested (Figure 1) had no V in it. In addition, we found no significant interaction between advertising, sales effort, and point-of-sales expenditures, a surprising but not an unacceptable result, and the results indicated that current levels of sales effort and point-of-sales expenditures were close to optimal. This last result was readily accepted.

No one found much difficulty in believing that a 50 percent increase in advertising produced a 7 percent increase in sales, but only Mr. Busch and Mr. Vogel were willing to consider seriously the possibility that a 25 percent reduction of advertising could produce a 14 percent increase in sales. Even they were not ready to act on this finding but they did want to analyze the situation further. Therefore, they asked us to design another experiment that would check these results and that would be more convincing to others.

We had to revise our theory before designing the next experiment. On the surface it appeared necessary to reject the theory but we had grown very fond of it. Therefore, we sought a modification of the theory that would make it consistent with the experimental results.

It occurred to us that there might be two or more distinct consuming populations in each market area with a response curve like the one we had assumed but that these might be separated along the horizontal scale (see Figure 4). The aggregated response curve would then have a V in it. When this possibility was presented to Mr. Vogel, he thought it quite reasonable and suggested that the markets might be segmented into three parts: heavy, moderate, and light beer drinkers. This made sense to us. One would expect heavy users of a product to be more sensitive to its advertising than moderate users, and moderate users more sensitive

Figure 3.   Results of first experiment (1962)

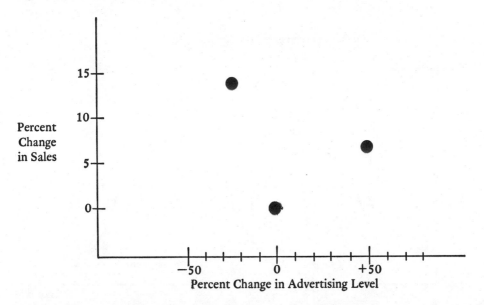

Percent Change in Advertising Level

than light users. We looked for some way of testing this assumption and we found one.

It would have been very time-consuming and costly to determine how many beer drinkers of each type there were in each market area. We had neither the time nor the money required to do so. But we did know from previous studies that beer consumption correlated positively with discretionary income within the range of such income in which most beer drinkers fall. Therefore, we determined the average discretionary income in each market area that had been used in the previous experiment and compared it with the average deviations from forecasted sales in each area. There was a positive correlation between these deviations and average discretionary income, thereby lending some credence to the user-level segmentation assumption.

We revised our theory to incorporate three response functions for each market area. This meant that the aggregated response functions for markets as a whole could differ significantly because of different proportions of heavy, moderate, and light beer drinkers.

The Second Experiment

In order to test the revised theory we decided that we needed seven different advertising treatments. We wanted to repeat the earlier experiment and add treatments further out on both ends of the scale. Seven treatments were selected: −100% (no advertising), −50%, −25%, 0%, +50%, +100%, and +200%. Because of improvements in our forecasting methods only six areas were required for each treatment. This design was accepted with only slight modification: the number of test areas in the two extreme treatments was reduced.

The experiment was conducted over twelve months in 1963 and 1964. Again data were collected monthly. The results obtained confirmed the findings of the

Figure 4. Response function of segmented population

Response

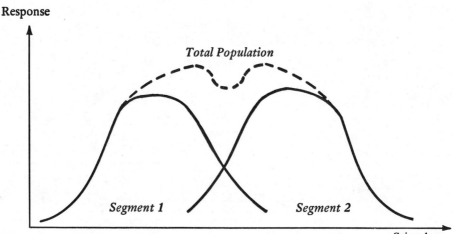

Stimulus

first experiment. When plotted the seven points fell on a curve such as is shown in Figure 5. There were two deviations from our expectations. First, only two, not three, peaks appeared. But this was not serious because the points out on the right were so far apart that there could well be a third hump concealed by the interpolation between the points. It was harder to explain the finding that the areas in which all advertising had been eliminated (−100%) survived the year with no significant difference in performance from the control areas (0%). Hardly anyone believed this result. Those who did attribute it to the long history, strength, and exposure of BUDWEISER in the marketplace. We suggested further tests of the effect of complete elimination of advertising.

Although a willingness to act on our findings had not yet developed, there was growing agreement on the desirability of continuing the research. The 1963-64 experiment was continued with particular attention given to the areas from which all advertising had been removed. The objective was to determine how long it would take before any deterioration of sales could be detected, at what rate it would take place, and how easily lost sales could subsequently be recaptured. We also initiated some research into the relative effectiveness of different media. While this research was going on; the first opportunity to apply the results already obtained presented itself.

Application of Results

In mid 1964 Mr. Busch wanted to make more cash available to meet some commitments he had made. He asked Mr. Vogel and us if this could be done. We jointly proposed that advertising be reduced by 15 percent in twenty-five of the smallest markets. The smallest markets were chosen in order to minimize any possible long-run harmful effects. The proposed change was capable of yielding more than the amount Mr. Busch asked for. We also pointed out that we could maintain

Figure 5. Results of second advertising-level experiment (1963)

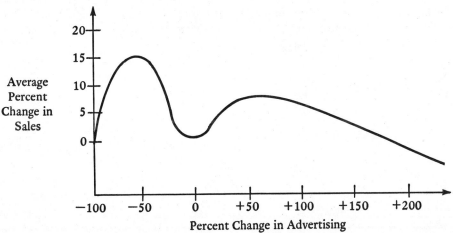

very close watch over the areas affected and report immediately on any reduction of sales that might occur in them. We predicted, however, that the proposed decrease in advertising would produce about a 5 percent increase in sales. Mr. Busch decided to go ahead.

The predicted results were obtained by the end of the year. As a consequence, the number of reduction areas was increased to fifty and the amount of the reductions was increased to 25 percent. From then on more and more areas were similarly treated and the reductions were gradually increased until the advertising expenditure per barrel was $0.80 in contrast to $1.89 which it had been when the research was initiated. During this period (1962-68) sales of BUDWEISER increased from approximately 7.5 million to 14.5 million barrels and its market share increased from 8.14 to 12.94 percent.

TIMING OF ADVERTISING

Returning to the experiment involving complete deprivation of advertising, the areas thus deprived showed no response until more than a year and a half later. From then on a small decline was noted each month. This was allowed to continue only long enough to provide good estimates of the deterioration rate. Moves to correct these markets were then made. They were restored to their normal growth rate in about six months with only their normal amount of advertising.

These results led to a new line of speculation. Would it not be possible to *pulse* advertising, using an on-and-off pattern, and obtain the same effectiveness that is obtained by continuous advertising? We came to think of advertising as a motion picture which, of course, is really a sequence of motionless pictures. If sixteen still photographs are taken and projected per second, the appearance of motion is created because images are retained in the retina between exposures. We felt the same should be true of advertising.

Two types of pulsing were considered. In one, advertising expenditures in all media are on or off together. In the other, only one medium is used at any time but the media are alternated. We designed an experiment to test the first of these types of pulse. It involved four treatments: one control (I) and three pulsing patterns (II, III, and IV) shown in Table 1. In addition, the level of expenditure in each was varied as is shown in Table 2. The market areas used in this experiment were classified by median income and growth rates.

One of the pulsing patterns was found to be significantly better than the others and slightly better than normal advertising when accompanied by a high level of expenditure. Another pattern was found to be best when accompanied by

Table 1. Pulsing patterns

	I	II	III	IV
Spring	X	X	0	X
Summer	X	0	X	X
Autumn	X	X	0	0
Winter	X	0	X	0

Table 2. Percent of local budget spent by pulsing pattern and advertising level

Advertising level	*Pulsing pattern*			
	I	*II*	*III*	*IV*
High	150%	100%	100%	100%
Low	100%	50%	50%	50%

a low level of expenditure. In addition, the pulsing patterns were found to interact significantly with median income level and the growth rate of the market area. Subsequent experimentation revealed no significant difference between time-pulsing and media-pulsing. Media-pulsing, however, was easier to administer.

These results were cautiously incorporated into small reductions of advertising expenditures that were made in series. It was only after one change was demonstrated to have the predicted effect that the next change was made. Regular monthly checks on the performance of each market area were initiated and continue to this day.

MEDIA SELECTION

In the early experiments on advertising expenditures, the budgets for experimental areas were set by the research team but the way in which additional moneys were allocated or reductions were made was left entirely in the hands of the advertising agency. Five media were involved: billboards, magazines, newspapers, radio, and television. We examined the relationship between the actual changes in media allocations and changes in sales. This preliminary analysis indicated no significant difference in effectiveness between magazines, newspapers, and radio, but it suggested that television was slightly superior and that billboards were substantially inferior.

An experiment was designed to test these tentative findings (see Table 3). Magazines were not included in this experiment because they could not be controlled within small areas. A distinction was made between *local* and *national* television. In each of twenty areas only one medium was used; in another twenty each medium was combined with national television. The results showed that national television was slightly superior to any local medium. Local television (with or without national television) and radio were more effective than newspapers or billboards. Billboards were the least effective.

To explain the poor showing of billboards, a number of observations were made to determine how much information could be conveyed by a billboard. We found that little more than the product name and a slogan could be communicated. This meant that billboards can do little more than remind one of the existence of an already familiar product; they cannot convey much, if any, new information about it. A second set of observations showed that the typical urban dweller in the United States saw but did not necessarily notice the word "BUDWEISER" on signs, displays, or beer containers almost ten times per day. He hardly needed additional reminding of its existence. On the basis of these findings virtually all billboard

Table 3.   Media experiment (1967–68): number and treatment of market areas

	Local TV	Billboard	Radio	Newspaper
No National TV	5	5	5	5
National TV	5	5	5	5

advertising was discontinued. The company had been spending about 20 percent of its advertising budget through this medium.

CONCLUSION

To summarize the results obtained by 1968, we note that volume had approximately doubled, market share had increased from 8.14 to 12.94 percent, and advertising expenditures were reduced from $1.89 to $0.80 per barrel, a 58 percent reduction. It would be foolish, of course, to claim that this improvement in performance was due entirely to changes in advertising. Other types of changes, some based on research and some not, were also made during this period. But one thing is clear: the changes induced by the research described here did not hurt Anheuser-Busch.

The strength of the opposition to the results of our early experiments is less surprising in retrospect than it was at the time. These results contradicted the strong beliefs of people who had good reason to believe they understood advertising and who had the success of the products involved to prove it. Furthermore, these people did not understand the logic of experimental design and the statistical analysis of the data yielded by experiments. They were convinced that sales were affected by a large number of complexly interacting and inherently qualitative variables and, therefore, that the effect of any one of these on sales could not be isolated or measured.

The greatest resistance came from those managers who had direct responsibility for the decisions to which the research was addressed and from the advertising agency people who were attached to the account. It was clear that the agency people felt that our research cast doubt on their competence and creativity. It also threatened the agency's income.

For these reasons it became apparent to us that three things had to be done if we were to gain acceptance, let alone support, of our efforts. First, we would have to bring those who had to deal with the research results to an understanding of the logic of experimental design and statistical analysis. Second, we would have to involve them actively in the design of the experiments and in the analysis and interpretation of their results. Finally, we would have to try to change the method of compensating the advertising agency so that its fee was not decreased as the efficiency of advertising was increased.

The process of education and involvement took time. It was carried out both informally and formally in sessions conducted specifically for this purpose. Managers at the highest levels were generally the first to approve of experimentation. They sometimes became impatient with their subordinates and tried to force early research results on them. Such pressure slowed acceptance at the lower levels.

But in general, when top managers felt compelled to act, as Mr. Busch did on the first reduction of advertising expenditures, they worked hard to make the implementation itself experimental and to carry it out as gradually and nondisruptively as possible. In all, it took about three years (1962–65) for the educational efforts to begin to pay off.

These efforts were facilitated by two other important changes. First, we proposed that the basis for the agency's compensation be changed so that it would benefit financially when the company did. As long as the agency was paid a percentage of A-B's expenditures on advertising, it naturally resisted research that had the potential of reducing its earnings. Therefore, we suggested a scheme by which the agency's fee was increased if either sales increased with no increase in advertising or advertising expenditures decreased with no decrease in sales. The agency was persuaded to try this scheme for a year with assurances that it would receive no less in fees during the trial year than it had in the previous year. In the trial year advertising expenditures decreased but since sales increased the agency's compensation also increased. The scheme was continued for another year with repetition of this outcome and then became permanent. Because of it the agency became increasingly interested in research, strengthened its research department, and encouraged it to collaborate with us. This was done to our mutual benefit. By 1968 the difficulties with agency acceptance of research results were largely a thing of the past. The agency has since initiated such a compensation scheme with other clients.

Acceptance of research as an instrument of management was greatly facilitated by the establishment of two very competent in-house groups, one in marketing and the other in corporate planning. Leon Pritzker, who was the initial director of the group in marketing, had a major role in the later phases of the research reported here. August A. Busch, III, then executive vice president but now president, observed: "The University and company units work together very closely...."[5] E. H. Vogel, Jr. continued: "Today we hardly make any decision of any consequence that does not involve our researchers in one way or another. This blending of research and management did not occur overnight. It developed slowly under careful guidance."[6]

Research results were built up slowly but accumulatively. The results of each piece of research were integrated with previous results where they were consistent. Where they were not, a more general explanation was sought, one that made integration possible, and then the integrating principle was thoroughly tested. No result was ever taken to be true for all time. As Mr. Vogel observed:

We did not try to impose [research-based] recommendations as though we had suddenly gained possession of ultimate truth. We usually initiated the application of recommendations on a small scale with close controls imposed on them. As confidence in results developed, we extended applications.

No matter how generally management accepted a research result it was never applied without a well-designed control system to tell us whether the recommendations worked as expected. We have learned as much from the feed-back such control provided as we have from the research that produced the initial recommendations.

More important, perhaps, is that we now design controls for evaluating decisions which management reaches without the benefit of research. This enables us to learn more rapidly and accurately from experience, and it has indoctrinated management with an experimental approach to decision making.[7]

NOTES

[1] See Busch [2] and Vogel [6].

[2] See "Computers Can't Solve Everything" [3], "Wharton Analyzes the Beer Drinker" [8] and "While Big Brewers Quaff, the Little Ones Thirst" [9].

[3] See Ackoff and Emery [1], Curtis [4], and Rao [5].

[4] See Waid, Clark and Ackoff [7].

[5] See Busch [2].

[6] See Vogel [6], p. 24.

[7] See Vogel [6], pp. 24–25.

REFERENCES

1. Ackoff, R. L., and Emery, F. E. *On Purposeful Systems.* Chicago: Aldine-Atherton, 1972, Chapter 8.
2. Busch, A. A., III. "The Essentials of Corporate Growth." Address given to Charles Coolige Parlin Marketing Award Banquet, May 9, 1973.
3. "Computers Can't Solve Everything." *Fortune,* October 1969, p. 126 ff.
4. Curtis, K. P. *The Modeling of Consumer Purchase Behavior.* Unpublished Ph.D. dissertation, University of Pennsylvania, 1969.
5. Rao, A. G. *Quantitative Theories in Advertising.* New York: John Wiley & Sons, 1970.
6. Vogel, E. H., Jr. "Creative Marketing and Management Science." *Management Decision,* Spring 1969, pp. 21–25.
7. Waid, C.; Clark, D. F.; and Ackoff, R. L. "Allocation of Sales Effort in the Lamp Division of the General Electric Company." *Operations Research* 4 (1956): 629–647.
8. "Wharton Analyzes the Beer Drinker." *Business Week,* 24 March 1973, p. 44.
9. "While Big Brewers Quaff, the Little Ones Thirst." *Fortune.* November 1972, p. 103 ff.

SOME SUGGESTIONS FOR FURTHER READING

Ackoff, R. L., and Emshoff, R. R. (1975), "Advertising Research at Anheuser-Busch, Inc. (1968–73)," *Sloan Management Review* (Spring), 1–16.

Montgomery, D. V. and Silk, A. J. (1972), "Estimating Dynamic Effects of Market Communications Expenditures," *Management Science* (June), 485–501.

——— and Weinberg (1973), "Modeling Marketing Phenomena: A Managerial Perspective," *Journal of Contemporary Business* (Autumn), 17–22.

Rao, A. G. (1970), *Quantitative Theories in Advertising.* New York: John Wiley & Sons, 60–79.

33 / CONFLICT AND COOPERATION IN MARKETING CHANNELS / Bruce Mallen

The purpose of this paper is to advance the hypotheses that between member firms of a marketing channel there exists a dynamic field of conflicting and cooperating objectives; that if the conflicting objectives outweigh the cooperating ones, the effectiveness of the channel will be reduced and efficient distribution impeded; and that implementation of certain methods of cooperation will lead to increased channel efficiency.

DEFINITION OF CHANNEL

The concept of a marketing channel is slightly more involved than expected on initial study. One author in a recent paper[1] has identified "trading" channels, "non-trading" channels, "type" channels, "enterprise" channels, and "business-unit" channels. Another source[2] refers to channels as all the flows extending from the producer to the user. These include the flows of physical possession, ownership, promotion, negotiation, financing, risking, ordering, and payment.

The concept of channels to be used here involves only two of the above-mentioned flows: ownership and negotiation. The first draws merchants, both wholesalers and retailers, into the channel definition, and the second draws in agent middlemen. Both, of course, include producers and consumers. This definition roughly corresponds to Professor Breyer's "trading channel," though the latter does not restrict (nor will this paper) the definition to actual flows but to "flow-capacity." "A trading channel is formed when trading relations, making possible the passage of title and/or possession (usually both) of goods from the producer to the ultimate consumer, are consummated by the component trading concerns of the system."[3] In addition, this paper will deal with trading channels in the broadest manner and so will be concentrating on "type-trading" channels rather than "enterprise" or "business-unit" channels. This means that there will be little discussion of problems peculiar to integrated or semi-integrated channels, or peculiar to specific channels and firms.

Reprinted from L. George Smith (ed.) *Reflections on Progress in Marketing*, published by the American Marketing Association in 1964, pp. 65–85.
Bruce Mallen is professor of marketing at Sir George Williams University in Montreal. He is an international authority in the field of distribution channels. He has contributed widely to scholarly publications and formerly headed his own firm, Bruce Mallen and Associates, Inc., a marketing consulting firm.

CONFLICT

Palamountain isolated three forms of distributive conflict.[4]

1. Horizontal competition—this is competition between middlemen of the same type; for example, discount store *versus* discount store.
2. Intertype competition—this is competition between middlemen of different types in the same channel sector; for example, discount store *versus* department store.
3. Vertical conflict—this is conflict between channel members of different levels; for example, discount store *versus* manufacturer.

The first form, horizontal competition, is well covered in traditional economic analysis and is usually referred to simply as "competition." However, both intertype competition and vertical conflict, particularly the latter, are neglected in the usual micro-economic discussion.

The concepts of "intertype competition" and "distributive innovation" are closely related and require some discussion. Intertype competition will be divided into two categories: (a) "traditional intertype competition" and (b) "innovative intertype competition." The first category includes the usual price and promotional competition between two or more different types of channel members at the same channel level. The second category involves the action on the part of traditional channel members to prevent channel innovators from establishing themselves. For example, in Canada there is a strong campaign, on the part of traditional department stores, to prevent the discount operation from taking a firm hold on the Canadian market.[5]

Distributive innovation will also be divided into two categories: (a) "intrafirm innovative conflict" and (b) "innovative intertype competition." The first category involves the action of channel member firms to prevent sweeping changes within their own companies. The second category, "innovative intertype competition," is identical to the second category of intertype competition.

Thus the concepts of intertype competition and distributive innovation give rise to three forms of conflict, the second of which is a combination of both: 1. traditional intertype competition, 2. innovative intertype competition, and 3. intrafirm innovative conflict.

It is to this second form that this paper now turns before going on to vertical conflict.

Innovative Intertype Competition

Professor McCammon has identified several sources, both intrafirm and intertype, of innovative conflict in distribution, i.e., where there are barriers to change within the marketing structure.[6]

Traditional members of a channel have several motives for maintaining the channel status quo against outside innovators. The traditional members are particularly strong in this conflict when they can band together in some formal or informal manner—when there is strong reseller solidarity.

Both entrepreneurs and professional managers may resist outside innovators, not only for economic reasons, but because change "violates group norms, creates uncertainty, and results in a loss of status." The traditional channel members (the insiders) and their affiliated members (the strivers and complementors) are emotionally and financially committed to the dominant channel and are interested in perpetuating it against the minor irritations of the "transient" channel members and the major attacks of the "outside innovators."

Thus, against a background of horizontal and intertype channel conflict, this paper now moves to its area of major concern: vertical conflict and cooperation.

Vertical Conflict—Price

The exchange act. The act of exchange is composed of two elements: a sale and a purchase. It is to the advantage of the seller to obtain the highest return possible from such an exchange and the exact opposite is the desire of the buyer. This exchange act takes place between any kind of buyer and seller. If the consumer is the buyer, then that side of the act is termed shopping; if the manufacturer, purchasing; if the government, procurement; and if a retailer, buying. Thus, between each level in the channel an exchange will take place (except if a channel member is an agent rather than a merchant).

One must look to the process of the exchange act for the basic source of conflict between channel members. This is not to say the exchange act itself is a conflict. Indeed, the act or transaction is a sign that the element of price conflict has been resolved to the mutual satisfaction of both principals. Only along the road to this mutual satisfaction point or exchange price do the principals have opposing interests. This is no less true even if they work out the exchange price together, as in mass retailers' specification-buying programs.

It is quite natural for the selling member in an exchange to want a higher price than the buying member. The conflict is subdued through persuasion or force by one member over the other, or it is subdued by the fact that the exchange act or transaction does not take place, or finally, as mentioned above, it is eliminated if the act does take place.

Suppliers may emphasize the customer aspect of a reseller rather than the channel member aspect. As a customer the reseller is somebody to persuade, manipulate, or even fool. Conversely, under the marketing concept, the view of the reseller as a customer or channel member is identical. Under this philosophy he is somebody to aid, help, and serve. However, it is by no means certain that even a large minority of suppliers have accepted the marketing concept.

To view the reseller as simply the opposing principal in the act of exchange may be channel myopia, but this view exists. On the other hand, failure to recognize this basic opposing interest is also a conceptual fault.

When the opposite principals in an exchange act are of unequal strength, the stronger is very likely to force or persuade the weaker to adhere to the former's desires. However, when they are of equal strength, the basic conflict cannot so easily be resolved. Hence, the growth of big retailers who can match the power of big producers has possibly led to greater open conflict between channel members, not only with regard to exchange, but also to other conflict sources.

There are other sources of conflict within the pricing area outside of the basic one discussed above.

A supplier may force a product onto its resellers, who dare not oppose, but who retaliate in other ways, such as using it as a loss leader. Large manufacturers may try to dictate the resale price of their merchandise; this may be less or more than the price at which resellers wish to sell it. Occasionally, a local market may be more competitive for a reseller than is true nationally. The manufacturer may not recognize the difference in competition and refuse to help this channel member.

Resellers complain of manufacturers' special price concessions to competitors and rebel at the attempt of manufacturers to control resale prices. Manufacturers complain of resellers' deceptive and misleading price advertising, nonadherence to resale price suggestions, bootlegging to unauthorized outlets, seeking special price concessions by unfair methods, and misrepresenting offers by competitive suppliers.

Other points of price conflict are the paperwork aspects of pricing. Resellers complain of delays in price change notices and complicated price sheets.

Price theory. If one looks upon a channel as a series of markets or as the vertical exchange mechanism between buyers and sellers, one can adapt several theories and concepts to the channel situation which can aid marketing theory in this important area of channel conflict.[7]

Vertical Conflict—Non-Price

Channel conflict not only finds its source in the exchange act and pricing, but it permeates all areas of marketing. Thus, a manufacturer may wish to promote a product in one manner or to a certain degree while his resellers oppose this. Another manufacturer may wish to get information from his resellers on a certain aspect relating to his product, but his resellers may refuse to provide this information. A producer may want to distribute his product extensively, but his resellers may demand exclusives.

There is also conflict because of the tendency for both manufacturers and retailers to want the elimination of the wholesaler.

One very basic source of channel conflict is the possible difference in the primary business philosophy of channel members. Writing in the *Harvard Business Review,* Wittreich says:

In essence, then, the key to understanding management's problem of crossed purpose is the recognition that the fundamental (philosophy) in life of the high-level corporate manager and the typical (small) retailer dealer in the distribution system are quite different. The former's (philosophy) can be characterized as being essentially dynamic in nature, continuously evolving and emerging; the latter, which is in sharp contrast, can be characterized as being essentially static in nature, reaching a point and leveling off into a continuously satisfying plateau.[8]

While the big members of the channel may want growth, the small retail members may be satisfied with stability and a "good living."

ANARCHY [9]

The channel can adjust to its conflicting-cooperating environment in three distinct ways. *First,* it can have a leader (one of the channel members) who "forces" members to cooperate; this is an autocratic relationship. *Second,* it can have a leader who "helps" members to cooperate, creating a democratic relationship. *Finally,* it can do nothing, and so have an anarchistic relationship. Lewis B. Sappington and C. G. Browne, writing on the problems of internal company organizations, state:

The first classification may be called "autocracy." In this approach to the group the leader determines the policy and dictates or assigns the work tasks. There are no group deliberations, no group decisions. . . .

The second classification may be called "democracy." In this approach the leader allows all policies to be decided by the group with his participation. The group members work with each other as they wish. The group determines the division and assignment of tasks. . . .

The third classification may be called "anarchy." In anarchy there is complete freedom of the group or the individual regarding policies or task assignments, without leader participation.[10]

Advanced in this paper is the hypothesis that if anarchy exists, there is a great chance of the conflicting dynamics destroying the channel. If autocracy exists, there is less chance of this happening. However, the latter method creates a state of cooperation based on power and control. This controlled cooperation is really subdued conflict and makes for a more unstable equilibrium than does voluntary democratic cooperation.

CONTROLLED COOPERATION

The usual pattern in the establishment of channel relationships is that there is a leader, an initiator who puts structure into this relationship and who holds it together. This leader controls, whether through command or cooperation, i.e., through an autocratic or a demographic system.

Too often it is automatically assumed that the manufacturer or producer will be the channel leader and that the middlemen will be the channel followers. This has not always been so, nor will it necessarily be so in the future. The growth of mass retailers is increasingly challenging the manufacturer for channel leadership, as the manufacturer challenged the wholesaler in the early part of this century.

The following historical discussion will concentrate on the three-ring struggle between manufacturer, wholesaler, and retailer rather than on the changing patterns of distribution within a channel sector, i.e., between service wholesaler and agent middleman or discount and department store. This will lay the necessary background for a discussion of the present-day manufacturer-dominated *versus* retailer-dominated struggle.

Early History

The simple distribution system of Colonial days gave way to a more complex one. Among the forces of change were the growth of population, the long distances involved, the increasing complexity of new products, the increase of wealth, and the increase of consumption.

The United States was ready for specialists to provide a growing and widely dispersed populace with the many new goods and services required. The more promitive methods of public markets and barter could not sufficiently handle the situation. This type of system required short distances, few products, and a small population to operate properly.

19th Century History

In the same period that this older system was dissolving, the retailer was still a very small merchant who, especially in the West, lived in relative isolation from his supply sources. Aside from being small, he further diminished his power position by spreading himself thin over many merchandise lines. The retailer certainly was no specialist but was as general as a general store can be. His opposite channel member, the manufacturer, was also a small businessman, too concerned with production and financial problems to fuss with marketing.

Obviously, both these channel members were in no position to assume leadership. However, somebody had to perform all the various marketing functions between production and retailing if the economy was to function. The wholesaler filled this vacuum and became the channel leader of the 19th century.

The wholesaler became the selling force of the manufacturer and the latter's link to the widely scattered retailers over the nation. He became the retailer's life line to these distant domestic and even more important foreign sources of supply.

These wholesalers carried any type of product from any manufacturer and sold any type of product to the general retailers. They can be described as general merchandise wholesalers. They were concentrated at those transportation points in the country which gave them access to both the interior and its retailers, and the exterior and its foreign suppliers.

Early 20th Century

The end of the century saw the wholesaler's power on the decline. The manufacturer had grown larger and more financially secure with the shift from a foreign-oriented economy to a domestic-oriented one. He could now finance his marketing in a manner impossible to him in early times. His thoughts shifted to some extent from production problems to marketing problems.

Prodding the manufacturer on was the increased rivalry of his other domestic competitors. The increased investment in capital and inventory made it necessary that he maintain volume. He tended to locate himself in the larger market areas and thus, did not have great distances to travel to see his retail customers. In addition, he started to produce various products; and because of his new multi-product production, he could reach—even more efficiently—these already more accessible markets.

The advent of the automobile and highways almost clinched the manufacturer's bid for power. For now he could reach a much vaster market (and they could reach him) and reap the benefits of economies of scale.

The branding of his products projected him to the channel leadership. No longer did he have as great a need for a specialist in reaching widely dispersed customers, nor did he need them to the same extent for their contacts. The market knew where the product came from. The age of wholesaler dominance declined. That of manufacturer dominance emerged.

Is it still here. What is its future? How strong is the challenge by retailers? Is one "better" than the other? These are the questions of the next section.

Disagreement Among Scholars

No topic seems to generate so much heat and bias in marketing as the question of who should be the channel leader, and more strangely, who is the channel leader. Depending on where the author sits, he can give numerous reasons why his particular choice should take the channel initiative.

Authors of sales management and general marketing books say the manufacturer is and should be the chief institution in the channel. Retailing authors feel the same way about retailers, and wholesaling authors (as few as there are), though not blinded to the fact that wholesaling is not "captain," still imply that they should be and talk about the coming resurrection of wholesalers. Yet a final and compromising view is put forth by those who believe that a balance of power, rather than a general and prolonged dominance of any channel member, is best.

The truth is that an immediate reaction would set in against any temporary dominance by a channel member. In that sense, there is a constant tendency toward the equilibrium of market forces. The present view is that public interest is served by a balance of power rather than by a general prolonged predominance of any one level in marketing channels.[11]

John Kenneth Galbraith's concept of countervailing power also holds to this last view. For the retailer:

In the opinion of the writer, "retailer-dominated marketing" has yielded, and will continue to yield in the future greater net benefits to consumers than "manufacturer-dominated marketing," as the central-buying mass distributor continues to play a role of ever-increasing importance in the marketing of goods in our economy. . . .

. . . In the years to come, as more and more large-scale multiple-unit retailers follow the central buying patterns set by Sears and Penney's, as leaders in their respective fields (hard lines and soft goods), ever-greater benefits should flow to consumers in the way of more goods better adjusted to their demands, at lower prices.[12]

. . . In a long-run buyer's market, such as we probably face in this country, the retailers have the inherent advantage of economy in distribution and will, therefore, become increasingly important.[13]

The retailer cannot be the selling agent of the manufacturer because he holds a higher commission; he is the purchasing agent for the public.[14]

For the wholesaler:

The wholesaling sector is, first of all, the most significant part of the entire marketing organization.[15]

... The orthodox wholesaler and affiliated types have had a resurgence to previous 1929 levels of sales importance.[16]

... Wholesalers have since made a comeback.[17] This revival of wholesaling has resulted from infusion of new management blood and the adoption of new techniques.[18]

For the manufacturer:

... the final decision in channel selection rests with the seller manufacturer and will continue to rest with him as long as he has the legal right to choose to sell to some potential customers and refuse to sell to others.[19]

These channel decisions are primarily problems for the manufacturer. They rarely arise for general wholesalers. ...[20]

Of all the historical tendencies in the field of marketing, no other so distinctly apparent as the tendency for the manufacturer to assume greater control over the distribution of his product. ...[21]

... Marketing policies at other levels can be viewed as extensions of policies established by marketing managers in manufacturing firms; and, furthermore, ... the nature and function can adequately be surveyed by looking at the relationship to manufacturers.[22]

Pro-Manufacturer

The argument for manufacturer leadership is production-oriented. It claims that they must assure themselves of increasing volume. This is needed to derive the benefits of production scale economies, to spread their overhead over many units, to meet increasingly stiff competition, and to justify the investment risk they, not the retailers, are taking. Since retailers will not do this job for them properly, the manufacturer must control the channel.

Another major argumentative point for manufacturer dominance is that neither the public nor retailers can create new products even under a market-oriented system. The most the public can do is to select and choose among those that manufacturers have developed. They cannot select products that they cannot conceive. This argument would say that it is of no use to ask consumers and re-tailers what they want because they cannot articulate abstract needs into tangible goods; indeed, the need can be created by the goods rather than vice-versa.

This argument may hold well when applied to consumers, but a study of the specification-buying programs of the mass retailers will show that the latter can indeed create new products and need not be relegated to simply selecting among alternatives.

Pro-Retailer

This writer sees the mass retailer as the natural leader of the channel for con-sumer goods under the marketing concept. The retailer stands closest to the consumer; he feels the pulse of consumer wants and needs day in and day out. The retailer can easily undertake consumer research right on his own premises and can best interpret what is wanted, how much is wanted, and when it is wanted.

An equilibrium in the channel conflict may come about when small retailers join forces with big manufacturers in a manufacturer leadership channel to com-pete with a small manufacturer-big retailer leadership channel.

Pro-Wholesaler

It would seem that the wholesaler has a choice in this domination problem as well. Unlike the manufacturer and retailer though, his method is not mainly through a power struggle. This problem is almost settled for him once he chooses the type of wholesaling business he wishes to enter. A manufacturer's agent and purchasing agent are manufacturer-dominated, a sales agent dominates the manufacturer. A resident buyer and voluntary group wholesaler are retail-dominated.

Method of Manufacturer Domination

How does a channel leader dominate his fellow members? What are his tools in this channel power struggle? A manufacturer has many domination weapons at his disposal. His arsenal can be divided into promotional, legal, negative, suggestive, and, ironically, voluntary cooperative compartments.

Promotional. Probably the major method that the manufacturer has used is the building of a consumer franchise through advertising, sales promotion, and packaging of his branded products. When he has developed some degree of consumer loyalty, the other channel members must bow to his leadership. The more successful this identification through the promotion process, the more assured is the manufacturer of his leadership.

Legal. The legal weapon has also been a poignant force for the manufacturer. It can take many forms, such as, where permissible, resale price maintenance. Other contractual methods are franchises, where the channel members may become mere shells of legal entities. Through this weapon the automobile manufacturers have achieved an almost absolute dominance over the dealers.

Even more absolute is resort to legal ownership of channel members, called forward vertical integration. Vertical integration is the ultimate in manufacturer dominance of the channel. Another legal weapon is the use of consignment sales. Under this method the channel members must by law sell the goods as designated by the owner (manufacturer). Consignment selling is in a sense vertical integration; it is keeping legal ownership of the goods until they reach the consumer, rather than keeping legal ownership of the institutions which are involved in the process.

Negative methods. Among the "negative" methods of dominance are refusal to sell to possibly uncooperative retailers or refusal to concentrate a large percentage of one's volume with any one customer.

A spreading of sales makes for a concentrating of manufacturer power, while a concentrating of sales may make for a thinning of manufacturer power. Of course, if a manufacturer is one of the few resources available and if there are many available retailers, then a concentrating of sales will also make for a concentrating of power.

The avoidance and refusal tactics, of course, eliminate the possibility of opposing dominating institutions.

Suggestives. A rather weak group of dominating weapons are the "suggestives." Thus, a manufacturer can issue price sheets and discounts, preticket and premark resale prices on goods, recommend, suggest, and advertise resale prices.

These methods are not powerful unless supplemented by promotional, legal, and/or negative weapons. It is common for these methods to boomerang. Thus a manufacturer pretickets or advertises resale prices, and a retailer cuts this price, pointing with pride to the manufacturer's suggested retail price.

Voluntary cooperative devices. There is one more group of dominating weapons, and these are really all the voluntary cooperating weapons to be mentioned later. The promise to provide these, or to withdraw, can have a "whip or carrot" effect on the channel members.

Retailers' Dominating Weapons

Retailers also have numerous dominating weapons at their disposal. As with manufacturers, their strongest weapon is the building of a consumer franchise through advertising, sales promotion, and branding. The growth of private brands is the growth of retail dominance.

Attempts at concentrating a retailer's purchasing power are a further group of weapons and are analogous to a manufacturer's attempts to disperse his volume. The more a retailer can concentrate his purchasing, the more dominating he can become; the more he spreads his purchasing, the more dominated he becomes. Again, if the resource is one of only a few, this generalization reverses itself.

Such legal contracts as specification buying, vertical integration (or the threat), and entry into manufacturing can also be effective. Even semiproduction, such as the packaging of goods received in bulk by the supermarket, can be a weapon of dominance.

Retailers can dilute the dominance of manufacturers by patronizing those with excess capacity and those who are "hungry" for the extra volume. There is also the subtlety, which retailers may recognize, that a strong manufacturer may concede to their wishes just to avoid an open conflict with a customer.

VOLUNTARY COOPERATION

But despite some of the conflict dynamics and force cooperation, channel members usually have more harmonious and common interests than conflicting ones. A team effort to market a producer's product will probably help all involved. All members have a common interest in selling the product; only in the division of total channel profits are they in conflict. They have a singular goal to reach, and here they are allies. If any one of them fails in the team effort, this weak link in the chain can destroy them all. As such, all members are concerned with one another's welfare (unless a member can be easily replaced).

Organizational Extension Concept

This emphasis on the cooperating, rather than the conflicting objectives of channel members, has led to the concept of the channel as simply an extension of one's own internal organization. Conflict in such a system is to be expected even as it is to be expected within an organization. However, it is the common or "macro-objective" that is the center of concentration. Members are to sacrifice their selfish "micro-objectives" to this cause. By increasing the profit pie they will all be better off than squabbling over pieces of a smaller one. The goal is to minimize conflict and maximize cooperation. This view has been expounded in various articles by Peter Drucker, Ralph Alexander, and Valentine Ridgeway.

Together, the manufacturer with his suppliers and/or dealers comprise a system in which the manufacturer may be designated the primary organization and the dealers and suppliers designated as secondary organizations. This system is in competition with similar systems in the economy; and in order for the system to operate effectively as an integrated whole, there must be some administration of the separate organizations within that system.[23]

Peter Drucker[24] has pleaded against the conceptual blindness that the idea of the legal entity generates. A legal entity is not a marketing entity. Since often half of the cost to the consumer is added on after the product leaves the producer, the latter should think of his channel members as part of his firm. General Motors is an example of an organization which does this.

Both businessmen and students of marketing often define too narrowly the problem of marketing channels. Many of them tend to define the term channels of distribution as a complex of relationships between the firm on the one hand, and marketing establishments exterior to the firm by which the products of the firm are moved to market, on the other. . . . A much broader more constructive concept embraces the relationships with external agents or units as part of the marketing organization of the company. From this viewpoint, the complex of external relationships may be regarded as merely an extension of the marketing organization of the firm. When we look at the problem in this way, we are much less likely to lose sight of the interdependence of the two structures and more likely to be constantly aware that they are closely related parts of the marketing machine. The fact that the internal organization structure is linked together by a system of employment contracts, while the external one is set up and maintained by a series of transactions, contracts of purchase and sale, tends to obscure their common purpose and close relationship.[25]

Cooperation Methods

But how does a supplier project its organization into the channel? How does it make organization and channel into one? It accomplishes this by doing many things for its resellers that it does for its own organization. It sells, advertises, trains, plans, and promotes for these firms. A brief elaboration of these methods follows.

Missionary salesmen aid the sales of channel members, as well as bolster the whole system's level of activity and selling effort. Training of resellers' salesmen and executives is an effective weapon of cooperation. The channels operate more efficiently when all are educated in the promotional techniques and uses of the products involved.

Involvement in the planning functions of its channel members could be another poignant weapon of the supplier. Helping resellers to set quotas for their customers, studying the market potential for them, forecasting a member's sales volume, inventory planning and protection, etc., are all aspects of this latter method.

Aid in promotion through the provision of advertising materials (mats, displays, commercials, literature, direct-mail pieces), ideas, funds (cooperative advertising), sales contests, store layout designs, push money (PM's or spiffs), is another form of cooperation.

The big supplier can act as management consultant to the members, dispensing advice in all areas of their business, including accounting, personnel, planning, control, finance, buying, paper systems or office procedure, and site selection. Aid in financing may include extended credit terms, consignment selling, and loans.

By no means do these methods of coordination take a one-way route. All members of the channel, including supplier and reseller, see their own organizations meshing with the others, and so provide coordinating weapons in accordance with their ability. Thus, the manufacturer would undertake a marketing research project for his channel, and also expect his resellers to keep records and vital information for the manufacturer's use. A supplier may also expect his channel members to service the product after the sale.

A useful device for fostering cooperation is a channel advisory council composed of the supplier and his resellers.

Finally, a manufacturer or reseller can avoid associations with potentially uncooperative channel members. Thus, a price-conservative manufacturer may avoid linking to a price-cutting retailer.

E. B. Weiss has developed an impressive, though admittedly incomplete list of cooperation methods (Table 1). Paradoxically, many of these instruments of cooperation are also weapons of control (forced cooperation) to be used by both middlemen and manufacturers. However, this is not so strange if one keeps in mind that control is subdued conflict and a form of cooperation—even though perhaps involuntary cooperation.

Extension Concept is The Marketing Concept

The philosophy of cooperation is described in the following quote:

The essence of the marketing concept is of course customer orientation at all levels of distribution. It is particularly important that customer orientation motivate all relations between a manufacturer and his customer—both immediate and ultimate. It must permeate his entire channels-of-distribution policy.[26]

This quote synthesizes the extension-of-the-organization system concept of channels with the marketing concept. Indeed, it shows that the former is, in essence, "the" marketing concept applied to the channel area in marketing. To continue:

The characteristics of the highly competitive markets of today naturally put a distinct premium on harmonious manufacturer-distributor relationships. Their

Table 1. Methods of cooperation as listed [27]

1. Cooperative advertising allowances	19. Delivery costs to individual stores of large retailers
2. Payments for interior displays including shelf-extenders, dump displays, "A" locations, aisle displays, etc.	20. Studies of innumerable types, such as studies of merchandise management accounting
3. P.M.'s for salespeople	21. Payments for mailings to store lists
4. Contests for buyers, salespeople, etc.	22. Liberal return privileges
5. Allowances for a variety of warehousing functions	23. Contributions to favorite charities of store personnel
6. Payments for window display space, plus installation costs	24. Contributions to special store anniversaries
7. Detail men who check inventory, put up stock, set up complete promotions, etc.	25. Prizes, etc., to store buyers when visiting showrooms—plus entertainment, of course
8. Demonstrators	26. Training retail salespeople
9. On certain canned food, a "swell" allowance	27. Payments for store fixtures
10. Label allowance	28. Payments for new store costs, for more improvements, including painting
11. Coupon handling allowance	29. An infinite variety of promotion allowances
12. Free goods	30. Special payments for exclusive franchises
13. Guaranteed sales	31. Payments of part of salary of retail salespeople
14. In-store and window display material	32. Deals of innumerable types
15. Local research work	33. Time spent in actual selling floor by manufacturer, salesmen
16. Mail-in premium offers to consumer	34. Inventory price adjustments
17. Preticketing	35. Store name mention in manufacturer's advertising
18. Automatic re-order systems	

very mutuality of interest demands that the manufacturer base his distribution program not only on what he would like from distributors, but perhaps more importantly, on what they would like from him. In order to get the cooperation of the best distributors, and thus maximum exposure for his line among the various market segments, he must adjust his policies to serve their best interest and, thereby, his own. In other words, he must put the principles of the marketing concept to work for him. By so doing, he will inspire in his customers a feeling of mutual interest and trust and will help convince them that they are essential members of his marketing team.[28]

SUMMARY

Figure 1 summarizes this whole paper. Each person within each department will cooperate, control, and conflict with each other (notice arrows). Together they form a department (notice department box contains person boxes) which will be best off when cooperating (or cooperation through control) forces weight heavier than conflicting forces. Now each department cooperates, controls, and conflicts with each other. Departments together also form a higher level organization—the firm (manufacturer, wholesaler, and retailer). Again, the firm will be better off if department cooperation is maximized and conflict minimized. Finally, firms standing vertically to each other cooperate, control, and conflict. Together they form a distribution channel that will be best off under conditions of optimum cooperation leading to consumer and profit satisfaction.

Figure 1.

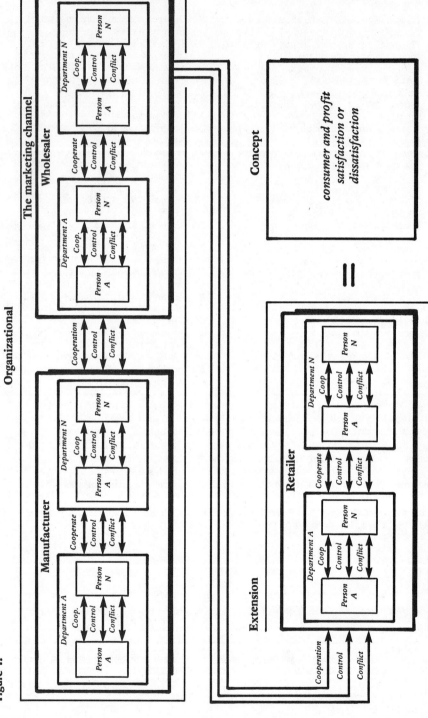

CONCLUSIONS AND HYPOTHESES

1. Channel relationships are set against a background of cooperation and conflict: horizontal, intertype, and vertical.

2. An autocratic relationship exists when one channel member controls conflict and forces the others to cooperate. A democratic relationship exists when all members agree to cooperate without a power play. An anarchistic relationship exists when there is open conflict, with no member able to impose his will on the others. This last form could destroy or seriously reduce the effectiveness of the channel.

3. The process of the exchange act where one member is a seller and the other is a buyer is the basic source of channel conflict. Economic theory can aid in comprehending this phenomenon. There are, however, many other areas of conflict, such as differences in business philosophy or primary objectives.

4. Reasons for cooperation, however, usually outweigh reasons for conflict. This has led to the concept of the channel as an extension of a firm's organization.

5. This concept drops the facade of "legal entity" and treats channel members as one great organization with the leader providing each with various forms of assistance. These are called cooperating weapons.

6. It is argued that this concept is actually the marketing concept adapated to a channel situation.

7. In an autocratic or democratic channel relationship, there must be a leader. This leadership has shifted and is shifting between the various channel levels.

8. The wholesaler was the leader in the last century, the manfacturer now, and it appears that the mass retailer is next in line.

9. There is much disagreement on the above point, however, especially on who should be the leader. Various authors have differing arguments to advance for their choice.

10. In the opinion of this writer, the mass retailer appears to be best adapted for leadership under the marketing concept.

11. As there are weapons of cooperation, so are there weapons of domination. Indeed the former paradoxically are one group of the latter. The other groups are promotional, legal, negative, and suggestive methods. Both manufacturers and retailers have at their disposal these dominating weapons.

12. *For maximization of channel profits and consumer satisfaction, the channel must act as a unit.*

NOTES

[1] Ralph F. Breyer, "Some Observations on Structural Formation and The Growth of Marketing Channels," in *Theory in Marketing*, Reavis Cox, Wroe Alderson, Stanley J. Shapiro, Editors. (Homewood, Ill.: Richard D. Irwin, 1964), pp. 163–175.

[2] Ronald S. Vaile, E. T. Grether, and Reavis Cox, *Marketing in the American Economy* (New York: Ronald Press, 1952), pp. 121 and 124.

[3] Breyer, *op. cit.,* p. 165.

[4] Joseph C. Palamountain, *The Politics of Distribution* (Cambridge: Harvard University Press, 1955).

[5] Isaiah A. Litvak and Bruce E. Mallen, *Marketing: Canada* (Toronto: McGraw-Hill of Canada, Limited, 1964), pp. 196–197.

[6] This section is based on Bert C. McCammon, Jr., "Alternative Explanations of Institutional Change and Channel Evolution," in *Toward Scientific Marketing.* Stephen A. Greyser, Editor. (Chicago: American Marketing Association, 1963), pp. 477–490.

[7] Bruce Mallen, "Introducing The Marketing Channel To Price Theory," *Journal of Marketing,* July, 1964, pp. 29–33.

[8] Warren J. Wittreich, "Misunderstanding The Retailers," *Harvard Business Review,* May–June, 1962, p. 149.

[9] The term *anarchy* as used in this paper connotes "no leadership" and nothing more.

[10] Lewis B. Sappington and C. G. Browne, "The Skills of Creative Leadership," in *Managerial Marketing,* rev. ed., William Lazer and Eugene J. Kelley, Editors (Homewood, Ill.: Richard D. Irwin, 1962), p. 350.

[11] Wroe Alderson, "Factors Governing the Development of Marketing Channels," in *Marketing Channels For Manufactured Products,* Richard M. Clewett, Editor. (Homewood, Ill.: Richard D. Irwin, 1954), p. 30.

[12] Arnold Corbin, *Central Buying in Relation to the Merchandising of Multiple Retail Units* (New York, unpublished doctoral dissertation at New York University, 1954), pp. 708–709.

[13] David Craig and Werner Gabler, "The Competitive Struggle for Market Control," in *Readings in Marketing,* Howard J. Westing, Editor. (New York: Prentice-Hall, 1953), p. 46.

[14] Lew Hahn, *Stores, Merchants and Customers* (New York: Fairchild Publications, 1952), p. 12.

[15] David A. Revzan, *Wholesaling in Marketing Organization* (New York: John Wiley & Sons, 1961), p. 606.

[16] *Ibid.,* p. 202 .

[17] E. Jerome McCarthy, *Basic Marketing* (Homewood, Ill.: Richard D. Irwin, 1960), p. 419.

[18] *Ibid.,* p. 420.

[19] Eli P. Cox, *Federal Quantity Discount Limitations and Its Possible Effects on Distribution Channel Dynamics* (unpublished doctoral dissertation, University of Texas, 1956), p. 12.

[20] Milton Brown, Wilbur B. England, John B. Matthews, Jr., *Problems in Marketing,* 3rd ed. (New York: McGraw-Hill, 1961), p. 239.

[21] Maynard D. Phelps and Howard J. Westing, *Marketing Management,* rev. ed. (Homewood, Ill.: Richard D. Irwin, 1960), p. 11.

[22] Kenneth Davis, *Marketing Management* (New York: The Ronald Press Co., 1961), p. 131.

[23] Valentine F. Ridgeway, "Administration of Manufacture-Dealer Systems," in *Managerial Marketing,* rev. ed., William Lazer and Eugene J. Kelley, Editors. (Homewood, Ill.: Richard D. Irwin, 1962), p. 480.

[24] Peter Drucker, "The Economy's Dark Continent," *Fortune,* April, 1962, pp 103 ff.

[25] Ralph S. Alexander, James S. Cross, Ross M. Cunningham, *Industrial Marketing,* rev. ed. (Homewood, Ill.: Richard D. Irwin, 1961), p. 266.

[26] Hector Lazo and Arnold Corbin, *Management in Marketing* (New York: McGraw-Hill, 1961), p. 379.

[27] Edward B. Weiss, "How Much of a Retailer Is the Manufacturer," in *Advertising Age,* July 21, 1958, p. 68. Reprinted with permission from the July 21, 1958, issue of *Advertising Age.* Copyright by Advertising Publications, Inc.

[28] Lazo and Corbin, *loc. cit.*

SOME SUGGESTIONS FOR FURTHER READING

Bucklin, L. T. (1973), "A Therapy of Channel Control," *Journal of Marketing* (January), 30–47.

Little, R. W. (1970), "Marketing Channel: Who Should Lead This Extra-Corporate Organization?" *Journal of Marketing* (January), 31–38.

Lusch, R. F. (1976), "Sources of Power: Their Impact on Intrachannel Conflict," *Journal of Marketing Research* (November), 382–390.

McCammon, B. C., Jr. and Hammer, W. L. (1974), "A Frame of Reference for Improving Productivity in Distribution," *Atlanta Economic Review* (September–October), 9–13.

Mason, J. B. (1975), "Power and Channel Conflicts in Shopping Center Management," *Journal of Marketing* (April), 28–35.

Robicheaux, R. A. and El Ansary, A. I. (1975), "A General Model for Understanding Channel Member Behavior," *Journal of Retailing* (Winter), 13–30ff.

34 / RETAIL STRATEGY AND THE CLASSIFICATION OF CONSUMER GOODS / Louis P. Bucklin

When Melvin T. Copeland published his famous discussion of the classification of consumer goods, shopping, convenience, and specialty goods, his intent was clearly to create a guide for the development of marketing strategies by manufacturers.[1] Although his discussion involved retailers and retailing, his purpose was to show how consumer buying habits affected the type of channel of distribution and promotional strategy that a manufacturer should adopt. Despite the controversy which still surrounds his classification, his success in creating such a guide may be judged by the fact that through the years few marketing texts have failed to make use of his ideas.

The purpose of this article is to attempt to clarify some of the issues that exist with respect to the classification, and to extend the concept to include the retailer and the study of retail strategy.

CONTROVERSY OVER THE CLASSIFICATION SYSTEM

The starting point for the discussion lies with the definitions adopted by the American Marketing Association's Committee on Definitions for the classification system in 1948.[2] These are:

Convenience Goods: Those consumers' goods which the customer purchases frequently, immediately, and with the minimum of effort.
   Shopping Goods: Those consumers' goods which the customer in the process of selection and purchase characteristically compares on such bases as suitability, quality, price and style.
   Specialty Goods: Those consumers' goods on which a significant group of buyers are habitually willing to make a special purchasing effort.

This set of definitions was retained in virtually the same form by the Committee on Definitions in its latest publication.[3]

Opposing these accepted definitions stands a critique by Richard H. Holton.[4] Finding the Committee's definitions too imprecise to be able to measure con-

Reprinted from the *Journal of Marketing*, published by the American Marketing Association (January, 1963), pp. 51–56.
Louis P. Bucklin has taught in business schools at the University of Colorado and Northwestern University, and is now professor of marketing at the University of California at Berkeley. He received his bachelor's degree from Dartmouth, his M.B.A. from Harvard, and his Ph.D. from Northwestern. He is an authority on marketing channels and channel management.

sumer buying behavior, he suggested that the following definitions not only would represent the essence of Copeland's original idea, but be operationally more useful as well.

Convenience Goods: Those goods for which the consumer regards the probable gain from making price and quality comparisons as small compared to the cost of making such comparisons.
Shopping Goods: Those goods for which the consumer regards the probable gain from making price and quality comparisons as large relative to the cost of making such comparisons.
Specialty Goods: Those convenience or shopping goods, which have such a limited market as to require the consumer to make a special effort to purchase them.

Holton's definitions have particular merit because they make explicit the underlying conditions that control the extent of a consumer's shopping activities. They show that a consumer's buying behavior will be determined not only by the strength of his desire to secure some good, but by his perception of the cost of shopping to obtain it. In other words, the consumer continues to shop *for all goods* so long as he feels that the additional satisfactions from further comparisons are at least equal to the cost of making the additional effort. The distinction between shopping and convenience goods lies principally in the degree of satisfaction to be secured from further comparisons.

The Specialty Good Issue

While Holton's conceptualization makes an important contribution, he has sacrificed some of the richness of Copeland's original ideas. This is essentially David J. Luck's complaint in a criticism of Holton's proposal.[5] Luck objected to the abandonment of the *willingness* of consumers to make a special effort to buy as the rationale for the concept of specialty goods. He regarded this type of consumer behavior as based upon unique consumer attitudes toward certain goods and not the density of distribution of those goods. Holton, in a reply, rejected Luck's point; he remained convinced that the real meaning of specialty goods could be derived from his convenience goods, shopping goods continuum, and market conditions.[6]

The root of the matter appears to be that insufficient attention has been paid to the fact that the consumer, once embarked upon some buying expedition, may have only one of two possible objectives in mind. A discussion of this aspect of consumer behavior will make possible a closer synthesis of Holton's contributions with the more traditional point of view.

A Forgotten Idea

The basis for this discussion is afforded by certain statements, which the marketing profession has largely ignored over the years, in Copeland's original presentation of his ideas. These have regard to the extent of the consumer's awareness of the precise nature of the item he wishes to buy, *before* he starts his shopping trip. Copeland stated that the consumer, in both the case of convenience goods and specialty goods, has full knowledge of the particular good, or its acceptable substitutes, that he will buy before he commences his buying trip. The consumer, however, lacks this knowledge in the case of a shopping good.[7] This means that the buying trip must not only serve the objective of purchasing the good, but must enable the consumer to discover which item he wants to buy.

The behavior of the consumer during any shopping expedition may, as a result, be regarded as heavily dependent upon the state of his decision as to what he wants to buy. If the consumer knows precisely what he wants, he needs only to undertake communication activities sufficient to take title to the desired product. He may also undertake ancillary physical activities involving the handling of the product and delivery. If the consumer is uncertain as to what he wants to buy, then an additional activity will have to be performed. This involves the work of making comparisons between possible alternative purchases, or simply search.

There would be little point, with respect to the problem of classifying consumer goods, in distinguishing between the activity of search and that of making a commitment to buy, if a consumer always performed both before purchasing a good. The crucial point is that he does not. While most of the items that a consumer buys have probably been subjected to comparison at some point in his life, he does not make a search before each purchase. Instead, a past solution to the need is frequently remembered and, if satisfactory, is implemented.[8] Use of these past decisions for many products quickly moves the consumer past any perceived necessity of undertaking new comparisons and leaves only the task of exchange to be discharged.

REDEFINITION OF THE SYSTEM

Use of this concept of problem solving permits one to classify consumer buying efforts into two broad categories which may be called shopping and nonshopping goods.

Shopping Goods

Shopping goods are those for which the consumer *regularly* formulates a new solution to his need each time it is aroused. They are goods whose suitability is determined through search before the consumer commits himself to each purchase.

The motivation behind this behavior stems from circumstances which tend to perpetuate a lack of complete consumer knowledge about the nature of the product that he would like to buy.[9] Frequent changes in price, style, or product technology cause consumer information to become obsolete. The greater the time lapse between purchases, the more obsolete will his information be. The consumer's needs are also subject to change, or he may seek variety in his purchases as an actual goal. These forces will tend to make past information inappropriate. New search, due to forces internal and external to the consumer, is continuously required for products with purchase determinants which the consumer regards as both important and subject to change.[10]

The number of comparisons that the consumer will make in purchasing a shopping good may be determined by use of Holton's hypothesis on effort. The consumer, in other words, will undertake search for a product until the perceived value to be secured through additional comparisons is less than the estimated cost of making those comparisons. Thus, shopping effort will vary according to the intensity of the desire of the consumer to find the right product, the type of product and the availability of retail facilities. Whether the consumer searches diligently, superficially, or even buys at the first opportunity, however, does not alter the shopping nature of the product.

Nonshopping Goods

Turning now to nonshopping goods, one may define these as products for which the consumer is both willing and able to use stored solutions to the problem of finding a product to answer a need. From the remarks on shopping goods it may be generalized that nonshopping goods have purchase determinants which do not change, or which are perceived as changing inconsequentially, between purchases.[11] The consumer, for example, may assume that price for some product never changes or that price is unimportant. It may be unimportant because either the price is low, or the consumer is very wealthy.

Nonshopping goods may be divided into convenience and specialty goods by means of the concept of a preference map. Bayton introduces this concept as the means to show how the consumer stores information about products.[12] It is a rough ranking of the relative desirability of the different kinds of products that the consumer sees as possible satisfiers for his needs. For present purposes, two basic types of preference maps may be envisaged. One type ranks all known product alternatives equally in terms of desirability. The other ranks one particular product as so superior to all others that the consumer, in effect, believes this product is the only answer to his need.

Distinguishing the Specialty Good

This distinction in preference maps creates the basis for discriminating between a convenience good and a specialty good. Clearly, where the consumer is indifferent to the precise item among a number of substitutes which he could buy, he will purchase the most accessible one and look no further. This is a convenience good. On the other hand, where the consumer recognizes only one brand of a product as capable of satisfying his needs, he will be willing to bypass more readily accessible substitutes in order to secure the wanted item. This is a specialty good.

However, most nonshopping goods will probably fall in between these two polar extremes. Preference maps will exist where the differences between the relative desirability of substitutes may range from the slim to the well marked. In order to distinguish between convenience goods and specialty goods in these cases, Holton's hypothesis regarding consumer effort may be employed again. A convenience good, in these terms, becomes one for which the consumer has such little preference among his perceived choices that he buys the item which is most readily available. A specialty good is one for which consumer preference is so strong that he bypasses, or would be willing to bypass, the purchase of more accessible substitutes in order to secure his most wanted item.

It should be noted that this decision on the part of the consumer as to how much effort he should expend takes place under somewhat different conditions than the one for shopping goods. In the nonshopping good instance the consumer has a reasonably good estimate of the additional value to be achieved by purchasing his preferred item. The estimate of the additional cost required to make this purchase may also be made fairly accurately. Consequently, the consumer will be in a much better position to justify the expenditure of additional effort here than in the case of shopping goods where much uncertainty must exist with regard to both of these factors.

The New Classification

The classification of consumer goods that results from the analysis is as follows:

Convenience Goods: Those goods for which the consumer, before his need arises, possesses a preference map that indicates a willingness to purchase any of a number of known substitutes rather than to make the additional effort required to buy a particular item.

    Shopping Goods: Those goods for which the consumer has not developed a complete preference map before the need arises, requiring him to undertake search to construct such a map before purchase.

    Specialty Goods: Those goods for which the consumer, before his need arises, possesses a preference map that indicates a willingness to expend the additional effort required to purchase the most preferred item rather than to buy a more readily accessible substitute.

EXTENSION TO RETAILING

The classification of the goods concept developed above may now be extended to retailing. As the concept now stands, it is derived from consumer attitudes or motives toward a *product*. These attitudes, or product motives, are based upon the consumer's interpretation of a product's styling, special features, quality, and social status of its brand name, if any. Occasionally the price may also be closely associated with the product by the consumer.

Classification of Patronage Motives

The extension of the concept to retailing may be made through the notion of patronage motives, a term long used in marketing. Patronage motives are derived from consumer attitudes concerning the retail establishment. They are related to factors which the consumer is likely to regard as controlled by the retailer. These will include assortment, credit, service, guarantee, shopping ease and enjoyment, and usually price. Patronage motives, however, have never been systematically categorized. It is proposed that the procedure developed above to discriminate among product motives be used to classify consumer buying motives with respect to retail stores as well.

This will provide the basis for the consideration of retail marketing strategy and will aid in clearing up certain ambiguities that would otherwise exist if consumer buying motives were solely classified by product factors. These ambiguities appear, for example, when the consumer has a strong affinity for some particular brand of a product, but little interest in where he buys it. The manufacturer of the product, as a result, would be correct in defining the product as a specialty item if the consumer's preferences were so strong as to cause him to eschew more readily available substitutes. The retailer may regard it as a convenience good, however, since the consumer will make no special effort to purchase the good from any particular store. This problem is clearly avoided by separately classifying product and patronage motives.

The categorization of patronage motives by the above procedure results in the following three definitions. These are:

Convenience Stores: Those stores for which the consumer, before his need for some product arises, possesses a preference map that indicates a willingness to buy from the most accessible store.
Shopping Stores: Those stores for which the consumer has not developed a complete preference map relative to the product he wishes to buy, requiring him to undertake a search to construct such a map before purchase.
Specialty Stores: Those stores for which the consumer, before his need for some product arises, possesses a preference map that indicates a willingness to buy the item from a particular establishment even though it may not be the most accessible.

The Product-Patronage Matrix

Although this basis will not afford the retailer a means to consider alternative strategies, a finer classification system may be obtained by relating consumer product motives to consumer patronage motives. By cross-classifying each product motive with each patronage motive, one creates a three-by-three matrix, representing nine possible types of consumer buying behavior. Each of the nine cells in the matrix may be described as follows:

1. *Convenience Store—Convenience Good:* The consumer, represented by this category, prefers to buy the most readily available brand of product at the most accessible store.
2. *Convenience Store—Shopping Good:* The consumer selects his purchase from among the assortment carried by the most accessible store.
3. *Convenience Store—Specialty Good:* The consumer purchases his favored brand from the most accessible store which has the item in stock.

4. *Shopping Store—Convenience Good:* The consumer is indifferent to the brand of product he buys, but shops among different stores in order to secure better retail service and/or lower retail price.
5. *Shopping Store—Shopping Good:* The consumer makes comparisons among both retail controlled factors and factors associated with the product (brand).
6. *Shopping Store—Specialty Good:* The consumer has a strong preference with respect to the brand of the product, but shops among a number of stores in order to secure the best retail and/or price for this brand.
7. *Specialty Store—Convenience Good:* The consumer prefers to trade at a specific store, but is indifferent to the brand of product purchased.
8. *Specialty Store—Shopping Good:* The consumer prefers to trade at a certain store, but is uncertain as to which product he wishes to buy and examines the store's assortment for the best purchase.
9. *Specialty Store—Specialty Good:* The consumer has both a preference for a particular store and a specific brand.

Conceivably, each of these nine types of behavior might characterize the buying patterns of some consumers for a given product. It seems more likely, however, that the behavior of consumers toward a product could be represented by only three or four of the categories. The remaining cells would be empty, indicating that no consumers bought the product by these methods. Different cells, of course, would be empty for different products.

THE FORMATION OF RETAIL STRATEGY

The extended classification system developed above clearly provides additional information important to the manufacturer in the planning of his marketing strategy. Of principal interest here, however, is the means by which the retailer might use the classification system in planning his marketing strategy.

Three Basic Steps

The procedure involves three steps. The first is the classification of the retailer's potential customers for some product by market segment, using the nine categories in the consumer buying habit matrix to define the principal segments. The second requires the retailer to determine the nature of the marketing strategies necessary to appeal to each market segment. The final step is the retailer's selection of the market segment, and the strategy associated with it, to which he will sell. A simplified, hypothetical example may help to clarify this process.

A former buyer of dresses for a department store decided to open her own dress shop. She rented a small store in the downtown area of a city of 50,000, ten miles distant from a metropolitan center of several hundred thousand population. In contemplating her marketing strategy, she was certain that the different incomes, educational backgrounds, and tastes of the potential customers in her city meant that various groups of these women were using sharply different buying methods for dresses. Her initial problem was to determine, by use of the consumer buying habit matrix, what proportion of her potential market bought dresses in what manner.

By drawing on her own experience, discussions with other retailers in the area, census and other market data, the former buyer estimated that her potential market was divided, according to the matrix, in the proportions [shown in Table 1].

This analysis revealed four market segments that she believed were worth further consideration. (In an actual situation, each of these four should be further divided into submarket segments according to other possible factors such as age, income, dress size required, location of residence, etc.) Her next task was to determine the type of marketing mix which would most effectively appeal to each of these segments. The information for these decisions was derived from the characteristics of consumer behavior associated with each of the defined segments. The following is a brief description of her assessment of how elements of the marketing mix ought to be weighted in order to formulate a strategy for each segment.

A Strategy for Each Segment

To appeal to the convenience store-specialty good segment she felt that the two most important elements in the mix should be a highly accessible location and selection of widely-accepted brand merchandise. Of somewhat lesser importance, she found, were depth of assortment, personal selling, and price. Minimal emphasis should be given to store promotion and facilities.

She reasoned that the shopping store-shopping good requires a good central location, emphasis on price, and a broad assortment. She ranked store promotion, accepted brand names and personal selling as secondary. Store facilities would, once again, receive minor emphasis.

The specialty store-shopping good market would, she believed, have to be catered to with an exceptionally strong assortment, a high level of personal selling and more elaborate store facilities. Less emphasis would be needed upon prominent brand names, store promotions, and price. Location was of minor importance.

Table 1. Proportion of potential dress market in each matrix cell

Buying habit	% of market
Convenience store—convenience good	0
Convenience store—shopping good	3
Convenience store—specialty good	20
Shopping store—convenience good	0
Shopping store—shopping good	35
Shopping store—specialty good	2
Specialty store—convenience good	0
Specialty store—shopping good	25
Specialty store—specialty good	15
	100

The specialty store-specialty good category, she thought, would require a marketing mix heavily emphasizing personal selling and highly elaborate store facilities and service. She also felt that prominent brand names would be required, but that these would probably have to include the top names in fashion, including labels from Paris. Depth of assortment would be secondary, while least emphasis would be placed upon store promotion, price, and location.

Evaluation of Alternatives

The final step in the analysis required the former dress buyer to assess her abilities to implement any one of these strategies, given the degree of competition existing in each segment. Her considerations were as follows. With regard to the specialty store-specialty good market, she was unprepared to make the investment in store facilities and services that she felt would be necessary. She also thought, since a considerable period of time would probably be required for her to build up the necessary reputation, that this strategy involved substantial risk. Lastly, she believed that her experience in buying high fashion was somewhat limited and that trips to European fashion centers would prove burdensome.

She also doubted her ability to cater to the specialty store-shopping good market, principally because she knew that her store would not be large enough to carry the necessary assortment depth. She felt that this same factor would limit her in attempting to sell to the shopping store-shopping good market as well. Despite the presence of the large market in this segment, she believed that she would not be able to create sufficient volume in her proposed quarters to enable her to compete effectively with the local department store and several large department stores in the neighboring city.

The former buyer believed her best opportunity was in selling to the convenience store-specialty good segment. While there were already two other stores in her city which were serving this segment, she believed that a number of important brands were still not represented. Her past contacts with resources led her to believe that she would stand an excellent chance of securing a number of these lines. By stocking these brands, she thought that she could capture a considerable number of local customers who currently were purchasing them in the large city. In this way, she believed, she would avoid the full force of local competition.

Decision

The conclusion of the former buyer to use her store to appeal to the convenience store-specialty good segment represents the culmination to the process of analysis suggested here. It shows how the use of the three-by-three matrix of consumer buying habits may aid the retailer in developing his marketing strategy. It is a device which can isolate the important market segments. It provides further help in enabling the retailer to associate the various types of consumer behavior with those elements of the marketing mix to which they are sensitive. Finally, the analysis forces the retailer to assess the probability of his success in attempting to use the necessary strategy in order to sell each possible market.

NOTES

[1] Melvin T. Copeland, "Relation of Consumers' Buying Habits to Marketing Methods," *Harvard Business Review* (April, 1923), pp. 282–289.

[2] Definitions Committee, American Marketing Association, "Report of the Definitions Committee," *Journal of Marketing* (October, 1948), pp. 202–217, at p. 206, p. 215.

[3] Definitions Committee, American Marketing Association, *Marketing Definitions*, (Chicago: American Marketing Association, 1960), pp. 11, 21, 22.

[4] Richard H. Holton, "The Distinction Between Convenience Goods, Shopping Goods, and Specialty Goods," *Journal of Marketing* (July, 1958), pp. 53–56.

[5] David J. Luck, "On the Nature of Specialty Goods," *Journal of Marketing* (July, 1959), pp. 61–64.

[6] Richard H. Holton, "What Is Really Meant by 'Specialty' Goods?" *Journal of Marketing* (July, 1959), pp. 64–67.

[7] Melvin T. Copeland, same reference as footnote 1, pp. 283–284.

[8] George Katona, *Psychological Analysis of Economic Behavior* (New York: McGraw-Hill Book Co., Inc., 1951), p. 47.

[9] Same reference, pp. 67–68.

[10] George Katona and Eva Mueller, "A Study of Purchase Decisions in Consumer Behavior," Lincoln Clark, editor, *Consumer Behavior* (New York: University Press, 1954), pp. 30–87.

[11] Katona, same reference as footnote 8, p. 68.

[12] James A. Bayton, "Motivation, Cognition, Learning—Basic Factors in Consumer Behavior," *Journal of Marketing* (January, 1958), pp. 282–289, at p. 287.

SOME SUGGESTIONS FOR FURTHER READING

Aspinwall, L. V. (1961), *Four Marketing Theories*. Boulder, CO: University of Colorado, article #22 in this book, and references cited there.

Bucklin, L. P. (1976), "Retrospective Comment on Retail Strategy and the Classification of Consumer Goods," *The Great Writings in Marketing*, ed., Howard A. Thompson, Plymouth, MI: The Commerce Press, 382–388.

Enis, B. and K. J. Roering (1980), "Product Classification Taxonomies: Synthesis and Consumer Implications," in Charles W. Lamb, Jr. (ed.) *Theoretical Developments in Marketing*. Chicago: American Marketing Association, 186–189.

Levitt, T. (1980), "Marketing Success Through Differentiation—of Anything," *Harvard Business Review* (January–February), 83–91.

Ramond, C. K. and H. Assael (1974), "An Empirical Framework for Product Classification," *Models and Buyer Behavior*, ed., Jagdish Sheth. Evanston, IL: Harper and Row, 347–362.

35 / BAYESIAN DECISION THEORY IN PRICING STRATEGY / Paul E. Green

Since the publication of Robert Schlaifer's pioneering work, *Probability and Statistics for Business Decisions*,[1] the Bayesian approach to decision-making under uncertainty has received much comment, pro and con, by theoretical and applied statisticians alike.

However, in contrast to the large number of theoretical contributions being made to decision theory in general and Bayesian statistics in particular, reported applications of these procedures to real-world problem situations have been rather meager. Applications appear especially lacking in the marketing field.

In highly oversimplified terms, the Bayesian approach to decision-making under uncertainty provides a framework for explicitly working with the economic costs of alternative courses of action, the prior knowledge or judgments of the decision maker, and formal modification of these judgments as additional data are introduced into the problem.

In the du Pont Company, the decision theory approach, often augmented by computer simulation, has been used experimentally over the past few years in a variety of market planning applications, ranging from capacity expansion problems to questions concerning the introduction of new products and long-range price and promotional strategy. The application to follow concerns the use of Bayesian theory in the selection of a "best" pricing policy for a firm in an oligopolistic industry where such factors as demand elasticity, competitive retaliation, threat of future price weakness, and potential entry of new competitors influence the effectiveness of the firm's courses of action. Although the content of this case is apocryphal, its structure has been compounded from actual situations.

No attempt will be made to describe even superficially all of the many facets of the Bayesian approach to decision-making under uncertainty. The content of this article is focused on only two main considerations.

First, in dealing with actual marketing situations, for example, pricing problems, the opportunity to obtain field information may be non-existent. Second, in dealing with actual marketing problems, the complexity of the situation may force

Paul E. Green, "Bayesian Decision Theory in Pricing Strategy." Reprinted with permission from *Journal of Marketing*, published by the American Marketing Association, January, 1963, pp. 5–14. This article was co-winner of the 1963 Alpha Kappa Psi award as best article of the year.
Paul E. Green is S. S. Kresge professor of marketing at the Wharton School of Finance and Commerce. He received both M.A. and Ph.D. from the Wharton School. Professor Green spent 12 years in industry with such firms as the du Pont Company and the Sun Oil Company. He is a leading proponent of Bayesian analysis in marketing; his current interests include the use of quantitative techniques in marketing planning and decision making, particularly multidimensional and non-metric scaling. He and his co-author D. S. Tull have the successful textbook *Research for Marketing Decisions*.

the analyst to develop a problem structure in much greater detail than has been described in the literature.

AN ILLUSTRATIVE APPLICATION

Since early 1955, the Everclear Plastics Company had been producing a resin called Kromel, basically designed for certain industrial markets. In addition to Everclear, three other firms were producing Kromel resin. Prices among all four suppliers (called here the Kromel industry) were identical: and the product quality and service among producers were comparable. Everclear's current share of Kromel industry sales amounted to 10 per cent.

Four additional end uses comprised the principal marketing area for the Kromel industry. These market segments will be labeled A, B, C, and D. Three of the segments (B, C, and D) were functionally dependent on segment A in the sense that Kromel's *ultimate* market position and rate of approach to this level in each of these three segments was predicated on resin's making substantial inroads in segment A.

The Kromel industry's only competition in these four segments consisted of another resin called Verlon, which was produced by six other firms. Shares of the total Verlon-Kromel market (weighted sums over all four segments) currently stood at 70 per cent Verlon industry, and 30 per cent Kromel industry. Since its introduction in 1955, the superior functional characteristics per dollar cost of Kromel had enabled this newer product to displace fairly large poundages of Verlon in market segments B, C, and D.

On the other hand, the functional superiority per dollar cost of Kromel had not been sufficiently high to interest segment A consumers. While past price decreases in Kromel had been made, the cumulative effect of these reductions had still been insufficient to accomplish Kromel sales penetration in segment A. (Sales penetration is defined as a market share exceeding zero.)

In the early fall of 1960, it appeared to Everclear's management that future weakness in Kromel price might be in the offing. The anticipated capacity increases on the part of the firm's Kromel competitors suggested that in the next year or two potential industry supply of this resin might significantly exceed demand, if no substantial market participation for the Kromel industry were established in segment A. In addition, it appeared likely that potential Kromel competitors might enter the business, thus adding to the threat of oversupply in later years.

Segment A, of course, constituted the key factor. If substantial inroads could be made in this segment, it appeared likely that Kromel industry sales growth in the other segments not only could be speeded up, but that ultimate market share levels for this resin could be markedly increased from those anticipated in the absence of segment A penetration. To Everclear's sales management, a price reduction in Kromel still appeared to represent a feasible means to achieve this objective, and (even assuming similar price reductions on the part of Kromel competitors) perhaps could still be profitable to Everclear.

However, a large degree of uncertainty surrounded both the overall attractiveness of this alternative, and under this alternative the amount of the price reduction which would enable Kromel to penetrate market segment A.

PROBLEM STRUCTURING AND DEVELOPMENT
OF THE MODEL

Formulation of the problem required a certain amount of artistry and compromise toward achieving a reasonably adequate description of the problem. But it was also necessary to keep the structure simple enough so that the nature of each input would be comprehensible to the personnel responsible for supplying data for the study.

Problem components had to be formulated, such as:

1. length of planning period;
2. number and nature of courses of action;
3. payoff functions; and
4. states of nature covering future growth of the total Verlon-Kromel market, inter-industry (Kromel vs. Verlon) and intra-Kromel industry effects of a Kromel price change, implications on Everclear's share of the total Kromel industry, and Everclear's production costs.

Initial discussions with sales management indicated that a planning period of five years should be considered in the study. While the selection of five years was somewhat arbitrary, sales personnel believed that some repercussions of a current price reduction might well extend over several years into the future.

A search for possible courses of action indicated that four pricing alternatives covered the range of actions under consideration:

1. maintenance of *status quo* on Kromel price, which was $1.00 per pound;
2. a price reduction to $.93 per pound within the next three months;
3. a price reduction to $.85 per pound within the next three months;
4. a price reduction to $.80 per pound within the next three months.

Inasmuch as each price action would be expected to produce a different time pattern in the flow of revenues and costs, and since no added investment in production facilities was contemplated, it was agreed that cumulative, compounded net profits over the five-year planning period would constitute a relevant payoff function. In the absence of any unanimity as to the "correct" opportunity cost of capital, it was decided to use two interest rates of 6 and 10 per cent annually in order to test the sensitivity of outcomes to the cost of the capital variable.

Another consideration came to light during initial problem discussions. Total market growth (for the Kromel or Verlon industry) over the next five years in each market segment constituted a "state of nature" which could impinge on Everclear's profit position. Accordingly, it was agreed to consider three separate forecasts of total market growth, a "most probable," "optimistic," and "pessimistic" forecast.

From these assumptions a base case was then formulated. This main case would first consider the pricing problem under the most probable forecast of total

Verlon-Kromel year-by-year sales potential in each segment, using an opportunity cost of capital of 6 per cent annually. The two other total market forecasts and the other cost of capital were then to be treated as subcases, in order to test the sensitivity of the base case outcomes to variations in these particular states of nature.

However, inter- and intra-industry alternative states of nature literally abounded in the Kromel resin problem. Sales management at Everclear had to consider such factors as:

1. The possibility that Kromel resin could effect penetration of market segment A if no price decrease were made;
2. If a price decrease were made, the extent of Verlon retaliation to be anticipated;
3. Given a particular type of Verlon price retaliation, its possible impact on Kromel's penetration of segment A;
4. If segment A were penetrated, the possible market share which the Kromel industry could gain in segment A;
5. If segment A were penetrated, the possible side effects of this event on speeding up Kromel's participation in market segments B, C, and D;
6. If segment A were not penetrated, the impact which the price reduction could still have on speeding up Kromel's participation in segments B, C, and D;
7. If segment A were not penetrated, the possibility that existing Kromel competitors would initiate price reductions a year hence;
8. The possible impact of a current Kromel price reduction on the decisions of existing or potential Kromel producers to increase capacity or enter the industry.

While courses of action, length of planning period, and the payoff measure (cumulative, compounded net profits) for the base case had been fairly quickly agreed upon, the large number of inter- and intra-Kromel industry states of nature deemed relevant to the problem would require rather lengthy discussion with Everclear's sales personnel.

Accordingly, introductory sessions were held with Everclear's sales management, in order to develop a set of states of nature large enough to represent an adequate description of the real problem, yet small enough to be comprehended by the participating sales personnel. Next, separate interview sessions were held with two groups of Everclear's sales personnel; subjective probabilities regarding the occurrence of alternative states of nature under each course of action were developed in these sessions. A final session was held with all contributing personnel in attendance; each projection and/or subjective probability was gone over in detail, and a final set of ground rules for the study was agreed upon. A description of these ground rules appears in Table I.

USE OF TREE DIAGRAMS

The large number of alternative states of nature which were associated with inter- and intra-industry factors necessitated the construction of "tree diagrams" for each pricing alternative. These diagrams enabled sales management to trace the impli-

Table 1. Subjective probabilities and data estimates associated with Everclear's pricing problem

1. If Kromel price remained at $1.00/pound and market segment A were not penetrated, what market share pattern for Kromel industry sales pounds would obtain in segments B, C, and D?

	Base assumptions—Kromel industry share		
	Segment B	Segment C	Segment D
1961	57.0%	40.0%	42.0%
1962	65.0	50.0	44.0
1963	75.0	80.0	46.0
1964	76.0	84.0	48.0
1965	76.0	84.0	50.0

2. If Kromel price remained at $1.00/pound, what is the probability that Kromel would still penetrate market segment A?

	Probability of penetration—Segment A
1961	.05
1962	.10
1963	.20
1964	.25
1965	.40

3. Under price strategies $.93/pound, $.85/pound, and $.80/pound, what is the probability of Verlon industry price retaliation; and given the particular retaliation (shown below), what is the probability that Kromel would still penetrate market segment A?

Pricing case (entries are probabilities)

Verlon industry retaliation	$.93 case	$.85 case	$.80 case
Full match of Kromel price reduction	.05	.15	.38
Half match of Kromel price reduction	.60	.75	.60
Stand pat on price	.35	.10	.02

Given a particular Verlon retaliatory action, the probability that Kromel would still penetrate segment A

	$.93 case			$.85 case			$.80 case		
	Full match	Half match	Stand pat	Full match	Half match	Stand pat	Full match	Half match	Stand pat
1961	.15	.20	.35	.20	.40	.80	.75	.80	.90
1962	.25	.30	.60	.30	.60	.90	.80	.85	.95
1963	.35	.40	.65	.40	.65	.95	.85	.90	1.00
1964	.60	.65	.75	.70	.75	.98	.90	.95	1.00
1965	.65	.70	.80	.75	.80	.98	.95	.98	1.00

4. If penetration in market segment A were effected, what is the probability that Kromel would obtain the specific share of this segment (a) during the first year of penetration, and (b) during the second year of participation?

Share	First year	Second year
25%	.15	.00
50	.35	.00
75	.40	.00
100	.10	1.00

Table 1. (Continued)

5. If Kromel penetration of market segment A were effected, what impact would this event have on speeding up Kromel industry participation in segments B, C, and D?

    Segment B—Would speed up market participation one year from base assumption shown under point 1 of this Table.

    Segment C—Would speed up market participation one year from base assumption shown under point 1 of this Table.

    Segment D—Kromel would move up to 85% of the market in the following year, and would obtain 100% of the market in the second year following penetration of segment A.

6. Under the price reduction strategies, if Kromel penetration of market segment A were *not* accomplished, what is the probability that Kromel industry participation in segments B, C, and D (considered as a group) would still be speeded up one year from the base assumption shown under point 1 of this Table?

Probability of speedup	
$.93 case	.45
$.85 case	.60
$.80 case	.80

7. If Kromel price at the end of any given year were $1.00/pound, $.93/pound, $.85/pound, or $.80/pound, respectively, *and* if market segment A were not penetrated, what is the probability that present competitive Kromel producers would take the specific price action shown below?

If Kromel price	*Action*	*Probability*
@$1.00/pound	$1.00/pound	.15
	.93	.80
	.85	.05
	.80	.00
@$.93/pound	.93	.80
	.85	.20
	.80	.00
@$.85/pound	.85	1.00
	.80	.00
@$.80/pound	.80	1.00

8. Under each of the four price strategies, what is the probability that competitive (present or potential) Kromel producers would add to or initiate capacity (as related to the price prevailing in mid-1961) in the years 1963 and 1964? (No capacity changes were assumed in 1965.)

Competitor	$1.00/pound	$.93/pound	$.85/pound	$.80/pound
R	.50	.20	.05	.00
S	.90	.75	.50	.20
T	.40	.10	.05	.00
U	.70	.50	.25	.00
V	.70	.50	.25	.00

Timing and amount available beginning of year

Competitor	1963	1964
R	10 million pounds	20 million pounds
S	12	20
T	12	20
U	6	12
V	6	6

cations of their assumptions. Figure 1 shows a portion of one such tree diagram.

A word of explanation concerning interpretation of the probability tree is in order. The two principal branches underneath the *$1.00 case* refer to the event of whether or not Kromel penetrates segment A in the first year of the planning period. Sales personnel felt that a 5 per cent chance existed for penetration, hence the figure .05000 under A.

However, if A were penetrated, four market participations were deemed possible; 25, 50, 75 and 100 per cent carrying the conditional probabilities of .15, .35, .40 and .10 respectively.

Multiplication of each conditional probability, in turn, by the .05 marginal probability leads to the four joint probabilities noted in the upper left portion of the chart.

Next, if Kromel did not penetrate segement A during the first year, a probability of .80 was attached to the event that competitive Kromel producers would reduce price to $.93 per pound. Multiplying the conditional probability of .80 by .95 results in the .76000 probability assigned to the joint event, "did not penetrate segment A and Kromel price was reduced to $.93 per pound."

However, if Kromel price were reduced to $.93 per pound, Verlon retaliation had to be considered, leading to the joint probabilities assigned to the next set of tree branches. In this way probabilities were built up for each of the over 400 possible outcomes of the study by appropriate application of the ground rules noted in Table 1.

A mathematical model was next constructed for determining the expected value of Everclear's cumulative, compounded net profits under each price strategy. See Table 2.

This model was then programmed for an electronic computer. The simulation was first carried out for the base case assumptions regarding total Verlon-Kromel market growth and cost of capital. Additional runs were made in which these assumptions were varied.

RESULTS OF THE COMPUTER SIMULATIONS

The computer run for the base case showed some interesting results for the relevant variables affecting Everclear's cumulative, compounded net profits position at the end of the planning period. These results are portrayed in Figures 2 through 4.

Figure 2 summarizes the cumulative probability of Kromel's penetration of market segment A (the critical factor in the study) as a function of time, under each pricing strategy. As would be expected, the lowest price strategy, the *$.80 case*, carried the highest probability of market penetration. However, the cumulative probability approached 1, that *all* price strategies would eventually effect penetration of market segment A by the end of the simulation period. This behavior stems from the impact of price decreases assumed to be initiated by Kromel *competitors* (if penetration were not initially effected under the original price strategies) which in turn changed the probability of Kromel's penetration of segment A in later years, since this probability was related to price.

Figure 3 shows the expected incremental sales dollars (obtained by subtracting the expected outcomes of the *$1.00 case*, used as a reference base, from the ex-

Figure 1. Portion of a "tree diagram"; Kromel price simulation

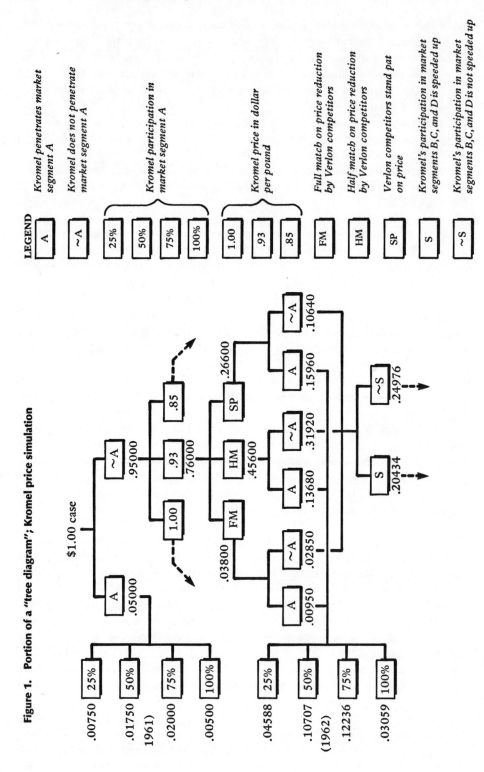

LEGEND

A	*Kromel penetrates market segment A*
~A	*Kromel does not penetrate market segment A*
25% 50% 75% 100%	*Kromel participation in market segment A*
1.00 .93 .85	*Kromel price in dollar per pound*
FM	*Full match on price reduction by Verlon competitors*
HM	*Half match on price reduction by Verlon competitors*
SP	*Verlon competitors stand pat on price*
S	*Kromel's participation in market segments B, C, and D is speeded up*
~S	*Kromel's participation in market segments B, C, and D is not speeded up*

Table 2.   Kromel model—expected value of cumulative, compounded net profits

The mathematical model used to determine the expected values of Everclear's cumulative, compounded net profits was as follows:

$$CCN(X_k) = \sum_{j=1}^{n} p_j \cdot \sum_{i=1}^{m} [(1+r)^{m-i} T \{ (D_{ij} - Z_{ij})(K_{ij}M_{ij}) \}]$$
$$Z_{ij} = \phi (K_{ij}M_{ij})$$

$CCN(X_k)$ = Expected value of Everclear's cumulative, compounded net profits under each X_k price strategy ($k = 1, \ldots, 4$).

p_j = Probability assigned to the j-th outcome ($j = 1, 2, \ldots, n$).

r = Interest rate per annum, expressed decimally.

T = Ratio of net to gross profits of Everclear's Kromel operation (assumed constant in the study).

D_{ij} = Kromel price in \$/pound in the i-th year ($i = 1, 2, \ldots, m$) for the j-th outcome.

Z_{ij} = Cost in \$/pound of Everclear's Kromel resin in the i-th year for the j-th outcome. (This cost is a function of the amount of Kromel pounds sold by Everclear.)

ϕ = Function of.

K_{ij} = Everclear's overall market share of Kromel Industry sales (in pounds) in the i-th year for the j-th outcome (expressed decimally).

M_{ij} = Kromel Industry poundage (summed over all four market segments) in the i-th year for the j-th outcome.

pected outcomes of each of the other three cases respectively) generated for Everclear under each price strategy. While some tapering off in average sales dollars generated from the price reduction cases compared to the *$1.00 case* can be noted near the end of the simulation period, this tapering off is less pronounced than that which would be experienced by the total Kromel industry.

The reason for this different pattern is that the price reduction strategies (by reducing the probability of future capacity expansion on the part of existing and potential Kromel competitors) led to gains in Everclear's market share, relative to market share under the *$1.00 case*. These increases in Everclear's market share, under the price reduction strategies, partially offset the decline in incremental sales dollar gains (experienced by the Kromel industry near the end of the period) and thus explain the difference in sales patterns that would be observed between Everclear and the Kromel industry.

Figure 4 summarizes the behavior of Everclear's average, year-by-year (compounded) net profits performance again on an incremental basis compared to the *$1.00 case*. As would be expected, time lags in the penetration of segment A, under the price reduction strategies, result in an early profit penalty compared to the *$1.00 case*. This penalty is later overbalanced by the additional sales dollars accruing from earlier (on the average) penetration of segment A under the price reduction strategies versus the *status quo* price case.

The overall performance of each pricing strategy on Everclear's cumulative, compounded net profits position (expected value basis) at the *end* of the five-year planning period is shown in Table 3. These values were obtained by application of the formula shown in Table 2.

Figure 2. Cumulative probability of Kromel's penetration of market segment A (As a function of time and initial price)

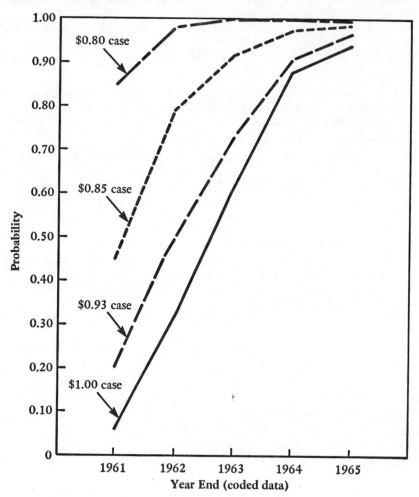

Table 3 shows that all of the price reduction strategies yield expected payoffs which exceed the *$1.00 . case.* These additional profits stem from two principal sources:

1. The higher profits generated in the middle portion of the planning period, as a function of the increased probability of effecting penetration of market segment A, and its associated effect on Kromel industry sales in market segments B, C, and D; and

2. The higher market share for Everclear, resulting from the influence of the price reduction strategies on lowering the probability of capacity expansion and/or entry by Kromel competitors (existing or potential). These combined factors overbalance the lower profit margins per pound associated with the price reduction strategies compared to the *$1.00 case.*

Figure 3. Kromel sales volume—Everclear Plastics Co. (Incremental sales dollars generated over $1.00 case)

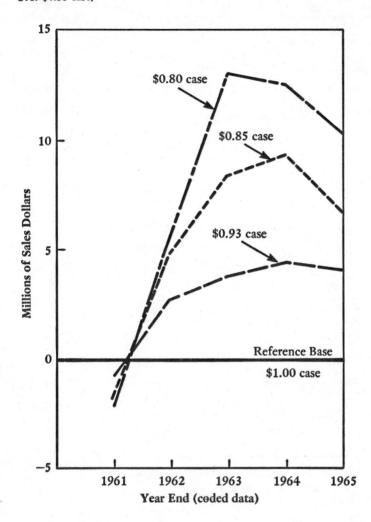

However, a relevant question arose concerning the influence of the more favorable market share factor (under the price reduction cases) on the outcomes of these strategies vs. the *$1.00 case.* Suppose that no favorable difference in market share were obtained under the price reduction strategies compared to the no-price reduction case. That is, suppose the probability that lower Kromel price would discourage future competitive expansion of Kromel industry capacity in the 1963–64 period were zero. How would this affect Everclear's profit position?

In order to test the impact of this variable on Everclear's cumulative, compounded net profits, the market share factor was held constant at the trend level estimated under the no-price reduction, or *$1.00 case* over the simulation period. This analysis resulted in the information given in Table 4.

It is clear from Table 4 that the market share factor is important in producing Everclear's higher profit position as associated with the price reduction alternatives

Figure 4. **Compounded year-by-year net profits of Everclear Plastics Co. (Compound rate equals 6% annually)**

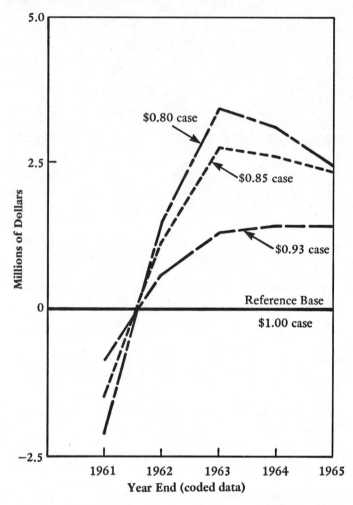

noted in Table 3. If increased share for Everclear were *not* obtained in the 1963–65 period (relative to the share expected under the *$1.00 case*), all strategies would yield close to equal payoffs. That is, over the planning period, the increased sales volume resulting from earlier (on the average) penetration of segment A under

Table 3. **Cumulative, compounded net profits— Everclear Plastics Co. (1961–65)**

Price strategy	End-of-period profit position
$1.00 case	$26.5 million
.93 case	30.3 million
.85 case	33.9 million
.80 case	34.9 million

Table 4. Profit position—market share help constant (Everclear's cumulative, compounded net profits; 1961–65)

Price strategy	End-of-period profit position
$1.00 case	$26.5 million
.93 case	26.9 million
.85 case	27.4 million
.80 case	25.2 million

the price reduction strategies just about balances the less favorable profit margins associated with these strategies.

However, beyond the planning period, all strategies have for all practical purposes accomplished penetration of segment A. The impact of *higher market share* for Everclear thus assumes an important role toward maintaining higher payoffs for the price reduction cases versus the *$1.00 case*.

When computer run results were analyzed for the sub-cases (varying the total market forecast and cost of capital variables), it was found that the study outcomes were not sensitive to these factors. Although the absolute levels of all payoffs changed, no appreciable change was noted in their relative standing.

In Summary. This illustration has shown two principal findings regarding the expected payoffs associated with the alternative courses of action formulated by Everclear:

1. All price reduction strategies result in higher expected payoffs than that associated with the *status quo* pricing case and of these, the *$.80 case* leads to the largest expected value.
2. The higher payoffs associated with the price reduction strategies are quite sensitive to the assumption that Everclear's future market share would be favorably influenced by reductions in Kromel price.

Everclear's management is now at least in a position to appraise the *financial implications* of its marketing assumptions in order to arrive at a reasoned selection among alternative choices.

IMPLICATIONS

The preceding illustration indicates the extent of problem detail which can be (and frequently must be) introduced to reflect adequately the characteristics of real market situations. Nevertheless, this illustration omits some important features of Bayesian decision theory.

First, payoffs were expressed in monetary terms (cumulative, compounded net profits) rather than utility, in the von Neumann-Morgenstern sense, as discussed by Schlaifer.[2] One assumes implicitly, then, that utility is linear with money. As tempting as this assumption may be, some small-scale studies at du Pont in which attempts were made to construct empirical utility functions raise some questions regarding the assumption of linearity. However, this feature of the Bayesian approach may well take many years of further education and development before it may find regular application on the industrial scene.

Second, while a plethora of Bayesian prior probabilities were used in this problem, no mention was made of analyzing sample data and calculating *posterior* probabilities. How does one investigate states of nature in problems of this type? Certainly the problems of conducting meaningful experiments are hardly trivial in pricing problems, or the general area of market planning.

Third, just how detailed a structure can be warranted, particularly when the inputs to the problem are largely subjective in character? One may obviously over-structure as well as under-structure a problem. This caveat, however, applies to all model building. While sensitivity analysis may be used to shed light on which variables "make a difference," the fact remains that the model-building process is still based largely on the builder's intuitive grasp of problem essentials and the interplay between analyst and decision-maker. The structure of the problem discussed in this article turned out to be complex precisely because the variables included *were* deemed important by the decision-maker(s). And part of the analyst's job is thus to examine the impact of supposedly important variables on the relevant payoff junction and then feed back his findings to the decision-maker.

Finally, in conducting this study, realistic problems have a way of generating quite a lot of arithmetic detail, for example, a multi-stage set of alternative states of nature and payoffs. Implementation of the Bayesian approach must, therefore, frequently be aided by recourse to a high-speed computing device. Moreover, a computer model also facilitates the task of running sensitivity analyses concerning either changes in the payoff values related to any particular combination of state of nature and course of action.

Our experience has indicated that the Bayesian approach, even coupled with the ancillary techniques of computer simulation and sensitivity analysis, does not offer any foolproof procedure for "solving" market planning problems. Still, it would seem that this method *does* offer definite advantage over the more traditional techniques usually associated with market planning. Traditional techniques rarely consider *alternative* states of nature, let alone assigning prior probabilities to their occurrence. Moreover, traditional market planning techniques seldom provide for testing the sensitivity of the study's outcomes to departures in the basic assumptions.

At the very least, the Bayesian model forces a more rigorous approach to market planning problems and offers a useful device for quickly finding the financial implications of assumptions about the occurrence of alternative states of nature. In time, this procedure coupled with a more sophisticated approach to the design, collection, and interpretation of field data appears capable of providing an up-to-date and flexible means to meet the more stringent demands of dynamic decision situations, so typical in the problems faced by the marketing manager.

NOTES

[1] Robert Schlaifer, *Probability and Statistics for Business Decisions* (New York: McGraw-Hill Book Company, 1959). In addition two excellent general articles dealing with the

Bayesian approach are: Harry V. Roberts, "The New Business Statistics," *Journal of Business* (January, 1960, pp. 21–30) and Jack Hirshleifer, "The Bayesian Approach to Statistical Decision—An Exposition," *Journal of Business*, October, 1961, pp. 471–489.

[2] Schlaifer, *op. cit.*, chap. 2.

SOME SUGGESTIONS FOR FURTHER READING

Brown, R. V. (1970), "Do Managers Find Decision Theory Useful?" *Harvard Business Review* (May–June), 78–89.

———— (1969), *Research and the Credibility of Estimates: An Appraisal Tool for Executives and Researchers*. Boston: Harvard Business School, Division of Research .

Cox, K. K. and Enis, B. M. (1972), *The Marketing Research Process*. Pacific Palisades, CA: Goodyear Publishing Co.

Myers, J. H. and Samli, A. C. (1969), "Management Control of Marketing Research," *Journal of Marketing Research*, 6 (August), 267–277.

Raiffa, H. (1968), *Decision Analysis*. Reading, MA: Addison-Wesley.

Wright, P. (1974), "The Harassed Decision Maker: Time Pressures, Distractions, and the Use of Evidence," *Journal of Applied Psychology, 59* (October), 555–561.

36 / THE DIALOGUE THAT NEVER HAPPENS / Raymond A. Bauer and Stephen A. Greyser

In recent years government and business spokesmen alike have advocated a "dialogue" between their two groups for the reduction of friction and the advancement of the general good. Yet, all too often, this is a dialogue that never happens. Rather, what passes for dialogue *in form* is often a sequence of monologues *in fact*, wherein each spokesman merely grants "equal time" to the other and pretends to listen while preparing his own next set of comments. Obviously, this is not always the case; and, if taken literally, it tends to minimize some real progress being made.

Our aim here is to try to facilitate and stimulate that progress by exploring what lies behind the dialogue that never happens and by suggesting what can be done—on both sides—to develop more meaningful and effective business-government interactions.

In this context, we link "government spokesmen" with "critics." Naturally, not all in government are critics of business, and vice versa. However, almost all critics seek redress of their grievances via government action and seek government spokesmen to present their views "in behalf of the public."

Our primary focus will be in the field of marketing—particularly selling and advertising—which is perhaps the most controversial and most frequently criticized single zone of business. Marketing seems to be the area where achieving true dialogue is most difficult and where business and government spokesmen most seem to talk past each other.

Before examining why this takes place, let us look at two comments on advertising that illustrate the lack of dialogue. The first comment is that of Donald F. Turner, Assistant Attorney General in charge of the Antitrust Division of the Justice Department:

There are three steps to informed choice: (1) the consumer must know the product exists; (2) the consumer must know how the product performs; and (3) he must know how it performs compared to other products. If advertising

Reprinted by permission from *Harvard Business Review*, Vol. 45 (November–December 1967), pp. 2–4, 6, 8, 10, 12, 186, 188, and 190. Copyright © 1967 by the President and Fellows of Harvard College; all rights reserved.

The late Raymond A. Bauer was professor of business administration at the Harvard Business School. He received a B.S. degree from Northwestern University and his M.A. and Ph.D. from Harvard, with social anthropology as his area of specialization. He wrote texts on American business and public policies and on advertising from the consumer point of view, including *Advertising in America*. Dr. Bauer was past president of the Association for Public Opinion Research. Stephen A. Greyser is professor of business administration at the Harvard Business School, where he teaches advertising and is executive director of the Marketing Science Institute. His M.B.A. and D.B.A. are from Harvard. He co-authored *Advertising in America* with R. A. Bauer and is a frequent contributor to scholarly journals on issues of marketing, advertising, and public policy.

only performs step one and appeals on other than a performance basis, informed choice cannot be made.[1]

The other comment is that of Charles L. Gould, Publisher, the San Francisco *Examiner:*

No government agency, no do-gooders in private life can possibly have as much interest in pleasing the consuming public as do . . . successful companies. For, in our economy, their lives literally depend on keeping their customers happy.[2]

DOUBLE-ENTENDRES

Why do business and government spokesmen talk past each other in discussing ostensibly the same marketplace? We think it is because each has a basically different model of the consumer world in which marketing operates. This misunderstanding grows from different perceptions about a number of key words.

The first word is *competition.* The critics of business think of competition tacitly as strictly price differentiation. Modern businessmen, however, as marketing experts frequently point out, think of competition primarily in terms of product differentiation, sometimes via physical product developments and sometimes via promotional themes. The important thing is that price competition plays a relatively minor role in today's marketplace.

Some of the perplexity between these two views of competition has to do with confusion over a second word, *product.* In the critic's view, a product is the notion of some entity which has a primary identifiable function only. For example, an automobile is a device for transporting bodies, animate or inanimate; it ordinarily has four wheels and a driver, and is powered by gasoline. There are variants on this formula (three-wheeled automobiles) which are legitimate, provided the variants serve the same function. Intuitively the businessman knows there is something wrong with this notion of the product because the product's secondary function may be his major means of providing differentiation (an auto's looks, horsepower, and so on).

Then there is the term *consumer needs,* which the business critic sees as corresponding to a product's primary function—for example, needs for transportation, nutrition, recreation (presumably for health purposes), and other things. The businessman, on the other hand, sees needs as virtually *any* consumer lever he can use to differentiate his product.

Next, there is the notion of *rationality.* The critic, with a fixed notion of "needs" and "product," sees any decision that results in an efficient matching of product to needs as rational. The businessman, taking no set position on what a person's needs should be, contends that any decision the customer makes to serve his own perceived self-interest is rational.

The last addition to our pro tem vocabulary is *information.* The critic fits information neatly into his view that a rational decision is one which matches product function and consumer needs, rather circularly defined as the individual's requirement for the function the product serves. Any information that serves that need is "good" information. To the businessman, information is basically any data or argument that will (truthfully) put forth the attractiveness of a product in the context of the consumer's own buying criteria.

Exhibit 1 summarizes our views of these two different models of the consumer world. We realize that we may have presented a somewhat exaggerated dichotomy. But we think the models are best demonstrated by this delineation of the pure views of contrasting positions, recognizing that both sides modify them to some extent.

VIEWS OF HUMAN NATURE

A review of our "vocabulary with a double meaning" and the two models of the consumer world shows that the critic's view is based on a conviction that he knows what "should be." In contrast, the businessman's view is based on militant agnosticism with regard to "good" or "bad" value judgments which might be made (by anyone) about individual marketplace transactions.

The businessman's view of human nature may be the more flattering, perhaps excessively so. Certainly, the marketer's notion of "consumer sovereignty" compliments the consumer in attributing to him the capacity to decide what he needs and to make his choice competently even under exceedingly complex circumstances. It also sometimes challenges him to do so. This perhaps undeserved flattery glosses over some obvious flaws in the market mechanism. It is rooted in the belief that this mechanism, even though imperfect in specific instances, is better than administrative procedures for regulating the market.

The critic takes a far less optimistic view of human nature—both the consumer's and the seller's. He thinks that the seller often (sometimes intentionally) confuses consumers with a welter of one-sided argumentation. Such information, in the critic's eye, not only lacks impartiality, but usually focuses on secondary product functions and is not geared to consumer needs.

Both sets of assumptions are, we think, at least partially justified. Customers do have limited information and limited capacity to process it. This is the way of

Exhibit 1. Two different models of the consumer world

Key words	Critic's view	Businessman's view
Competition	Price competition	Product differentiation
Product	Primary function only	Differentiation through secondary function
Consumer needs	Correspond point-for-point to primary functions	Any customer desire on which the product can be differentiated
Rationality	Efficient matching of product to customer needs	Any customer decision that serves the customer's own perceived self-interest
Information	Any data that facilitate the fit of a product's proper function with the customer's needs	Any data that will (truthfully) put forth the attractiveness of the product in the eyes of the customer

the world. Furthermore, there is no reason to believe that every seller has every customer's interest as his own primary concern in every transaction, even though in the long run it probably is in the seller's own best interest to serve every customer well.

All of this disagreement comes to focus on a point where both business and government are in agreement; namely, modern products are sufficiently complex that the individual consumer is in a rather poor position to judge their merits quickly and easily. The businessman says that the customer should be, and often is, guided in his judgment by knowledge of brand reputation and manufacturer integrity, both of which are enhanced by advertising. The critic argues that the customer should be, but too seldom is, aided by impartial information sources primarily evaluating product attributes.

These conflicting views of vocabulary and human nature are reflected in several specific topic areas.

BRANDS AND RATING SERVICES

One of these areas is the relationship of national branding to consumer rating services, the latter being a traditional source of "impartial information" for consumers. Somehow the crux of this relationship seems to have escaped most people's attention: Consumer rating services are possible *only because* of the existence of a limited number of brands for a given product. In order for a rating to be meaningful, two conditions are necessary:

1. *Identifiability*—the consumer must be able to recognize the products and brands rated.
2. *Uniformity*—manufacturers must habitually produce products of sufficiently uniform quality that consumer and rating service alike can learn enough from a sample of the product to say or think something meaningful about another sample of the same product which may be bought in some other part of the country at some later time. This is a seldom realized aspect of national branding.

It is generally assumed by both groups that the "consumer movement" is basically opposed to heavily advertised branded goods. The stereotype of *Consumer Reports* is that it regularly aims at shunting trade away from national brands to Sears, to Montgomery Ward, or to minor brands. Yet the one study made of this issue showed that, contrary to the stereotype, *Consumer Reports* had consistently given higher ratings to the heavily advertised national brands than to their competitors.[3]

Ideological Blindness

What we have here is an instance of the consumer movement and brand-name manufacturers being ideologically blinded by different models of the market world. The consumer movement concentrates on the notion of a product having a definable primary function that should take precedence over virtually all other attributes of the product. True, some concessions have recently been made to aesthetics.

But, on the whole, the consumer movement is suspicious of the marketing world that strives to sell products on the basis of secondary attributes which the consumer movement itself regards with a jaundiced eye.

The evidence available to the consumer movement is that, in general, national advertising is *not* accompanied by poorer performance on primary criteria. But the consumer movement fails to realize that it *takes for granted* the central claim for advertised branded products—namely, that by being identifiable and uniform in quality, they offer the customer an opportunity to make his choice on the basis of his confidence in a particular manufacturer.

But the manufacturers of nationally branded products and their spokesmen have been equally blind. First of all, we know of none who has pointed out the extent to which any form of consumer rating must be based on the identifiability and uniformity of branded products. The only situation where this does not apply is when the rating service can instruct the consumer in how to evaluate the product —for example, looking for marbleizing in beef. However, this is limited to products of such a nature that the customer can, with but little help, evaluate them for himself, it cannot apply to products for which he has to rely on the technical services of an independent evaluator or on the reputation of the manufacturer.

Moreover, except for such big-ticket items as automobiles, consumer rating services usually test products only once in several years. In other words, they rate not only a *sample* of a manufacturer's products but also a sample of his performance *over time*. Thus, if one "follows the ratings" and buys an air conditioner or a toaster this year, he may buy it on the rating of a product made one, two, or three years ago. Similarly, if one buys a new automobile, he depends in part on the repair record (reported by at least one rating service) for previous models of that brand.

In large part, then, consumer rating services are devices for rating *manufacturers!* This is not to say they do not rate specific products. Sometimes they even draw fine distinctions between different models from the same company. But in the course of rating products, they also rate manufacturers. What more could the manufacturer ask for? Is this not what he claims he strives for?

Basic Dichotomy

More to the point, what is it that has kept the consumer movement and brand-name manufacturers from paying attention to this area of shared overlapping interests? Neither will quarrel with the exposure either of factual deception or of product weaknesses on dimensions that both agree are essential to the product. This is not where the problem is. The problem is that the manufacturer *sells* one thing and the rating service *rates* another.

The concept of a "product" that dominates the thinking of rating services and the thought processes of those who suggest more "impartial evaluation information" for consumers (e.g., Donald Turner of the Department of Justice and Congressman Benjamin Rosenthal of New York) is that a product is an entity with a single, primary, specifiable function—or, in the case of some products, such as food, perhaps a limited number of functions, e.g., being nutritious, tasty, and visually appealing. The specific goal of many proposed ratings—with their emphasis on the physical and technical characteristics of products—is to free the customer from the influence of many needs to which the marketer addresses himself, mostly particularly the desire for ego enhancement, social acceptance, and status.

The marketer, oddly enough, tends to accept a little of the critics' view of what a product is. Marketing texts, too, speak of primary and secondary functions of a product as though it were self-evident that the aesthetic ego-gratifying, and status-enhancing aspects of the product were hung on as an afterthought. If this is true, why are Grecian vases preserved to be admired for their beauty? And why did nations of yore pass sumptuary laws to prevent people from wearing clothes inappropriate to their status?

We shall shortly explore what may lie behind this confusion about the nature of products. First, however, let us examine another topical area in which similar confusion exists.

"MATERIALIST SOCIETY"

The selling function in business is regularly evaluated by social commentators in relationship to the circumstance that ours is a "materialist society." We could say we do not understand what people are talking about when they refer to a materialist society, beyond the fact that our society does possess a lot of material goods. But, in point of fact, we think *they* do not understand what they are talking about. Let us elucidate.

At first hearing, one might conclude that criticism of a materialist society is a criticism of the extent to which people spend their resources of time, energy, and wealth on the acquisition of material things. One of the notions that gets expressed is that people should be more interested in pursuing nonmaterial goals.

The perplexing matter is, however, that the criticism becomes strongest on the circumstance that people *do* pursue nonmaterial goals—such as ego enhancement, psychic security, social status, and so on—but use material goods as a means of achieving them. Perhaps the distinctive feature of our society is the extent to which *material* goods are used to attain *nonmaterial* goals.

Now there are many ways in which societies satisfy such needs. For example, there are ways of attaining status that do not involve material goods of any substance. Most societies grant status to warriors and other heroes, to wise men who have served the society, and so on. Often the external manifestation of this status is rigidly prescribed and involves signs whose material worth is insignificant: A hero wears a medal, a ribbon in his lapel, or a certain type of headdress, or he may be addressed by an honorific title.

However, in societies that value economic performance, it is not uncommon for material goods to be used as status symbols. Indians of the Southwest, for example, favor sheep as a symbol even to the extent of overtaxing the grazing lands and lowering the economic status of the tribe. As a practical matter, this might be more damaging to the welfare of the Navaho than is the damage that many low-income Negroes do to their own individual welfares when, as research shows, they insist on serving a premium-priced brand of scotch.

Many of the things about which there is complaint are not self-evidently bad. Art collecting is generally considered a "good thing." But take the worst instance of a person who neurotically seeks self-assurance by buying art objects. Clinically, one might argue that he would do himself a lot more long-run good with psychotherapy even though, when one considers the resale value of the art objects, he may have taken the more economical course of action. Similarly, it is not self-evident that the promotion of toiletries to the youth as a symbol of transition to manhood is inherently cruel—unless the commercials are especially bad! It is clear, however, that there is no societal consensus that the transition to manhood should be symbolized by the use of toiletries.

What seems to be the nub of the criticism of our society as a materialist one is that simultaneously a great number of nonmaterial goals are served by material goods, and there is no consensus that this should be so. Behind this is our old friend (or enemy): the concept of a product as serving solely a primary function. In the perspective of history and of other societies, this is a rather peculiar notion. Who in a primitive society would contend that a canoe paddle should not be carved artistically, or that a chief should not have a more elaborate paddle than a commoner?

Much of the confusion over the words on our list seems to be a residue of the early age of mass production. The production engineer, faced with the task of devising ways to turn out standardized products at low cost, had to ask himself, "What are the irreducible elements of this product?" This was probably best epitomized in Henry Ford's concept of the automobile, and his comment that people could have any color they wanted so long as it was black. Clearly, Ford thought it was immoral even to nourish the thought that a product ought to look good, let alone that it should serve various psychic and social functions.

But all this was closely related to the mass producer's effort to find the irreducible essence of what he manufactured. This effort broke up the natural organic integrity of products, which, at almost all times in all societies, have served multiple functions.

Many writers have called attention to the fact that in recent times our society has passed from the period of simple-minded mass production to that of product differentiation on attributes beyond the irreducible primary function. As yet, however, we do not think there is adequate appreciation of the impact of the residue of the early period of mass production on thinking about what a product is. In that period even very complex products were converted into commodities. Since each performed essentially the same primary function, the chief means of competition was pricing.

PRODUCTS AS COMMODITIES

At this point, we shall argue that the thinking of those who criticize the selling function is based on a model for the marketing of commodities. This factor does not exhaust the criticism, but we believe it is at the core of present misunderstandings over the concepts on which we have focused our discussion.

On the one hand, to the extent that products are commodities, it is possible to specify the function or functions which all products in that category should serve. It follows that a person who buys and uses such a commodity for some purpose other than for what it was intended has indeed done something odd, although perhaps useful to him (for example, baseball catchers who use foam-rubber "falsies" to pad their mitts). In any event, it is possible both to specify the basis on which the commodity should be evaluated and the information a person is entitled to have in order to judge that product. A person searching for a commodity ought first to find out whether it serves this function and then to ask its price.

On the other hand, to the extent that products are *not* commodities, it is impossible to expect that price competition will necessarily be the main basis of competition. Likewise, it is impossible to specify what information is needed or what constitutes rational behavior. Is it rational for a person to buy toothpaste because its advertiser claims it has "sex appeal"? Presumably people would rather look at clean than dingy teeth, and presumably people also like to have sex appeal —at least up to the point where it gets to be a hazard or a nuisance.

But it does not follow, insofar as we can see, that ratings—or grade labeling— should discourage product differentiation or the promotion of products on a non-commodity basis. If the consumer were assured that all products in a given rating category performed their primary functions about equally well, could it not be argued that those attributes which differentiate the products on other functions would then become increasingly interesting and important? Or, to be more specific, what makes it possible for "instant-on" TV tuning to be promoted—other than a presumed agreement, by both manufacturer and consumers, that the TV set performs its primary function little better or worse than its competition?

This is a facet of competition not appreciated by the opponents of grade-labeling, who have argued that it would reduce competition. Perhaps it would be more helpful if the opponents of grade labeling first gathered some evidence on what has actually happened to competition in countries where grade labeling has been introduced. (The head of one major relevant trade association recently told one of us that he knew of no such research.)

TOWARD MORE INFORMATION

Readers will note that we have indulged in considerable speculation in this article. But most of the issues on which we have speculated are researchable. Relatively little, for example, is really known about how businesses actually see themselves carrying out "the practice of competition," or even about the actual competitive mechanisms of setting prices. Furthermore, in all of this, there is no mention of the *consumer's* view of these various concepts or of his model of the marketing process. To be sure, we can be reasonably certain of some things. For example, we know that consumers do regard products as serving needs beyond the bare essentials. Yet it would be helpful to know far more about their views of the overall marketing process.

What we propose as a worthwhile endeavor is an independent assessment of the consumer's view of the marketing process, focusing on information needs from his point of view. Thus, rather than businessmen lamenting the critics' proposals for product-rating systems and the critics bemoaning what seem to be obvious abuses of marketing tools, both sides ought to move toward proposing an information system for the consumer that takes into account *his* needs and *his* information-handling capacities while still adhering to the realities of the marketing process.

For those who have the reading habit, it will be obvious that this proposal is but an extension of the conclusions reached by members of the American Marketing Association's Task Force on "Basic Problems in Marketing" for the improvement of relations between marketing and government.[4] In brief, along with suggested studies on the influence of government policies and programs on corporate marketing decisions, a special study was recommended in the area of consumer-buyer decision-making and behavior:

It is of the highest importance to investigate the impacts of the host of governmental regulations, facilities, aids, and interventions upon the quality and efficiency of consumer-buyer decision-making.[5]

The report went on to state that, particularly in light of the generally recognized drift from *caveat emptor* toward *caveat venditor*, "abundant basic research opportunities and needs exist" in the area of government impact and consumer-buyer behavior.

WHAT CAN BUSINESSMEN DO?

Certainly there is a crying need for more information and, as we have tried to illustrate, for fresh analytic thinking on almost all of the issues on which government and business are butting heads. We have elaborated on the different models of how the marketplace does, and should, work because we think their existence explains the largest part of why marketers and their critics often talk past each other, even when they have the best intentions of engaging in a dialogue. The other part is explained by the relative absence of facts. As we have noted, the consumer's view of the market-advertising process and his informational needs represent an important (and relatively unprobed) research area.

Returning to the "dialogue," we should add a further problem beyond that of business and government spokesmen talking past one another. Inasmuch as many on both sides see themselves as representing their colleagues' views, partisanship becomes mixed with the aforementioned misunderstanding. Since such partisanship is likely to address itself to stereotyped views of "the other side," the comments become irrelevant. That many well-qualified firsthand commentators are regarded as self-serving by their critics is a point aptly made by Denis Thomas. Equally apt is his corollary observation that those "who view business ... from a suitably hygienic distance lose no marks for partiality even if their facts are wrong."[6]

How then can effective interactions take place? Obviously, the key parts will be played by:

1. Thoughtful business and government leaders.
2. Marketers and their critics who take the time to consider and to understand

(even if they do not agree with) each others' premises and assumptions.

3. Those who engage in meaningful dialogue oriented to fact finding rather than fault finding.

4. Those on both sides who address themselves to solving the problems of the real, rather than the presumed, public.

Beyond the parts played by thoughtful business and government people, we see a distinctive role for schools of business in bringing about meaningful interaction. Business schools are a unique resource both in their understanding of the business system and in their capability to conduct relevant research. Other faculties, at least equally competent and objective in research, generally do not have the depth of understanding of why things are the way they are—a necessary precursor to relevant study. We hasten to add that grasping how something *does* operate implies no consent that this is how it *should* operate, now or in the future.

Both in research and as participants (or moderators) in dialogue, business school faculties can play a significant role.

Business and government should sponsor the necessary research. The particular need for business is to recognize that the era of exclusively partisan pleading must end. . . . Academic "insurance" of the objective conduct of the research and presentation of findings should bring about a degree of governmental acceptance and set the standard for any subsequent research.

We can use more of this, and more of it is beginning to take place. A dialogue is always most profitable when the parties have something to talk about.

NOTES

[1] Statement made at the Ninth Annual American Federation of Advertising Conference on Government Relations held in Washington, D.C., February 1967.

[2] *Ibid.*

[3] Eugene R. Beem and John S. Ewing, "Business Appraises Consumer Testing Agencies," *Harvard Business Review*, Vol. 32 (March–April 1954), pp. 113–126, especially p. 121.

[4] See E. T. Grether and Robert J. Holloway, "Impact of Government upon the Market System," *Journal of Marketing*, Vol. 31 (April 1967), pp. 1–5; and Seymour Banks, "Commentary on Impact of Government upon the Market System," ibid., pp. 5–7.

[5] Grether and Holloway, *Ibid.*, p. 5.

[6] *The Visible Persuaders* (London: Hutchinson, 1967), p. 11.

SOME SUGGESTIONS FOR FURTHER READING

Etzioni, A. (1978), "Public Affairs," *Human Behavior*, 14.

Hughes, G. D. and Williams, E. C. (1979), *The Dialogue That Happened.* Marketing Science Institute, Cambridge, MA. (August).

Leone, R. A. (1977), "The Real Costs of Regulation," *Harvard Business Review* (November–December), 57–66.

Stigler, G. J. (1971), "The Theory of Economic Regulation," *Bell Journal of Economics and Management Science* (Spring), 3–21.

INDEX